G000061205

201526194

Touché

Thomas Couture, *Le Duel après le bal masqué*, 1857. © By kind permission of the Trustees of the Wallace Collection, London.

Touché

The Duel in Literature

John Leigh

Harvard University Press

CAMBRIDGE, MASSACHUSETTS • LONDON, ENGLAND

2015

First printing

Library of Congress Cataloging-in-Publication Data
Leigh, John, 1969–
  Touché : the duel in literature / John Leigh.
      pages cm
  Includes bibliographical references and index.
  ISBN 978-0-674-50438-7 (alk. paper)
  1. Dueling in literature.   2. Dueling—History.   I. Title.
II. Title: Duel in literature.
  PN56.D84L45 2015
  809'.933559—dc23

                                          2014042689

In memory of my father, James Ronald Leigh

Contents

Touché

Introduction

To the highly reasonable writers of the eighteenth century, as to their readers, the continued existence of the duel offered a living instance of the way the past might linger and lodge, uninvited, in the present. Duellists were supposed to belong to the Dark Ages, yet their swords flashed in the face of the Enlightenment's most searching objections. Even by the late nineteenth century, when the monarchy in France had, once again, been abolished, the slave trade concluded, and divorce permitted, Guy de Maupassant declared duelling, possibly with a hint of wistfulness, to be "the last of our unreasonable customs."[1] In ages better known for their bourgeois and democratic commitments, this privilege endured, little daunted. Indeed, the prestige of the duellist seemed only to have been enhanced, or even assured, by all attempts to outlaw and to discredit him. Maupassant's mentor, Flaubert, laid out a chain of non sequiturs when, in his satirical *Dictionary of Received Ideas*, he offered the following "definition": "DUEL: Thunder against it. Not a proof of courage. Prestige of the man who has had a duel."[2] The final sentence empties the first two of all their force. The contradictions in this little huddle of lazy assertions are highly characteristic of the responses provoked by duelling in the previous two centuries. Whether timidly hesitant or overtly paradoxical, ambivalence is a signature key to the reactions provoked by duelling in the works of the many influential writers who took an interest in these affairs. Few authors overtly condoned, let alone lauded, duelling in the eighteenth and nineteenth centuries, yet it intrigued those same thinkers, even if their fascination often wears the mask of indignation.

This fascination was surprisingly widespread; duels pervade the literature of the period. They occur in famous plays as various as *Le Cid* and *The Rivals*, poems such as *Eugene Onegin*, and novels as dissimilar as *Clarissa* and *The Three Musketeers*. They beguile and attract the most influential writers of every generation. Duellists confront one another in the pages of strikingly disparate writers, whose common interest in the phenomenon brings them into a perhaps unsuspected proximity to one another.

This catalogue is not a series of accidents or coincidences. Duels, self-contained dramas with a beginning, a middle, and an end, seem particularly hospitable to literature. Writers are drawn to duels, in the interests of discovering something fundamental about human beings and the way they variously organize and delude themselves, the way they face one another, their fears, and, ultimately, death. We are not talking just about a narrative fact or a simple plot device, although of course it is that too, but, variously, a conundrum, a scourge, a trope, which, at different times and for different writers, will assume varying guises. For some authors, it was an inexplicable, alien phenomenon; for others, a test they did, or would need to, face. The duel which their personages fight, or refuse to contest, illustrates their character and that of the societies they inhabit.

One reason for which quite so many duels occur in the pages of literature was the continued failure of the law to deter duellists. Louis XIV of France counted the abolition of duelling as one of the glories of his reign. But the legal contrivances, in France as in most other countries, that rendered participation in a duel punishable in the most severe ways were known, if not always openly acknowledged, to be ineffectual. The threat of capital punishment understandably did not discourage gentlemen who were evidently prepared to die in combat. Writers might, however, ridicule such men or expose, with more compassion, the damage they inflicted on one another, themselves, and their families. Their texts were deemed an indispensable part of the apparatus, as the social and moral case against duelling was built. Yet literary texts also assume a privileged role in honoring the ambiguities of the act. For writers were no less drawn to the duellist as a figure of intrigue, a man embodying freedom beyond the law yet subordinating himself to cruelly inexorable rituals, a hero recalling an age of chivalry or a madman reminiscent more of its follies. Several writers were drawn to the act itself: Richard Steele survived a duel and went on to oppose the practice for the rest of his life; Lermontov perished in a duel, as, of course, did Pushkin.

Throughout these years, the duel was, for those who fought it, an illegal obligation, forbidden by law but demanded by custom, setting conscience against reputation. The resulting tensions were bound to interest writers, themselves engaged in an effort to ennoble their innermost convictions and impressions by translating them into socially acceptable forms. A sometimes elusive set of converging factors renders the duellist peculiarly sympathetic to the writer's mind or sensibility. As a form of preordained combat, governed by rules and by conventions, a duel is a set piece, insulated to an extent from the disorder and impulses of real life. Particularly when fought by pistol, the deed requires space and seclusion and as few witnesses as possible. So how would duellists know how to act when their time came or how to interpret their actions? They would, of course, rely on writers. In a dizzying circle of self-reference, writers often portray their duelling protagonists doing just that. In Chekhov's short story about a duel, the characters rely on their hazy recollections of Lermontov's *Hero of Our Time* as they go about the practical arrangements necessitated by a duel with pistols. Russian novels, like Russian dolls, contain their forefathers, and Lermontov's description of the duel is itself in turn highly self-conscious. And no doubt he was conscious of it himself when he entered his own fatal duel. So, rather like Mafiosi who draw on the very films that purport to mock them, the fictional portrayals feed back into the practices of the duellists.[3] These texts end up advertising the duellist. They invest their act with meaning and dignity. Literary depictions of duels make them seem honorable. The conventions and the style associated with the duel are not just endorsed but endowed by texts.

When would duelling ever end? A response to this exasperated question potentially presupposed an answer to another, more scholarly inquiry. When had it begun? The origins of the duel were agreed to date back to the half-remembered, half-imagined days of single combat. Epic poems tend to depict hand-to-hand combats when the battle raging all around seems, suddenly, miraculously, to be suspended. All eyes are, momentarily, trained on this crucial bout. Those passages in which Hector and Achilles (*Iliad*, Book XXII), Aeneas and Turnus (*Aeneid*, Book XII), Tancred and Argantes (*Jerusalem Liberated*, Book XIX) cross swords remained canonical, perhaps surprisingly so, throughout the early modern period. These fights were enjoyed on their own terms but were also admired as an example of the poet's own combat with noble antecedents. The descriptive challenges entailed by successive single combats provided a leading criterion for the comparison and evaluation of poems from different countries across different ages. The sobriety of the Enlightenment did not preclude a reverence for these passages, which were deemed to be a final certificate of authorial skill. John Hoole, as he opens the preface to his eighteenth-century translation of *Orlando furioso*, tells us, "All the battles and single combats in Ariosto are excellent: in the last he is greatly superior to Tasso, and indeed to most other poets; for in this respect there appears some defect even in the poems of Homer and Virgil, in which there are few good descriptions of this kind." Ariosto's art in managing the turns of fortune and keeping up the reader's "attention between hope and fear" is saluted as preeminent, excelling even that of the Ancients.[4] In fact, the single combats in the works just mentioned seem to have been all that some readers remembered. "What else is all Mr. Pope's Homer full of but duels? . . . Nay, and in Dryden's Virgil, is there any thing almost besides fighting?"[5] The colonel who asks this question, in Fielding's late novel *Amelia*, is venturing an implicit apology for modern duelling. This practice had, it could be contended, its origins in a humane expedient, designed to spare "the greater effusion of blood," the violence of all-out war. In some famous cases, a clash between enemy forces was indeed apparently spared by the single combat engaged by respective champions.

However, in *Amelia*, Dr. Harrison, a learned clergyman, puts the colonel right. These epic poems, he remarks, speak of wars between nations and not private duels, of which there is not one single instance in the works of ancient Greeks and Romans. Richardson's Sir Charles Grandison likewise enumerates famous encounters in ancient times, such as the battle of the Horatii and the Curiatii or of Tullus and Albanus, which, however, are public, national combats. True, Augustus apparently received a challenge from Mark Antony, but he politely suggested "that, if Antony were weary of his life, he might find many *other* ways to end it than by *his* sword."[6]

Mouthpieces of their respective authors, these wise gentlemen each typify an early modern wish to decouple the duel from single combat and judicial combat, its venerable ancestors. This wish nevertheless remains anxious, for that noble pedigree of the duel as a Homeric bout between selfless champions representing a greater number is never quite effaced. Even in subsequent ages, when the duellist fights uniquely in his own interests, he may profit from that aura. Duellists might be deplored as monstrous, lawless egotists, but the same individuals could be admired for donating their lives in the name of the sacred ethos that was honor. The duellist represented interests other than, or at least supplementary to, his own. That nimbus of generosity remains in place, long after the introduction of modern arms and new causes. Indeed, the tension between the duellist's wish to understand his act as a variant form of single combat and therefore a prestigious neoclassical confrontation and the need for his critic to denounce it as barbarous, by privileging its medieval provenance, is one of the currents running through this book.

There was somewhat less pressure, among critics, to divorce the modern duel from judicial combats or ordeals, which had been instituted in medieval times, as a proof of God's truth. In more secular ages, such trials by combat did not enjoy the continued prestige of those heroic, classical duels.[7] In fact, Ariosto's single combats appealed in subsequent ages since these bouts, sometimes ostensibly designed to be judicial, rapidly, often ironically, mutate into more recognizable modern duels. Rinaldo aborts a judicial combat, skeptically reasoning that it cannot vindicate the honor of the falsely accused Ginevra. But he decides anyway that he fancies a duel on her behalf, telling himself,

> The other knows not if he's wrong or right.
> To his bold heart this is of no import;
> For that which moves a noble, valiant knight
> Is beauty in distress of any sort.

Meanwhile, Ariodante hears that no knight has come forward to defend Ginevra, who continues to languish under suspicion. But, far from suspecting that she might actually be in the wrong, they just dread the strength and skill of Lurcanio, their prospective adversary.[8] Ariodante's presentiments, together with the subtleties of Ariosto's commentary, suggest that the duel is perceived to reward skill or obey chance, rather than expressing divine justice. Yet, once again, the intelligence of subsequent secular ages did not entirely dispel a residual feeling that the duel vouchsafed a definitive, mysteriously transcendent verdict. Unfortunate gentlemen would, after all, continue to be killed *in* a duel, not *by* a duellist. Indeed, when the pistol modernized the duel, it paradoxically restored to prominence that primal sense of an inscrutable, God-given outcome.

From the seventeenth century onward, the duel is consistently claimed, and perhaps perceived, to be moribund, if not already defunct. It is already viewed as an anachronism, perhaps acceptable (so works such as Pierre Corneille's *Le Cid* [1637] seem to say) in medieval times and in Iberian backwaters but not in contemporary France—yet it is, of course, happening there and elsewhere. Paradoxically, the senescence of the duel, its vulnerability in the modern bourgeois world, may endow it with the transcendent force of a time-honored ethos. The duel harks back to an age without strangers, when resolution had to be reached, an age before that "new aristocracy," composed of bankers and lawyers, was empowered. Particularly in postrevolutionary France, the duellist is fondly observed or imagined to harbor a cultivated disdain for money in particular and a distaste for bourgeois calculations in general. For these reasons, duelling could appeal no less to those of a Republican stamp. It is suffused with a nostalgic glow, even as it is happening in the present. The duellist is often fanatically fixated on the past, to the extent that he may be seen to be living in it—all the more so if he actually belongs to a shrunken present. Honor is his one vestige, a consolatory excuse for poverty, an answer to "the insolence of wealth," as Dr. Johnson called it.[9] In thrall to the social norms of his period, the duellist is nevertheless typically a stranger to his present, at an angle to his age. Genealogy and lore are the ingredients that combine to form his sense of honor. Indeed, a certain strain of pessimism is integral to the ethic of chivalry that underpins the ritual.[10] Yet, for all this commitment to the past, the interest often lies in the way the anachronistic rite adapts itself to the exigencies of the modern world and thereby reveals characteristics of its age. No one duel is quite the same as another. An improvisatory spirit is often brought to the rubric. A famous duel was, for instance, fought in France by principals who ascended, at a short distance from one another, in a hot air bal-

loon. It testifies to a sort of joyous death-defying creativity, an ingenuity which almost excuses the fatalities that followed.

It is by changing that the duel stays the same. It proves resilient
and elastic, stretching to accommodate new weaponry, handled by
different kinds of people. The challenge to come up with a new sort of
duel and embed its rigid formulae in a modern context is taken up by
a number of writers. Jules Verne is among them. While Phileas Fogg is
crossing the United States in a train, availing himself of the latest mode
of transport in the New World, he is drawn into a duel. The duel is
fitted into the tight confines of the timetable, while a railway carriage,
emptied of its passengers, provides the perfect *champ clos* for this
shoot-out.[11] Beneath the appearances, nothing is really new. Indeed, the
antique marbled room where Fogg reclines all day, obedient to an immutable routine, is located, perhaps ironically, in the Reform Club.
This meeting of past and present, continuity and change, in the incongruous clash between means and ends is often represented in a comical
mode. Cartoons in recent years have shown duels conducted by mobile phone (at a signal, the word "bang" is typed out, and the adversary whose phone rings first loses) or in dump trucks, yet we are never
far from poignancy and cruelty.

The shape of the book is designed to honor this spirit with a combination of chronological and thematic perspectives. Because one text
often presupposes another, when it comes to the depiction of duels, it
seems sensible to proceed chronologically, but the text zigzags somewhat on its way to a thematic conclusion in order to emphasize recurrent ideas and preoccupations. Our own tour begins in France, toward
the end of the lengthy reign of Louis XIV (1643–1715). Measures against
duelling had, of course, been promulgated in previous ages. Victor Hugo
and Alexandre Dumas will remind us, for instance, of Cardinal Richelieu's dogged pursuit of the duellist, in the reign of Louis XIII. But never
before had such absolute and concentrated power been directed, with
so little effect, at the practice of duelling. The failure of duellists to
desist, even under the pressure of a king as potent and effective as
Louis XIV, provokes a degree of anxiety among those thinkers not content to pretend that the much-vaunted "ordonnances" were actually
working. The terms on which the opposition to duelling is framed

change in response to this impasse. While seventeenth-century critics of the duel drew largely on theological and biblical arguments to make their case, eighteenth-century commentators, while remaining aware of those lines of attack, prefer to prick the duellist in a different spot. The duel is now discredited less as an irreligious outrage than as a pseudomedieval anomaly. The duel, it is argued, had no precedent or equivalent in the Classical world. It cannot, therefore, be necessary to a definition of honor or integral to an idea of civilization, both of which manifestly existed and prospered in Antiquity. Indeed, such is their conduct that duellists can be counted the modern embodiments of the enemies threatening those civilized societies. They are, in a word, barbarians. This is the term recycled insistently when duels and duellists are to be deplored. The vocabulary, highly pejorative yet less morally strident, testifies to the developing criteria by which duellists are attacked and to the changing terrain on which these assaults occur. Commentators thereby emphasized the non-Classical nature of a practice, which nevertheless draped itself in Classical idioms and imagery (with, among other things, its high-minded talk of "satisfaction" and its cultivation of swordsmanship). Against this grain, though, runs Corneille's masterpiece, *Le Cid*, which, dating back to 1637, nevertheless remained a crucial focus for some of the arguments that swirled about the irrepressibility of duelling. The play's continuing popularity and prestige pose a challenge for the detractors of the duel. Eighteenth-century campaigners and critics will continue to wrestle with this famous precedent.

Corneille's genius in investing Rodrigo with such nobility and virility must be answered by the countervailing efforts of modern writers. In writings designed to find a way to eliminate duelling, the Abbé de St. Pierre (whose religious affiliation allows him to rage with impunity against the codes of honor) urges the authorities in France to sponsor an annual parody of *Le Cid*. Across the Channel, in the same years, Richard Steele earnestly sets about writing a comedy that will attempt to demystify the duel in a similar vein.

Comical depictions of duels duly abound, above all on the stage, in the early modern period, as Chapter 2 will show. Although their quality is variable, there is no evidence whatsoever that any of these works succeeded in mobilizing opinion against duelling in any significant way.

Ridicule, it is acknowledged by a number of thinkers in the period, can be a mischievous weapon to handle, at risk of recoiling and blowing up in the face of those who try to deploy it. Ridicule may sometimes contrive to legitimate the very people or practices it means to deride. By showing us the absurdity of a duel without a real cause or a bout fought for the most risible of reasons, writers may merely gratify an image of noble insouciance and unaccountability. Aristocrats are seen to play by different rules—comical, incomprehensible rules maybe—but these standards, and the sacrifices they sometimes demand, may reconcile the rest of us to the distance and distinction that nobles enjoy from the lower orders. Above all, though, such authors miss their target when they depict bourgeois or lower-class would-be duellists, for it is not the duel itself but those "bourgeois gentilhommes" incapable of going through with it that constitute the chief satirical object of the text.

Some of these comedies, however, deplore the folly of duelling with a darker side. That is, some pathos may be savored amid the comedy. Writers had tended hitherto to view duels and duellists essentially from the perspective of spectators, but now they are more likely to imagine or to remember (in the case of Sheridan) what it might actually feel like to be a man in a duel. The nobleman is not irremediably other. If you prick him, does he not bleed? But, in fact, the boundaries between classes become increasingly porous, as confusion over the duel suggests.

In a context of toothless laws and largely conciliatory comedies, a new literary strand may be seen to emerge, in Chapter 3. The novel, itself still sometimes distrusted in the eighteenth century as a frivolous and effeminate genre, could tackle these intractable social problems with privileges of its own. Opposition to duelling always required some courage. No critic would want to claim that honor did not matter or even exist. And a critic of the practice would run the risk of condemning himself, while he denounced the duel, as a man lacking the courage or the class to defend his own honor—unless, of course, that critic happened to be female. Two ambitious, enormous novels, Richardson's *Clarissa* (1748) and then *Julie* (1761) by Rousseau, both extraordinarily subtle and brilliant expositions of the way our most intimate feelings meet and must negotiate social norms, unsurprisingly devote some space to a critique of duelling. Unprecedentedly, that careful critique is voiced, in each case, by the eponymous female character. Laclos, meanwhile, sets himself up as a self-conscious heir to Richardson and to Rousseau, and the duel that crowns his novel can be understood as a continuation of their dialogue, an agon, rather than a "realistic" documentary act.

The duels variously contested and proposed in these famous novels reveal the appeal of this practice to men who cannot otherwise give expression to intense feelings of love or anger or some combination of these emotions. It would be natural, given those itineraries, to assume that the duel should be an act prized by writers and readers in the Romantic age. We might be inclined to think of duellists as Romantic heroes, ready to brandish their sword and perish for their lovers. I try to explain why the duellist is not highly regarded in this era. Upon reflection, however, it does not seem so unaccountable. In fact, the duel appeals more to the Enlightenment, even as it irks the thinkers of this age, because it is scrupulous, rule bound, equitable, and, above all, temperate. It is logical—absurdly so.

It may also come as a surprise that the French Revolution and reform movements in its wake appear to have had little or no effect on the incidence of duelling. Duels cease to be a dominant or serious concern of the writer wearily inured to them. In the early Romantic period, a new urgency and spontaneity characterize the violence that writers choose to depict. The courtesies conventionally extended by combatants to one another just look like so many hypocrisies, that etiquette a risible sham. For a while, a horrified interest in murder supersedes the rather bemused fascination exerted by duelling.

It seems fair to agree with the verdict that men and women of the eighteenth century favored *l'amour-goût* over *l'amour-passion*, in Stendhal's neat codification.[12] This former sort of love was not really compatible with Romantic duelling. Whenever they take place in the course of eighteenth-century texts, duels are seldom chivalric and hardly heroic, or they are, at best, ambiguously so. Vanderk fils, Valmont, and Casanova fight duels with apparent disregard for the fair sex, in a mode that decouples the point of honor from its chivalric pedigree, while Roderick Random is an inveterate duellist, to whom the language of chivalry becomes momentarily expedient.

These duels nevertheless transform their protagonists, not only socially but emotionally. The duel may be seen to evolve in tandem with the increasingly sophisticated duet. At the same point, in the latter half of the eighteenth century, the full emotional and musical potential of the duet was developed in opera. Previously, the "duetto metastasiano"—in the mode of the librettist Pietro Metastasio (1698–1782)—was rare and static, but, thanks to Gluck, Mozart, and, subsequently, Rossini, duets were through-composed.[13] The genre of opera seria had made duets more or less redundant. Opera, in particular those pieces written for castrati, remained above all a music of arias, in which the splendors of the individual voice could be appreciated. Castrati were seldom involved in duets (or duels). The duet now changed existing positions; emotions were modified in the process of their performance. The duel, in common with the duet, becomes a transformative experience for each of the principals. In the writings of Michel-Jean Sedaine, Smollett, and Casanova, duels are envisaged as a way of marking one's social progress. Provided they do not turn out to be fatal, duels help their participants in the process of acquiring knowledge about the world or themselves. This had not always been the case hitherto.

The duel both illuminates and intensifies man's character. A new set of extremes comes into play, sharpening and polarizing our vision in various ways. The world becomes attractive to the duellist; he becomes attractive, or at least interesting, to us. But quite what is it that the duel brings into focus? In nineteenth-century texts, the grandeur of the natural world may expose the pettiness of man's pretentions. This can be seen graphically at times, as the principals perch on a vertiginous cliff edge or, as in one of Goya's black paintings, they trade blows against a magnificently grim and desolate landscape. Their vengeful squabbling is belittled by such backdrops. But somehow at one and the same time, there may emerge a contrary sense: the duel shows the grandeur of man, even against that same hinterland. Only man is cursed, or perhaps blessed, with the capacity to kill politely.

If the location of duels in eighteenth-century texts is more or less incidental, the nineteenth century ensures that it becomes part of the picture, literally, in the forested backcloths to the paintings of Thomas Couture and Jean-Léon Gérôme. Nineteenth-century authors try strenuously to understand whether the practice of duelling may be authorized by nature or whether the ritual exists in defiance of it. From Rousseau onward, nature looked more beautiful, or at least more pertinent, to writers and their readers. Accordingly, whereas eighteenth-century writers were inclined to ask whether duelling had occurred in the Classical world (confident that the answer was negative), their nineteenth-century counterparts wonder whether it is happening in the natural world. Equally, the temporality of the duel assumes a new interest for nineteenth-century writers. "Pistols At Dawn" is essentially a literary phrase that appears to have emerged in the nineteenth century. The occurrence of duels at dawn seems first to have acquired a significance in nineteenth-century texts. The topos triggers at least two responses. First, dawn, its pristine air, its chorus of birds, provides a contrast, if not a reproach, to man's wanton destructiveness. It is a singularly poignant, cruelly ironic moment to die. Even if the author refrains from an overt critique of the folly of duellists, de rigueur in the previous century, we feel that this practice must be denatured, counterintuitive. The beauty of the world becomes visible and, with it, the preciousness of life, by which time it is too late to honor them adequately. "Pistols At Dawn" meets practical needs but spawns a poetry of revelation and regret. Things come to light at dawn, a metaphor for clarity of thought and a vision of the world as it is. Duels at this hour stage an epiphany, as the folly and transience of human lives dawn belatedly on those at risk of losing theirs. Dickens's *Nicholas Nickleby* (1844) provides a fine example of these ironies and incongruities at work:

> It was already daybreak. For the flaring yellow light within, was substituted the clear, bright, glorious morning; for a hot, close atmosphere, tainted with the smell of expiring lamps, and reeking with the steams of riot and dissipation, the free, fresh, wholesome air. . . .
>
> Fields, trees, gardens, hedges, everything looked very beautiful; the young man scarcely seemed to have noticed them before, though he had passed the same objects a thousand times. There was a peace and serenity upon them all strangely at variance with the bewilderment and confusion of his own half-sobered thoughts, and yet impressive and welcome. . . .

The sun came proudly up in all his majesty, the noble river ran
its winding course, the leaves quivered and rustled in the air, the
birds poured their cheerful songs from every tree, the short-lived
butterfly fluttered its little wings; all the light and life of day came
on, and, amidst it all, and pressing down the grass whose every blade
bore twenty tiny lives, lay the dead man, with his stark and rigid
face turned upwards to the sky.[14]

Other authors will, at this juncture, point us to a cooing bird, a prancing
deer in the distance, testimony to the rhythms of a peaceful life that
this ritual dares to defy, but Dickens is unique in the telescopic swoop
down onto the abundance of "little lives" inhabiting the grass.

Secondly, the development of "Pistols At Dawn" permits and promotes an associated motif: "The Night Before." Again, nocturnal anxieties are not a feature of any eighteenth-century text to which duels
are nevertheless central (in part because the timing of the duel is more
incidental). A capacity for sleep had, traditionally, been a topos before
battle in historical accounts (sound sleep indicating good prospects and
a clean conscience, a restless night suggesting the reverse). The nearest
equivalent to the duellist's agonizing wait for dawn would be that of
the condemned prisoner. Hugo, whose play about duellists, *Marion de
Lorme*, embraces a nocturnal scene prior to an execution, imagined the
final day of a man condemned to hang. Indeed, at least one other author explicitly brackets the eerie, false calm common to both preludes.[15]
But the prospective duellist offers new and distinct possibilities. Hugo
and such writers invite us to imagine or sympathize with the man
about to be executed. Either he deserved to die and that might limit
reserves of sympathy, or, if he did not, the text becomes a moral tale,
designed to provoke indignation, even anger. Likewise, the soldier on
the eve of the battle will not die alone. He may, or may not, be accompanied by fellow men at arms, but he has his nation and, in consequence, some consolatory notion of solidarity. The duellist, waiting
ahead of his particular assignment, is more solitary, his predicament
less morally obvious. A particular blend of bravery and timidity, defiance and conformity, comes into focus, lending the inspection of these
figures a new intensity.

Whereas duels in eighteenth-century works tend to occur toward
or at their end—*Clarissa* and *Les liaisons dangereuses* offer supreme

examples—in the works of their nineteenth-century successors, the duel moves nearer to the beginning. For the writer will draw on the duel to support insights about these men and their society. As in *The Pickwick Papers*, Flaubert depicts a duel of little consequence in his *Education sentimentale* (1869). The duel can provide a step to the upper echelons, but in this mockery of the linear Bildungsroman, Frédéric Moreau's duel does not move him up any ladders. But participation in a duel is essential to his self-esteem, his self-constructed notion of what it is to be sentimentally literate. At the same time, in this often painful parody of novelistic clichés, the duel is exposed as a rite of passage no less resistible to the ironically self-aware author.

The pressures incurred by serial publication were perhaps responsible to an extent for the formulaic approach. Trollope confessed to a weakness for including a hunting scene in every novel he wrote, whatever the demands of plot and character. The duel, similarly, furnished an *obligato* part, a literary set piece. It forms part of the codes and apparatus of signs that a reader learns to bring to the experience of reading. It constituted a challenge for aspiring writers, particularly Russian novelists, as they at once paid homage to their forerunners and exhibited an ability to elaborate on their craft. Each discrete duel, building on previous examples, provided another twist. These novelists tended to consult their precedents as assiduously as they drew on their own lived experience. Laclos's duel recalls that in *Clarissa*; Dickens's those of Smollett, himself steeped in Cervantes. Lermontov is, naturally, ever aware of Pushkin; indeed, there seems hardly to be a novel without a duel in nineteenth-century Russia. And it is this interplay of formula and variant, the former as rigid as the latter is unpredictable, that accounts for the pleasures furnished by the duel in an endless sequence of literary texts.

In Chapters 4 to 6, we shall witness a return to duels as they apparently once were and ought to have remained: Kleist, Hugo, and Dumas, among many others of course, introduce us to intrepid, chivalrous gentlemen. In these cases, it always seems necessary to recollect or envisage the duellist as a swordsman, in order to retrieve that pristine sense of adventure and gallantry. In the nineteenth century, the heyday of the historical novel, duelling seems to be easily consignable to the past. In the twentieth century, too, the duel becomes a shorthand for the deluded and decaying mores of a self-destructive, defunct age. Duelling is repeatedly presented as an epitome of the sclerotic and complacent culture of the dying Austro-Hungarian Empire. It is therefore an irresistible part of the classic retrospect about that society. And yet something admirable or appealing in the mores that symbolize this decadence guarantees a continuing interest in these brilliant works. In the historicizing accounts of the nineteenth century, however, the fate of the duellist functions, or seems to function, as an analogue. The past is a veil. Once discovered, questions of legitimacy, autonomy, and freedom that the duellist asks of society turn out to be troublingly modern. The duellist is now a persecuted hero who speaks eloquently to and for his contemporary age. Again, writers engage in a literary dialogue with their counterparts from the past. Hitherto the object of moral revulsion or satire, the duel can now serve as the vehicle for psychological or social considerations.

The story then is that of the inexorable embourgeoisement of the duel. When fought with pistols fired by principals drawn from the middle classes, the duel is more likely to take the form of a bloodless affectation. The Italian historian Jacopo Gelli could observe in 1899 that duels fought by pistol were generally little more than a "grotesque comedy" (commedia grotesca).[16] Nevertheless, as the duel's protagonists become more bourgeois, so its causes become more patriotic. In the 1870s, literary texts testify for the first time to duels that are contested on nationalistic grounds. True, Casanova declared himself a valorous Venetian as he duelled with a Pole, but that identification was secondary to an initial contretemps provoked, unsurprisingly, by a lady. Smollett's characters use the duel as a vehicle to vindicate national honor, but, likewise, their combats, while colored by sentiments particular to their nations, are initiated in private discord. It is from 1815 onward, when sporadic "Waterloo duels" were contested between French and British combatants, that private, individual reprisals appear to have served as an informal means of winning back national pride.[17] A nation might be appraised by the way its men conducted their duels. This approach, more common in the later nineteenth century, places duels at the service of an anthropological inquiry, reducing them to an epiphenomenon of wider mentalities, so no longer does the duel, however troubling and morally ambiguous it might remain, command such attention of itself.

Chapter 5 discusses "Romantic" duels, although they cannot be qualified with this adjective unambiguously. Even as the texts featured here dwell on duels associated with lost or wasted love, they innovate and ironize. Pushkin's *Eugene Onegin* provides perhaps the first detailed inspection of duelling pistols in a poem; Mérimée's story is one of the first accounts in which a duel masks a suicide. Chapter 6 considers the duel under a different light. Smollett is one of the first writers to view the duel as a means rather than an end—we will see this expediency clearly in Thackeray and Dumas and elsewhere throughout the nineteenth century. Anything punctilious, such as a code of honor, is always going to be richly exploitable by cynics and susceptible to parody. Casanova, like Smollett, shows how the duel is instrumental in the construction of the self, for it is, to a great extent, by facing up to an opponent that one gains understanding. These nonchivalric duels turn out, in all the texts just discussed, to provide a transformative experience, moving the protagonists up or down (usually up) the social scale. Just as importantly, the duel brings psychological benefits too. The duellist has in effect to become someone other than the man he was, yet, in so doing, he becomes truer to himself.

In Chapter 7, the continuing vitality of the literary duel even in periods during which the credibility of the duel remained seriously under question and in which the custom was all but defunct comes into focus. Indeed, it is the strange persistence of a convention among people who do not subscribe to it that forms the paradoxical core of a number of these texts. In literary manifestations, the duel has always been made to reveal, under pressure, latent weaknesses, otherwise hidden resentments, and unacknowledged inadequacies. In the stories of Mark Twain and Maupassant, we shall meet, for the first time, an obviously nationalistic element at work in their depiction of duels. Yet, in each case (*A Tramp Abroad*; "A Duel"), the writer proceeds to a more disturbing and equivocal depiction of the duel (*Pudd'nhead Wilson*; "A Coward"). The duel has become a strange compulsion. The attention accordingly falls more and more onto the man who feels the need to fight and initiates the process, rather than his opponent who decides, under duress, to adhere to the codes of honor. These figures, in Maupassant, Conrad, and Schnitzler, cannot square with themselves their wish or need to duel. They send the reader off on a perplexing journey. The duel seems to have become an inexorable, mechanistic, and autotelic process, independent of rational volition. We witness a progressive isolation of the duellist, as the idea of honor becomes less palpable for him, and the person or persons in whose name he fights recede. Duels do not, however, drop out of literary texts at this point. On the contrary, they become all the more unsettling, the result of some sort of idiopathic disorder. They occur in a haphazard manner, conducted by men who do not believe in the rituals of the *point d'honneur* or in anything for that matter. These latter-day duellists seem to enjoy or to need the process and the excitement it brings, and this, rather than any reward or benefit they anticipate, is the self-contained purpose of the duel. Whereas the earlier nineteenth century tended to polarize the principals, in the interests of some antithetical display, the combatants of the later period are largely seen to be fighting themselves. This had been an inference or deduction to be drawn from many of the earlier texts, as the duellist defies and steels himself (or fails to do so), but, in the accounts of Maupassant, Schnitzler, and Pirandello, the idea is now literalized. Ultimately, the boundaries between self and others collapse under the gaze of these writers.

The duel then not only brings together two lives in conflict, but it permits us to savor a beguiling mixture of politeness and violence, deference and defiance. These and other paradoxes I endeavor to explore further in Chapter 8. Many literary representations of duels leave us trying to decide whether the participants deserve sympathy or warrant ridicule. The line between tragedy and comedy is seen to be dangerously thin. Indeterminacy and irony find expression in a particular sort of vocabulary, used both by and of the duellist. He may disguise his fears or his misgivings under an evasive, sometimes arcane vocabulary that dignifies or downplays the violence of the act. Particularly curious is the term "satisfaction," which duellists solemnly expect and give. Critics of the duel, but also those authors merely amused or intrigued by the practice, do not take this vocabulary for granted, and it helps to shape a sense that the duellist plays by different rules and belongs to an exclusive, even exotic breed apart.

The equivocal response to the duellist is, in the eighteenth and the nineteenth centuries, a subset of wider doubts about the merits of chivalry, a set of values and assumptions often considered laughable yet admirable at once. The popularity of the duel is attributable by certain authors to changes in the conduct of warfare, which leave the duelling field as the last arena for hand-to-hand combat. The extent to which the duel offers an analogue to war, or a contrast to it, provides a recurrent question, as does the duellist's relationship to women. In the texts under consideration, duels generously fought on behalf of women often enforce female passivity and, perhaps counterintuitively, reinforce male bonds.

Scores of other texts, in which a duel, incidental to the plot or to the fortunes of the chief characters, occurs, have clamored for attention. That duel in *Nicholas Nickleby* is an especially redundant bout which pits two rather inconsequential, albeit colorful characters against each other. Indeed, the presence of superfluous duels in nineteenth-century novels, exemplifying the profligacy of those who fight them, might have warranted further analysis of itself. As it is, my rationale for the choice of the texts here, from among many others, requires each to be unimaginable without the duel or duels which occur in its pages. It is an indispensable part of the text's economy. By that, I do not mean that a duel is a sine qua non in terms of the work's machinery on the level of narrative. It is, for instance, difficult to imagine *Eugene Onegin* without the duel between Onegin and Lenski, less because it advances the plot or moves the characters into states of mind and places otherwise unattainable to the author than because this encounter and the motivation for it, as well as its consequences, are central to understanding their attitudes to life and to love. Death could have come to the personages discussed here in all sorts of ways imaginable to their fertile authors, but a fatal duel is always accompanied by a unique pathos, its author necessarily raising questions about society and its codes, as well as simply disposing of a principal. Although its outcome may be heavily indebted to chance, a duel never happens to occur. It is always the product of decisions.

I was first surprised then delighted and, at length, almost dismayed by the incidence of so many fictional duels. They constitute a pervasive, persistent phenomenon in European literary culture. I want to look closely at these texts, rather than just using them as a prism. While this book will, I hope, shed some light on the actual practices of duelling, its interest may lie above all in the variety of forms with which writers chose to depict and dramatize duels, with which their texts, or they themselves, were variously deemed responsible for the propagation of duelling or made to assume a burden of responsibility for its abolition.[18]

Duelling has, from the late twentieth century onward, spawned a substantial critical literature, albeit "critical" in our more tepid, academic sense. For the most part, these studies have been sociohistorical in their emphasis, although not averse to drawing on literary sources in order to map the changing fortunes of the duel;[19] others focus on the phenomenon within the parameters of a particular nation or century; still others interrogate the duel as a psychological or social matter.[20] The reasons for the stubborn durability of the phenomenon, the no-less-intriguing causes of its eventual decline and eclipse, the forms of masculinity it promoted, and the national characteristics this propensity exposed have all engaged critics, yet no study to date has offered a detailed consideration of the duel as the recurring subject of novels, plays, and short stories, by turns comic and tragic, absurd and horrific, or, of course, both at once.

As it turned out, it sometimes felt right to talk about, say, peculiarly German or irritatingly French or embarrassingly English predilections, but I have not quite succumbed to the temptation to organize this book along national lines. Many writers discussed here saw themselves self-consciously as votaries of a republic of letters to which European frontiers were porous, if not irrelevant. Besides, duelling was itself a cosmopolitan practice: commentators often deplored the duel as a custom exported by irascible continental neighbors; among duellists themselves, there remained a sense, even in the increasingly patriotic and democratic air of the nineteenth century, that their allegiance to an aristocratic caste mattered at least as much as their own nationality; and, incidentally, after a fatal duel, the survivor would often find that it was a good idea to spend some time abroad. It would therefore be a pity to segment a truly pan-European phenomenon into discrete realms that were often of little or no consequence to the duellists themselves.

By the same token, I cannot claim to be exhaustive or fully impartial in my attentions. Readers are asked to forgive the omission of works written in Spanish and Portuguese, although ever since Cervantes "smiled chivalry away" on the Iberian Peninsula, works featuring duels appear to have been few and far between. This is not, of course, the case with Russian literature. But Irina Reyfman's fine study of the duel in Slavonic culture makes me feel less uneasy about depriving you of a more detailed discussion of those works.[21] If considerable emphasis rests on canonical texts, this is because it was, in part, through these familiar writings, which enjoyed the visibility of landmarks within and beyond their respective cultures, that responses to duelling were shaped. But perhaps some of the dusty, undistinguished works which, a while ago, were written in the utterly vain hope of persuading duellists to stop fighting may be excused a new form of redundancy, now that gentlemen have, finally, refrained from doing so.

CHAPTER ONE

Honored in the Breach

VISITORS to the Hall of Mirrors in Versailles who can resist looking at themselves may make out a series of inscriptions painted up on the vault. Each proclaims a notable achievement of the reign of Louis XIV. One of them carries the words "De l'abolition des duels." Courtiers gazing up at them will, in some cases, have afforded themselves a discreet smile, as they thought of the duels they had just fought. Lesser mortals out in the street also learned of this accomplishment. On the plinth of the equestrian statue of Louis XIV in the Place des Victoires, dedicated in 1686, Parisians were told that duelling had been vanquished. The inscriptions on the bas reliefs of the pedestal commemorate

> The hegemony of France recognized by Spain, 1662;
> The peace of Nijmegen, 1678;
> The crossing of the Rhine, 1672;
> The final conquest of the Franche-Comté, 1674;
> Duels abolished;
> The extirpation of heresy, 1685.[1]

Duelling had long been illegal in almost every European country. But Louis XIV reimpressed the ban in a number of ordonnances. The juxtaposition of martial triumphs and legal measures helped to make the point that the abolition of duels, far from sapping a military ethos by inducing cowardice and effeminacy in the nation at large, was, on the contrary, integral to the power and prestige of the nation. Strikingly, indeed rather ominously, "Les duels abolis" alone bore no date. In fact, there were many dates on which it had already been abolished. The legal proscriptions of duels introduced by Louis XIV were neither the last nor indeed the first attempt to abolish the practice, which would continue throughout the following two centuries to pose a potent challenge not only to royal authority but to reason and good sense.

The chaste historical "fact" is supplemented by laudatory verses inscribed on the statue:

> Pour bannir des duels de l'Empire des Lis,
> En vain nos plus grand Rois ont tout mis en usage:
> Le Ciel au seul Louis réservoit cet ouvrage;
> Il parle, & pour jamais on les voit abolis.

> [To banish duels from the realm of the fleur-de-lis,
> Our greatest Kings in vain did all they could:
> Heaven left this work alone to Louis;
> He speaks, and duelling is abolished for good.]

The verse sounds more definitive still (although possibly not in my translated doggerel). Duels, it sings with lapidary certainty, have been abolished for ever more.

One way of abolishing duels was that of telling everyone, in every form available, that they had been abolished. A poem titled "Le duel aboli," submitted by Bernard de La Monnoye (1641–1728), naturally carried off the first poetry prize ever awarded by the Académie française in 1662 for its celebration of this fait accompli. It seems that this outcome may have been the product of a political calculation, on the part of both poet and jury, wonderful as the poem may have been.[2]

But for all Louis XIV's self-trumpeted victory over the practice of duelling, he had, at best, won a battle; he would not win the war on duelling.[3] Many commentators considered the punishments inflicted on those found guilty of duelling to be unenforceably severe. Even witnesses and providers of arms were officially subject to strict sanctions. Laws that were neither obeyed nor enforced appear to have been integral to the functioning of the state in the ancien régime at all levels.[4] However, once Louis XIV had celebrated the abolition of duels by associating it with his personal prestige, its continuing vitality became a particular source of chagrin. It practically became a crime of lèse-majesté to assert that duels were in fact still going on and to acknowledge thereby that the king's wise ordonnances were not working. The ordonnances, then, succeeded largely in muzzling critics of duelling or at least in rendering awkward their earnest attempts to discuss possible ways of eradicating a practice that had, of course, already been eradicated.

In his *Discours contre les duels*, written toward the end of the seventeenth century, Jean Frain du Tremblay's tiptoeing around this dilemma is clearly visible. He admits that His Majesty's ordonnances are not observed, yet he duly steadies his reader with the assurance that "nothing is rarer these days than such quarrels." Moments later, he blames those responsible for overseeing these laws. They are guilty of failing to appreciate the gravity of the offense when the laws are transgressed, or rather, of course, were they still to be transgressed. "With prudence, the King has then entirely abolished this fierce custom, or this barbarism of fighting duels. But although His Majesty has done everything that the wisest and shrewdest legislator could do in this matter, yet those entrusted with the observation of these measures are perhaps not persuaded of the justice of the measures themselves nor of the enormity of the crime that is duelling."[5] The executive arm of the kingdom, and not its legislative brain, would appear to be at fault, by this reckoning. As the passage shows, it is evidently hazardous, once the official line insists that duelling has been abolished, to suggest further ways of abolishing it. The force of Louis XIV's edict against duels did not prevent them, but it contorted the terms in which the supposedly irreversible achievement could be discussed. Du Tremblay appears to be protesting too much when declaring duels to be "entirely abolished." Yet in both the *Dictionnaire universel*, compiled by Antoine Furetière in 1690, and the officially sanctioned *Dictionnaire de l'Académie* (1694), the same pleonastic adverb surfaces in one of those ostensibly insignificant, arbitrary examples of usage, which nevertheless provides the reader with a subliminal prod: "le Roy a fait des Edits si sévères contre les duels, qu'ils sont entièrement abolis."[6] These dictionaries are interdependent, and this official line runs, as a leitmotiv, through the different texts.

Even comparatively outspoken writers in the eighteenth century, once Louis XIV had died (largely unregretted by them), continued to assert that, against all the evidence, duelling had ceased, entirely. Perhaps they had started to succumb to a mechanism characteristic of absolutist regimes: a spurious "fact" is repeated so often that at length it attains the status of an unquestionable truth. Louis-Sébastien Mercier reported in the *Tableau de Paris* (1781–88) that duelling was no longer in vogue and had all but ceased, again clinging to the official line.[7] These writers maintain that progress has been achieved not on account of legislation but as a result of an imperceptible, gradual change in opinions and sensibilities. However, we can detect a tension between Mercier's wish to observe another facet of daily life in Paris and his eagerness to see off an element that has faded from the tableau he purports to be painting in words. Duels do not exist, he confidently asserts, yet they warrant a chapter in a book that, he claims, is a plain record of the sights seen by his roving eye in the streets of Paris.

"A Barbarous Custom"

Du Tremblay denounced duelling as "this fierce custom, . . . this barbarism." The repeated demonstrative suggests that, however heartfelt his own indignation might be, he is drawing on a settled consensus in alighting on these adjectives. It is an agreed, acknowledged fact. Duelling was repeatedly characterized as "barbarous," not only in the predictable terms of this insistent official line but also in the more imaginative and unrestrained words of contemporary writers. From the Abbé de Saint-Pierre to the *Encyclopédie* to Fielding and Laclos, from Flaubert to Queen Victoria, this is the universally agreed adjective of choice. This term is still being flung in the direction of duellists in the late nineteenth century.[8] Just as duellists drew on a time-honored transnational ethos, so their opponents, otherwise separated by nationality and by age, draw on a similarly long-lasting antiduelling discourse.

Those who use this adjective are implicitly registering the origins of the duel in the Middle Ages. A Greek term for those who are not Greek, the epithet "barbarous" is widened to mean "non-Classical," "medieval," or "gothic."[9] The deployment of this adjective is designed to tell us that the duel belongs, or ought to belong, to the Dark Ages. The emphasis falls more heavily on notions of civilization than on matters of morality. "Barbarous" does not, of itself, mean sinful. Eating meat without using cutlery might be "barbarous," but it is not immoral per se. Duelling is therefore cast as an essentially retrograde, uncivilized custom.

A shift in the terms by which duelling is opposed may be charted. Writing in the seventeenth century, du Tremblay argues that it is the worst of all possible crimes in that the duellist condemns both himself and his opponent to hell. Of course, there remained religiously inspired attacks on duelling in the eighteenth and nineteenth centuries. But even Rev. William Scott, responsible for *The Duellist, a Bravo to God and a Coward to Man; and Therefore, Impossible to Be "A Man of Honour"* (1774), argues, more pragmatically than dogmatically, that soldiers should hold the fire of their courage for those who really deserve it—namely, the enemies of king and country.[10] Nevertheless, this appreciable shift carries us from theological arguments against duelling to philosophical, humane reasoning against the practice. In the eyes of many eighteenth-century critics, the duellist sins not so much against God as against himself. The duel is now to be discredited less as an irreligious outrage than as a medieval anomaly. The choice of the adjective "barbarous," with its emphasis less on immorality than on delinquency, helps to explain the new role with which plays and fictional stories were to be invested. By invoking these criteria when denouncing the duel, moralists and writers invited the duel to become the province of literature. Readers would not only be told that duelling was immoral; they could be shown that duels were barbarous. This is designed to be a more stinging accusation. A duellist might not mind acting lawlessly or irreligiously—some libertines rejoiced at the very thought of doing so—but he could well be hurt by the suggestion that his action was uncivilized, inelegant. This obligatory epithet made it clear that the duel had nothing to do with civilization and, therefore, with France. Yet the word "barbarous," so often encountered here, seems particularly ill suited to describing duellists. Duellists deferred to carefully circumscribed rules. They were not to act rashly or wildly and, in making and meeting an appointment, exhibited a capacity for restraint, courtesy, and self-control. Barbarians, on the contrary, could be defined as people without honor or even the concept of honor.[11]

By branding it "barbarous," critics signaled the duel as a non-Classical monstrosity. Unknown to the Greeks and Romans, it grew up among the tribes that conquered the Roman Empire or its remains. Critics suggested that it remained essentially foreign to civilization. Writers had a common wish to locate the origins of the duel beyond their own borders. The impulse was no doubt forgivably patriotic, but, in disavowing its origins, they also expressed a hope that a custom separable from their national history and destiny might, painlessly enough, be uprooted. It was, however, unanimously agreed that the duel was a medieval vestige, a tributary of that vast current of gallant literature and chivalric effusion which swept France from the thirteenth century onward. The duel provided a residual but essential expression of the chivalric spirit. In the course of the eighteenth century, critics prefer to prick the duellist in a different spot. The duel, they argue, had no precedent or equivalent in the Classical world. It cannot, therefore, be essential to a definition of honor or integral to an idea of civilization, both of which manifestly prospered in Antiquity. Particularly as neoclassicism took hold, and noblemen not only validated themselves by going to Rome and to the sites of the ancient world but drew their moral and aesthetic ideals from these civilizations, the absence of duelling in Classical times became all the more conspicuous.[12] This observation was advanced by numerous writers, as they laid out their arguments against duelling.[13] "The ancient Romans would scold and call names filthily yet there is not an example of a challenge that ever passed among them."[14] Even Dr. Harrison, the good Anglican churchman in Fielding's last novel, *Amelia* (1751), draws on the Classical reference point to face down Colonel Bath, when, inevitably, they discuss duelling: "What were all the Greeks and Romans?—were these cowards?—and yet, did you ever hear of this butchery, which we call duelling, among them?"[15] The murkily medieval origins of the duel therefore discredited it. It may come as a surprise to see the fervor with which this argument is adduced as a compelling reason for opposition to the duel. Fougeroux de Campigneulles, one of the more moderate, informed critics of duelling, felt the need to go further. The Classical world, he maintained, obviously did not fight duels. But what is more, the Ancients could not even begin to suspect or imagine that duels might possibly exist.[16]

As the eighteenth century advanced, another term enlisted in the battle against duelling is strikingly recurrent. The custom of duelling was not vilified as a "habit" or castigated as a "crime"; it was a *fureur*. This term implied, optimistically, that it might be a passing phenomenon, a fashion. We might say that duelling was all the rage. Each of these terms, *barbare* and *fureur*, were designed to expose duellists as irrational hotheads unbridled bucks out of control. Yet neither of the terms seems quite right. In fact, they each seem well wide of the mark. The duellist prided himself on not acting impulsively, on meeting his opponent on level terms, at a prearranged time and place. He was scrupulous about the courtesies preliminary and indeed subsequent to the duel itself. Neither rage nor pique were to be displayed or, ideally, to be harbored at any point. The protocols of the duel had been settled precisely in order to distinguish its exponents from people in thrall to their rage, such as barbarians.[17]

It became permissible to show gentlemen who were less than completely impious drawn into fighting duels.[18] While victorious or surviving duellists could be vilified as murderers, the losers too would stand accused of throwing their lives away, much as suicides did. But attitudes to suicide relaxed in the course of the eighteenth century, to the extent that this very term began to circulate, in preference to the more morally strident "self-murder" or "self-slaughter," English versions of the infamous felo-de-se. The German Enlightenment popularized a word, *Freitod*, that seemed to advertise suicide as a potentially virtuous or courageous decision, as opposed to *Selbstmord*. As religiously motivated or inspired arguments began to lose some of their force, so the responsibility for showing instead the distress inflicted by and on the duellist mounted. And these circumstances, imagined and exemplified, fall more into the province of the arts. From the late seventeenth century onward, increasingly, in common with suicide, duelling is seen as a medical problem, with scientific explanations replacing those based on morality and religion. The intervention of state and church into the relationships of people began to be resented and resisted.[19] Responses to both the predicament and the punishment of those guilty of duelling appear to run on parallel lines.

The fiats from on high, expressed in edicts sanctioned by the highest authorities, were now succeeded by arguments appealing more to a sympathetic or imaginative intelligence—hence the increasingly prominent role of the duellist in novels and in plays. "The stage will compleat what religion began," observes a French critic visiting England, noting that "no opportunity is there neglected to turn duels into ridicule, and make those who fight them appear contemptible."[20]

Such responses to duelling testify to the increasing need in the eighteenth century to see and to feel for oneself that matters might be awry, although there remained many discursive texts deploring duels on rational grounds.

In fact, far from echoing those who had condemned the duel as an affront to the church, a violation of one of the Commandments (for the duellist betrayed a willingness to commit a murder), and an arrogant wish to risk and take lives that were the gift of God, it was now sometimes emphasized, conversely, that the duellist was in fact heir to biblical combatants. When Cain called out Abel, the brothers thereby became the original protoduellists (although David and Goliath also had this honor bestowed on them).[21] Far from showing freedom from and disdain for religious mores, the modern duellist was deferring to ancient, biblical precedent. Indeed, the continued penchant for duelling could be denounced as a variant form of fanaticism: "There is a warlike fanaticism [fanatisme guerrier] just as there is an ecclesiastical fanaticism [fanatisme ecclésiastique]. While the latter relies, against all the evidence, on spirit, the former pits honor against the most convincing reasoning."[22] The weaponry of the Enlightenment was being turned onto the duellist from a new front. As the sun set on the reign of Louis XIV, there was, at last, more candor about the continued extent of duelling. In July 1715, as Louis XIV lay on his deathbed, the first, most forthright and original of many petitions flowed from the pen of the Abbé de Saint-Pierre.

Abbé de Saint-Pierre

Undaunted by the most intractable difficulties jeopardizing the stability of early eighteenth-century society, the abbé de Saint-Pierre (1658–1743) was, and remains, best known for publishing a project for perpetual peace in Europe, in 1713, at the close of the War of the Spanish Succession. It caught the attention of the *philosophes* and earned him a reputation as a morally sound, if fanciful, utopian thinker. But he turned also to subsidiary questions, no less knotty in their own way but perhaps soluble on a smaller scale. After sorting out world peace, he launched into a project to improve and standardize the spelling of European languages. It should come as no surprise that he turned his

attentions in due course to the no-less-recalcitrant scourge that was duelling. The abbé was honest and uninhibited about the resurgence of
the duel during recent wars. Silently doing as much damage as ever, it
is—here is that adjective—"a barbarous custom reviled by nature."[23]
He is one of the few undeceived writers to have observed an "illness"
afflicting Europe and France in particular. Indeed, the image of the duel
as an illness or epidemic allows for the possibility that its perpetrators
are also its victims—duellists were not simply arrogant aristocrats disdainful of the laws but pitiable, ailing figures unable to change their
behavior. In French dictionaries of the period, "DUELLISTE" designates
a man given to fighting duels, habitually, compulsively—or at least to
talking about them frequently. "He who professes to fighting duels
often."[24] Unusually, the abbé brings to his *Mémoire* a semblance of insight into the predicament of the man challenged to a duel. Such compassion had been largely absent from previous treatises. The term
maladie did have jurisdiction in figurative senses, beyond physical
illnesses and infirmities.[25] Nevertheless, the abbé de Saint-Pierre is
one of the first writers to pathologize the duellist.

The duellist is denigrated in these texts to the point where exculpatory pity may be felt for him. It turns out that he is fundamentally
powerless, however courageous he may seem, a victim of his character
and his passions. The duel may exemplify an action to which an agent
feels committed without the consent of his will. This is not a response
only to the dictate of honor or to the force of custom and opinion but
answers a more mysterious and profound inner compulsion. Gentlemen
continued to be compelled by honor to fight; but a sense of the stubborn sovereignty and might of honor, or noblesse oblige (enforced by
monarchies), makes way for two different sorts of obligation. First, duellists are seen to be compelled to fight by the promptings of some
congenital insistence. Particularly in the later eighteenth century, we
see young men recycling the errors of their fathers in a vicious circle.
Likewise, the duellist, absurdly and hopelessly, exemplifies the absolutely inexorable mechanistic nature of the codes governing the conduct of duels, rules that brook no possible deviations or exceptions. The
duellist may go to his death, proud neither of his valor nor of his independence but desperately conscious that those rules have acquired a
life of their own.

Equally, in keeping with the temper of a century in which the principal arguments and primary considerations are no longer deontological (the duel often results in murder; it is plain wrong; and the church says so), the abbé appeals to a pragmatic form of reasoning, centered on the numbers of soldiers lost to the custom. Assuming that an officer is worth ten men, he estimates that about four thousand brave soldiers are lost to death, while the same number flee into exile. He invokes a criterion that begins to be heard for the first time in the eighteenth century: "the emergence of 'population' as an economic and political problem."[26] Indeed, such was the concern for the dwindling numbers, whether they were perceived to be down to forced marriages, monasteries, or wars, that Maurice de Saxe followed up his reflections on the art of warfare with a compensatory set of *Réflexions sur la propagation de l'espèce humaine.*[27]

Like his contemporary Fénelon, Saint-Pierre realized that it might be useful to allow men who needed to serve in wars to fight during peacetime and that it would be fanciful simply to ask men to cease to be belligerent at such moments. Duelling offered an outlet. Fénelon, for his part, thought of a solution that obviated any need for duelling. In a remote reserve full of wild animals, men would be able to slake a natural thirst for violence.[28]

The abbé proposed various measures to curb, or at least to reduce, the incidence of duels. He recommended the removal of swords from daily dress. But he realized that the nobility would be loath to lose this marker of their status. To this end, he proposed that, instead of wearing a sword, an aristocrat could have embroidered in silver letters the name of his military allegiance or, failing any military connections, the abbreviation "NOB."[29] He argued that it was imperative to make attempts, beyond the legislative measures hitherto, to tackle this custom. The very terms of his grievance provide a hint as to his modus operandi. Duelling was, he maintained in less morally stringent terms than his predecessors, a *custom*. Customs began to be rehabilitated in the eighteenth century, thanks largely to the typically unstinting efforts of Rousseau. Jean-Jacques was perhaps inspired by the work of the abbé when, in *Du contrat social,* he emphasizes the indifference, indeed the resistance, of customs to laws.[30] Rooted in our social lives, customs are not easily amenable to legislation. Plays seen by the public and novels read by those who nourished that capricious "queen known as public opinion" therefore had a role to play in adjusting social mores and practices. The abbé anticipates Rousseau in indicating that philosophical or discursive argument of itself would hardly be sufficient to effect a transformation in mentalities rooted in customs, for, as Rousseau wrote, "customs form the morality of the people."[31] It would then be desirable to devise or at least encourage different customs, rather than simply making the laws ever more severe.

In the *Mémoire*, the abbé accordingly addresses a number of points designed to show duelling as risible, rather than simply reiterating that it was illegal. He recommended that those found guilty of duelling should appear in public, sporting "bizarre" clothes. Identifying Pierre Corneille's *Le Cid* as the foremost challenge, he recommended, in another measure, that every year a prize should be awarded to the author of the best parody of this masterpiece. It would continue to dominate eighteenth-century thinking about the duel and its manifestations on stage and page alike. Vexed, but not surprised, by the continuing failure of the law to stop duelling, Rousseau remarked that the same people who attended the execution of a duellist would nonetheless still applaud the Cid onstage.[32]

Corneille, *Le Cid* (1637)

Corneille's tragicomedy, based on a Spanish play by Guillén de Castro, became the great popular success not only of his lifetime but of the century, while it provoked a long-lasting argument about dramatic practice, known as the *Querelle du Cid*. Writing *Le Cid*, Corneille robed in the impeccable pleats of a stylish French mantle an essentially gothic story, turning a legend set in medieval Spain into a work more conformable to Classical ideas and tastes. Ever since the advent of *Don Quixote*, Spain could be regarded as a nursery of nonheroic, comical subjects. For, as Byron later observed, "A single laugh demolished the right arm / Of his own country;—seldom since that day / Has Spain had heroes."[33] *Don Quixote* had evidently done its work. Spain was thought to be the country where the fewest duels were fought. Corneille, however, recalls a Spanish hero from pre-Quixotic times, only he is endowed with the qualities of a rational man, and the nobility and courage of the duellists in *Le Cid*, condoned (but not approved of) by the monarch at whose court they fight, allow the play to be seen potentially as an implicit apology for the practice.

Two duels, each eminently rational, as prosecuted and justified by different characters, are at the heart of this play. Rodrigo finds himself having to avenge his father's honor. The Count, Chimène's father, has been passed over for the post of Governor of the Prince of Castille. Don Diego, Rodrigo's father, has instead acquired this position. The Count, having suggested that his rival has not earned the position on merit, gives Don Diego the "soufflet," or slap, the preliminary to an inevitable duel. The cause of this duel is timeless: a slight, an affront to honor. If the duel is a medieval vestige, then the cause here is not quintessentially medieval or even residually chivalric. This is an argument about promotion and merit. These recriminations over administrative capabilities and prospects seem more pertinent to the modern world than does gallantry on behalf of a damsel in distress.

Indeed, the deliberations about the freedom to duel suggest that the play is located on the borders between a feudal and an absolute monarchy. While it is apparent that Rodrigo can hardly refuse his father's command without incurring disgrace, the Count, for his part, could and should give verbal satisfaction by an apology. He knows that duelling is illegal, but it is also implied that the ban—part of the king's move toward an absolutist stance—is recent and hence is not established. Animated by feudal convictions, he sees honor and glory as greater stimuli than service to the king.[34] He agrees to fight, reassuring himself with the sort of familiar French sentiment that has since echoed in picket line and lecture hall alike: "Désobéir un peu n'est pas un grand crime" (It's not such a crime somewhat to disobey).[35]

Don Diego, for his part, sees the duel equivocally. With the first of many elegant oxymorons, he speaks of the "glorious crime" that he has authorized. The duel occurs, offstage, in accordance with Classical conventions. But before long, Rodrigo appears at Chimène's house carrying the sword that his father had solemnly transferred to him, still dripping with her own father's blood, a tangible trophy of his triumph offstage. In another of those beautifully tensed oxymorons in this play, Rodrigo announces that henceforward he goes "then to drag out a dying life" (une mourante vie). But, in the acrimonious exchanges that follow, tellingly, Rodrigo and Chimène use each other's names frequently, a countervailing sign perhaps of their enduring intimacy, and indeed they confess their love for each other.[36]

We witness a familiar collision of duty and love, a staple of tragic conflict (seen in no less brilliant a light in Corneille's *Horace*, for instance), but here his duty to the state as a soldier comes into conflict less with his love for Chimène than with his duty as a son. Meanwhile, the Moors are menacing Seville. Their presence in the background to the duel and to the central conflict between the two families does not provide incidental color. Dying in battle offers a convenient way out of emotional or moral impasses, an early modern form of euthanasia, while combat against Moors provides the possibility of a specifically Christian salvation. Even a defeat of the English would not have quite the same expiatory value. This dimension allows Corneille to broach criteria sometimes considered by those who preferred to condemn the duel on pragmatic grounds. Duellists, whether those who died or the victors who fled into exile, were expending energies otherwise usefully employed in combat against the nation's enemies. In due course, we learn that Rodrigo has been valorous and victorious in battle against the Moors. This spectacular victory and the rich extravagance of the terms in which both Rodrigo's prowess and the Moors' catastrophic failure are celebrated prepare us for a particularly poignant detail. It is a nice irony (the product of an adjustment which Corneille made to previous stories of the Cid's heroics) that, having rushed into war, in order to spill expiatory blood after slaying Chimène's father, Rodrigo does not kill the Moorish kings; he takes them alive.[37]

The Infanta decrees that "the good of the country" and, invoking a surprisingly modern-sounding criterion, the interests of the "public" mean that the life of this duellist should be spared. Duels turn out to have been a good training ground for warfare. Indeed, war, as waged and then recounted by Rodrigo, is essentially an aggregate of individual duels or, as Conrad will later put it, a form of "gregarious duelling."[38]

Given that the war with the Moors is a composite of single combats, it would seem that the duellist's skill and valor would be serviceable attributes in battle. The king knows of Rodrigo's supremacy both in duels and on the battlefield. And his prowess in each of these discrete forms of combat is no coincidence. These are compatible skills or, as we might, elegantly, put it these days, transferrable competences. The king does not want to consent to another duel, because he fears losing Rodrigo to this risky business (or "sort capricieux").[39] It is, however, because he can duel so formidably that Rodrigo is useful in battle. The king's hesitation reveals, as indeed does that of Chimène, the intrinsically equivocal character of the duel. It requires and rewards courage and strength, recommending the victor, yet its outcomes also seem to be determined by blind chance. On the one hand, the duel debilitates the state, by depriving it of soldiers, yet, on the other hand, the duel seems also to strengthen it, by fortifying those soldiers who survive.

Chimène now appeals to the king's justice: Rodrigo should be put judicially to death. When he refuses, she asserts her right to name a champion, whom she agrees to marry in recompense, an "old custom" that appeals to feudal honor rather than to royal justice. In order to avenge her father, whoever will challenge Rodrigo to another duel and defeat him will earn her hand in marriage. The king pauses to regret, pragmatically, without the obligatory indignation, that the custom may weaken the state in this case. A nobleman by the name of Don Sanche boldly steps forward and offers to fight Rodrigo. The opening line of his speech is promisingly nerveless, but the bold self-assertion of the verse that follows is somewhat less auspicious:

> Faites ouvrir le camp, vous voyez l'assaillant,
> Je suis ce téméraire, ou plutôt ce vaillant.[40]

> [Prepare the field, here stands the challenger,
> I am that bold or, rather, brave man.]

Fighting "téméraires," or unduly bold figures, usually come to grief. Don Sanche's self-correction comes too late to efface the suspicion that he was probably right the first time. The successive nouns testify to a certain hesitation concerning the respective value of knowledge (or "science") and courage, when undertaking a duel.

The duel now takes place, offstage of course. A second sword, likewise "dripping with blood," is now brought onto the stage by Don Sanche, to Chimène's renewed chagrin. It would seem that the blood of Rodrigo has been spilled on it. Happily, it turns out that Rodrigo is safe, and the play can proceed to a secure resolution. Nevertheless, *Le*

Cid raises unsettling questions about the form and the scope of the duel. At the heart of the play are divergent understandings of its purpose and possibilities, for Chimène feels that her father's death needs to be avenged, whereas Rodrigo, more conventionally, is content to feel that honor has been satisfied.[41] Numerous subsequent authors implicitly ask a simple, related question: When is a duel over? Clarissa, perhaps like Chimène, sees the prospect of an endless chain of reprisals, while Kleist provides a more literal complicating twist in response. Rousseau's *Julie*, meanwhile, will suggest that the effects of a duel can reverberate both widely and indefinitely beyond the death of a principal.

For now, Corneille's audience (and, unfortunately, his censors) could not fail to be aware that a play set in medieval Spain contained a contemporary analogue. Duelling was outlawed, its exponents pursued and brought to justice with unprecedented rigor by Cardinal Richelieu in these very years, a campaign resentfully remembered or imagined in the literary works of subsequent ages. Richelieu (who had lost an elder brother to a duel) made it known that he did not approve of this play, which could be seen as an apology for aristocratic attributes. *Le Cid* became a battleground between a noble ethic and the bourgeois values evidently promoted by Louis XIV.[42]

Such is the tension between aristocratic formality and raw violence embodied by the duel that it mirrors and magnifies the forces at work in French tragedy. The artifices governing the procedures of the duel—the interval between challenge and act, word and deed, the formality and the polite regard of the antagonists for each other, and the characteristics it imposes on the combatants, such as a heightened, lucid awareness of the unforgiving nature of the process—all these aspects fictionalize the duel and risk turning it into a spectacle, a constructed work of art, a "game of death." Thanks to the deliberate, inexorable form of the duel, the grandeur and nobility of the protagonists, the duellist may plausibly be tempted to feel that he is an actor or, worse still, a character in a miniature tragedy. This feeling may protect him from an otherwise potentially bitter, bleak awareness of the brutality and horror of an unnecessary yet obligatory event. The formalization of violence, indispensable to the duel and integral to so many tragedies, aligns duel and the tragedy as neighboring pursuits. Duels channeled and ennobled violence, as tragedies provided a purgative outlet for its horrors. Indeed, it was suggested that, because visible violence on the French Classical stage was proscribed, by contrast with practices then current and popular in British theaters, aggressive impulses could not be gratified or sublimated anywhere other than in the self-staged spectacle of the duel. Theorists such as the abbé Batteux, who had reinforced these conventions and turned them into prescriptions, were then partially responsible for the abiding popularity of duelling across France, where "duellomanes" in effect staged themselves.

Duelling was not a pursuit that could be accounted regrettably timeless or lamentably intrinsic to the human condition. It was all the more dispensable and contemptible as a result. But in the teeth of these arguments, Corneille's masterpiece had made the duel more classically plausible and respectable. Indeed, both his previous play (*Médée*, 1635) and his subsequent play (*Horace*, 1640) were located in ancient settings. *Le Cid*, like these tragedies, broadly followed the rules recommended or prescribed by seventeenth-century French theorists, drawing on Italian Renaissance reconstructions of Greek practice. Like Classical tragedy itself, the duel obeyed a set of internally consistent, preestablished rules. Each set or system of rules was therefore, aesthetically at least, sympathetic to the other. Furthermore, the characters depicted conform to Classical notions of idealized, forceful archetypes, devoid of particularized attributes. And they are certainly not "barbares" or, as they weigh their alexandrines, given to "fureur."

The abbé de Saint-Pierre sensed that, as long as *Le Cid* continued to cast its long shadow over the endeavors of French playwrights, duelling would necessarily remain a troubling phenomenon. Rodrigo was a paragon of heroic valor. The Abbé calculated that, in order to quell or merely limit duelling, it was urgently necessary to contend with this play, first performed some eighty years earlier. It is safe to say that subsequent duellists in France were conscious of the duels in Corneille's masterpiece, for the simple reason that *Le Cid* was, over centuries, the most famous play in France. The thrill of its armed combats, the cool lucidity of its protagonists recommended the play to a wide range of constituencies. A century or so later, *Le Cid* reportedly remained popular even among soldiers and mathematicians.[43]

CHAPTER TWO

The Comical Duel

THE Abbé de Saint-Pierre's proposal met with no success. Indeed, years after his death, the authorities were still exercised by the sort of questions that he had raised. The Académie française, for instance, proposed an essay title in 1753 that took the form of the following question: *Is ridicule a corrective or an inhibitive force?* An aversion to ridicule as improper and undignified remained in place. A suspicion of the nature and the value of ridicule could be dated to at least the seventeenth century, when it was not sanctioned by the prestigious academies, and Boileau, notably in his *Art poétique,* expressed disappointment that the great Molière, whom he otherwise so admired, had stooped to showing farcical characters onstage.[1] As La Rochefoucauld put it in a characteristically tight maxim, "ridicule dishonors more than dishonor itself."[2] For the likes of Boileau, however, it unfortunately dishonored the author of the ridicule as well as its object. Not only derision but laughter itself could be considered undignified, even vulgar, and it was, in all seriousness of course, that Lord Chesterfield warned his son against laughter, while assuring him that "nobody has ever heard me laugh."[3]

Later in the eighteenth century, Rousseau argued that, of all forms, comedy was especially normative and cruelly effective in persuading people to conform to agreed norms of behavior. Long before the contrivance of canned laughter, Rousseau understood how, contagiously begetting more laughter, comedy was able to induce people to laugh not at what was actually wrong but at what was merely abnormal. The derision of bourgeois audiences leveled at aristocratic behavior onstage was, as Saint-Preux comments in *Julie,* but a transitory response, before they went on to adopt the mores they had mocked. Thus Molière managed to "correct" the court but only by "infecting" the town.[4] The gratification of bourgeois audiences by making them laugh at the practices of the nobility was, in Rousseau's eyes, counterproductive.

Rousseau's stance was, as usual, exceptional though. *Castigat ridendo mores*, a phrase attributed to Jean de Santeul (1630–97), applied across the board. Indeed, in the ongoing struggle against the duel, particularly cogent reasons commended ridicule as the most appropriate form of attack. It was clear that the most draconian tariffs, including capital punishment, were unlikely to work on a duellist who, by definition, was prepared, if not willing, to run the risk of premature, violent death.

Deterring the Duellist

When he visited Valetta in the 1760s, Patrick Brydone found that conversations frequently turned to the fate of a gentleman currently languishing in a dungeon. This unfortunate man had already completed the first part of his sentence—the paying of *amende honorable* in St. John's church for forty-five successive days—and after being confined to a dungeon without light for five years, he would remain a prisoner in the castle for life. Yet this "poor wretch" was not a gentleman who had fought a duel but a man who, "after an argument by a billiard table," had refused to do so. As Brydone learned, uniquely in Malta, not only were duels permitted by law, but a refusal to fight one was punished by it. Custom and law, then, combined both to entitle and to enjoin gentlemen to duel. People on the island of Malta were, as a result, exceedingly polite. As Brydone evidently appreciated, they were "very exact and circumspect, both with regard to their words and actions." The effects of these measures also prompted him to think more widely about the wisdom of penal legislation elsewhere, leading him to conclude that "the punishment for fighting ought never to be a capital one, (but rather something ignominious) and the punishment for not fighting should always be so, or at least some severe corporal punishment; for ignominy will have as little effect on the person who is willing to submit to the appellation of a coward, as the fear of death on one who makes it his glory to despise it."[5]

The punishment should then fit the crime, not by meeting it with a retributive *contrappasso* but by exposing the motivation or stimulus that lay behind the willingness or refusal to duel. The duellist, acutely aware of his social standing and just as careless of death, needed to be deterred by ridicule. This idea echoes in the prefaces of earnestly comic authors and well-intentioned moralists. It is perhaps Brydone of whom the anonymous author of *The Duellist* (published in 1822) is thinking, when he avers, in a similarly neat formulation, that "ridicule would perhaps be the best weapon to correct this mania, for those who fight through the dread of being laughed at, may be induced to avoid it from fear of the same impending punishment."[6]

Alternatively, the sentiment may be inspired by an even sharper aphorism chiseled by Joseph Addison in one of his essays, earlier in the eighteenth century: "Death is not sufficient to deter men who make it their glory to despise it."[7] But if death itself, seemingly the ultimate sanction, were insufficient, what could possibly act as a more potent deterrent? Writing in *The Tatler*, a Mr. Sage suggests that duellists should, after a first offense, ride the wooden horse in the tilt yard; for a second, stand in the pillory; and, in the case of a third transgression, be sent for life to Bedlam.[8]

By the nineteenth century, the grim prestige with which certain noble victims of the guillotine were invested suggested to certain writers that it was now sufficient to be subjected to capital punishment in order to qualify, by association, as a de facto aristocrat. The scaffold "qui fait tomber la tête . . . fait surgir le nom."[9] As heads rolled, reputations rose. A duellist who endured this fate would be adding luster to his reputation for honor and bravery. An Italian lawyer exercised by the scourge of duelling, Vincenzo Marcucci, was concerned that sending a duellist onto the scaffold, where he would be the passive victim of the executioner, could only increase his renown. He who had respected his opponent in a fair contest now found an anonymous, implacable foe, against whom he had no possible chance. This perhaps seemed unjust or, at the very least, inelegant. Accordingly, Marcucci devised a project, by his own admission, a rather extravagant and unusual plan, whereby two gentlemen condemned for fighting a duel would instead fight each other, in the town square, to the death. This would afford a distinctly more edifying, less pathetic example in which viewers would withhold pity at the sight of a powerless victim and see for themselves the horrors of the duel.[10]

Marcucci strikes an unusually serious note, among numerous outlandish proposals for antiduelling legislation in the literature of the period. In the absence of effectual laws, there emerges a sort of sub-genre, consisting of ever more ingenious, facetious suggestions, the joyous impracticality of which betrays a respect for the spirit of the duel.[11]

Duel and Ridicule

Noblemen with a propensity to duelling were not easily embarrassed by the exposure of their conduct as illegal or immoral. But ridicule was a response they both understood and feared. Duelling did not gener-ally suffer the scrutiny of reason for very long before it looked like an indefensible, hare-brained idea. But gentlemen were not particularly in-terested in the promptings and pleas of reason. That is an essentially bourgeois scruple, rather like spelling correctly or counting one's money. The best-known philosophers who disliked duelling in the name of reason were not themselves from the nobility: Joseph Addison and Richard Steele, Voltaire, Rousseau, Diderot, and (in breeding, if not by birth) d'Alembert. It was all too easy for them to condemn that which their social status would not allow them anyway. Eighteenth-century crusaders against the duel met with little or no opposition on their own philosophical terrain. With few exceptions, no writer seri-ously proffered an argument in favor of duelling or even an apology for the practice. There was perhaps a possibility that the daylight of reason might expose the essentially irrational nature of other traditions and privileges on which aristocratic authority rested. On the contrary, it was the irrational, incomprehensible, and inexplicable nature of the duel that recommended it, as an aristocratic spectacle for uncompre-hending bourgeois—the chief constituents in the theaters where these comedies took place. The fact that duelling, on the terms of any cost-benefit analysis, looked otiose was its virtue. It exhibited, if nothing else, a splendid indifference to cost-benefit analysis.

The very gratuitousness of the duel that rendered it risible also made it admirable. Perhaps it was comically inexplicable, stupidly reckless, but those same facets could make the duel look innocent and pure, be-cause it was fundamentally disinterested: the duellist was, usually, not tainted by self-interest or darkened by the shadows of calculation.

These questions were (in common with many other vexing inquiries about the role and responsibilities of literature) provoked by Don Quixote, when the motivation for his actions, or antics, was broached and gently interrogated by Sancho Panza. Whereas other knights and lovers had once fallen into fury and madness, on account of unrequited love or some such cause, he seemed to be doing it for no reason whatsoever. However, since the Don does not recognize the impeachment as such, he sees no need to deny it. On the contrary, he explains, "a knight-errant who runs mad upon a just occasion deserves no thanks; but to do so without reason is the business, giving my lady to understand what I should perform in the wet, if I do this in the dry."[12] Don Quixote's dry run may have been provisional, but there remains a distinct sense that it is ennobled by not enjoying the sanction of immediate interests. There is no negative reason for the Don's love of chivalry—he has not been fired from a job or rebuffed by anyone, nor does he fear being thought a coward. He feels obliged to answer a call to quest and to combat, out of the pure love of chivalry. The duels that result are not instrumentalized but represent duelling for the sake of duelling.

In the ancien régime, the more gratuitous the duel, the more irrational, hence the more aristocratic it will appear, for recklessness could be misconstrued as a proof of valor, folly a sign of class, and wanton self-destructiveness a bizarre token of largesse. But when no aristocracy remained or had ever existed (such were the respective conditions in postrevolutionary France and in America, which so intrigued Tocqueville), the abidingly gratuitous nature of the duel can henceforward only be an index to some profound absurdity. Since there is no good reason for such duels in the first place, there is, by the same token, no good reason for them to stop. The more inconsequential its causes, the more durable the feud, nourished, as it is, by self-perpetuating hostilities. Accordingly, attempts to ridicule the duel tend to succeed only in dignifying it, by ridiculing less the practice of the duel itself than protagonists manifestly unworthy of it or, as it often turns out, incapable of going through with it. Ridicule ends up enhancing a practice that defies and transcends comprehension. A ridiculous duel may well serve only to validate those duels that are not.

Moreover, as Casanova observed, in an aphoristic aside embedded in his memoirs, "We rid ourselves more easily of our vices than of our ridiculous traits."[13] His maxims and aphorisms are often particularly well turned. Writing these memoirs, he was no doubt mindful of Rousseau's unprecedented candor in his *Confessions*. It was unusual in reckoning shame at the ridiculous, rather than the immoral, moments in one's life to be the most potent and intractable force, yet such was Rousseau's avowal early on in his account: "It's not that which is criminal that is hardest to talk about; it's that which is ridiculous and shameful."[14]

Counterintuitively for the purposes of the reforming satirist, duels, when shown to be ridiculous, are often seen to stem from an incorrigible habit or compulsion. The duellist, we have seen, has a congenital compulsion to fight. In showing this to be ridiculous, its immutable character is merely reinforced. Moreover, there is something curiously affirmative, even bizarrely life enhancing, about these inveterate duelling addicts, probably because they love duels more than they hate the men they meet in them. It is tempting to try to assign all works in which comical duels take place to one of two categories:

Genus A: In which either or each of the combatants (or, in fact, merely would-be duellists) is ridiculous, because they are not sufficiently valorous or, often by way of explanation, aristocratic.

Genus B: In which we see a ridiculous custom, which impairs and wastes the lives of otherwise decent, serious individuals.

Type A consists of works that mock the pretensions of the duellist, while B embraces those in which the duel itself is the object of mockery. It is possible, but rare, to encounter A and B at once. Duelling may be considered, from a rational point of view, a ridiculous practice. From the bourgeois perspective, it is obviously an expensive one—honor is not worth the price of one's life. But the parvenu or the coward, whose failure to fight properly, or indeed at all, merely validates the duel as the preserve of men of quality and distinction. Condemned in general, particular encounters could nevertheless be tolerated and enjoyed.

Discussions of duels in particular attract stories of aristocratic nonchalance. Unflappable insouciance is a particular stock-in-trade of the aristocrat in the face of death, hence the interest commanded by the collected wit and wisdom of those speaking at the scaffold or under the blade of the guillotine. Sainte-Beuve's supposed appearance at a duel with an umbrella, lest he should catch a cold, shows the nineteenth-century author preserving that noble tradition. The duel provides the true gentleman with a splendid opportunity to show off his irrepressible sense of humor. These duellists only harmed their own or themselves. This seemed irrefutable, until, in part thanks to Rousseau's emphasis on collateral damage to family, new criteria came into play in the course of the eighteenth century.

So the duellist actually prides himself on conduct that might be perceived to be aristocratic or ridiculous, insofar as this denotes a resistance to the norms of common sense and reason. Derisive detractors of the duel only play into the hands of those whom they think they are mocking. For duellists and their apologists, the accusation that conduct might be "ridiculous" merely betrays a failure to understand notions of honor. The duel is the privileged expression of the practices of a caste, insulated from the opinions and tastes of other classes. So their disapproval only seems to validate and protect its worth, rather than chasten its devotees. The duel detaches the aristocrat from other spheres and provides a confirmation of their essential difference in motivation and conduct.

Accordingly, the absurdity of so many duels is widely acknowledged, but not with embarrassment or shame. On the contrary, its absurdity may, on occasion, be vaunted by the principals themselves. A particularly dependable fount of proud absurdities, Sir Lucius, in Sheridan's *The Rivals*, maintains as he organizes a duel for which there is no obvious just cause, "The quarrel is a very pretty quarrel as it stands— we should only spoil it, by trying to explain it."[15] Indeed, duellists are seen to thrive on and exult in that absurdity, which keeps it out of the reach of bourgeois common sense. A duel is its own justification. A demand for an explanation constitutes an affront to or indignity for an aristocrat. Ridicule of the nobleman is therefore flattering to him. It constitutes a certificate of acceptance, if not resignation, when faced by unaccountable conduct. Ridicule is the response when society and its custodians are faced by people who do not need to be called to account.

Unlike some of Molière's monomaniacs, ridiculous, duel-obsessed characters, such as Sir Lucius, are saturated with self-consciousness.

They are not obsessed to the point that they cannot see their own obsession; on the contrary, it is the nature of their idée fixe that it requires them to talk about it, with lucidity, ad nauseam, often with a degree of satisfaction and pride. This may render all the more frustrating their inability to escape the compulsion. The clumsy, contradictory nature of this self-knowledge is well seen and aped by Faulkland, when, once again in Sheridan's *Rivals*, he tries to pass himself off as a penitent duellist. Lavishly lamenting his own "restless, unsatisfied disposition" and the "natural fretfulness" of his temper, he aligns himself with delusional duellists, like General Gantlet, who are utterly enthralled with themselves.[16]

Molière, *Le bourgeois gentilhomme* (1670)

A few comical duels punctuate the plays of Molière, but none has proved as memorable as the scene in which Monsieur Jourdain, the eponymous *bourgeois gentilhomme*, realizes that he ought to acquire some gentlemanly savoir faire, now that he has come into some money. A swarm of opportunistic personal trainers promptly descends onto his household (as in Hogarth's second plate of *The Rake's Progress*), ready to grant his wish—and to take his money. Monsieur Jourdain "wants to dream of learning the beautiful things," such as music and dance and, naturally, fencing.[17]

Fencing and duelling are of course discrete, if related, activities, but there were concerns, especially as hitherto exclusively noble pursuits became (or were perceived as) accessible to the most successful, acquisitive bourgeois, that it was now in a sense essential to convert the skill of fencing into the practice of duelling. John Locke, writing in this period, saw the danger: "Young men, in their warm blood, are forward to think they have in vain learned to fence, if they never shew their skill and courage in a duel; and they seem to have reason."[18]

It soon becomes apparent that Monsieur Jourdain intends not only to acquire the noble art of fencing as a man of leisure. More dramatically, he wishes to prepare himself for the eventuality of a duel—and a mortal combat at that. He is not just learning to fence but preparing and intending to kill his adversary. He promptly moves into an emphatic register, envisaging his lessons with the *maître* as a rehearsal for a rencounter. Yet, betraying a bourgeois disposition, he wishes to learn to fight only with the proviso that "a man, without any courage, can be sure of killing his man without himself being killed."[19] Jourdain's wish to subscribe to such a life-insurance policy anticipates more literal exploitations of this dynamic in the nineteenth century. But if Molière takes pleasure in deriding bourgeois calculations, he also enjoys mocking the inane "wisdom" of the métier, or "mystery," when the *maître d'armes*, in an attempt to allay Jourdain's fears for his life, confides that the whole "secret" amounts to just two things, "giving and not receiving." The philosophical pretensions of the "science" of swordsmanship are debunked, while we may perhaps catch an ironic echo of pious Christian *dicta* concerned to emphasize the superiority of giving over receiving. The master veers from this unhelpfully self-evident observation to the obscurely technical pointer, an axis on which Molière's charlatan doctors also move. Molière recycles the joke: "As I have already told you, the entire secret of fencing consists in doing just two things, giving and not receiving; and, as I showed you the other day through demonstrative reason, it is impossible for you to receive, if you can deflect your enemy's sword from the line of your body."[20]

Molière ridicules the pretensions of the teacher who can guarantee results, as well as the fears of a bourgeois drawn to the each-way gamble. Aristocrats watching the play would not need reminding that the attraction and the prestige of duelling with swords were guaranteed by the uncertainties and the dangers that attended any bout. Honor was housed in these very hazards. Molière satirizes not only the risk-averse stance of the bourgeois but also the opportunism, the obfuscatory hocus-pocus, and the petty, conspiratorial jealousies of these masters. Alluding to reason, a perhaps Cartesian mania for unduly simple rationalizations also comes into satirical focus. Indeed, such is Molière's mobility as a satirist that the different constituencies in town and at court could each choose to dwell on the satire in operation elsewhere.[21]

Class inheres no less stubbornly than the credulity, avarice, or misanthropy of Molière's other famous comic creations. After the humiliations of the Fronde, noblemen could at least satisfy themselves that they were not bourgeois. The attitude to death, betrayed by an exposure to swords, is among the most telling indicators of class, and here it assures us that Monsieur Jourdain will always be more *bourgeois* than *gentilhomme.*

The phrase most prominent in the patter of the *maître d'armes* is the "ne . . . que" exceptive construction, his equivalent to that devious adverb "simply," which always precedes complex instructions in modern booklets: "The entire secret of fencing consists of just two things" (Tout le secret des armes ne consiste qu'en deux choses). The fencer should deflect his opponent's sword from his bodyline, a movement that "depends solely on a movement of the wrist" (ce qui ne dépend seulement que d'un petit mouvement du poignet). The disingenuous syntax is duly assimilated and echoed by Jourdain:

> When your opponent thrusts in quarte, you only have to do this, and when he thrusts in tierce, you just have to do this. That's the way never to be killed.[22]
>
> [Quand on pousse en quarte, on n'a qu'à faire cela, et quand on pousse en tierce, on n'a qu'à faire cela. Voilà le moyen de n'être jamais tué.]

The construction only serves, however, to show with what difficulty skill in fencing and, no less imperative, a correspondingly nerveless temperament can be acquired, even for those born to such tasks. Money alone cannot buy the right or indeed the character to duel. Indeed, an ability to fight a duel remains an index or signifier of class, all the more so after the Fronde, when some aristocrats have lost their fortune and other distinguishing traits such as their estates, and a certain degree of social mobility was exemplified by the rise of such figures as Charles Colbert, of whom Monsieur Jourdain was, by repute, a version.

Le bourgeois gentilhomme remained a prototype for the depiction of the aspiring but deluded duellist. It is fundamentally a work of type A but not without type B components. Shaftesbury, writing toward the beginning of the eighteenth century, approved of the raillery and ridicule now aired more freely than hitherto. "Exceeding *fierceness,*" he observed, "with perfect *inability* and *impotence,* makes the highest ridicule."[23] Monsieur Jourdain provides an excellent example of his observation, as he ineptly swishes a sword, yet he and similarly hapless butts did not ultimately serve the antiduelling cause.

More Wretches and Cowards

Around the beginning of the eighteenth century, a rash of comedies produced either side of the Channel continued to carry the fight. Sir Richard Steele was among the most energetic of commentators, as the numerous discussions of the intractable scourge of duelling in his prose indicate. Steele's plays at the beginning of the century are overtly sententious. In his play *The Tender Husband* (1705), the fifth act is devoted entirely to a "maudlin condemnation of duelling." The play did not meet with success and, as he later claimed, with a hint of bitterness, was "damn'd for its piety."[24] By the 1720s, he was still trying to find a solution to this quandary, the moral equivalent to finding the Northwest Passage. Steele went further, producing an eminently rational play, *The Conscious Lovers* (1722), expressly to depict an averted duel. It forms a dramatic companion piece to earlier essays in *The Tatler*, in which reason tempers and finally vanquishes the urge to duel. But the play betrays its sententious impulse, so sometimes the characters seem to be reading, rather than speaking, to one another. And of course it is extracts from *The Tatler* that they would appear to have memorized. For example, at the end of act 4, Myrtle, who, moments earlier, had challenged Bevil Junior to a duel, now says to him, "Dear Bevil, your friendly conduct has convinced me that there is nothing manly but what is conducted by reason and agreeable to the practice of virtue and justice. And yet, how many have been sacrificed to that idol, the unreasonable opinion of men!" The scales then fall with implausible speed from Myrtle's eyes, leaving him suddenly self-critical and instantly articulate, while providing him with an ability to extemporize rhyming couplets on the theme of doomed duellists:

> Betrayed by honour, and compelled by shame,
> They hazard being, to preserve a name:
> Nor dare inquire into the dread mistake,
> Till plunged in sad eternity they wake.
>
> That I could be such a precipitant wretch![25]

There is something self-defeatingly blunt about such nakedly programmatic endeavors to portray ridiculous behavior. William Kenrick's *The Duellist*, performed at Covent Garden (on one night only in 1773), is typical. The prologue tells us that duelling deserves to be ridiculed; the play obligingly does ridicule duelling; the epilogue confirms that duelling has been ridiculed. Kenrick comes up with the highly English expedient of dressing up the inveterate duellist in women's clothes, complete with bonnet and fan. Emasculating the duellist seems like a good way of discouraging him. But the circumstances and the character of this duellist seem at once too particularized and too comically general—he does not appear to be the verifiable butt of a satirical intention—to admit of the possibility of change or reform.

Diderot, like Rousseau, was concerned to distinguish well-meaning but ultimately ineffectual comedies, whose depiction of human foibles would never sting any particular reader or spectator, from satirically dangerous and virulent forms, which were instead trained on a specific verifiable target, sure to recognize him- or herself. Swift characterized satire, unless it went for the jugular of a specific target, as "a sort of glass, wherein beholders do generally discover everybody's face but their own."[26] Or we could switch metaphors: such innocuously generalized comedy is but a blunted sword.

The principal personage in Kenrick's play, the eponymous duellist, General Gantlet, is, as the other characters remind one another, "unaccountably exceptious" (the adverb acknowledging the sketchiness of the underdrawing that might have helped us to understand mitigating circumstances), "as captious and quarrelsome as ever," and "tenacious of honour."[27] He is the first to recognize these attributes in himself. We would call him a duelling addict. His desire to duel does not result from the exercise of a will exaltedly free of legal, theological, and indeed medical considerations but responds to the demands of a visceral urge. No explanation as to why he should be so is forthcoming. There are no excuses for him. Nor is there any sense that his behavior might be corrigible. Equally, we have no clue as to whom he has been fighting or why. Notorious as he may be in polite society for his propensity to fight duels, his monomania seems to be confined to him. He appears to inhabit a world entirely of his own, as though it did not take two men to fight a duel. Kenrick is perhaps underlining the point that General Gantlet is a sort of forlorn quixotic figure, tilting at illusory enemies, on the most frivolous or specious of grounds. As one of his acquaintances exclaims, "What a captious mortal! Could he find nobody else to quarrel with, he would certainly take exceptions at himself and tilt with his own shadow!"[28] "Tilting" carries unmistakable echoes of Don Quixote's endeavors. A rather tepid conclusion, uttered in the last lines of the play, when we are told that it is preferable to forgive rather than to resent injuries, does not quite allay the General's sense, which remains intact until the very end of the play, that he has a right to a certain level of resentment.

In the latter half of the eighteenth century, the production of moralistic antiduelling comedies continued, undaunted, unabated. Let us take, as an example, *Jacquot et Colas duellistes*, a comedy from the 1780s, by a now all-but-forgotten playwright called Louis Hurtaut Dancourt. The original sense of the duellist as compulsive fighter, by the later eighteenth century largely dormant, is still stirring here, even though the duellists in question are not from the usual constituency. They decide, deliberately and self-consciously, to contest a duel by swords:

> JACQUOT: *Il tire une botte.*
>   *Colas, de meme, tirant hors de portée*
> COLAS: Flin!
> JACQUOT: Flan!
> COLAS: Zigue!
> JACQUOT: Zague![29]

The stage directions are supplemented by cartoon-like vocalizations, as their swords cross. But then the peculiar politeness of the duel's language and etiquette is replicated. These two cowards mutate, linguistically, into noble heroes. All the accompanying language and gesture and trappings have been borrowed. But they have the panoply of courtesies, the honorable emotions, down to a tee. After the vernacular remarks they have made, the language is promptly ennobled. After Jacquot "kills" Colas, he exclaims, "Ah! My poor Colas, if only I were in your shoes" (Ah! Mon pauvre Colas, que ne suis-je à ta place?).[30]

These folk are patently unable to wield this noble arm, but they can handle an alexandrine. And this point is emphasized by the fact that one of the "champions" is a gamekeeper, a professional marksman. This reputedly trigger-happy gamekeeper cannot manipulate a sword. Sheridan's saber-rattling Irishman, Lucius O'Trigger, arouses the same suspicions. Duelling honorably necessitates skill, courage, and savoir faire. Not only are their cowardice and *maladresse* risible, but they think themselves fierce and dangerous. Each assumes, wrongly, that he has killed the other. When they then happen on each other in a later scene, each naturally assumes that the other is a ghost.

This comical scene could just as easily have been written in 1683. The same archetypes are to be seen, the same comic resources are deployed. This is a comedy that, no doubt to the delight of a Parisian audience, draws on an ancient distinction of town and country, seigneurial temperance and peasant panic. They are a long way from being as murderous as they think are. The play delivers a vision of satisfyingly naïve yokels. It is obviously a type A play, in that, as usual, the comedy exposes the duellists as ridiculous, not the duel. Its charm rests on the familiarity and the predictability of the characters and their respective antics.

Country duelling provides a farcical echo to the serious duels fought in the cities. Ireland, an essentially rural society detached from the mainland, behind the times, is perceived (by the English) to be a natural habitat for such comical characters. As the nineteenth century ages, however, the comic foil is more likely to be a man stuck in a dead-end office job.

This comic template proves remarkably durable, particularly in France. In 1834, an enjoyable example could be seen on the French stage when *Les duels; ou, La famille Darcourt,* by the prolific double act Mélesville and Carmouche, was first performed. The braggart who dominates this particular comedy, Monsieur Beauchan, hails from Bordeaux, not far north of the traditional nursery of such people in Gascony. He could be a figure drawn from any previous century. Beauchan, who wears a black cravat, yellow gloves, and a "moustache moyen âge," is a sort of bravo ready to duel at the drop of a hat. His aunt is entirely worthy of him. She arrives with her luggage: "silks à la Louis XIII, feathers à la Henri III, porcelain à la Louis XV, Gothic jewels. . . . All the very latest get-up!"[31] Yet, because they are a confection of different cultures and ages, they embody a malaise typical of the nineteenth century that becomes especially acute, for obvious reasons, under the second Restoration, in the France of Charles X. A year later, in a volume on duelling, Fougeroux sighs, "there is nothing new in this century."[32]

The harmless would-be duellist is all the more innocuous for being a recognizable stage type. In one respect, though, this archetypal comical buffoon is brought up to date. Whereas, in the eighteenth century, he is likely to have been a harmless peasant or a deluded churl, he may now be a bureaucrat (to use an English noun first recorded in 1842). The duellist manqué is now a man nursing his delusions behind a desk. In a stroke of authorial genius, Beauharn, the die-hard duellist, is employed by a company that specializes in life insurance.

In a similar vein, comic responses to duelling find new resources when, in the later eighteenth century, the default duelling weapon begins to change from sword to pistol. A peasant brandishing a sword may yet seem innocuous; a peasant wielding a pistol is a potential psychopath.

It is against this background of plays, which set themselves the ambition of ridiculing and discountenancing duellists, that Michel-Jean Sedaine's sober depiction of the dilemmas that a duel might provoke in and around duellists themselves deserves to be appreciated.

Sedaine, *Le philosophe sans le savoir* (1765): Vanderk *fils* versus d'Esparville *fils*

The twenty-first of October 1765 was to have been the opening night of *Le duel*, a new play written by a playwright named Michel-Jean Sedaine. It was, however, postponed when the censor, Marin, intervened, requiring extensive revisions. When, in December of that year, the reconstituted play was finally performed, the first, and most apparent, casualty of this intervention was the title: *Le duel* had become *Le philosophe sans le savoir*.[33]

Like *Le Cid*, Sedaine's play is a hybrid drama in the modern taste. It too centers on the predicament of a young man (Vanderk fils in this case) who undertakes to defend the honor of his father by fighting a duel. This time, mercifully, his opponent is not his prospective father-in-law. A wedding has, however, been planned—that of Vanderk père's other child, his daughter. It is on her wedding day that he learns of his son's own particular engagement. Far from trying to obstruct his son, fulminating against duels in general, or indeed preparing his speech for the wedding, the father calmly, indeed optimistically, sees to the practical arrangements that will prove necessary, should his son win the duel. But then Vanderk is a merchant. His son, he realizes, may need enough money to escape and support himself abroad, until such time as he can return. In accepting the obligation of fighting a duel, a duellist had also to be ready to leave for exile after it.

The censor was concerned that the father's tacit assent to his son's actions might be seen to provide an implicit apology for duelling. Unlike contemporaneous comedies, the play does not obviously belong to genus A, in which a patently ridiculous figure—a fop, a drunkard, or an Irishman (or all of them wrapped into one)—plays the duellist, unconvincingly. The characterization and the actions of the characters embroiled in circumstances that move toward a duel remain largely dignified.

The duel, always potentially tragic but equally susceptible to farce, constituted a highly suitable action at the heart of this new, rather indeterminate form. Sedaine was perhaps trying to appease those members of his audience and readership who preferred to know quite whether this was a comedy or a tragedy when he decided to include a handkerchief in the opening scene, in which we see Victorine, a young lady, wiping away her tears. The humble handkerchief had been responsible for controversy when *Othello*, to which it is of course indispensable, was to be performed in French translation. The stately and sublime diction of a French tragedy did not admit of quite such a banal, workaday object. This allusion might instantly provide a guarantee that the play will be keeping a safe distance from the world of high tragedy. Sedaine, who collaborated with composers, provides with this handkerchief an opening chord, plangent but major, like that of an overture, which will set the mood. But it may, just as quickly, alert us to elements of pathos in this comedy, perhaps depending on the intent and temper of the given actress. It was the presence of such elements that attracted the support of Diderot, who saw in Sedaine's works the imprint of a dramatic artist working at the same level of technical accomplishment and moral finesse as the painters Chardin and Greuze.

The father, unaware at this stage of his son's arrangements in the immediate future, sits him down in order to reveal details of the past. They emerge, now that the marriage contract is to be signed. Vanderk's own father, he explains, was killed when serving as a young soldier.

Vanderk then reveals that, years ago, he himself incurred the wrath of a young officer billeted in their quarter. They therefore fought a duel. As he explains to his nonplussed son, he is actually the scion of a family of *qualité*, no less than the "baron de Salvières, de Clavières etc." (The impatient, unimpressed "etc." is an especially aristocratic touch.) He does not confess to having killed his opponent, but the implications are obvious. Following the duel, he fled to Holland. There he was taken under the wing of a kindly Dutchman, who, upon his death, bequeathed the French fugitive both his business and his name. The French nobleman, having gone Dutch, went on to become the successful merchant his son knows him to be. Vanderk is then, in every sense, an *homme d'affaires*, a perfect "bourgeois gentilhomme," or perhaps rather a "gentilhomme bourgeois," for the eighteenth century.[34]

Arabella, in Charlotte Lennox's *The Female Quixote* (1752), has difficulty accepting that a good-looking gardener is not actually a nobleman in disguise, for, as she observes, "these things happen every day."[35] They do in the literature of the period, at any rate. Goldsmith's *She Stoops to Conquer* (1773); Captain Absolute disguised as Ensign Beverley in Sheridan's *The Rivals* (1775); Count Almaviva posing as the musician Lindor in Beaumarchais's *Le barbier de Séville* (also 1775); Mozart's *La finta giardiniera* (still 1775); they follow on from similarly vertiginous social abseiling or rappelling in Goldoni's plays and Marivaux's comedies. These recurrent revelations tickle a bourgeois fantasy that one's husband or father may suddenly be about to reveal that he too is, after all, of noble blood. These epiphanies, surprising as they may seem on the stage, constitute a sort of formula that is rarely as radical as it may appear.

Granted the conventionally surprising nature of this revelation, we still should not understate the originality of the play's dynamics. Unlike those examples of nobility unveiled, the gentleman has not been masked momentarily for the purposes of proving love. For once, no women have been tested in the process. What is more, unusually, perhaps uniquely, the fugitive nobleman has permanently adopted the shell of the businessman in which he had found a hermitage. He has not only donned a merchant's mask but grown into it. Vanderk voices an eloquent paean to the class of traders to which he now belongs: "It is not a people, it is not a single nation that he serves; he serves them all, and he is served by them; he is the man of the universe. . . . We are, on the surface of the earth, as many silk threads which unite the nations and bring them to peace by means of the necessity of commerce: that, my son, is a respectable merchant."[36]

The image of merchants as so many silken threads establishes both their preciousness and their vulnerability. Commerce furnishes luxury, but it necessitates risks. Above all, there is honor in commerce. And of course folly and affectation attend the practices of the nobility. The notion that trade and commerce could be considered reputable remained provocative in mid-eighteenth-century France. English writers had been quicker to bestow on merchants the laurels reserved elsewhere for soldiers and poets. A bust of Thomas Gresham featured among the English worthies in Lord Cobham's famous gardens at Stowe. Gresham, an inscription tells us, "who, by the honourable Profession of Merchant, having enriched Himself and his Country, for carrying on the Commerce of the World, built the Royal Exchange."[37] Concentric circles extend beyond the self, and the nation, to the world.

Such a regard for commerce as a bringer of unity to nations, rendering boundaries porous, percolates from Voltaire's enthusiasm for Gresham's Royal Exchange (on display in the *Lettres philosophiques* [1734]) and his hymn to the worldly pleasures bought by commerce in his poem "Le mondain" (1736).[38] Under these influences, "the honourable profession of Merchant" was ceasing to sound oxymoronic in French. Indeed, the abbé Coyer penned the *La noblesse commerçante* in 1756. But Sedaine is discreet, as Voltaire could never be. Voltaire had the audacity not only to dedicate his tragedy *Zaïre* (1732) to an English merchant but to follow that by dedicating *Mahomet* (1736) to Pope Benedict XIV. Presumably, the French nobleman, in order to adopt his name and his business, has had to embrace his religion too. Whereas Voltaire's chief argument for commerce rests on the capacity of trade to bring discrete parts of the world together, which religion sets against one another, and commerce is Voltaire's ersatz religion, the play remains silent in this regard.

This eulogy of commerce is rather ironic, for Vanderk's son, to whom it is addressed, hardly needs convincing. As the father soon learns, his son is now, in turn, about to fight a duel. The circumstances of this duel to which Vanderk fils finds himself committed are highly original. Having happened, while in a café, to overhear contemptuous remarks about merchants, he has challenged the young man responsible for them to a duel. He is therefore not only defending the honor of his father, who is one such merchant, but championing the integrity of the merchant class to which he belongs.[39] It is less clear than hitherto where the boundaries between gentlemen and others lie. Indeed, the duel is attributable to a struggle in remapping this territory and the resentments excited by that upheaval.

In a brilliantly original scenario, the dignity of merchants is to be vindicated by the aristocratic art par excellence. This seems curious, perhaps paradoxical. It may be a case of upstart emulation, but there remains a possibility that the younger Vanderk is piqued by insecurities in an environment that remains contemptuous of business.[40] The duel would then satisfy a secret need to prove his credentials, perhaps as a consequence of the latent promptings and pulses of his noble blood.

Sedaine voices the disturbing idea that the growing prosperity and confidence of the commercial classes results not in a marginalization of the aristocratic pursuit that is duelling but in an annexation of the practice, with its own new rationale—and indeed with its own weapons. At all events, the pistol may play a part in encouraging this appropriation of a hitherto aristocratic preserve. Against the grain of conventional comic depictions, the bourgeois, embodied and epitomized by Vanderk fils, is no less capable of courage and self-sacrifice. Sedaine extends the jurisdiction of the duel to a middle class, albeit one that has come from the aristocracy. Indeed, it was a duel that caused Vanderk to become a bourgeois in the first place, a delicious irony. So the father lends financial support to his son, in whose position he had once found himself. The handkerchief at the outset seems to have been a red herring. Vanderk senior does not succumb to tears at the thought of losing his son in a duel. But then "a threepenny piece is always better than a tear."[41]

Once the father has embraced his son who departs, maybe never to return, he does, however, pour grief and anger into a soliloquy. Vanderk père directs his ire at the absurd cruelty of duelling and "the shackles of honor." The speech expresses the conventional indignation that duelling is supposed to provoke. Once again, duelling is descried as "barbarous." In an apostrophe launched at the duel, he declares, "You could only survive at the heart of a vain and self-satisfied nation, a people consisting of individuals who each count their own person for everything and their country and family for nothing."[42] This reflection, voiced on behalf of the nation and family, is more modern and constructive. It seems to carry the imprimatur of Rousseau, just as the earlier praise of commerce was Voltairean in spirit, minus the anticlerical sting. The father inveighs against the duel in the name of family values. Although he is denigrated for his apparent quiescence, there is no doubt about the mutual affection of father and son. Perhaps this intimacy is underlined by the fact that we do not learn the first name of either of the men. All that matters is the family name common to them. They face the same predicaments, across generations otherwise sundered by sensibility and convention.

It is not possible to run away from the past, however full and accomplished Vanderk's self-renewal may appear to have been. Vanderk is able to change his name, to shed his identity and, it seems, religion, but he is powerless to stop the resurgence of the past in the present, as his son's actions recall his own. Here we meet with a notion, increasingly common in the second half of the eighteenth century, that the child induces the parent to address his or her own past. The marriage of Vanderk's daughter first forces the details out; but the prospect of his son falling into the same trap reconciles himself more fully to his own past. Sedaine surely draws on the pathos briefly glimpsed in Rousseau's *Julie*, published a few years earlier. Rousseau was mocked for suggesting that the victor of a duel would suffer pangs, after getting Julie to warn Saint-Preux off duelling by telling him of her father's ongoing torment. He had fought a fatal duel decades before, but even this hardened soldier is tormented by guilt. His unduly possessive, intractable stance is attributable in part to that misadventure.

Vanderk, an apostle of moderation, can see the extremities to which the duel carries its participants. But, true to his character, he does not issue an outright condemnation of the duel, as demanded of eighteenth-century writers. They are supposed to say, first, that it is barbaric and, secondly, that it is not happening. Vanderk obliges with that epithet, in the corrected version, but the inclusion of a serious duel in this domestic context constitutes an audaciously original move.

The lonely despair of a penitent duellist who lost his father, fled his country, and is now about to lose his son is indeed poignant. Both Vanderk's predicament and his diction ensure that the play is now colored in darker, seemingly tragic tones. Sedaine explained, in his apologetic missive to the censor, that he had wished to reproduce the predicament of Brutus, who in the tragedy by Voltaire is to be seen wrestling with a cruel duty to which he can only assent with the greatest pain.

Sedaine offers an unusual vista onto the duellist's predicament. The son is destined to repeat the sins of the father. This lends the duel a hereditary aspect: the young man may be destined to fight not only owing to lateral, social dictates but also on account of vertical, familial imperatives. It emerges also that the duel is essentially a young hothead's prerogative, on the evidence of this play, although we may be admiring in Vanderk's remarkable sang froid and restraint, as he waits to hear of his son's fate, those same qualities that once helped him to win his own duel. Indeed, remote as the nobleman may seem to be from the merchant, the same boldness in speculation may have made the successful duellist a good businessman.[43]

All is well, however. First, Vanderk père is visited by a gentleman who urgently needs to borrow some money. It turns out that he has in mind the same sort of contingency package for his son, who, they learn, is Vanderk fils's opponent. Then both sons arrive, safe and well, and, naturally, they are now the best of friends. They have fought a duel with pistols. The bullets flew through the air, grazing Vanderk's hat but mercifully sparing the combatants. As Vanderk père explains to d'Esparville fils, his son's adversary, "After what has happened, Sir, you can only be the greatest foe or the greatest friend of my son, and you do not have the freedom to choose."[44]

However earnestly Sedaine attempts to condemn duelling, the duel is seen to push the life of comfortable moderation, vaunted by the Enlightenment, to extremes of intensity and intimacy that foreshadow Romantic ideals. The duel is not merely the prerogative of a recklessly self-centered aristocracy, on this evidence. After all the innocuous encounters, numerous botched and blunted swordfights, a prospective duel rings an alarm that has sounded too often to remain alarming.

Sedaine renders the duel dangerous again—to the extent that the censor felt he had to intervene. Sedaine does so not through granting us a privileged insight into the feelings and anxieties of the young man about to fight the duel—we do not even know his first name—but through exploring the predicaments and the fears of the people around him: his lover, Victorine (whom George Sand later married off to Vanderk fils, in a continuation of the play) and, above all, his father. He is the hero and the philosophe of the play's title. The damage the duel wreaks in families is felt keenly here. The duel, ultimately, happily, a farce, is nonetheless conducive to pathos rather than to ridicule. It has the trappings of an archetypal comedy, finishing, inevitably, in marriage. It seems destined to be one of the A-style plays. But it is, triumphantly, a B. That is, it successfully debunks the practice of duelling, rather than ridiculing duellists.

Works written in the hope of deterring duellists had tended, almost invariably, to show duels as pointlessly destructive, violent, and barbaric. But, in so doing, duels looked like ordeals too terrifying for bourgeois cowards, like Monsieur Jourdain. The duel has caused Vanderk père to become a better person, but only by becoming a different man. He has had to try to efface his true identity. Even if this comedy proceeds to a happy ending, it unfurls a dark past. Comedies hitherto tend not to recall deaths in duels. But, dark as it may be in places, it is not a play without lighter moments. These often seem rather peripheral to the play. Sedaine throws in, perhaps dutifully, as though the form demanded it, a frightful comedy aunt, who maintains that "commerce diminishes the soul."[45] Sedaine demystifies any aura around the duel by allowing us to witness banal preliminary arrangements. There can be few antecedents in which so much time is given to looking for keys. Of course, this delay, which occurs when Vanderk fils wishes to sally forth out to the ramparts for the duel, is integral to the functioning of the plot, but it is an enjoyably ordinary circumstance, tempering momentarily the duellist's more exalted sense of what he is undertaking.

The language with which the arrangements for the duel are made is characteristically euphemistic. Sometimes—when, for instance, Vanderk declares that he has in mind only his wife's "satisfaction"—this permits a frisson.[46] But, more profoundly, the whole play, from the scene in which he hurls his apostrophes at the "fatal prejudice" to that devoted to a description of the duel, never features that unspeakable word.

Sedaine self-consciously points to the kinship between his play and a tragedy, when Vanderk fils, anxiously pacing up and down prior to the duel, is thought to be rehearsing a tragic role for the stage. Victorine is in tears, as the play opens, but, with a prompt recoil from the sensibility it seeks to elicit in its audience, we are immediately advised that "young girls weep sometimes to give them something to do."[47] Yet at no point does the playwright deride the duellist. He contrives to inveigh against the duel without mocking the duellist. True, the sons engage in an ultimately risible encounter, as they fall off their horses, but this scene unfolds offstage and does not detract from the pathos. Ultimately, the duellists owe their salvation in the end to good fortune. Such are the margins between tragedy and comedy.

Sedaine's play turns on the inner life of one man marked by two duels, the former fatal, the latter futile. In so doing, Sedaine shows how a vicious, if ridiculous, custom provides, by turns, a crisis of regrets and a drama of reconciliation. Yet, when faced by possibly the first play to attend seriously to the woes entailed by duels, after numberless self-defeating comedies, the censor ultimately succeeded in compromising it, *sans le savoir* of course.

Sheridan, *The Rivals* (1775): Bob Acres versus Ensign Beverley; Sir Lucius O'Trigger versus Captain Jack Absolute

While gentlemen were taking the waters at Bath to restore their health, they were prone to fighting duels to preserve their honor. The risks incurred by the latter activity seem to have been greater even than those that the former involved, cruel jibes about the popularity of burials in the Abbey every year notwithstanding. By the 1770s, the wearing of swords had therefore been strictly prohibited in spa and city. Not only had they caused fatalities during struggles in the fashionable assembly rooms and on the parades, but they evidently frightened the ladies circulating in and around the Pump Room.[48] Richard Brinsley Sheridan's *The Rivals*, first performed in 1775, is a comedy to which the local, changing circumstances of late eighteenth-century Bath, where the play is set, are absolutely integral.

> "SIR LUCIUS: We wear no swords here, but you understand me."
>   So Sir Lucius O'Trigger informs his friend Bob Acres, who does
>   not fully understand him:
> "ACRES: What! Fight him!
> SIR LUCIUS: Aye, to be sure: what can I mean else?"[49]

In the absence of swords, those indispensable props and signals of class, the English language has instead to assume a greater burden in communicating identity and intention. The result is, however, a veritable pileup of mistakes and obfuscation. This is a highly verbose play in which the only objects we see are books and weapons. *The Rivals* is celebrated, above all, for having bequeathed to us the character of Mrs. Malaprop, the ridiculous aunt of Lydia, Captain Absolute's intended. But her extravagant misprisions are rivaled by the linguistic idiosyncrasies of other characters, who speak in their own bizarrely inventive, exuberant ways. None is stranger than the idiolect of Acres, the yokel who, in spite of himself, will be drawn into a duel. He is given to cursing, which is not that unusual for an Englishman, only his self-minted oaths all refer to and jumble up weapons and their component parts:

> I grow full of anger, Sir Lucius!—I fire apace! Odds hilts and blades!
> . . .
> Odds flints, pans and triggers!
> . . .
> Odds balls and barrels!
> . . .
> Odds bullets and blades![50]

As the prospect of a duel with Acres's rival, Ensign Beverley (Captain Absolute's alias for the purposes of courting Lydia), approaches, the strange exclamations, and the particular form they take, are perhaps attributable to fear and confusion, but Acres is already attached to these odd metonymies when we meet him. "Odds! Triggers and flints," he declares, a little earlier.[51] The self-consciousness with which these eccentric habits are presented is remarkable. Acres himself proudly draws attention to his neologisms. But then swearing in the eighteenth century seems widely to have been regarded as an art form, a creative act.[52] Jargons in this city of fashions are adopted and discarded as quickly as styles of clothing. And no area of a language ages more quickly than its oaths. But this does not entirely account for Acres's odd scrambling of the lexicons particular to sword and pistol. Nor is he alone in this creative confusion.

When Acres's servant, David, hears of the prospective duel, he indignantly speculates about some fellow confronting his master "with his damned double-barrelled swords, and cut and thrust pistols!" and, a little later, when that duel is about to take place, he is duly upset by the prospect of "bloody sword-and-gun fighting."[53] These may be the words of a simpleminded soul, who does not understand the weapons of his social superiors and likes to ape his master's voice, but perhaps they translate more profound uncertainties as to how people will be going about their affairs. Indeed, this confusion of weapons is epitomized by the pugnacious Irishman Sir Lucius O'Trigger. His name is a meeting place for the ancient and the modern, a site where things chivalric and ballistic collide. He reminds us of that swaggering oxymoron Ancient Pistol and, in turn, Roderick Random. But he will have also brought to the mind of eighteenth-century audiences the figure of Sir Dermot O'Leinster, the hero of *A Duel*, the English version of Sedaine's *Le philosophe sans le savoir*. Whereas Sedaine's play proceeds in a calmly chronological trajectory from father to son, swords to pistols, and from duelling disputes to their resolution, Sheridan's play is altogether more tumultuous. Indeed, the comedy thrives throughout on confusion between the rival forms of weaponry.

O'Trigger challenges Captain Absolute to a duel later that day. These gentlemen are therefore double booked, because, in the guise of Ensign Beverley, Absolute has already been challenged by Bob Acres, for whom O'Trigger is acting as a second. As the play moves toward this pair of simultaneous duels, it becomes apparent that Sheridan's approach to these farcical affairs is at odds, in a number of respects, with that of other comic writers. Sheridan, for a start, attends to the practicalities of a duel by pistol with unprecedented attention. He shows, even in this joyous comedy, the terrors particular to a gunfight. He is also one of the first writers to pay heed to the eager complicity of the seconds, and, while his criticism of the fallacious understanding of honor promoted by duelling takes a reasonably familiar form, we also learn that O'Trigger has secret, serious reasons for wanting to fight a duel. There is method in his madness. These insights and innovations are themselves secondary to, and possibly explained by, another novel feature to this play. Sheridan himself had fought two duels, with a rival suitor, and this biographical information, while confined to the background, no doubt added a slight frisson to the comedy.

The absence of blades from the streets of Bath is redeemed by their figurative prominence. The language and the imagery of the sword classicize and dignify a duel in which pistols are to be fired. Urging Acres to fight a duel, Sir Lucius invokes Achilles and Alexander the Great, who "drew their broadswords" before worrying about the legality of their actions. O'Trigger then steels Acres into being valorous with the helpful advice, "Let your courage be as keen, but at the same time as polished as your sword."[54] When, finally, Acres sends off his cartel for the attention of Beverley, it carries his crest, "a hand-and dagger seal."[55] Acres is made to feel that, in contesting a duel, he will belong to a genealogy of valiant swordsmen, although, when it comes down to it, he will be fighting with pistols. And even when bullets are, eventually, discussed, Sir Lucius's allusion to the "quietus" one might bring with it maintains the altitude of the register and preserves the illusion of honor and dignity.[56]

O'Trigger, meanwhile, has his own illusions.[57] Sir Lucius brandishes figurative swords when he speaks about duels. Yet both his surname and the address of his ancestral home, Blunderbuss Hall, suggest, conversely, an affiliation to firearms. A blunderbuss denotes bluster in the eighteenth century, and we await another example of the stage Irishman, talkatively obsessed with his pedigree and faded Milesian splendor. Sir Lucius is not, however, the archetypally irascible, garrulous Irishman of tradition but a highly courteous, cool figure. When, killing two birds with one stone, he arranges simultaneous duels, such economy demonstrates swagger worthy of d'Artagnan. Nevertheless, destitute of land and wealth, he clings to a past and to the consolations of genealogy. Claims to distinction and to a record of ferocity in duelling seem often to be the refuge of the dispossessed man. These resentments and bogus claims to antiquity were already familiar motifs for an English audience, and they will resonate in the works of Thackeray and Byron inter alia.

So O'Trigger is busy on two scores. First, he is the second to Acres; second, he intends to fight a duel with Absolute. Both engagements show him proceeding without a hint of passion and always with impeccable courtesy. Sir Lucius is a rather subdued sort of rodomont. He does not have the bombast, the *enflure,* of his predecessors. His currency is oblique elegance, even as he contrives an argument, and consequently a duel, with Absolute. This is one of the most marvelously inane, utterly gratuitous provocations to a duel to be enjoyed in all literature. Sir Lucius approaches Absolute, as he strolls along North Parade, and, in medias res, declares,

> SIR LUCIUS: With regard to that matter, Captain, I must beg leave to differ in opinion with you.
>
> ABSOLUTE: Upon my word then, you must be a very subtle disputant: because, Sir, I happened just then to be giving no opinion at all.
>
> SIR LUCIUS: That's no reason. For give me leave to tell you, a man may *think* an untruth as well as *speak* one.
>
> ABSOLUTE: Very true, Sir, but if the man never utters his thoughts, I should think they *might* stand a *chance* of escaping controversy.
>
> SIR LUCIUS: Then, Sir, you differ in opinion with me, which amounts to the same thing.[58]

Sir Lucius has picked and found a fight through a set of maneuvers that forces his interlocutor to contradict him. It is a triumph of circular, syllogistic logic. And it results in a duel being arranged for six o'clock that evening. Yet, remarkably, behind this ridiculously contrived and redundant duel, there actually lies, disguised, a real reason for it. O'Trigger reveals, in a momentary but telling aside, that Absolute had insulted him about Ireland on a previous occasion.[59] O'Trigger prefers to submerge this resentment in order to fight under the cover of a pointless rather than a partisan matter. "A very pretty quarrel as it stands," it appears to be a duel for the sake of duelling, a combat sanctified by the nobility of purposelessness. He would seem to be more concerned with what the duel looks like, not what it is for, rather than answering a purpose or settling a score, which would be so routine by comparison. Yet that aside tells us that Sir Lucius nurses a serious resentment and has not forgotten the insults to his nation. This patriotic feeling, given expression and justification in a duel, is unusual at this stage in the eighteenth century. That it should, furthermore, be disguised in this manner makes it rarer still. Sir Lucius evidently knows the value of seeming dispassionate. Perhaps he is strategically aware that, as in some subsequent depictions of duels, simmering anger might not actually help the principal to compose and acquit himself properly in a bout. It makes sense to conceal that resentment, to oneself and to others. In all likelihood, though, it seems that he is chiefly concerned with appearances. Genteel duels, fought for the love of duelling itself, rather than out of hatred for the other man, commend themselves as especially stylish. That combination of dignity and poverty, Sir Lucius's shabby chivalry, is likely to have rendered him a quixotic figure in the eyes of an English audience.

As Sir Lucius prepares for his own duel, he is pushing Bob Acres into engaging a duel with Ensign Beverley, who, unbeknownst to the Irishman, is the same fellow he is going to fight. In act 3, scene 4, we see the second dictating terms, literally, to his principal, a rather labile rustic type. For it is of course imperative first to master the correct formulae in order to compose a suitably courteous challenge. Sir Lucius accordingly dictates a pro forma letter on behalf of his principal. Acres wishes the ink were red, in order to convey, or rather to ignite, his rage and passion, yet this is tempered by Sir Lucius, who insists on the need for impeccable civility. Acres protests, as he takes down in dictation the words "I shall expect the honour of your company," that he is not asking his adversary to dinner. But Lucius advises Acres "to do everything in a mild and agreeable manner," upon meeting his antagonist.[60]

Meanwhile, Absolute's second, his friend Faulkland, aware of the forthcoming duel, is also stirring. He loves a young lady by the name of Julia but is not sure of her feelings for him. We know that he is unduly, comically insecure about her tenderness for him, partly because, as an audience, we hear her confessing to the warmth and authenticity of her feelings and partly because, as readers, we know that a girl called Julia will not let him down. Promoted by the pious sensibilities of Rousseau's *Julie* (1761), the name Julie, or Julia, is an irresistible choice for a writer in need of a young heroine, who has undoubted moral qualities among her high endowments.[61] Faulkland will test her feelings for him by pretending to be the principal, not the second, in the forthcoming duel. This will be "the touchstone of Julia's sincerity and disinterestedness."[62]

Faulkland borrows this duel, to be fought by others, for his own "romantic" purposes. This expedient is itself borrowed by Sheridan from Smollett's *Roderick Random*, one of the works that Lydia has borrowed from the circulating library (and is seen throwing down the toilet).[63] The ruses of Absolute and Faulkland and the dissimulation of Captain Absolute, disguised as Ensign Beverley, help to suggest that people may be at their most eloquent when speaking for or as someone else. But all the languages of this play are, in one way or another, appropriated and derivative. Amid the Babel of idiolects, oaths, and, of course, malapropisms, there is something suspiciously smooth, disconcertingly dulcet about Faulkland's sighing valedictions. Faulkland's fluency does look inversely proportional to his sincerity.

This is a comedy which moves inexorably to two duels, without ever suggesting that this is an illegal or, God forbid, immoral pursuit. It is a genus A play in which Acres is seen to be cowardly. Indeed, he does not mind being called a coward.[64] But he overcomes his fears by intimidating David and, transferring the accusation down the social scale, calling him in turn a coward. Sheridan suggests that Acres is entitled to be a coward in these circumstances. Fear is legitimate; poltroonery is not. Acres and David are not, however, the archetypal poltroons of comedies past. Rustic cowardice has been a staple of comedies in which duels featured. David, unusually, avows his fears. He is right and reasonable to be afraid, and it is folly to pretend otherwise. He may remind us of Rochester's dictum, "For all men would be cowards if they durst."[65] David deplores the duel from a new perspective. Rather in the manner of his contemporary and fellow valet Figaro, David exclaims, "this *honour* seems to me be a marvellous false friend, . . . a very courtier-like servant."[66] He voices robust, earthy common sense in demystifying the duel, rather than venting the rational, moral objections advanced sententiously by Steele's characters: "Put the case, I was a gentleman (which, thank God, no one can say of me); well—my honour makes me quarrel with another gentleman of my acquaintance. So—we fight (pleasant enough that). Boh!—I kill him (the more's my luck). Now, pray who gets the profit of it? Why, my honour. But put the case that he kills me!—by the mass! I go to the worms, and my honour whips over to my enemy!" The surest way of not disgracing one's ancestors, he adds, is "to keep as long as you can out of their company": "Our ancestors are very good kind of folks; but they are the last people I should choose to have a visiting acquaintance with."[67] He does not invoke the laws, whether judicial or moral, that the duel transgresses. He simply envisions what could happen: death. And he seems to bring to bear Rousseau's line of argument in conjecturing a female reaction to this disaster: "How Phyllis will howl when she hears of it!" Only Sheridan gently debunks the Rousseauesque tactic, by adding, with a stroke of comic genius, "aye, poor bitch, she little thinks what shooting her master's going after!"[68]

David has, in common with Figaro, a robustly simple attitude to life and the absurdity of his social superiors. He tries to dissuade his master from going to his ancestors "with an ounce of lead in [his] brains."[69] Other comedies would tend to mock the uncomprehending or fearful servant, when faced by the antics of his aristocratic employers. But the mood was turning. Certain that it could be made more relevant and edifying, Diderot called for servants to be replaced by children onstage. Sheridan still employs servants in his theater, but he refrains from the usual sort of condescension. Discretion is the better part of valor, and David is worthy of his name, itself that of a famous victor in single combat. He is not afraid of duels but disdainful of them. David simply states, "I never knew any good come of 'em."[70] Instead, he suggests an obvious English alternative—a boxing match or a bout with staffs. David's unsophisticated dismissal of duelling (rather than a more polished critique of duelling in an authorial mouthpiece) offers Sheridan a way of showing the evident absurdity of duelling, without running the danger or incurring the discomfort of seeming to be sanctimonious or, worse still, hypocritical when broaching an activity in which he himself had indulged. For the play's initial success was attributable in part to the way it both presupposed and disguised some knowledge of Sheridan's own duels, fought in Bath.[71]

In the final act, the scene now transfers to Kingsmead Fields, where the dual duels have been prebooked. First O'Trigger and Acres appear. The sword is the only weapon really adequate to the braggart's pretensions. But the pistol does offer him new possibilities, and the mechanisms of this new kind of duel have their own dramatic appeal. Cowardice may take shelter under extravagant promises of precision: "the farther he is off, the cooler I shall take my aim." Acres, true to his name, reckons that forty yards is a good distance. The distance is arranged to make marksmanship look impressive but, in practice, to make the duel less likely to be fatal. Sir Lucius, however, prefers a "pretty gentleman's distance," asserting that "three or four feet between the mouths of your pistols is as good as a mile."[72]

This is the first play in which we see the actors pacing out on the stage with the intention of staging a duel by pistols, a spectacle obviously unavailable to Shakespeare or to Sheridan's seventeenth-century predecessors. Yet the vocabulary that precedes this modern dressage recycles a fairly traditional repertory of images and tropes. Indeed, after the highly genteel detachment of Sir Lucius's epistolary style and his polished references to epic heroes and swordsmanship, his intention to arrange a duel for Acres, at merely four yards apart, that will bring the principals face to face, frowning brow to brow, is all the more shocking. That contradiction between Classical grandeur and prosaic modernity is there in his name, Sir Lucius O'Trigger. He seems a cruel sadist, if he is serious about such a distance. We may, however, excuse Sir Lucius in suggesting that he is organizing a duel by pistols as though it were a duel by swords. *Mano a mano* has simply turned into muzzle to muzzle.

Sheridan is one of the first writers to show the increased influence of the second, an influence attributable to the rise of the pistol as the chief duelling arm. Faulkland finds it easy to upgrade his role as a second to that of a principal in the duel, for the sake of impressing Lydia, in part perhaps because the role is no longer that of the entirely passive bystander; Sir Lucius, meanwhile, is decidedly keener to act as Acres's second rather than fighting his own duel (with Absolute). Indeed, his interaction with Acres is a sort of ersatz duel.

Sir Lucius is very concerned that this should all be done properly, with due ceremony, at a suitably reduced distance, which is very good of him. Sir Lucius, like Faulkland, is using someone else's duel to make a statement about himself. Sir Lucius prefers to fight by sword, leaving Acres and the Ensign to lug out with pistols. They are engaged in a form of second-class duelling, leaving the really noble weapons in his care.

But just as Sir Lucius's first name is undercut by his surname, so there
is a tension in his language between rather grandiose expressions (such
as the "quietus" that may come with the bullet) and less exalted detail (as in the question to Acres, should he die: "would you choose to
be pickled and sent home?").[73] The euphemisms and elegant circumlocutions coexist with unsparingly direct phrases. This sublimely euphemistic register cannot be sustained indefinitely. From speaking in
this highfalutin manner, Sir Lucius plunges us into the mud and soil
of actuality. The euphemisms are so extravagant that they call attention, all the more worryingly, to that which they purport to conceal.
Then the duellist's stance has to be discussed: "Let him see the broad
side of your full front—there—now a ball or two may pass clean through
your body, and never do any harm at all. . . . and it is much the gen-
teelest attitude into the bargain."[74]

O'Trigger's considerations of style remain uppermost. This is a prospective duel whose absurdity combines and exceeds the elements of
all the other unnecessary duels of previous comedies, for Acres manages to be ignorant of the reasons for which he is fighting and of the
identity of his opponent. Nor, of course, does he know how to fight.
For an eighteenth-century audience, the comically clueless rustic duellist is familiar, but this situation, in which he will have to stand and
face a gunshot, is an especially sinister, highly unnerving feature of
the modern duel.

"Valour will come and go." It is "sneaking off! . . . oozing out as it
were at the palms of my hands."[75] Perhaps because Sheridan had himself fought duels, he offers a somewhat more nuanced perspective on
cowardice, which is no longer a unitary block, a congenital weakness,
but a fluctuating property. This comedy suggests that cowardice is contingent on the social context. In front of Sir Lucius, Acres is allowed,
indeed expected, to be cowardly, whereas it is his social duty to be
braver than David and indeed to accuse him, through a transferal or
sublimation of his own fears, of cowardice. In fact, Sir Lucius probably
busies himself with Acres's duel in order to allay fears raised by his
own engagement.

Sheridan's comedy then compasses, within a small social circle, a
wide range of responses to the duel, all of which are delicately shaded:
there is the traditional fear of the servant, complemented by his good

sense; the young lover's aim to exploit the romantic possibilities and the reflected glory of the duel, without actually fighting it; O'Trigger's desire to duel, ostensibly to pursue the noble absurdity of a disinterested quarrel but actually to settle scores and assuage real resentments.

Yet Sheridan makes conspicuously absent any grievances about the duel on the part of the authorities. And even the coda or epilogue (traditionally the space where, in rhyming couplets, an eighteenth-century audience will be regaled, and sometimes surprised, by a speech telling them just how improving the play has been) keeps its own counsel on the scourge of duelling and the folly of duellists. Compared to French works, such as those of Sedaine beforehand and Laclos shortly after, the play voices hardly a scruple about the legality of duelling.

Indeed, even as they move around an evolving city, where the New Room is yet new, in which the latest fashions are sported, the most recent novels are read, and, as we have seen, the weapons of choice are changing, the characters in The Rivals, apparently aspiring to improve their health, remain hopelessly incorrigible. There is, however, possibly one exception—Mrs. Malaprop. Just before the end of the play, in the final scene, she gives voice to her chagrin: "O Sir Anthony!—men are all barbarians—."[76] After the morass of circumlocutions, pleonasms, and idiolects to which this comedy has treated us, Mrs. Malaprop's final words are, on one level, inapposite, given the peaceful conclusion to the play, yet her simple indictment, subject and object linked by the most rudimentary of verbs, is finally à propos. "Barbarian," that ubiquitous, mandatory term attracted by duellists, resonates here. We may instinctively assume that we ought, once again, to adjust and correct Mrs. Malaprop's word, only, on this occasion, she means exactly what she says.

Dickens, The Pickwick Papers (1836): Mr. Nathaniel Winkle versus Dr. Slammer (of the Ninety-Seventh)

The report of Sheridan's comic pistol duels echoes long into the nineteenth century. Thackeray's inflammable Captain Costigan has been playing the role of Lucius O'Trigger.[77] Dickens takes further the rather sinister elements of Sheridan's comedy when, in his turn, he depicts a farcical duel, pitting Mr. Winkle against Dr. Slammer (of the Ninety-Seventh Regiment) in an early chapter of *The Pickwick Papers*. In fact, it is the first day of the journey into the Kent countryside of the Pickwick Club: Messrs. Tupman, Snodgrass, Winkle, and, of course, Pickwick. Mr. Tupman and a stranger to the party have decided to attend a ball. Tupman, who has brought no attire suitable to the occasion, furtively borrows Winkle's dress suit while he is asleep. At the ball, the stranger upsets one Dr. Slammer by winning the attention of a little old lady whose "fat countenance" he admires.[78] The following morning, Winkle is fetched from his room and challenged to a duel. Dr. Slammer's assistant has established that the man wearing the dress suit must be him. Winkle, who, obviously, has no recollection of the contretemps that has caused this duel, checks his bag to see whether his suit has been stolen. But it is there all right (returned and neatly replaced by Tupman), and he concludes that he must have been drunk. He will have to fight the duel with Dr. Slammer.

The premise of the duel is absurd and provincial enough, even were it to be contested by the relevant men, but Dickens supplies an additional farcical dimension in contriving a duel between two persons who have never met or corresponded. As in Stendhal's *Le rouge et le noir* (1830), come the following morning, the challenger can remember only what the man was wearing, and now that he has changed, he is no longer recognizable. Fortunately, the duel is aborted just in time, when Dr. Slammer realizes that he is confronting the same coat but a different man in it.

This is a duel in the comic tradition, featuring bourgeois chaps out of their depth, incapable of going through with a duel, supported by supposed friends who can enjoy the thrill from a safe vantage point. This misadventure mixes all the well-loved ingredients of the traditional farce: comically apt names (Dr. Slammer, who has a second by the name of Payne); an utterly frivolous cause (a fat lady); the provincial setting (Rochester); the hint at bourgeois affectation and thrift (the pistols are not bought or inherited but hired "with the satisfactory accompaniments of powder, ball, and caps" from a shop);[79] and, above all else, an ignorance of what precisely to do. Snodgrass's notions of loading a pistol were "rather vague and undefined": the narrator means that the second has not the first idea.[80]

The emphasis falls not only on the fears, or the cowardice, of the principals—a familiar enough butt of comic depictions—but on the schadenfreude of the seconds (or supposed friends). This dimension had not been represented by eighteenth-century authors when they came to depict duels in their fiction, although eager O'Trigger, in *The Rivals*, announces the tendency for the second to appoint himself the impresario of the duel.

First, a virile, staccato conversation is recorded, as the preliminaries of the duel are orchestrated. Mr. Winkle's friend Mr. Snodgrass loyally and unhesitatingly agrees to serve as a second.

> "I want your assistance, my dear fellow, in an affair of honour," said Mr. Winkle.
> "You shall have it," replied Mr. Snodgrass, clasping his friend's hand. . . .
> "I will attend you," said Mr. Snodgrass.
> He was astonished, but by no means dismayed. It is extraordinary how cool any party but the principal can be in such cases. Mr. Winkle had forgotten this. He had judged of his friend's feelings by his own.[81]

After reproducing the dialogue of the characters, with minimal interruption, the narrator's brief sententious observation about the insouciance of other participants is all the more striking and expansive. The second's coolness, and indeed his pleasure in seeing his friend at risk, may mirror and authorize the reader's own morbid curiosity and interest. The second would then be a sort of surrogate for the reader, who can enjoy danger close by at no cost. Or the second corresponds to the author, dispassionately moving his characters into different positions. Dr. Slammer's second tells his counterpart, "we may place our men . . . with as much indifference as if the principals were chess-men, and the seconds the players."[82] The seconds turn into the principal characters here.

Dickens pursues this facet of the modern duel as the bout approaches. Winkle is more vexed by his friend than by his unknown adversary. Indeed, his friend becomes the de facto adversary in these circumstances. Winkle's oblique attempts to induce him to call it off, met by that friend's evasions, make for a virtual duel. Winkle, "perceiving that he had not alarmed his companions sufficiently, changed his ground." He asks his friend to pass a note on to his father, should he fall. "But this attack was a failure also." He then reminds Snodgrass that if the Doctor should fall, he could be tried as an accessory and would run the risk of transportation for life: "Mr. Snodgrass winced a little at this, but his *heroism* was invincible. 'In the cause of friendship,' he fervently exclaimed, 'I would brave all dangers.' "[83]

As Winkle internally curses "his companion's devoted friendship" while they walk along in silence, it becomes clear that the faithful and assiduous Snodgrass has left no stone unturned:

> "Have you got ev'rything?" said Mr. Winkle, in an agitated tone.
>
> "Ev'ry thing," replied Mr. Snodgrass; "plenty of ammunition, in case the shots don't take effect. There's a quarter of a pound of powder in the case, and I have got two newspapers in my pocket, for the loadings."
>
> These were instances of friendship, for which any man might reasonably feel most grateful. The presumption is, that the gratitude of Mr. Winkle was too powerful for utterance, as he said nothing—but continued to walk on—rather slowly.[84]

The timing of Dickens's prose is brilliantly suited to the pace of Mr. Winkle's deliberate steps. Dickens is now rather more explicit in expressing his interest in the duties of friendship.

Since we have barely acquainted ourselves with these characters, who are essentially weightless at this stage, the duel seems all the more gratuitous, a fight between utterly interchangeable men. There is of course a danger of reading this farcical adventure too seriously. It is not intended to evoke the violence and ferocity of men in Kent, which indeed proves to be the blessed nursery of "apples, cherries, hops, and women."[85] Besides, the respective roles of Snodgrass and Winkle are replicated comically when, in the next chapter, the latter has to ride a restive horse, while the former sits comfortably in the back of the carriage pulled by it. Yet the duel here exposes paradoxes and surprises latent in male friendship. Dickens's exploration of male interaction has been chiefly seen through the lens of homosocial theorizing.[86] Dickens pauses, while reflecting on the love of Nicholas Nickleby for Madeline, only nourished by absence and sustained by mystery, on the sad failure of friendship to command such loyalty. Not only does it easily fade in absentia, but it may prove fickle in close proximity.[87] In the post-

Revolutionary age, when traditional social bonds no longer necessarily held people together, friendship was highly idealized as the last, unique repository of trust.[88] In this context, Dickens's preliminaries to the duel will perhaps have seemed all the more amusingly cruel.

If the schadenfreude of the second matures into one motif, another, not without precedent in eighteenth-century comedies, is his own inordinate fear. His intrusive interest may reproach us, as we ourselves eagerly read the story, but his cowardice when faced by a duel contested by others is likely to amuse us with impunity. In an unfinished comic story by Jules Renard, the poor second complains that he is having to do all the work, while this ironic tendency perhaps reaches its zenith in the account of a "grand duel" related by Mark Twain, when the second graduates into the story's principal protagonist and its hero.[89] The second had evolved from the role of the "stickler," or moderator, at tournaments, who parted the combatants when they had been deemed to have fought long enough, and seconds continued to be known as "sticklers" throughout the early modern period.[90] But the pejorative sense, denoting a meddlesome, unduly fastidious presence, has now emerged, as the second's role in supporting and protecting the combatant shades into that of devising, implementing, and insisting on points of duelling etiquette. As Dickens's comical account suggests, the seconds, to all intents and purposes, faced the task of calibrating the extent of the resentments and converting that into the distance between the principals. Alternatively, it was, in effect, up to the seconds to decide how much they would miss their friend.

Astonishingly and puzzlingly, projected or threatened duels continue to accumulate in the chapters of *The Pickwick Papers* that follow. The absurd assumption that Mr. Pickwick and Peter Magnus are about to meet in a duel, after little more than an embarrassing misunderstanding, rests on provincial suspicions of the wicked, sophisticated ways of the metropolis—"A duel in Ipswich! . . . Nothing of the kind can be contemplated in this town."[91] But the officials want to believe that a duel is about to happen, if only so they can cancel it with a display of righteous self-importance, for a duel reflects glory even on those who prevent it. In chapter 32, Bob Sawyer's guests, Messrs. Noddy and Gunter, ludicrously think of fighting a duel. In chapter 38, Winkle and Dowler go to lengths to avoid meeting in a duel that they think inevitable. Winkle runs off, worried that he will kill Dowler in a duel, but it is clear that the humane action is first and foremost cowardly. It is no use if those who object to duelling are themselves known poltroons.[92]

These episodes all belong securely to genus A, and Dickens's readers may have been by turns amused and reassured to see the fanciful fears and the mannered indignation on the part of pompous but harmless middle-class chaps wholly innocent of the convulsive social and political movements announced by the Industrial Revolution and the recent Reform Act. On the cusp of the Victorian age, in 1836, as the first trains pull out of London, the Pickwickians can be seen bumped about the country in (and on) old-fashioned coaches and horses. Naturally, they head for Bath, a setting favored by the Georgian bucks of Sheridan and Smollett. The continuing popularity of the duel, if only in threats or fantasies, is symptomatic of a genteel age more concerned with good form than with reform. It paradoxically presupposes a stable society in which people know their place and the present still resembles the past.

The farcical duel in *The Pickwick Papers* had been reworked from an episode in an earlier theatrical version by Dickens, and the bizarrely genteel brutality would draw him back subsequently, but in a different key.[93] The duel between Sir Mulberry Hawk and Lord Verisopht in *Nicholas Nickleby* seems superfluous to the design of the novel. It looks like a display of gratuitous violence, unless the cool artifice of the duel allows us to appreciate, by contrast, the honesty and transparency of Nicholas's spontaneous bursts of fury, when he resorts, at intervals, to fisticuffs. Drawing on the likes of Smollett's *Roderick Random*, Dickens would then be using the duel in order to emphasize Nicholas's unpretentious violence and to advertise his simple, robust dignity. But the duel evidently intrigues and unsettles Dickens beyond that strategic role, exemplifying what his friend and biographer John Forster called "a profound attraction of repulsion" to which he was subject.[94]

CHAPTER THREE

The Poignant Duel

A gentleman deficient in courage and conviction, as he faces up to a duel, may find that the surest way of slipping out of his obligation, with his honor intact, is to inform his wife (or, failing that, his mother) of the business in hand, inadvertently of course. Some females duly fail the test, when their vanity encourages a duel to be fought in their name. In the comic tradition, however, women are, for the most part, sweet, sensitive creatures easily moved to compassion or feeble beings incapable of discretion. Either way, their involvement will generally forestall a duel. The resourceful servant Scrub, a forerunner to Smollett's Strap, in Farquhar's comedy *The Beaux-Stratagem* (1707) outlines the successive steps guaranteed to result in the cancellation of a duel. He is speaking with one of the beaux, Archer:

> SCRUB: If our masters in the country here receive a challenge, the first thing they do is to tell their wives; the wife tells the servants, the servants alarm the tenants, and in half an hour you shall have the whole county in arms.
> ARCHER: To hinder two men from doing what they have no mind for.[1]

By the second half of the eighteenth century, female characters, when faced by the prospect of a duel, may, however, be characterized by a new moral seriousness. While comedies exposing the pretensions and the folly of the duellist were often bluntly counterproductive instruments in the campaign against duelling, two women in particular take themselves seriously and require the reader to do so too. They are the heroines of two stupendous novels, which must dominate any account of the shifting sensibilities in eighteenth-century Europe. Their signal importance may be registered by not only the number of readers they instantly attract but also the volume of parodies that assail their lofty moral vantage points. In both *Clarissa* and *Julie*, the eponymous characters now bring to duelling, as they do to all the social questions of their time, their own privileged capacity for refined sensibility and intelligence. For the first time, then, female characters are enlisted as rational yet compassionate critics of the custom.

The traditional opposition to duelling voiced by men always ran the risk of looking like sour grapes, for they were necessarily vulnerable to accusations of lacking the class or the courage to stomach such forms of combat. By entrusting a critique of duelling to women, neither allowed nor expected to duel in any circumstances, such objections were necessarily silenced.

Both Richardson and Rousseau entrust cogent condemnations of duelling to exceptionally "pervivacious" young women, in these novels.[2] They reveal a new tactic, a different sensibility, in the struggle of authors with the scourge of the duel. Rousseau, in the guise of Saint-Preux, observes a self-defeating dimension to the exposure of noble follies on the stage, when authors take it upon themselves to ridicule the mores of their society. He would, accordingly, tackle the problem of the duel in his novel with a new degree of seriousness. But the case against duelling had already been spelled out, with great cogency, by another fictional woman of intelligence and sensibility: Clarissa Harlowe.

Richardson, *Clarissa; or, The History of a Young Lady* (1747–48): Mr. Lovelace versus Colonel Morden

Samuel Richardson's gigantic novel ends, as it begins, with a duel. These two actions form emphatic punctuation marks at either end of a novel immediately recognized as essentially plotless, its interest guaranteed more by the intricacies and subtleties of thoughts and feelings, whether the "indigested self-reasonings" of Clarissa Harlowe or the "extravagant volubility" of her tormentor, Robert Lovelace.[3] Like other writers, Richardson seems aware of the difficulty in bridging a gap between an indisputable discursive position on duelling in general that he might like to take and a more ambiguous standpoint from which the efficacy of particular duels may be appreciated.

In the very first letters that acquaint us with the protagonists of the novel, we learn of a "rencounter" between James Harlowe, Clarissa's brother, and Lovelace.[4] Their antipathy dates back to a "College-begun" resentment, but it has been compounded by Lovelace's interest in James's sisters. During their bout, Lovelace, we learn, finds himself in a position to kill Harlowe, but he "gives him his life." The duel that opens the novel therefore establishes the character of Lovelace in an ambivalent manner. Evidently a libertine ready to resort to violence, he is nevertheless a gentleman capable of, indeed given to, acts of generosity. Skill is matched by restraint in this case. That composite of aggression and courtesy, violence and charm, so characteristic of the duel immediately suggests itself.

Such gracious condescension does not pass unappreciated by Clarissa, who admits to being grateful that this notoriously "very revengeful man" did not do her brother all the "mischief he could have done him, and which [her] brother had endeavoured to do *him.*"[5] This swordsmanship tempered by restraint foreshadows and mirrors, as we soon see, his dexterity in teasing, tricking, and ultimately securing power over the sister. A "finished libertine" like Lovelace probes and prods just as he manipulates his sword, waiting for his moment before surprising his adversary. Duels provide a motor for events in the text and the behavior of its characters, so, for instance, Lovelace's acquaintance Belton dies, regretting a duel fought long in his past, while Lovelace himself, hiding at a tavern to spy on Clarissa, satisfies suspicious locals with the explanation that he is on the run after a duel.[6] Moreover, Lovelace sees himself as a figurative duellist, his life a sort of extended duel. He casts himself on occasion as a "principal" in the actions he conducts, ever conscious of occupying center stage. Less conventionally, he pays a tribute, in one of many typically self-enthralled passages reviewing his conduct, to his "old friend CHANCE, which has many a time been an excellent second" to him.[7] The usual italics are supplanted by capital letters here, such is Lovelace's largesse, but it is clear that he regards his own initiative and agency as sovereign and that, grateful as he is to it, he does not see himself as beholden to the workings of chance. Lovelace manipulates metaphors deftly (hence his acute chagrin when Clarissa outwits him with a double meaning of her own), and this duelling analogy may appear to be somewhat trite: with whom, or with what, does this figurative duellist contend? Lovelace is, as we know, bent on avenging humiliation at the hands of a woman, given to a ferociously competitive outlook, while his provocative rapier wit shows off that disposition more generally. Ultimately, then, the conclusive combat he fights now provides a literal manifestation of a hitherto figurative bout, as a protracted duel with life itself comes to a close.

Appalled and exhausted by the series of violations to which Lovelace has subjected her, Clarissa is also ready to expire. Her cousin William Morden is returning to England from Florence, and she knows that he will certainly challenge Lovelace to a duel in order to avenge her. This premonition prompts a letter to Morden in which she provides an extremely lucid, rational critique of duelling in general, even as she implores him to refrain specifically from fighting a duel on her behalf.

Clarissa airs her objections to duelling, one by one, with philosophical clarity. First, mindful of the church's stance, she warns Morden that "vengeance is God's province" and chides him for thinking of invading it. Secondly, more pragmatically, she points out that her cousin would, in the event of a duel, be "running an *equal* risk with a *guilty* man." (Clarissa is fond of italics.) Thirdly, as a gentleman who has "adorned a public character," his challenge would amount to "an insult upon magistracy and good government." Fourthly, were he to win the duel, he would lend his adversary the merit of falling by his hand. Fifthly, this act of revenge might initiate a potentially endless chain of vengeful acts: "where should the evil stop?" she asks rhetorically: "And who shall avenge on you?—and who on your avenger?"[8]

She foresees both guilt and shame as a result of a duel, irrespective of its outcome. It is a remarkable epitome of philosophical and theological arguments rehearsed hitherto. Clarissa can be assumed to have assimilated them at church from the intelligent preachers whom she makes a point of hearing. Here, spelled out in the second person, the arguments acquire a new urgency. Her inventory of points ranges from theological wisdom to impeccably rational arguments. Indeed, they are, literally, unanswerable: the letter in which they are enumerated is "to be delivered after [her] death."[9] Clarissa's ailing, dying state lends the objections to duelling a numinous quality. She addresses her cousin, as he reads the letter, from beyond the grave, with prima facie certainties as to the sinfulness of the act.

Nevertheless, amid the coolly catalogued grievances is a slight hint that her objection to the prospective duel might also be attributable to a tacit wish for no harm to come to the man for whom she may harbor what her friend Anna Howe calls a "lurking love." She remarks that Lovelace does not deserve to forfeit his life and soul after rendering her "miserable for *a few months* only."[10] This ad hominem argument does not particularly convince, given that she is dying as a result. In her young life (for Clarissa is only nineteen years of age), it is a considerable interval. In the very last words of her last letter, no doubt calculating that Morden will need to be dissuaded from pursuing Lovelace, she takes her leave, addressing "dear cousin Morden, my friend, my guardian, but not my avenger," affectionately but admonishingly taking care to add, in a final exclamatory, perhaps despairing parenthesis, "(Dear Sir! Remember that!)."[11]

But Morden will not remember that, or rather, worse still, he chooses to countermand her pleas. Morden quite deliberately disobliges his cousin, taking great trouble to seek out Lovelace. Clarissa is extremely scrupulous when it comes to the arrangements to be put in place after her death. Indeed, the care and consideration with which she proceeds constitute further evidence both of her essential goodness and her evangelical calm. This disposition is exemplified by her appointment of John Belford, Lovelace's reformed friend, to the role of her executor, providing an opportunity for him to rehabilitate himself further, while confirming herself above the verdicts of public opinion. The "preparation" she invests into her funerary arrangements is marveled at by all who know her. But her fastidiousness renders Morden's undaunted resolve to pursue Lovelace all the more striking and unsettling. This willful prosecution of plans, running contrary to Clarissa's intentions, lends further substance to any assumption that this is a world in which men hold sway, even those well-disposed toward women. Relatives have never understood or respected Clarissa's self-determination, and Morden turns out to be no different. It is a final affront, as her dying wish is overlooked. For Morden hears the call of honor but is deaf to Clarissa's plea.

The reward for reading to the very end of this unprecedentedly enormous novel is then the death of Lovelace, at the hands of Morden, in that duel. The duel is undertaken, unabashedly, with no regard to the dishonored, dying lady's fervent wishes. There is no suggestion that Morden did not receive her letter (as Thomas Hardy might perhaps have contrived things). Indeed, the duel is pursued actively against these wishes. It is not as if the duel were a regrettably inevitable evil, imposed on Morden by the circumstances. On the contrary, Lovelace has left the shores of England, although he has been careful to avoid going somewhere very remote, like Spain, lest that choice raise suspicions that he is attempting to flee from retribution. The trail of letters, as the novel reaches its conclusion, allows us to track Lovelace, who means to head to Venice (for the Carnival, naturally), across northern Europe, where he is followed purposefully by Morden. Finally, the duel takes place at Trent. This being the case, the outcome vouchsafed by Morden cannot possibly be described as chivalric. The final act that is the fatal duel can be put down to a cruelly unforgiving male logic— these men need to sort out their differences in this way, the strength of female objections notwithstanding; or the economy of the novel has to ignore the claims of reason. We move inexorably toward a dramatic and cathartic ending, which requires retribution for the villain and the restoration of order, even if reason does not insist on or even permit this outcome. As eighteenth-century moralists continue to downplay the impact of *Le Cid* and its duels, along comes a no-less-clinching, climactic duel. By placing the duel at the very end of a seemingly interminable novel, Richardson, in spite of the nicely worded grievances about the folly and futility of duelling, surely honors the duel. He honors it as an act responsible for bringing about the finality of a resolution, the solaces of closure, indeed of affording, for reader and challenger alike, satisfaction. Moreover, this ending honors not only the duel but the infernal man who perishes in it, Lovelace.

Richardson may have wanted both the satisfaction of condemning the duel and the pleasure of concluding his novel with a retributive bout. The equivocation recalls Rousseau's remark about those who, after applauding the Cid on the stage, are content to watch him hang in public for the crime of duelling.[12] The play is but a diversion that does not actually interfere with our own moral and legal intelligence. Puzzlingly, we can applaud what we deplore, and vice versa.

The duel could be condemned implicitly by the sort of men who contest it. Lovelace, the veteran of several duels, may confirm a suspicion that duelling is for disreputable types. But if he proves to be the archetypally cynical, cunning libertine, his adversary, Morden, is, beyond doubt, cultured, kind, rational, and decent. In fact, for all the horrors of Lovelace's conduct toward Clarissa, he too can behave with unfeigned integrity. Unlike Valmont, later on, his generosity to simple folk is not staged. His hatred of hypocrisy, his distaste for and refusal of money, indeed his love of writing all paint a picture of a man free from all forms of dependence and transparent in his dealings with other men. He claims that he "never lied to man, and hardly ever said truth to woman."[13] As the novel moves to a potentially redemptive conclusion, Richardson lavishes detail on the practical arrangements that precede the duel. Of course, this forms part of the craft of the professional writer, attentive to authenticating detail of the sort that captivated his readers. But that detail also allows us to see how some of the courtesies and scruples integral to the process may also conceal more sinister maneuvers.

In an exchange of polite letters, Lovelace and Morden conduct a detailed discussion about the weapons best suited to their forthcoming encounter. Scruples, shared by each of the principals, with regard to timing and the choice of weapons appear to indicate the utmost care and regard for the adversary. And the duel would seem to offer an inspiring example of impeccable gentlemanliness. It is clear that the debate about the choice of weapons amounts to an extended negotiation about their respective commitments, abilities, and class. Lovelace, who seems rather enthralled with his own cheerfulness, tells his correspondent that he is no "unfleshed novice" and speaks of his supreme confidence.[14] But, in reminding himself of this, he is possibly protesting too much. Moreover, in telling his opponent, there is perhaps another motivation at work. Lovelace is so confident in his mastery of the sword that he is loath to exploit what he sees as his advantage. This would seem to be the honorable expression of a wish for equal opportunities and fair play. They fix on the rapier: "Yet I repeatedly told him that I value myself so much upon my skill in that weapon, that I would wish him to choose any other."[15] Lovelace is ostensibly trying to warn Morden off the sword, leaving him (and us readers) with the suggestion that he is magnanimously reconciled to dying in the imminent contest. This would be impressively generous unless it is, perhaps at the same time, complacently hubristic. But it is also, in all likelihood, a sort of mind game, by which the declaration of his mastery puts pressure on his opponent to emulate, rather than to evade, it. Lovelace's apparent generosity seems tactical and manipulative. The more he insists that this is the weapon in which he has supreme confidence and is therefore to be avoided by his adversary, the more he goads Morden into accepting it. Morden, after hearing these protests, is bound to look like a coward or less of a gentleman if he does not agree to it. He could not innocently opt for pistols without now looking evasive or fearful. So the freedom to choose only adds psychological complications and constraints. Just as the preceding letters lead us through labyrinths of desire and denial, so these letters expose the subtleties involved in these apparently generous offers and decisions, as no writer examining the process had done so before.

The letter that follows does quietly betray new uncertainties. Lovelace sounds confident of his chances with the pistol too, writing, "No man, I'll venture to say, has a steadier hand or eye than I have."[16] Between the commas, however, a telling little parenthesis is allowed to surface.

The duel that follows, on the morning of 15 December, offers a model of good conduct, taste, judgment, tact, and modesty. The principals also know the virtue of punctuality. As Lovelace's French servant, F. J. De la Tour, reports in a translated letter,

> The two chevaliers came exactly at their time: they were attended by Monsieur Margate (the colonel's gentleman) and myself. They had given orders overnight and now repeated them in each other's presence, that we should observe a strict impartiality between them. . . .
>
> After a few compliments, both the gentlemen, with the greatest presence of mind that I ever beheld in men, stripped to their shirts and drew.

Several passes follow, before Lovelace is mortally wounded. "His sword dropped from his hand. Mr. Morden threw his down, and ran to him, saying in French—Ah monsieur, you are a dead man!—Call to God for mercy!"[17]

It may seem curious that two Englishmen abroad communicate in French at this desperate juncture. And they are not even in France. But they speak in French in order that their duel may be understood, as well as observed, by De la Tour. He can then commemorate this duel

Illustration after a design by Daniel Chodowiecki from Richardson's *Clarissa*
(Geneva: Barde, Manget & co., 1786). Reproduced by kind permission of the Syndics
of Cambridge University Library.

for posterity. A duel, however violent, can be read and appreciated like a text.

A fatal duel might not necessarily be preferable to a nonfatal bout in persuading us that duelling is evil or wrong. It would seem that the former does advertise the virtues of courage and fortitude. It risks turning the malefactor into a martyr. We are perhaps inclined to feel that it is dangerous before thinking it sinful. Besides, the duel seems final and clean by comparison with the "dejected whimpering and terror" elicited by the lengthy scenes in which, by turns, Belford's father, Belton, and other characters die. A few months before, Lovelace has also described a nightmarish dream in which Morden "all of a sudden flashed in through a window, with his drawn sword" before him.[18] Lovelace then finds himself hurtling through a black hole. This premonitory dream, one of several vividly gothic episodes, helps us to feel that this outcome is not only inevitable but, in a sense, right.

Fascinatingly, the novel that delivers this definitive, dramatic finale has contained, within its own pages, a seemingly irrefutable, literally unanswerable set of objections. But the imperatives of reason and the dictates of the novel ultimately send *Clarissa* in opposing directions, for the duel continues to provide an irresistibly elegant ending, whether to the narrative of a novel or to the trajectory of a life.

Rousseau, *Julie; ou, La nouvelle Héloïse* (1761): Lord Bomston versus Saint-Preux, Canceled

Rousseau's *Julie* could be construed as a riposte to Richardson's *Clarissa*, one epistolary novel replying to the other, in a sort of extended RSVP. Here, programmatic objections to duelling, among many other observations, are again voiced by the eponymous heroine. But while Richardson shows the redundancy of even compelling philosophical arguments, Rousseau's men obey the female call for the duel to stop.

Julie, anxiously aware that her lover, Saint-Preux, intends, after a drunken escapade, to challenge Bomston to a duel, takes it upon herself to discourage him from doing so. Julie intercedes, urging him to resist engaging a duel by appealing to his reason. The discrepancies in their class undoubtedly facilitate this intervention, but the letter, with its calmly enumerated objections to duelling, indicates that she is a morally worthy heir to Clarissa. As in *Clarissa*, a few years earlier, there follows a set piece, which, thanks to its philosophical clarity and tendency toward abstraction, is detachable from the surrounding novel.

The belief or conviction that the novel might ideally fortify philosophical reflections, sugaring the moral pill, remained axiomatic among many eighteenth-century writers. By integrating rational arguments and homilies within the space of a novel, those ideas would, potentially, attract attention otherwise denied to them. However, the converse might turn out to be true. Purely rational objections to such a predicament as that of Saint-Preux risked looking pallid and slight, in proximity to the intense experiences and emotions conveyed by the novel.

Rousseau, who wishes (so he claims) that he had not needed to write this novel yet manfully writes a text almost as long as *Clarissa*, redeems the contradiction central to that work. That is, the fatal duel which defies and disobliges the heroine in whose name it is fought also guarantees the shape and splendor of a conclusion. This subsequent duel is, happily, averted thanks to Julie's objections. Rousseau's novel organizes a set of objections to the duel, without then questioning or negating these words with deeds. But the predicament of Saint-Preux is also somewhat different from that of Colonel Morden. As Julie recognizes, he is, in the first instance, insufficiently noble and practiced to cross swords, his chivalric nickname notwithstanding. In fact, Richardson's subsequent novel, *Sir Charles Grandison* (1753), seems designed to apologize for the spectacular duel that brought *Clarissa* to a close. Sir Charles, when challenged to a duel by Sir Hargrave, declines with a series of well-aimed and well-received maxims: "to *die* like a man of honour, Sir Hargrave, you must have *lived* like one."[19] Even if the objections are sound per se, the repartee form in which they prevail constitutes a sort of surrogate duel. Grandison dominates this battle of wits thanks to verbal thrusts that are both sharp and spontaneous. The speed and pertinence of his responses are integral to their efficacy.

An ecumenical chorus (consisting of a Jew and a Roman Catholic, among others) chirps approvingly at intervals, authorizing our own admiration of Grandison. "I had rather be Sir Charles Grandison in this one past hour, than the Great Mogul all my life," exclaims

Mr. Bagenhall, one of the assembled gentlemen. The scene risks turning into one of Steele's more sententious dramas which weary us with their wisdom. However, the usual moral and historical objections to duelling are accompanied here by both a revelation and an action. Grandison reveals that, after his father was wounded in a duel, his mother, "within a year after falling into fits," died. He also acts in grabbing a pair of duelling pistols, which lie temptingly on a nearby table, and discharging them out the window, presumably after opening it. Such additional dimensions will be seen again in Rousseau's novel.[20]

A potentially tedious lesson devoted to the evils of duelling is camouflaged by the urgency and pathos of Grandison's circumstances, yet the epistolary form allows a range of essayistic forays into moral and philosophical realms. Smollett includes in his epistolary *Travels through France and Italy* a discussion of duelling, unprovoked by anything like an actual duel, and it enjoys the ease and autonomy of a detachable pamphlet.[21] Unusually, a table of contents enumerated the "matières" or the themes of the letters, allowing them to be consulted for Rousseau's wisdom on various philosophical and moral points. *Julie* is indeed a heavy vehicle for the dissemination of Jean-Jacques's ideas and ideals, a panorama, from an alpine altitude, of eighteenth-century manners and moral questions. But it is of course much more than that. This is an extraordinarily moving, sometimes frustrating, always absorbing, ultimately tragic story. And, as in *Clarissa,* the fictional, epistolary form allows a powerfully different sort of critique, supplementing rational argumentation, to emerge. Strikingly absent from the society in the Valais that these characters inhabit is any formal or official religious authority. Until the very end of the book, no priest or pastor is to be seen. This is a world where the characters are largely self-reliant, even as they find themselves at odds with different forms of authority. Friendship, whether in its male (Bomston and Saint-Preux) or female (Julie and Claire) variants, provides the surest means by which the hazards of life are negotiated. Letters to friends are the confessionals for these Protestant personages. Julie's letter, like that of Clarissa, brings to bear a largely secular, philosophical understanding of the woes entailed by duelling.

Richardson has preceded Rousseau in looking at a prospective duel through the eyes of the person on whose behalf it is supposedly fought, that is, the lady whose honor is to be vindicated. The discursive points familiar from philosophical arguments gain urgency and immediacy. Rousseau's writing, however detached and purportedly objective, assumes the form of a first-person account, just as Voltaire's work, even at its most confessional and intimate, is essentially an oeuvre in the third person. Julie's letter is an impressive tapestry in which objections, variously local and universal, are skillfully woven together. In the first case, Julie has not the slightest doubt about the outcome. Bomston is the veteran of several duels, and Saint-Preux is not.

The novelistic form allows the rational argument to be supplemented by two further emotive approaches to the question. First, Julie provides a moving insight into the chagrin of her father, who, she confides, killed his friend in a duel when they were young men. The highly intractable, buttoned-up Baron allows Rousseau to exemplify the lasting damage that the successful duellist may inflict on himself. This event in the prehistory to the text accounts for, and may to an extent mitigate, both the Baron's inordinate attachment to his daughter and his exceptional reserve. The idea that a duel might, far from providing the expected "closure," leave a lasting and terrible impression on its victor may have been inspired by a disturbing passage in *Clarissa*.[22] Rousseau is also no doubt remembering the consequences of his own father's clash with a gentleman, which occurred in 1722, when Jean-Jacques was a child. Although the proposed duel did not take place, Rousseau's father, Isaac, sentenced to imprisonment, fled the family home in Geneva, preferring a lifelong exile than an insult to his honor, an "accident," as Rousseau recalls in the *Confessions* "the effects of which have reverberated for the rest of my life."[23] Secondly, once Julie has completed her philosophical letter, she then writes *ad hominem* to Bomston, making it clear that, if the duel should go ahead (and to form), she will not survive. In this remarkable letter, she therefore acknowledges the limits to the power of Saint-Preux's reason and that of Bomston but also the insufficiencies of her own rational argument. It is as though she were aware of the failure of Clarissa to persuade Morden through reason alone to desist from the duel.

Rousseau's master stroke consists in allowing Julie to diversify the objections to duelling in an affective register. Her subsequent letter, abandoning the rational approach, supplements it but also possibly

exposes it limits. It therefore epitomizes Rousseau's approach in writing
a novel. The temptation to duel may be removed by the graces of sensibility, if not by the force of reason, and would-be duellists, undeterred
by a tract, might be more embarrassed by a novel.

The prospective clash of Lord Bomston and Saint-Preux promises
to be a spectacular mismatch. An Englishman who cannot take his
drink, a Yorkshireman liberal with his money, Bomston does, however,
behave predictably here—he duels because that is simply what noblemen
do; Saint-Preux is a different sort of man. He wants to duel because he
sees a chance of crossing swords with a nobleman. The dispute turns
not so much on actual insults to the honor of Julie but on Saint-Preux's
hidden resentments and on the dark and, as it turns out, utterly justified sense of his own social inadequacy. This rootless, penniless, indeed nameless man is obsessed, to a degree that might surprise even
eighteenth-century readers, with his honor. Saint-Preux may, at little
or no financial cost to himself, measure up to a nobleman, while, like
Werther, in the following decade, his tastes in music, learning, and
sensibility convince him of his own worth.

The most extraordinary part of this affair is, however, about to
occur. Saint-Preux in his subsequent letter to Julie describes what has
just happened, as he was poring over her letter to him and pondering
his next move. Eighteenth-century readers would have seen a plethora
of comically aborted duels. Rousseau realizes that it is not sufficient
simply to call off this engagement too, which will leave either or both
of the nonduellists looking feeble or risible. Indeed, Rousseau was of
the opinion that any play in which a man turned down a duel was destined to fail.[24] Shakespeare's Richard II rather arbitrarily aborts a duel
(about to be contested by Bolingbroke and Mowbray), thereby demon-
strating his authority and possibly disappointing the audience. But it
takes a writer as gifted as Shakespeare to lend the frustrated duellists
vivid, dramatic verse that will assuage those feelings of disappointment. The pathos of exile that they duly envision fully compensates
for the withheld action. Rousseau's characters do not live under a monarchy. Resistance to such a custom cannot be coerced with such a fiat,
but they must assent to an inner compulsion. Rousseau ensures that
they duly act out a self-staged ersatz duel. Saint-Preux hears a knock
at the door. It is Bomston. Saint-Preux, alert to the symbolism, notes

that his prospective adversary arrives without a sword, carrying a cane. He is accompanied by a little retinue, his prospective seconds redeployed as witnesses. He thereby recognizes that ceremonious solemnity is integral to the process of reparation. A ritualistic shell remains in place. There follows a moving, rather tense scene, in which Bomston falls to his knees and asks for forgiveness. When Grandison fires the pistols, he does so in a symbolic gesture, but it is, above all, a prudent act, removing any temptation to duel there and then. By contrast, the genuflection here fulfills no practical purpose. Nevertheless, it represents a form of active abstention, as the duel declined is elevated into an admirable, pivotal act. Indeed, Rousseau chose this drama of conscientious objection for one of twelve carefully prescribed engravings, by Hubert-François Gravelot, adding to the picture a caption: "the heroism of virtue."[25]

The duel that costs Lovelace his life would seem to point to the redundancy of the most persuasive of arguments, as against an internalized compulsion to fight at any price. Gentlemen seem destined to remain deaf to the pleas of a lady, even as they purport to act chivalrously on her behalf. Rousseau, both alert to this sequence of events in Richardson's novel and mindful of the self-defeating character assumed by comic exposés of the duellist, stages, as a consequence of Julie's critique, a highly original solemn nonduel, a ceremonious act of contrition that honors her words. Moreover, when, later, Saint-Preux is confronted by a challenge from Julie's father, he unhesitatingly brushes off the proposition, dismissing it as an example of a bizarre and unduly delicate conception of honor.[26] There will be no reprise of Le Cid here. Saint-Preux has assimilated Julie's wise words, which remain no less valid at this subsequent point.

Rousseau provides explanations of his own modus operandi in this work not only through one *avertissement*, two prefaces, and an appendix but in the letters themselves. Saint-Preux dilates on the ineffectual, self-defeating nature of ridicule and comic responses to vice: "In depicting the ridiculousness of classes that serve as role models to others, writers only succeed in extending rather than effacing it, and . . . the people, always given to aping and imitating the rich, go to the theater less to laugh at their folly than to study it, in order to become madder still by imitating them."[27] Thanks to Clarissa and to Julie, two

L'héroisme de la vertu. Illustration engraved by Jean Ouvrier after a design by Hubert-François Gravelot from Rousseau's *Julie; ou, La nouvelle Héloïse* (Paris: veuve Duchesne, 1788). Reproduced by kind permission of the Syndics of Cambridge University Library.

of the most celebrated novels of the eighteenth century, sentiment col-
laborates with reason in an attempt to defeat the duel. A second prong
in the onslaught against duelling is forged in this way. The would-be
duellist is not, as in those comedies, cowed by public opinion into re-
jecting duels; he has instead internalized an opposition, at once rational
and heartfelt, to the custom.

Julie is a moral mediatrix here, relying on the strength of her own
arguments but trusting also in the depth and sanctity of her feelings.
Only by listening to the promptings of our own hearts and consciences,
instead of tightening (or indeed relaxing) laws, suggests Rousseau, can
customs mature and change. These novels were not, of course, written
expressly and programmatically with the exclusive aim of exposing the
folly of duelling. Nevertheless, their response to the moral difficulties
of their society necessarily encompasses the problem of duelling. Both
texts suggest, with an unprecedented depth of feeling, that duels may
be the product of a hereditary malaise, episodes in a cycle of violence
that repeats itself, beyond the control of the agent. They each examine
the long-term damage (the guilt, the emotional stunting) that duelling
may inflict, perhaps counterintuitively in their day, on the victors, as
well as on secondary victims such as offspring. The haunted duellist
is a figure we shall meet again.[28] Concurrently, his sense of an obligation to his own family, or that of his adversary, grows into a more decisive criterion.[29] Rousseau's *Julie* is then a younger sister and heir to
Clarissa, but, to the chagrin of those concerned to demystify duels,
among her own numerous novelistic progeny was an enfant terrible by
the name of *Les liaisons dangereuses*.

Laclos, *Les liaisons dangereuses* (1782): Vicomte de Valmont versus Chevalier Danceny

As the last great epistolary novel of the eighteenth century, *Les liaisons dangereuses*, comes to a close, Madame de Rosemonde, the wise,
if frail, elderly aunt of the notorious Vicomte de Valmont, opens a letter,
addressed to her by one Monsieur Bertrand. She reads the following
words: "It is with great regret that I fulfill the sad duty of announcing
to you news that will cause you great sorrow." Like every other move
in this supremely crafted novel, Laclos's decision to entrust this duty

to a hitherto unknown character wraps these words in a semblance of objectivity. But the key promptly changes. The formalities make way for a febrile register: "Your nephew, Madam . . . My God! Must I distress such a respectable lady! Your nephew, Madam, has had the misfortune to succumb in single combat, this morning with M. the chevalier Danceny. I am entirely ignorant of the subject of the quarrel: . . . it appears, I say, that he was not the aggressor. And yet must it be he that the Heavens have permitted to succumb!"[30] Dangerous liaisons have now turned fatal: Valmont, his aunt learns, has died in a duel. Yet in dignifying it as a "combat singulier," Bertrand selects an archaic term which, aligning Valmont with warriors of yore, spares Rosemonde the thought that her nephew has been killed in another avoidable duel. Likewise, rather than prosaically "dying," Valmont is instead allowed to "succumb." Both semantic choices elevate the squalid, illegal death of her nephew to a higher plane. The remarkably twisted chain of subjunctives at the end of the paragraph, culminating in an exquisitely pompous imperfect subjunctive, emphasizes the extraordinariness of tragic events, which not only defy comprehension but resist expression. They seem to call for a higher register than that summoned by more ordinary occurrences. Bertrand's reluctance to call a duel a duel is mirrored by a similar reticence, common to all the other protagonists, including Danceny himself. It seems to be a dirty word, a taboo, not only because duels were illegal but because the notion that duels were never being fought had become ingrained.

Paradoxically, the duel appears to rejuvenate the Vicomte de Valmont, even as it kills him. Valmont could, at this stage, be considered an old rake, who, in the course of the novel, has taken advantage of younger people, including the man who now slays him. Yet this exchange of letters in which we learn of the duel guarantees an aura of youth around Valmont, as his "precocious" death liberates him from his cynical, older self. If details of his fate were instead communicated by relatively youthful characters, say, Danceny to Cécile, Valmont would look like an old roué, who has finally met his match. But, in reading this letter in the company of Rosemonde or, in a sense, on her behalf, the reader is implicitly encouraged to feel that Valmont's death is premature. His death is thereby romanticized. Rosemonde must endure the sorrow of outliving her younger relation. But it is not only relative to Rosemonde that Valmont seems young, his death a tragic waste. Bertrand too turns out to be an older figure who remembers Valmont with affection: "Good God, when, after his birth, I held in my arms this precious scion of such an illustrious family, little did I predict that he would expire in my arms and that I would be weeping over his death. Such a premature and such an unfortunate death! My tears flow in spite of myself."[31] He is then by no means the objective on-looker we might first have supposed him to be. The letter celebrates and affirms a skein of enduring loyalties, stretching between Bertrand, evidently an old retainer, and Rosemonde; between Rosemonde and her errant nephew; and, most significantly, between Valmont and Danceny, who part with mutual, gentlemanly respect.[32] The Vicomte is then embraced by the concentric circles of household, family, and class.

Valmont and Danceny have stepped out of doors in order to enter a male world, where, free from a claustrophobic society governed by plea-sure, they seem to breathe a different, more natural air. For the first time, Valmont's vulnerability can be appreciated. Valmont acquires a past in the eyes of the reader, who can see that he too was once the object of hopes and aspirations. Even if no man is a hero to his valet de chambre, Bertrand's abiding loyalty and affections seem beyond doubt here.

These intimate connections appear to redeem the dangerous liai-sons of the previous pages, rendering redundant any recourse to law or any appeal to other forms of compensation. Never, since Corneille's *Le Cid*, has the efficacy of the duel in providing resolution, or what would now be termed "closure," been more manifest—in French lit-erature, that is, for this conclusion obviously recalls that of *Clarissa*. The duel furnishes both texts with the splendor of a definitive ending.

More specifically, the form of Bertrand's letter recalls De la Tour's announcement of the death of his "dear chevalier" and master, Lovelace, in Richardson's novel. Indeed, it so happens that they are written on the same date, the seventh of December. In fact, the duels may have taken place on the very same day.[33] At all events, both novels proceed to wintry ends.. If Rousseau in *Julie* purged the duel from the pages of his epistolary novel, Laclos reinstates it. The duel, like that which kills Lovelace and terminates *Clarissa*, delivers the "right" result, pos-sibly with the complicity of a penitent malefactor. Laclos includes no programmatic objections to duelling beforehand. There is a set of arguments about the legality and justice of the bout, but, unlike *Clarissa* and *Julie*, where objections are rehearsed prior to a duel, here they are belated and therefore futile. By comparison to that of Lovelace, Valmont's death seems more redemptive, even heroic, at first glance. Valmont is described as a sort of warrior or soldier throughout, from the first letters. The scene is therefore set for him to die a heroic death, whether as a real or parodic figure.

Valmont's death seems then to be a luminous moment. His is a beautiful death, one of many in the fictions of this era. Mlle. de St. Yves's passing in Voltaire's *Ingénu* sustains a tradition of "belles morts," sanctified by sentiments and embalmed with tears, inaugurated by the lengthy deathbed drama in Rousseau's *Julie*.[34] This letter exalts Valmont, and it honors the duel as a redemptive conclusion to a life of disreputable, unseemly pursuits, repairing fractured relationships. The act appears to have expiated Valmont's crimes rather than adding to them. Borne and lamented by the figures around him, Valmont is the hero of a secular pietà. He dies in receipt not of extreme unction but of those secular sacraments vital to the later eighteenth century—tears, the badge of sensibility. He moves to tears not only good old Bertrand but also his opponent, Danceny. Valmont expires with a valedictory sigh ("soupir")—*soupirant* being a "suitor" in French—so it appears to be the final bow of a lover. *Les liaisons dangereuses* is seldom visual until the aftermath of this duel, described in graphic detail, perhaps ironically, given Bertrand's avowed wish to spare Rosemonde the worst. Yet when we learn that Valmont expires, bathed ("baigné") in blood, the term, with its baptismal flavor, yields further evidence of renewal. Indeed, the scene may recall the moment at which Orlando inflicts a mortal wound on the pagan Agricane, who asks to be baptized.[35]

The duel, in which two gentlemen, obeying the same rules, meet each other as peers may come as a relief and a redemption for the reader. The touching description penned by an ordinary man, Monsieur Bertrand, makes accessible an aristocratic prerogative to a wider community, which embraces anyone with a core of sensitivity. After all, as he avers, with disarming simplicity, "in every social station, people have a heart and some sensibility."[36]

Both the outcome and the means by which it is reached seem eminently fitting and satisfying. Having lived by the sword, Valmont is apparently reconciled to dying by it. Valmont loses the duel, but he wins the respect of Danceny. Death by duelling is a socially, if not legally, acceptable way of allowing Valmont to recognize and expiate his wrongs. Moreover, his death, it would seem, may have been a form of assisted suicide. The death of Valmont is indeed impressively stoical. He dies, without all the ceremonies of extreme unction, in a manner that is not conventionally Christian. Strikingly, his apparently mundane concern for the arrangements of documents, even as he dies, recalls the story of Seneca, who interrupted his protracted death in the bath by dictating a speech. It offers a marked contrast with the undignified, abject failure of Saint-Preux to take up stoic examples when he is thrown out of Julie's household. But Saint-Preux fails to live up to that ideal, as he hammers the floor, convulsing on the staircase. Here, however, the stoic model is intact and impressive. Laclos was supposed to be debunking the ideals of his exalted forerunner, *Julie*, but here it is inverted. From the epigraph onward—"j'ai vu les mœurs de mon siècle et j'ai publié ces lettres"—in which Rousseau's rather portentous prefatory remarks ahead of *Julie* are echoed, there is a challenging relationship with this parent text.

Valmont dies with dignity and with charity, it seems. But he gives away not only his life but those papers. These documents, it turns out, are the letters and private records of the Marquise de Merteuil, which will seal her downfall. The name of the lady he apparently loved is not on his lips as he dies (as it is, albeit ambiguously, on those of the expiring Lovelace). Nor, as he succumbs, does Valmont mention his loving aunt. There is no hint of chivalry in this scene. It is a useless death, equivalent to that of Mme. de Tourvel. On the contrary, he is preoccupied with the wish to expose and damage another woman—the Marquise de Merteuil. This moment seems to be pivotal. It precedes and permits the publication of damning details, a strategy more common in nineteenth-century literature. This spectacular encounter seems designed to deflect our attention from another duel. But, however compelling it might be, it is a duel that cannot happen. The battle of wits and of wills, contested throughout the novel by Valmont and Merteuil, necessarily cannot be a duel of equals, as Merteuil points out, and will never result in reconciliation. Indeed, while men of different ranks, from Bertrand to Danceny, loyally rally around one of their own, women, without exception, shun Merteuil. *Clarissa* and *Julie* are each animated by female friendships (Clarissa with Anna; Julie with Claire) that are models of resilience and intelligence. These relationships offer, in the deepest darkness, countervailing warmth and light. But women in this novel are not allowed the consolations of friendship. The opening letter, from Cécile to her friend Sophie, may mislead readers familiar with *Clarissa* and *Julie,* for it will quickly be forgotten, and that relationship is not seen to mature. Cécile and Sophie instantly present symptoms of the follies of the French educational system, whereas those other pairs of female friends provide articulate commentaries on the predicament of women, not merely evidence of its urgency. Hence, Laclos's authorship of a discrete, discursive work, *De l'éducation des femmes,* for a critical discussion of the educational deficiencies in society cannot be entrusted to characters who are too manifestly the products of the system to be its critics.

Valmont's actions, including this final one—the duel—are comprehended by a society inured and reconciled to libertinage. However refractory, they can be considered natural, or at least second nature, to someone of his station. Indeed, Valmont's least expected, and perhaps most costly, action is that of falling in love with Madame de Tourvel (or seeming to do so).

Another detail suggests that the duel may have been less than chivalric. Under the idealizing gloss of Bertrand's account, we learn that Valmont sustains *two* wounds to his body. Honor would normally have been satisfied by one blow. Danceny allows himself, or is possibly encouraged, to administer a coup de grâce, which will, in the event, kill his adversary. This seems not to indicate a *boutade* by which a score can be settled but to translate a cruel intention to fight to death or a duel *au dernier sang.* It verges on cold-blooded murder.

Here the duel forms part of a two-pronged climax. Valmont's death is one of twin cataclysms that bring this text to a close. The other sees the Marquise de Merteuil struck down by smallpox and, as a consequence, lose an eye. Whereas Valmont loses his life and is acclaimed as "truly grand," she loses an eye and is accounted "really hideous."[37] Bertrand testifies to the unaffected benevolence shown to him by Valmont over the years, whereas, disfigured, Merteuil provides for some people definitive evidence of an inner ugliness. The novel may have warned us to discount such facile assumptions and obtuse equations, but it too ultimately tempts us with such a conclusion.

Merteuil reads partially and selectively—a few pages here, a fragment there. She seems, unfortunately, to have skipped the eleventh letter of Voltaire's *Lettres philosophiques* devoted to the benefits of inoculation. Impressive as her self-directed curriculum may be, the Marquise, the most autonomous and enlightened of women, appears to have neglected this obvious measure.

Les liaisons dangereuses is, like *Julie*, headed by two prefaces. They are signposts to different places, located in opposite directions. In the "avertissement de l'éditeur," we are told that the work, evidently a mere novel, could not possibly be set in the eighteenth century, insofar as "Enlightenment, which has gained ground universally, has, as everyone knows, made all men honest and all women so modest and reserved." This novel could not possibly be set in this vaunted "siècle de philosophie," in part on account of its preposterous ending, the stuff of fictions, a novelistic cliché. The "rédacteur," for his part, assures us that the letters have been assembled recently.[38]

These twin cataclysms, supposedly outlawed by 1782—smallpox by inoculation; duelling by reason, if not legislation—appear to side with the editor's view and afford contemporary readers a complacent sense that this story can be consigned to an unthreatening past. Valmont and Merteuil are anachronisms, the world they inhabit a sort of time capsule, an hypostasized ancien régime, wholly indifferent to the changes occurring beyond it. Danceny and Cécile, for their part, flee to inviolate cloistered societies—a convent for her; for him, Malta, that safe haven for errant knights and, as it happens, "the only country in the world where duelling was permitted by law."[39]

Inoculations, such as Louis XVI's public inoculation just after his coronation, in a sort of modern edition of the *sacre*, gave Louis-Sébastien Mercier the confidence to assert, in 1790, that the reign of smallpox was over.[40] These details are ironizing elements that would be identified to contemporary readers as such, gratifying them that the age in which they lived was different and better. This allows Laclos's late eighteenth-century readers to look on earlier decades with comfort and condescension. Both endings provide the solace of a putatively providential intervention (itself regarded as a fondly outmoded set of beliefs). This dimension is emphasized by the vocabulary (the "combat singulier," in which God will decide) and smallpox (that remark confirming a miraculous restoration of order). They seem to be representative of a society that promptly resorts to metaphysical explanation.

These apparent archetypes of modernity, driven by their unforgiving materialism and apparent atheism, ironically, each fall victim to increasingly retrograde threats—smallpox and a sword. These characters already belong to the past, thanks to the manner of these events. This may in turn allow the readers of the novel to feel that they inhabit a different, better sort of world. Valmont and Merteuil dare to think they can lift themselves out of their age. Far from heralding a future, they are claimed by the past.

Both the duel by sword and the exposure of smallpox apparently promise the relief and the pleasure of manifest justice in a world of duplicity and deception. Indeed, the progression from the first to the second half of the novel testifies to a transition from what might be called an essentially Voltairean conception of writing, where letters are semianonymous exhibitions of esprit, opportunities for the display of an ironic intelligence, to a Rousseauesque *furor scribendi*, in which the written word, now more earnest, even heartfelt, provides, after all, a window onto the mental state of its author, who may be called to account. The letters can, after all, be traced back to their writers and read as expressions of their intentions and of their character.

Laclos depicts a self-regulating society in which honor and shame administer a justice of their own, a society from which the Président, Madame de Tourvel's husband, and the rule of law he supposedly oversees, are conspicuously absent. Ironically perhaps, his absence from Tourvel's day-to-day life and from the book is provoked by his preoccupation with a seemingly interminable legal case. We never see the Président, no letter of his is conserved. Valmont then offers an indictment of a society where laws are silent. This ending also points to the sovereignty of customs over laws, urgently adduced by Rousseau.

Les liaisons dangereuses terminates then in a classic libertine duel, harking back to the dénouement of *Clarissa*, with its impeccably genteel bloodshed, but this terminal encounter also foreshadows duels in the following century. The duel is contested not only as a result of the sexual liberties Valmont has been taking, but it is tied to Valmont's decision to make public Merteuil's letters. This act of Valmont's takes us back ironically to the first letter Merteuil addressed him, in which she promised to write his memoirs for him. But it also looks forward to an age when, increasingly, duels will be fought over insults and accusations aired by the printed word.

Readers are likely to sense that they are bystanders to a duel that symbolizes the wintering sensibilities of a moribund age. We learn that the noble name of Valmont will seemingly die out with him.[41] Danceny and Cécile remain childless at the end of this sterile novel, notwithstanding the efforts of the film *Valmont* (1989) to provide the prospect of a baby (and a sequel). But in fact Laclos's work places a hinge (or creates a liaison) between the eighteenth century's moral nervousness about the duel and the more descriptive attitude subsequently embraced by texts. Valmont himself bestrides the boundary between ancien régime libertinage and an unprecedented form of listlessness. This disaffected man, mechanically repeating "it is not my fault," foreshadows the dark nihilists of the following century, superfluous men whose principal seat is located in Russia. But nineteenth-century texts will also reorient us, in transporting readers to a past seemingly innocent of the Enlightenment. Heinrich von Kleist inaugurates this new chapter with a story of love and self-sacrifice in which the duel's medieval roots are exhumed, even as he poses serious questions all the while about such values and ideals as it might enshrine.

CHAPTER FOUR

The Judicial Duel

Kleist, "Der Zweikampf" (1811): Graf Jakob der Rotbart
versus Herr Friedrich von Trota

Many a story spun around a duel is entertaining; some are troubling,
but, of all, Heinrich von Kleist's "Der Zweikampf" is perhaps the most
puzzling, such is the reticent, understated fashion in which the tale is
told. After successive eighteenth-century representations of duels, this
story is among the first to depict a duel without also trying overtly
to persuade us that the custom was, or remains, morally wrong. Kleist
brings to the account of a duel a sober, apparently dispassionate attitude that will, in subsequent texts, become more typical. Kleist's own
motivation and deductions remain alike opaque.

In the story's opening sentence, we learn of the enmity between
Count Jakob der Rotbart (Redbeard) and his half brother, Duke Wilhelm
von Breysach, who is assassinated one evening when hit by an arrow
fired from the dark. His widow commissions her chancellor, Godwin,
to trace the provenance of the arrow, a rare, well-manufactured specimen, and he duly establishes that Rotbart had acquired such arrows.
He is accordingly under suspicion. However, when questioned under
oath, he produces an alibi that surprises everyone. On the night in
question, he claims that he was in fact in the arms of Littegarde von
Auerstein, a widow who enjoys a reputation as one of the most virtuous
ladies of the land. Rotbart produces a ring which, he maintains, she
gave him that night, even though she claimed to have lost it while out
walking. Humiliated, she is thrown out of her house. Among her suitors
and admirers is, however, Friedrich von Trota, who is persuaded of her
innocence. He makes for the court to serve as her advocate and champion. He throws down a gauntlet and challenges Rotbart to a duel to
ascertain the truth.

Kleist drew on Jean Froissart's chronicles in writing the story, which is set toward the end of the fourteenth century. In taking seriously a medieval tale at this early point in the nineteenth century, 1811, Kleist is precocious. Walter Scott's medieval reconstructions, for instance, first date from 1819, when *Ivanhoe* was published (although Schiller's plays set in the Middle Ages precede). If, say, Voltaire and his epigones had noticed or chosen to relate this story, they would have found it typically unedifying, at best amusing. Kleist does not, however, condescend toward his characters, as they try to come to terms with the results of a trial by single combat. On the other hand, such is the narrator's reticence and the tone of his voice, this medieval story also lends itself to being generalized and applied to Kleist's own age. While the story is suggested by Froissart, and the universe in which it takes place is medieval, the language of the protagonists seems contemporary. Equally, the anxieties provoked by the apparent arbitrariness, the silent indeterminacy of God, seem modern. Kleist relates a medieval trial to which the scrutiny of an enlightened, doubting, secularized mentality is brought.

Commentators had tended to be embarrassed, if not anguished, by the survival and indeed the continuing prosperity of a medieval practice in a modern world. Conversely, Kleist chooses to depict in the figure of Trota, one of the duellists, an essentially modern mind astray in a stubbornly medieval world. Kleist is fascinated by people who do not fit into their place or time, those who, anticipating Nietzsche, can be called "unzeitgemäss" or "untimely." There is little medieval coloring, whether the length of the swords or the nature of the costumes, such as the hats worn by medieval ladies which delighted so many nineteenth-century painters. Instead, Kleist's story resembles a medieval sculpture from which the color has faded and the paint peeled off, leaving it to be read as a more generic and concentrated account of a duel.

Throughout his oeuvre, Kleist is interested in the way that the processes by which justice is sought take on a life of their own, only to negate the good intentions that first prompted them. Thus in "Michael Kohlhaas," Kleist charts the progressive degradation of a good man, justifiably angered by the detention of his horses at a border crossing. His

pronounced sense of justice is corroded by the need for personal revenge, and the more persuaded he is of his own righteousness, the
more appalling he becomes. The ferocity of Kohlhaas's need for justice
removes the good grounds he had in wanting it, and the means vanquishes the end. But the story suggests that justice and law can also
be out of tune with each other, and the law only makes it harder to
establish what, as well as who, is right and wrong. In "Die Marquise
von O . . . ," Kleist similarly investigates the curious consequences of
a noble lady's attempts to deal with the mystery of her unaccountable
pregnancy. The crime committed by the prisoner in "Das Erdbeben von
Chili" is likewise of negligible interest compared to the fact that God
or nature, or whatever causes the earthquake, seems to trump the judicial judgment by which he had been incarcerated. Kleist is then interested less in human fallibility as such than in flawed or failed attempts to administer justice in response. It should come as no surprise
then that Kleist pays attention to the machinery of a judicial duel, an
archetypal human attempt to summon God's verdict. Kleist had already written a rather pallid fictional account of a judicial duel titled
"Geschichte eines merkwürdigen Zweikampfs." It turns out to be but
a hors d'oeuvre, a skeletal tale when compared to the fleshed-out version we encounter in "Der Zweikampf."

The duel takes place, authorized by the Holy Roman Emperor, in
front of an audience including Littegarde herself. Kleist first refrains
from telling us what actually happened on that fateful night, and now
he referees the bout with scrupulous impartiality. Or so it seems. The
duel itself occupies but a relatively short section of this story. We are
told that, first, Rotbart is wounded in the wrist, and then, after an unfortunate stumble in the sand, of which Rotbart takes advantage, Trota
sustains a very serious wound. He is at the mercy of Rotbart. The duel
is over. Rotbart has apparently been vindicated. Puzzlingly, Friedrich
has been completely passive all the while.

We are, however, likely to conclude that the outcome of this duel
is simply random and contingent, all the more so because a mishap *(ein
Unglück)* is responsible for the outcome. There is no suggestion that
this result might reflect their respective abilities as swordsmen, let
alone do justice to them in some more profound sense. Kleist's reflec-

tions on the fallibility of humans in "Über das Marionettentheater" are substantiated here.

The silence of the narrator is especially telling at this point. He has the resources to describe in detail the injuries inflicted, yet he restrains himself from supplementing this unblinking narrative with the sort of moral commentary that, almost invariably, had been supplied in the previous century. We are left to make of this duel what we will. The narrator of this story does not assist us very obviously. Nor, as he relates the story, does he himself seem to know what had, in actual fact, occurred.

Kleist dares to depict a duel that is divorced from justice and profoundly meaningless. His abstemious style seems to correspond to a fog-bound world from which absolute, God-given verdicts are absent. This understated style not only is crucial to the effects of suspense and the accompanying ironies but contributes to a profound sense that authority is not definitive but collapsed or hollow. The aspirations of German idealism—human progress, peace between nations and individuals, a society based on justice—are negated here, as in Kleist's other works.

Nevertheless, however dispassionate the tone of the narrator, we are perhaps quietly invited to take sides, thanks to subliminal hints. Rotbart, for instance, sounds as though he could be as disreputable as Bluebeard or Blackbeard. Beards suggest an absence of transparency; the red suggests spilling of blood. These redbeards (like Barbarossa or the Sorcerer Rothbart in *Swan Lake*) are rarely the nicest of men. Rotbart is a mute protagonist, a closed book. He is confronted by an articulate, open-minded sort of Enlightenment philosopher *avant la lettre*. Friedrich is a gentleman, whose faith in the lady does not rest on any God-given evidence. He perhaps could be described then as a sort of proto-Protestant in a world that still credits miraculous interventions from God and theophanies. Indeed, Friedrich von Trota comes across as a proto-Protestant hero, such is the prominence and authority of his inner spiritual condition. An inner voice confides Littegarde's innocence to him. He has a joyous affirmative belief in her goodness. "Do not waste a word in defending and justifying your innocence! In my heart a voice speaks in your favor, much more compelling and more convincing than any assurance, indeed more so than all reasoning and any proofs that you could summon together and bring to the court at Basel."[1] There is, characteristically, a quiet irony at work. Trota urges Littegarde not to waste a word in defending herself. Littegarde, withdrawing into total silence, hardly needs to be encouraged. The chancellor's name, Godwin, is ironically pertinent or quietly impertinent. Kleist plays throughout with allusions to light. Moons are the units of time mentioned here. People are in the dark, literally and figuratively, from the moment of the murder until the very end, when daylight *(Tageslicht)* is invoked. "They agree to the holy verdict of weapons, which will infallibly bring the truth to light."[2] That adverb *(unfehlbar)* betrays a slight soupçon of irony, while the final words derive their force from following another little adverbial push.[3]

The duel occurs in an exclusively male world onto which women are at best onlookers. Kleist's story takes an unusually attentive interest in the fate of the lady who is the duel's raison d'être. In previous stories, female characters have tended to remain passive and silent, even when their destiny turns on the outcome of the duel. This lady is also silent, yet she is at the center, rather than the margins, of the story. Littegarde retreats into seclusion and silence (as did the eponymous heroine in "Die Marquise von O. . . ."), rather than challenging the verdict or seeking some sort of judicial review. However, by retreating to and espousing a state of greater passivity (that is, not talking, seeing anyone, sleeping), she can gainsay the passivity to which she is condemned. She is resolutely passive, actively so. She does not simply challenge the verdict but rejects speech itself, that fickle vehicle for truth. At the same time, by refusing to speak, she is perhaps brought closer to us, for silence is the same whether kept by a medieval or by a modern mouth. We may read into her response our own imaginative reconstructions, aided by a refusal of omniscience on the part of the narrator.

The duel is resolved by an accident and some rather ungentlemanly opportunism. But, as we have said, the reticent narrator offers no moralizing or salutary reflections on the folly of duels. Trota is simply defeated and may not survive his injuries, while the victorious Rotbart appears to be in good health. An eerie passivity now descends over the story, as the combatants each wait while their wounds get better and

worse respectively. The reconciliation that often follows and redeems the duel, either between men or between men and their God, is
withheld. Trota starts to feel better, as Rotbart's injury deteriorates in
turn. Trota's recovery seems to be a Resurrection. Less dramatically,
though, one injury simply takes as long to take effect as the other does
to heal. The right result is achieved by the wrong means. It is not that
a duel is never right.

So Rotbart wins the duel, but he loses the case. Littegarde, meanwhile, is vindicated less by the skill and valor of her champion than
by an unexpected turn of events. Kleist's drama is built up by the slowly
delivered outcome. The ending pronounces doubt as to the efficacy of
the judicial duel but also shows an unwillingness to revolutionize or
abandon it. The kaiser builds in a condition: "If God so wishes" ("wenn
es Gottes Wille ist"). The tweaking of the terms represents a judicial
fudge, rather than a moral shift, but then this is a story whose currency
is understatement. Much virtue in "if"—this is a world in which God
himself seems fallible and capricious. The declarative final sentence,
with conditional appended, resembles an unresolved chord, and the effect of this final sentence and strangely reversed outcome is to wrong-
foot us as the duellists themselves were, albeit figuratively. Just as this
story exemplifies for Kleist "die gebrechliche Einrichtung der Welt,"
the fragmentary nature of things is a hallmark of Romanticism, by
contrast with an eighteenth-century taste for Classical completeness.
Moreover, we are not told that Littegarde and Trota marry and live happily ever after.

This idea evidently intrigued Kleist. Similar ironies can be savored
in a piece written late in Kleist's life. A "Portsmouth man" and a
"Plymouth man" confront each other in a boxing match, the British
equivalent of the duel. The Pompey pugilist prevails in the bout after
administering a fatal blow to his adversary. On the very next day, however, he himself dies of a hemorrhage.[4]

Richardson and Rousseau were among the first writers to expose,
counterintuitively, the pity of the winning duellist. "You could not
have been happy, had you prevailed over me. Think you, that a murderer ever was an happy man?" Grandison asks his challenger, Sir Hargrave.[5] Several penitent males in *Clarissa*, in common with Julie's
gloomy father, suggest that he is right. The victor becomes the loser in

these cautionary tales. Kleist, however, downplays the moral sanction to these stories in order to pose questions that are both more literal and more indeterminate. When exactly is a duel over? What counts as the outcome? Jakob's immediate triumph or Trota's remote victory? Trota's health or Rotbart's mortal illness? Kleist's emphasis on irony rather than morality sets the tone for subsequent accounts. Wilkie Collins's story "Miss Bertha and the Yankee" (1877) recycles Kleist's conceit in a gothic idiom. Vying for the same young woman, Stanwick and Varleigh fight a duel. Stanwick pulls off an ungentlemanly sword trick, for which he has paid a fencing master (appropriately called Bender) fifty pounds, and he passes his blade clean through Varleigh's breast. Varleigh, however, survives, recovers, and, literally, haunts the victor, who obligingly commits suicide at the very spot on which he had attempted to kill his rival.

The duel has often been perceived as a means of reaching the truth. It evolves as a conclusive test that delivers an irrevocable result. And this sacred certainty may exercise an attraction that is all the more potent in ages, such as that of the Enlightenment, which advertise the necessity of doubt and prize the compromises of toleration. The duel promotes the illusion that we can achieve outcomes which definitively detach black and white. That halo will remain in place, even after Kleist's story; but here the expedient of the duel sheds no light, and humans are necessarily condemned to dwell in a penumbra of meaning. The conclusion, satisfying insofar as good triumphs over evil, remains provisional and hollow. We are told that the kaiser, reviewing his judicial procedures, inserts a new clause into the statutes. The duel will still decide the fate of two disputants "if God so wishes." The ending remains poised between a reluctance to abandon rules that uphold the sanctity of the duel as a time-honored method for determining the will of God and a realization that God's will is inscrutable. It is either an enlightened redraft or, more likely, a meaningless gesture.[6]

Ironically perhaps, Kleist's story provides an all-the-more-subtle exposé of the injustices associated with duels in showing that justice has been served in this case. The story deprives us of the indignation that Rotbart's triumph might have sanctioned but without really allowing us the solace of a providential outcome either. For, moments earlier, we were perhaps frowning at the crude injustice of such a duel.

The hedged "if" clause is an appropriately muted ending to a story in which there is little consolation to be derived from the workings of justice and authority.

Kleist's irony takes a perhaps unexpected form. Rather than delivering a trite conclusion such that the duel fails to resolve the legal and moral matter satisfactorily, it turns out that the duel does, at length, winnow right from wrong and achieve the desired result. It is by flattering enlightened readers into thinking that this story is likely, or even certain, to show that the duel is a travesty that he may then surprise them when it is not. God seems to change his mind in the course of this short story. The meaning of the duel is God given, but only if God is in the mood for giving. The story ends on this conditional note.

Kleist is interested in the duel as a vehicle for the consideration of a crisis in human affairs, when faced by a silent or inscrutable God. The duel is robbed of any value here. It is arbitrary and contingent, even if the result can ultimately be squared with justice. Few of Kleist's readers are likely to have needed persuading that judicial duels were fallible. But he may also shake modern complacency about such a tool, for the duel leaves us hostages to irony. In its latter, secular form, the duel yet retains some residual appeal as the expression of a definitive judgment, which swallows all previous discord. Kleist shows how, even in a devout age, the duel remains an immanently human act, whose outcome testifies to the mysteries of fate rather than to the word of God. "Der Zweikampf" then captivates Kleist above all as a small but significant tributary of the never-ending, incalculable duel between life and chance.[7]

CHAPTER FIVE

The "Romantic" Duel

THE curtain has barely opened onto the scene in *Così fan tutte* (1790) by Da Ponte and Mozart, when Ferrando and Gugliemo, young tyros, outraged at Don Alfonso's suggestion that their ladies could ever be unfaithful, challenge this "old philosopher" to a duel. But he is not interested. He is a practical, peace-loving man who "achieves satisfaction only at the dining table."[1] So the young gentlemen promptly resort to another expedient, and off they go to disguise themselves and test the validity of the contention. In no previous work has a duel threatened to occur quite as promptly. Works hitherto have tended to move toward a conclusive duel, but the early position here confirms its status as little more than an inconsequential piece of plot machinery. The philosopher dismisses, without reply, the duel as a puerile impulse. Never has it seemed easier to cry—or to laugh—off a duel.

"These days duels are infrequent, thanks to philosophy," Mercier had announced in his *Tableau de Paris*, with little doubt and less nostalgia.[2] A century on from the acclaim with which Louis XIV's supposed abolition of duelling was greeted, the extinction of the duel is just as confidently ascribed to philosophy this time. The Enlightenment, vexed by duelling, seemed at length to have done its work.

It may, then, seem curious that those who took part in the French Revolution and its legislative aftermath did not actually succeed in, or even incline to, taking measures to abolishing duels, an aristocratic pursuit par excellence. Nevertheless, in 1791, François Gorguereau published a work under the title *Le duel considéré dans tous les rapports historiques, moraux et constitiuonnels, et moyens de l'anéantir radicalement*. The title amply indicates the extent to which the dutiful antiduelling indignation of the Enlightenment has mutated into the angrier ambition of the French Revolution, leaving previous projects

looking rather meek. Instead of just abolishing it entirely, the revolu-
tionaries would now radically annihilate the duel. Yet their efforts, and
their rhetoric, would avail no more than had the reasoning of the calmer
rational philosophers of the previous decades.

On the contrary, early nineteenth-century France instead witnessed
an embourgeoisement of the duel, rather than its abolition. Instead of
deploring the duel as an aristocratic abuse of power that needed to be
extirpated, the middle classes deemed it a privilege they might henceforward share with the nobility.[3] Indeed, the right to duel was perhaps
the chief marker of class available at no, or little, material cost to the
humbler citizen. The bourgeois, even if he could never quite live like
the ci-devant nobleman, could at least aspire to die like him.[4]

Honor was now for hire. It was possible, according to *The Pickwick
Papers*, to borrow a set of duelling pistols from a shop. But many works,
like that novel, will show that the bourgeois gentleman is not fully
capable of duelling *comme il faut*. Impoverished and disenfranchised
though the aristocrat might be, his fearlessness in the face of death is
the final, residual element to remove. François I's lament—"Tout est
perdu sauf l'honneur"—turned out to be an adaptable phrase.[5]

In circumstances under which it would be reasonable to expect the
point of honor to disappear, along with sedan chairs, red heels, and peri-
wigs, a continuing willingness to duel, often on a whim, offered evidence of an utterly absurd, bewildering world, rather than another
symptom of a necessarily confusing, stratified society. The propensity
to duel, in short, becomes less a social than an existential problem. As
long as an aristocracy thrived, it was possible to assert, as did Jane
Austen, that one half of the world could not understand the pleasures
of the other.[6] The maxim could equally apply to the nation's various
vices. The horrified yet fascinated bourgeois onlooker might not understand why duels had to happen, but he or she could yet assume that it
made sense to those whom they engaged. In a less stratified society,
however, the impulse to duel could no longer be dismissed, or indeed
enjoyed from afar, as some exotic upper-class ailment.

Many writers in the Romantic generation, however, marginalized duels in their works. A duel with a fatal outcome contested by
Karl Moor is mentioned only cursorily in Schiller's *The Robbers*.[7] His
meditations provoked by the sight of his pistol and the temptation to

kill himself with it are of more weight. Such introspection supplants the action of a duel as the chief emphasis. Even French writers, whose (often ambivalent) concern with duelling has been greater than that of other nations hitherto, now mention duels only *en passant*.

Many Romantic writers prefer to turn their attention to the fever of anticipation, although others dwell more on the inertia of the aftermath. Xavier de Maistre's ingenuity in relating the *Voyage around My Room* (1794) is perhaps all the more mischievous, indeed perverse, since he resists the facile pleasure of describing the duel that caused him to be detained, for days on end, under house arrest in that same room.[8]

Octave, in Alfred de Musset's *Confession d'un enfant du siècle* (1836), barely mentions a duel he fights, while his continued angst provoked by the woman on whose behalf it is contested is explored in detail.[9] Similarly, in Benjamin Constant's *Adolphe* (1816), a duel takes place within one short sentence, when Adolphe steps out on behalf of a lady, Ellenore, whom he knows he does not love.[10] The duel has become an everyday occurrence, the ritual a routine. In this period, Romantic fervor seldom results in duels. Both Adolphe and Octave, in Stendhal's *Armance* (1826), brooding, listless figures, fight a duel because they find themselves unable to contrive a good reason for not doing so. These are archetypally romantic young men, yet each duel contested occurs in the name of the flings society expects, not the love they feel. The duels are, in each case, tangential to these feelings. Adolphe and Octave duel with men whose unique role in the text is to provide the opposition. These duels each permit the conventional expression of a regard for an older woman, while the intensity of love finds no equivalent accommodation. In *Armance*, which describes the duel in some detail, there prevails an irony that militates against feelings, whether of sympathy or of revulsion. It is an irony that the worldly Mme. d'Aumale, and not the cousin (namely, Armance) whom Octave loves, should be the secondary cause of the duel, which is provoked by a spat at the theater; an irony that the somber, suicidal young man should thereby become a murderer.[11] These Romantic acts are empty, conventional gestures.

Of course, there is no surer "love-broker" for women than a "report of valour."[12] It would be tempting to regard a duel fought for the right woman as a quintessentially romantic act. Romantic intensity, however, demands real over symbolic action, spontaneity over ritual, improvised rather than intended, codified conduct and, *in extremis*, death over injury. It validates all things natural in preference to mannered and artificial behavior. Romantics prefer the uncertain exhilarations of the infinite, whereas the duel brings closure and, even when fatal, reconciliation of sorts. Above all, though, whether German, British, or French, Romanticism disdains the antiquated prerogatives of class. Romanticism is not that hospitable to duels, because its writers cherish the notion that the individual is sovereign and self-sufficient, not in need of the reference points of his wider family and bloodline to lend him vigor and meaning. These individuals are supposedly invulnerable to the dictates of genealogy, the props and the consolations of wealth, the weight of honor and the dignity of history.

Accordingly, a guiding aesthetic seeks to account for this new preference. Often inspired by Shakespeare's tragedies, Romantic writers are now increasingly entranced by bona fide murderers, whose acts, while deprived of the apparently redemptive concern for honor, or of the regard for their victim instantiated by duels, are nevertheless felt to be characterized by a perversely ennobling, transcendent aspect.[13]

Early nineteenth-century texts and images tend to favor the depiction of murder over the representation of duels. None was more arresting, chilling than David's unforgettable picture of Marat in his bath, perhaps the most famous painting of a murder ever. That the perpetrator, Charlotte Corday, was a descendant of Corneille, author of *Le Cid*, provided an almost unbearably poignant example of the shift from a culture of polite and noble killing to brutal opportunistic slaughter.

Noncodified, nonaristocratic ways of killing now caught the eye and chilled the spine. The writers of this period became specialists in depicting intensely resentful and vengeful men, whose birth, status, or mere impatience deprived them of the possibility of fighting a duel. They may, technically, find themselves beneath adopting such an aristocratic rite, but, more pertinently, they feel that an action more urgent, authentic, and individualistic is called for. The result is often a peculiar air of tension, as they refrain from the formalities of the duel, only to launch spontaneously into violence. In two of Goethe's plays, *Clavigo* (1774) and *Torquato Tasso* (1790), a duel, however expected or

desired, turns out to be inadequate to the intensity of their protagonists. Inspired by a true story that had occurred a few years earlier,
Clavigo centers on domestic tensions among the French community
in Spain. Goethe sets himself up as a German referee of a Franco-
Spanish clash. This is a home of the chivalric duel, and ideal conditions prevail. A duel between Beaumarchais and Clavigo is variously
suggested, proposed, and expected throughout the play, before it proceeds to a bloody conclusion. Beaumarchais, however, seeking to
avenge his sister, bypasses the conventional *bienséances* and discards
the usual weapons. "Ah! No swords, no weapons! I want to throttle him
with my bare hands, so that that bliss will belong entirely to me! And
the feeling that I have annihilated him will be all mine."[14]

Beaumarchais does not want to feel that a weapon, above all a pistol
aimed from a distance, has done the work for or instead of him. Critics
did not approve of this blunt immediacy: Christoph Martin Wieland
thought Goethe had turned Beaumarchais into a cannibal.[15] A duel
might well have taken the sting out of such an accusation and restored
Goethe's play to a safer place within the canon. Clavigo himself wel-
comes this blow as redemptively fraternal. It is more intimate and
authentic than would be his death, in consequence of a rencontre. A
strange intimacy, almost of an erotic quality, results from inflicting
revenge without the support of seconds or the intermediary aid of a
weapon. Romantics are, in short, too impulsive and impatient, their
feelings too urgent, to fight duels. They would rather kill one another
without thinking twice, or even once, about it. They are too individualistic to conform to a code of conduct, even if that code commends
itself by being proscribed, under pain of death, by the law.

The ritualized formalities of the codes of honor, resulting in the
resemblance of one duel to another, ideally temper or alleviate hatred. Rituals may comfort, substituting resentments with manners,
replacing grievances with fears. But some men were reluctant to deny
themselves the full intensity—whether of horror, joy, or relief—that is
the privilege of the assassin.[16]

Nature's Aristocrats versus Darwinian Imperatives

Schiller's William Tell and Hugo's heroes Didier and Hernani enjoy no
social distinction, but they are characterized by a nobility of spirit and

a natural sense of justice, enforced by their courage. These authors helped to make it clear that honor was no preserve of the nobility. "A drover may be touched upon a point of honour," advises Walter Scott, in his short story "The Two Drovers" (1827). Indeed, a concern for honor was no longer always considered the exclusive product of a noble blood-line; it was contingent on regional and national circumstances. Scott recognizes a regard for honor peculiar to mountainous lands. "Inacces-sible to laws," the Highlands have necessarily developed their own codes of honor.[17] Scott was no doubt indebted to Rousseau's descrip-tions of Swiss societies that subsisted in remote corners of the Alps and to Jean-Jacques's characterization of the prickly, honor-obsessed Saint-Preux, wandering fretfully in his native Valais. The further one traveled from cultures policed by laws, the more weight honor carried.

In Scott's story, the Highland understanding of honor collides with its English conception. These traditions diverge in part because of the particular weapons to which each nation remains attached, the High-lander jealous of his skein dhu, the Englishman accustomed to using his fists to defend his honor. There results a strange, misbegotten duel fought between the drovers following a petty dispute.

Scott's sensitivity to the manifestations of honor either side of na-tional frontiers is matched when he inspects its fluctuations across in-visible temporal boundaries. His third novel, *The Antiquary* (1816), is set in the 1790s. When the impetuous Hector M'Intyre is injured in a duel with Major Neville (under his assumed name of Lovel), Scott dis-patches Lovel into exile abroad and rehearses familiar objections to du-elling. Jonathan Oldbuck, the eponymous antiquary, observes that the duel has no basis in antiquity; it is therefore a dispensable, deplorable act. Scott inherits an eighteenth-century bent in pitching this argu-ment, but he deftly ascribes it to an antiquary who lives in the past whether, through birth, in the eighteenth century or, by taste, in the age of Classical civilization that enthralls him. But a new context by which duelling may be relativized and criticized is soon seen in the same work. M'Intyre, still smarting from the wounds he sustained in the duel at the hands of Lovel, takes his frustrations out on a seal on the shore. The struggle between man and beast is described as a duel. The seal too gets the better of him, and after he meets the phoca (as Old-buck insists on calling it), ridicule rings out remorselessly throughout the rest of the novel.[18] Of course, his name, Hector, merely points up the risible, mock-epic quality of this bout. Lovel, meanwhile, comes within an ace of being a libertine, but he is nowhere as dastardly as Richardson's villain.

Combat between two men is now brought into comparison with a clash of animals. Such analogies are without precedent in the previous century. Diderot, writing in the 1760s or 70s, sees the duel as a metaphor for human interaction in a world that is inherently adversarial. "Duels," he observes, "recur in society in all sorts of forms, between priests, magistrates, hacks, philosophers." Figuratively speaking, we are all duellists. If rivalry is an important stimulus to genius or talent, duels are an inevitable, sometimes laudable, byproduct of a prosperous society. Although at least one eighteenth-century writer describes sexual congress in terms of a mortal duel, Diderot's vision is characteristic of an overriding tendency to see duelling as a specifically social, rather than a natural, phenomenon.[19] It is an armed manifestation of wider civil and social practices. Now, however, the analogies help to shape the argument that duelling is both primal and natural. Men were only acting on the demands of highly natural impulses that inhered in the human race, as in all other species. According to Darwinian theories, natural selection resulted in restless competition among individuals. That struggle for life was most severe between members of the same species. Four years after the publication of *The Origin of Species* (1859), Jules Verne depicted in the *Voyage to the Center of the Earth* a struggle that appalls and absorbs the humans who chance to see it. An ichthyosaurus and a plesiosaurus are locked in a "battle of monsters."[20] Dinosaurs, deep in the heart of our planet, are fighting one another in a primal duel. Strikingly, the combat is not attributable to any observable purpose. It is obviously not the act of a predator, nor, in a vast inland sea, would it seem to concern territory as such; but it emerges as the result of some vague and terrible compulsion. Of course, a struggle between different species may not, strictly speaking, meet the criteria for a duel, but here the description of the combat between two monsters, resulting in one indistinguishable, writhing ensemble, is depicted in those terms. Duelling then is, after all, as old as the hills. Duels on this scale, in the proto-Darwinian sense, both legitimate the duel and dwarf it. Intestine struggles are diminished by the emerging, wider picture of a global competition. There can be nothing especially heroic or noble about such combats, which must be construed not as the prerogative of punctilious aristocrats but as the consequence of evolutionary drives. This does not vindicate the duel so much as relegate it to a facet of the perpetual, tooth-and-claw struggle to which all of nature's creatures are subject.

John Lyde Wilson, a U.S. senator, in the preface to his *Code of Honor* (1838), advanced an argument in favor of duelling that could never be sounded in the eighteenth century. Whereas the insufficiencies of the laws devised by men had apparently necessitated duelling, now it was possible to declare that natural laws enjoined and insisted on it:

> The history of all animated nature exhibits a determined resistance to encroachments upon natural rights,—Nay I might add, inanimate nature, for it also exhibits a continual warfare for supremacy. Plants of the same kind, as well as trees, do not stop their vigorous growth because they overshadow their kind; but, on the contrary, flourish with greater vigor as the more weak and delicate decline and die. Those of different species are at perpetual warfare. . . . The elements themselves war together, and the angels of heaven have met in fierce encounter. The principle of self-preservation is co-extensive with creation.[21]

The duel provided, then, a classic example of social Darwinism. Indeed, the ritualized resolution of a conflict can be seen in the natural world when, for instance, two males of the same species meet in combat, as the females look on, with polite interest. Such natural "duels" are invoked by Charles Mackay in his influential study (1841) of fashionable delusions, among which duels and ordeals take a prominent place: "Two dogs who tear each other for a bone, or two bantams fighting on a dunghill for the love of some beautiful hen, or two fools on Wimbledon Common, shooting at each other to satisfy the laws of offended honour, stand on the same footing in this respect, and are each and all mere duellists."[22]

But the analogue can only take us so far, for, while natural selection might be expected to result in all-out, fatal struggle between males, "intraspecific conflicts are usually of a 'limited war' type, involving inefficient weapons or ritualised tactics that seldom cause serious injury to either contestant."[23] Darwin himself observed that such bouts did not typically result in death.[24] Male snakes often fight one another without using their fangs. Animal weaponry is sometimes particularly well suited to nonfatal outcomes—the backward-pointing horns of the oryx, for instance, require males to kneel gently down with their heads between their knees in order to fight. Those oryx with forward-pointing horns evidently fought themselves into extinction instead of evolving.

At all events, a more benign, Rousseauesque view of nature makes way for a Darwinian perspective, as nature is seen as the arena of cruel and ruthless actions. Internecine fighting between members of the same class was natural and inevitable, no less so among those with whom one was intimately close. It was therefore entirely natural to fight the closest of relatives, those to whom one was most attached—even literally. Indeed, Ang and Cheng, the original Siamese twins, were depicted fighting in a contraption that toured around the United States and Europe.[25]

However, if analogies with struggles in the natural world emptied duelling of much of its aristocratic grandeur, even as they provided a sort of implicit vindication of the practice, this evolving consideration did not result in the extinction of literary interest in duelling. On the contrary, the increasing sophistication, availability, and popularity of the duelling pistol helped to persuade authors, and those with authorial pretensions, to adopt the previous prerogatives of the nobility.

Pushkin, *Eugene Onegin* (1823–31): Eugene Onegin versus Vladmir Lenski

It is tempting to regard *Eugene Onegin* as the first, mighty work of the modern era to leave a heavy footprint on the virgin snow of the Russian language. The novel in verse has long been hailed as a new dawn for writers hitherto in thrall to English, German, and, above all, French authors. *Eugene Onegin* may also be saluted as the work that opens a new chapter in the portrayal of duels in literature. What is more, its author, by dying as a result of a duel in 1837, was to become a laureate of duellists, beyond the frontiers of Russia.

In emphasizing, sometimes exaggerating, the originality of this poem-cum-novel, it is, however, possible to underplay the self-consciousness of a bifocal work, moving elusively between extremes of poetic exaltation and satirical desperation, between a Romantic sensibility and ironic recoils. Pushkin presents a poetic persona who seems wearily aware of precedent at every juncture. An anxiety of influence hangs all the more heavily on poets, as we know. This poet's retrospects are often despondent, even grudging. On one occasion, when he attempts to describe one of the female protagonists, Olga, he can hardly bear to go through with the description. This is a poem full of yawning. On other occasions, he registers some fatigue with the obligatory timeworn topoi of poetry, such as the moon, sung by Leopardi et al. W. H. Auden would in time moan that the U.S. landing on the moon had spoiled it as a resource for poets, but Pushkin is already regretting the modern, disenchanting encroachment of gas lanterns. It was, above all, in the light of Napoleon's victories, and indeed his defeats, that inherited notions of poetry and heroism would have to be revised. In chapter 2, the poet sings,

> Having destroyed all prejudices, we
> Deem all men naughts
> And ourselves units.
> We all aspire to be Napoleons;
> For us the millions of two-legged creatures are but tools;
> Feeling to us is weird and ludicrous.[26]

Thinkers as various as Hegel and Tocqueville agreed that the postaristocratic culture ushered in by Napoleon, or, if that verb should seem too gentle, imposed in the Empire, was less hospitable to poetry. Napoleon had made life cheaper. Tocqueville perceived a shift by which a heroic, mythical view of man, integral to the imaginings of writers working under aristocracies, would necessarily be supplanted by an idealization of nature. It was here alone that sublime effects, heroic or monstrous, frightening or awesome, were now to be retrieved.

The principal shadow cast over the poem is, however, that of Byron, and in particular *Don Juan*, published a few years earlier. Pushkin claims to distance himself from Byron, but the arch way with which he does so seems itself to be mischievously Byronic. He competes with Byron throughout, from the first chapter onward. In *Don Juan*, Byron had joked about the length of the English winter ("ending in July, / To recommence in August"); Pushkin can trump that with his allusions to the Russian seasons. Above all, his description of a duel recalls Byron's evocations of a pistol duel in that poem.[27]

Structured by eight chapters, the novel in verse could be compared to an octagonal edifice sculpted with its depiction of the cycle of seasonal labors. Miniatures of timeless peasant life punctuate the story. This difficult business of survival throws into relief the mad expenditure of life that is the duel. The progress of the seasons and the respective labors that are attuned to each of them form a backdrop, against which the duel seems all the more counterintuitive.[28]

A seemingly inconsequential detail may help us to see this particular Pushkinian marriage of romance and realism. In one of many beautifully tangential, potentially or partially symbolic details characteristic of this work, the poet describes women in the fields picking the berries, singing as they work. And "The Song of the Girls" is duly integrated into the poem.[29] But Pushkin does not allow us to enjoy the music of the maidens without reserve, for we have already been told that they are singing by decree, so that their masters can be sure that they are not eating those berries. The poem behaves similarly. Even as we hear the poet's music, we remain aware that it is not, nor can be, an effortless pastoral. There always remains an inhibiting consciousness of the limits to or costs of lyricism. That alternation between an indulgence of lyricism and a dispassionate regard for the calculations and economies necessitated by real life continues throughout the novel-poem, which is itself advertised, unusually, as a formal hybrid.

When it comes to chapter 6, and the duel between Eugene Onegin and Vladimir Lenski, this equivocation reaches a new pitch. Unlike contemporary, Romantic accounts by Musset and Constant, this poem-cum-novel seems to honor the duel, on account of the precision with which the poet observes the event. Moreover, the duel constitutes, to all intents and purposes, the only event in the book.

The asides, the knowing, ironic gestures, are packed away, until, after the duel, Pushkin can revert to playful self-consciousness. It is about to become deadly serious. On the one hand, the poet is relentlessly modern, sardonic, knowing, bringing to his poem his own version of a disillusioned, splenetic Byronic cynicism. On the other, the duel, its preliminaries, and its aftermath subordinate all the intelligence, virtuoso rhymes, and wit to an overriding pathos before death, fate, and courage. The pulse changes radically. This episode as a result may seem detached from the poem, as the event is isolated from the life of the people.

In eighteenth-century works, authors tend to show, sometimes with irony, sometimes with intent to ridicule, and on other occasions, with grudging respect, how the duellists, while notionally adversaries, stand alone together in defiance of the law. It is the similarity of the two duellists, their common allegiance to values, that the duel exposes and emphasizes. Although the duels in which they participate are concluded in contrasting fashions, the adversaries of Sedaine's play and those of Laclos's novel, for instance, meet and fight each other fraternally. The French duel hitherto tends to allow the author to celebrate the similarity of two individuals, ironically inclined to eliminate each other. But the Russian duel typically pitches a pair of highly contrasting individuals against each other, perhaps representatives of antithetical Weltanschauungen.

Eugene Onegin seems to provide us with a highly coherent order structured about two complementary couples: Olga and Tatiana; Onegin and Lenski. The very structure of the poem and its versification insist on a binary understanding of the world it depicts. And a duel provides a satisfactorily pungent encounter of two competing sensibilities. The duel will become a favorite literary device for pitting irreconcilable figures against each other, potentially embodiments of different viewpoints—the libertine versus the poet; the older versus the younger man. This duel appears to stage a trenchant opposition. On one side, there stands Eugene Onegin. Inauspiciously, Onegin has been introduced to us as a "deep economist." He is a prosaic man versed only in Adam Smith, of all people.[30] In describing this hero, Pushkin contrives, like Byron, to lasso recalcitrant terms such as "mortgages," breaking them into the meter of his poetry. On the other, Vladimir Lenski. Here appears a doomed poet par excellence. While Onegin dresses like a London dandy and expresses himself in elegant French, Lenski has studied at the University of Göttingen, a nursery of idealism. Adolphe, Constant's brooding creation in a story first published in 1816, studied there. Like another doomed poetical alumnus of a German university, Lenski wears black and muses on skulls.

The poet proposes a set of dichotomies, but the appositional coupling that follows is teasingly unclear. It seems verse might be equated not with flame but with ice.

> They got together; wave and stone,
> verse and prose, ice and flame,
> were not so different from one another.[31]

The dancing apposition suggests a false dichotomy. The text invites us, on occasion, to respond, like Tatiana, to a world full of portents and symbols, but, at other times, these signs seem little more than clichés, displayed self-consciously.

Pushkin indulges in digressions, and he apologizes for them (pushing the digression in another direction as he does so). But, like Byron's avowed digressions, they do not stray as purposelessly as all that. In these apparent digressions, Pushkin sows the seeds of future events. A modern duel, cruel in its efficiency and finality, is integrated within the fabric of poetic imagery. Poetic metaphors become literalized. Pushkin's interest in ballet, and in ballerina's feet above all, foreshadows the paces measured out by the duellists. Nabokov calls it the "pedal digression."[32] All these portents induce a sense that Lenski's death is inevitable, demanded, if not by God, then by the patterning of the poem itself. It is barely possible to recount such a story retrospectively without becoming susceptible to the ironies warning us that this was going to happen.

But the pistol also helps to secure this impression. The adversaries have not even given each other a passing glance. The outcome of the duel will not offer a tribute to the bravery or the skill of the principals but provides a subset of some higher truth bound with the inscrutability of fate and thus the vulnerability of man.

> A brace of pistols,
> two bullets—nothing more—
> shall in a trice decide his fate.[33]

The duel is provoked at a ball when Lenski chivalrously, if self-regardingly, steps in to defend Olga from the attentions of Onegin. His overheated vocabulary may put us on our guard.

"I," he reflects, "shall be her saviour.
I shall not suffer a depraver
With fire of sighs and compliments
To tempt a youthful heart, nor let a despicable, venomous
Worm gnaw a lily's little stalk,
Nor have a blossom two morns old
Wither while yet half blown."

The stanza is replete with metaphors: the worm, the stalk, the blossom, and, indeed, fire. Lenski is too busy with the metaphorical fire to be aware of the dangers of the real one. This is a set of poetic tropes that disguises to himself the brutal yet also banal event he has decided to undertake. Pushkin, deflating the overblown sentiments mercilessly, now impatiently proceeds to encapsulate the preceding verses for our benefit:

All this, friends, meant:
I have a pistol duel with a pal.

Indeed, the poet seems exasperated with a desire to poeticize the banality of the duel:

Should they not burst out laughing while
Their hand is not yet crimsoned?[34]

The horrors of a duel are never that remote from ridicule. Pushkin succeeds both in dignifying the event and exposing its horror. This stanza epitomizes that alternating current, switching us between lavish poetical expression and a more economical commentary.

Lenski's response to his own challenge is drawn more vigorously than that of Onegin. As in subsequent works, such as Maupassant's "A Coward," his calling a man out possibly answers a need to test his own nerve, to challenge himself. Furthermore, the same obscure reasons for making the challenge in the first place also account for the resulting malaise. The duel may lend Lenski the intensity his poetry lacks. Inspiration, alas, does not result. His desire for some form of self-assertion is hopelessly derivative. He does not have the ironic self-awareness, that ability to overhear himself, that the poet has evinced.

Lenski makes all the right gestures, making us feel that issuing a challenge is just one of those poetic gestures and moves, in the hope that content, and talent, will follow. But it refuses to do so. He opens, first, his case of pistols and, then, by candle, his copy of Schiller. But he shuts the book and takes up his pen.

> Upon the fashionable word
> "ideal," Lenski dozed off gently.

The poet now includes the verses that Lenski penned that night. He deems them worth reproducing in full:

> "Whither, ah! Whither are ye fled,
> My springtime's golden days?
> What has the coming day in store for me?
> In vain my gaze attempts to grasp it;
> In deep gloom it lies hidden.
> It matters not; fate's law is just.
> Whether I fall, pierced by the dart, or whether
> It flies by—all is right:
> Of waking and of sleep
> Comes the determined hour;
> Blest is the day of cares,
> Blest, too, is the advent of darkness!"[35]

As Nabokov remarks, the image of the springtime recalls the poetry of André Chénier, among others. Perhaps Chénier is not the sort of poet Lenski should be emulating given that Chénier was writing on the eve of his execution during the French Revolution.[36]

In the following stanza, Lenski burns no less ardently.

> The ray of dawn will gleam tomorrow,
> And brilliant day will scintillate;
> Whilst I, perhaps—I shall descend
> Into the tomb's mysterious shelter,
> And the young poet's memory
> Slow Lethe will engulf;
> The world will forget me; but thou,
> Wilt thou come, maid of beauty,
> To shed a tear over the early urn

And think: he loved me,
To me alone he consecrated
The doleful daybreak of a stormy life! . . .
Friend of my heart, desired friend, come,
Come: I'm thy spouse!"[37]

Substituting the epithet "young poet" for his name, he indulges in the conceit of antonomasia. Nabokov's English brings out an archaic quality in Lenski's expressions ("whither," "ye," "thy," etc.) and thereby evoke an aching for a vanished past. Lenski can imagine his death but only in the vaguest of anachronistic terms. It is a strange confection of François Villon ("où sont les neiges d'antan?") and Alexander Pope ("Whatever IS, is RIGHT").[38] Or, perhaps, it is ironic that he is already being called away from the present, linguistically. He has already joined the dead.

Lenski resorts to anachronism to denote seriousness and solemnity; He does not allow himself to imagine falling, prosaically, under a bullet. He dreams, in an appropriately literary idiom, of being pierced by the dart—*strjela* [/strji'la/] in the Russian text: стрелой (strjeloj). Those who translate this as "bullet" surely compromise Lenski. It seems ironic or fanciful that Lenski dreams of being pierced by a dart—St. Sebastian style—when he will face a pistol shot. Pushkin, by contrast, refuses the romanticizing imagery of darts and will find poetry in the pistols. He allows us to behold, intently, these objects of terrible beauty.

Lenski earnestly attempts to come to a literary understanding of the duel, to insert it into a set of poetical acts. The course taken by sleep, poetical inspiration, love, and indeed a duel by pistol all lie somewhere on the unmapped boundaries between the realms of fate and the landscape of our will. Unable to articulate his feelings to Olga, to play more than a few chords at the clavichord, and to read Schiller, the poet's attempts to confer some literary meaning on the imminent act fail. At length, he falls into slumber at his own word—"ideal." Romantic expostulations are soporific. The duellist is ironically sent to sleep at the thought of the romantically dignified nature of the act he is to commit. Dormant in his very name is an idea of indolence—"Len," or Лень. But, ultimately, what interests and invigorates is the duel itself, not its significance. The pangs of "the night before" weighed less in earlier accounts of duels. Their nineteenth-century counterparts are more likely to revel in the nocturnal anxieties that creep over the prospective duellist, who is advised, "Should he feel inclined to sleep when he retires to rest, and troubled images disturb his imagination, let him take some amusing book—one of Sir Walter's novels, if a lover of the romantic; or Byron's 'Childe Harold' if he delights in the sublime; and read until he drops asleep, leaving word with a trusty servant to call him at five, and provide a cup of strong coffee, to be taken immediately on rising."[39]

The duel possibly represents an attempt to implant the intensity of risk into a predictable life of routines. Nevertheless, Lenski's inchoate verses, like the mood that led him to issue the challenge, seem overheated. Such jejune ardor cannot find expression. He does not enjoy the tranquility necessary to recollect and articulate his emotions. There is a mismatch between intense but undigested real feelings and the stilted formulae for expressing them.

That contrast between the two men is brilliantly sustained through Pushkin's evocation of the night before the duel. Onegin sleeps deeply, dreamlessly, and, ironically, "like the dead."[40] We are granted no access to his feelings or presentiments. Possibly, he is not troubled by any. Or the poet chooses to maintain a respectful distance from them. We merely see what he does. How prosaic is his own anticipation of the duel. The economist wastes no time on the sort of effusions to which Lenski is vulnerable:

> Now he awakes at last
> And draws apart the curtain's flaps;
> Looks—and sees that already
> It is long since time to drive off.[41]

Lenski seeks, with the help of Schiller and his own verse, to account for the duel as an episode of poetical moment. By contrast, Onegin is resolutely mundane: Pushkin does not interrupt Lenski's feverish poetical rhapsodies by mentioning anything as humdrum as curtain flaps. All these terms point to the practical and specific grounded world that he inhabits. Even the phrase "drive off," with the means of transport implied, suggests this in preference to a more grandiose journey "to meet my fate." He is thinking more about the means; Lenski about the end. He looks and sees, while Lenski thinks and doubts.

The description of the duel generates considerable pathos, such is the waste of young talent, and the silly paradox that these men could have remained friends, while it provokes a commentary on the tyranny and folly of public opinion that permits the duel. Pushkin also has an eye trained keenly on what happens when two duellists meet, as though the poet were himself looking unblinkingly through the sights of a pistol.

The pistol is not incidental, nor is its role in this duel minimized, as in certain descriptions previously. In stanza 29, the poet affords us a detailed inspection of the weapons. This stanza is a reproach to the poetical excesses of stanzas 21 and 22. The "ray of dawn will gleam," sang Lenski, but the pistols, attracting that same word in turn, now mock the poet's efforts:

> The pistols now have gleamed. The mallet clanks
> Against the ramrod. The balls go
> Into the polyhedral barrel,
> And the cock clicks for the first time.
> The powder in a grayish streamlet
> Now pours into the pan. The jagged,
> Securely screwed-in flint
> Anew is drawn back.[42]

With its evocation of the gleam, the click of the cock, and the powder, this stanza successively invites the participation of the respective senses of sight, hearing, and touch. The appearance of the protagonists themselves, even Eugene himself, has not been described in such loving detail. Nor do we see the hand in this or whose hand it is. The passive voice reigns in this description, suited to the fact that the pistols will no doubt have been loaded by the seconds (one of whom seems considerably more enthusiastic about the arrangements than either of the protagonists and the other whose very name, Guillot, seems to be a harbinger of death). But the combination of this vivid detail and an invisible, anonymous human presence loading the pistol again may help to make us feel that the duellists themselves have little or no agency. The weapon acquires a sinister life of its own, as one action leads mechanistically and remorselessly to another, before the final, fateful event is triggered.

This is remarkable poetry, unprecedented in its mechanistic detail. These specifications resemble those of a manual or recipe. Never had the workings of a pistol been turned into poetry. *Eugene Onegin* is not a particularly long work, yet this account, when we know the duel to be running late and the poet to be given to impatience, is especially leisurely.

Pushkin initially describes the contest with the hushed, impartial tones of a reporter commentating live on a golf match. As the duellists pace, the poetry echoes their tread in its monosyllables. This is a highly numerical stanza. The poet enumerates with precision the numbers of paces the principals take. Then, at length, the outcome is decided:

> Onegin fired. . . . The clock of fate
> Has struck: the poet
> In silence drops his pistol.

Now the commentator gulps, as the ellipsis provides a refuge for the poet confronted by the ineffability of death. But no sooner has the duel claimed a life than the commentator takes us to more familiar poetical ground. By contrast, we are now treated to a stanza of overtly poetic beauty. Lenski falls, laying his hand on his breast as he does so. The dying man is honored with a serene image:

> Softly he lays his hand upon his breast
> And falls. His misty gaze
> Expresses death, not pain.
> Thus, slowly, down the slope of hills,
> Shining with sparkles in the sun,
> A lump of snow descends.
> Deluged with instant cold,
> Onegin hastens to the youth,
> Looks, calls him . . . vainly:
> He is no more. The young bard has
> Found an untimely end!
> The storm has blown; the beauteous bloom
> Has withered at sunrise; the fire
> upon the altar has gone out! . . . [43]

Lenski's fall is commemorated in what the poet has earlier called "luxurious language," as snow descends meltingly down the slope of the hills.[44] The poet, reaching for a simile, finds that he now needs nature. Hitherto, the poet has tended to be disdainful of folkish willingness to read symbols into nature's movements (such as Tanya's response to the falling star or a passing hare).[45] This is an analogue rather than a prophecy, but the poet has sometimes found himself to be rather embarrassed by similes, that poetic staple, and he was dismissive of portents.[46] This poet is too modern and knowing, cynical, and Byronic for that.

In honor of the dead man, the poet moves into a more generous, poetical flight of fancy. The terms and imagery conspire to make the death, however untimely and however tortuous the procedures that led to it, seem natural as well as painless. Good poetry carries the aura of inevitability, and, as Lenski falls, the language takes on a more obviously exalted poetical quality. It is as Lenski dies that this novel in verse bursts out of prose into poetry.

Or is the poetry drawing on Lenski's own inchoate, rather hackneyed efforts, of which we just had a specimen? The poet may momentarily have borrowed Lenski's own overblown imagery in his honor. Is Pushkin experiencing, and wanting us to experience, pathos naturally and sincerely, or is he possibly indulging in it and self-consciously overdoing its effects in tribute to the fallen "bard," a perhaps slightly unkind or facetious synonym for the "poet," which Pushkin has saved until this moment: a defunct term now suited to this deceased man. As Pushkin later asks his readers, including perhaps himself, "Might he not be, in fact, a parody?"[47]

There is another little trick or delicate irony in this stanza devoted to the death of Lenski: a surprising jolt is conferred by the poet's word order, such that the man "deluged with instant cold" should be not Lenski but Onegin. Indeed, it may seem to be Lenski who wins. This stanza commemorates a moment of serenity and seems to celebrate the capacity of poetry to vanquish death, to decide for itself, to offer a result of its own. The poet, then, is destined to fall. But therein lies his victory. Even a poet as remote in time and in type as Seamus Heaney has, writing of Osip Mandelstam, conceived of poetry as a lost cause, the poet raising his voice "like a pretender's flag."[48] Is this man a poet?

Or is he rather a poem? His most poetical accomplishment would appear to be his death. Lenski is faithful to all the clichés of the poetic life—he likes the moon, he falls in love, yet he does not really succeed in composing poems, leaving us to wonder whether it is somehow possible to be a poet without actually writing poetry. Thomas Chatterton did not write any serious poetry of his own, it turned out, but by dying "a poetic death," he rose to an exalted quasi-poetical status.[49] Lenski, we were told, "wandered . . . under the sky of Goethe and Schiller."[50] However, this may be Pushkin's deft way of saying that, while he is in their thrall, he is not at their level. Besides, this formulation suggests that he may not necessarily have gone to the trouble of reading their words.

Just as Lenski's poetical credentials and the poetry of his death are questioned by this poem, so Eugene Onegin leaves, in his deserted house, the traces of a man perhaps unexpectedly devoted to poetry. A portrait of Byron adorns his wall. While Schiller and Goethe reign in Lenski's sky, less nebulously, Byron presides over his desk. There, is after all, poetry in his life and ideals, indeed love. Eugene Onegin turns out, in the event, to be a more assiduous reader.[51] We would have been wrong to dismiss him simply as the prosaic inverse of the poet Lenski.

Wobbling on the thin line between the sincerity of imitation and the cynicism of parody, the poet moves between expansive poetry that is full of wonder, pathos, and compassion and asking for that back, almost apologizing for the effects he has just achieved. In other words, the reader may savor the experience, but there is a sense in which its container is always the poet's, and we will have to return it to him, in exchange for our deposit. We encounter a rich paradox here: the tension between what a duel involves and what it signifies, what it is and what it seems. Pushkin's verses remove the poetry from the duel, yet they do so poetically.

Pushkin distanced himself from potential associations with any of the characters from *Eugene Onegin*, maintaining that the subject of this novel in verse was no biographical version of himself, although the disclaimer may merely raise the suspicion it is supposed to quell. But, of course, ironically and tragically, Pushkin contributes to the poetry of the duel by dying in a duel, even though his poem complicated the equation between self-conscious gestures and the poetic vocation. This irony only helped to make the conjunction between work and life more memorable.

Lenski's death, however unhappy and inglorious, is integral to his own reputation as a poet, and perhaps, cruel as it is to say, this remains his greatest poetical achievement. Pushkin, by his own death, casts the poet as prophet and turns the duel into a tragic totem of the inscrutability of fate in the modern age. *Eugene Onegin* inaugurates a new chapter in the portrayal of duels in literature. Pushkin shows us what a duel might look and feel like. His close, mesmerized attention to the weapons is essential to that achievement. Or perhaps it would be more accurate, if less analytically proper or prudent, to say that Pushkin himself was responsible for this new chapter. Or, to be precise, it was Georges d'Anthès. On 25 January 1837, Pushkin fought a duel with d'Anthès, his brother-in-law, a Frenchman in forces based in St. Petersburg. On 27 January, Pushkin died of the wounds he sustained from a pistol shot. On 13 February, d'Anthès and Pushkin were each sentenced to hang, the latter, obviously, in absentia.

The tortuous events leading to this famous, fatal duel have been exhaustively detailed in Serena Vitale's study. One of the obstacles she and other historians have encountered, in trying to reconstruct the precise nature of these mysterious events, is that of disentangling the actual events from those that Pushkin invented and sang in his great poem. Many details in the contemporary and subsequent descriptions of Pushkin's death appear to have been plagiarized from *Eugene Onegin*.[52] Pushkin's passing was rapidly mythologized into a poetical death. As he lay dying, Pushkin, it was observed, found himself in the semirecumbent posture he assumed when he wrote his poetry, even though the excruciating pain was less poetical.[53] But this tendency to conflate fact and fiction, allied to the fatalistic bent of so many Russian thinkers, seems to have been encouraged by Pushkin's own fears and confessions. As he lay dying, he appears to have remembered the prophecies of one Mrs. Kirchhof and his own fears and premonitions about the number 6. The fatal duel he described takes place in the sixth chapter of *Eugene Onegin*. Pushkin had, unfortunately, turned into Lenski.[54]

One of the first translators of Pushkin into French was Prosper Mérimée, who, in 1828, had himself survived a duel with Félix Lacoste, outside Paris. Later, in the 1860s, he would sit in the Senate alongside Georges d'Anthès, Pushkin's adversary. But in the interim, he wrote his own Romantic yet absurd story about love gratuitously brought to an end by a duel.

Mérimée, "Le vase étrusque" (1830): Saint-Clair versus Thémines

Auguste Saint-Clair, a timidly introspective young man, has been harboring a secret passion for a beautiful Countess. To his dismay, he learns one day, while conversing with friends, that she was once the mistress of the late Monsieur Massigny, by common consent the most boring man in the world. Saint-Clair can barely believe that the treasured object of his love shared similarly exalted feelings for such an obviously dissimilar man. Her past attachments indeed distress him more than her present arrangements, for he is fully reconciled to sharing his lover with her husband—an example of the nineteenth-century physiology of marriage. Yet this highly distasteful rumor is lent substance by the presence (and prominence) in her home of an Etruscan vase, which Massigny had given her as a token of his love, upon returning from a sojourn in Rome. Saint-Clair has noticed the piece upon every visit to her home. Indeed, it is into this vase that she has always placed the flowers which he has brought her.

Saint-Clair regards his love for the Countess as irremediably tainted. D'Albert, a similarly idealistic figure in Théophile Gautier's novel *Mademoiselle de Maupin*, published a few years later, in 1835, expresses a passionate desire to find a mistress without "a past."[55] He wants his ideal woman to have known no man at all, let alone one who was famously boring. By tradition, or at least according to Oscar Wilde, a man wants to be the woman's first love, while a woman is more concerned that the man should be her last. But perhaps the dismay these young men have in common mirrors wider yet also more localized concerns, felt acutely in Restoration France, about the persistence of an uncomfortable, sometimes compromising past. The sanctity of Saint-Clair's love is sapped by his contempt for Massigny. Disgusted with himself, he takes it upon himself to initiate a duel and to die in consequence. To this end, he willfully provokes a quarrel with a seasoned marksman that, sure enough, leads to an engagement at dawn. The duel here suggests itself to the gentleman in despair as a form of assisted suicide. He lacks the moral independence, or perhaps the courage, to kill himself, but, by outsourcing it thus, an honorable exit is assured.

On the eve of the duel, Saint-Clair learns, however, that there never was the least rapport between his lover and Massigny. Indeed, she thinks the idea utterly preposterous. When challenged about the vase, she drops it, scoffing, and it shatters into a thousand pieces. Saint-Clair bursts out laughing too, but, as the narrator quietly observes, "a tear enters his eyes as he laughs."[56] His love and its object are vindicated, but he also knows that backing out of the duel, no matter how fatuous its cause and fatal its prospects, is unconscionable.

Mérimée does not tell the story of the duel that now follows in his own voice or describe it from the vantage point of an omniscient narrator. Instead, he entrusts the account to Saint-Clair's debonair second, Colonel Beaujeu, whose name surely betrays his insouciance. Beaujeu duly informs us that the social circle, of which Saint-Clair formed a part, met, as usual, in the café Tortoni, where Beaujeu relates what happened. Saint-Clair generously proposed that Thémines (the marksman he had sought out) shoot first—an honorable man will always wait before firing.

> Thémines fired; I saw Saint-Clair spinning round once, before he dropped down stone dead. I've already observed that often when soldiers are shot, they do this strange spin before they die.
>
> That's really extraordinary, said Roquantain. And what about Thémines: what did he do?
>
> Oh! What you have to do on such occasions. He threw his pistol to the ground with an air of regret. He threw it so hard that he broke its hammer. It's an English pistol, by Manton. I don't know whether he'll be able to find an armorer in Paris who can get him another one.[57]

The colonel exemplifies the difficulty of describing any occurrence with (military) precision, without also sounding callous. The accent is always apt to fall on ancillary matters. Nevertheless, the death of Saint-Clair is accepted all too easily after this cruelly dispassionate account. Roquantain registers interest in a scientific curiosity rather than a horrific tragedy. Saint-Clair's premature death is added to a familiar catalogue. Even Thémines's dramatic action, designed to exhibit bitter regret or to disown the pistol, is likewise ascribed to his sense of duelling propriety. It is recognized as a conventional gesture duly performed only with an *"air* of regret." Most tellingly, the second dwells on the value and rarity of the damaged pistol, in preference to discussing the destroyed life. A Manton, the Rolls Royce of pistols, would admittedly have been a prized possession, but the remark betrays the cruelty of the second, rather than honoring the prestige of the pistol. The quiet retrieval of a weapon, discarded in dutiful despair, appears to have been one of the second's unofficial tasks.

Far from providing an obituary of Saint-Clair, the text inherits the characteristics of the gentlemen it describes, with its strenuous bonhomie and worldly detachment. Related in this nonchalant fashion, the duel seems emptied of any romantic verve. The story gives us access to a world-weary, unimpressed Parisian *monde*, incapable of surprise or sorrow. Moreover, the narrator, with his wry, aphoristic tone, seems at home in this milieu.

However, at length, the narrator and the society that he evokes seem to diverge. The final paragraph of this elegant story may take us by surprise. We learn that the Countess, devastated by the death of her lover, becomes a recluse. Withdrawing from the fluent flippancies of her circle's conversation, she falls silent. Readers will remember the silence and solitude embraced by Littegarde in Kleist's story, a couple of decades previously.

> For three whole years the Countess did not see anyone: winter and summer alike, she stayed in her country house, barely leaving her room, waited on by a mulatto woman who knew about her relationship with Saint-Clair and to whom, day in day out, she hardly uttered a word. After three years, her cousin Julie returned from a long voyage; she forced the door open and found poor Mathilde so thin and so pale that she thought she was looking at the corpse of the same woman she had last seen looking beautiful and full of life. . . . The

Countess languished . . . for another three or four months, before she died of a chest illness attributed to domestic troubles, as Dr. M . . . , who looked after her, says.[58]

This sad, secluded end recalls that of *La princesse de Clèves*, in which the sincerity and intensity of love must negotiate the norms of a worldly society. With comparable restraint, Mérimée respects the inner life of the Countess.

Like other stories dominated by a duel, this account does justice both to the absurd and the touching facets. The causes of the duel are, even by the standards of nineteenth-century France, utterly ridiculous. Far from vindicating female honor, as in Kleist's story, the young duellist acts, with unwarranted chagrin, on a perceived lapse in her taste. Yet this conclusion transforms a risible story into a heartbreaking account of love thwarted and thrown away. That worldly tone of restrained, elegant irony, a signature key of the French short story, is supplanted by a sober account of the Countess's last days. Saint-Clair is, after all, remembered and cherished, to say the very least.

Even the choice of title suggests that the text purports to interest itself in a smashed vase, just as it pays attention to the damaged pistol, in each case skirting the human costs. It is obvious that a broken heart is ultimately pulsing at the core of the story, which is not really about an Etruscan vase.[59]

Amid the sociable chatter in which this story abounds, one of Saint-Clair's acquaintances asks whether there might be some sort of "general formula for singularity." If he were a hunchback, he claims that, in order to distract attention from this impediment, he would kill someone in a duel and take laudanum. No one would see the hump after he achieved such notoriety.[60] Alcibiades had tried to purchase a similar reputation after cutting a dog's tail to distract from a reputation with which he was unhappy. The effort to stand out as different from the others merely emphasizes how indebted that individual is to social trends. The duellist, consulting his own rules, while ignoring those of the law, embodies the Romantic aspiration to live a singular, even unique life, but it is a pity that he has this wish in common with everyone else. The duel exemplifies the paradox that is regulated singularity or formulaic individuality.

Saint-Clair, in a seemingly inconsequential detail, undergoes a "strange spin" just before dying in the duel. A few years later, in 1834, when Alexandre Dumas fought a duel with one Frédéric Gaillardet, he reports that his second, a doctor by the name of Bixio, inspired by this story, was fascinated to see whether Dumas might fall in the same way. But the question would be resolved only when Bixio was himself shot dead in 1848, not before spinning three times and declaring, "Now I know one turns round." Dumas's writings exemplify the continued shift from a moral to a preponderantly scientific interest in the duel; yet this supposedly true story draws explicitly on Mérimée's literary antecedent, and the same cool worldliness is in evidence. Villiers de l'Isle Adam's "Sombre récit, conteur plus sombre" (1877) also ends with its own little sophisticated spin on Mérimée's fatal encounter. A duel accounts for a sudden urgency in reuniting schoolmates who have not seen each other for ten years. Their reunion is destined to be momentary, for this duellist also falls with a spin, and the old friend, after acting loyally as a second, turns into a debonair storyteller.[61] Just as the dying combatant twists back on himself, so these authors turn back, in an involuted fashion, to their fictional antecedents.

But the tone of Mérimée's story is ultimately difficult to secure, for just when we thought it was safe to stay on its surface, unsuspected depths need to be plumbed. The Countess's silent grief may reproach us as readers who came to this story expecting merely to find amusement. A duel makes for a good story, as Mérimée well knows, but that story invariably seems to impose hidden costs.

Mérimée's story announces the emergence of a new strand in works devoted to duels. Now that the duel, having survived the Revolution and other upheavals, has acquired a sort of wearied respectability, such that it is widely tolerated, even tacitly admired, it can provide a socially acceptable screen for bitter resentments and shameful despair. Under its elegant veneer, the duel can conceal and permit acts of murder and of suicide.[62] Diverse as the causes of duels may have been in the eighteenth century, such dissimulation is not imagined in eighteenth-century accounts. But the idea will recur, culminating in the *demi-assassinats* or de facto suicides dressed up as duels in the works of Kuprin and Pirandello, while rendering all the more grievous Maupassant's coward, who, committing suicide to avoid a duel, reverses that trajectory.

But Saint-Clair's willfully self-destructive duel deserves to be contrasted with a body of literary works given rather to portraying the duel as a means of self-realization. This sometimes takes the form of a crude professional ascent—a duel survived may amount to a sort of qualification, a ladder, rather than a snake, in a militarized society where respect is earned by courage or extracted by fear—but it can also stir deeper spiritual and moral intuitions.

CHAPTER SIX

The Duel and Self-Realization

Smollett, *The Adventures of Roderick Random* (1748):
Roderick Random versus the World

The collected novels of Tobias Smollett amount in essence, it some-times feels, to one overgrown narrative, chopped up into different books. Roderick Random, Peregrine Pickle, Ferdinand Fathom, and the hundreds of characters whom they each encounter all inhabit the same, tumultuous region. The alliteration with which their respective pairs of names slide toward one another offers but an initial taste of the ten-dency for distinctions of different kinds to blur, for one adventure to lead restlessly to another. We may seem to be reading slightly differing versions of the same book again and again. Yet Smollett's oeuvre in its totality is highly diverse and, as such, characteristic of the eighteenth century. He first trained as a surgeon, like many of those writers who took an interest in duels over the following century. He wrote poetry and completed a tragedy *(The Regicide)* which, for ten years, he failed to persuade anyone to stage. More successfully, Smollett was, like his contemporaries and compatriots, Hume and Robertson, a historian of his own age, keen to train a historiographical stethoscope on the changing pulse over the past centuries. His history of England came to a close in 1748, a few years after the disaster of the '45 and the battle of Culloden that compounded it.[1] Completed in the same year, *The Ad-ventures of Roderick Random*, his first novel, acts as both a supple-ment and a challenge to that history. Here Smollett gives expression to a more intimate, affective history of one particular Scotsman, who, inevitably but erroneously, was recognized as a fictional version of Smollett himself.

Among these various achievements, Smollett also contrived to translate *Don Quixote*, possibly without knowing any, or much, Spanish. His interest in the legacy of chivalry in modern times was, however, by no means confined to that project. The eponymous hero of *Sir Launcelot Greaves* (1760) styles himself self-consciously on Don Quixote, while remaining fully alert to the potential futility and absurdity of an attempt to resurrect that knight in a country and in an age cynically aware of the Don's haplessness. The name that Smollett chose for his hero—Sir Launcelot Greaves—conveys some of the jarring ambivalence of this figure, who is pulled between chivalrous aspiration and humbler roots. With one foot in the past and the other in the present, he is a gentle heir to Shakespeare's contradictory Ancient Pistol and a forerunner to Sheridan's Lucius O'Trigger. The chief protagonist of *The Adventures of Roderick Random* instantly offers us a similar friction. The name Roderick is not entirely random. It recalls and resurrects Rodrigo, the famous Cid. Roderick Random is a Scottish warrior, a Cid in tweed, in quest of honor and dignity, to whom duelling provides a vital form of self-expression. But then nor, for that matter, is the name Random random. The substantive designated, in the eighteenth century, the range of a piece of ordnance, especially "the long or full range obtained by elevating the muzzle of the piece."[2]

If this affiliation to the Cid is submerged and may seem coincidental, Roderick Random later gives us reasons for thinking that it is not fanciful. Not long before the novel's conclusion, Random makes, as the heading of the chapter announces, "a very interesting discovery": by an "amazing stroke of Providence," he comes across his long-lost father.[3] No less improbably, this chance reunion takes place in South America, where his father goes by the name of Don Rodriguez. Having left Scotland many years previously, he settled in Paraguay, where he found his fortune and lived comfortably ever since as a Spanish *hidalgo*. So, Random's name notwithstanding, blind chance is ultimately subordinated to benign Providence. Roderick is not only integrated into the society from which he has been alienated, by an advantageous marriage at the end of the story, but he also acquires a pseudo-Spanish pedigree as the son of a noble *picaro*. This is an entirely fitting conclusion for a man who fights his duels with both a punctilious concern for honor and unremitting Scottish bluntness.

It is apparent from the opening of the novel that Random's angry desire for revenge and his irascible defensiveness are preordained. From the very start, Random is seeking redress and looking to get his

Frontispiece to the second edition of Smollett's *The Adventures of Roderick Random* (London: Osborn, 1748) engraved by Charles Grignion after a design by Francis Hayman. Reproduced by kind permission of the Syndics of Cambridge University Library.

deserts from a society that cruelly withholds them from him. This resentment is prompted by his exclusion and disinheritance, having been born illegitimately. Justice is not to be obtained from the law. On the contrary, injustice is perpetrated by the legal apparatus. Random's cruel, grudging grandfather is a lawyer, a fact that hammers home this point. Duelling is then the expression of a natural urge to bypass the law. In subsequent novels by Smollett, the desire to supply the deficiencies of an ineffectual legal system is an explicit motivation among those, such as Sir Launcelot Greaves, who challenge and combat others. Random soon realizes that any chance of self-improvement lies beyond the scope of the law. *Roderick Random* appears to endorse the duel as a salutary form of self-defense, a vindication of one's rights in a society where justice is not administered reliably.

Random's wish for revenge on the forces of cruelly arbitrary authority is pronounced from the start and expresses itself in the crudest way imaginable. Young Random plots to capture his tyrannical schoolmaster, a proto-Dickensian figure, already lurking in the pages of this eighteenth-century novel, in order to spit in his face. Random is sorely troubled by his illegitimate birth. Whereas Tom Jones, Candide, and Figaro are natural-born and, to varying degrees, joyously free in their thoughts and their actions as a consequence, this bastard, who has entered the world earlier than any of them, feels acutely the pain and exclusion of his birth.

The aptronyms in which Smollett delights—Mr. Syntax, the teacher, or Mr. Vulture, the bailiff—may divert us from the unremitting cruelty and crudity of a world in which men are continually at odds with each other. Smollett's remorseless savagery and scatology, which we encounter, earlier, in Swift and, later, in Voltaire's *Candide,* lack the compensations furnished by the elegance of their irony or the gloss of their stylistic patina. Voltaire, in particular, allows us to look at violence through the safety of a pane of clear glass, a French window. Smollett, his admiration for the French stylist notwithstanding, does not quite afford us that distance and that light. The violence in the world described by Smollett is hellishly pervasive and, in modern terms, "disproportionate." Nor is such aggression the predictable prerogative of obviously vindictive or resentful people. For instance, Roderick's benign uncle, his kind, wealthy benefactor from the navy, Tom

Bowling, who would appear to be a fictional counterpart to Hogarth's hearty Captain Tom Coram (1740), promptly chops the head off a dog and slays the other, as soon as they threaten him. All men are armed against the world and both required and ready to come to blows in their defense and in their interest. Ironically, the only man with an aversion to blades, and other weapons, is the barber, Hugh Strap, Random's loyal servant and friend.[4]

It is a world in which people, and the actions that they perpetrate, are repeatedly described as barbarous. Duelling, which continued to attract this epithet throughout the eighteenth century, seems, on the contrary, necessary to temper, rather than to exemplify, the barbarities of the world. Duels, in which this story abounds, provide a universal way of restraining this violence. They are, if you pardon the expression, not part of the problem but its solution.

Random, a disinherited gentleman, in due course, a stray Scotsman, and a man in want of an honorable wife, tries to assert his status and defend his pride through fighting duels. But everyone else seems to be doing the same or threatening to do it. An extraordinary mania for duelling, with whatever weapon comes to hand, for whatever slight perceived, can be seen throughout this volume. There appear to be more duels per square mile than in any other volume, including even Dumas's *Three Musketeers*, although the formula recurs almost as insistently in Smollett's subsequent novels. Let us enumerate, as concisely as possible, these numerous duels, between which a plotline occasionally breaks out:

1. Random challenges his treacherous countryman, Gawky. Gawky misses the appointment.[5]
2. Random's page, Hugh Strap, is challenged by Captain Weazel, but weapons are not agreed upon.[6]
3. Weazel challenges Random to a duel in a kitchen. (He defends himself there and then with a spit.)[7]
4. Random, seeking revenge on Odonnell, an Irish fortune hunter who has assaulted him, entertains "thoughts of demanding satisfaction in an honourable way," but Random pursues "a middle course": he and his friends strip Odonnell naked and scourge him with nettles.[8]

5. Miss Williams tells her story: Lothario, as she calls him, is apparently killed by Horatio, in a duel fought with swords in defense of her honor. She accordingly "yields up" her body "as a recompense for the service he had done" her, only to learn that the story is a fiction.[9]

6. Random learns that his kindly uncle, Tom Bowling, has apparently killed the captain of his ship in a duel.[10]

7. Midshipman Crampley ridicules Random about Scotland, and a fight breaks out. They are advised "either to leave [their] difference undecided till [they] should have an opportunity of terminating it on shore, like gentlemen, or else chuse a proper place on board, and bring it to an issue by boxing." This last expedient is "greedily embraced," and there ensues a "furious contest" in which many "cross-buttocks . . . and pegs on the stomach" are sustained.[11]

8. Random challenges Crampley, now the captain of his ship, presenting his pistols: "He took one without hesitation, and before I could cock the other fired in my face throwing the pistol after the shot. . . . I . . . , flying upon my antagonist, knocked out several of his fore-teeth with the butt-end of the piece."[12]

9. The cook wench and dairy maid, who both fancy Random, fight each other: "if their sentiments had been refined by education, it is probable that one or other of them would have had recourse to poison or steel, to be revenged of her rival." As it is, their enmity is "confined to scolding and fisty-cuffs."[13]

10. A coachman challenges Random to single combat. He offers to box him for twenty guineas. Random responds, "I would not descend so far below the dignity of a gentleman, as to fight like a porter; but if he had anything to say to me, I was his man at blunderbuss, musket, pistol, sword, hatchet, spit, cleaver, fork or needle."[14]

11. Random, now enlisted as a soldier, falls out with a Frenchman. Random clenches his fists "to give him a hearty box on the ear." Thinking better of that, Random instead agrees to "do him the honour of measuring his sword" with his own, "like a gentleman." This is the first proper duel. Random is defeated. He is "ashamed at the pitiful figure of [his] antagonist, who was a poor,

little, shivering creature descrepid with age, and blind of one
eye," but his pity is wasted: the Frenchman promptly wounds
and disarms him.[15]

12. Random wishes to claim satisfaction with his musket: "at which
    weapon we should be more upon a par than with the sword, of
    which he seemed so much master." He decides, however, to
    takes lessons in the "noble science" of swordsmanship, and he
    gains revenge when he reverses the result, in the aftermath of
    the battle of Dettingen.[16]

13. Bragwell boasts of a recent "affair" with Tom Trippet.[17]

14. Random decides to fight a duel with Bragwell, in order to im-
    press Melinda.[18]

15. Random receives a written challenge from an Irish adventurer,
    Rourk Oregan, a rival for Melinda's hand. They fight a farcical
    duel by pistols at the back of Montagu-house.[19]

16. Random treads on the toes of a tall, raw-boned fellow with a
    hooked nose. He insists on gentlemanly satisfaction, and
    Random is prepared to fight; but the invitation is refused.[20]

17. Random encounters another admirer of Melinda: "instead of re-
    senting my address in what is called an honourable way, [he]
    threatened to prosecute me for an assault, and took witnesses
    accordingly."[21]

18. At last, Random is challenged by, and duly duels with, Lord
    Quiverwit, by sword. Quiverwit is seriously wounded. They are
    reconciled.[22]

Smollett depicts a tiring world in which nothing is trivial. The pro-
liferating frequency of these duels becomes draining for the reader, all
the more so when they are circular and self-generated. Insofar as they
have a cause, these solipsistic duels are sometimes about the right of
the combatant to duel, or they may be designed to prove that he is
worthy of that weapon. Thus Random fights a second duel with a
Frenchman, in part to avenge his insolence after the previous fight but
also to show to him that he too can handle a sword.

Random's feelings of inadequacy are undoubtedly compounded by
his self-awareness as a Scot, born not long after his nation's union with
the English crown. It leaves him orphaned twice over, as it were. He

keeps alive a residue of chivalry, a warlike spirit that now cannot be directed to the interests of his land but must be rerouted in the defense of his own fortunes. The Jacobites, after the abortive rebellion of 1715, had been disarmed ever since. Random's adaptability in helping himself to whatever he can get his hands on, and his unfamiliarity with traditional weapons, may be characteristically Scottish. There is a hesitation between validating the duel as a rightful expression of manly courage and dignity, robbed by Culloden, and deploring it either as a self-defeating compulsion, which leads only to further duels, or, worse still, after the wars that have convulsed Britain and Europe, as nothing more than a sham, a game in which boys play men. The frequency of these duels banalizes and devalues each and every one of them. They are not the expression of a code that these gentlemen honorably feel compelled to follow but merely a pastime, an affectation. They become gestures and postures. They certainly lack the terrible finality of the single, conclusive duel that terminates *Clarissa,* published that same year. Smollett depicts a society in which men are engaged in a perpetual combat with one another, usually a nonfatal jockeying for preeminence. Such are the conditions of eighteenth-century society, in which fighting has a central place, not least among the gentlemen in its higher echelons. But Smollett is also not painting an entirely "realistic" picture of his society—the names of his characters alone should warn us off that. He is updating Don Quixote for his century and his nation.

It is apparent from the brief summaries of the aforementioned duels that, concerned as Roderick Random is to patrol the line between duel and brawl, his experiences reveal that it is extremely thin. A duel is little more than a civilized, glorified, brawl—a brawl, an inglorious duel. The invitation to the first duel, as Random avows, masks and excuses an intention to brawl. After composing a written challenge comme il faut, he recollects, "I betook myself to the field, though not without feeling considerable repugnance to the combat. . . . There I waited an hour beyond the time appointed, and was not ill pleased to find [my adversary] had no mind to meet me; because now I should have an opportunity of exposing his cowardice, displaying my own courage, and of beating him soundly wheresoever I should find him, without any dread of the consequence." "Elevated with these suggestions," as Random ironically puts it, he then hurries to the lodgings of his elusive adversary, Gawky, in order to carry out this beating, only to find that he has scarpered.[23]

Random comes close to admitting that he challenged Gawky in the hope that he would be too cowardly to respond and that a good old-fashioned assault suits better his modus vivendi. In other words, we sense that Random is born to brawl, not to duel, and it will take him some effort to adjust to the higher level. But he seems less interested in taking revenge on Gawky, a rather innocuous character, than in "displaying [his] own courage." The admission confirms a suspicion that hangs over so many of the duels enumerated. It is not the case that these duels result, unfortunately and inevitably, when men take against each other; instead, men take against each other, in order that they may fight a duel. Enmity is but a pretext in some cases, and it is partly for this reason that it so rapidly melts into friendship, upon the conclusion of the duel.

The reader may well despair of discerning a pattern or program in this succession of duels, which are sometimes haphazard, usually grotesque, always just about nonfatal. Random challenges opponents as often as he is challenged by them; he uses pistols or swords or whatever comes to hand, and he is prepared to fight for whatever reason. Nevertheless, there is a clear progression from initial duels, or pseudoduels, with marginal, risible figures, whether a feeble Scot such as Gawky or dubious Irish schemers such as Odonnell or Oregan, to the concluding bout by swords with an English grandee, Lord Quiverwit. The evolving form the duel takes would seem broadly to correspond to the escalation in Random's fortunes. Important as friends and patrons may be, the choice of the right enemies is also essential to one's progress and prosperity in this society.

These duels betray social instability on a large scale, as people fight for recognition and, in a lawless society, defend their own claims and rights. The successive fights reveal a desperate struggle for preeminence and respect among people on edge, rather than the meeting of gentlemen sorting out particular differences. The earliest fights (1–15) are explicitly poor man's duels. However, the duel is not palely imitated or parodied but, on the contrary, comes to life in these boisterous encounters. These imaginative pranks and improvised brawls bring their own satisfaction, to the writer as well as to the combatants. They are an integral part of Smollett's comical, mock-epic arsenal. The eighteenth century has been said to mark the final hurrah of the mock-epic genre, an era when readers could yet be expected to recognize the epic antecedents to which these episodes were the comical heirs.[24] Smollett's instincts as a writer, whetted by his work as a translator and satirist, lead him to show adventures that are essentially mock-epic. Duels between lowly, cowardly figures, who cannot manipulate their weapons, abound. But Smollett typically shows us duels in which, far from denoting the clumsiness or the stupidity of the lower orders, the earthier touches provide both the actual damage and the real resolution. For example, the apex of Random's career as a duellist would appear to be his final duel, his bout with Lord Quiverwit, who has issued a courteous challenge. Random recollects the duel in detail. Random eventually prevails, but, poised to administer the coup de grâce, he inverts the sword and thrusts the hilt into Quiverwit's mouth, costing him several teeth. This sort of behavior would later cause the "docteurs en duel" to frown and fret before devising explicit rules.[25] Random is, however, unapologetic in describing this improvised coup de grâce. Are we to understand that, schooled in the tough lower reaches of society, he betrays himself momentarily? Or, just as plausibly, he feels that, as Clarissa tells Morden, the Lord, whatever his rank, does not deserve the honor of being killed by him. This injury is more humiliating and fitting.

In the 1750s, after the great fright of the '45, a British fear of being overwhelmed by a French army, which was, numerically speaking, vastly superior, manifested itself in several ways.[26] Britain concentrated its efforts on naval strength, in order to deny the French a route across the sea to its shores. Smollett, a captain in the navy, was well aware of the particular importance of the navy to British self-assertion. But in depicting duels, sometimes regarded as a deplorable French habit par excellence, conducted in this roughshod manner, he satisfies a perhaps peculiarly British fantasy: that of beating the French at their own game or, more precisely, outmuscling them, less through skill and professional savoir faire than by improvisatory ferocity and daring. The strength of the British would not lie in military skill and accomplishment but rest on the readiness of everyone to take up arms, with native aggression. There might be fewer soldiers in Britain than in France, but the sons of Albion were more belligerent. And until it came to another Franco-British war, internecine jockeying and duelling between the constituent parts of the United Kingdom might provide, as the crudely effective ragbag of Welsh, Scots, and Irish soldiers in Shakespeare's *Henry V* had testified, an excellent interim experience.

A duel-cum-brawl is the optimal way of capturing Random's equivocal sense of his place in the world, poised between the "extravagance of hope" and a despairing anxiety about his straitened circumstances, his unwavering belief in the advantages and entitlements of his birth and class failing to be deterred by tainted nobility, desperate poverty, impatience, and resentment. These duels are then fought less in the interests of righting particular wrongs than in order to redress, or mitigate, the profound anomaly that is Random's disinherited social position. The causes of these duels are secondary to the reason for them—his all-consuming resentment. In allowing Random to measure himself against apparent superiors, the duel may give full expression to his hostility and bitterness. Since the duel retains a noble aura, fighting it, rather than winning it, becomes an end in itself. The inadequacies of his birth, the humiliations of his nationality, the privations of his purse can be effaced by the act of fighting a duel. Injuries inflicted are a mere bonus. A simpler aim animates him and drives him to fight duels: the conquest and prize of an otherwise unavailable woman. There is, then, an additional hint at sexual frustration that is sublimated by the duel. In chapter 22, Miss Williams, Narcissa's servant whom Random befriends in an attempt to get closer to her, tells him of her misadventures at the hands of two men whom she calls Lothario and Horatio. The former turned out to be no gentleman in his conduct toward her; the latter, chivalrously taking up arms on her behalf, informed Miss Williams that he had avenged her and wounded Lothario in a duel. Accordingly she "yielded up [her] body as a recompense" to this champion, only to learn later that both his regard for her and the veracity of the duel were entirely illusory. Horatio made up the story, in league with Lothario. They turn out to be as dastardly as each other. Her disillusionment and despair are complete.

Touched as Random is by Miss Williams, he seems only to have been strengthened in his view that, provided he can avoid being killed in the process, participation in a duel is likely to yield him the prize of the lady whose hand otherwise eludes him. The duel is the one noble prerogative that is affordable to such an impoverished scion. He himself now proceeds opportunistically to seek out a suitably glamorous duel on behalf of Narcissa. The enchantingly beautiful Narcissa, in common with Smollett's other heroines, is dainty and demure. She does not express any vigorous views until the point at which she learns that Random has wounded Lord Quiverwit in a duel on her account. She calmly expresses her opinion in a letter to him. Unimpressed, she writes with concision, "As I am fully convinced of your honour and love, I hope I shall never hear of such desperate proofs of either for the future."[27]

Random's duel may have flattered Narcissa more than she cares to admit. It certainly does not compromise her love for him. Nevertheless, she is quick to see this duel as his way of compensating for a lack of confidence in his own merits, a wish to supply his perceived shortcomings, a self-defeating bid to shore himself up against his insecurities. Like Richardson and Rousseau, Smollett entrusts to a female character disapproving remarks with regard to duelling. She puts her finger on the problem. Random's constant wish, or need, to duel is indeed desperate. It is the action of a man whose grievances cannot otherwise be heard, a man anxious to be taken seriously. Yet the duels only sink him further into the contemptibility he is eager to escape. But then, as his confidence grows, he derives pride and strength from being a blunt Scotsman, rather than kowtowing ceremoniously. The duel that terminates in a blow to the face, the sword upended, and the duel that shades into a brawl are his way of expressing himself, embellishing the formal ritual with touches of his own personality, showing his dual allegiance to an upper class, whose forms and rituals he wishes to imitate, and a tough, direct, and brutal lower class that has formed him too.

This is a society in which even apparently innermost natural emotions—love and hatred—may be understood as expressions of one's social place and are accordingly subject to negotiation. Careful consideration of the means by which one fights is required. Déclassé, Random feels free to use either weapon, but he remains conscious of the statement he is making to others when choosing his enemies and his weapons. The novel concludes with Roderick achieving satisfaction of a lasting, fulfilling kind—the satisfaction of loving, and of being loved by, a beautiful (and wealthy) lady, whose looks are then duly "improved by matrimony." No wonder that Random heads the final chapter with these words of his own: *"I am more and more happy."*[28] The self-applause may be irksome, the providential dénouement convenient, but in the preceding pages, Smollett's vision of a society in which fighting is paramount disconcerts. If his views on duelling seem conventionally "correct" in discursive works, such as his *Travels*, here, in his novels, they are more nuanced—at once exciting and disturbing.

This novel, highly contemporary, even documentary in its concerns and observations, is nevertheless always as aware of the splendors of Cervantes, Tasso, and, albeit obliquely, Corneille's *Le Cid* as it is of its remoteness from them. In turn, it will prove to be a well-placed stepping-stone, carrying us between those works and the comedies of Sheridan, before leading us onto the novels of Thackeray, Dickens, and, of course, Walter Scott, Smollett's compatriot and biographer.

Casanova, "Il duello, ovvero Saggio della vita di G. C. Veneziano" (1780): Casanova versus Branicki

In June 1780, there appeared a short text, published in Venice, that took its place among a series of volumes titled *Opuscoli miscellanei*. In these rather leisurely disquisitions, the author, Giacomo Casanova, reflects on subjects as various as forthcoming theatrical productions and the troubles that have punctuated Poland's military history, amid sundry philosophical and political matters. It is while he is describing the death of a famous Polish general, by the name of Count Giovanni Branicki, that the author tantalizes his reader with a little footnote: "The other Branicki of great renown, now a grand general, is a Polish gentleman, who was never related to or a friend of the grand general to whom we allude. The king made him principal hunter, while he was injured in a duel, fought with the author of this memoir, who, exiled at that time from Venice, his homeland, was sojourning in Warsaw. If the reader wishes to know the story of this duel, he will find an account of it here in the next memoir."[29]

So the story of Casanova's duel, which enhanced his fame in Europe, first emerges, as if by accident, when he was actually in the process of talking about another, quite different man called Branicki. Curiously, indeed modestly, a story of which Casanova will be the hero is seemingly prompted by a coincidence of names and launched by a footnote. It is with his adversary, and not with himself, that the story seems to start. Sure enough, the next essay in the miscellanies, interleaved inconspicuously between the ongoing history of the "Turbolenze della Polonia" and its sequel, is titled "Il duello, ovvero Saggio della vita di G. C. Veneziano." In keeping with the considered, philosophical tone of the other essays, the story of Casanova's duel is underpinned by an unusual subtitle. A *saggio* is an essay. Casanova was possibly hiding a scandalous story under the cover of a morally respectable title or maybe promoting a sense that life and duel are coextensive, that the latter might stand for the former, that this story is a crossroads in his life or an epitome, which is therefore worthy of philosophical scrutiny. The duel is a structuring event in his life, if not an allegorical expression of the challenge that is life itself.

No less curious is the name of the author, or lack of it, on the title page: G. C. Veneziano. Casanova's name is thinly disguised. This is but a small or sham mask, a verbal equivalent to the *larva*, that incomparable Venetian specialty. But the abbreviation of the name and the seemingly proud avowal of his citizenship are similarly interesting. The autobiographical account that follows is written in the third person. This is by no means an unusual step. Voltaire's brief *Mémoires*, for instance, take this form, a refuge from accusations of egotism. But Casanova, by viewing himself in the third person, is able to describe himself simply as "il Veneziano"—the Venetian.

In 1753, Casanova had escaped from his confinement in the Leads, situated in the east wing of the doge's palace. His account of the escapade was, like the relation of the duel, published as a story in its own right. He gained his freedom but lost his home and spent the subsequent years in restless exile. Casanova, calling himself simply "the Venetian," sets himself up, rather ironically if not grandiosely, as a champion of his nation. He is unlikely to have expected this story of a duel to restore honor to himself and his nation. After all, the Republic of Venice had, in 1739, renewed extremely severe laws against duels, threatening not only those who fought them but also those who carried cartels with capital punishment. Duellists were to be decapitated on St. Mark's Square, between the two famous monolithic columns. Besides, the laws extended to anyone who published details of a duel or even a rebuffed challenge, a measure designed both to encourage a man to dare to decline a challenge and to protect him from public derision after doing so.[30]

First-person accounts of a duel are bound to be weighted in favor of the man who has lived to tell the tale, betraying, through their very form, something of the eventual outcome. Casanova, by describing himself in the third person, seemingly becomes a more indeterminate object of scrutiny. It does not seem impossible that he might be killed in the duel, for attentive readers of the previous opusculet know that his adversary, the Count Branicki, is, as the story is being written, alive and prospering as a "gran Generale."[31] These maneuvers help us to appreciate that Casanova is not bound to win this duel and may persuade us to perceive him as a man fighting against the odds. Indeed, in the first sentence, Casanova emphasizes his humble, poor background. But by observing himself in the third person, Casanova can also avoid shouldering full responsibility for his actions, which may thus be described as though they were those of someone else. Moreover, an inspection of the other opuscules reveals another intriguing element. One of them is titled "La vergogna [Shame], opera postuma di G.C.V."[32] Casanova, using the same initials as those of the title page to "Il duello," is possibly entertaining the idea that he could or might have died, looking at his life from the perspective of someone who is now irremediably different from his previous self.

Other people were also looking at Casanova. The debonair Charles-Joseph, Prince de Ligne, painted the following portrait, which summons up some of the fascinating contradictions embodied by this man:

> He would be a really handsome man, if he were not ugly; he is tall, with a herculean build, but an African complexion, lively eyes, full of intelligence to be honest, but, always suggesting susceptibility, anxiety, or resentment, they lend him a rather fierce appearance. He is easier to be provoked into anger than into good spirits. He laughs only a little, but he makes people laugh; he has a way of saying things that is reminiscent of a clumsy Arlequin or Figaro and makes him very agreeable. Only those things that he claims to know does he not know. He believes in nothing, except that which is the least believable, since he is superstitious on so many scores. . . . He is proud, be-

cause he is nothing and he has nothing. . . . He is always on the lookout for slights to his pride.[33]

The prince does not allude to the pursuits for which Casanova became notorious, indeed synonymous. The equation of Casanova with Figaro and Arlequin helps to show how porous the line between historical person and theatrical personage has become. Casanova was destined to be an actor. Born on the little Calle della Commedia, the son of an actor and an actress, Casanova was acutely aware of the disreputable status of that profession (actors and actresses continued to be denied Christian burial in France well into the eighteenth century). With the instincts of a playwright, Casanova, very cleanly and precisely, divides up his life into three sections, describing it as "my play in three acts." At the age of thirty-eight, the first act closed in London; the second act was concluded by his departure from Venice in 1783; the third will be closed by his memoirs.[34]

It is in a theater that Casanova's duel originates, in 1766. While at the theater in Warsaw, Casanova is visiting one of the boxes to pay his respects to a Venetian dancer. When another gentleman calls at the box to see her, it would be customary to depart and allow him his turn, and, very politely, this gentleman beseeches Casanova, " 'I flatter myself that you will have the grace to concede your place,' said the Blue Cordon, a Knight of the White Eagle and of St. Stanislas."[35]

Casanova describes the man, metonymically, by his decorations. Presumably, the fellow is, on this night out, wearing the sash and medals to which he is entitled, and Casanova is merely recording what he recognized there and then. However, the description of these honors allows us to appreciate the full grandeur of this gentleman, whom Casanova has had the honor and good fortune to rile, and this in turn establishes an immediate contrast between one sort of courtly, ostentatious honor and another kind, which will be embodied by Casanova. For the latter has already, toward the beginning of the story, confided that he had recently sold his Roman order of the Cross, awarded to him in 1770 by the pope. Casanova sells it not, he says, to raise funds but because he is disgusted by the quality of other people sporting the same decoration. But it allows us to appreciate a contrast. Certain honors may be bought and sold but not honor itself. The detail may also support the idea that Casanova will tell us the plain, undecorated truth.

Even though Casanova later acquired a title—it turned him into the Chevalier de Seingalt—he recorded, with some satisfaction, a verbal joust with Emperor Joseph II on the subject of purchased nobility: " 'I do not respect those who buy nobility,' said Emperor Joseph II to Casanova one day: And he, whose every word is a flash of wit, whose every thought is a book, said to him—'and what about those who sell it, Sir?' "[36]

Back in the theater, a tense exchange follows in which Casanova, departing, hears himself accused of cowardice by the Polish grandee. Casanova is already on his way home, on the staircase, but, with a punctual example of l'esprit de l'escalier, he ripostes, "A Venetian coward could still kill a courageous Pole." Tempted, he remembers, to draw his sword, he shows the Pole his guard.[37] After this exchange of quips, recorded verbatim in the text, Casanova now considers his next step. He needs to decide whether these remarks warrant a duel. It is perhaps symptomatic that he first recollects Plato's strictures about honor in Gorgias, before he then proceeds to Christian considerations. If he is to fight a duel, it will not be in ignorance of the philosophical and theological insights into the practice or out of barbaric impetuosity. Casanova instead makes it clear that duelling is de rigueur for an eighteenth-century courtier. Haughty philosophical condemnation of the practice is, Casanova asserts, the prerogative of those who live away from the courts. He is probably alluding to the privileges enjoyed by a famous Genevan of a republican disposition and solitary moods. Indeed, in the next pages, he takes on Rousseau's "singular idea": "he says that those really vindicated by the duel are not those who kill but those who force their attackers to kill them."[38]

Casanova, in the moments that follow the brief exchange of remarks, rehearses objections to the duel, whether philosophical or theological, ancient or modern. He demonstrates not so much the inadequacy of these various arguments but the irrelevance of this anthology, given the predicament in which he finds himself, for the demands of honor at court are intransigent. Unusually, Casanova acknowledges quite candidly that he is assenting to the force of opinion, rather than acting on his own impulse or convictions. Yet, in admitting to feeling these pressures, Casanova does not discredit the duel as meaningless or demeaning. In fact, he follows the outer rituals all the more ostentatiously, even as an inner belief in their sanctity has been sapped.

The redundancy of philosophical arguments is attributable in part to the mores that prevail in such an environment but also, substantially, to the "wretched pride inherent to human nature." Nor is the advice of friends in this case availing. Now quoting Cicero, he spells out the dangers of receiving advice from so-called friends. The only wisdom he values is the brief and stark alternative proposed by an acquaintance. According to him, whatever Casanova chooses to do, it should be much or nothing: "Molto, o nulla."[39] This spirit may appeal to an eighteenth-century readership, inclined on occasion perhaps to weary of the moderation and good sense blandly preached by some writers of the Enlightenment. Casanova will, of course, opt for "molto," anticipating a more Romantic polarization, although, being an eighteenth-century writer, he is not quite ready for "tutto o nulla." The duel will take Casanova perilously close to death, that "monster" that he loathes.[40] Death, however, becomes negotiable if life means living without liberty or without honor. The duel therefore permits a reprise of Casanova's daring escape from the Leads. In an essentially libertine conception of life, he is prepared, like Valmont, to die in his prime.

So Casanova has a servant run with a letter for Branicki, in which a duel is solicited. The choice of location and of weapons will rest with Branicki. For his information, Casanova's sword is thirty-two inches long. A reply is promptly forthcoming. Branicki wants to fight a duel as soon as possible. But Casanova cannot fight later that day, as proposed. It is a Wednesday, the day on which the post goes. Moreover, with that perfectly balanced mixture of bombast and understatement, he has a will to write. He is unassuming yet unruffled too. Such gentlemanly unconcern for the duel, absorbed by the day-to-day business of life, is elided with a modest, self-deprecating approach to the forthcoming *affaire*. Branicki prefers to fight with a pistol, claiming that he does not want to fight by sword with a stranger. Casanova, for his part, does not wish to fight with pistols. This is a barbaric, ungentlemanly weapon that he is, obviously, bound to hate.[41]

In an age when titles indicative of class distinction were increasingly fluid and marketable, class is revealed in part by one's taste in weapons, as well as one's skill and confidence in handling them.

Scruples about the morality of duelling and, more practically, a hesitation about the weapons with which the duel is to be contested can
mask fears. But they are also an ideal way of deferring the events for
the reader and building suspense. Casanova is a seductive storyteller.
At length, the duel takes place. Two or three seconds pass, as the
Pole takes aim and conceals his head behind his pistol. Meanwhile,
Casanova just shoots, for taking aim is not very gentlemanly. Branicki
falls to the ground. Casanova rushes up to him. The Pole has not been
killed, but he is seriously wounded: not quite *tutto* but certainly *molto*.
He has enough energy to utter a few words: "You've killed me."[42]

Casanova departs the scene *à la polonaise*, that is, on a galloping
horse. But, rather than suggesting that he takes flight in desperate
haste, the language here makes Casanova look like he is just fitting
in—when in Rome. Again, he knows the required *bienséances*. The
nobleman knows no national boundaries; the duel is a cosmopolitan
practice, conducted, naturally and properly, in flawless French. But
here the backdrop is decidedly exotic. The ruffians in attendance ready
to chop off the Venetian's head; the snow, the sabers, those symbols of
malice and cruelty in the Italian imagination.[43] Casanova's restraint
and politeness are thrown into relief by this hostile environment. Casanova's account anticipates Russian stories featuring duels (pardon a
virtually tautological remark), in that gentlemanly breeding and
impeccable manners are shown off against a backdrop of Eastern
savagery—snow, poverty, impulsive violence. Even a defenestration is
threatened at one point.

Bernardo Bellotto (1721–80), Casanova's fellow Venetian, painted
Warsaw in the bright shades with which he had depicted Venice. It
seems always to be summer chez Bellotto, as in Canaletto's pictures.
Here, though, the descriptions obey Western expectations of Sarmatian
cold and brutality. After the duel, Casanova takes refuge in a Franciscan
friary. Without its walls, chaos and confusion reign. Rumors that the
Venetian has killed Branicki now circulate and prompt ulans to run
amok in the streets of Warsaw, lashing out with their sabers at anyone
who does not look as though he might be Polish. "Great was the fear
and uproar in Warsaw."[44] The impeccable good manners, the restraint,
and the regard of the duellists for each other mark a contrast with the

utter turmoil that follows. It is compared to an imminent invasion of Turks. Casanova, naturally horrified by, although seemingly rather proud of, these scenes for which he is in part responsible, depicts himself in the eye of the storm. A series of grand visitors pay visits (and homage) to the brave refugee. Finally, one comes bearing a letter from the king himself. He reveals that Casanova will be pardoned.

The duel has barely finished, yet another sort of duel is about to begin. Casanova's nerve and independence of mind will be tested anew, first by a Jesuit and then, more sorely, by a surgeon. The Jesuit, Confessor to the Bishop of Poznań, is, as Jesuits are supposed to be, accommodating.[45] Together, they painlessly find a formula by which Casanova can avoid excommunication. By contrast, the surgeon, a Frenchman, is more exacting. He decides that the afflicted hand needs to be amputated. So Casanova now has to face the medical equivalent of excommunication. Exhausted and weakened by hunger, Casanova nevertheless stands firm. When asked why he will not consent to losing his hand, Casanova replies, in French, that no one can object to his wish to keep his hand, because he is its absolute master.

It is a struggle for control and sovereignty over oneself. Just as Casanova controlled the hand that fired the gun supremely well, so he is reluctant to relinquish his power over his own body. When, a few years later, Immanuel Kant, in nearby Königsberg, answered his own question, "What is Enlightenment?" (1784), the examples of presumptuous figures from whom we need to win autonomy are, not unexpectedly, priests but also doctors.[46] Just as the duellist has defended his honor without recourse to other authorities, so in the aftermath, he retains his autonomy and independence. After the narration of the duel, just as much detail and tension pulse through the description of these scenes. Casanova recollects verbatim the dramatic exchanges with the surgeon, as they fight over his hand:

> SURGEON: But, Sir, the gangrene will set in.
> VENETIAN: Is is there?
> SURGEON: Not yet, but it is imminent.
> VENETIAN: Very good. I want to see it; I'm intrigued by it. We will talk about it once it has made an appearance.
> SURGEON: It will be too late by then.

VENETIAN: Why?

SURGEON: Because it spreads extremely quickly, and in that case it
will be necessary to amputate your arm.

VENETIAN: Very good. Go ahead and amputate my arm; but for the
time being, return the bandages to me and be off with you.[47]

The contrapuntal rhythm of these exchanges acts as a verbal equivalent to the cut and thrust of the duel by swords Casanova would like
to have fought. He and the doctor clash in brusque terms, as each
parries the other's moves, but Casanova not only assumes a defensive
stance. He responds by asking questions, probing and thrusting in reply
to the doctor. The scene helps to cast Casanova as the possessor of an
empirical mind, warding off those whose scientific certainties are not
grounded in observation.

So Casanova chances his arm once again. The same polite hostilities, the same heroic steadfastness, are in evidence. The amputation of
a hand looks so certain that (in the French version) it is even announced
in the *Gazette de la cour*.[48] The king, for his part, is of the opinion
that Casanova is a fool to sacrifice his arm, and that evening Casanova
is visited by no fewer than three surgeons ready, happy, and willing to
perform the operation. But the three surgeons who pay a visit to Casanova's bedside in a humble convent are no wise men. When the bandages are duly removed, to their consternation, the wound is clean.
Casanova is ready to be resurrected. "In three weeks the Venetian
went out with his arm in a sling and having lost a lot of weight; but he
was well. It was Easter Day."[49]

After the successive trials and torments that Casanova endured, in
the third week, he rose again. In the same idiom, Casanova, after paying
his respects to the king, duly makes a miraculous appearance, to the
astonishment of all, in the house where his erstwhile adversary is re-
covering. These visits, in which the two men solemnly pledge friendship to each other, echo Christ's appearances after the crucifixion.

Casanova's duel is then not merely a defiant, heroic bout with a
nobleman on his own terms, in his own backyard, but also the prelude
to an act of revenge on the disadvantages of his own past. His defiance
of the wisdom of the doctors and his self-defense and self-reliance in
chancing his own arm take on particular significance when we read
the accounts of Casanova's childhood in the *Histoire de ma vie*: "My

vocation," he resentfully explains early on in his account, "was the study of medicine, so that I might go into the medical profession, a career to which I was very attracted, but no one listened to me."[50] No one listened to him back then; now it is Casanova who enjoys the privilege of not listening to the doctors. So the duel, or rather its aftermath, permits a revenge on physicians and all those who ignored his vocation. The duel fulfills a destiny but also adds an ironic twist to it, in pitting him against doctors whose colleagues he was to have been.

Casanova reveals skill in the negotiation of hazards and perils. It is his mastery of the calculated risk that wins the day, rather than superior skill, let alone God-given, providential blessings. In that sense, the duel serves once again as a metaphor for the wider transactions and encounters of which life is a series. Casanova considered this episode central to his conception of himself, to the extent of using it as the title for the memoirs themselves. The duel, once again, represents a way of renegotiating, if not actually moving, the boundaries between classes. Casanova was de facto ennobled after fighting the duel. But that risks understating his transfiguration, for, as was later remarked, the duel had transformed Casanova from a pupa into a butterfly. Later, incorporating this story within his memoirs, Casanova switched into the first person and wrote them in French. Like Frederick the Great or Edward Gibbon, he was self-consciously adopting the language of civilization. He was also distancing himself from the tradition of dubious Italian memoirs that stretches from the incredible, but incredibly amusing, account of Benevenuto Cellini to the fantasies of Pinocchio.

Casanova would have us believe that challenging someone to duel is "the natural impulse of anyone who has been brought up to be moderate and check his brutal reactions."[51] Horace, quoted in the epigraph, is enlisted as a proleptic sponsor of the duel. "Animum rege: qui nisi paret imparet" (Control your passion, or it will control you).[52] Not only is Casanova keen to show that he is an erudite, if vagabondish, man, but the duel and his evocation of its deliberate processes aligns it with Classical good taste and ethics. Just as Venice, a city-state without a Classical past, was lavishly decorated with Palladian temple façades, so the Venetian here becomes a spurious heir to Classical thinkers, and the duel becomes the epitome of restraint. Even the dilemma that confronts him is seen through a classicizing lens: *molto o nulla*. We can perhaps hear an echo of a motto attributed to Cesare Borgia: "aut Caesar aut nihil"; Casanova's refusal of compromise or conciliation also recalls Machiavelli's admiring remarks about Roman abstention from half measures.[53] Casanova records Cicero's thoughts on friendship, which occur to him as he contemplates his next move. This reverses the trend, widespread among Enlightenment detractors of the duel, whereby its non-Classical, barbaric provenance is emphasized. Instead, Casanova explicitly contrasts the duellist with the barbarian.[54]

Casanova fights the duel as a champion of Venice, against the accusations of a Pole, a proud and loving gesture to the nation that had exiled him. Both nations represented here were poised to forfeit their proud histories of self-government, surrendering them to foreign powers (Venice in 1797; Poland circa 1772–95). The duel, as in Ireland, appeals to a higher value and ethic, not quantifiable in financial terms. The nation may have lost its power but not its honor, which may be the only residue, once one has lost everything else. Honor cannot be prised from a truly honorable man. Casanova, or the Chevalier de Seingalt, is keen to present himself as a gentleman. Failing wealth and pending a title, duelling is one of the ways he can show this. But Casanova also shows himself, before, during, and after the duel, to be a shrewd man of calculations. The concern with money, so antithetical to the esprit of the duellist, has to be hidden. Casanova of course waves away a donation offered to him after the duel to help with his flight from Poland. But the story is essentially a string of astute calculations, from the careful decision to fight a duel to the nerveless firing of the pistol to the rebuttal of the surgeon.

Duels had traditionally been fought on behalf of ladies. Here, however (perhaps surprisingly, given Casanova's reputation), chivalry, that residue of medieval mores, is relegated in the interests of Classical erudition and enlightened poise. The Venetian dancer, the duel's initial raison d'être, soon fades from view. This is a duel fought explicitly for negative reasons, to counteract insulting accusations, but it is also a bout, fought with full knowledge of the enlightened, rational opposition to duelling, that ennobles Casanova, before he felt obliged to buy a title. Staged against a snowy backdrop, it follows the template of *Clarissa* in its commitment to civility, if not in the outcome. Regrettably, a true gentlemanly duel by swords could not be arranged to Casanova's taste. But a duel by pistols does at least allow him one further opportunity to display his exquisite sense of propriety and style. Honor has been amply satisfied, the story concluded, but Casanova, when he finally takes leave of Branicki, does not forget to return him (by hand, of course) his bullet. He might as well be placing, in its rightful berth at the end of a sentence, a full stop.

Hugo, *Marion de Lorme* (1829): The Marquis de Saverny versus Didier; Richelieu versus the Duellist

"The pen is mightier than the sword." Before this statement adorned library façades and books of quotations, it belonged to the unsuspecting, fictionalized Cardinal de Richelieu, to whom it was assigned by Edward Bulwer-Lytton, in his play *Richelieu; or, The Conspiracy*, first performed in 1839.[55] Here, the line is tinged with an ironical hue. Now frail and elderly, the Cardinal has just failed to lift a large broadsword he had previously wielded in battle. He turns instead to a pen, in order to sign some papers. That this paean to the pen should come from an author manqué, a dismal connoisseur of the arts, an infamously cruel potentate, seems almost an irony too far.[56] Far from refraining from violence, in order to pursue a peaceful vocation as a writer, Richelieu used the pen in question against perceived enemies of the realm. Victor Hugo's *Marion de Lorme* shows Richelieu to be ruthless and unsparing in his pursuit of these enemies, among whom none was more hostile to his designs than the duellist.

Written around 1829, in the throes of the restored monarchy under Charles X, this is a play about duellists, about their honor, loyalty, and courage, by contrast to the covert machinations of political and religious agents. The duellist is an emphatically free and vital man who belongs outdoors, while his real enemy—unlike his adversary and equal in the duel—remains confined or concealed. The persecution of the duellist by the stern Cardinal and his henchmen appears then to be an unfair form of revenge exacted on the young and healthy by the elderly and infirm. Duellists in Hugo's vision come across as secular Huguenots—a busy, innocuous minority, sustained by their own codes of conduct, repressed by an uncomprehending state. As King Louis XIII, powerless next to the Cardinal, himself laments,

Puis ce sont tous les jours quelques nouvelles listes.
Hier des Huguenots, aujourd'hui des duellistes[57]

[Every day he draws up some new lists.
Today it's Huguenots, tomorrow duellists]

So the pen that is mightier than the sword is asked to draw up long lists, inventories of prospective victims. These indiscriminate lists are the cruel inverse of the poetic spirit, incarnated by Hugo's rhyming verse.

Cardinal de Richelieu was a figure that fascinated and often appalled nineteenth-century writers, but he could, depending on their perspective, be cast as a canny administrator ahead of his time, who, in dispensing with royal fiat, became the architect of the modern French state. Alternatively, he could be seen as a sinister cleric, intent on introducing dogmatic, unforgiving mores to a nation hitherto celebrated for its easygoing *galanterie*. Bulwer-Lytton explicitly responded to Hugo's play by allowing us to see Richelieu under a more favorable light and in fact by allowing us to see him. Richelieu dominates Hugo's play, yet, however ubiquitous his influence, he never actually makes an appearance. The Cardinal, in common with other famous stage ecclesiastics, keeps us waiting: Molière's Tartuffe (1664) does not appear until act 3; Schiller's Cardinal Grand Inquisitor in *Don Carlos* (1787) remains offstage until act 5, scene 10. The latter in particular serves as a model for Richelieu's sinister magnificence, but Hugo, taking a step further, reserves the entry of the Cardinal to the very last scene, and even then he remains invisible behind the curtains of the enormous "litière," or palanquin, on which he is carried.

The theater is a particularly good place to portray a man conspicuous by his absence. Richelieu's invisibility lends his tyranny a particularly sinister aspect. Hugo's duellists embody the very inverse of this closet tyranny. This spectral presence permits a chiaroscuro contrast (replicated by Dumas in his *Three Musketeers*, set in the same era) between the transparency or loyalty of the duellist and the invisibility, the inscrutability, of the cryptic Cardinal, in the company of père Joseph, the original éminence grise. Hugo thereby emphasizes the "sublime detachment" or the "abstract arrogance" with which the ascetic Cardinal conducted his reforms.[58] As in Dumas's novels, the numerous, local duels which oppose duellists are incidental to that grand opposition between pairs of gentlemen and a repressive state.

Hugo's play unfolds in a highly specific setting, temporally and geographically. It is September 1638, and we are at Blois, a town on the Loire, where the Marquis de Saverny is enjoying the company of the beautiful young woman and notorious courtesan Marion de Lorme. Much to his chagrin, however, he is swiftly ushered out of her house, in order that she might meet a mysterious young man with whom she has an assignation that night. The man in question, an orphan by the name of Didier, duly appears. He loves Marion, who is known to him as Marie, and has no idea that the object of his adoration is none other than that scandalous figure. But Didier's heartfelt declarations of love do move Marion, who, ashamed and remorseful about her promiscuous past, is in love— with Didier. Their tryst is interrupted by noises offstage, the "cliquetis" of blades, that music to French ears. Didier, without thinking, rushes to the aid of Saverny, who has been accosted by a band of thieves. After more offstage commotion, Saverny reappears, both amazed by and grateful to the dexterity of his mysterious benefactor who, against the odds—"six larges poignards contre une mince épée"—has repelled the dozen thieves, before fleeing, incognito, into the night.[59]

The next act now brings duelling to the center of the stage. The prevailing mood is giddy and gallant. The soldierly banter among nobles stationed in Blois, gossiping about combats in Paris and teasing one another to the brink of duels, is innocuous. Duels form an unobjectionable part of the social whirl in Paris.[60] The outcomes of recent duels in Paris are discussed with the enthusiasm and insouciance of people discussing football these days. We witness irascibility and impetuosity among these assorted, interchangeable men but also loyalty, courage, and, above all, opinionated freethinking. Nor are these duellists meatheaded bullies. Their duels are fought over the respective merits of literary works, and in act 2, a pair of hotheads, Villac and Montpesat, cross swords after disagreeing about Corneille's Le Cid, a play known to have earned the disapproval of Richelieu.

MONTPESAT: Le Cid est bon!
VILLAC: Méchant!
    Ton Cid, mais Scudéry l'écrase en le touchant![61]

[MONTPESAT: *The Cid* is cool!
VILLAC: You fool!
   Your *Cid*, it's Scudéry that will rule!]

Only in France can a literary discussion turn quite so easily into a duel.
But their fun is about to be threatened and eclipsed. On a lamppost at
the center of the stage, a notice is pinned up. It makes clear that the
punishment for duels will be severe, capital, and merciless. It is signed
by both Louis XIII and Richelieu. It takes the form of rhyming couplets,
not an obvious vehicle for articulating a moral or rational argument
against duelling. The rigor of the ordonnance only looks more unreasonable. Moreover, far from instilling fear into freethinking noblemen,
this severe, rhyming ordonnance ironically assumes a part in provoking
a duel, for Saverny, suggesting that Didier, still in disguise, might be
illiterate, goads him into spelling its message out, and this provocation
inevitably results in a duel. Didier admits that he is not a nobleman and
that he has no seconds at his disposal. However, the utter abjection of
his birth, far from shaming him, confers an inverted, virtual nobility
(as it did for Figaro, until, finally and disappointingly, he meets his parents), and the mystery leaves aristocratic possibilities intact. A foundling, he could be noble, and the two men agree to fight without delay.
There is, however, another potential obstacle to the duel. Night has
now fallen. Conveniently, the very lamp on which the order is posted
will serve as a means of illumination. More romantically, Didier,
casting his coat off and doffing his hat to his opponent, declares,

> On y voit assez clair,
> Vous dis-je! Et chaque épée est dans l'ombre un éclair![62]

> [It is sufficiently bright,
> I'm telling you! And each sword cuts through the dark with a flash
> of light!]

The sword is, as ever, made to be seen, unlike the insidious dagger or
the furtive pistol.

   Saverny and Didier proceed to cross swords and fight a nocturnal
duel "en silence et avec fureur." Illuminated by the "lanterne de l'édit,"
this duel is not reluctantly breaking but joyously flouting the prohibition. The transgressiveness of the duel is, once again in the French

tradition, an essential part of its charm. After years of offstage, reported bouts, the French theater is at last graced by an honorable,
proper duel, however spurious its grounds.[63] What a shame then that
it should end prematurely, as the Cardinal's men arrive to apprehend
the combatants. Didier promptly flees the scene, as Saverny falls to the
ground, feigning death.

In the next act, Didier, rejoined by Marion, has insinuated himself
into a troupe of actors, in order to escape detection. Dressed as Span-
iards, Didier and Marion join these players, who, of course, welcome
them, not in the least concerned as to why they might be needing to
seek refuge. Guards and officers, under the supervision of the creepy
Laffemas, come looking for the fugitives and have their suspicions: by
asking the players to do a brief turn, they hope to catch out those who
are not bona fide actors. Corneille's genius has, up to this point, reigned
in the background, as implicitly present as the grip of Richelieu. But
now, under the scrutiny of Laffemas, Marion takes the part of Chimène,
and she rehearses the moment when Chimène beseeches Rodrigo to
fight and win the duel against Don Sanche for her. It is an inspired
appropriation of Corneille's poetry. The pertinence of this speech to
Didier and Marion's own situation is obvious. If they are Rodrigo
and Chimène, she knows that the opportunistic Laffemas is ready to
be Don Sanche. But it is also a moving tribute to the way one writer
may resurrect an antecedent and how a play apparently about one age
may speak to another or others. Le Cid, set in medieval Spain, was of
course relevant to the age of Louis XIII, but it now appealed specifically
to that of Charles X and Hugo's contemporaries too.[64]

Then it is the turn of Didier, who has been encouraged to pass himself off as the Cid himself. Desperately, he has been learning his lines.
To the surprise of everyone, however, he refuses to play the game by
stepping up to the challenge as Rodrigo. Instead, volunteering his own
name, he gives himself up for arrest. In an interesting twist, Hugo
stages a man who is unwilling to play a part. For Didier has, in the interim, finally learned that the love of his life is none other than the
notorious Marion de Lorme and, horrified and betrayed by this revelation, sees his imminent death by execution as a relief.

If this last act has a Shakespearean flavor, with the embedded drama
designed to catch the conscience of the malefactors, so too does the

next act, in which we see the care-worn king agonizing over the fate of the arrested men, lamenting his responsibilities and the weakness they expose. Marion pleads with Louis XIII on Didier's behalf, while Saverny's elderly uncle evokes memories of the gallant and free-spirited court of Henri IV, the king's father, in an attempt to free his nephew. Henri IV remains a byword for gallantry, adaptability ("Paris vaut une messe"), and tolerance. The king at length shows clemency, but his decision is countermanded by the Cardinal, so the men must go to their deaths. It is clear that the duellists will go into the night together. Thanks to the intercessions, each prisoner has enjoyed an opportunity to save himself, but both men nobly refuse to abandon the other in saving themselves.

As the final act opens (we now move from Chambord to Beaugency— with an excursion to the castle of Nangis, the play follows the Loire upstream), the Shakespearean accent remains no less pronounced. Workers, as jocular as the gravediggers in *Hamlet*, are preparing the scaffold on which the arrested duellists are to die. The sentence to hang has been commuted to execution by axe. This news prompts characteristically cheerful nonchalance on the part of Saverny, who then falls asleep, a sign of aristocratic insouciance perhaps but also a guarantee of this duellist's essentially childlike innocence.

Didier, however, remains awake. Before the axe descends at the appointed hour, Marion de Lorme makes a sudden appearance. She has come to save him. Hugo appears to be recycling but modulating the "rescue scene," cherished on the Romantic stage, where, latterly, the woman is rescued by her lover. Didier, however, refuses her assistance. He realizes that she has bought his freedom by selling her body to the sinister lawyer. Steadfastly, he refuses to save himself. Humiliated, Marion despairs. But in the final, touching moments of the play, as a cannon signals Richelieu's imminent arrival, Didier renews his declaration of love for Marion. Ironically, the man refused clemency himself forgives her both her past and her misguided attempt to win his freedom. The man persecuted and punished by the haughtily unforgiving Cardinal himself assumes a Christ-like role opposite her Magdalene. Marion, or Marie, as he calls her once again, is forgiven and redeemed, as the *litière*, borne by twenty-four soldiers, majestically transports the Cardinal hidden from our view.

First titled *Un duel sous Richelieu,* before falling victim (like Sedaine's *Un duel*) to revisions, this then is a play intrigued and enchanted by the fashion for duelling and its appeal in the twilight years of the reign of Louis XIII, the 1630s. But Hugo also hails the duellist as a more timeless rebel, a hero of self-sufficiency and honesty, in the face (the hidden face) of censorship and repression, a standoff understandable to Hugo's audiences in the deeply reactionary 1820s. Saverny is an aristocratic archetype—insouciant, flippant—but a man of his word, the sort of privileged and irresponsible yet endearing figure from the upper echelons traditionally associated with duelling. But Monsieur Didier is a different sort of inveterate duellist, born to this art by inclination and nature, if not by birth. He is an honest and sincere ordinary man, who acts on principle and sticks to his convictions. The duellist then emerges as an epitome of self-reliance. This truth is made clearer still in the case of Didier, who is not merely, like other Hugo heroes (Ruy Blas and Hernani come to mind), a self-made man in a world of vested interests and ancestral privileges but an orphan and foundling *ex nihilo.* He is, he proudly declares, Didier "de rien," an heir to Figaro, if anyone, whose patron was St. Anonymous.[65]

The duellist stands in contrast to those in society whose influence derives from lending and borrowing the power of others. A self-reliant individual in pursuit of justice, he represents his own interests and will defend them himself. In that sense, then, the duellist, hitherto deplored as an archetypal, unreconstructed aristocrat, turns out to be a sort of modern democrat, a believer in the sovereignty of the individual, who takes matters to the bar of his own judgment. He contrasts here with the king, who has allowed his powers to be signed off to another man, a monarch whose inertia and fatigue, rather than any spirit of devolution, account for the delegation of his power. As for Richelieu, he relies on intimidating a team of proxies who increase his aura of godlike inaccessibility. He is deplored as somber and sinister. But his strategic withdrawal from the social stage is also designed to render him invulnerable to others. He has, Marion points out, never set eyes on Didier, a man who both looks and is, obviously, transparently good.[66] Face to face with Marion and Saverny's uncle, Louis XIII shows his humanity—that is his weakness, or vice versa. Richelieu's abstentions allow him to pursue his cruelly undeviating line, leading him to implement and execute his policies without a second thought. These decisions depend on bureaucratic invisibility. While the duel necessitates the courage of meeting eye to eye, the pyramid of persecutions seems a feature of modern oppression. A similar form of ruthlessness may be seen in Beethoven's *Fidelio* (1805, revised 1814), where orders, descending from an invisible tip, must be obeyed by those who mediate them.

Hugo's play, like *Le Cid*, rather eludes obvious categorization. At first, thanks to the pacey rhyming couplets, it may seem comical, even shallow. The rhymes do not always flow effortlessly; the historical color is sometimes daubed and blotchy. For example, in the castle of Chambord, Saverny's uncle is advised, "En attendant que je vous avertisse,/ Regardez ces plafonds qui sont du Primatice" (While you are waiting to be shown in,/ do look at Primaticcio's great frescoing).[67] The desire to emulate a Shakespearean common touch sometimes results in bathos—the king, after enumerating his woes, suddenly and redundantly, complains that it is also raining.[68]

Nevertheless, rhyming couplets, with their proposal and response, a sonic thrust and parry, are a privileged vehicle for the evocation of this culture of deft and nimble ripostes, as the same sound is answered and *touché*. The propensity to duel over bagatelles or to take up arms as a way of continuing literary discussions seems the height of frivolity and immaturity. But that may cause us to underestimate the seriousness with which the play describes the persecution of duellists. Didier is, evidently, a different, modern sort of young man, a "singular" individual, fighting duels for mature, earnest reasons, just as his love for Marion is loyal and sincere.

The duel in which men cross swords is at the other extreme from political machinations. Theirs is a state of utter transparency, the sword a shaft of light, an "éclair." Duels are recommended here by the fact that they are proscribed by faceless legislation. Here the tragedy is that the duel, an expedient which seems to be essentially self-regulating, is put down with inhuman cruelty neither known to nor imagined by the duellist. The conspicuously, theatrically transparent duellist, who fights *mano a mano*, is subject to edicts issuing from above. Even if these orders emanate from individuals who incarnate theological virtue, that haughtiness and invisibility negate such virtue. Indeed, it is in the same years of the seventeenth century that Milton, as he defends the freedom of writers against licensing, expresses his famous disapproval of "a fugitive and cloistered virtue . . . that never sallies out and sees her adversary."[69] Virtue is personified as a sort of duellist coming out to take on vice. In the mere act of standing up to and looking one's enemies in the eye, credit and merit are already in evidence.

Ultimately, the play turns on the duel between individual and state, between royal and ecclesiastical authority, between humans and their conscience. Whereas the contrast between army and church is often expressed by the twin metonymy of "le sabre et le goupillon" (the sword and the aspergillum), here the duality opposes the sword of the duellist and Richelieu's engines of artillery. Richelieu, the audience is reminded, commanded the artillery at the siege of La Rochelle. When he then makes his grand entry at the end of act 5, it is, appropriately, to the sound of cannons.

Nineteenth-century Romantics were fascinated by the early decades of the seventeenth century, and their beguiling mixture of candour, immediacy, and *désinvolture* in love. This era comes to mark the last hurrah of the nobility before its defeat in the "Fronde" and its subsequent emasculation by King Louis XIV. The old charms and gallantry of a chivalrous order come up against the stern and steely resolve of Richelieu and his men. So the play also stages a duel between an old order and what seems a modern administration, symbolized memorably by the respective forms taken by the rival notices brandished by the representatives of king and Cardinal, as the duellists' destiny hangs in the balance: the clemency, confirmed by the king, is inscribed on a piece of parchment, while the warrant for their death, promulgated by the Cardinal, is written on paper.[70] The victory of the latter seems a cruelly foregone, inevitable outcome.

Dichotomies of this sort are typically painted in memorable and vivid colors. Every detail signifies and symbolizes in the works of Victor Hugo, a talented amateur painter and watercolorist.[71] Two primary colors duel with each other throughout this spectacle. Didier, sounding and looking like Hamlet, despairs that his heaven is black.[72] Later, he describes his heart as black as the night.[73] The black of the raven ("le corbeau")—or perhaps that of the crow or Corneille—is his guiding light.

By contrast, scarlet is, of course, the color cardinals wear. Hugo anticipates the interest in the so-called cardinal painting popular in the

1800s.[74] The scarlet donned by the cardinals was not only a gift to painters but a reminder to the faithful of the blood spilled by the martyrs (even though, with the exception of John Fisher, in 1535, no cardinal had ever been martyred). Here, though, it is the blood of duellists for which Richelieu thirsts. As L'Angely, the king's fool, dares to observe,

> Le ministre est puissant;
> C'est un large faucheur qui verse à flots le sang;
> Et puis, il couvre tout de sa soutane rouge,
> Et tout est dit.[75]

> [The minister has power;
> He is a large scythe who spills much blood;
> And then he covers it up under his red vestment,
> And all is said and done.]

But this river of blood coursing through the play is seen in other little tributaries. After consorting with Laffemas, Marion feels her lips to be burning as though branded. Hugo specifies that the gigantic "litière" should be scarlet. Marion exclaims in the final verse of the play, "voilà l'homme rouge qui passe!"[76] With *Marion de Lorme*, Hugo creates, in the same period which saw the publication of Stendhal's famous novel a *Rouge et le Noir* (1830) for the stage.

In a stage direction at the beginning of *Le roi s'amuse* (1832), Hugo specifies that he wishes the king, François I, to appear as Titian had portrayed him.[77] His theatrical mind moves here in painterly ways too. By the end of *Marion de Lorme*, Marion ceases to be a marionette, a disreputable, passive toy of men, and, redeemed by love, she achieves a sort of saintly grandeur in the final scenes. When, not long before the curtain falls, Hugo's stage direction asks this fallen woman to appear disheveled, on her knees, in a plea for forgiveness, the tableau and the attitude she strikes seem designed to evoke images of the penitent Mary Magdalene, whom her pseudonym, Marie, also surely recalls. Hugo perhaps had in mind Antonio Canova's neoclassical sculpture, completed in 1809, well-known in France. Or, casting it back to the first decades of the seventeenth century, he was thinking of the great tenebrist image of the penitent Magdalene, painted by Georges de la Tour, dated to 1638.[78]

Hugo may seem preposterously precise in specifying that Saverny should be dressed in the latest fashions of that year, 1638. However, even if audiences failed to recognize that exact date via the fashions current nearly two hundred years previously, he wants his readers and audiences to know that the play was set in this year of special significance in the annals of French history, for in 1638, after years of hoping, praying, and waiting, a male heir was born to Louis XIII and Anne of Austria, on 5 September, to be precise. The play, we learn as Saverny observes a departing swallow, is set in this very month. The baby boy would grow to become Louis XIV.

The year 1638 therefore marked the dawn of a golden Classical age, when arts "most approached perfection," an age, in the influential opinion of Voltaire, more illustrious still than Augustan Rome, Periclean Athens, and Medici Florence.[79] But, as one era opened, so another closed, and, with the passing of Louis XIII, some writers in the nineteenth century saw an end to tolerance, indulgence, and laissez-faire. Instead, there arose and prospered a form of prescriptive, rule-centered Classicism, against which Hugo's play now constitutes a series of rebellious acts. Hugo, whose love of the grotesque, tragicomic hybrid, contempt for the unities, and veneration of Shakespeare were given theoretical expression in the preface to his play *Cromwell*, removes the duellist from the hallowed plinth erected to him by *Le Cid* and, replacing him in a Gothic niche, finally turns him into an exalted romantic hero.

However, the duellist's privilege, that of cheerfully settling his scores and flourishing his sword, marks a contrast with the predicament of women or, rather, the one woman here. Hugo assembles a huge motley of soldiers, noblemen, guards—a sort of colorful frieze—to emphasize all the more tellingly the utter isolation and vulnerability of Marion de Lorme, the only female character in this teeming cast (with the momentary exception of her maid, Rose). Most of the numerous males treat Marion as though she were the only woman in the world. They have to have her. They do not seem to have loyalties to other women. She is by turns loved and reviled by men who have little sympathy for her actual needs and wishes. But Didier wants to marry her, and in this final heartbreaking scene, as in previous acts, he addresses her as "mon amour, mon épouse."[80] Audiences might think back to

Jean-Nicolas Bouilly's *Léonore*, the model for Beethoven's *Fidelio*, a
generation earlier in 1798, in which the eponymous heroine rescues her
husband from prison at the death. However, her name Marion (or "mar-
iant") only permits an irony. She is destined not to marry him.

The duel, conversely, brings together in fraternal intimacy men of
polarized backgrounds, outlooks, and appearances. Saverny is fair-
haired; Didier a saturnine figure, dressed in black. Hugo follows Laclos
in subordinating a vigorous superficial contrast to a curiously intense
union, as he emphasizes the paradoxical complicity and intimacy of
their antagonism, a motif that Conrad will also pick up, as he brings
two contrasting but complementary personalities together to duel.
From opposite extremes, each of Hugo's pair of duellists negates bourgeois values of thrift and caution. As Saverny, accused of always being
in debt, declares, "My blood, that's my only money."[81] Didier, meanwhile, bypasses bourgeois presentiments from below.

So the duellists die together, fraternally, martyrs to the duel, as to
the freedom to defy and to disobey. Just as Saverny is loyal to his rival
in defiance of a blood relation, Didier chooses to die with his adversary rather than live with his lover. It seems, summarized in such
terms, to be a preposterous choice, yet it is also the ending somehow
demanded by the logic of the play, as the duel mutates from actual
knockabout combats to a wider struggle between the individual's right
to self-expression and the imposition of state control. This particular
finale also then allows Didier heroically to choose death, even as he is
condemned to it.

Haunted by the lurid horrors of the scaffold, Hugo reveals the folly
of inflicting capital punishment on gentlemen who are evidently reconciled to a violent death. Persecution only dignifies and unites these
gentlemen in their defiance. Didier remarks, as he prepares to die, that
"death has a thousand faces."[82] Hugo exposes in *Le dernier jour d'un
condamné* (1829) the horrors of waiting and wondering that are imagined and depicted here.

These ordonnances themselves pose a challenge to free-spirited
duellists and afford the prestige of transgressing unreasonably severe
laws. But Hugo also suggests that duelling brings people together—not
just, as other works have suggested, the two adversaries brought together by the duel but a collective class. Duellists in this play are like

adherents to a minority religion, held together by a common set of values.

In Corneille's *Le Cid*, for all the noble miens in this medieval arena, the dispute that provokes the first duel is in essence recognizably modern. It turns on the merits of the future governor and the right to promotion. It is a matter of state that then becomes a fiercely contested private matter. Hugo, inverting this trajectory, shows how duels, which are fought over individualistic, even idiosyncratic, matters of personal taste and opinion, come to attract the punitive attentions of an interventional state. The risible disputes that lead to duels often constitute a reason for discrediting those who fight them, but here that very frivolity is cherished by Hugo as a salutary expression of freedom, however eccentric or unguarded. Hugo is concerned to defend the rights of the individual in a centralized state, which, here, resembles a panopticon. This preoccupation about the extent to which state and private interests can and should intersect is already evident in *Le Cid*, and it remains a chiefly French concern. In English fictions, this is not a facet that exercises the likes of Smollett, Sheridan, and Thackeray. Indeed, there is barely a sense that duels might actually be illegal. True, the police make a brief appearance in Smollett's *Humphry Clinker*, but no charges are brought;[83] equally, in Russian novels, this dimension remains largely secondary. Here, however, the competing forces of individual discretion, religiously ordained edicts, and royal fiat swirl around the duel.

The attitude to duelling is a balance in which rival conceptions of freedom and competing views of the role of the state over individual rights may be weighed. Richelieu remains acknowledged as the chief architect of the centralized French state. But he achieved his "raison d'état" and administrative improvements at considerable expense. Accompanied by père Joseph, Richelieu exercised a tyrannical force, all the more objectionable for being invisible. As a result, Richelieu's reforms and methods threatened "the French people's aptitude for joy, games, and celebration, which even in times of danger, they have been reluctant to give up."[84] Indeed, it was then, above all, that frivolity proved salutary. A significant shift should be registered here. For the first time in over a century at least, the duel can now be represented and advertised by a French writer as a quintessentially French act. This exhibition of bravura on chivalric grounds or frivolous pretexts has become a vital expression of an individualistic esprit. Duelling is an honest and honorable way of settling differences, the prerogative of the noble individual, noble because individual, asserting his rights against the edicts of an invisible, inhuman state. French writers hitherto had insisted that duelling was neither French in origin nor, somehow, in character. Now it may be considered an act of rebellion, in defiance of and by contrast with the dark machinations of Richelieu and the administrators whom this "Bismarck of the Counter-Reformation" would empower henceforward.

The duellist's sword is, tragically, not as mighty as the statesman's pen, but Hugo, inspired by Corneille's embattled drama *Le Cid*, defends the individual's freedom both to fight and to write as salutary expressions of defiance. *Marion de Lorme* in turn bequeaths to generations of French authors, from Alexandre Dumas to Edmond Rostand, the seductive conceit that the pen and sword are congenial sisters.

Thackeray: *The Memoirs of Barry Lyndon, Esq.* (1844): Redmond Barry versus Captain Quin etc., etc., etc.

If Hugo returned imaginatively to September 1638 in order to disinter a culture of self-expression promoted and protected by the sword yet under threat from the dictates of the state, William Makepeace Thackeray turned, closer to home, toward the eighteenth century in his pursuit of largely vanished codes of chivalry. Thackeray, born in 1811, had a particular enthusiasm for the apparent contradictions and excesses of the flagging, decadent ancien régime. As the Victorian age dawned, the prosperity of a culture in the previous century that was apparently more concerned with honor than troubled by virtue became all the more conspicuous and puzzling. The increasing prominence of patriotism, a product of the greater power and prestige of the nation-state, and the reassertion of notions of Christian piety made certain eighteenth-century codes of conduct seem all the more outlandish. The peculiar mixture of punctiliousness and recklessness necessary to the flourishing of the duellist in earlier times looked alien to nineteenth-century eyes. Even if duels continued to be fought, as indomitably as ever in Thackeray's own day, the reasons for them appeared to have changed. If, in the eighteenth century, a duel largely provided an opportunity to show one's class or one's right to join that class, the nineteenth-century duel is more loosely tied to notions of liberty and opportunities for self-expression.

Thackeray enjoys the equivocal reputation of being a brilliant author "in spurts," but, according to Anthony Trollope, "in imagination, language, construction, and general literary capacity, Thackeray never did anything more remarkable than *Barry Lyndon*."[85] That verdict has not helped the novel to become popular, even though Trollope was earnestly paying it a sincere compliment, rather than stealthily denigrating the rest of Thackeray's oeuvre in this fashion. Stanley Kubrick's film (1983) has no doubt absolved some people of the toil of reading the book. But even Thackeray's critics have tended to pay more attention to *Vanity Fair* and *Henry Esmond*, regarded by his contemporaries as the most excellent and representative work, and, since the Victorians preferred his "later, staider works," these texts have come to be seen as the incarnations of his talent, his true accomplishments.[86] Thackeray's own hesitation between different versions of the text has not helped matters. The novel was first published serially in *Fraser's Magazine* in 1844 under the title *The Luck of Barry Lyndon: A Romance of the Last Century*. In 1856, Thackeray adjusted the title to the *Memoirs of Barry Lyndon*.

In Smollett's *Roderick Random*, fighting is the chief conduit by which the disenfranchised Scot can make his way until, at length, he achieves legitimacy and gains respect. Redmond Barry is an Irish counterpart to Roderick.[87] He too relates his memoirs in the first person, and his story constitutes a similarly extended catalogue of fights, whether, like Random, while engaged as a mercenary in the army or as an irascible pseudochivalric campaigner serving his own interest. But while Random finally integrates into society, achieving success and happiness, Barry's tale is considerably darker and bleaker. Random's first-person account is calmly retrospective, recounted by a balanced, contented, mature man, but Barry takes continued pleasure, as he relates his story, in brazen lies and self-glorification. We will understand only toward the end of his tale the reasons for which he may feel the need to perpetuate the illusion of his own prowess. Moreover, whereas the present of Random's account is essentially a continuation of the past that it relates, Barry's narrative commemorates a history that seems irretrievably distant, sundered from the present by the Napoleonic age.

Redmond Barry is itching from the outset to cross swords, on the most frivolous and specious of grounds. Like Random, from an early age he sees that social distinction and prestige in the eyes of ladies may be won by fighting with suitable panache. In chapter 2, after his pedigree has been laid out, he now duly shows himself to be "a man of spirit." He decides, at the age of fifteen, to fall in love with a woman called Nora Brady, his cousin in fact. She is not the most beautiful of ladies—"When I come to think about her now, I know she could never have been handsome; for her figure was rather of the fattest, and her mouth of the widest" (Thackeray has learned from Dickens that a safe way of debasing the duellist is that of inflating the lady on whose behalf he is fighting), but that matters not to him. Barry realizes he is in competition for her favors with an older man, and an Englishman to boot, Captain Quin. So his "first affair" beckons (he is referring to the duel, not the relationship), and Barry is, he admits, "as proud of it as of a suit of laced velvet." However dubious the cause and empty the threats, the terms of his first challenge are impeccably polite: "'Mr Quin,' said I, in the most dignified tone I could assume, 'may also have satisfaction any time he pleases, by calling on Redmond Barry, Esquire, of Barryville.' At which speech my uncle burst out a–laughing." He himself cannot quite stay in the same key of restraint and dignity, when assuring his acquaintances that he is deadly serious:

> "Mark this, come what will of it, I swear I will fight the man who pretends to the hand of Nora Brady. I'll follow him, if it's into the church, and meet him there. I'll have his blood, or he shall have mine; and this riband shall be found dyed in it. Yes! And if I kill him, I'll pin it on his breast, and then she may go take back her token." This I said because I was very much excited at the time, and because I had not read my novels and romantic plays for nothing.[88]

The effect worked by the passage depends on a contrast between the noble ferocity of the oath and the apologetic candor of the explanatory statement that follows it. Barry owns up to the fact that his words are provided by fictional texts. Because duelling took place, by and large, out of sight, those stories provided the principal means of understanding what was supposed to happen. Yet, far from proceeding to take an ironical distance from those inflated feelings and bold words, in recollecting them, he only goes on to reflect on the contrast between past and present and the degradation of manly values in the interim.

When returning home, Barry knows that his mother should not hear of the affair. He reckons, however, that she probably knew all, "but she said not a word about the quarrel, for she had a noble spirit, and would as lief have seen any one of her kindred hanged as shirking from the field of honour."[89] It is a wonder, then, that she comes from Bray. This noble reticence prompts a wistful reflection on the differences between past and present forms of valor. Curiously, the expedient of the duel seems to have gone from being reviled to being regretted, without any intermediate stages. Barry opens this passage with a resolutely rhetorical question:

> What has become of those gallant feelings nowadays? Sixty years ago a man was a *man*, in old Ireland, and the sword that was worn by his side was at the service of any gentleman's gizzard, upon the slightest difference. But the good old times and usages are fast fading away. One scarcely ever hears of a fair meeting now, and the use of those cowardly pistols, in place of the honourable and manly weapon of gentlemen, has introduced a deal of knavery into the practice of duelling, that cannot be sufficiently deplored.[90]

A true gentleman, a real man, does not fire pistols. And, ironically, as we shall see, nor will Barry in this instance. The sword and the pistol are appointed emblems of past and present, indicative of the different ways of duelling, as the conduct of duels themselves betrays a change in mentality across the divide. Barry sounds like an eighteenth-century residue, a "faithful remnant" astray in nineteenth-century Britain.

So the duel is eagerly embraced as a rite of passage. It turns Barry into a man, he feels. And he immediately seizes the opportunity to assume a different persona, that of a leader, as he orders the staff about. "Six hours previous I would as soon have thought of burning the house down as calling for a bottle of claret on my own account; but I felt I was a man now, and had a right to command."[91]

Barry is careful to spend the night before the duel writing, in the time-honored fashion, and seeing to his affairs, should he perish. He leaves to his mother his charger (a mare that happens also to be called Nora), and he generously bequeaths his silver-hilted hanger to Phil, the gamekeeper, which Phil is unlikely to find very useful as he discharges his duties. These gestures are impressive but rather undermined in the detail.

At last, the eagerly awaited duel takes place. Barry shoots Captain Quin, "flaming in red regimentals, as big a monster as ever led a grenadier company," in the neck. Quin drops down dead. "I did not feel any horror or fear, young as I was, in seeing my enemy prostrate before me; for I knew that I had met and conquered him honourably in the field, as became a man of my name and blood." On the contrary, the death of Quin gives birth to Barry: "I began so the first day of my life, and so have continued."[92] This combat sends Barry out into the world and inaugurates the adventures that now ensue. First, Barry makes in all haste for Dublin. However, it turns out, several pages later, that the pistols were not loaded with real ammunition. Barry had fired his pistol loaded with a plug of tow. The duel costs neither party anything. The ribbon was the only thing to dye. Captain Quin was therefore not even slightly wounded. "Resurrected," he promptly marries Nora. Barry, beguiled by the thought of his own valor, in turn misleads his readers by telling them not what actually transpired but what he thought had happened then. Barry's virility and dignity have been purchased by a fraud. This sets the tone. He seldom lets the truth obtrude into a good story. Barry continues to tell anyone who will listen that he did indeed kill a man in a duel, an honorable preface to the tale of his European adventures.

These adventures, outlined in the chapters that follow, are breathtakingly ignoble. Like Roderick Random, Barry enlists as a mercenary soldier, first in the British forces and then under Prussian colors, where he finds himself fighting in the Seven Years' War, for Frederick the Great, in an army "composed for the most part of men hired or stolen, . . . from almost every nation in Europe." Naturally, "the deserting to and fro was prodigious."[93] The duellist's particular values and scruples would normally distance him from the mercenary's venal opportunism. Barry stumbles aimlessly around the battlefields. After serving for a while as a footman, he manages, by pretending to be insane (and claiming to be Julius Caesar) to pass himself off as a soldier aptly called Fakenham, whose clothes he steals.

If Quin's resurrection amazes or amuses us, more disagreeable revelations lie in wait. Weapons in this story have hitherto served as little more than toys—objects for play and display, loaded with harmless pellets or mounted high up on walls for show. But just as Barry overstates his duelling prowess, so he downplays his ugly complicity in the miseries of war. Barry soon finds himself at the battle of Minden, one of the exchanges that devastated Westphalia, Candide's stamping ground. He recollects, with horror, the death of his comrade Captain Fagan: "Some of our people had already torn off his epaulets, and, no doubt, had rifled his purse. Such knaves and ruffians do men in war become! It is well for gentlemen to talk of the age of chivalry; but remember the starving brutes whom they lead—men nursed in poverty, entirely ignorant, made to take a pride in deeds of blood—men who can have no amusement but in drunkenness, debauch and plunder." These details and the indignation they prompt constitute a sort of rejoinder to Thomas Carlyle's hero worship, of which Frederick was one of the objects, published in 1841:

> While, for instance, we are at the present moment admiring the "Great Frederick," as we call him, and his philosophy, and his liberality, and his military genius, I, who have served him, and been, as it were, behind the scenes of which that great spectacle is composed, can only look at it with horror. What a number of items of human crime, misery, slavery, go to form that sum-total of glory! I can recollect a certain day, about three weeks after the battle of Minden, and a farm-house in which some of us entered; and how the old woman and her daughters served us, trembling, to wine; and how we got drunk over the wine, and the house was in a flame, presently: and woe betide the wretched fellow afterwards who came home to look for his house and his children![94]

This tirade, couched in sententious terms familiar from Enlightenment histories, reads as entirely justified. But the description of the torched house that follows is alarmingly nonchalant. The personal pronouns eventually go missing, as though the soldiers bear no responsibility—"and the house was in a flame, presently." The syntax that follows, even that exclamation mark, the vernacular "woe betide," the familiarity of "fellow" all fail to accommodate sufficient shame and contrition at an inhuman act. It seems to be written as though uttered, a moment after, by one of the drunken soldiers. With time, one would hope that the syntax and texture of this episode might have matured into a more considered reflection.

There is also a somewhat awkward leap from the generalized, sententious reflection ("what a number of items . . . glory!") to the specificity of the anecdote that bears that out. Far from owning up to a terrible crime, the reminiscence is merely an "item" conveniently assigned to the role of illustrating a wider, indeed universal tendency. The obfuscation is then compounded by the vocabulary of the sentence that opens the next chapter—"After the death of my protector, Captain Fagan, I am forced to confess that I fell into the very worst of courses and company." The heartfelt confession occurs only after Barry has described the slaughter of innocents; and the superlative he now sees fit to use ("the very worst of courses") surely contrives to minimize the horrors that have just been evoked.[95]

Throughout, these accounts of imposture and cowardice are interspersed with brief but ennobling references to Barry's sword; he speaks of his "unrivalled skill with the sword": "my sword had . . . got such a reputation through Europe that few people cared to encounter it."[96] The "sword" is a magical, talismanic term for Barry, buoyed by its associations with justice, immediately suggesting honor and nobility until, by repetition, it becomes a lazy metonymy.

Duels, particularly by sword, are designed to provide the ideal counterweight to this indiscriminate brutality. People talk about them frequently. They have happened often in the past; they are threatened often in the future, but they never actually come to pass, unless the pistols are loaded with a plug of tow. This proliferation of duels, as in Smollett's works, is comical. Like excuses, as they multiply, they weaken and ultimately discredit the narrator. On one occasion, after Barry stupefies his interlocutor, he owns up to his creativity:

"Mine is the first sword in Europe. . . ."

"Boy!" said Lord George, "I am not four years younger than you are."

"You are forty years younger than I am in experience. I have passed through every grade of life. With my own skill and daring I have made my own fortune. I have been in fourteen pitched battles as a private soldier, and have been twenty-three times on the ground, and was never touched but once, and it was by the sword of a French *maître d'armes*, whom I killed. . . ."

This speech was not exactly true to the letter (for I had multiplied my pitched battles, my duels, and my wealth somewhat); but I saw that it made the impression I desired to effect upon the young gentleman's mind.[97]

Charm is a sort of refined insincerity. Candor about one's dishonesty produces its own ambiguous seductions. We run the risk of feeling that, unlike Barry's interlocutors, including no less a person than his own mother, we, his readers, are the uniquely privileged trustees of his confidences. Paradoxically, the more dishonesty to which he owns up in our presence, the more flattering he becomes and the more we risk trusting and liking him. The pace of the text is such though that Thackeray ensures that the duel, described in chapter 2, soon leaves readers with their fingers burned—which is more than can be said of either of the duellists.

Usually invisible from the text, the editor nevertheless feels obliged to add a footnote: "And as for the duels which Mr Barry fights, may we be allowed to hint a doubt as to a great number of these combats? It will be observed, in one or two other parts of his Memoirs, that whenever he is at an awkward pass, or does what the world does not usually consider respectable, a duel, in which he is victorious, is sure to ensue; from which he argues that he is a man of undoubted honour."[98] The duel has a magical expiatory effect, wiping away whatever sin preceded it. But the observation also potentially winks self-consciously at the reader. The duel is summoned by the author to provide momentary suspense and excitement until he works out what next to do and the reader buys the next installment of the newspaper in which it is serialized.

At all events, Barry, armed with his pedigree, soon establishes him-self, like Launcelot Greaves and Roderick Random, as a self-deceiving braggart, except he seems to stand at more of an angle to his past. He narrates an essentially eighteenth-century story of adventures from a vantage point in the nineteenth century, when, after the French Revo-lution and other convulsive transformations, Quixote seemed more quixotic than ever. Writing, like Barry, in the first person, Roderick is supposed to be a credible narrator, however implausible his adventures may be. If they do stretch credibility, that is because Providence moves mysteriously and unpredictably, not because the hero is a congenital liar. But, in the interim, Baron Munchhausen has materialized. Barry is an avowed liar, and he hails from Ireland, a "nation," Thackeray once wrote, "of liars." If the Irish were good liars, they therefore made good storytellers, and novelists are perhaps bound to be drawn to liars. Barry remarks, "If they tell more fibs than their downright neighbours across the water, on the other hand they believe more."[99] It anticipates, to a degree, the rueful observation, "if one could only teach the English how to talk, and the Irish how to listen . . ."[100]

This self-dramatizing Irish swaggerer is, by the 1840s, a well-established stock figure of comedy—Dick Sheridan (as Barry calls him) perhaps most famously sculpting or at least polishing the archetype, in the form of Sir Lucius O'Trigger, with his bloated pride in the meager vestiges of his family and his wish to avenge the slightest insults to name and nation. As James Kelly has outlined, Ireland became associ-ated with duelling and "fire-eating," all the more so after the (Dublin-born) Duke of Wellington, famously, fought a duel. Threats to duel, pointless challenges, and, above all, hyperbole in reminiscence are the stock-in-trade of the Irish. Ireland, it was said, was "the garden of duel-lists."[101] The idea of the Irish duellist tickles the sensibilities of English writers for two principal reasons. First, by Thackeray's age, the Irish could be considered pugnacious but harmless, a combination attribut-able to a reputed fondness for drink (usually claret, which is what Red-mond flings in the face of Quin to initiate their duel). Secondly, less fancifully, the Irish record of fighting as mercenaries lent a particular flavor to images of the Irish duellist. The Irish supplied armies with soldiers across the length and breadth of Europe and indeed beyond. They were known to be tall and strong, thanks, in part, to a diet of potatoes, apparently. Duellists of course never fight for money; they defend their honor. There is, then, something intrinsically comic when the Irish mercenary (which is what Barry has become) aspires to fighting honorably in this fashion.

Barry allows English readers not only to deride Ireland's hopeless obsession with antiquity and honor but also, in the manner of Scott when writing about Scotland, to see, not without pathos, how the duel becomes the privileged vehicle for reasserting wounded nobility and retrieving a broken continuity with the past, an inevitable symptom of their losses.

Barry identifies two giant historical figures, who, looming over the age, have each rendered the adventurer extinct, chivalry untenable, duels unfashionable: his resentment is fixed on Beau Brummell and Napoleon Bonaparte, in that order. Brummell may have been the first person ever to advocate the idea that a gentleman need not be armed. At any rate, he is duly denounced by Barry as "a nobody's son: a low creature . . . who never showed himself to be a man with a sword in his hand: as we used to approve ourselves in the good old times, before that vulgar Corsican upset the gentry of the world!"[102]

There follows a series of mournful Burkean reflections on the embourgeoisement of all values. How ironic then that, in the following stages of the book, Barry should bring to the courtship of Lady Lyndon, whose name he will adopt, those same standards. Disgracefully, Barry decides to pursue a match with an older lady, the Countess of Lyndon, whose husband is ailing. But she is wealthy. Barry cannot disguise his impatience at the husband's stubborn refusal to die. He gallantly tries to persuade her to have an illegitimate heir to remove the prospective heirs, the Tiptoff family, from the inheritance. Barry and his wife flee (disguised as Mr. and Mrs. Jones) to Bristol.

Thackeray thus brings together two characteristic, perhaps seemingly incongruous elements of ancien régime mores: on the one hand, a concern for honor, with the accompanying propensity to duel; on the other, a devotion to profitable arranged marriages. Thackeray finds himself intrigued by the capacity of people in the past to defy our ready comprehension when they choose to live by codes of conduct seemingly at variance with one another.[103] However, tempting as it may be to see the duel as a natural ally of love and romance, here, once again,

it is enlisted as a guarantor of good business and the protector of reputation. In *Pendennis* (1848–50), Thackeray brings together within the
same comical scene these two disparate ideas of a match. Although
this novel is set in the nineteenth century, Captain Costigan, another
pleasingly "typical" Irishman, like Barry, is passionately committed
both to loveless, financial matrimony ("only your low people . . . marry
for mere affection," opines Barry) and to the point of honor.[104] These two
codes of conduct converge when Costigan tries to enforce a marriage
of convenience by threatening a duel: "Captain Costigan . . . composed
a letter of a threatening nature to Major Pendennis's address, in which
he called upon that gentleman to offer no hindrance to the marriage
projected between Mr. Arthur Pendennis and his daughter, Miss Foth-
eringay, and to fix an early day for its celebration; or, in any other case,
to give him satisfaction which was usual between gentlemen of
honour."[105] He then asks Mr. Garbetts, an actor, "Principal Tragedian"
indeed, to run this errand and deliver the letter.

Sure enough, Barry too, aggrieved that the Tiptoffs stand to inherit
the estate and castle on which he has his own eyes trained, challenges
these parvenu upstarts to a duel. It is what he does. Whereas in *Pendennis*, the tragedian chooses to avert a tragedy by neglecting to pass
on the cartel to the prospective adversary, here Tiptoff, having been
challenged, refuses to meet Barry on the "field of honour"; instead, he
answers Barry "by a lawyer" and declines his "invitation which any
man of spirit would have accepted." Barry, in response, roars words
reminiscent of those shouted out when Nora Brady's hand was on offer
("I'll have his blood" etc.): "as sure as I am a man of honour, and have
tasted your blood once, I will have your heart's blood now." He draws
his sword, placing his back to the door. But he is on this occasion confronted by a dozen constables, armed with bludgeons and pistols. Lawyers and policemen, those embodiments of modern order, are arraigned
against him. "Take down his words, constables; swear the peace against
him!" screamed the little lawyer, from behind his tipstaffs." And then
something extraordinary happens. For the first time since Barry's account, and indeed his life, began, he is honest enough to admit, "I was
no longer the man I was at twenty, when I should have charged the ruffians sword in hand, and have sent at least one of them to his account.
I was broken in spirit, regularly caught in the toils, utterly baffled and

beaten by that woman. . . . I put down my sword upon the lawyer's desk."[106] The past conditional, highly characteristic of Barry, ensures that the braggadocio remains partially intact. Of course, he would have behaved differently at the age of twenty. But the simple ingenuousness of that last indicative sentence is without precedent.

The duellist is once again claimed by the law, as Thackeray follows some famous precedents. While Clarissa is ultimately but equivocally avenged, her brother is engaged in lifelong litigation. The law defers indefinitely a satisfactory outcome. Dickens too provides an implicit contrast between duelling in the traditional manner and that of the legalistic variety, when writing *The Pickwick Papers*. The posturing of the duellist, seen early on in the novel, seems affirmative by comparison to the more protracted and expensive legal duels, beginning, within a few chapters, with Bardell versus Pickwick.

Thackeray listened to the hinges as they creaked between the old and the new world. Barry's sword is sequestered by lawyers and policemen. And it is the transfer of this hallowed arm to a lawyer's desk that completes and colors in this pivotal moment. "My strength of mind and body were no longer those of the brave youth who shot his man at fifteen, and fought scores of battles within six years afterwards. Now, in the Fleet prison, where I write this, there is a small man who is always jeering me and making game of me, who asks me to fight, and I haven't the courage to touch him."[107] The avowal seems candid, even painfully honest, but then he is still convincing himself that that first duel he fought with Quin, at the age of fifteen, was real and meaningful. And, even as he acknowledges that he is in terminal decline, he compares himself to Hannibal, resting after his career.

The revelation that the incredible account we have been reading has been written in prison may come as a shock. We might find ourselves having to reread that muted sentence. But the editor, adding a note to the memoir, confirms that Barry was an inmate of the Fleet prison (abandoned in 1844) for nineteen years, after which he died of delirium tremens.[108] It is a brilliantly paced, incidental admission, handled, after all the confessional candor and extravagant self-exposure, with wonderfully casual understatement. Thackeray is indeed a master of subordinate clauses and parenthetical detail. In fact, a no-less-brilliant manipulation of adjectives and commas soon follows it, when we learn that Barry's niece is "a great heiress, of strict principle, and immense property in slaves in the West Indies."[109] Barry's ruminations on the effects of "time, illness and free-living" acquire a retrospective pertinence and pathos, written, as they are, in captivity.

But the revelation also makes sense of another curiosity. Throughout this text, readers may have felt, against their better judgment, that Barry speaks as though duels were not continuing to be fought in his age, in the nineteenth century. But then what can he know, in his secluded gouty retreat, of his contemporary society? It is no wonder that, ignorant of the world around him, he finds himself doomed to living in and off the past. The revelation accounts for his willingness to admire the vitality of the past, as opposed to a colorless present, as he perceives it. Prison has forced him to inhabit the eighteenth century.

Of course, we will have realized that his fond reminiscences are composed of a *nostalgie de boue*. Nevertheless, the disclosure also casts a retrospective pallor over that same vitality, the account of which is not ultimately redeemed by any wisdom, peace, or prosperity. In prison, Hugo's idealistic duellist, Didier, faced execution head-on, a dramatic dénouement by no means alien to his fearless spirit, but Barry languishes in prison indefinitely, without the dignity and compensation of a good cause or an injustice to nurse. *The Memoirs of Barry Lyndon* may be garrulously Irish, but they seem also to be a sort of ersatz Protestant confessional. Here, Barry's words, confided to the page, seem the product of loneliness, an expression of pessimism. The title of the memoirs, when first published, looks more hollow than ever: *The Luck of Barry Lyndon.*

Thackeray not only draws on his own knowledge of Smollett and of Scott but enjoys presupposing our probable experience of their novels. We are warned that Redmond Barry is "not, we repeat, a hero of the common pattern."[110] Barry forsakes violence, not because he comes to his senses but because, as he candidly admits, he is lacking in courage and vigor. It is an abject end. Roderick Random and Walter Scott's Guy Mannering come back to their rightful place, after tortuous journeys, in which an ability to duel proves its worth. But Barry Lyndon is not redeemed. His impostures are exposed at the end, leaving him sunken. We have a sense that this is a man adrift in the wrong century. No successive centuries hitherto were probably as different from each other as the eighteenth and nineteenth, as a result of the French Revolution and the accelerating pace of change in its aftermath. It is not just Barry who has aged; the era itself seems less colorful, "more moral and matter-of-fact," leaving behind an age whose incommensurate passions and conventions challenge our comprehension.[111] There is no sense in Smollett that the present is much different from the past he recounts. But Barry shows us the poignancy and the pain that result when the times change too rapidly to carry a man with them.

Random and Greaves are claimed and disarmed by the law but, in each case, with their own blessing. This deluded duellist is neither impressively autonomous nor radically defiant but is timidly rebellious, grudgingly honest. A Protestant in Ireland, like a Jacobite in England, Barry Lyndon is as compassless as Scott's Waverley, only he is not troubled by principles. Yet, as long as we are reading his words, we implicitly acknowledge his capacity to entertain us. If we remain disinclined to credit his self-vaunted skills as a swordsman, we cannot doubt his talents as a wordsmith, and readers may find themselves curiously touched by Barry, no matter that he is, indisputably, a rogue, a braggart, a Quixote without ideals, a foiled, failed d'Artagnan.

Dumas père, *Les trois mousquetaires* (1844): D'Artagnan versus Athos, Porthos, and Aramis, inter alia

Alexandre Dumas's most celebrated novel, *The Three Musketeers*, is blessed with a doubly misleading title. It seems rather pedantic to point out that the book interests itself ultimately in the fortunes of four musketeers. Certainly, d'Artagnan achieves the honor only at the close, as the others, Athos, Porthos, and Aramis, retire from active service, but the young man thinks himself a de facto musketeer from an early point in the story. He might not have the uniform, but he is proud to possess, in his own words, the heart of a musketeer.[112] It would, however, be less forgivable to suppose that those three (or four) musketeers actually carry muskets. At length, rather grudgingly, the musketeers do take up these weapons, but such arms are really better left to the *valetaille,* all the more so, given that one of their four respective valets happens to be called Mousqueton.

The arm with which we are likely instantly to associate the musketeers is not the musket but, of course, the sword. This observation
is likely to seem drearily obvious. *The Three Musketeers* is one of those
familiar novels that we think we might somehow have read, although
without quite remembering when. This is possibly an effect of the hundred or so films into which the novel has been turned. *The Three
Musketeers* is a story that commends itself to children. Its improbable
adventures and literally dashing heroes guarantee an exuberantly pictorial quality to the story. Above all, this is a world of soldiers as children might imagine them to be, a costume drama, of which the sword
is an indispensable part. The décolletés of beautiful ladies serve as
mailboxes for billets-doux. Equally present are tapestries, the index of
serious ancien régime splendor, especially, as is often the case here,
when they have a secret entrance cut into them. We are transported to
a realm where the characters, without realizing it themselves, seem
to be decked out in fancy dress. The *-os* and the *-is* endings of the musketeers' names inoculate them against any real danger and us against
any potential scruples about the pain and suffering that they, not to
mention their adversaries, might have to endure. Yet the swords that
they wield do administer fatal wounds. Dumas's narration is diverting,
in that it encourages readers to avert our gaze from the serious consequences of armed combat. When they hack one another to bits, somehow
they do so innocently. Soldiers are nothing but "big children,"[113]
swords their toys.

The sword as a weapon worn routinely in civilian contexts was disappearing, along with the ancien régime, from living memory. By 1844,
after the rise and fall of Napoleon and then that of Louis Philippe, the
prerevolutionary age has begun to recede, leaving the sword to enjoy
a certain innocence. The sword no longer represents the same sort of
danger to the typical reader in the mid-nineteenth century. A child's
passion for dinosaurs, in which an even safer thrill can be indulged,
perhaps relies on similar presuppositions. A duel by pistol would
simply be unconscionable in this milieu. But the charm of these duellists depends to an extent on our knowledge that their instruments
have been superseded by weapons and by concomitant mentalities that
are more matter-of-fact. Schiller's Karl Moor disdains "puerile sword-
play" (bubisches Degenspiel), as he nurses his pistol.[114] In Victor

Hugo's tragedy *Hernani* (1830), the eponymous hero is asked at one point to hand over his cape and sword. He readily gives up the former, but will not surrender the latter. Hand on hilt, he declares, "No. This is my other friend, innocent and faithful."[115] How quite can a sword be *innocent?* Perhaps it is yet to slay or maim anyone. But in a mechanized world, where guns rule, the personification of the sword is itself telling.

D'Artagnan acquires his trusty sword (swords, like steeds, always seem to attract this particular adjective) when, within sentences of the opening, it is solemnly handed from father to son. This homespun accolade carries echoes of the scene in *Le Cid*, in which the Count entrusts his son Rodrigo with his own sword. D'Artagnan's father too has schooled his son in the fine arts of swordsmanship. His words of wisdom are recollected in direct speech: "Fight at every opportunity; fight all the more so because duelling is forbidden. That means it takes twice as much courage to fight."[116] This is taking the Count's nonchalance in *Le Cid* to new, flagrant lengths. D'Artagnan père is endearingly unabashed as he launches his son on a life of crime. But this is honorable crime. Dumas and Hugo are joint heirs to Corneille in their enthusiasm for the duellist as a reputable outlaw. The aura conferred on him by lawless defiance is, as ever, more conspicuous in French texts than in their English counterparts. Transgressing the laws of a heavily centralized state is good, flouting them better still.

Unusually, if not paradoxically, d'Artagnan decides to become impulsive. His spontaneous irascibility is authorized from the start as a matter of policy and a question of honor. Mindful of his father's advice but perhaps taking it further than intended, d'Artagnan goes on to take "every smile for an insult and every look directed at him for a provocation," with the result that "his hand reached for the hilt of his sword ten times a day."[117] He has successfully turned himself into an inveterate, serial duellist.

This sword-toting impulsiveness, this propensity of d'Artagnan to draw his sword and fight duels is not explored, let alone explained, unless the paternal influence is emphasized as a factor. However, the novel opens in the little town of Meung, where, we are reminded, the author of the *Roman de la rose* (or at least one of them) was born. This is a cradle of chivalry. A susceptibility to this sort of romance has, by long tradition, been not only mediated but initiated by books. Francesca da Rimini, in Dante's *Inferno*, who fell in love upon reading about a kiss in the company of Paolo, has been identified as the prototype of this sort of reader.[118] We have encountered such readers, memorably, in *Don Quixote* and, more recently, in *Madame Bovary*. But d'Artagnan appears not to have been guilty of reading the kind of novels of which he is to become the hero. This is a novel about the last age before novels, that is, an age innocent of Cervantes and Descartes, whose rationalizing, ironizing perspectives corrode the fantasies of old.[119]

D'Artagnan's love of duelling is attributable above all else to the fact that he is a Gascon. Dumas seems only to be half joking when he maintains that Gascons can see in the night.[120] Gascons are "the Scots of France," such is their ferocious pride, even if, when it comes to a fondness for duelling, the Irish seem the preferred candidates appointed by the English to such a role.[121] It seems that d'Artagnan, like other young blades, may feel the continual need to fight, in order to stop himself from thinking about why he might be fighting or indeed from thinking *tout court*. In the eighteenth century, this record would alone confirm him as an execrable or, more likely, a comical character. George Farquhar's character Brazen, a sort of honorary Gascon, outlines his modus vivendi: "I always fight with a man before I make him my friend: and, if once I find he will fight, I never quarrel with him afterwards."[122] This ethic, entrusted to Brazen—a comical character—is taken seriously, once it comes to Dumas's attention. The duel by sword guarantees a bond, forged by courage and honor. That ethic is under assault from, on the one hand, the uncomprehending, even resentful edicts of absolute power in the form of haughty religious diktats but also, on the other hand, from encroaching bourgeois notions and norms of honor. A legal contract, Tréville (the patron of the musketeers) asserts, is not worth as much as a swordsman's word of honor.[123]

Athos, Porthos, and Aramis choose their names to cloak their aristocratic provenance. They fight duels not to prove their class and to defend their honor but out of disinterested pleasure in the sport. By becoming musketeers, they celebrate belonging to a class unto itself, whose esprit de corps transcends all other allegiances and loyalties. The musketeer elite is not determined by affiliations to class or by a common commitment to denominational values. The duellist belongs to a caste that can look past these. This class embraces people of quite different persuasions (Aramis is, for instance, devout) and ambitions.[124] A propensity to duel seems the chief prerequisite for membership of the musketeers and for the friendship between members of this elite. This is a society built on valor. It obviously appeals to monarchists, but the emphasis on equality and virility, characteristic of the duel, renders it palatable too to those of a republican bent.

In this long, tireless text, fate and fatality are not invoked or mentioned once. The novel celebrates the courage and the daring of the self-made man, in harmony with his sword. Gentlemen do not, supposedly, rush or run. But wherever d'Artagnan goes, it is with "miraculous celerity." As he races to the first of many duels, d'Artagnan "flew rather than walked toward the convent."[125] Had Dumas contented himself with the first verb alone, the metaphor would be dead, but the next few words breathe literalizing life to it, by telling us to imagine the verb he has thought fit not to use. Dumas does, on occasion, find the time to marvel at the alacrity of his own characters: "all the events we have just related have taken place within half an hour."[126] In the same vein, d'Artagnan watches with "all his eyes" and "listens with all his ears."[127] Such is the tone of the book, this does not seem hyperbolic or misjudged. Horses only ever gallop in this novel. At one point, it is true, more contemplatively, "d'Artagnan admired how fragile and unknown were the threads by which the destinies of a people and the life of a man might hang," but "he was just immersed in those reflections, when the goldsmith entered." Momentarily, Dumas gestures toward an inner, ruminative life, but it lasts a sentence and a half, before the action resumes. Then again, "time passes quickly, when it is spent in attacking and defending."[128] In this breathless world of dashing, cavalier figures, the protocols of duelling are bound to pose a particular problem here. Romanticism had no truck with the formalities, the artifices of the cartel, the ossified rituals and the self-important prerogatives of the gentry. The rituals of the duel look unnecessarily staid and ceremonious, and they necessitate a delay, during which doubts and, God forbid, even fears risk implanting themselves. Dumas shares a Romantic impatience with the ceremony, pomp, and punctilio of the duel, and he inherits their distaste for rules and the impatient wish to be free of them.

In the code published in 1836, the comte de Chatauvillard is largely concerned to proscribe actions that lie beyond the presumed limits of gentlemanly conduct and to tighten regulations in response to the increasing frequency and uncertainty with which pistol duels were being contested. Nevertheless, he largely leaves the duellist by sword carte blanche. In article 16 of the code, after numerous negative, punitive formulations, it comes as a relief to read that "lowering oneself, making oneself bigger, throwing oneself to the right and to the left, striking off, throwing oneself forward, flitting about one's opponent, is within the rules of combat."[129] While the count prescribes the "most perfect immobility" for the pistol shooter, the swordsman may, with absolute impunity, lead his opponent on a merry dance.[130] The extravagant *gambades* with which d'Artagnan and company pirouette around their adversaries suddenly look neither so fictive nor so fanciful any more.

The pistol slowed down the duel, petrifying the principals. But d'Artagnan's exuberance does not allow him to wait for long. For him, duelling is a joyous vocation, not an ugly compulsion. Whereas, in Russian texts, the night before an encounter seems interminable (permitting doubts and misgivings to fester), here no sooner is the duel arranged than it has to happen. The musketeers go to the usual lengths and observe the courtesies, of course, but that Romantic urgency has been imparted to their arrangements. There is an extemporaneous quality to these duels.

Pushkin, and many of his successors in Russia, matched the deliberate and scrupulous nature of the duel by pistol with a commensurately detailed description, emphasizing the suffering there is in waiting, the agony of anticipation, and the cruel games the mind plays with itself when trying to catch up with a previous impulse. With ceremonious, indeed funereal slowness, the loading of pistols is completed and described. Dumas accelerates the duel, with his dynamic narration and hard-pressed superlatives.

Not only are the three musketeers—Athos, Porthos, and Aramis—mentioned unfailingly in that order (like the partners of some prestigious estate agency), but this sequence governs, no less infallibly, the order of their appearances in various situations. For instance, when d'Artagnan needs to call on them, quite naturally "he visited, in succession, Athos, Porthos, and Aramis." The sequence literally connotes an imperturbable order, in a changing, challenging world. Athos, Porthos, and Aramis fight successive duels against three English adversaries in this order, each duly vanquishing his opponent in turn.[131] The rhythm and assonance won by the unerring sequence of these three otherworldly names may recall those produced by the biblical triumvirate of Shadrack, Meshak, and Abednego. It possibly helps the reader to intuit an unshakeable, unassailable stability even in an arbitrary hierarchy. It is never adjusted or compromised. The ethos of loyalty and steadfastness under a monarchy, threatened in Dumas's time by unremitting political turmoil, is commemorated by the immutability of this order among the friends and colleagues.

If men continually pair off in duels, there is also an insistence on triads throughout this book. Chapter 1 of *The Three Musketeers* is, for a start, titled "The Three Presents of M. d'Artagnan Père." At the end of the novel, d'Artagnan fights three times. This patterning emphasizes tacitly just how difficult it will be for d'Artagnan, the fourth man, to earn a place in this exalted, settled elite. Yet he can fight his way to the top. This is a work preoccupied with social mobility, if not in quite the same vein as Friedrich Engels's *The Condition of the Working Class in England*, also published in 1844. In nineteenth-century Europe, when class became more fluid, more susceptible to redefinition, rooted less in property and dynasty, nobility was, in some cases, not so much manifested as earned by a readiness to participate in a duel. Flaubert's Frédéric Moreau, nineteenth-century bourgeois par excellence, is naturally enchanted by the idea of fighting a duel, as he swishes an imaginary sword in the kitchen: "the idea of fighting for a woman aggrandized and ennobled him, in his eyes."[132] Frédéric's fond "idea" is highly generic—he is fighting for an indefinite woman. The duel, in other words, becomes an instrument of social mobility, no longer an expression of one's higher class but instead a means of access to it.

D'Artagnan soon contrives to arrange successive duels with each of the three musketeers in turn. It is therefore no surprise that he should agree to the following trilogy of appointments: Athos at noon, Porthos at one p.m., and Aramis at two p.m. An hour is allocated to each encounter. The timing of these arrangements is of course a tribute to d'Artagnan's swaggering self-confidence, which trumps even a need for lunch. The duels are prearranged, the formalities in place. But there is a new haste and bravura. Their swords flash with the sort of opportunistic daring that characterizes the pistol drawn from the holster, shot from the hip, the very staple of the wild Western tradition, where self-control and precision need to be allied to brilliant impetuosity and quick reflexes.

Dumas's friend the painter Eugène Isabey was enthralled by duels. Isabey skillfully sets his duels in locations that suggest spontaneity. He had a particular predilection for painting steps and stairs. These flights lend his paintings movement and perspective, but, no less importantly, they provide a background narrative detail for the duel. A duel fought on steps is necessarily unorthodox, and it therefore leaves room for imagination and improvisation. As in Dumas's works, the duel, even when preordained, rewards spontaneous daring and creative ingenuity. It is while rushing down stairs, four at a time, that d'Artagnan, ever in haste, first brushes into Athos and provokes a duel with him.

D'Artagnan measures up successfully and honorably to each of these three seasoned musketeers in turn. He has served a de facto apprenticeship ahead of joining their ranks. Dumas manages to suggest that he is extremely impulsive and irascible, in the best Gascon tradition, while succeeding in displaying the restraint and the patience required of the duellist. This trilogy, a form of speed duelling, allows d'Artagnan and the musketeers to make the acquaintance of one another. Satisfactory progress in these duels provides not only guarantees to d'Artagnan's prowess with the sword but a moral warranty. D'Artagnan understands honor and fair play.

Amid the numerous duels d'Artagnan goes on to fight, another comic innovation on the part of Dumas stands out. Later in the novel, under the chapter "An impossible duel," d'Artagnan finds himself drawn into a bout that he is unable to contest.[133] D'Artagnan agrees to fight a gentleman by the name of de Wardes, and a date and time are accordingly fixed. However, de Wardes is the alias assumed by d'Artagnan himself, when, disguised, he is visiting the royal apartments. He has then arranged to fight this duel with himself. Whereas subsequent writers, above all in the twentieth century, play with similar conceits, as the duellist comes face-to-face with himself, here it offers triumphant evidence of d'Artagnan's ingenuity. D'Artagnan is not, like Barry

Eugène Isabey, *Après le duel*, 1866. By kind permission of the Museum of Art and Archaeology, University of Missouri–Columbia.

Eugène Isabey, *Le duel* (date not known). Courtesy of the Trustees of the Cooper Gallery, Barnsley.

Lyndon, a profoundly divided self, yet all duels necessitate some sort of self-confrontation. Here the duel to be fought against himself pays another tribute to his "eternal gaiety."[134]

The conflict in this book is not to be found within d'Artagnan but occurs when he comes against sinister, inscrutable forces at work. As in Hugo's *Marion de Lorme,* the duellist is a model of transparency. Once again, the insidious Cardinal Duke de Richelieu, with his Cardi-nalistes, are ranged against the duellists and musketeers, loyal subjects of the king. Furthermore, Dumas contrasts the perpetual motion of the duellist with the guarded introspection of the mysterious Milady. That ethic of transparency, celebrated by Hugo, is conserved by duellists brandishing their swords. In a wonderful validation of this ethic, the musketeers are described as "good people, proud in the sunlight, faithful in the dark."[135] The swordsman looks his opponent in the eye and may understand him better than he does himself. As in Hugo's drama, the vigor and vitality of the swordsmen is pitted against the furtive machinations of the Cardinalistes, again steered invisibly by the éminence grise. Milady speaks "mechanically," as "the cardinal's satellites" adhere, unthinkingly and unimaginatively, to his edicts.[136]

Balzac's novel *Illusions perdues*, completed a year before Dumas's work, charts the fortunes of Rastignac, after his arrival from the Provinces in Paris. But this time, as the provincial naïf sets foot in Paris, there is to be no forlorn tale of lost illusions. On the contrary, it is a novel in which we witness the fulfillment of d'Artagnan's dreams and the vindication of his efforts, complete with the awareness that reality, which can stretch "six feet taller than dreams," may turn out to be stranger and more fantastic than was imaginable, so illusions are only dispelled insofar as they turn out to be realized.[137] This is a story that reverses the trajectory of Don Quixote, as d'Artagnan sees windmills turn back into knights.

As d'Artagnan sets out for Paris, his long sword awkwardly brushing his ankles and rubbing against his mount, when he is in the saddle, this picture recalls Honoré Daumier's paintings of the Don, spindly legged, dwarfing the mule on which he rides.[138] D'Artagnan is the proud owner of a long sword, that traditional index to self-delusions or to an old-worldy innocence. His weapon, brushing against a leg, does not fit him. He has only fifteen écus and a ridiculously small horse. But when Dumas says that his hero, d'Artagnan, is an "exact copy" of Don Quixote, both morally and physically, the line seems disingenuous. He turns out not to be an exact facsimile, for his heroism is actually commensurate with the world of intrigues and injustices about him. We see an unquestioning, quasi-feudal relationship to Tréville and to Louis XIII, in which the chivalric qualities of boldness, bravery, and loyalty—to a king in need of protection—are in abundance. This is an era in which absolutism, as embodied here by Richelieu and experienced under Napoleon, has become unpalatable. D'Artagnan belongs to a preenlightened, preindustrialized, quasi-feudal era when innocence and joy may yet characterize these combats.

Dumas casts a retrospective glance on this age, with wonder and with envy, marveling at "the curiously easy morals of this gallant era," when "people were less inhibited . . . than they are now." There was, "in that age, less freedom yet more independence."[139] There were perhaps more rules but therefore more potential for, and more fun in, breaking them. The novel offers a fond evocation of aristocratic nonchalance and self-assurance before they were expunged by both the Revolution and the advent of Napoleon. In accordance with the intuited logic of aristocrats, duelling must be right, simply because they are doing it. Equally, because Richelieu was such a ferocious opponent of duelling, those given to it may readily be identified with freedom from his unforgiving rigor and his punitive stance. This syllogism allows duellists to be celebrated as sponsors of liberty, embodiments of freethinking and Gallic generosity. They are, far from resting on a privilege of aristocracy and exclusivity, rebels who champion the freedom of the individual.

D'Artagnan now fights in troops loyal to the king. The action moves from the streets of Paris to the ramparts of La Rochelle. Here duelling is entirely consonant with the skills required of a good soldier. It provides a rehearsal before fighting in battle, an interlude during it, and a relief or recreation after it. In fact, the book barely distinguishes between those duels fought within the context of a war and those duels provoked by affronts to one's honor.

La Rochelle is a last bastion of Calvinism. But the ease and exuberance with which the musketeers defend themselves contrast with the inordinate influence wielded by Richelieu, "a man who, instead of a sword, holds in his hand the forces of a whole kingdom."[140] The odds are unfairly stacked against the musketeers. Richelieu does not stand tall holding the sword in a duel. Instead, at the siege of La Rochelle, the preface to the revocation of the Edict of Nantes and the reversal of Henri IV's tolerance of Protestants, the destructive forces unleashed by the "orifice of the immobile cannon" are uppermost.[141]

D'Artagnan's sword must make itself felt among all the arquebuses and guns, clumsily wielded by the nameless assassins around him. The true test of aristocratic nonchalance is the nobleman's ability, even in the presence of death, to retain his sang froid. "Extreme anxiety can only be combated by extreme insouciance."[142] This is often best exemplified by a timely bon mot, a witty, pithy remark to relieve pressure and pain. Understatement in particular is a badge of noble fearlessness. Dumas's novel celebrates an ethos that is as endearing as it is mythical. Such "memories" of fearless nonchalance appealed to a more bourgeois age, painfully conscious of having lost it. The story of Francis Drake's bowls match, played on Plymouth Hoe, a fine example of this mentality, was first recorded and popularized in the nineteenth century.[143] The English anecdote plausibly has Drake concentrating on his sport. It should come as no surprise that the French variant on this would instead involve food. D'Artagnan and colleagues agree that there is ample time to finish their dinner and drink their wine, as enemy soldiers advance, five hundred feet away, adding that "nothing is disagreeable like being disturbed over dinner."[144] The negated adjective "disagreeable" is typical of the lexicon—a more assertive term would risk conveying sincerely moral indignation, whereas the intrusion of the enemy is only momentarily troublesome. Their nonchalance gratifies notions of French panache and their unique capacity to savor the fleeting sensual pleasures conferred by food, wine, and duelling. This joie de vivre, interrupted occasionally by a *joie de tuer*, testifies to their self-confidence and a decidedly hedonistic ethos, no longer countenanced by the professionalized armies of the Napoleonic era and its aftermath.

But these duels are often interrupted or aborted, not to spare blood and relieve the reader, as in the eighteenth century, but so that they might turn on a common enemy (that archenemy of all duellists, Richelieu and his Cardinalistes) and see them off. The threat posed by this nemesis of the duellist is more sinister than embodied by either duellist. As Hugo's *Marion de Lorme* has shown, the persecution to which the duellist was subjected by Richelieu could easily be read as the repression experienced under the Restoration. The duellist stands for anyone who seeks justice courageously on his or her own terms.

Hugo's reconstruction of the age of Louis XIII has a more overtly ideological edge than Dumas's return to it, which may seem prompted by innocuous nostalgia for the innocence of a pre-Classical age. *The Three Musketeers* would, however, be a wholly unconvincing pastiche, were it not for some elements that remind us, self-consciously, that it is the work of a nineteenth-century pen. There are occasional interjections, where, briefly, the narrator sighs or perhaps frowns at the changes that time has wrought. Some pervasive yet less conspicuous elements are discernible. There is a typically nineteenth-century, nonchivalric interest in the cost of everything. D'Artagnan, within a chapter or two, sells his steed. He declares his wish to be a millionaire, as well as a musketeer.[145] Sometimes these elements mix uncomfortably or comically. Monsieur Bonacieux approaches the dashing young man in the hope that he can locate his wife who has been abducted. This d'Artagnan agrees to do, in lieu of rent, for, it turns out, Bonacieux is none other than his landlord. This is not a lord, to whom he owes feudal honor, but a landlord, with whom he is in arrears. In addition to these quietly dissonant chords is another innovative element: d'Artagnan is knight-cum-detective, a sleuth with a sword. D'Artagnan is the forerunner of the gentleman spy, chivalrously restoring order where there is chaos.[146]

The attitude of the duellist in love is the same as in combat. The affectionate sparring common to both is more nourishing and fulfilling, above and beyond the deadening jurisdiction of the law. It is fitting that d'Artagnan's love interest throughout the story should be Madame Bonacieux. Dumas harks back to a mythical age of *amour courtois* when duelling and flirting with other people's wives, far from being frowned on, was a recommendation in some quarters. Marriage is a contractual matter, legalizing but also domesticating love and desire, whereas the libertine wish to duel and to love is gratified beyond the law.

But, alas, all that vigor and joy cannot last. At first the narrator confesses to being carried away by his own account.[147] Ultimately, however, the novel seems exhausted and defeated by its own descriptive verve. In the epilogue, we are told in an uncharacteristically perfunctory sentence that "d'Artagnan fought Rochefort three times, and three times he injured him."[148] (As ever, this book favors triads). In the final words, Monsieur Bonacieux, Constance's charmless husband and d'Artagnan's disagreeable landlord, a figure who, amid the motley of swordsmen, spies, aristocrats, and priests, seems already to be a gray nineteenth-century bourgeois, receives the honor of a sinecure at the expense of his generous Eminence, the Cardinal de Richelieu. Flaubert ended *Madame Bovary* (1837) on a discordant note, by remarking that

Homais has just been awarded the cross of the Légion d'honneur.[149] In turning its attention away from the principal personages, to acclaim the latest worldly success of Monsieur Bonacieux, Dumas seems to have performed a similar valedictory trick. Honor has taken a decidedly bourgeois turn.

CHAPTER SEVEN

The Grotesque Duel

Twain, *A Tramp Abroad* (1878) and *Pudd'nhead Wilson* (1894):
Gambetta versus Fourtou; Judge Driscoll versus
Count Luigi / Angelo Capello

When he traveled to Europe, ostensibly to appreciate its culture and learn the German language, Mark Twain headed for Heidelberg, seat of a venerable university. Concluding that German should be "set aside among the dead languages, for only the dead have time to learn it," Twain immediately interests himself instead in the wordless duels contested by the students.[1] Germans impress him when they fall silent. If man-to-man combat is a universal phenomenon, its grammar and its accents are regionally diverse. It becomes apparent that the *Mensur* (as the Germans call their student duelling ritual) gives expression to a virile culture, by comparison with a decadent, effeminate French society. "A successful attempt to combine the ludicrous with the unpleasant," it appalled Jerome K. Jerome, when he and his two friends set out on their "Bummel" (1900): "In favour of the duel, seriously considered, there are many points to be urged. But the Mensur serves no good purpose whatever. It is childishness, and the fact of its being a cruel and brutal game makes it none the less childish. . . . The Mensur is, in fact, the *reductio ad absurdum* of the duel; and if the Germans themselves cannot see that it is funny, one can only regret their lack of humour."[2] This critique may offer a clue to the attractions of the *Mensur* in Twain's wide eyes. It has some of the quiet intensity, incomprehensible to adults, of the child's adventures evoked in *Huckleberry Finn* and *Tom Sawyer*. Indeed, Twain finds actual duelling to be more laughable. Student duelling does deserve to be taken seriously. Twain admits in *A Tramp Abroad*, his account of that tour, to being confounded by the spectacle that unfolds in front of him. He first establishes the seriousness of this phenomenon with a correspondingly careful, forensic account of the context. The details and dimensions suggest that the imperative is that of accurate, credible observation. But the meticulousness also suggests an intake of breath, a setting of the scene, the better to show off the action that is to follow:

> We crossed the river and drove up a bank a few hundred yards, then turned to the left, entered a narrow alley, followed it a hundred yards, and arrived at a two-storey public-house; we were acquainted with its outside aspect, for it was visible from the hotel. We went upstairs and passed into a large whitewashed apartment, which was perhaps fifty feet long, by thirty feet wide and twenty or twenty-five high. It was a well-lighted place. There was no carpet. Across one end and down both sides of the room extended a row of tables, and at these tables some fifty or seventy-five students were sitting.[3]

The unpretentious ordinariness of this setting renders all the more outlandish the violent encounters, unprovoked by any hostility, that duly take place. Twain's eagerness to tell us exactly what the place looked like renders all the more plausible and sincere his failure to account for what then happens there. He is describing manners utterly alien to the American mind, but these students are also strangers to those whom they fight and, in a sense, to themselves, by the time they step out, covered in protective gear, their faces alone exposed: "These weird apparitions had been handsome youths, clad in fashionable attire fifteen minutes before, but now they did not resemble any beings one ever sees unless in nightmares."[4]

Twain is restrained, refraining from speculation as to the causes or effects of this practice within the traditions of Germany.[5] But then he finds he takes pleasure in observing the skill of the combatants in their bouts, paraphrased as "wonderful turmoil." He observes himself as he watches these duels, perhaps surprised to find that he watches the engagements "with rapt interest and strong excitement." Twain cannot take his eyes off this compelling spectacle, even though it makes him flinch and blanch with every blow. Captivated by "the stir and turmoil, and the music of the steel," he finds it more satisfying than *Lohengrin*, a performance of which he had seen just before. It is in part the ability of these fencers to move seamlessly between urbanity and ferocity that impresses him. He is moved to remark that "the world in general looks

upon the college duels as very farcical affairs." By contrast, he prefers
to conclude that "it is a farce which has quite a grave side to it." The
same mismatch of form and content, cause and consequence, is at
work: "All the customs, all the laws, all the details pertaining to the
student duel are quaint and naïve. The grave, precise and courtly ceremony with which the thing is conducted, invests it with a sort of
antique charm." These anonymous, self-effacing figures transfix
Twain. Student duelling ought to be ridiculous. Yet for rather mysterious reasons, it commands his respect. Twain, for once rather tongue-
tied, can only confess limply that "the duel has a singular fascination
about it somewhere," in part because honor by no means compels students to fight. This scene, and the silent gravity it manifests, prompts
an exclamation confined to a footnote:

> How strangely are comedy and tragedy blended in this life! I had not
> been home a full-hour after witnessing those playful sham-duels,
> when circumstances made it necessary for me to get ready immedi-
> ately to assist personally at a real one—a duel with no effeminate
> limitations in the matter of results, but a battle to the death. An ac-
> count of it, in the next chapter, will show the reader that duels be-
> tween boys for fun and duels between men in earnest are very
> different affairs.[6]

Suddenly the reader is transported, on a footnote, across the Rhine.
Twain seems, all of a sudden, to be in Paris, where he is invited to
attend a duel as a second, a signal honor. Twain begins by telling us
that the modern French duel "is in reality one of the most dangerous
institutions of our day: "Since it is always fought in the open air, the
combatants are nearly sure to catch cold." Courageously, Twain agrees
to act as a second for a gentleman by the name of Gambetta in a duel
he is to fight with Fourtou. After the silent gravity of the student
encounters in Germany impressed itself, now the verbosity of the
would-be French duellists is all the more striking. Gambetta is agonizing over the choice of his dying words, assuming that he will be
giving a valedictory speech, but trusting that he will have time to deliver it. The last words that he rehearses are ironically at odds with the
status of the duel itself: "I die for my God, for my country, for freedom
of speech, for progress, and the universal brotherhood of man!" Twain

persuades Gambetta to cut down his antemortem words to a simpler formulation: "I die that France may live."[7]

Prolixity is in inverse proportion to potency, as subsequently in Westerns. Twain, no doubt playing up to the American reputation for uncomplicated savagery, now proposes that the two men duel by axe. He next proposes Gatling guns, at fifteen paces, as conducive to a verdict. He then moves from proposing rifles to suggesting double-barreled shotguns and Colt's navy revolvers, all of which are, by turns, rejected. The author emphasizes the self-consciousness with which the duel is fought and the way peripheral questions of detail have replaced the fight itself. This is a burlesque duel, in the tradition of Flaubert and Stendhal. The duel has degenerated into a composite of clichés and set pieces. Accordingly, it is solemnly agreed that the duel will not be fought at dawn but at half past nine, presumably allowing for a large *petit déjeuner.*

This evocation of a French duel foreshadows the risible encounter described in an unfinished comical story by Jules Renard.[8] Both writers seem to place the accent on a vainglorious French disposition, all the more flagrant after the humiliation of the Franco-Prussian War. The duel, a mannered, precious custom, is hopelessly at odds with the efficiencies required of modern warfare.

Sword fighting in Europe may seem to be a curious pastime. Americans are perhaps particularly unimpressed by such a way of dignifying violence. Twain's contemporary and compatriot Ambrose Bierce included an entry on the duel in his *Devil's Dictionary* (published from 1881 onward), which, after defining it as "a formal ceremony preliminary to the reconciliation of two enemies," adds this laconic observation: "A long time ago a man lost his life in a duel."[9]

Twain's mockery is inventive. He belittles the French by scaling down their weapons to ridiculous proportions. Many texts have featured men who do not fit their weapons. Smollett's works feature men whose swords are far too long for them. Here, for the first time, but with the same comical payoff, the pistols are minuscule: "He fished out of his vest pocket a couple of little things which I carried to the light and ascertained to be pistols. They were single-barrelled and silver-mounted, and very dainty and pretty. I was not able to speak for emotion." Twain manages to argue for a reduction in the proposed distance from sixty-five to all of thirty-five yards. He hands the pistol back to his principal, placing it "all lonely and forlorn, in the centre of the vast solitude of his palm."[10]

Shots are exchanged. Gambetta, a portly man, falls back on Twain, leaving him with a broken rib, among other injuries. Twain, however, makes a good recovery, in time to hobble onto a reception and triumphal march, after which he concludes," I would rather be a hero of a French duel than a crowned and sceptred monarch."[11] This is a telling jibe in the 1870s, implying that the French had shed their kings, only to obsess themselves all the more with honor and pomp. Twain declares himself to be "the only man who had been hurt in a French duel in forty years." The piece ends, like *Madame Bovary* and *The Three Musketeers*, with the announcement that "the Cross of the Legion of Honour has been conferred" on him. But, as he adds, "few escape that distinction."[12] Twain suggests that the duel provides a personal compensation for national misfortune. Honor is the refuge and the balm for a defeated people. The Légion d'honneur, initiated by Napoleon in 1802, is the ultimate bourgeois accolade. The award conferred on the author at the end seals the new status of the duel and confirms the descent of the point of honor from noble prerogative to bourgeois farce.

The effects of these two duels are, in each case, inversely proportional to the causes. While the grandeur of the "proper" duel slides into pomposity and then bathos, a mere sport can, conversely, be endowed with surprising gravitas and nobility. The duel illuminates and exaggerates national characteristics. We could ascribe the contrasting scenes to the fact that Twain, readily impressed and enchanted by sword fighting, was perhaps always less susceptible to the European way with guns. Or perhaps he admires and praises German duellists largely in order to mock the pretensions of their French counterparts. On this evidence, the French fight serious duels frivolously, while the Germans fight frivolous duels seriously.

It was not, however, essential to travel from the United States to an imagined past or to contemporary Europe in order to see the appeal of an antiquated form of honor to individuals incapable of bearing its weight. For even in the New World, there were those who, obsessed by ancestry and class, took inordinate pride in anything preceded by the word "old," harking back to a world that never was. Some American gentlemen, although (or perhaps because) they could not be festooned with noble titles, strenuously kept up the notion of the gentleman.[13] The skein of absurdities and delusions that supports chivalry, or a debased contemporary version of it, is pilloried no less in Twain's later, even darker story *Pudd'nhead Wilson*, published in 1894.

We are introduced at the outset to the chief denizens of the small slaveholding town of Dawson's Landing, in Missouri. York Leicester Driscoll, judge of the County Court, his profession and title notwithstanding, is devoted to the "code." Such is his embodiment and caricature of medieval European practices, Driscoll is bound to be devoted to the ethic of duelling: "To be a gentleman—a gentleman without stain or blemish—was his only religion, and to it he was always faithful."[14] Another lawyer and old Virginian grandee by the name of Pembroke Howard, the judge's best friend, is, likewise, "a man always courteously ready to stand up before you in the field if any act or word of his had seemed doubtful or suspicious to you, and explain it with any weapon you might prefer from brad-awls to artillery."[15] Percy Northumberland Driscoll, the judge's brother, is the only one of these gentlemen to have had a child, after losing a succession of boys and girls to illness and disease. The little boy, named Thomas à Becket Driscoll, is born into this childless, sterile world, only to be exchanged with Valet de Chambre, a boy born on the same day to one of Driscoll's slaves, Roxy.

In this story, nothing takes its rightful place. Babies are exchanged; Pudd'nhead Wilson, the brightest character in the town, is derided for his foolishness (hence the unkind nickname). Chivalry amounts to a set of strange scruples in an otherwise insensitive society. Thackeray was amused by the conjunction of rapaciously worldly actions alongside high-minded pretensions to honor. In *Barry Lyndon*, he briefly alluded to the coexistence of high principles and slavery. Twain's novel amplifies that incongruity to a deafening degree, hearing another such dissonance in the slave-owning, duel-fighting dominions of the southern states.

These proud descendants of the First Families are bound to be confounded by the redheaded young man from New York State, a lawyer by the name of David Wilson, who settles one day in their midst. His collection of fingerprints, with which he will solve the mystery of the

murder that takes place by revealing the true identity of the perpetrator, is a source of ridicule and bafflement in the small town. Just as
the precision of Colt's modern guns blasts away the pompous practices
of the knights in *A Connecticut Yankee in King Arthur's Court* (1889),
so the latest forensic methods, promoted by Francis Galton, secure the
truth and guarantee justice in a society where duelling merely accen-
tuates divisions in class and perpetuates confusion and folly.[16] In this
world where people are chattels, duelling is an appropriately ostentatious and exclusive way of showing one's class and one's commitment
to honor. Its conjunction with slave owning is particularly ironic and
grotesque; its contrast to the quiet precision of fingerprinting is stark.

A strange farcical duel now occurs when the town receives a visit
from a set of noble Italian twins, Counts Luigi and Angelo Capello. One
of them kicks Tom Driscoll (who is actually Roxy's son, Chambers),
and, when he refuses to fight a duel, his supposed father, Judge Driscoll,
outraged at the stain to his family honor, steps in. It is *Le Cid* back to
front, as father deputizes for son. A duel ensues. Shots are exchanged
but to no effect.

The town of Dawson's Landing is delighted and honored to have
staged this duel and aches to see a rematch. The provincial thrill conferred by the duel in this sleepy town on the Mississippi anchors Twain's
account within the long comical tradition of duels that elicit bourgeois
or rural stupefaction. Yet, even Roxy, a black, enslaved woman, who is
canny and undeceived, can find the duel a marvelous source of excitement. Her breathless vernacular account of the fight is unique in the
literature devoted to duelling yet also characteristic in the way the action eclipses and renders the actors anonymous, as the bullets ricochet.

> Happen dis-away. I 'uz a-sett'n' here kinder dozin' in de dark, en *che-
> bang!* goes a gun, right out dah. . . . En treckly dey squared off en give
> de word, en bang-bang went de pistols, en de twin he say, "Ouch!"—hit
> him on de han' dis time—en I hear dat same bullet go spat! Ag'in' de
> logs under de winder; en de nex' time they shoot, de twin say, "Ouch!"
> ag'in, en I done it too, 'ca'se de bullet glance on his cheek-bone en
> skip up her en glance on de side o'de winder en whiz right acrost
> my face en tuck de hide off'n my nose.[17]

The duel is a counterproductive farce, as it was in *A Tramp Abroad*.
And, once again, the injuries are sustained not by the participants but

by the spectators. Roxy's son, with incredulity, asks whether she stood there all the time, watching this dangerous showdown: "Dat's a question, ain't it! What else would I do? Does I git a chance to see a duel every day?"[18] Not for the first time, any moral reservations provoked by the institution of the duel are forgotten amid the raw excitement of the spectacle. Excluded from participation in a duel by her class, gender, race, and civic status, Roxy nevertheless fully shares the town's enthusiasm for this event. Moreover, when her son, whom she exchanged with that of the slave-owning family, refuses to fight, she suspects that it is the slave blood in him that is rebelling against this act. She turns out to be no less concerned with honor and decorum than the little town's pompous patricians.

The duel, once again, polarizes in fascinatingly equivocal ways. This is a world where black and white, literally on this occasion, turn out to be interdependent, even if they appear to be utterly distinct and remote from one another. Twain's story flowed from, but flooded out, a comical account inspired by Ang and Cheng Bunker, the original Siamese twins, who had settled in the States, where they too kept slaves. In the story "Those Extraordinary Twins," a version of *Pudd'nhead Wilson* which was superseded by it, the duel between Judge Driscoll and the twins takes on an even more farcical form. In this version, the twins, Angelo and Luigi, are conjoined, so there are, in effect, three principals in this duel. Ang and Cheng raised numerous practical questions about the day-to-day management of their lives. Twain tries to envisage how a duel with just one of the twins might take place.

In these texts, the movement between comedy and tragedy occurs with disconcerting suddenness, leaving the misshapen text to resemble the grotesquely deformed body of the quarrelsome Siamese twins it is evoking. *Pudd'nhead Wilson*, admits Twain, seemingly both surprised and disconcerted by the rebellion against his sovereignty as author, "changed itself from a farce to a tragedy while I was going along with it, . . . a most embarrassing circumstance." But the latter does not supplant the former, and we are left, ultimately, with "two stories in one, a farce and a tragedy."[19]

Twain's story, like the others, is an avowedly grotesque hybrid. The author's interest in interchangeable duplicates and in divided or rival selves accounts, in part, for his attention to the duel. Fundamental to these texts is, in each case, a duel that, tragicomical and Janus-like, is itself a set of embattled, conjoined twins. Of course, this interest extends to, or rather stems from, his own creative duplication, in which the authorial persona chosen by Samuel Clemens not only is a doppelgänger but says so: Twain.[20]

Renamed Mark Twain, Samuel Clemens has also been dubbed the "American Cervantes."[21] If Cervantes mounted a lethal assault on chivalry, his American successor aspired to finishing it off with bullets to its head, just as it risked twitching back into life. But Twain would not be the last writer to administer such blows. The death of chivalry would continue, periodically, to be announced. In fact, as Twain himself might have said, killing off the spirit of chivalry is the easiest thing in the world—it has been done hundreds of times.

Maupassant, "Un duel" (1883) and "Un lâche" (1884): France versus Prussia; Vicomte de Signoles versus Himself

First published in 1883, "Un duel," the short story of a Franco-German encounter, could not be further away from the French and German duels experienced, five years earlier, in *A Tramp Abroad*. A little over a decade has lapsed since the Franco-Prussian War, in which Maupassant was conscripted. Writing in the aftermath of a humiliating defeat for France, Maupassant rations his words. Indeed, thanks to its economy, the short story is an eminently suitable vehicle for depicting a modern duel. A duel contested with pistols is over quickly, defying descriptive capacities, terminated before the reader can quite understand what has happened.

The short story is a form typically without heroes, in which the prevailing mood is often loneliness.[22] "Un duel" offers us an unlikely hero. Duels can place an ordinary man in an extraordinary situation. Yet the rules and restrictions render it impossible to regard him as a hero of any traditional variety. In "Un lâche," seemingly a pendant to this story, Maupassant inverts the trajectory—a reputable gentleman is dismally unable to fight a duel he has nevertheless engineered.

France has been defeated and occupied by the Germans. The first trains have started to leave Paris for the newly drawn-up borders. On one of them sits Monsieur Dubuis, reading his newspaper; opposite him, a pair of English tourists, reading aloud from their guidebook. The

train is carrying them through a devastated, war-torn landscape to
Switzerland, where Dubuis will meet up with his family, which has
taken refuge there. When their train makes an intermediate stop at a
small town, a strapping, red-bearded Prussian soldier, a member of the
victorious occupying forces in France, enters their compartment, his
saber brushing the running board as he enters. Kleist's Rotbart rides
again. The Prussian soldier begins to brag. As they pass a village, he
tells the company that he killed twelve Frenchmen and took one hundred prisoners there. He boasts (in grammatically perfect French) of
Prussia's supremacy and revels in the misery of France. Then, suddenly,
he rests one of his jackboots on one of Dubuis's thighs. When the train
comes to a halt at another station, the Prussian asks Dubuis to fetch
him some tobacco, promising a tip for his trouble. Dubuis runs along
the platform and enters another compartment. At the next stop, the
German finds the Frenchman and attempts to cut his moustache to
smoke the whiskers in his pipe. There follows a struggle as the portly
Monsieur Dubuis wrestles with him. When it finishes, and the German
officer has got his breath back, he demands a duel by pistol. They have
now arrived in Strasbourg, and they each agree to alight, find two seconds, and duel before the train sets off again. While the Prussian finds
two fellow officers, the two English onlookers agree to act as Dubuis's
seconds, although they are rather anxious about missing their connection. Swiftly, then, they make the arrangements. Dubuis is promptly
placed at twenty paces from his adversary:

> A voice shouted:
> "Fire!"
> Mr. Dubuis fired, randomly, without waiting, and he noticed to
> his amazement that the Prussian standing opposite him tottered,
> threw his arms up, and fell flat onto his face. He had killed him.[23]

The English pair escorts Dubuis back to the station and, joyously, they
step back onto the train.

Death greets the Prussian in the pluperfect tense. An accidental
hero, Dubuis slays the nameless Prussian, without ever having held a
pistol before. Typical of Maupassant's stories, the style is unobtrusively
chaste. All the more striking then are the occasional similes in this
story. In its first sentence, France, defeated and occupied, is described

as "palpitating, like a defeated wrestler at the knee of the victor."[24] By personifying the nation thus in the opening sentence, Maupassant perhaps licenses the reader to view the ensuing fight between two persons in turn as a rematch between the nations, which will gratify his French readers by restoring their pride. Maupassant would seem to have appointed Dubuis as an unlikely champion for his vanquished nation. His first name is never revealed. Nor does the narrator relax the formality as the story unfolds and start, as one might expect, to call him plain Dubuis. The narrator thereby maintains throughout a respectful detachment from this character, while emphasizing that he is a bourgeois gentleman who deserves to be treated with dignity. This distance also helps to preserve him as a French archetype, rather than as a specific character. The Prussian soldier is not allowed a name, so he too may be seen as a representative of his nation's forces.

The title "Un Duel" promises the encounter of two individuals, but a trinity of nationalities is in play here. The English spectators, appointed as seconds, join the ensemble. The addition of these English folk provides a pair of *repoussoir* figures, observers who might mirror and authorize our own response to the fight. However, it also reinforces a sense that this story has the potential to allegorize the wider struggle of nations, just as Twain's Gambetta seems to offer a fictional version of the historical personage.

Yet the duel could hardly be described as heroic. Dubuis's paunch, his robotic movements as he is moved into position before firing, and his apparent incompetence all render grotesque the events described. Dubuis exacts revenge on the Prussians but also perhaps retaliates against Twain, with a portly counterpart to his fat Gambetta. Nor is the outcome an affirmation of Anglo-French warmth. There is no real entente here. The Englishmen are entirely self-serving, amoral observers who do not come to the assistance of their beleaguered neighbor. The Englishmen are described as portly types, a familiar French tribute to the hefty English diet, as in Huysmans's *A rebours*, although the French were not alone in being impressed by the appetite and the corresponding girth of Englishmen in this period.[25] One of the Englishmen, opening an umbrella in order to protect his pale skin against the sun, watches this miniature Franco-Prussian struggle, curious, eager, and, naturally, ready to place a bet on the outcome. A first attempt at constructing a Channel tunnel was discontinued in 1881, two years before the publication of this story, owing to fears that the French might use such a tunnel to invade England. Relations between these two sides of the triangle were barely less tense, while British fears of a possible German invasion were in turn exploited by George Tomkyns Chesney's best-selling book, *The Battle of Dorking* (1871).

It would seem facile, however tempting, to conclude that Dubuis's victory allows a fantasy of defeat reversed and honor regained or should lead us to infer that we are all latently heroic. Rather than avenging the defeated French, Dubuis's single, fatal shot points instead to the cruel arbitrariness of the armed struggle. The duel then is a subset of a wider war. Indeed, Alain Corbin has shown how Prussians could, in the minds of ordinary French people, stand for higher authority and, however perverse it may seem, come to be interchanged with counter-revolutionary aristocrats.[26]

So the duel is triumphantly appropriated by an ordinary man, a humble merchant, in an emphatically modern bourgeois setting, where umbrellas are carried and honor is satisfied, as trains are changed. The duel, inserted into the train timetable with an efficiency that might impress the Germans and with a speedy nonchalance that would have delighted Dumas, is comically abbreviated. Modern bourgeois life can still just about accommodate a duel.

Maupassant uses the railway carriage as a vehicle to instigate social collisions, as he would do in "Boule de suif." Maupassant, no doubt indebted to Jules Verne's railway duel in *Around the World in Eighty Days*, contrasts the modernity of the setting with the archetypally timeless, not to say anachronistic, nature of the contest. But this duellist is a guileless, artless hero, who is indebted to the randomness of the pistol, rather than any unsuspected skill.

"Un lâche" was first published a year after "Un duel," in 1884. It is tempting to see these two stories as complementary parts of a diptych. Indeed, perhaps relying on the simple transparency of his previous titles, such as "Un duel," Maupassant establishes an ironic effect with this title, both apposite and inadequate. It is an unforgiving title, when the story under its heading will show compellingly, perhaps even sympathetically, the pressure exerted by fear. "Un lâche" is a story in which the challenge of exploring and nuancing the psychological complexity of the duel is triumphantly met.

Viscount Gontran-Joseph de Signoles is the polar opposite of Monsieur Dubuis. He is handsome, noble, and experienced. Handsome Signoles's reputation for prowess with both arms is well established. It is, however, the pistol that he favors. " 'When I fight,' he would say, 'I shall choose the pistol. With this arm, I am sure to kill my man.' "[27] His assurance is rendered all the more indubitable by the verbatim quotation, as though having uttered them so often, these words were now axiomatic. But when his thoughts are vocalized to himself in an inner monologue, it perhaps also betrays a certain obtuseness. The dream of Monsieur Jourdain, the *bourgeois gentilhomme* (that of killing, with certainty, complete with the associated warranty of not being killed), has apparently come true. But this is a story of a *gentilhomme* turned *bourgeois*. Maupassant's predecessors have shown numerous examples of bourgeois would-be duellists, prone to fears, vulnerable to a lack of savoir faire. Maupassant is famous for his bourgeois and lower-bourgeois characters. Unusually, his interest is focused here on an aristocrat of undoubted pedigree, but he brings to his understanding of this man the same merciless acumen. Moreover, the setting of this initial encounter is unmistakably bourgeois. The scene unfolds in Tortoni's ice-cream parlor. The Vicomte does not like the way a man is looking at the ice cream of one the ladies present. Her own husband does not react, underlining the strangely tangential nature of what follows. It is the most fleeting, melting, absurdly perishable of pretexts for a duel. And yet the duel will commemorate and freeze this moment, lending it retrospective significance. But the ice cream serves also as a metonymic equivalent of the man's courage and substance. A "glace" can be a mirror as well as an ice cream, and the pages that follow confirm an impression that Signoles is confronting himself and his own narcissistic fears in embarking on this duel.

Now the narrator proceeds to place the emphasis on the mechanized, automated responses of the patrons in the restaurant privileged to see this encounter. The inexorable process has been initiated. After the offending man swears, "three waiters pivoted on their heels like spinning tops," while women at the bar turn round in unison "as though they were two automata responding to the same handle."[28]

Wound up, the mechanism of the duel is ready to unwind. A scene designed to testify to noble freedom acquires a mechanistic element, and thanks to "the mechanical superimposed onto a living thing" (le mécanique plaqué sur le vivant), as Henri Bergson famously defined it, the scene descends into comedy.[29] The duel inflicts onto the proudest, freest men inexorable conditions that turn them variously into chessmen, puppets, and robots.

Our Viscount retrieves a card with the name of the man, "Georges Lamil, 51 rue Moncey." The narrator tells us simply that, upon his return home, "he took a penknife and pricked the printed name in the middle, as though he had stabbed someone."[30] It is a beautifully telling detail. As we will soon appreciate, his aggression is reserved for and sublimated in this innocuous action. It is the only harm he will ever cause Lamil. It is a classic instance of transferal, an action characteristic of the narcissist who, unable to commit himself as he should, resorts to another action in its place. Just as Lenski dreamt of a dart nobly piercing its victim in a duel that he knew would be fought by pistols, so the Vicomte subconsciously favors this means of attack over the actual prospective duel by pistol, about which he has presentiments to which he now begins to admit: "So he would have to fight! (Il fallait se battre) Would he choose the sword or the pistol, for he considered himself to be the man insulted. With the sword, he would run fewer risks; but with the pistol, he had a chance to make his opponent shrink back." Maupassant's free indirect discourse starts to reveal fissures in the Vicomte's mind. Even the exclamation mark betrays a forced attempt at cheerfulness and, in conjunction with the purposeful "so," a slightly strenuous effort at enthusiasm, betrayed by the impersonal "il fallait." In the subsequent inner deliberation, a first hint of fatal hesitation announces itself.

> "Is it possible to be afraid, in spite of oneself?"
>   And that doubt came over him, that anxiety, that terror; what would happen if a dominant, irresistible force, more potent than his own will, were to tame him?[31]

The prominence of synonyms (inquiétude, épouvante; dominatrice, irrésistible), all delaying the formulation of the question, let alone an answer to it, evoke a prevaricating, irresolute mind and suggest restless

obfuscation. His doubts are such that he needs to find different words
for them. The circumlocutions betray that fatal propensity to over-
complicate. No less ironic is the verb "discuss" in the narrator's next
inconspicuous sentence, which is followed by a series of terse, intransi-
tive verbs:

> They discussed the conditions.
>   The colonel asked:
>   You want a serious duel?
>   The Count responded:
>   Very serious.
>   The Marquis replied:
>   Are you keen on pistols?
>   Yes.
>   Count: Twenty paces to order and raising the arm instead of
> lowering it. Exchange of bullets until a serious injury occurs.
>   . . . and they left.[32]

The stichomythia—a sequence of bullet points—in this staccato dialogue is itself an ironic premonition. This is to remain the only exchange in the story. Unlike "Un duel," which could go either way, the
title hanging over the short story creates its own relentless pressure.
There follows a passage notable for the pileup of reflexive verbs: "When
he felt he was alone once again, it seemed to him that he was going
mad. . . . He got up again with a start and went away, feeling incapable
of putting two ideas together, of making his mind up, of making any
kind of decision.[33]

But this story, swimming in reflexive verbs, is crowned by the most
apposite reflexive of all: *se battre*. Maupassant seizes the potential of
this reflexive verb. To fight is to fight against oneself. "So, he was going
to fight [se battre]! He could avoid that no longer. What then was happening inside of him? He wanted to fight, he had that intention and
that resolution firmly held."[34] The verve and energy in that exclamation mark are promptly dissipated by the following sentence. The
multiplication of the nouns, or near synonyms (not content with an
"intention," he also has a "resolution") again hints at procrastination.

The farcical situation that occurs when Russian duellists resort to
some fictional account to work out how to go about the practicalities

risks recurring here. Signoles does not look to poetry or novels for inspiration or information, but he does turn to a little library of duelling manuals. He takes up *Le code du duel* by Chatauvillard and, in a nice recursive self-referential gesture, Baron de Vaux's volume, to which Maupassant himself supplied the preface. Georges Lamil fortunately does not feature in this gallery of sharpshooters. Ironically, the few volumes that show, quite dispassionately, how to go about duelling seem to have acted as a greater deterrent than all the previous books that never tired of pointing out its horrors and condemning its exponents. " 'It's impossible. I cannot fight in this way.' "[35] The sense of loneliness is compounded by the quotation marks—for there is no one to whom he is speaking. Equally, the quotation marks make the reflection seem rather ponderous. The Vicomte's counterparts in the past (such as Farquhar's Brazen) were big talkers, swaggering braggarts. Their cowardice is redeemed by their linguistic exuberance. Their stories of feats, imagined rather than described, turn them into rather splendid trumpeters of their own glory. Here, on the other hand, Maupassant depicts a character who, in the middle of Paris, is alone. He has no audience, no interlocutors. He speaks to himself. And he fights himself. An atomized individual, a Vicomte seemingly divested of relations, an embodiment of anomie. His oscillation between strident assertion and self-doubt recalls the agonies evoked by Pushkin. Yet he cannot even enjoy the pathetic consolation of Lenski, who feels, however absurdly or inarticulately, that he is fulfilling some sort of poetic destiny, as he leafs through Schiller. Instead, "He looked down the muzzle at the little, deep black hole that spits out death."[36] But another German writer is spectrally present here. As Nietzsche wrote, a few years later, "He who fights with monsters should be careful lest he thereby become a monster. And if you gaze long into an abyss, the abyss will also gaze into you."[37] The barrel of a gun is just such a little abyss. Maupassant's depiction of failing or illusory willpower collapsing under irrational and self-destructive fears seems almost to be an enactment of Nietzsche's aphorisms designed to expose fallacies of free will. For Nietzsche, the genealogy of our decisions necessarily remains mysterious. We underestimate, at our peril, the primacy of the unconscious and the affective elements that go into apparently moral decisions and judgments. Even our most seemingly deliberate thoughts are not summoned imperiously by the self, for, as he puts it, with seductive simplicity, in *Beyond Good and Evil*, "A thought comes when *it* wants, and not when *I* want."[38]

This story strips the duellist of his will, freedom, and autonomy, proud bulwarks (particularly in the French tradition) both against repressive laws and against the ordering dictates of bourgeois convention and public opinion. For the Germans, ridding oneself of the duel and its mannered, anachronistic ways liberated them from the corset of French *courtoisie*. But for the French, the duel remained the most beautiful celebration of self-determining defiance, be that of one's adversary, the law, or oneself. It had inspired Chateaubriand, Hugo, and Dumas, all literary descendants of Corneille, to venture onto the same territory as him. Maupassant's subversion (like the comical bout related by Jules Renard) is, then, all the more brilliant and daring, such is the accumulated weight of assumptions according to which the duel remains the privileged expression of noble freedom.

"Il voulait se battre." Grimly and literally, this wish is met. The reflexive verb realizes itself in all its majesty. The Vicomte kills himself. He had elected to fight the duel by pistol, fortified by the thought that, with this arm, he was sure of killing, as he called him, "my man" man. Unfortunately for him, the patronizing possessive is all too true: he cannot miss. And he does kill his man, in killing himself. Suicide would seem to be at once a product of cowardice and courage, which weep into each other, like two scoops of ice cream.

In a review of the "progress" of duelling, published in 1822, the anonymous author already observed a tendency toward isolation, as the duellist, hitherto a figure who sought publicity and engaged in combat in the presence of spectators, becomes an essentially solitary figure. While the knight of chivalry engaged to protect and defend the honor of others, "the modern champion fights for himself alone, unmindful of those to whom his life is valuable."[39]

The nobleman here, conscious of family and of ancestry, has, to our knowledge, no friend or companion, neither brother nor sister, in whom he might confide. Monsieur Dubuis, we know, has a wife and children, as well as compatriots, in the form of the humiliated French. Dubuis acts as a champion for the nation, but in "Un lâche," Signoles is not fighting to redress a wrong in which he has little personal interest. On the contrary, he is fighting to redress a nonwrong in which he has a highly, unaccountably personal interest. While the duellist of old entered combat "for the honour of conquest only," the modern duellist engages largely for negative reasons: that is "to avoid the imputation of cowardice, of which perhaps he was never suspected."[40] The modern duellist is then substantially more suspect than were his medieval progenitors. Smollett and his ilk depicted a society in which men were engaged in a perpetual combat with one another; Freud diagnoses a society in which people are engaged in an inner combat with themselves. By the time that Maupassant and Conrad are penning their stories, the duel has become inexplicable to the duellists themselves. The frivolous duels of the eighteenth century might not be comprehensible to the reader, but he or she could yet assume that these aristocrats enjoyed some higher sense of the mysteries and rites that escaped them.

André Breton declared a random pistol shot, fired into a crowd, to be the ultimate surrealist act.[41] The count is sending us on our way to André Gide's *acte gratuit* and eventually Meursault's incomprehensible act in Albert Camus's *L'Étranger*, the work of a man estranged from himself as from others, even if the Arab whom he kills is, technically, the "foreigner" to which the title could be alluding. These men take up arms in order to satisfy some part of themselves that cannot be understood. They are ultimately unaccountable to themselves. Signoles is an ancestor of those murderers, even if he "only" kills himself.

In "Un duel," Maupassant represents a more or less impromptu encounter, in a story from which his taste and talent for irony seem momentarily to have lapsed. But they are, after all, effaced the better to emphasize these very aspects in the other story. The Count appears to fear the duel more than death. Or he fears fear itself more than death. Fear and valor are no longer distributed according to class. Maupassant offers us a brilliant pathology of the coward. It is not just the sovereignty of fear but its intermittence, its own uncertain duel with courage, that intrigues and disconcerts here. A born coward would perhaps not challenge someone to a duel in the first place. A thoroughgoing poltroon would be one-dimensional. As Acres recognizes in *The Rivals*, "Valour will come and go."[42] Its flux seems hard to predict. This leads to further questions. When is our will our own? When is a man himself? Rousseau asserted, controversially, that, whereas women are always women, men are only, properly, men on occasions.[43] He may be unmanned at the most inconvenient junctures.

Maupassant's story anticipates by a decade or so Conrad's examination of cowardice in *Lord Jim* and Schnitzler's famous monologue, "Leutnant Gustl" (both 1900): Gustl, like the Vicomte, finds himself in an impossible situation from which only suicide will extract him. While he is fetching his jacket from the cloakroom, after attending an oratorio (for which he has a free ticket and in which he is otherwise not interested), he jostles another member of the audience, a baker in fact, who calls him a silly lad ("du dummer Bub"), a verbal gauntlet.[44] He roams the streets of Vienna all night, realizing, with horror, that, in accordance with the code's prescription, he will have to kill himself because the baker is too lowly to be *satisfaktionsfähig*. However, in a grotesquely comic twist, he is spared the need to commit suicide, an act for which he does not have the heart, by the surprising and gratifying news that the baker, the man responsible for the insult and the only witness to it, has died from a heart attack that very night.

In each case, we see a man tormented, to the point of having to commit suicide, by an internalized social obligation, yet we see no society. The Vicomte is not seen in conversation with friends or colleagues; Gustl, likewise, drifts around the empty streets of Vienna at night on his own. The first-person form of the *monologue intérieur*, in which his story takes expression, makes him seem lonelier yet.

The Count, in common with Gustl, appears to be suffering from what Heinz Kohut has called "narcissistic rage."[45] This may manifest itself in the need to right a perceived wrong or to take revenge on someone, unnecessarily. Narcissists love their image, not their real self, and, as in the case of Narcissus himself, this preoccupation can lead to their deaths. The prospective duel has exposed a mighty gap between self and image. The Vicomte has an exaggerated investment in his image, ultimately at the expense of the self. Under the pressure of these demands, the narcissist can barely come to terms with the realization that he is not quite the man others might think he is or indeed the man he himself thought he was. Suicide is the ultimate self-oriented, self-absorbed act. By killing himself, no one can threaten that image he has constructed. That adjective in the very first sentence, "le beau

Signoles," is already quietly deferring to his grandiose self-image and, thanks to the understated magic of free indirect discourse, is borrowing a term that seemingly conveys the accepted social description. It is essential to destroy himself in order to preserve that picture everyone has of him. Maupassant's little story anticipates by just a few years Oscar Wilde's drama of narcissism, *The Picture of Dorian Gray* (1890).

In some cultures, such as that of the samurai, suicide is honorable, a badge of courage. Many critics of duelling maintained that duellists were cowards, not brave enough to stand up to public opinion. In Maupassant's story, as in his own *Bel-ami* and in Schnitzler's "Leutnant Gustl," it is emphatically not their conscience that makes cowards of these men. Neither man claims to have been persuaded that the prospective duel might actually be unnecessary and illegal. Neither man has qualms or inhibitions about such costs. They are not even enlisted as excuses or disguises to camouflage their fears. Fears take them by surprise. In an earlier story, "Sur l'eau," Maupassant's first-person narrator describes vividly how paralyzing and estranging the sudden advent of fear can be. Stranded on a boat, as a mist descends, fear takes hold of the first-person narrator, and there ensues a sort of duel between his will and that fear, which leaves him in a cataleptic sort of state: "I tried to reason with myself. I could feel very strongly the will not to be afraid, but there was in me something other than my will, and this other thing was afraid. I asked myself what I could be dreading; my brave *self* scoffed at my cowardly *self*, and I have never conceived as well as on that particular day the opposition of the two beings that are in us, one willing, the other resisting, and each prevailing by turns."[46] Fear divides the self into two, leaving it prey to an internalized battle, a civil war. Maupassant charts the way in which fear insidiously takes hold of the imagination and unmans its victim once it has crept over him. No wonder then that fear comes, usually, as a feminine noun. Maupassant, Flaubert's prodigious protégé, has then not only substantiated but surely also challenged the scantest of received ideas recorded by the master in his *Dictionary of Received Ideas:* "SUICIDE: Proof of cowardice."[47] Maupassant's brilliant short story, among its other achievements, furnishes a grand footnote to this dictionary "definition," as the received idea is given a new, cruelly ironic twist.

Conrad, "A Duel" (1908): Feraud versus D'Hubert

Napoleon, reports the narrator at the outset of Joseph Conrad's short story "A Duel," "disliked duelling," even if his "career had the quality of a duel against the whole of Europe." The emperor's hostility to the practice did not result, as we might assume, from his rational, reforming impulses but can instead be explained by two notable deficiencies: he simply "was not a swashbuckler"; likewise, he "had little respect for tradition."[48] These negative remarks immediately help to endow duelling with an aura of time-honored prestige. Duellists are cast as defiant custodians of tradition, gentlemen of flair. On these terms, it is the detractors of duelling who are found wanting.

Amid the "universal carnage" of the Napoleonic wars, two cavalry officers, by the names of Feraud and D'Hubert, pursue a private contest that is renewed over several years. In these circumstances, they fight each other "like insane artists trying to gild refined gold or paint the lily."[49] There is something mad and prodigal about the duel against a backdrop of war, yet the kinship of duellist and artist proposed by the analogy allows us to appreciate the duel as a pursuit that may be seen as curiously creative, rather than wantonly destructive. To those who have assumed that duelling was essentially an ersatz form of warfare, an occupation for officers bored by peace (hence the popularity of duelling in France throughout the peaceful period from the Napoleonic wars to the Crimean War), these duels are especially perplexing. Fought while wars are being waged on a European scale, these private duels may seem deplorably self-indulgent yet fundamentally disinterested. Conrad's soldiers may seem to be locked in petty, internecine squabbling. Alternatively, they could be seen engaging in a series of bouts, which, neither propelled by nationalistic prejudice nor driven by territorial ambition, resurrect examples of ancestral largesse and bygone valor.

These insane artists are both cavalry officers: "their connection with the high-spirited but fanciful animal which carries men into battle seems particularly appropriate," the narrator points out. This affiliation renders them eminently well suited to the demands of the duel and disposed to assimilating the curiously chivalrous element integral to single combat.[50] The duellist may be a deplorably hotheaded and irascible individual, but the more illusory his pretexts for fighting, the more imaginative the duellist.[51] Literature is then hospitable to duellists as kindred artists, who are recognizable, even from behind the writer's desk, as creative counterparts.

One of these officers, Lieutenant D'Hubert, has been deputed by his general to recall the other, Lieutenant Feraud, from his quarters, in order that he might answer claims that he has wounded a citizen in a duel. D'Hubert stops by at Feraud's quarters only to learn from a pretty girl that he is not there. Feraud is eventually traced to the salon of a smart hostess, Madame de Lionne. D'Hubert enters her elegant house and, simply by summoning Feraud away from the gathering, while he is talking to a lady, enrages him to the point that he in turn finds himself challenged to an impromptu duel. D'Hubert, astonished at the rage and impulsiveness of Feraud, nevertheless realizes that he is not at liberty to refuse to fight. In short order, they cross swords, and Feraud soon falls to the ground, wounded but not mortally.

This first duel and its preliminaries are—even within the modest compass of this short story—described in considerable detail. That detail allows us to appreciate a marked contrast between a feminine, domesticated world of delicacy and tenderness, on the one hand, and, on the other, an uncouth, even brutal male realm. The narrator fondly describes the fresh complexion and long eyelashes of the pretty girl at Feraud's house, yet she has no significant role to play in the story. The application of seemingly irrelevant detail evidently offers one canonical way of building up a realistic effect in the story. Yet these superficial details—of uniforms, spurs, polished boots, and dolmans—may also lull us into subscribing to an innocent, perhaps nostalgic view of the army as a repository of elegance and gallantry. The scene, at this early stage of the story, is painted with substantially the same palette we have seen in Dumas's *The three Musketeers*. Female grace and delicacy not only contrast with but also complement male brusquerie. The ladies are ladylike; the men are virile. But there is of course another obvious, no less satisfyingly simple antithesis in play here. The combatants are polarized in every imaginable way: D'Hubert is tall, Feraud short; the former is a restrained Picard, the latter a characteristically fiery Gascon; D'Hubert has a moustache "the colour of ripe corn," Feraud "a twisted-up jet black little moustache." This is a classic meeting of north and south and of their respective temperaments. These differences explain and are explained by their respective drinking habits: "The little Gascon, who, always sober in his potations, was as though born intoxicated with the sunshine of his vineripening country" versus "the Northman, who could drink hard on occasion, but was born sober under the watery skies of Picardy."[52] As the story unfolds across the early decades of the nineteenth century, it is clear that, politically, they are also at odds with each other. Conrad's story sticks closely to the historical account of the duelling officers, but these contrasting details were supplied by his imagination.

Conrad pits against each other two gentlemen whose respective temperaments seem to serve as test cases for the optimal duellist. Ferocious Feraud's vigor and spontaneity are formidable, but, even as he ascends to the rank of general, he remains nothing more, and nothing less, than a "fighter." The son of a blacksmith, he too strikes while the iron is hot and trusts in his instinct, careless of the consequences. Feraud is the dislocated individual yet curiously vital and affirmative in his own way. Like some Russian duellists, he is a loner, without relations, whether amorous or familial. D'Hubert, for his part, is known by his colleagues as "The Strategist."[53] His composure and sang froid will allow him to measure up to the intensity of his adversary. Each man finds in his adversary an opposite, who is complementary as well as hostile. Together, they are complete; on their own, but half of something. In that sense, the meeting of these contrasting temperaments resembles the internal duel of northern and southern impulses, warring within an individual, as traced by Conrad's contemporary Thomas Mann, author of *Tonio Kröger*, published in 1903. It is, moreover, tempting to see these polarities occurring within the same envelope as a privileged concern of an avowed *homo duplex*.[54]

The text indeed offers us this agreeable contrast in color and in style partly in order to complicate it in the pages that follow. From these polar positions, the two men gradually become linked in what D'Hubert acknowledges to be an "intimate connection."[55] Maddeningly, he finds that his hatred of Feraud assumes the intensity of an attachment. So the readily assimilable pleasures of antithesis are duly supplanted by the mysteries of a clash, which is held together by less visible, less discernible forces. The duel offers a level playing field where competing attributes, contrasting polarized personalities, meet and dissolve. Duels have been seen to be perpetuated by loathing, which cannot be appeased by the law, but Conrad brings to this story a diagnosis of hatred as an amalgam of intimacy, respect, fear, and resentment, a self-generating, self-justifying condition.

The duel gradually turns these gentlemen, attentive to females, well attired in their uniforms, when we first encounter them, into animals. They were both initially compared to the horses on which they ride into battle. But now, when Feraud fights, it is with "a fierce tigerish agility fit to trouble the stoutest heart." He sets about his opponent, snarling like an "enraged animal," an image that recalls those evocations of combat in Dumas. But Conrad cannot rest on this cliché; and he duly qualifies it, for there is, he suggests, a form of ferocity proper to humans: "He meant it with an intensity of will utterly beyond the inferior faculties of a tiger."[56]

These fights lack the effortless charm and élan of Dumas's combats. They seem more dangerous, even grotesque, and they seem less obviously relished by their narrator. Theirs is a need to fight, no mere wish. Nevertheless, the absurd unaccountability of the duel renders it human, by contrast to the struggles of animals. The single-minded concentration that it necessitates and promotes is saluted by the author. "What was more appalling than the fury of a wild beast, accomplishing in all innocence of heart a natural function, was the fixity of savage purpose man alone is capable of displaying."[57] It may seem paradoxical or grimly ironic, but the act of trying to kill a member of one's own species in cold blood appears to be a human prerogative.

The one dichotomy that Conrad does not mean us to see as an organizational principle in this story is that of right and wrong. We may be inclined to resent the hotheaded Feraud for initiating the process, but the incident that ignites the rivalry is so utterly inconsequential as to be forgotten more or less as soon as it has occurred. The duel, to which both participants have agreed, perpetuates a rivalry with no real basis. It eclipses right and wrong. Conrad's story exposes a paradox. The duel perpetuates and commemorates the subject of a disagreement but also makes it forgettable. The means outgrows the end. No one, not even the closest friends and colleagues of the two rivals, can quite understand the reasons for which this duel is renewed at intervals over so many years. Each of the participants refrains from explaining to anyone the reasons for the duel. No doubt, this is, in part, a tribute to their gentlemanly discretion, but the reader may suspect that the protagonists themselves cannot quite account for the absurdity of duels that have become their own justification.

The colonel in charge of Lieutenant D'Hubert, for one, dismisses the ongoing duel as "some silly woman story," glibly assuming that it is fought on behalf of a woman. *Cherchez la femme,* he thinks, but this turns out to be a pedestrian assumption, for the causes of the duel are immaterial. Later, when the venerable Chevalier de Valmassigne is called upon to be a second by D'Hubert, he likewise thinks it must be a *galanterie*.[58] These common misconceptions allow us to appreciate that this series of duels is prolonged for reasons that make chivalry look quaintly secondary. It is more intense and ontological than that. The duel, often a self-regardingly circular practice, acquires a life of its own, beyond the ostensible need to address grievances. It allows its protagonists to feel that they are alive, on the brink of death, and it raises their existence to a new pitch. For Feraud, the feud is integral and essential. It becomes his raison d'être, as the chivalric, gallant context—the salon, from which he is fetched at the beginning of the story, a vestige of eighteenth-century culture—is transcended. The duel seems sustained by negative reasons, the fear of being seen to be a coward. But this negative reason means that no other parties are defended or appeased. It lends an intensity to the duel that its critics perhaps fail to comprehend. This is a deadlock that cannot be broken by anyone else. Nor is the duel amenable to any mediation or arbitration.

This first inconclusive duel, itself provoked indirectly by a duel previous to this story, in turn leads to further encounters. Every duel is the same yet unique. There is no real sense that they are incremental, as the men renew their acquaintance, relying on accumulated knowledge of each other. Their experiences in the interim, of promotion through the ranks, of war, ageing, death, and indeed of each other, count for nothing. Conrad depicts the duels as discrete events, like matches in which the rules that apply elsewhere are supplanted. Therein lies some of the appeal of the duel. It rejuvenates its combatants, lifting them out of a linear existence, forcing them to live in the moment. A progression of sorts is, however, observable in the pacing of Conrad's narrative. The descriptions become more abbreviated, almost impatient. The second duel is fought in Silesia, and the antagonists, now each promoted to the rank of captain, confront each other with cavalry sabers. This bout is explicitly signaled to us as the clash of a rational mind and an instinctive approach, but both finish up in a state of utter savagery. "Dishevelled, their shirts in rags, covered with gore and hardly able to stand, they were led away forcibly by their marvelling and horrified seconds."[59] The third duel pits the men against each other on horseback, on a plain not far from Lübeck. This bout is terminated prematurely when Feraud is temporarily blinded by the blood that flows from a wound inflicted by his opponent's saber.

Meanwhile, the epic of the Napoleonic wars is transforming the political and moral landscape of Europe. Feraud and D'Hubert are swept along, upward and toward each other by the events that convulse Europe. Now we glimpse them retreating, side by side, from Moscow, gallantly supporting each other as they beat off attacks and struggle through the snow back to France. Yet Feraud's resentment never thaws. The Napoleonic wars transformed Europe, yet they cannot change these individuals. This is not just a tribute to Feraud's Gascon stubbornness but a testimony to the inexorable demands of honor and—a theme cherished by Conrad—the lack of resolution in life. The impeccable gallantry and companionship of the soldiers coexists with remorseless savagery, as these unsparingly bloody duels have shown.

The Napoleonic wars now run their course, and the two men have each reached the rank of general. Indeed, by contrast with the personages of Smollett, Dumas, or Thackeray, these figures win promotion in order to fight duels. Soldiers were not supposed to duel with opponents beneath their rank (if we overlook the fact that they were not allowed to fight anyone). Feraud is concerned that when D'Hubert becomes a captain, his rival might now elude him; D'Hubert is accordingly nettled when Feraud becomes an aide-de-camp. Now that the wars have subsided, they find themselves in highly contrasting situations. While D'Hubert is engaged to be married and contemplating a life of domestic bliss, Feraud leads a lonely, degraded existence, shambling about different cafés. Rather as Pushkin shuffles the cards, showing us the poetical side to the economist and banal or self-deceiving elements in the poet's character, so here the archetypal northerner, cold, willing to follow rules, finds himself in love and fear of losing that to a duel, while the Gascon, supposedly of a sunnier, more innocent disposition, slips into nihilistic despair.

The specter of Feraud, purposeless and disheartened now that peace has returned, recalls the eponymous forgotten warrior of Balzac's short story "Le Colonel Chabert" (1832). If the deserter became an archetype in the eighteenth century, in the subsequent decades, it is the returning soldier, deserted by civil society and domestic life, who attracts more attention. There is a new emphasis on the threshold between civilian and military life, on occasions, literally, as we see the soldier in the act of forsaking the tender, domestic charms of his wife or lover for an utterly antithetical existence. Dislocated and unrecognizable, the battle-weary soldier is the source of pathos. We can see why Feraud might want to renew combat with his old foe, but D'Hubert, the calm embodiment of reason, the calculating northern mind, is strangely susceptible to the unaccountable appeal of duelling: "He felt an irrational tenderness towards his old adversary and appreciated emotionally the murderous absurdity their encounter had introduced into his life. It was like an additional pinch of spice in a hot dish. He remembered the flavour with sudden melancholy."[60] The adjective "murderous" may mislead, for, unlike the wars that rage in the background, the duels do not kill but provide a curiously life-enhancing facet.

The final scenes contrast the intensity of male rivalry with the contentment to be found in domestic harmony. The first names of the adversaries, Armand and Gabriel, emerge eventually, as enmity matures into intimacy. D'Hubert comes to the realization that the "intimate connection" provoked by the former circumstances may offer some sort of equivalent to the intimacies offered by conjugal relations. Perhaps Conrad had been influenced by E. M. Forster's *The Longest Journey*, published a year previously in 1907, in which the generosity of male friendship is memorably contrasted with the constrictions of marriage.

A fourth, final duel now beckons between these two contrasting individuals, whose respective circumstances now polarize them yet further. After a trilogy of inconclusive clashes of blades, this duel will be fought with pistols, to the death. The two retired generals head into a wood to shoot at sight. Their duel is a reprise of war. "It was like going into battle."[61] Feraud wastes one of his bullets, as D'Hubert takes cover behind a tree. Then, in a highly unorthodox approach, D'Hubert sinks down to the ground, gently lays his pistols down, and stealthily takes out a little mirror in which he can detect any approach from behind. Feraud advances and sees his opponent prostrate on the ground, concluding that he has killed him. But when D'Hubert jumps up and Feraud, agitated, misses again, they are face-to-face, and D'Hubert has two shots to spare. It is just a shame for him that he has sprung up without remembering to pick up his pistols. Feraud stands at his mercy, though, and D'Hubert has contrived to win a duel by pistol, without firing his.

The duels, fought at first in front of people, in a pleasant garden, then recede from view; finally, stealthily, they meet in a wood. The progress of the duels perhaps mirrors, in this short story, the wider development of duels from sword to pistol and, in the same vein, from public spectacle to private affair. Conrad's short story encapsulates a variety of duels, each fought in different circumstances and, eventually, with different arms, but these iterations only underline the obduracy of the male need to fight or to hold a grudge.

We progress, in the Hogarthian sense, through successive iterations of the duel, each more brusque and unforgiving than the previous bout. This story ostensibly charts the degradation of both cavalry officers, who become increasingly grizzled and exhausted. As these men are promoted, so they are degraded. Commensurately, the descriptions of the duels accelerate. In the first clash, the attention to detail and an emphasis on appearance, both that of the protagonists and the milieu in which they move, is somewhat more leisurely. More adjectival expenditure occurs early on.

The degradation comes as a shock after the evocation of the material splendors of the military uniforms and habitats in the opening chapter. But there is a trajectory in the other direction. The brutalization constitutes a form of purification. Duels fought by sword, by saber, on chargers lose their chivalric aspect, as the duel is stripped down to its simplest form. Finally, the pistol is discarded. The duel becomes wilder, signified by the move from a garden to a forest. But it still rewards guile and intelligence.

We may have been tempted to construe the duel as a sort of luxury afforded by the Empire, a romantic act. By the end of the story, the duel

seems to respond to a different sort of imperative. It epitomizes a
need to fight that outlives patriotic duty and transcends other commitments, whether in peace or in war. In an age that still despaired
of abolishing the duel, Conrad's story is a testimony both to the unchanging nature of brutal man and to the salutary, even invigorating
quality of such challenges.

A fascination with violence when it comes draped in courtesies may
be understood against a backdrop of ugly, opportunistic attempts on
life. Conrad's earlier novel *The Secret Agent* (1907) turns on the violence of assassination, after an anarchist, Marcel Boudin, was blown
up by his own explosives in February 1894; in that same year, French
President Carnot was stabbed to death while riding through Lyons in
an open carriage; Empress Elisabeth of Austria (Sisi) was stabbed with
a four-inch needle at Geneva in 1898; Umberto I, King of Italy, was murdered in 1900; President William McKinley was shot in Buffalo, 6 September 1901. Assassinations and anarchism were rife in these years,
leaving the rituals and conventions of the duel to seem all the more
genteel by contrast. Indeed, in G. K. Chesterton's novel *The Man Who
Was Thursday* (1908), the hero, Gabriel Syme, prevents a suspected anarchist from catching a train for Paris, where (it is thought) he intends
to explode a bomb, by engaging him in a duel.[62] The protracted sword
fight that follows, complete with time-consuming courtesies, is exuberantly described. This may be a sham duel, contrived only to kill
time, but it both represents and guarantees civilization against dark
forces. Along the same lines as Verne and Maupassant, Chesterton is
tickled by a duel in a distinctly modern setting, but this salvific duel
embodies an innocent leisureliness amid threats of chaos.

"A Duel" may strike us as a rather perfunctory title for a story
which, tracing a series of encounters, fought at intervals over some
fourteen years, is stretched over a Tolstoyan canvas, but then Conrad
allows the inference that "A Duel" is indeed devoted to one ongoing
mental and ontological struggle. The successive duels are subsidiary
to and symptoms of one wider contest. The duel is once again a labo-
ratory for an inspection of the human qualities, the doses of reason and
of instinct, necessary to survival and success. Whereas eighteenth-
century writers tend to ask anxious questions about the duel, that
persistent scourge of reason, their counterparts in later decades prefer

to invite the duel to pose questions about society and man. Conrad's story, careful as it is in observing the years of the Empire, offers not so much a sociological survey of that period or place as a pathology of duellists, as men prey to a human compulsion, proud of a human prerogative. The opening sentence casually points to a characteristic symmetry between duel and war. If Napoleon's campaigns can be circumscribed in these terms, a duel can by the same token be inflated into a war. Equally, this duel between two otherwise unremarkable men acquires the grandeur and the significance of a war. It seems to symbolize and incarnate something bigger than either of them. The narrator eventually cannot resist making this analogy clear: this duel is a form of "private warfare."[63]

Conrad's story yokes together the apparently antithetical worlds of Dumas and Maupassant, the former's carefree abandon and the darker introspection of the latter. On the one hand, it is a miniaturized history of France from the height of Napoleon's success to the Restoration of the monarchy; on the other, it provides an insight into an unchanging male psyche, into the nature of fear and the almost comical absurdity of the compulsion to duel. Unusually, Conrad's story ends on a redemptive note. But that does not entirely mute the previous sequences which revealed troublingly dissonant aspects to human nature.

Conrad's tale perhaps suggests that it is ourselves we loathe when we oppose others; it is versions of ourselves rather than the opposites of them that threaten and that we feel the need to destroy. Chesterton, again, has a short story (1905) in which Dr. Hirsch is due to fight Mr. Jules Dubosc in a long-awaited duel. These gentlemen are, in every way, polar extremes. But intuiting that "things made so opposite are things that cannot quarrel," Father Brown doubts that antithetically different figures should want to seek to cancel each other out.[64] Theirs is just too improbably beautiful, schematic, and simple an opposition. Dr. Hirsch and Mr. Dubosc, he deduces, must be one and the same man. So it proves: Hirsch leaves his house on the Champs Elysées by the front door; Dubosc returns to the same place by the back.[65] In Conrad's "The Duel," the superficial polarities in the duellists make way for a sense of their common drives and needs. Either side of Conrad's story those of Maupassant and Schnitzler show, in their turn, the most compelling, harrowing, yet plausible of duels to oppose individuals who are highly similar; and the person whom we resemble, fear, and need to challenge, above all others, is, of course, our self.

It is tempting to look forward from Conrad's life and times to Ridley Scott's cinematic version of the story, *The Duellists* (1977), but it might be as helpful to look at an echelon in the other direction. Conrad may have read a short story by Mérimée, called "Le coup de pistolet" (1856). Although famous as the Frenchman who "invented" Spain thanks to his short story "Carmen," Mérimée set this story in Russia and took it from Pushkin. Here the characters live as austerely and, of course, drink as uncompromisingly as Russians are supposed to. And they obey all the clichés endowed by a combination of Russian novels and the Crimean War, which had just ended. It would be right to assume that the story will involve duelling.

Indeed, Silvio, the chief protagonist of the story, is ominously celebrated for his skill and precision in firing pistols. The walls of his spartan room are pockmarked with shots. He has the aloofness or timidity of those Russian men. No one quite knows who he is. One evening after playing at faro, an officer unfamiliar with Silvio's ways quarrels with him and flings a candlestick at his head. To the surprise and indeed the dismay of the party, Silvio does not exact the satisfaction to which he is entitled. No duel ensues. But not long after this incident, Silvio receives a letter that, mysteriously, requires him to leave with immediate effect. He does go to the trouble of explaining himself to the narrator before leaving. It turns out that he has unfinished business with another gentleman. This potential quarrel would have interrupted a more important ongoing matter, and it was this matter that stopped him from prolonging a quarrel with the man who hurled the candlestick at him. It risked exposing him to death, when he has another appointment to keep. He had, he explains, fought a duel with a count. He offered his opponent the first shot, not honorably but, as he candidly avows, because passion and hatred were seething to the extent that he did not believe that his hand would be sure. His opponent first refused but then fired, and the bullet grazed Silvio's hat. He shows the hole in it to the impressed narrator. As Silvio prepared to fire back, the count nonchalantly ate some cherries, spitting out the pits. He felt he could not fire, and, justifying the delay by claiming that his opponent's life does not mean enough to him but also enraged by this display of nonchalance, he keeps his powder dry. Several years later, he decides he is ready to take his shot and exact his revenge. The count has now married a beauty, and they live in an elegant villa. Gruff and bearded, Silvio appears at the door. The count soon overcomes his surprise, and they prepare to fight. Silvio courteously offers his opponent the first shot, but it whistles past and hits a painting behind him. It is now his turn to shoot, and he is about to fire when the Countess comes running in, fainting as soon as she realizes what is happening. Silvio insists, even in these circumstances, on having his shot. The Count, like a brave man, takes up his position. Silvio aims, but he does not fire. He then shoots deliberately into the painting, sending a bullet into a rather fine Swiss landscape.[66]

Duels by pistol foresee some delay between one shot and the next (assuming that there is a next shot). This new facet of the duel is exploited to barely credible lengths in the stories of Conrad and Mérimée. This story's pace anticipates the tempo of Conrad's story, with its long, brooding intervals punctuated by sudden rapid encounters. As Andrew Steinmetz warns, "unless a man fires quickly, he can never fire well."[67] The stories also explore the capacity of these men to resume relations, whether amicable or hostile, indifferent to the time that has lapsed in the interim. They pay testimony to the unyielding demands of honor among males, even when they cut across obligations to women and collide with domestic responsibilities. As in Conrad's tale, there are two speeds or itineraries here—a linear progression, as D'Hubert, his temples graying, intends to "settle down," while France progresses through the vicissitudes of the nineteenth century. Against this, the duel gains an aura of atemporality, which may render irrelevant all other considerations. Here we see an early example of the pathos engendered by the "impossible retirement"—the predicament of the man who, older and wiser, nevertheless cannot bring himself to hang up his guns—a motif much favored by Westerns in the century that followed.[68]

Silvio's earnest wish is to fight a consequential duel. The seriousness of his wish to purge himself and exact revenge is shown by his dismissal, at the risk of damage to his reputation and honor, of an everyday duel. Mérimée's story shows that there are run-of-the-mill duels, clichéd encounters, soon forgotten, whereas this duel stems from a burning resentment. The cause of the duel is incidental to the reason for it. Indeed the two are sometimes inversely proportional: the more trivial the cause of the duel, the more significant and profound the torment of the man going ahead with it.

Mérimée shows us an interrupted duel, Conrad an interrupted series of duels, but the point is substantially the same. By Conrad's day, the duel was already an obviously retrograde way of sorting out one's differences. And to D'Hubert, thinking about the future and consigning the memories of the Napoleonic wars to the past in a peaceful and prosperous present, the thought of resuming it is more than a little unnatural and exasperating; but Feraud's life needs this fear and intensity to lend it shape and meaning. We learn nothing of Feraud's last days, as Conrad leaves the story, on a note in a major chord. But in Mérimée's story, we are told, briefly, that Silvio was soon killed. It is no surprise that this dogged soldier should die as he lived, but there is also a sense that, having fulfilled the demands of honor, he is free to die, and his death does not call for reflections or regrets beyond that.

As in Conrad's story, in which the definite article is belied by an extended series of duels, a meek singular ("le coup de pistolet") turns out to have harbored a plural, prolonged series of missed, abortive, delayed shots, until perhaps the final, fatal one that claims the life of Silvio. He wants the duel to signify. He needs it to remove the happiness and accomplishments of the more mature man or, rather, to threaten them. The relentlessness and the patience of Silvio, like that of Feraud, seem obsessive and perverse, and his desire to extract the maximum value out of the duel seems cruel. However, when it transpires that he behaves honorably and does not kill this gentleman endowed with all the domestic and social accomplishments that he himself lacks, it is clear that he chiefly wanted to see his opponent fear him. That outcome can deliver revenge and guarantee satisfaction, as his death cannot. The story then redeems him and also the wasted life of Mérimée's earlier story "The Etruscan Vase."

Whereas in Conrad's story, the cool northerner, D'Hubert, is the man who spares his rough opponent and tempers his ardor with restraint, here the story derives its force from the fact that Silvio, the grizzled loner, is the man who, at odds with his instincts, suddenly shows clemency. Both stories pay a tribute to the curious ethic that duelling entails. The need to fight is sometimes complemented by a wish to avoid killing, the wish to fight the duel when it will matter, the need to see out one duel instead of fighting another. As these stories attest, the duel involves the skill of waiting as much as that of shooting: waiting while the other man shoots and waiting for a moment to renew hostilities. And it is the essence of chivalry to know when and how to wait. Mérimée's story shows how even in the toughest and crudest male environments, in a God-forsaken Caucasian barracks, a code of honor has its sway.

The story, published in both the series of *Blackie's Educational Texts* and *Rivington's Intermediate French Readers*, was, around 1900, present on reading lists for pupils learning French in British schools. This particular work of Mérimée's evidently commended itself not only on account of its specimens of irregular verbs and subjunctives. For once the story had been translated and comprehended, a claustrophobic, violent world, governed by a code of conduct which fostered courage yet restraint and offered virile solutions to puerile predicaments, revealed itself to those schoolboys, growing up unsuspectingly on the eve of the First World War.

Schnitzler, *Casanovas Heimfahrt* (1918): Casanova versus Lorenzi

Of all writers, Arthur Schnitzler seems highly representative of, even synonymous with, his place and time: Vienna, as the nineteenth turned into the twentieth century, resplendent in all its corruption and charm. Schnitzler's literary excursions beyond this realm have been deemed less successful, yet a story of his, set in eighteenth-century Venice, constitutes a fascinating addition to his oeuvre, as to our collection of works devoted to the art of the duel.[69]

The first sentence of this story tells us, simply and unsparingly, that Casanova was fifty-three years of age. A great evocation of weariness and disillusionment, of verve surpassed and exhausted, suitable to 1918, follows. He has, rather like the rituals of the duel themselves, outlived his chief raison d'être and come to see time risk stranding him. But, in a story of otherwise highly sober, measured descriptions, Casanova is honored by a rare simile in this opening. He is compared to a wounded bird circling down from the skies, looking to return home. This image also allows or encourages a sense of things coming home to roost, an imminent reckoning of some sort.

Casanova, we learn, is indeed hoping for and dreaming of a return to his birthplace, Venice. La Serenissima promises to be his final destination, provided the Supreme Council agrees to forgive him previous indiscretions and allow him back. Venice is of course associated, in the literary imagination, with death and decay. "Everyone dies in Venice."[70] Thomas Mann's masterpiece *Death in Venice* dates to 1912, a few years earlier, and Schnitzler's story shares with Mann's novella certain preoccupations. Here, from the outset, a distinctly autumnal atmosphere prevails: even the leafless chestnut trees seem long since deflowered; his clothes are ragged.[71] Casanova has no money, little clothing, and just a few teeth.

He finds himself, to his frustration, at Mantua, in a state of limbo. While keen to move nearer to the Venetian territories, he is keeping himself busy by writing a work that will defend Christianity against Voltaire's onslaughts. He is walking along, pondering the degradation of his fortunes, when an old acquaintance by the name of Olivo happens upon him. Olivo persuades Casanova that he ought to come and stay with his family at their castle. Casanova had once helped Olivo to marry his wife, Amalia, thanks to a financial contribution. He had, in a variant on the mythical droit du seigneur, exacted a sort of remuneration from her, which they had both discreetly enjoyed.

Olivo, a trusting and sincere fellow, is the proud epitome of bourgeois productivity, with his three girls, growing up on an idyllic estate and vineyard inherited from a Count, which he has turned to profit. He is everything that Casanova is not. We learn subsequently that Olivo has won a lawsuit against a neighbor, the bourgeois counterpart to a duel. His very name is redolent of fertility. The world he inhabits is fecund and sunny. Schnitzler's style evokes the neatness of the surrounding countryside, in coupling every noun with an adjective: "bright meadows, golden fields, white roads, light-colored houses." It is a bourgeois idyll, in which nouns and adjectives are cheerfully conjugal. But "Casanova concerned himself little about the view."[72] Indeed, it forms a contrast with the seeming narrowness of Casanova's prospects and the sterility of Casanova's libertinage, which, rather than being devoted to the service of joyous transgressions, leveled against conventions, is henceforward largely designed to prove to him that the present is the same as the past. The conquests he hopes still to achieve are not a passport to the exposure and destruction of the hypocrisies of a society but a means of confirming certainties for him, over which he has an increasingly faltering command. These are the certainties of the old world—the certainties that a woman would yield to him—but also the eternal verities supported by an unchanging social, hierarchical order that underpinned and was underpinned by them. Casanova is therefore naturally aligned against Voltaire's scoffing mockery, his cynical disdain for the truths of revealed religion. Championing religion and virtue, Casanova has set himself the task of proving that Voltaire was an atheist, and it is in particular Voltaire's mock-epic poem, a caustic, scurrilous history of Joan of Arc, *The Virgin (La Pucelle)*, that, irony of ironies, Casanova is seeking to attack. Casanova thereby becomes the self-appointed champion of virginity and asceticism.[73]

Olivo's wife, Amalia, is delighted to see Casanova again, after sixteen years, and she hints that she would be ready to resume with him the transgressions of the past. She feels that his presence promises to transport her to those days (or nights) and rejuvenate her. But Amalia is now too old for him, even the oldest of her three daughters too young. Like the bird spiraling down from the air back to the earth, Casanova is variously caught between places, ages, states of mind, and definitions of himself. This feeling is aggravated by the rather aloof, cool presence of a beautiful young lady, Marcolina, Amalia's niece, in the midst of the family. Marcolina's haughty presence is supported by a reputation for spotless virtue and prodigious intelligence. She has turned down several proposals of marriage; she is studying higher mathematics in Bologna. Casanova is at once intrigued, aroused, and vexed by this cool young woman, who is utterly indifferent to his name and reputation, completely immune to his charms. Indeed, she is rather hostile to his ideas on Voltaire and the Kabbala. She gently mocks and parries his views, revealing herself to be a more accomplished freethinking person than is Casanova, whose thirst for intellectual credibility and his *libido sciendi*, exhibited repeatedly in his memoirs, are frustrated here. His desire to win immortality, less through immorality than authorial glory, seems doomed to failure. Casanova needs to be taken seriously.

He is not just some kind of old seducer but an ambitious author keen to make his mark. Unfortunately, he is also a "dethroned prince," little more than a beggar, reduced to penury.[74]

Amalia and Casanova both wish to delude themselves that time has not changed them. Amalia would like to be intimate with him again, in order to relive that time. But he admits that he wants the younger woman, Marcolina, whether that represents a way of avenging her intellectual aloofness, of simply gratifying himself, or of pretending to himself that he has not changed. He acknowledges though that, whereas he could, first, depend on his looks alone and, latterly, trade on his name in order to make conquests, he now requires assistance. Shamelessly, he asks Amalia to assist him in getting Marcolina into his bed, for Casanova is now contemplating the young woman with fantasies and longings reminiscent of those that Aschenbach directs at Tadzio in *Death in Venice*, desires that are similarly untrammelled by his awareness of their futility and foolishness. Schnitzler shares a fin-de-siècle fascination with the desires of an older man projected in the direction of a young woman or girl, as manifested, for example, in George Bernard Shaw's *Pygmalion* (1916) and Frank Wedekind's "Lulu plays," *Erdgeist* (1895) and *Die Büchse der Pandora* (1904).

Casanova's feelings toward Marcolina are needled further by his awareness, and then the actual sight, of a dashing, young soldier, Lieutenant Lorenzi, who, so Casanova rapidly intuits, is evidently in some sort of relationship with Marcolina. Casanova already resents Lorenzi, but all the more so when they meet, and Casanova is reminded, as he considers this handsome young man's chiseled face and sharp features, of himself in years past. "For a moment, Casanova was in doubt as to who it was that Lorenzi reminded him of. Then he realized that his own image stood before him, the image of himself as he had been thirty years before. 'Have I been reincarnated in his form?' Casanova asked himself. 'But I must have died before that could happen.' It flashed through his mind: 'Have I not been dead for a long time?' "[75]

Amalia has already hinted that Lorenzi is as handsome as Casanova had once been, possibly more so. Casanova is immediately jealous of his doppelgänger and previous incarnation. He wants both to become and to destroy his previous self. However, as he tells his stories, he seems to be the old Casanova again, "the joy-blessed, shameless, ra-

diant Casanova" (the adjectives are momentarily more prodigal), forgetting that he is thinking of going back to Venice "as a scribbler, a
beggar, as a nobody to see out his once splendid days."[76] But, he recognizes, the stories are all about the past and fill the void of the present
and the future. Casanova, at dinner that evening, is rueful and melan-
cholic, absorbed by thoughts of Marcolina. Gloomily, he reflects on the
futility of his project to outsmart Voltaire and bemoans his incomplete
Streitschrift. "Only where he evoked memories could his words, his
voice, his glance, still conjure; apart from this, his presence was empty
of interest. His day was done!"[77]

Marcolina is a new, less suggestible sort of woman to Casanova. She
refuses not only to be taken in by anyone, but to believe in anything.
She is, in this context, the niece, or *Nichte*, of the family, and perhaps
this designation punningly suggests a sort of nihilism.[78] Marcolina is
mentioned again and again in relation to windows (a motif we see in
Schnitzler's play *Liebelei*).[79] But she looks through windows not in the
confined, claustrophobic manner of Emma Bovary. She can see through
Casanova.

The axioms of mathematics are pitted mercilessly against the creeds
of religion, of which Casanova mounts an unimpressive defense. But
Marcolina is not, it turns out, a pure mathematician. The following
morning, before dawn, as Casanova prowls outside the house, he spies
Lorenzi leaving her room surreptitiously. Casanova is furious, indignant, and humiliated, not only because he is jealous of Lorenzi and his
youth but because he more or less subscribed to the fantasy that she
was indeed unattainable. He has been close to being fooled by her appearance of and reputation for chastity, as well as trumped by her, when
it comes to their verbal duel over Voltaire and freethinking. Her secret
relationship with Lorenzi confirms that Casanova is confronting a new
sort of enemy; it is not virtue or faith that opposes him, but she is armed
with the weaponry of the Enlightenment against his charms. But what
makes Casanova sad, not without reason perhaps, is the sense that she
is hypocritical or duplicitous, as he, in actual fact, is not. He is not
claiming to be pious—his reputation precedes him. He intends to profit
from that reputation, rather than to insinuate himself into the confidence of others by other means. We are all pious in our own ways,
Casanova assures her.[80]

Casanova, back in his room, finds himself facing his reflection in the mirror. Preoccupied with mortality, resentful of Marcolina's youth as of Voltaire's immortality, he is disgusted at himself and his wan, ageing countenance. In a scene reminiscent of Aschenbach's visit to the barber in *Death in Venice*, he is transfixed by his grotesque appearance: "In a self-tormenting mood he allowed the corners of his mouth to droop as if he were playing the part of the pantaloon on the stage."[81]

Casanova now receives a letter, not only permitting him to return to Venice but summoning him back as speedily as possible. He is invited to serve as an undercover informer for the police in the Republic, reporting on conspirators. Casanova feels demeaned to have been invited to undertake this task. He nevertheless accepts and reconciles himself to leaving Marcolina and the others as soon as possible.

Meanwhile, there is time for a last evening of cards. Lorenzi, after incurring terrible losses at the gaming table, owes one of the party, the Marquis, two thousand ducats and has until the following morning to find them. Casanova offers him the money if Lorenzi will enable him to spend the night with Marcolina in his place. "Who regains wealth regains youth. Wealth is everything!" But Marcolina must not suspect that they have swapped places. To this end, Casanova will borrow Lorenzi's dark-blue riding cloak. That night, furnished with the cloak, Casanova makes his way to Marcolina's room. She opens the window expectantly, and swinging himself in, he insinuates himself into her arms, where a night of bliss follows. His pleasure is complete: "Was he not a god? Were not youth and age merely a fable, fictions invented by men?"[82]

Casanova flatters himself that she too must feel pleasure (in his memoirs, he honorably emphasizes the importance of conferring, as well as taking, pleasure) and that his imposture can be transformed into some higher register: "Would not the ineffable bliss of this night transmute into truth what had been conceived in falsehood?" His questions, paradoxes, and exhilarated fantasies seamlessly turn into a brilliantly delirious dream sequence thanks to which Casanova and Marcolina are now in Venice, then gliding along canals, next dancing at the masked ball, and, finally, he is crying to a gondolier, swimming, and drowning. Then the spell is suddenly broken by this devastatingly simple sentence: "Between the curtain and the window frame, dawn was making its way through in a narrow strip of light."[83] Schnitzler uses the term "Dämmerung," which is feasible for half light at any time but normally reserved for the fading light of the evening. And that fading or decline is what Casanova now acutely feels. He awakens brusquely to find Marcolina at the foot of the bed, looking at him "with unutterable horror." His tumble from ecstasy into delirium, from ingenuity to excess is brilliantly described: "His expression was one of rage and shame; hers was one of shame and disgust."[84]

But, worse still, he sees himself "in the mirror of the air." He beholds "a yellow, evil face, deeply lined, with thin lips and staring eyes." Casanova looks at himself, his gnarled wrists and yellowing skin, as though he were observing a portrait of himself by Egon Schiele. He reads in Marcolina's face the worst possible judgment. He is condemned neither as a thief nor as a libertine. Horror of horrors he finds himself, "in a definitive verdict," culpable of being an old man.[85]

Casanova flees the room without saying a word. He promptly discovers that, outside, the gondolier of the dream awaits him. It is none other than Lorenzi, who draws his sword. He demands satisfaction and proposes to fight Casanova at this very moment. The Venetian explains in response that he is not really dressed for the occasion: "I should like to bring to your attention the fact that I am unfortunately compelled to appear in a wholly inappropriate costume." Then, casting the cloak to the ground, Casanova stands opposite Lorenzi, stark naked. Lorenzi in turn strips and presents himself, "splendid in his nakedness like a young god." The gray *Dämmerung* has now mutated into a silvery *Morgenlicht*. It is a beautiful description of a potentially farcical adventure. "The next moment they crossed blades, and the steel glittered like silver in the morning sun."[86]

Medieval chivalry is wrought from the most disreputable of deceptions, won by a bribe. Casanova tells himself that this is no ordinary fight: "A fight? No, a tournament." Casanova can believe again in his own myth and invulnerability, and, as he does so, he administers a fatal blow: "At that, Lorenzi sank to the ground, a stab wound to the heart. His sword fell from his hand, his eyes stared wide open, as though he were in the greatest state of shock, he raised his head once again, his lips painfully quivered, his head drooped, his nostrils opened wide, a quiet murmuring, and he died."[87] With sang froid but tenderness too,

Casanova closes the man's eyes and kisses him on the forehead. It is seductively described, yet even as the text seems to admire Casanova, as it records his tender gestures and invests the moment with a sort of poetic aura, it still calls this act for what it is. Justice might not be served, but honor has been satisfied. The text continues to alternate between brilliance and sordidness, a neomedieval fantasy and crude opportunism. It is the interplay between surgical detail and fanciful, extravagant transformations.

This final duel is a sort of pristine encounter, a naked dance or *gymnopodie.* The duel, in the eighteenth and nineteenth centuries, often testified to some sense of progression, but by the late nineteenth / early twentieth century, in common with composers of the era (such as Erik Satie), the emphasis is on multiple perspectives, by which the same subject may be seen, rather than development. It is a reprise of the duel at the end of *Les liaisons dangereuses,* such is the contrast between older libertine and younger gallant, but here the duel is not expiatory.

Venetians invented mirrors, and Casanova makes repeated use of them, even when they are virtual or furnished by other presences. Moments earlier, he saw himself, in the "mirror of the air," as a grotesquely old, wizened man. Now Lorenzi mirrors him. By entering a duel, the adversary is honored as an equal, assenting to the opponent's provenance but also taking part in an imaginative transferal. It is a memorable moment. It is perhaps the first depiction of a duel in an age for which duelling now belonged to the past. A golden aura suffuses this duel. These duellists are not naked but nude.[88] Casanova is fighting a hero. However, even at this moment, Casanova ironically pays homage to the man he is laboriously trying to prove wrong—Voltaire. In perhaps his most impious work of all, *La Pucelle,* invoked approvingly by Marcolina, Voltaire stages a duel between two knights, La Trimouille and Christophe Arondel, who fight each other stark naked.[89]

So Casanova graduates into a mock-epic character from the work of which he so disapproves, *La Pucelle.* Whereas Voltaire looked at the duel as a medieval vestige, the laughable runt of an outmoded chivalric practice, and a way of deriding the chivalry and gallantry of that age, Schnitzler looks back to the eighteenth century to find a residue of honor. Schnitzler is not, of course, attempting to re-create a realistic eighteenth-century duel but is staging a metaphorical encounter. The rising sun, the *champ clos*, the Edenesque garden and air all permit an *épuration*.

The duel represents a face-to-face, man-to-man confrontation and a reckoning with oneself. This duel, fought in the nude, is the honorable duel par excellence. Although duellists were advised to strip to avoid wounds from being touched by clothing, this would appear to be a secondary motivation here. On one level, having acted dishonorably thanks to the disguise of the coat, there is something redemptive about stripping and self-exposure—for the man who lent the coat as well as for the man who took it. More generally, this is the glorious inverse and antithesis of the shady spying that Casanova is expected to engage in, upon his return to Venice, a final display of the self, in all its honesty, before entering a modern subterranean world of hidden intelligence. It is also a form of engagement, within eye contact, naked, that is at the other extreme, for that matter, from trench warfare.

Conducted with a sword, the duel is a beautiful sight and an engagement in which mutually intuitive understanding and imaginative anticipation of the other will be rewarded. Casanova's exaltation during the duel replays terms we heard when he was in sexual congress with Marcolina. The duel offers, similarly, an exaltation of the self but also a negation, a way of expiating his imposture in the darkness.

Casanova wonders, during the card game, whether he might be the victim of an intrigue only to come to the realization that he no longer has enemies. The attention of enemies is a flattering sign that one is worth hating. Enmity is a sign of vitality, the provocation of hatred, a proof of vigor. It is not just love that he needs but enmity, not just sex but a duel. The duel with the young man that follows the sexual act with the young lady is no less integral and essential to this recovery of the self's vitality.

Casanova's libertinage is the product of intelligence and of sympathy and of rare insight. He plots, casts himself into a role. He is at once an author and his own hero. Because of his own faltering capacities, his search and need for intimacy look less self-indulgent than self-effacing. Casanova is doubtless opportunistic, even malicious, but this largely results from his acute observations of humans, of life itself. Imagining and predicting the conduct of others are at the basis of Casanova's libertinage. As he pays close attention to what people say,

Arturo Martini, *Il duello*, 1917. Galleria Internazionale d'Arte Moderna, Ca'Pesaro, Venice. Courtesy of MUVE Photo Archive, Fondazione Musei Civici di Venezia.

understanding and anticipating their moves, this guile serves him well in the duel.

Freud regarded himself as an analogue of Schnitzler, exploring the recesses of the desiring self on the sofa, as Schnitzler examined them in his fiction.[90] There is, unquestionably, a homoerotic dimension to this naked duel. Casanova had also seen Lorenzi in his dream. But, as Freud suggested, desire for the other was, in certain contexts, essentially narcissistic. Casanova loves and resents, in the form of Lorenzi, his own previous self. The duel pits interchangeable selves against each other, as in the print, produced in 1914, by Arturo Martini.

Casanova can see in the dark, the inverse of Maupassant's nihilist. He is blessed with an elephantine memory. The narrator borrows from Casanova some of his supernaturally penetrative vision. All these descriptions play with the reader. Leisurely descriptions of trees, dust on the road, furnishings, his room all help us to feel that same impatience, as he tries to head back to Venice. Casanova, whose age is mentioned in the first sentence, is running out of time. He is an older man in a hurry, losing, as we all will, his duel with time. For death is the only sure victor. The duel has become another episode in the universal "Dance of Death."

Older, uneasier duellists seem to command more interest latterly (witness the stories by Conrad and Schnitzler and, in a precocious example, the nobleman fought by Silvio in "Le coup de pistolet"). They are not wiser, penitent former combatants but weary, reluctant participants, paying a debt to the past. Their bouts are all the more perversely honorable for being fought without any belief in their essential meaning. Perhaps these older figures, acting impeccably yet with no inner assent to the culture, mirror the ageing of the duel itself as an institution. It plods on, beyond its natural life, like the offenses that the duel aims to avenge.

The older duellist has, numerically speaking, less to lose than his younger counterpart. But he has become domesticated and responsible. Duels fought by young men are not as intrinsically interesting. The duel barely interrupts a boisterous and vigorous, perhaps violent life. For the older man, however, it is an epiphenomenon, an appendix to a book, a delayed or deferred chapter, which seems to belong to an earlier part of the narrative or, at worst, a premature conclusion.

Venice at last beckons, almost on the horizon. For Casanova, Venice may be said to assume the role of the wife we see in other stories (by, for instance, Mérimée and Conrad); La Serenissima will gratify the feelings of comfort and domesticity for which he has pined. After the duel, however, the story moves in a somewhat anticlimactic way, slowly and deliberately, the thoroughness of the description again making us feel some of the impatience and anxiety of Casanova, as he tries to flee

Albert Besnard, *Le Duel*, from the series *Elle*, 1900. The Richard Harris Collection.

back home. Schnitzler, whose fellow Austrians had built the bridge from the mainland to Venice in 1846, enjoys evoking the frustrations of travel in earlier ages. Schnitzler constructs a text that is the inverse of Mann's *Death in Venice*. Aschenbach cannot leave Venice; Casanova has trouble arriving there. The former is an ascetic, the latter a libertine. But both are frustrated, struggling writers: Aschenbach is trying, laboriously, to write about Frederick the Great; Casanova, with no less ambition and difficulty, is trying to refute Frederick's sometime friend and courtier Voltaire; but both remain more or less overtly aware of their feeble attempt to comprehend a genius greater than their own. Writing is a battle against oneself, no less.

This short story expresses the seductive, dangerous fluidity of living in the past, off one's memories. In a lovely expression, Amalia throws an *"erinnerungstrunknen Blick"* Casanova's way—"drowned in memories."[91] All serve as tributaries to the central destination of Venice, that place where the flow of time perhaps lends itself most poignantly to our appreciation. Yet it turns out to be a strange waterless Venice to which he returns. The return to Venice is a return to mother sea, not just the sanctuary abroad but a sort of womb where he can be an innocent libertine once again.

The descriptions, leisurely yet focused, transmit a sense of how Casanova might look at the world. Like a detective, he notes whether windows are open and constantly assimilates information that might prove useful to him later, while quarrying his memory. The sober, realistic detail yet serves the purpose of evoking an eighteenth-century libertine at work. The descriptive style seems to borrow from and defer to Casanova's own keenly observational gaze, the impressions that play in his "sharp eyes." On other occasions, the text sometimes leans toward him with the ironic sympathy of free indirect discourse. "Had he not experienced on numerous occasions that in every truly living human soul not only various but also apparently hostile elements cohabit in the most peaceful way?"[92]

Ultimately, such a duel, set against the static horror of the trenches, may seem impossibly gallant, ridiculously quaint. There is little more fanciful in 1918 than eighteenth-century Europe, at least as it was remembered or imagined *avant le déluge*, with its elaborate codes of honor, its epicurean proclivities, its blend of tender sensibility and imperturbable libertinage. Schnitzler's story, in which the reign of swords is untroubled by pistols, allows Casanova, some 140 years on from his actual encounter, finally to fight the duel of his dreams.

Pirandello, *Il giuoco delle parti* (1918): Guido Venanzi versus Marquis Migloriti; or, Leone Gala versus His Wife

Schnitzler's play *Liebelei* (1900) centers on an "essentially frivolous" character by the name of Fritz. It becomes apparent as the play draws toward its conclusion that "he neither fully understands, nor is able to respond to, an essentially serious situation—the situation of love." But this superficiality does not take the form of carefree, joyful libertinage. It is stimulated by a fear of death, which is heightened by a duel he must fight. As J. P. Stern observes, such fears of death are fundamental to Schnitzler's depictions of human character; but his figures are by no means heroic, and their fears are abject and desperate. They are killed fighting a duel and respecting the code of honor, "yet they are robbed of all dignity because it is an obligation they themselves know to be a sham."[93]

Pirandello's play *Il giuoco delle parti* likewise brings together a claustrophobically narrow range of characters—all bored, frivolous, urban bourgeois figures. The play opens in Silia's apartment, where she and her lover, Guido, are conversing. It becomes apparent that Silia is utterly exasperated by her estranged husband, Leone. She is vexed not by his hostility to her or to her lover but by what we would recognize as his passive aggression, even when absent. She hates the chairs that belong to him, for instance. She wishes he were dead and seems to be serious in realizing her dreams. Indeed, she sees her chance to rid herself of him when a group of quite innocuous drunkards makes its way by chance into her house. While Guido slips into another room offstage and remains hidden from these visitors, Silia deals with them. Among these boorish revelers is Marquis Migloriti, a celebrated swordsman. She contrives to acquire his card. The following day, she presents it to her husband, declaring herself insulted by this nobleman's actions and inviting her husband to defend her honor and meet the redoubtable Marquis in a duel.

Leone readily assents, even though, avowedly, he has no experience whatsoever of duelling. He has in fact never held a sword. So the duel promises to amount to a death sentence; the Marquis is more henchman than adversary. This duel, carefully contrived as a vehicle of revenge, recalls a similarly cool Italian execution, assuming the form of a duel, that takes place in Chesterton's "The Sins of Prince Saradine" (1911), witnessed by Father Brown. Antonelli, a Sicilian, disembarks at the house of Prince Saradine with two rapiers, in order to avenge the murder of his father and the abduction of his mother, many years previously. Hamlet's failures appear to be decisively overcome here, until we learn that Antonelli's actual nemesis, the real prince, is actually the butler to (and brother of) the man whom he slays in this duel. He has wisely calculated that it is better to have two enemies rather than one and has set his brother up against the vengeful Sicilian.

A similar twist in which the characters fighting the duel are reshuffled like a pack of cards will occur in Pirandello's play. For now, though, we register the fact that Leone, in order to keep up appearances, visits his wife's apartment for half an hour every day. He is punctilious in observing this daily rite. Leone's scrupulous observation of that ritual, concluded by a chiming clock, seems ostentatiously shallow. His record of acquiescing and keeping up appearances seems auspicious for wife and lover alike. Why would he not go along, just as complaisantly, with fighting a duel?

Leone's name connotes courage. Yet the chief constituent of that courage would appear to be indifference. He does not seem to fear losing his life, because he has little or nothing to lose. Courage on these terms then is essentially a manly form of indifference. Paradoxically, his belief in and pursuit of honor are sanctioned above all else by world-weariness. The nonchalance that vexed Silvio (in both Pushkin's and then Mérimée's novella), when he aimed his pistol at the Count, seems to be in evidence here too. While Silvio nibbled grapes, Leone's apparent pleasure in eating and sleeping, unperturbed by the prospect of dying violently and imminently, seems to betoken insouciance. That indifference, the belief in the cheapness of life, seems all too credible in 1918. What does Leone have to live for anyway but a loveless, humiliating marital life? As Leone declares, "I try my hardest to exist as little as possible."[94]

The duel then simply intensifies a confrontation that Leone sees as inherent. That confrontation is a duel with the world, with all others. Leone has sharpened his main weapon, indifference, an "inexhaustible source of courage—not merely to face one man, that's nothing—but to face the whole world, always." He seems equipped for the duel thanks largely to an inner armory of cynical convictions. "I live in a realm where nothing whatsoever can trouble me, my dear. Nothing at all, whether it's to do with death or with life! Just look at the ridiculousness of men and their silly little opinions! Don't you worry! I understand the game."[95]

To an audience, these trouble-free words issued from the stage may seem innocuous. Life is a game, even our mortal clashes part of a human comedy. Thus far, the prospective duel, no matter how absurd and contrived its premise, seems conventional enough. This lineup of characters is not unfamiliar. A duel always calls to mind duels of the past. By the turn of the twentieth century, it is an especially self-conscious act, heavy with history. In *Liebelei*, Schnitzler treats us to a telling little premonition when a character by the name of Lenski makes a fleeting appearance. This latest duel brings an opportunity to stage a foolish doctor, Dr. Spiga in this case, who, no more enlightened than Molière's physicians, frets selfishly about what he should wear at the duel, as though it were a wedding or indeed an evening at the theater. As for Leone, he does not believe in this drama. He does not believe in anything. Yet he will play his role to perfection. So the artificial mechanisms of the duel remain, as they were chez Corneille, allied to the conventions of the theater.

Leone appears then to take up his place in a long line of demonstrably disaffected, inert characters: avowedly superfluous men, such as Bazarov, Fritz, or Des Esseintes.[96] He is a *qualunquista*, washed up from the fin-de-siècle. We think we know where he is coming from. Only he is not the man we thought he was. He will in fact liberate himself from going along with his wife's plans by not fighting the duel. That is a decisive step, a revelation, for this is the first occasion on which we meet with a man who, deliberately and remorselessly, fails to acquiesce in the duel. Yet by doing so, he achieves revenge. For Leone has cooked up a plan. His indifference was just an act, a sham. The duel is, after all, more than a game.

Leone first asks his rival, Guido, to be his second but then demands that he replace him. Leone has been second string in the relationship, the shorter side in this love triangle. So there is a sort of ironic pertinence in asking Guido to step into his shoes and replace him. It is a *coup de théâtre*, a shock to honor, yet it neatly replicates the marital configuration.

Silia immediately voices a question that will occur to perplexed members of the audience. Is her husband not going to be dishonored by evading the duel? But he brushes off this accusation: "You are my dishonor," he says to his wife.[97] Touché! He is prepared to forsake the obligation to his wife, just as easily as she seems to have neglected him as husband. This volte-face exhibits an unprecedentedly calculated attitude to the demands of honor.

It is at this point that Leone's apparently incidental interest in cooking starts to look pertinent, even significant. Leone's principal avowed interest lends him an understanding of life as well as a love of it. Materially speaking, it shows that he too has an appetite, a capacity for pleasure. More symbolically, an ability to cook seems to inform his approach to his wife and her lover. He has understood the psychological ingredients of fear, pride, and vanity that contribute to their characters.

This then is a comedy that is deadly serious in the end. It takes the side, perhaps somewhat unconventionally, of the married man, against the desperate claims of romantic or, at least, illicit love. He cannot be construed as villainous, because Silia's pain seems largely self-induced. No one appears to have forced her to marry Leone in the first place; nor is Leone demonstrably unfair or unpleasant in his interactions with her. She is not even unhappy; she just wants to be happier. But nor, for that matter, is he a moral hero, purposefully defending and vindicating the sacrament of matrimony. That might be vouchsafed by the husband killing the adulterous lover with his own hands. This indeed happens when fatal duels take place both in *Effi Briest* and in *Liebelei*. But Leone, for all the courage promised by his name, kills no one. His act of revenge is engineered and achieved by proxy. As in those stories of Fontane and Schnitzler, Pirandello's duel does not embody chivalry of the traditional variety, in which the honor of a lady is defended, but the duel is a glorified assassination of the lover, on behalf of a disgraced lady, carried out by a "hired" expert. Indeed, Pirandello, who studied for a doctorate in Bonn for several years, is likely to have been influenced by these German precedents.

The title, the "rules of the game," and the nonchalance of the characters all may persuade us to subscribe to an essentially frivolous view of love and of life itself. The duel appears to be the epitome of such a game, bound by rules in which people do not believe yet feel somehow obliged to follow. Mark Twain and Jules Renard, among others, inherit and perpetuate the view of the bourgeois duel as a contradiction in terms, an affectation, at best an amusing spectacle. But, while their representations are safely comical, Pirandello's drama is tragicomical or tragic. Famous for his grotesque drama, Pirandello is drawn to a practice the elegance of whose form, married to the brutality of its end, guarantees a tragicomedy.

The duel, as in *Liebelei*, takes place offstage. We do not need to see the actual combat. In fact, such a spectacle would be a distraction working against the design of the play. The duel does not constitute the drama; what matters is the presentiments that the duel sets into play. The duel is a lens trained onto human nature, its fears, and its desires for dignity and honor. Or rather it is a magnifying glass in which those inherent drives and emotions are enlarged. Furthermore, in this case, the location of the duel offstage permits an ironic symmetry: condemned to returning offstage, Guido ends up where he was in act 1. The duel now takes place. On the stage, meanwhile, the doctor has placed his array of instruments on the table, to the distress of the servant Philip, who wants to lay out breakfast, as Leone's routine demands. But then the tables are turned. The doctor comes rushing in, pale faced, and grabs his instruments. Guido has evidently been killed. Breakfast can now be served.

Pirandello hereby perpetuates a tradition of debunking extravagant epiphanies by invoking baser appetites, as greed trumps grief. In the famous challenge thrown down to Paris, Balzac's Rastignac declares, "A nous deux maintenant!" But these "grandiose words," as the narrator calls them, do not quite constitute the final chord of *Le Père Goriot:* "And for his first act of defiance aimed at society, Rastignac went round to the house of Mme. de Nucingen for dinner."[98] Eating is a measure that the usual demands and the normal rhythms of life can be reasserted.

Pirandello's figures are divested of contextualizing factors. They are Italian but only because that is the language of the play and of Pirandello. They enjoy a universal status. Jean Genet protested that his play *Les Bonnes* (*The Maids*) (1947) should not be seen as written on behalf of the union of domestic staff but seen as an abstracted game.[99] The duel likewise becomes the focus, as in Schnitzler, of a psychological drama, not a social problem.

No one believes sincerely in the demands of honor, but, equally, they seem unable not to believe in them and to cast them off entirely. A gradual degradation of the code of honor, an erosion of its sanctity, may, however, be observed: first, the Comte in Maupassant's "Un lâche" (1884) cries off a duel he cannot face, albeit by killing himself, and perhaps thereby salvaging some honor. Then in Fontane's masterpiece *Effi Briest* (1895), Geert von Innstetten decides he needs to fight a duel, after learning that his wife had an affair with Major Crampas, several years previously. It therefore seems to be both a belated and contrived gesture.[100] He knows that, in order to steel himself to fight a duel with his wife's lover, he ought to tell someone else. Communicating the details of her adultery to a third person, a colleague at the Berlin Foreign Office, he knows that, once the affair is common knowledge, he will not be able to go back on his word. He cannot trust himself entirely. The wish to fight the duel is not an entirely self-enforced reflex. In this case, honor is not internalized as an inherited dictate to which one naturally and spontaneously responds, but it requires the assistance of external pressures. Finally, Leutnant Gustl in Schnitzler's story of 1900 finds himself in paroxysms as he faces up to the prospect of having to kill himself, since he is not allowed to meet an obligation to duel. He is, however, unwilling to commit suicide, as in the earlier Maupassant story.[101]

However, the text of which Pirandello's play is most reminiscent is Alexander Kuprin's *The Duel* (1905). Both texts resolve a love triangle by devising a duel in which the lover is killed. Damocles-like, Kuprin's title hangs over the novel, yet the duel (engineered by Alexandra so that her husband, who has twice failed army exams, can win some respect and progress in his career) is far from inevitable. Her lover, Romashov, the latest listless victim of the duel, could easily resign his commission from an army where he knows himself to be unhappy, yet he fights reluctantly and self-destructively. It is, as in Pirandello's drama, at once a romantic and a squalid event.

Honor in its traditional guises now commands only the most brittle and shakable of devotees. There is no honor among gentlemen. In fact, there may be no gentlemen. But Leone takes an audacious step further in degrading the point of honor by quite deliberately and willfully side-stepping a commitment to which he had seemingly promised himself and by thrusting an unsuspecting *ingénu* in his place. This step is without precedent in the texts concerned with duels. He has, in the absence of the virile courage associated with duelling, the temerity to arrange a duel for his rival and to dispense with the code of honor. He first appears to be a cynical, complaisant gentleman, whether in his approach to the duel or his attitude to his marriage. However, the final act reveals him to be a melodramatic avenger of old. It would be easy to assume that divorce legislation would by now have done for duels of this kind. But, as the eponymous hero of Saki's collection of stories *Reginald* (1904) opines, even in Britain, "The fashion just now is a Roman Catholic frame of mind with an Agnostic conscience: you get the medieval picturesqueness of one with the modern conveniences of the other."[102]

No one emerges from this misadventure with any credit. Leone goes back on a promise we thought he had made. Likewise, he only succeeds in persuading the lover to duel by tricking him into doing so. The Marquis too may be deplored for compliantly picking off a vulnerable and deluded opponent. In Pirandello's *Six Characters in Search of an Author* (1921), perhaps his most famous play, the characters are in the process of rehearsing *The Rules of the Game*. This work indeed enjoys much in common with that comedy—humans seek to become the authors of their life but turn out to be characters trapped in the plot of a figure more authorial than themselves.

The duel is a highly intriguing phenomenon, not only because, potentially leading to a fatal outcome, it obviously pushed those whom it involved to extremes of emotion but also because it remained, even at the beginning of the twentieth century, the lingering expression of a social and moral code of conduct. A murder could only take place beyond the bounds of society, whereas even an illegal duel was still authorized and enforced by the norms of honor. When those norms were in the process of collapsing, the futility and the absurdity of the point of honor, the object of rational contempt and virtuous indignation throughout the years that are the span of this study, were sensed all the more keenly, as the duel exacted from the detached bourgeois figures it henceforward engaged a more than usually inglorious sacrifice.

The duel then finds itself back at the end of the work, its preferred, prominent position in decades past, but, as in Kuprin's novel, it now occurs invisible to us, divested of all poetry and drama. On the surface, a fatal duel fittingly brings down the curtain on an archetypal story of love and revenge, but even as this terminal duel cuts down a young lover, the text resists romance in the interests of a more complex, bitter irony.

CHAPTER EIGHT

Paradoxes of the Duel

A Tragicomedy

A discrepancy yawns between the historical or forensic treatment of duelling and its numerous fictional instances. Indeed, conflicting responses could cohabit under a common title. J. G. Millingen, author of *The History of Duelling* (in two volumes), published in 1830, announces himself as a stern critic of the pursuit, but his earnest moral stance at the outset of the work is later given the lie by his apparent enthusiasm for this extravagance. Volume 2 of his work seems to mock the ambitions of volume 1.[1] The anecdotes that abound in the latter part of the book seem to tell another tale. Such anecdotes tend to celebrate nonchalance in the face of death, on occasion as a tribute to courage, at other times as a product of vanity. Max Beerbohm quotes Baron d'Orsay, on the eve of a duel, bemoaning the odds in favor of his opponent: "We are not fairly matched. If I were to wound him in the face it would not matter; but if he were to wound me, *ce serait vraiment dommage!*"[2] It is not an especially bon mot, but it may appeal, because it allows us to acquiesce in an image of the nobleman, above all a French example of the species, as definitively other. The duellist is typically cast, both in literary and historical accounts, as a paragon of style, a miracle of poise in the face of death. The emphasis falls on looks rather than on life as the supreme value. These gentlemen are, of course, playing. The more austere commentator may deplore such artifice—these duellists are not confronting death with sufficient solemnity. These noblemen deceive themselves in death, as they have in life, never doubting their supremacy in an unquestioned social order. Others, however, see this playful adherence to form, even in mortal danger, as redemptively gallant, knowing, and, above all, touching. If, eventually, duelling was "laughed into extinction," it took many centuries to do so, for writers, captivated by those whom they would deride, often laugh with duellists, not at them.[3] Like the dyer's hand, even the most joyless critics seem to favor a facetious or ironic mode oddly commensurate with the spirit of duelling.

If declining a duel entailed social death, deploring it, however rationally and persuasively, carried its own risks. The thought that their objections to duelling might be attributable to a deficiency of courage or of class, or indeed of humor, probably stayed the hands of some potential critics, leaving some of the fiercest and the most interesting criticism entrusted to personages in fiction or else to those who had themselves fought a duel.

Sir Richard Steele (1672–1729) could speak against duels with the authority of experience. Yet the critic necessarily remains at a remove from the objects of his critique. In one of the installments of *The Tatler*, he puts it nicely: "He comes upon action in armour, but without weapons: he stands in safety, but can gain no glory."[4] Particularly when it comes to duelling, the critic risks looking like a timid bystander, equipped to observe but not prepared to act. Steele, in the guise of Isaac Bickerstaff, not only discusses the scourge of duelling in numerous installments of *The Tatler* and (with Joseph Addison) in its successor publications, but he also exposes to the reader his own hesitation as to the most suitable line of attack. He claims to be working on a treatise that will rigorously prove how fallacious and offensive to reason is the practice of duelling. He professes, however, that he is just as tempted to make it possible to "laugh at things in themselves so deeply tragical as the impertinent profusion of human life."[5]

Because the duel is staged at an appointed hour, in front of an invited audience, it naturally gravitates toward the spectacle of a play. Comedy and tragedy, apparently polar extremes, could turn into each other, at the slightest hint from fate. The dénouement to a duel alone ultimately tended to determine whether it was a comedy or a tragedy, in one act. "Finita la commedia," says Pechorin tersely to his second, after sending Grushnitsky to his death in their duel in Lermontov's *A Hero of Our Time*.[6] The party wall shared by life and stage, tragedy and farce, seems precariously thin. The duel is a piece of theater, its principals playing parts conceived in a dark and distant past. The timeless rituals of the point of honor seem to fictionalize even those duels we know to have been real. These rules and mores carry the duel into a vacuum, where a different set of conventions applies. A duel is the most deliberate, self-conscious of acts. A duellist is always implicitly consulting previous duels; it is a kinship with those duels from the past, from age-old chivalric literature, that, hazily, lends meaning and dignity to an event which will, as it often turns out, be lacking in both. Overtly stylized, deliberately, even proudly artificial, the ritualized combat would appear to belong to the realms of fiction. This is in part attributable to the fact that a physical, violent act owes its continued existence to the most intangible of notions, honor. And honor, after all, exists "because everyone believes that everyone else believes that it exists."[7]

Leigh Hunt commented that duelling "has received hundreds of banters, and (consequences apart) has a natural tendency to the burlesque."[8] That is a particularly worrying little parenthesis. As Chesterton's Father Brown (in "The Sins of Prince Saradine") witnesses the fatally conclusive duel, and "the whole green theatre of that swift and inexplicable tragedy," he is perplexed by the intersection of theatricality and brutality and slightly troubled by his own correspondingly ambiguous interest in it: "Somehow he had not seen the real story, but some game or masque. And yet people do not get hanged or run through the body for the sake of a charade."[9]

A painting by Jean-Léon Gérôme may exemplify the attraction of this paradox. His work, exhibited to great acclaim in 1857 at Paris and then, a year later, in London, depicts a fatal duel that has followed on from a masked ball. Critics and commentators thought it a moral piece, apparently reflecting scandalous French mores, a response to recent duels conducted in the Bois de Boulogne. The popularity of this moving, intriguing picture was soon attributable to its timeliness in exposing the horror and frivolity of contemporary duellists. But if the painting tells a story, its precise shades of meaning remain shrouded in the half light of a cold dawn.

Gérôme allows us to appreciate a play of contrasts, a meeting of incongruities. The Pierrot's soft shoes on the hard ground suggest that one man has been called, literally, out by another. The restrained grisaille of the background, the muted, slightly dirty white of the terrain, the sober black-and-white costumes of the two gentlemen who support the dying duellist, all throw into relief the outlandish variegations of

Jean-Léon Gérôme, *Suites d'un bal masqué* (The Duel after the Masquerade), 1857. Musée Condé, Chantilly.

the costumes donned by the other men and the few but costly specks of blood on the tunic of the fallen man. How little it takes to kill a man, the painting seems to suggest—whether it be the trivial incident that doubtless provoked the duel or the seemingly slight wound that has terminated it. That blood, the duellist's pallor, and his posture, as he slumps to the ground, allow Gérôme to tell us that the clown is, beyond doubt, about to die. The outcome is unmistakable. Moreover, it seems inevitable. The skeletal trees and the shroud-like carpet of snow seem ready to embrace the victim.[10] Snow, thanks to François Villon's famous unanswered question, provides a poignant image of transience. "Where are the snows of yesteryear?"[11] Nature does not rebel in horror at this action. On the contrary, she seems prepared to collaborate with the idea that a cold-blooded killing may occur with impunity.

Yet that certainty does not dispel a number of other unanswerable questions. There remains, of course, an ambiguity as to what may have provoked this duel. Our only clue is the masked ball that preceded it, an occasion for jollity, now a source of irony. The combatants have evidently left the ball in haste, not allowing themselves time to change their costumes. Nor does the outcome of the duel provide answers. Thanks to the victorious duellist turning away from us, we cannot be sure what he concludes. Gérôme does not, at the risk of melodrama, show us a repentant, horrified, or victorious face. The victor's sword may have been discarded with insouciance or arrogance—or, perhaps more likely, in exasperation and despair. Then there is the figure of the dying man himself, a Pierrot or Gilles, the clown from the commedia dell'arte tradition, as ambiguous as Watteau's famous figure. The painting brings tragedy and comedy within the same frame. Indeed, its frame, also designed by Gérôme, carries engraved masks representative of comedy and tragedy, as if to emphasize the point. A tragic event is clothed in the garb of a comedy. Yet these incongruities somehow do not detract from the solemnity of the composition. It echoes distinctly a Lamentation or perhaps a Deposition from the Cross.

Whereas moralizing critics were quick to see this as an indictment of recent, reckless duellists who had made headlines in France, others preferred to register the painting less as a moral condemnation than a quasi-literary commemoration. Not until the twentieth century, however, did a critic, Francis Haskell, suggest that the painting (in common with the image of duelling figures from the commedia dell'arte by Thomas Couture) may have illustrated a story by Jules Champfleury.[12] Théophile Gautier, meanwhile, admired the painting as a pictorial equivalent to a page from a story by Prosper Mérimée. Other writers and artists took up the peculiar pathos in this scene in their own ways. They saw it as a painting about duels, not about clowns.

The background is appropriately blurred and hazy, an analogue to the unknown and now irrelevant events that have led to this encounter. This contrast between the occluded background and the unforgivingly conclusive event at the fore dramatizes a progression intrinsic to the duel. The effect always mocks and supersedes the cause. All the previous rights and wrongs, pleasures and pains of a life are effaced at the moment of a duel. They are reduced to, excluded by, and forgotten in a simple matter of life and death.

The mismatch of content and form, the latter comically rigid or wooden, when the former is tragic, is characteristic of duelling. Even the most sober critics succumb to that frisson when politeness manages to prevail under the greatest strain. The adherence to these formulae can be by turns touching, consoling, or hilarious. But when they lead to a fatality, they seem all the more perplexing and hollow.

Perhaps inspired by the poignancy here, Gautier, in one of his own novels, *Capitaine Fracasse* (1863), likewise blurs the boundary between theater and life beyond. The hero, Fracasse, an actor in a ragbag troupe, seizes a blunted sword from the wardrobe where it lives as a prop, and he conducts a fierce duel with a nobleman.[13] They fight in costume. It is difficult to calculate the exact seriousness and danger of this bout, because its status as actual or theatrical event remains indeterminate. Gérôme's painting succeeds in depicting this duel (and perhaps duelling in general) as at once absurd and dignified.

If Gérôme had indeed been inspired by Mérimée's writing, the painting was to resonate in the pages of his contemporary authors. In one of Villiers de l'Isle Adam's stories, characters are accused of turning themselves into a pendant to the famous Gérôme painting.[14] Another of his short stories, "Sombre récit, conteur plus sombre," walks us along the same perilous line between theatrical spectacle and hideous actuality just as ambivalently. A group of playwrights, gathered in a café, listens with rapt attention to a story told by one of their colleagues. He was asked, he relates, to be the second to an old friend. He obliges, and on the morning of the following, wintry day, they turn up at a spot in the Bois de Boulogne, outside Paris, as agreed. The friend is shot and drops down dead. The group of authors, having listened to the story, greet it with a spontaneous round of applause. Never was a *conte cruel* better named.[15]

A conflict between content and form is often fundamental to texts that feature duels, for, while the duel was acknowledged to be a medieval rite in origin, it could, insofar as it is rule bound and binary, equitable and balanced, readily assume a supremely Classical form. Duellists were brutally civilized or courteously violent, a bewildering and compelling conjugation. The duel, the prerogative of noble, Western gentlemen, marries politeness and brutality in ways that disconcert throughout the eighteenth and nineteenth centuries.

The Savage Noble

The eighteenth-century appreciation of the *noble savage* is well-known. Indeed, it has been magnified and distorted into a mythology, for that precise combination of adjective and noun seems not to have been used as such in that age. Nevertheless, if figures approximating to the noble savage begin to intrigue eighteenth-century writers, from Rousseau onward, so their corollary—what we might call *savage nobles*—necessarily unsettle to a similar extent. It was impossible to appreciate so-called savages without, at the same time, deploring the soi-disant civilized gentlemen supposedly at the other extreme. Richardson's *Clarissa* is notable for the way in which Lovelace's machinations are deplored as the actions of a savage. This is not an inert analogy but a sustained comparison. Belford, his reformed friend, brackets Lovelace with his "fellow-savages in the Libyan wilds and deserts."[16] But in other texts, more provocatively, the exotic savage and the European nobleman are not grouped together but take each other's places. In Diderot's *Supplément au voyage de Bougainville,* the head of the Tahitian people, Orou, declares to the civilized Frenchmen who have arrived in Tahiti, "you are more barbaric than we are," as the tables are turned.[17] Diderot's friend and collaborator the abbé Raynal pauses, as he relates his own history of colonial troubles, to offer the reader a troubling rhetorical question upon the meeting of Cortés with the Aztecs he is about to conquer: "Reader, tell me, have civilized people arrived in the lands of savages, or have savages arrived in the lands of civilized people?" These good and gentle Mexican natives are archetypes of good sense, embodiments of self-sufficiency, for they are observed to be "without any vengeful feelings, almost without any passion."[18] The *esprit de vengeance* that the institution of the duel gratified was not, on this reading, intrinsic to human nature; this esprit was itself, never mind the duel that refined and sublimated it, a dubious privilege of European "civilization." Vengeance was supposed to be a primitively natural impulse refined and tempered by the duel, just as it was quelled by Christianity. But natural man, as imagined by Rousseau and his followers, stood tall, without any wish or need for vengeance.

The duel is a form of civilized, ordered violence, ostentatiously different from brawls and other, lower forms of aggression. This is especially apparent when duellists fight with swords, for the lower orders did not wear or know how to manipulate them. The pistol will bring the duel closer to other, ordinary forms of violence, hence, often, an accompanying insistence on, even a need for, more ceremony yet when that is the weapon of choice.

A duel is necessarily intraspecific, fought between members of the same class or, latterly, the same peer group. It is always an affirmation of a common bond, a shared privilege, even as those peers oppose or seek to eliminate each other. A duel presupposes a state of total equality, whether in social standing or through the parity of weapons, yet there is likely to follow a steep, rapid descent to the ultimate inequality, the greatest of all: one man lives; the other dies.

The duel then provides the pleasures of antithesis, while always implicitly paying tribute to the shared class and culture of the antagonists. Equally, accounts of duelling, even as they place emphasis on this anomaly, may in a complementary fashion draw attention to the antagonism within the apparently unitary individual defending himself, his own self-estrangement. The self can harbor inner opponents. The duellist has, on occasion, turned out to be his own worst enemy.

The duel epitomizes, perhaps magnifies, the hubris against which Augustine warned when writing that no one is so well-known to himself that he can be sure as to his conduct the day after.[19] Augustine's admonition resonates in Rousseau's writing. In a magisterial letter toward the end of *Julie*, the heroine identifies as a primary human weakness an overconfidence that leads us to read the symptoms of a moment as the signals of a permanent state. This is a foible that, sadly, characterizes humans of every stripe, in all possible guises, but the duellist's bravado is a supreme example of this generic human weakness. Indeed, the example Julie then provides is that of the flow and ebb of courage, from one day to the next: "The modest language of valor runs: 'I was brave on a given day'; but he who says 'I am brave' does not know what he will be tomorrow."[20]

The man who has challenged another to a duel trusts or assumes that, as the following day dawns, he is bound still to feel, first, the need to fight and, secondly, both the inclination and the strength to do so. But many literary texts show how the evaporation of the first desire, overnight, precedes a rapid weakening and decline of the latter feelings. Over time, the urge to fight, almost invariably, becomes less urgent. "La nuit porte conseil." But it is too late to heed that advice. He hears but cannot take it. The duel not only enacts honor imposed by peers and by society on an individual powerless to resist them; it exposes the way the individual himself internalizes these pressures and chooses, willfully, to invite them onto himself. It is not merely a struggle between society and individual which we have witnessed (although that is present); it is a combat within the individual, between the way he sees himself and is, between the way he feels on one day and the way he feels the day after, between his words and his deeds, between the experience of a moment and the replacement of that moment in time.

The challenge to duel, with the crucial delay that entails, opens a gap both between present and future and between intention and action or cause and consequence. These particular fears, fueled by the imagination and confirmed when a self fails to recognize itself from the preceding day, therefore reveal something archetypally hubristic and delusional in the human psyche.

The duellist can be considered an outlaw, and therefore an antisocial being, yet he is acutely susceptible to opinion and to honor, criteria that exist only in social contexts. It seems highly unlikely that two men would arrange to fight a duel on a desert island.[21] He has, at once, no regard for laws and a heightened awareness of norms. He is necessarily an outsider and an insider, an outlaw who is part of the establishment. Duelling is a practice that does not happen to be against, or rather above, the law; its exponents always celebrate the fact that it is liminal, conducted beyond the reach of the law and on the margins of social acceptability. If it is contested on the edge of society, the duel nevertheless remains a social act. Brecht states that "the smallest social unit consists not of one person but of two."[22] The presence of two people is sufficient for them to regulate each other, and duellists accordingly form a social unit, bound by custom and convention. The duel is then emphatically a social encounter, even if its purpose, or at least its effect, may be to eliminate half of that unit, leaving us with this paradox: the duel is a quintessentially social act, tending to result in an antisocial outcome.

The duellist is apparently trying to kill another man yet not wanting to do so. He seeks, ideally, to prevail in a duel by inflicting a symbolic wound. But then nor does the victor really win a duel; he survives it. Duels are, almost invariably, seen to be followed by feelings on the part of the victor of instant regret or relief, depending on the outcome. This apprehension may possibly be self-interested (because a fatal duel could be a massive inconvenience to the survivor), but it stems from a more profound sense that an equal has been killed. By killing a man, his right to have lived as an equal is recognized. Nevertheless, if the intention were to kill a particular man, the duel provides a hugely inefficient, not to say insecure, way of carrying this out. Duellists tend to face each other as opponents, not enemies. The vast majority of duels, at least in their literary and fictional manifestations, are elicited by haphazard, unguarded comments, casual offenses, rather than resulting from grudges nursed over the years.[23] The duel not only relegates and redeems the causes of a quarrel but unites two men in a collective experience that transcends their discrete wishes and needs. The peculiarity of duelling is ultimately attributable to the fact that it is necessarily a composite of resentment and respect, ingredients mixed and distributed in proportions that sometimes surprise the combatants themselves.

The Cult of Style

The fascination of duelling lies partly in the way that words turn into deeds, to be betrayed by them. Writers may be particularly drawn to duellists on account of a common preoccupation with style, at a cost, if necessary, to life itself. Honor—the duellist's raison d'être—is essentially a sort of style that, "concerned with harmonious appearances as much as with desirable consequences," tends "therefore toward the denial of life in favor of art."[24] Honorable as he may be, the duellist must remain morally ambiguous because, for all his noble punctilio, he is, ultimately, prepared to kill.

Violence in various arenas may be disguised and dignified by the vocabulary that grows around it, even if the terms first enlisted start out by being transparent. For instance, the *matador* is, as that noun tells us, notwithstanding the elegance of his attitudes, plainly and simply, a "killer." Yet, particularly in languages other than Spanish, the brutality it connotes has been diluted. Likewise, the duellist's willingness to kill, in cold blood, is often veiled under the lexicon used both by and of him. The moral code leads the duellist into highly delicate situations. He is prepared to kill, or to be killed, in the name of some stain on honor. But by killing with honor, a compound of stylishness and courtesy, he may be forgiven and redeemed.

Life, to which each and every creature clings by its instincts, could, it was assumed and asserted, be discarded with style only by an élite remote from and superior to such base promptings. It was not sufficient then merely to take part in a duel to prove one's membership of such an exalted élite; the duellist ought, ideally, to play his part with style, to invite, bring on, and toy with death. This meant not only proceeding with impeccable politeness, evinced by a mastery of the courtesies in issuing and accepting a challenge, but also, if possible, accompanying the performance with sallies of esprit and witty repartee, since an ability to think on one's feet is paramount, while understatement may indeed be counted the very essence of gentlemanliness.

It ought ideally to look as though the duellist were taking pleasure in the duel. In the seventeenth and eighteenth centuries, fighting was not just regarded as an occasional duty to be undertaken; it could be reckoned among the "pleasures and gratifications" of gentlemen. Steele cites a Frenchman who wondered how aristocrats, now that King Louis XIV had "taken away gaming, and stage-playing, and now fighting too" asks, "How does he expect Gentlemen shall divert themselves?" Duelling, from this perspective, was not exclusively a means to settle scores for these leisured gentlemen; it also provided a way of killing time. If the English hanged themselves to while that time away, their French counterparts apparently preferred to slaughter one another.[25] "Living? Our servants will do it for us."[26]

The duellist is, not just by tradition but by definition, the antithesis of the bourgeois, because he fights not for gain from his adversary but to declare who or what he is. Duels therefore do not produce losers and winners in quite the sense that prevails in other contests. Duellists gamble with the asset that is life itself, as members of the nobility gamble with their money, not so much for profit as to show their allegiance to a caste.[27] The duel for French noblemen, deprived of the immediacy of violence on the English stage, enabled them to divert themselves in combat of their own. But, of course, they not only furnished themselves with a spectacle but diverted the other classes that were expected to provide a suitably intrigued, dumb-founded audience for these self-staged characters. Their fearlessness, nonchalance, and good humor in the face of death were de rigueur.

Form and content, means and end, often find themselves in contra-diction. In 1835, it was, for instance, observed that "these days we slaughter one another more politely than in the past."[28] Verb and ad-verb pull in opposite directions. The particular effect may also be as-cribed to the coupling of a resolutely nasty and brutish verb with a more refined Latinate adverb, emphasizing, once again, that the duel offers an apparently civilized means of achieving a base end.

One of Smollett's countless duellists, Rourk Oregan, was, we read, "determined, in an honourable way, to cut the throats of all those who stood between him and his hopes."[29] The commas administer a little jolt, a momentary, muffled embarrassment about putting it in these terms. The adjective is left looking rather discomforted by the verb that follows. A similar effect is won by this description, again from Gautier's pen, of a spot carefully chosen for a rencontre: "The ground was firm and solid, without any stones or mounds or tufts of grass that might get in the way of the feet, and it offered the men of honor all the facili-ties necessary for cutting each other's throats correctly [pour se couper correctement la gorge entre gens d'honneur]."[30] Just as it is be-ginning to sound as though an estate agent were describing this highly sought-after duelling field, Gautier comes up with a brilliant touch, daring to insert the adverb "correctly" between verb ("cut") and object ("throat").

Even critics of duelling tend, on occasion, to resort to the same ar-senal of ironies and elegant evasions apparently favored by the duel-lists whom they would deplore. A strangely day-to-day, bizarrely mun-dane lexicon is often enlisted in order to conceal the true nature of events but also to mitigate the brutality that is about to occur. Oblique elegance soon forgives reckless violence. Discussions of duels, owing to their illegal status, often draw on a reservoir of euphemisms. Those euphemisms often take the form of understatement. And under-statement communicates a spirit of nonchalance, useful in in-timidating one's opponent. Thus, gentlemen with a reputation for duelling were said, in English-speaking lands, simply to have been "out" on occasions.

The formulae of the duel mean that the duellist need never be sin-cere; therein lies both his horror and his charm. The emphasis on style liberates gentlemen from scrupling about candor and honesty. Osten-tatiously polite euphemisms in this vocabulary tell us that style is of more consequence than the precise meaning of the act. Immediately after the duel that concludes Richardson's *Clarissa*, the principals, Lovelace and Morden, exchange their parting words in French. Two En-glishmen, fighting on Austrian territory, move into this language to communicate a shared sense of savoir faire and mutual regard for each other. The switch into French helps to promote an accompanying sense that the duel did not give sincere expression to a personal animus or realize intentions in the most literal, direct ways. Irrespective of the actual, innermost feelings harboured by these gentlemen about each other, both have played their roles.

French may well have been the most suitable tongue for adieux, the courtly language of civilization. It was also emphatically the language of diplomacy. The duel amounts to some business to be transacted. It is not, therefore, a crime that they have committed. The French lan-guage detaches them from their own action. The duel itself is, as it were, a foreign tongue, acquired and perfected by learning and experi-ence, and not merely the expression of innate and natural capacities.

Demanding Satisfaction

Sir Richard Steele seems to have felt strongly about the folly of duel-ling. No doubt drawing on his own experiences, he declared himself sure that it was not a practice to which any man ever willingly con-sented. It was, he asserted, a "custom which all men wish exploded, though no man has courage enough to resist it." If public opinion and custom were responsible for contriving the duel, which rested on the triple foundation of "cowardice, falsehood and want of understanding," the particular, indeed peculiar language with which its protocols were issued and discussed was responsible for colluding with the practice. Indignant at the dishonest, vacuous terms that mitigate "the science of quarrelling," Steele fantasizes about a simplification of its vocabulary. By stripping the rite of its ceremonious aspects and the attendant pomposities, duelling might be seen for the horror it really was. One "unintelligible" word vexes Steele's persona, Bickerstaff, in particular. It defies sense and challenges all explanations: the term *satisfaction.* He cites the case of an honest, unworldly country gentleman who, one day, fell into a disagreement with some "modern men of honour." When he received a letter the following morning, summoning him to a duel, he was puzzled: "This is fine doing (says the plain Fellow): Last night he sent me away cursedly out of humour, and this morning he fancies it would be a satisfaction to be run through the body."[31] Once again, the Latinate noun *satisfaction* sits uncomfortably with the blunt verb that follows.

That same tension vibrates in English works depicting or decrying duels throughout the century. In a comedy by Thomas Holcroft from the other end of the century, his vacillating nobleman, Lord Vibrate, has to check and interrupt himself, when he too ponders *satisfaction:* "He shall give—and what yet is satisfaction? Is it to be run through the body? Shot through the head? A man may then indeed be said to be satisfied—I had forgotten my doubts on duelling."[32]

Fielding's *Tom Jones* contrives to makes the word sound utterly vacuous. After Tom runs the jealous Fitzpatrick through with his sword, the latter memorably declares, "I have satisfaction enough; I am a dead man."[33]

The same meeting of plain English vernacular and smart Latinate terminology continues to resonate in nineteenth-century works. In Dion Boucicault's popular comedy *London Assurance* (1841), the contrasting consequences of the duel, abstract and physical, permit a sort of zeugma when Sir Harcourt Courtly explains that, after his wife eloped with an intimate friend of his: "Etiquette compelled me to challenge the seducer. So I received satisfaction—and a bullet in my shoulder at the same time."[34]

Such words as *satisfaction* helped to ennoble the act and make the duellist feel that he was performing a ritual that was honorable and antique. Yet satisfaction of this sort was unknown to the Classical ages in which the noun was minted. Duelling, it was agreed, was a medieval invention. If only plain Anglo-Saxon terms, remote from the discourses of the writers of Antiquity, could be used, much of the stylistic gloss integral to the prestige of the duel might wear off. Accordingly, Steele drafts a sort of specimen letter, a model cartel which, shorn of the usual linguistic garlands, conveys the sordid, grim reality that will confront the duellists. Turned into "downright English," a challenge would run like this:

> Sir,
>
> Your most extraordinary behaviour last night, and the liberty you were pleased to take with me, makes me this morning give you this, to tell you, because you are an ill-bred puppy, I will meet you in Hyde-Park an hour hence; and because you want both breeding and humanity, I desire you would come with a pistol in your hand, on horseback, and endeavour to shoot me through the head, to teach you more manners. If you fail of doing me this pleasure, I shall say, you are a rascal on every post in town: and so, Sir, if you will not injure me more, I shall never forgive what you have done already. Pray Sir, do not fail of getting every thing ready, and you will infinitely oblige, Sir
>
> Your most obedient humble servant, &c[35]

Even this challenge may seem to us to be worded rather politely; but it is supposed to be an exemplar of unceremonious bluntness, and it goes to show just how delicate and euphemistic such invitations were in normal circumstances. The language of this letter exposes, in the cold light of day, the stupidly contradictory, self-defeating nature of the enterprise. The recipient must "endeavour to shoot" his opponent "in the head," to teach *himself* more manners; if he "will not injure" him further, his opponent will not forgive him. The absurdities of the causal relationships here, the strange non sequitur fallacies in the logic of the duel are flagrant irregularities that the plainer language allows us to spot. Words such as *satisfaction* were among those that lent a supposedly barbaric practice a Classical dressing and antique pedigree, and a noble language of the sword remained largely in place even when the pistol replaced it.

Steele reckoned that the peculiarities of the vocabulary both concealed men from and reconciled them to an action that was ugly and cruel. Perhaps by using pistols, rather than swords, there would be an equivalent process of demystification. But it would not quite work out that way. On the contrary, as the rules circumscribing duels by pistol came into force in the nineteenth century, so a new, still-more-arcane vocabulary emerges. First recorded in 1836, coincident with Chatauvillard's new duelling code, is the very convenient verb to express the act of firing into the air and deliberately missing one's opponent: to *delope*. For example, "after his opponent had missed, the other principal immediately *deloped*"; "Upon a *delope*" (for the term exists as a substantive too), "the affair immediately terminates, and the seconds should never permit another discharge." The neologism to *leech* (to "step up" or to "advance") emerges likewise in response to the conditions of duelling by pistol, although the noun *releager* (or place of meeting) may owe its existence to the same mock-serious, semiprécieux disposition that gave us collective nouns, probably at around the same time.[36] Such arcane vocabulary serves the purpose of disguising the actual circumstances and events from members of the public who do not need to know what has been happening, but it also binds the duellists, who are necessarily social equals, linguistically within the tight confines of a shared code, thanks to which the literal and prosaic details of a fight become the mysteries and beauties of a duel.

Euphemism and Understatement

It is possible to read about duels without once encountering the term *duel.* Indeed, the term *encounter* may be more likely. In the first instance, the duellist will not wish to vaunt his achievement, if successful in a duel, or to alert the police or scare ladies if he has to talk about it beforehand. A standard synonym for a duel, whether in French or in English, German, or Italian, is an *affair(e).*

At a potentially high price, the duellist insists on or agrees to emphatically direct, unmediated redress, in the form of personally obtained satisfaction, as opposed to legally administered justice, yet his action is mediated in and accompanied by words that, not just for practical reasons but on stylistic grounds, belong to a culture of evasion. The authors of these euphemisms collude with a culture that pretends that this violence does not matter. Their elegance renders acceptable that violence and may redeem it. *Meiosis* is the stylistic deity here. By recognizing what has really happened, the authorial wink may persuade us that it does not need to be talked about seriously, if indeed at all. Euphemism neutralizes and apologizes for that which it does not quite describe.

Understatement is the stylistic preference of the duellist who quietly absorbs a brush with death into the fabric of his daily life. But that tendency is also the basis of some comic misprisions. In Dickens's short story "The Great Winglebury Duel" (1836), the hapless young fellow Trott nervously informs the mayor of the village that, to his regret, he has agreed to commit a "rash act," as he calls his prospective duel with Horace Hunter.[37] He begs the local dignitary to help him out of his predicament. The mayor naturally assumes that Trott is to be married and duly packs him off to Gretna Green with a bride promised to a different man. Trott therefore misses his appointment at the duelling field and marries the woman instead. Dickens's story may hinge on a silly, implausible misunderstanding, but it is grounded in the culture of understatement central to the ethic of duelling.

Elegant evasions are useful in diverting the attention of the censors but also in allowing those gentlemen, in turn, to pretend that they are themselves not unduly troubled. For this reason, no doubt, Lovelace designates the duel that he is about to contest an "interview."[38] There is also a pleasure in evasion, a wish to play along with the illusion that the gentlemen might be engaged in something other than a duel. These periphrases are polite alternatives, minimizing the fears to which the duellist may be subject but also extending in the same breath some grace to the opponent. Fear appears to be tamed in these formulae. An adversary will be bound not only to acknowledge the gentleman's right to challenge him but to recognize his savoir faire. The courtesies cool and anonymize the individual who uses them, yet they are also intimidatingly calm.

Sir Lucius O'Trigger, in Sheridan's *The Rivals*, would, of course, never be so vulgar as to call a duel a duel, even if his surname gives the game away. As he says, bowing to a bemused Captain Absolute, "I humbly thank you, Sir, for the quickness of your apprehension— you have named the very thing I would be at; . . . I should take it as a particular kindness, if you'd let us meet in Kingsmead Fields, as a little business will call me there at six o'clock, and I may dispatch both matters at once."[39] His "little business" is, of course, another duel that he has previously orchestrated. The sort of euphemism in which the duel is clad here is reminiscent of similarly downbeat evasions in Smollett's texts. For instance, toward the end of the *Life and Adventures of Sir Launcelot Greaves,* Captain Crowe, spoiling for a duel, intends to "balance accounts" with Mr. Dawdle.[40] Curiously, for all the insistence on the nobility of duelling and the good name of those who were suited by class to fighting the duel, this lexicon turns the duel into a transaction, which aligns them with a mercantile class from which they would normally want to be distanced.

The abstruse duelling vocabulary comprises circumlocutions and euphemisms so extravagantly delicate that, like a figleaf, they reveal as they conceal. English-speaking writers of course may resort to French terms to dignify and polish acts of violence, although Latin too may be serviceable. Once again, O'Trigger comes to mind. He memorably suggests to Bob Acres, ahead of his duel, that "if an unlucky bullet should carry a *Quietus* with it," it would be useful if he had sorted out his "family matters." "A *Quietus!*" responds Acres, drawing attention to the preposterously euphemistic quality of the Latinism, an abbreviation of *quietus est,* which may be translated, literally, as "he is at rest."[41] On this occasion, the faux-antique patina that coats the vocabulary of duelling outdoes bogus medieval terms in suggesting that even a bullet may come endowed with a Classical pedigree.

Laws and Rules

"The Law has no power over heroes," asserts Arabella, the "Female Quixote"; "they may kill as many men as they please."[42] Lawless violence is an inevitable byproduct of chivalry, and the sort of honor exemplified by duelling necessitated a brush both with the law and with death.

Duelling was a crime, more or less wherever and whenever it occurred. Yet, uniquely and intriguingly, in breaking the law, the duellist nevertheless had to adhere to rigorous rules. He could boast of his freedom and autonomy in defying the law, the state, common sense itself (not to mention the instinct for self-preservation universal among creatures), but he must also exemplify utter subordination to prescribed rules. The resulting tension means that a duel bears, in both form and effect, a natural resemblance to a French Classical tragedy. Defiance and obedience occur at the same time; freedom is achieved within a structure that subordinates the individual. And the duellist somehow contrives to appear at one and the same time a monster of selfishness and a prodigy of selflessness.

The laws of the realm and the dictates of honor not only failed to converge; they were diametrically opposed in most countries. In cases of murder or manslaughter, a passionate impulse or momentary lapse would usually mitigate, in the eyes of the law, while, by the standards of duellists, such conduct was evidence of a weakness that only debased the duellist and discredited the outcome. An Old Bailey trial after a fatal duel fought in 1694 shows how impulsive or passionate actions were looked at with more indulgence. However, the "malice propense," deplored and punished by the law, was no different from the sang froid expected of and admired in the duellist. The ambivalence embodied by the duellist, a criminal who seems to obey a higher code, is equivalent to that elicited by other attractively lawless figures, such as rakes, highwaymen, and pirates, whose heyday appears to have been the eighteenth century.

There are, schematically speaking, four principal types of duellists, at least in the pages of the works we have encountered. The *dutiful* duellist—that is the gentleman drawn, against his better judgment and at odds with his inclinations, into a duel that he regrets is illegal and that he fears he will lose; the *inveterate* duellist—the psychopathic man who, wholly indifferent to the law, lives in pursuit of strife and excitement, one of those men "that put quarrels purposely on others, to taste their valour";[43] the *vain* duellist—the self-regarding libertine who chooses not only to break but to flout the law; and finally, the *quixotic* duellist, whose priority is chivalry, whose concern is justice. All four have their own attractions and frustrations, but the latter is perhaps the most vexing.

Smollett was evidently fascinated by the duellist as a paradoxical figure bent on breaking the law, the better to enforce justice. Smollett's would-be Don Quixote, Sir Launcelot Greaves, styles himself, rather grandly, as a self-appointed "co-adjutor to the law."[44] It is over that vast, uncharted region beyond the reach of laws that he means to range, sword in hand. Such self-righteous duellists could then commend themselves to writers, who might, in turn, see themselves as supernumerary lawyers, charged with the same task of addressing those several wrongs and grievances that remained invisible to the law. Some writers claimed, more or less plausibly, that this was the raison d'être underpinning their work. Such was Laclos's stance when defending *Les liaisons dangereuses:* "the rightful province of the moralist, whether he be playwright or novelist, begins where laws have no effect [se taisent]."[45] The novelist provided an extralegal form of public justice, be that by ridiculing human foibles or by exposing human vices, which, possibly immoral, were nevertheless not ipso facto illegal. Laclos cites as a sponsor of this idea Molière's *Tartuffe.*[46] Tartuffe has not acted illegally at any point, but his behavior asks for the opprobrium of a writer. Accordingly, then, one of this novel's conclusions and resolutions is afforded, seemingly to the satisfaction of all parties, by a fatal duel, to which the law turns a blind eye. However, what remains less clear is the role of the duel in this supposedly moral quest. Laclos may be suggesting either that, in the absence of effectual laws or indeed in areas of interpersonal conduct that cannot possibly be regulated by the law, a duel provides a valuable, alternative enforcement service, in common with the novel, or, conversely, that the novel, unlike the law, refuses to disregard the devastating effects of the abuse that is duelling itself. So either the novelist supplants the lawyer, monitoring wrongs and chastising foibles beyond the realm of the law, and thereby recognizing a similar impulse in the duellist, or, in this case, the duel is actually one of those wrongs that the authorities have not successfully outlawed. This idea had been floated, notably in the terms of a prize question framed in 1761 by the Académie des jeux floraux, based in Toulouse: "Has the wisdom of literary works done more against the folly of duelling than the jurisdiction of laws?"[47]

If poets were famously to be appreciated as "unacknowledged legislators," certain duellists feel impelled to act as supplementary lawgivers. Particularly in the eighteenth century, duelling provides a test case not only for the strengths of the laws of the land, when weighed against the customs of a class or caste, but also for the competing claims of philosophy and the arts, each in its own way promoted as an implicit legislator.

Ultimately acquiescent, Smollett's Sir Launcelot Greaves learns, under the influence of his fair lady Aurelia, to accept the sovereignty of the laws, and, finally hanging up his lance and sword, he chooses instead to pursue his enemies through the courts: "Sir Launcelot was not now so much of a knight-errant, as to leave Aurelia to the care of Providence, and pursue the traitors to the farthest extremities of the earth. He practised a much more easy, certain, and effectual method of revenge, by instituting a process against them, which, after writs of *capias, alias, & pluries,* had been repeated, subjected them both to outlawry."[48] Sir Launcelot ultimately recognizes due process, and the new method of revenge he pursues is recommended as "easy, certain and effectual," even though the accumulated writs, festooned with their Latin names, hardly suggest that the law is any less anachronistic or obfuscatory. Smollett might have added that the new method was also "legal," except his hero would never think of subordinating himself to the law to that extent. Nor does Smollett tarry in order to describe these legal adventures in any detail. The vindication of the law and the assumption of good sense by the pseudo-Quixote necessarily spell the end of the story. The triumph of the law appears then to be definitive, but the novel does not take as much interest in it.

The duel shows man to be the autonomous arbiter of his own experience, without recourse to higher authority. Privilege, its etymology rooted in "private law," was measured and manifested by the nobleman's contempt for the laws that applied to others. Moreover, the resolution of a conflict by means of a duel, without recourse to third parties, was responsible for a sense that, even when fatalities occurred, relationships could be restored. The duel was then the privileged expression of a society that was essentially sedentary and secluded, a society where there were no strangers to whom cases in need of resolution could be entrusted. Whereas the law might provide solutions without reconciliation, the duel would offer conclusive outcomes, allowing for reintegration. The contrast between the mechanisms of the law and the rituals of the duel looks favorable to the latter and can

induce a certain nostalgia for a society in which relationships between individuals could yet be restored by them.

Continued instances of duelling provided an opportunity to lament,
or to enjoy, the insufficiencies of the laws of the land. Flaubert is supposed to have remarked that "every lawyer carries the wreck of a poet,"
and it evidently consoled poor poets to think that pettifogging lawyers
were all writers manqués.[49] But, in fact, the converse would appear to
be just as true: Petrarch, Ariosto, Tasso, Milton, Pierre Corneille, Voltaire, Walter Scott, Balzac, Maupassant, among many others, took seriously to writing, once it was obvious that the law would not appeal.
As Balzac complained, laws were like spiderwebs in that they detained
the smallest objects, while allowing the largest to pass through. For
many writers, the persistence of duelling seemed to point to massive
legal toothlessness or plain incompetence. Indeed, the reason some
duellists gave for their actions was the indifference or impotence of the
law in the face of aristocratic license and impunity. Famously interminable legal cases, such as *Jarndyce and Jarndyce*, are often associated with Dickensian London, but the legal embroilments of other ages
and places were no less tortuous. In these circumstances, the appeal
of the duel is unmistakable. In the eighteenth century, the recourse to
the point of honor by demonstrably controlled, intelligent gentlemen
directed a reproach at the legal system. The duellist exposed not only
the unenforceable nature of the particular legislation against duelling,
which repeatedly proved powerless to prevent or deter it, but all other
laws that required expenses and patience beyond the capacities of most
people, before justice could be attained. Dying in a duel is surely preferable to being "slowly murdered by the law."[50]

The duel is made to look all the more conclusive and satisfying
when we come to the very last words of *Clarissa*, which follow immediately from the description of Lovelace's death at the hands of Morden.
We already know that virtuous and wise Clarissa, however fearful of
the duel and implacably opposed to the practice she might be, is no
less determined to avoid proceeding with a case at law and thereby
handing responsibility to the apparatus of the state. We now learn
that Clarissa's brother, James Harlowe, having married inadvisedly, is
engaged in an endless process of litigation, even though he lacks "so
much patience as is necessary to persons embarrassed in law." As in

Candide, where, buffeted by successive misfortunes, Martin wonders in the end whether violent convulsions might ultimately be preferable to the lethargy of ennui, the ending here offers a contrast between the finality of the bout and the limitlessness of litigation, between the deadly yet dignified duel and the harrowing ungenerosity of "a lawsuit for life."[51] The incidence of duelling was, in most places, an open secret. An overwhelmingly indulgent attitude to a lawless yet prestigious pursuit was by no means exceptional in the early modern period. Gambling, in the eyes of the law, was not allowed but tolerated, with the result that gambling debts (or "playdebts," as they were known in the eighteenth century) were afforded no legal status.[52] In Britain, until the Night Poaching Act of 1800, the vast majority of people did not take poaching seriously as a crime, and illegal trade in game was profitable. The contradictory responses elicited by duelling also recall the range of reactions excited by castrati around the same time. Charles Burney, compiling his *Dictionary of Music,* was sent ever farther south while he traveled in Italy, in search of the location of this "vocal manufacture," as he delicately called it, for it was, officially, illegal.[53] Yet the practice was deplored no more than its products were admired, often revered. There was no necessary tension between these attitudes. It seemed possible to entertain both views at once and to protect oneself against accusations of hypocrisy, by adopting the neat Augustinian practice of contriving both to hate the sin and love the sinner. Jonathan Swift renewed that idea in his own endearingly homespun terms when writing to Alexander Pope: "I hate and detest that animal called man, although I heartily love John, Peter, Thomas, and so forth."[54] This idea seems to have been particularly operative whenever the privileged predicament of the duellist comes into view. Even as duelling was despised and deplored, duellists would often command affection and admiration.

An illegal obligation, the duel then both subordinates and frees its exponents. It thus exemplifies, in vivid colors, the spirit of chivalry itself, which, as celebrated by Edmund Burke, is nothing less than "that proud submission, that dignified obedience, that subordination of the heart, which kept alive, even in servitude itself, the spirit of an exalted freedom."[55]

The Duel over Women

In the third act of Arthur Schnitzler's play *Liebelei*, first performed in 1895, Christine is shocked to learn that her lover, Fritz, has been killed in a duel:

> CHRISTINE: But I must be allowed to find out who has killed him, and for what reason . . .
> THEODORE: It was . . . for no real reason . . .
> CHRISTINE: You are not telling the truth . . . Why, why . . .
> THEODORE: Dear Christine . . .
> CHRISTINE: [*She goes up to him, as though she means to interrupt— at first she says nothing, looks him in the eye, and then suddenly screams*] Because of a woman?
> THEODORE: No—
> CHRISTINE: Yes—for a woman. . . . [56]

The hesitation between prepositions, and the corresponding movement from genitive to accusative, indicates the indeterminacy of the act of duelling, when ostensibly fought *over* a woman or on her behalf. "Because," and the duel was provoked or caused by a woman; "for," and the duel was fought, perhaps more generously or gratuitously, with her in mind. The former is perhaps intelligible and forgivable, caused by a scrape; the latter implies a more deliberate donation of Fritz's life, in her name; the former connotes a past that has been shared, the latter the prospect of a future.

Christine could, it seems, live with the idea that Fritz had died for her or even because of her. But death on behalf of another lady is a betrayal greater than that of sleeping with her. Redress is always possible, in the second case, but the great honor and privilege of having a man die on one's behalf constitute an irrevocable, unequivocal proof of love: greater love hath no man than he should give his life in a duel. Indeed, Christine is evidently concerned less by Fritz's death than by the reasons for it. Her understandably urgent need to know the details of this case suggests that the duel does signify yet. It retains, even in the cynical urbane world of Vienna at the turn of the century, the capacity to yield potent symbolic truths.

Dying *for* a lady seems almost impossibly gallant, yet the preposition may also militate against that sense, because it potentially denotes a willfully reckless act, a perhaps self-conscious, self-regarding statement, rather than an unavoidable scrape: "What well-born woman could possibly deny her heart to a man who has risked his life for her?" asks the narrator of Gautier's *Mademoiselle de Maupin* (1834).[57] It is a resolutely rhetorical question, yet it also implies that honor places demands on women, who might prefer to reject the claims of the gallant gentleman, even as they feel—or are supposed to feel—beholden and obliged to him. Indeed, in one of the stories interlarded in the *Adventures of Roderick Random*, Miss Williams tells the story of Horatio, as she chooses to call him. He is a mysterious "gentleman," quite unknown to her, who suddenly steps out to defend her honor when it is threatened. However, she realizes, when he returns victorious from the duel to claim her as his prize with ungentlemanly haste, that he has fought the duel for her, rather than on her behalf. His concern for her honor does not outlive the duel. He lays claim to her in the crudest way imaginable, winning her simply because he won the fight, without consulting her or considering honor in the process.[58]

The prestige of the man who has fought a duel, as Flaubert's received idea suggests, was well established, in spite or indeed on account of the legal objections to the practice; at least as great, however, was the prestige conferred on the lady in whose name a duel was fought. The female response to duelling, as imagined by literary texts in the eighteenth and nineteenth centuries, is often at once compassionate and reasonable, yet in these pages are women who not only dreamed of causing a duel to be fought over them but swooned at the thought of a man expiring, her name on his lips. Just as suspect as the sexual avidity and opportunism of the man winning a woman by a duel was her own vanity in allowing or encouraging him to fight it.

"The blood that is shed for a lady, enhances the value of her charms," declares Arabella, the "female Quixote," who has been reared on romances and tales of chivalry. Yet even her cousin and foil, Miss Glanville, the more sober and knowing of the ladies throughout, confesses for her part, "I should not be sorry to have a duel or two fought for me in *Hyde-park*," only to add concessively, "but then I would not have any blood shed for the world."[59] Such a bloodless duel epitomizes an ideal of harmless violence that meets the Enlightenment need for good sense and moderation, while gratifying its taste for self-sacrifice and politeness.

Smollett's hero Roderick Random takes a fancy to a lady by the name of Melinda and proposes to fight a duel over her with one of many doltish braggarts we meet in the pages of eighteenth-century novels, Bragwell. Random runs the idea of his chivalric duel by her, hoping and supposing that she might care enough for him to fear for his life. But he need not have worried, for, on the contrary, he reports, "I could perceive by the sparkling of her eyes, that she would not have thought herself affronted in being the subject of a duel. I was by no means pleased with this discovery of her thoughts, which not only argued the most unjustifiable vanity, but likewise the most barbarous indifference."[60] She ought really to have swooned or wept at the thought of his possible death, while bemoaning the barbarousness of duelling. But she has failed his shibboleth. Happily, Narcissa, his eventual wife, passes a similar assignment toward the end of the novel.

When women (on whose behalf the duel was supposedly waged) declared themselves unimpressed, there were new possibilities for demystifying and deterring the duel. Clarissa and Julie, as we have seen, are invested by Richardson and Rousseau with the character and the capacity to talk about the evils of duelling from a vantage point that looks objective. Rousseau was, he wrote, convinced that changes in opinion could only take effect if women, "on whom, to a great extent, the thinking of men depended," could be allowed to intervene.[61] Female writers could speak out about the follies and perils of duelling. Susanna Centlivre is one such writer who demystifies the duel as a virile pursuit. In Centlivre's comedy *The Beau's Duel; or, A Soldier for the Ladies* (1702), foppish William Mode, "a mere compound of powder, paint and affectation," purports to fight a duel, while Colonel Manly looks on in dismay, validating the idea that duels are not fought by proper soldiers and real men.[62]

Paradoxically, in an instant, duels may turn the most implacable of enemies into the best of friends. Typical of such metamorphoses is that of the wild Irishman Rourk Oregan, who makes a momentary appearance in Smollett's first novel. After duelling inconclusively with Roderick Random, he "threw away his pistols, and hugging [Random] in his arms, cried, 'Arrah, by Jesus, now you are the best friend I have met with these seven long years.'"[63] The duel, a practice unique to gentlemen, reinforces what they have in common, even as they stand at odds with each other. This rapprochement may occur in any circumstances, but duels caused by or fought over women are naturally and particularly conducive to these expressions of fraternal fondness.

The duel turns out, surprisingly, to be a conduit for male friendship, between the combatants. This friendship, founded on a shared experience, is also built on their common distance from women, and the duel may encourage them to measure and sometimes magnify the profound chasm between themselves and women. In Pushkin's *Eugene Onegin*, this dynamic is in evidence. The enmity between men can seem to be more intense than the intimacy between them and women. Conrad's short story "A Duel," among others, explores this imponderable discrepancy. Indeed, when the cause of a duel does not implicate women, and particularly when this cause is utterly frivolous, the dispute, by the curious logic of the duel, may prove more durable.

Even those duels fought in the defense of female honor can paradoxically unite the rivals in contempt for women. Indeed, should the duel prove fatal, there is still time on occasions for men to express to each other fond feelings of warm regard and mutual respect. The dying Valmont, reconciled with his opponent Danceny, ensures that Merteuil's reputation is ruined. There is no lingering allusion to women with whom he has been intimate, Madame de Tourvel, let alone Cécile de Volanges, or any word of those to whom he is related, such as his loving aunt, Madame de Rosemonde. As Lovelace expires, likewise reconciled with and embraced by his opponent, he utters highly ambiguous exclamations about Clarissa. These violent, virile clashes, whether in Laclos, Casanova or Schnitzler, cannot quite dispel the feeling that they are actually a distraction from or perhaps a sublimation of the impossible, yet eternal duel between male and female.

Women seemed quite capable of surviving without duelling, and they could be the source of more conciliatory wisdom: Vengeance was incompatible with happiness, warned the Marquise Du Châtelet in her *Discours sur le bonheur*.[64] It is, however, clear in many novels that vengeful impulses were not necessarily less present or pronounced among women. The Marquise de Merteuil, after all, initiates *Les liai-*

sons dangereuses with her bid to take revenge. But her need for revenge cannot be sated through violence of her own, and it is necessarily through a series of mediated actions, perpetrated by the proxies whom she appoints for the purpose, that she schemes. Equally, the text ends on an unsettling note. Madame de Rosemonde, vexed at the fatal duel that has robbed her of her nephew, declares that she will not avenge Danceny and that his troubled conscience need be her only consolation. But we should perhaps not take her exactly at her word. Her revenge is the work itself: she seems likely to have passed on the letters that now form this book. The act of publishing, or indeed that of reading, turns out to be a less-than-innocent pursuit. We are ultimately indebted to a female form of revenge for the pleasures of learning about the duel that is its more extravagant male incarnation.

Epilogue: 1918

Time cools, time clarifies; no mood can be maintained quite unaltered over the course of hours.

—THOMAS MANN, *DER ZAUBERBERG*

VISITORS to the Hall of Mirrors in Versailles who can resist looking at themselves or up at the inscriptions on the vault may observe the precise spot at which, on 28 June 1919, the Treaty of Versailles that ended World War I was signed. It is tempting to venture an uncontroversial half truth in asserting that the First World War was the war to end all duels. Never such punctilio again. The inglorious drudgery of trench warfare surely cast into the darkness of a total eclipse any exalted notion of face-to-face combat. The extinction of the duel presented a small, secondary symptom of the "immense castration of Europe" entailed by the Great War.[1]

Thomas Mann's momentous, epochal novel *The Magic Mountain (Der Zauberberg)*, published in 1924, stages a descent, literally, from the ritualized combat that is a duel into the unprecedentedly amorphous, anonymous violence of World War I. At the Berghof Sanatorium, perched high in the Swiss Alps, Hans Castorp, initially paying a visit to his cousin, has ended up becoming a patient, having accustomed himself to a cycle of eating, sleeping, and talking, such that he has forsaken the rhythms that characterized the world below and cannot face its demands. Mann's novel brings together a number of patients from all over Europe and beyond who engage in garrulous expostulation. Eventually, yet suddenly, however, two of those loquacious patients, Ludovico Settembrini, an apostle of progress, a freemason who believes in the Enlightenment, and Leo Naptha, a Jesuit who subscribes to the medieval worldview, square up and find themselves committed to a duel.

This duel, eight hundred or so pages into the novel, is positioned toward the end of the book and, no less precariously, at the end of an era. It takes place, in all senses, on a precipice, almost teetering over into another world. The duel reaches a new height, a height of absurdity in these pages. Indeed, it constitutes a veritable *nec plus ultra* of the genre, capping and condensing all the contrarieties encountered hitherto: the symbolic representation of antithetical weltanschauungen, the tension between intellectual distinctions and personal animus; the bizarrely obligatory, inexorable nature of the duel, as the present obeys a past in which it cannot believe.

The occurrence of this duel seems inordinately contrived, because of both the improbably intellectual argument that engenders it and its prominent position at the end of the book, which turns it into a deus ex machina. This text, which contrives to turn its readers into patients, such is its absorbing, unremitting quality, cascades into violence. A surpassingly verbose text, this novel of ideas descends steeply into a dizzying spiral of actions. Austere, confined, and airless, it rushes, at the death, to a conclusive action, in a manner that recalls the sudden sovereignty of deeds over words in *Clarissa* and *Les liaisons dangereuses*. As in those novels, the duel takes place in a wintry setting. A frozen waterfall provides a chilly backdrop. Indeed, a crystallization of the duel can be said to occur, for this is a superlative encounter: it is to be contested at the highest level, above even the Berghof Sanatorium; fought at the shortest distance (for three paces is, astonishingly, the proposed distance at which the principals are to shoot); its cause is as ridiculous as any of the past; it promises, ostensibly, to be the ultimate duel. Held back until the final pages of this novel, it would seem to certify definitively the infirmity and the absurdity of soi-disant civilized Europeans. It is an encapsulating moment of utter madness.

The duel is also frozen in time. Something strange seems to happen to time, upon the arrangement of a duel. The duel is inherently backward looking—not only does it draw meaning from noble roots in single combat, its participants remaining necessarily conscious of their ancestry, but, more locally, by arranging a duel, they contrive to stop the clock ticking. The offense is suspended in time. Prospective duellists find themselves obliged to endeavor, in order to lend any real meaning to their enterprise, to keep present an event in the past. The folly of the duel is not just murderous; it is ontological, for it attempts to defy the natural rhythms of time. Here, an especially protracted lapse of time between the insult that is the duel's cause and its occurrence stretches out. It will be three long days before the gentlemen meet again. That tardiness is duplicated by a sense that this is an age, on the cusp of World War I, sacrificing to a deity in which no one believes, playing out a hollow ritual with no conviction.

By filtering the duel through the gaze of Hans Castorp, the passive and impressionable young German, the novel allows suspense to attend not just the outcome of the duel but its occurrence. Ought he to be able to prevent it? Will reason or madness prevail? Castorp is not really a participant, just as he is not really a patient. Yet the duel sucks him in too. Settembrini is an utterly characteristic latter-day duellist, in that he does not need to be told that the duel is an absurdity. Indeed, he is capable of telling us this. Yet he will take part, his theoretical disapproval notwithstanding. Settembrini wishes to fight with swords, but Naptha opts for pistols, preferences that seem ironic, given their respective standpoints and contrasting commitments to progress.

Madness prevails and the duel goes ahead, but, as it turns out, the violence is tempered by a perverted form of dignity. Settembrini, who has the first shot, decides to *delope*, the first time he has been seen to back down or compromise. He appears to have seen sense; Naptha, for his part, turns the pistol on himself. He sinks to the ground, blood trickling in the snow. It is a lesson we may have learned from Mérimée and Pirandello: duellists called Leo or Leone are usually killed. Something hubristic in the name evidently invites that outcome. In this case, there also lingers a suspicion that the duel was to have provided a form of assisted suicide for the devout Jesuit.

Even at this late stage, Mann provides a now familiar scenario with a new twist, for, uniquely, this proves to be an encounter in which both principals fire, without shooting at each other. Neither duellist has engaged with the other sufficiently to be seriously challenged, let alone persuaded by him; they continue to wrestle with their own demons. It is a modern tale of Narcissus, with the mountains providing the echo as the shots ring out. The *delope* and the suicide that result here confirm the sense that neither man required the presence of the other in this parody of a duel, an encounter in which the principals do not meet. The duel would then seem to epitomize the self-destructive, narcissistic folly of European civilization. It merely completes a *dialogue des sourds.* The duel marks the failure of dialogue, imprisoning them in their own prolix arguments.

Yet the duel exhibits a curious, counterintuitive chivalry that rapidly looks precious, even quaint by comparison with what follows immediately in the concluding pages, for Castorp now descends to the flatland to take up arms for the Germans. World War I has broken out. There follows, in the final pages of this novel, a compelling evocation of the horrors that overtake the soldiers. The indiscriminate nature of this warfare elevates the duel into an indulgence, a privileged form of aggression, a luxury of violence afforded by a complacent society. The principals, dwarfed by a conflict of national and global dimensions, look like toy soldiers. They seem to be fighting over nothing. But the inverse may possibly apply—the duellist faces his death with dignity and pride. He always makes a decision to fight, albeit conditioned by social norms, whereas the soldier in World War I is compelled and embroiled. Mann's staccato style conveys the consternation these terrors bring, as the complex ruminations of the intellectual sparring partners make way for childlike questioning. "Where are we? What is that? Where has this dream led us to?"[2]

So Castorp duly disappears into a nameless crowd, swallowed by the national interest and by the turmoil of war. Mann has hitherto advertised the names of the protagonists, even those of little or no consequence in the text, so that they are sometimes obtrusively present.[3] Mann now describes a veritable block of men, marching toward their target, unless they first stumble to their deaths: "They are three thousand, so that they can be two thousand when they reach the hills, the villages; that is the meaning of their number. They are a body calculated as sufficient, even after great losses, to attack and carry a position and greet their triumph with a thousand-voiced huzza."[4]

In such circumstances, it does not matter whether Castorp lives or dies. The author suggests that he will probably die, but he cannot be sure. He abdicates responsibility for his character, just as the machinery of the war propels itself, indifferent to him. So the real sickness rages not up there on the mountain but down here. The sanatorium may have seemed nearer to Babel than to Basel. But that ceaseless polyglot chatter which fills the dining room and balconies of the sanatorium, exasperating though it may be, is now bathed in a civilized aura. As ever, the duel has proved to be an emphatically cosmopolitan affair, not a nationalistic bout.

As it turns out, the duel not only stages a binary opposition; it itself forms one half of an antithesis. It represents the past; World War I announces the present. The duel embodies some semblance of dignity, even in a state of sickness, while the Great War summons horrors into the deepest recesses of a supposedly progressive world. If the duel is preposterous, the war is diabolical. The duel offers a privileged, exalted way to die, in retrospect.[5]

The cosmopolitan society hosted by the Berghof Sanatorium is comparable to the polyglot, multiethnic peoples encompassed by the vast Habsburg Empire. Indeed, the routines of the Berghof (thanks in part to its suffix) invite analogies with life at court, its ceremonies, perhaps its hypocrisies, certainly its infantilizing character. In the *Radetzkymarsch*, written within a decade of Mann's work in 1932, Joseph Roth likewise devotes considerable space to describing a duel or, to be more precise, its agonizing preliminaries, even as his novel moves with great economy across three generations of the Trotta family and evokes the gradual collapse of the Habsburg Empire. Roth also explicitly aligns duel and war in a mutually questioning relationship, just as Mann's novel transports us vertiginously from a duel into the jaws of World War I.

Trotta's grandfather earned the gratitude of the Emperor Franz Josef and gained a barony after saving him from death at the battle of Solferino in 1859. Indeed, he is henceforward known as "the Hero of Solferino." Solferino haunts the story, and it is, of course, that act of heroism notwithstanding, the abiding memory of a defeat. The hero's son settles, unheroically, behind his desk into an ordered existence as district commissioner. His own son, partly to assuage his disappointed father, joins the army, but unlike his disciplined father and austere grandfather, he is soon taking to a disoriented, indolent life, punctuated by extramarital liaisons. One of these relationships results in a duel, contested by Dr. Demant, with whose wife Trotta has been having the affair, and Captain Taittinger, who makes a distasteful remark about her conduct. Young Trotta is then indirectly responsible for the duel, but, like Castorp, he feels at once estranged from the values of the previous generations, doomed to feel complicit with the duellists, yet powerless to stop them, no doubt incapable of going through with a duel himself or of subscribing to its code of values. Trotta and Castorp are both younger, bemused onlookers, beholding a rite that they cannot emulate or comprehend, authorizing the reader's own detached confusion. And we, for our part, are not encouraged to identify with the principals or take sides; we are invited rather to share the bewilderment, compounded by guilt and anxiety, of the main character observing it.

Roth evokes, with particular potency, the agony to which time subjects humans in such a predicament. Unusually, the duel is prearranged for the following morning at 7:20 a.m. That may be the precise moment at which the sun rises, but those twenty minutes carry their own supplementary torment. The precision of this timing and the accuracy of the pistols are, unfortunately, not matched by a corresponding moral efficacy. This is a society that knows exactly when and how matters are to be administered but has lost any understanding it ever had as to why it is concerned with them. The duel, depicted in this light, provides a focus for the doom-laden anticipation by the empire of its own overdue demise. It is apparent throughout the text that this is a society waiting impotently for death—that of the elderly, infirm Emperor Franz Josef, that of itself. Roth depicts the agony of a society living off the past, incapable of reform, willfully deaf to the rumblings of the approaching storm (the metaphor with which this text, like that of Mann, approaches the First World War), when violence will be taken into national ownership. Meanwhile, the text echoes with the jangling of unearned spurs. We learn, in a laconic, secondhand message conveyed to Trotta, that Taittinger and Demant have shot each other dead. Simultaneous deaths in a duel, although not without precedent historically, have never occurred in the pages of all the works hitherto. The futility and absurdity of the duel are emphasized here by this outcome, which, in common with Mann's rencounter, is neither remotely retributive nor redemptive.

Indeed, a downward trajectory exerts a pull in this text, as at the end of *The Magic Mountain*. The duel occurs at the apex of a social pyramid. But World War I carries conflict to the base of that mountain. Young Trotta steps down, literally, from the cavalry (to the acute disappointment of his father) and joins the infantry, before dropping out of the army altogether. But, eventually, when World War I beckons, he is recalled and killed, while crawling up an embankment, a couple of pails in his hand, an inglorious death suitable to this troglodyte conflict.

The Habsburg Empire, an uneasy amalgam of races and peoples, is by no means recollected by Roth as a peaceful idyll. The assortment is not always harmonious, yet there seems to be a residue of grudging respect; and the violence enshrined by the duel at least takes place on a human scale. Indeed, Taittinger's insult to Demant, a Jew, is duly compounded by an anti-Semitic slur. But this detail helps to make Roth's point. Taittinger insults Demant enough to provoke a duel but respects him sufficiently to fight it. Later, as German nationalism gathered force, Jews would be excluded from the privilege of duelling.

While Mann's juxtaposition of duel and war suffices, structurally and symbolically, Roth's narrator allows himself a leisurely disquisition on the duel as the insignia of an age in which the death of even one human being was yet endowed with some significance.

> Back then, before the Great War, . . . it was not yet a matter of indifference whether a person lived or died. If a life was snuffed out from the host of the living, another life did not instantly replace it and make people forget the deceased. Instead, a gap remained where he had been, and both the near and distant witnesses of his demise fell silent whenever they saw this gap. . . . Anything that grew took its time growing, and anything that perished took a long time to be forgotten. But everything that had once existed left its traces, and people lived on memories just as they now live on the ability to forget quickly and emphatically.[6]

It may seem puzzling that a duel, gratuitously resulting in a loss of life, should provoke this nostalgic reflection. Yet, however absurd a duel may be, the memory of the man fallen in homage to it is cherished. The duel is, perhaps, reassuringly binary, providing familiar evidence that the world is not, after all, changing. The duel provided a constant source of consternation to its critics, but, once eclipsed in the tumult of World War I, they are able to see its workings as integral to a paternalistic society. The same unbending rules, elaborate rituals, and the sense of obligation that underpinned a cruelly inexorable practice may take on a more appealing air. Such mechanical formulae, which "re-place thought and anticipate decisions," spare individuals the strenu-ousness of constantly improvising and making up one's own rules. They relieve them of the effort of attempting to come to terms with the uncertainties of present and future without the compass of the past.[7]

These two novels each show the combined absurdity and poignancy of duelling on the eve of the world war, an epitome not only of the cul-ture that preceded and contrasted with that war but also of the unfor-giving, self-destructive mores that resulted in it. Only with irony can we now begin to comprehend such strangeness. Historical reconstruc-tions may bridge the gap opened by World War I, but the novelistic imagination may be more incisive. Neither author is asserting that World War I spelled the end of duelling as a historical causation or fact, but it is clear that the duel both appalled and suited that society. Now it is, above all, a strange relic, a curiosity. Both writers are very quick and, as it happens, equally right, to conclude that, although duels had been happening in living memory, their demise would be irrevocable. They saw not only that duelling had ceased to occur but also that it could never happen again. Indeed, it is those phenomena which have just ceased to be that can seem most irretrievable.[8] So asserts the nar-rator of Gregor von Rezzori's *An Ermine in Czernopol (Hermelin in Tschernopol)*, a novel (1958) set just after World War I, likewise in Cen-tral Europe. Czernopol is a fictionalized version of Rezzori's birthplace, Czernowitz, located in Romania after the world war but hitherto at the eastern edge of the Habsburg lands and home to a variegated collection of different ethnic groups—Germans, Jews, Ukrainians, Russians, Ruthenians. Rather aloof from this motley crowd moves the "ermine" in question, Major Nikolaus Tildy de Szolonta et Vöroshàza, a gentleman whose appearance, bearing, and conduct announce his allegiance to the defunct Austro-Hungarian monarchy under which he had served, while confirming him, in the wide eyes of the narrator when he was a child, as the mysterious hero of a fairytale.

Offended by the remarks of a young man, Năstase, about the pro-priety of his serially unfaithful sister-in-law, Tildy sends his seconds to challenge Năstase to a duel, only to receive by return a letter that declines the challenge. When Tildy is summoned by his commanding officer, Colonel Turturiuk, to explain himself, he then challenges the colonel in turn. Tildy is duly called to the office of General Petrescu. Outraged at the major's conduct, Petrescu too makes an offhand remark about the cause of the proposed duel:

> At that, Tildy jumped up, picked up his shako and gloves, clicked his heels together, and left the room without uttering a word or waiting to hear another one.
>
>   One hour later his challenge was delivered to General Petrescu.
>
>   That same afternoon Tildy was arrested and placed under observation at the municipal asylum for the insane.[9]

Tildy's compulsion to duel has, of course, carried him beyond the jurisdiction of the law, but it has now also taken him to a realm beyond the comprehension of society. What is worse, his actions cannot be understood as those of a rational human being. The ascending status of Tildy's prospective opponents calls to mind a number of texts (by Smollett and Dumas, for example) in which successive duels guarantee progress and promotion, while, more specifically, Conrad shows how one duel may unleash another. But Tildy is not strategic or opportunistic like the heroes of those novels. He simply cannot envisage a different response. Steadfastly, he refuses to believe that times have changed, so, like the ermine once its white fur is stained, he proceeds to destroy himself.

Of course, the rapid progression to the asylum is related comically. Laughter and irony are the refuges of uncomprehending citizens when faced by this display of chivalry, wooden and fixed, in a modern world, but the child's instinctive appreciation of his nobility is, to an extent, vindicated when, later, the derisive general oversees a brutal suppression of unruly football supporters and Tildy, released at length from the asylum, dies under the wheels of a runaway tram.

Literary texts—previously tasked with debunking the duellist then, in the nineteenth century, inclined to defend him—now become a privileged form for responding to his demise. By the same token, the duel perhaps offers itself as one way in which a human need to confront and engage with death may be expressed. A taboo is tamed in these instances. History may give us the statistics about the numbers of duelling, but novels such as these summon up the peculiarity of duelling, its mixture of absurdity and pathos. It is through a novelistic shimmer that the ethos of the duel, and the vanished world of which it is an emblem, can best be appreciated, if not fully understood. As Tarangolian, the omniscient yet urbane gossip in Rezzori's novel, explains, humans are comparable to the housing of an hour-glass: "Our consciousness is its narrow waist, barely able to hold on to what passes through. Only the widest unfilled spaces cast back a vague reflection. In order to perceive something so that it will not be forgotten, we have to become aware of its presence without looking at it. You have to look past something in order to see it in full."[10]

The novel, in depicting this thwarted, frustrating gentleman, astray in the modern age, evokes the passage of time. But Czernopol is also a city of laughter. The dislocated, would-be duellist in its midst cuts a resolutely humorless figure. He is therefore very amusing. Tildy, in common with these other duellists, is a flawed sort of hero, suitable to an age that favors the ironic mood, an era in which the hero's power of action is now less than ours. Once noble and free, the duellist is henceforward frustrated and absurd.[11] After World War I, the duel is bound to seem utterly trivial and laughable. Those who had survived the Great War would not now want to throw away their lives on a whim. A duel would seem, more than ever, to be a form of self-indulgent playacting. When Luis Buñuel, in *La voie lactée (The Milky Way)* (1969), suddenly throws in a duel between a Jesuit and Jansenist, a prolongation, by sword, of an argument on the subject of prevenient grace, the debt to Mann's terminal bout seems unmistakable. That same, familiar frisson occurs, as abstruse, abstract causes take physical effect. But while that duel was fatal, this is not; while that was dangerous and symbolic, this seems merely innocuous and archaic. The duel seems just as surreal an element of Buñuel's world as the other grotesque fantasies.

When asked about the eventuality of a challenge, Guy Crouchback, in Evelyn Waugh's *Officers and Gentlemen* (1955), dismisses it with one word:

"Guy, what would you do if you were challenged to a duel?"
"Laugh."
"Yes, of course."[12]

In the modern age, now that people live longer, collect pensions, and may invoke incitement to hatred in court, the idea of risking one's life gratuitously can only be a self-conscious anachronism, an irresponsible stunt or a limp joke. It would be nice to think that enlightenment, rather than disillusionment, pacifism and not cynicism, were responsible for its eclipse. But it seems literary texts choose to privilege the more negative causalities at work, allowing readers to look back at duelling with a certain nostalgic fondness.

Sightings of the duel since the First World War indeed confirm it as an intriguing rarity, rather than a menacing scourge, a colorful vestige rather than an appalling custom. From our vantage point on the other side of World War I, it may now be difficult for us to understand that people could once take notions of honor and self-sacrifice, their good name and the demands of blood, and ultimately themselves so seriously, indeed more seriously than life itself. It has, in short, become difficult to take ourselves seriously, without taking ourselves too seriously. This danger was of course apparent to writers in the eighteenth century, even if it was a malaise from which the nineteenth century made a brave, momentary recovery.

But there remains some freedom, conferred by our half truth, for uncertainty, and we should also be wary of identifying the Great War as the terminus, because, well before 1914, duelling had begun to decline. In early nineteenth-century Britain, legislation annulled the pension of those soldiers who had died in a duel, thereby removing the aura of romanticism that wafted around duellists, whose wife and family would now possibly face a lifetime of poverty. But equally, the First World War did not offer a definitively closing bracket. One inveterate duellist in the 1920s was Benito Mussolini, who, like his friend Gabriele D'Annunzio, was repeatedly called out to the field or at least built himself some notoriety in not discouraging rumors to this effect. At home, he needed to be more discreet though. With the creatively euphemistic jargon deployed by duellists, he would tell his wife to prepare spaghetti for his eventual return. The Duce's blood-stained shirt would presumably invite less attention among the children, if tomato sauce was being splashed about.[13] Mussolini's counterpart in Spain, General Franco, drew on ideas of chivalry in shaping his nation. In an attempt to align one of the insubordinate Catalan cities and to inspire it with ancestral ideas of Spanish grandeur, plain and simple Valencia was buffed up as "Valencia del Cid" after the Civil War. Even in

Europe's more politically temperate spots, a passion for bygone ages of chivalry remained no less intensely spurred by literary texts. P. C. Wren followed up his best-selling novel *Beau Geste* (1924) with the story of *Beau Sabreur* (1926), its hero a gallant, duelling swordsman.

In a few privileged theaters of the Second World War, renewed opportunities to contest individual duels, as a subset of national conflict, were granted. The thrills of single combat seem, briefly, often fatally, to have been gratified in the air during the Battle of Britain. The Australian Spitfire pilot Richard Hillary wrote in his book *The Last Enemy* (1942), "In a fighter plane, I believe, we have found a way to return to war as it ought to be, war which is individual combat between two people, in which one either kills or is killed. It's exciting, it's individual and it's disinterested. I shan't be sitting behind a long-range gun working out how to kill people sixty miles away." Patriotism might have replaced the duellist's punctilious regard for honor, but the idiom could remain intact. "The fighter pilot's emotions," he wrote, "are those of the duellist—cool, precise, impersonal": "He is privileged to kill well, for if one must either kill or be killed, as one must, it should, I feel, be done with dignity. Death should be given the setting it deserves; it should never be a pettiness; and for the fighter pilot it never can be."[14] It is therefore disappointing, as well as tragic, that Hillary should meet his death after a training accident, in 1943.

Nor did writers after World War I promptly and obligingly cease to be interested by the drama and trauma of the duel. However, henceforward, such attributes as honor and courage, given expression by the duel, seemed to be located in an irrevocably vanished past, or they had to be retrieved beyond the frontiers of old, aristocratic Europe.[15]

But duels are never quite out of date for the simple reason that they are, from the outset, anachronistic. The duel, even at the height of its prosperity, remains an antiquated practice. Seventeenth-century France and medieval Spain are interchangeable in the eyes of *Le Cid*'s critics; Pushkin's Lenski and Laclos's Valmont go to their deaths self-consciously, as though heroes of a bygone age.

It is symptomatic that, when, in 1904, the Alliance of Honour (an organization which would eventually boast branches in sixty-five nations) was founded in Britain, it was a society that did not engage with duelling but strove to combat masturbation. It was one of many crusading social purity organizations, like the White Cross Army (founded in 1883), that sought to inculcate in young men the virtues of self-control. Chivalry was, in the final decades of the nineteenth century and the run-up to the First World War, focused overwhelmingly on sexual purity.[16] The vocabularies of honor and chivalry could safely be expropriated for these purposes.

The Alliance of Honour, one of whose founding members was Robert Baden Powell, encouraged sport in particular as an outlet for male energies. Toward the end of the nineteenth century, the impulse to violence once gratified by the duel could be sublimated and domesticated in sport. In 1895, a conference was held in Italy to discuss the continuing scourge of duelling. A year later, in 1896, Baron Pierre de Coubertin, a keen fencer himself, arranged the first Olympiad of the modern era. The evolution of the Olympic Games illustrates the way in which sport first advertised and then disavowed its origins in noble pursuits. One of the events was advertised as "Men's Single-Shot (or Double-Shot) Running Deer." The marksmen who fired at the mobile deer-shaped cut-out targets could yet pretend that they were heirs to the noblest huntsmen; but, by 1928, the event was dropped and henceforward events of this kind were known by the more prosaic "Rapid Fire Pistol." Similarly, the 1906 games, held in Athens, featured an event called "Duelling Pistol." Olympians fired their duelling pistols from distances of twenty or thirty meters at stationary targets sporting frock coats. Even if these dummies never sent out a cartel or returned fire, they superficially preserved some of the thrill and the nobility of the duel. Predictably and irrevocably, the nomenclature and the weaponry soon changed in favor of disguising any residual connection between sportsman and duellist, and the pseudoduellist turned into a small bore.

If the Olympics formalized ersatz duels anywhere, it was in fencing. In 1924, when the conduct and the results of an Olympic fencing bout were disputed, an actual duel—between a member of the Hungarian team and an Italian fencer—followed. The ersatz duel was followed by a real one, leading us to suppose that the Olympic ethos had, at this point, still not entirely superseded the codes of duelling. Of all sports, soccer probably allows some sort of approximation to the conditions of the duel: in particular, the penalty shootout, for, even if the striker is trying to miss his opponent, the penalty spot remains fixed at twelve yards, the "gentlemanly distance," as Byron deemed it.[17] Like the duellist, the goalkeeper was once supposed to remain stationary as he awaited the shot.

But of course penalty shootouts were themselves deemed ungentlemanly in certain quarters, hence the abstention from them by the legendary Corinthian Casuals. Sport offers a domestication of violence. Death inflicted by one competitor on the other is not an eventuality in modern sport. A duel, however, requires death to remain a distinct possibility. A bout deprived of that possible outcome is no proper duel, hence the German *Mensur* cannot be considered in quite the same vein. Perhaps then there was another arena for the thwarted duellist. The race between Captain Scott and Roald Amundsen was construed as a sort of duel "au dernier sang."[18] Meanwhile, in the 1920s and early 1930s, the duel between man and mountain assumed greater importance than ever before. The mountain was a giant to be slain rather than an equal engaged in a duel. Nevertheless, the idea of a totally unyielding yet ever fair opponent, the attack on whom required courage and brought honor, perhaps intersected with the ideals incarnated by duels. Indeed, in his poem "Knight Errantry," the climber Geoffrey Winthrop Young saw the mountaineer as the embodiment of chivalric spirit and daring, the knight's lance now supplanted by the "ashen shaft" of the ice axe.[19]

The law, it was pointed out in one of the few apologies for duelling, may dissipate suspicions, but it is not capable of removing hatred. The duel, in the interests of achieving this, substitutes brute force, violent and impetuous anger by aggression that is controlled and regulated carefully by norms. According to this nineteenth-century, post-Darwinian argument, circumstances may prevail in which two people simply cannot coexist, or, in the words of the Western, a town ain't big enough for two men. According to natural laws, one person must die, since he obstructs the happiness of another.[20] The face-offs that follow became a hallmark of the Western. The duel in Westerns offers a sanitization of frontier violence. The duel, or in Western parlance, the showdown, channels, orders, and tempers the lawlessness in the Wild West. The Western "is probably the last art form in which the concept of honor retains its strength."[21]

Perhaps the most famous Western of all, *High Noon* (1952), makes explicit, already in its title, its affiliation to the noble ethos of duelling: the fight is prearranged for the appointed hour. Fighting under the midday sun, the cowboys embody that transparency and visibility that characterize the duellist facing up to his opponent. The dusty street of the frontier town becomes the "champ clos" of the past, a little theater, a concentrated enclosure in which the duellists may trade their shots unremittingly yet honorably.

Of course, this is a privilege of the genre. It seems highly unlikely that violence actually took quite this idealized, stylized form. The duels in these Westerns, with their ritualization of ugly violence and chaos, hark back to a golden age of duelling (an unspecified, if not utterly mythical, era), rather than looking at the past as it was. Above all, they perpetuate the illusion that the duel is an honorable bout between equals, each giving the other a fair chance. They would appear to be depicting duels as they ought to be, rather than gunfights as they were. After all, the majority of Wyatt Earp's 150 victims were shot in the back: "Careful men, if violent ones, real Westerners preferred to gun their enemies down with a shotgun from behind some convenient shelter; but in fantasy they walk towards each other for ever, face to face, down sun-bright streets—ready for the showdown, which is to say, the last form of chivalric duel."[22] Such Westerners may seem characteristically, uncompromisingly American, yet they bow to time-honored rituals endowed by literature.

The duel's extinction seems also to have fostered its prosperity in the wider, figurative sense. As the dramatic content of duels in literary representations thins out, the physical combat makes way for internalized, psychologically complex duels. Already in the works of Conrad, Maupassant, and Schnitzler at the turn of the twentieth century, the gap between duellists closes to a point where they become, or seem, indistinguishable, however antagonized they may be. The duel is fought with a doppelgänger or with oneself, and the outcome may be suicide, as one part of that self overcomes another. But then, even in less obviously violent contexts, life may take the form of a duel in which the younger self is always challenging its older version. In choosing our path through life, and in order to become ourselves, we each need to kill off potential versions of ourselves, the persons we might have become. But the duel could also be envisaged as a collaborative endeavor, a challenge to avoid or minimize greater violence. In W. G. Sebald's *Austerlitz* (2001), the eponymous hero, who was transported to safety in the West as the Second World War took hold in Central Europe, is transfixed in later years by a photograph of his younger self as a boy. He tells the narrator that he continues to be disconcerted by "the piercing, inquiring gaze of the page boy who had come to demand his dues, who was waiting in the gray light of dawn on the empty field for me to accept the challenge and avert the misfortune lying ahead of him."[23] In this challenge posed by past to present, the vocabulary (the gray dawn and the empty field) lends renewed figurative life to the otherwise generic, bloodless trope of the duel as any troublesome inner struggle of drives or wishes.

After Freud, we are, then, all duellists, "en garde" against ourselves. But the most gifted imaginative writers must fight an especially painful inner duel with themselves. A sensibility to and interest in the mechanisms of duelling is, for such writers, but a facet of a wider struggle, the bout between the writer and "an inner enemy," for, as Maupassant avows, writers lead a double life that is both the strength and the misery of their existence.[24]

But if these inner duels with ourselves may be more protracted and agonized, as well as more frequent, than their literal equivalents, the increasingly bizarre irrelevance that is the actual duel does retain some appeal to those who are perhaps particularly given to hopeless nostalgia. Now that duellists have long since lapsed from experience and memory, literature and film are all the more potent in filtering our image and understanding of duelling.

Safely consigned to an increasingly remote past, the duel can threaten no longer. The possibility of a duel now rests on the highly improbable chance that two men, who are each at the same time inordinately attentive to their good name and utterly insensible to prevailing social mores, can find and insult each other. It is difficult these days for anyone to believe that a duel might be proposed sincerely, and the recipient of a challenge would surely not fail to be aware that he had been challenged in the expectation that he would decline. Besides, the

"Touché!"

publicity, were he to accept the offer, would, in all likelihood, generate a momentum of its own at odds with the serious fulfillment of the duel's ostensible purpose.

Nevertheless, now that it is possible to decline a duel without bringing dishonor to oneself, it is correspondingly easier to issue a challenge with impunity. By calling another man out, a modern-day gentleman may find a way of laughing off a dispute with him and of thereby ensuring that it is taken no further. A challenge to duel has become, at best, a vehicle for registering outrage beyond the conventional channels. Whereas the duel of the past necessarily staged a meeting of equals, now, conversely, it means that the prospective opponent cannot be dignified by opposition through respectable, rational refutation. Olivier Pétré-Grenouilleau's book on the slave trade (2004) caused Claude Ribbe to challenge the editor to a duel.[25] Ribbe evidently felt that such revisionist views deserved only to be challenged in a form that, like those views he confronted, belonged to a discredited past. Once again, the invitation to duel here was a grand gesture, calculated to result in nothing more substantial than publicity, likely to cost nothing to the gentleman making it.

In 1948, the inaugural Bollingen Prize for poetry was awarded at Yale University to Ezra Pound, then still confined to a mental hospital. The critic Karl Shapiro suggested that the choice betrayed fascist and anti-Semitic sympathies. Allen Tate, a member of the jury that had awarded the prize, responded to the accusation by challenging Shapiro to a duel. His honor had been impugned, but since it was a mannered, marginalized practice, the duel will also have served as a fitting homage to his twin vocations as poet and southern gentleman, vocations that converge in his "Ode to the Confederate Dead." The invitation was, of course, laughed off as a ludicrous enterprise by his detractor.[26] Loyal to the dictates of a vanished ethos, Tate was no doubt mindful of an earlier farce. Ezra Pound had himself challenged a poet, Lascelles Abercrombie, to a duel in 1913, averring that "stupidity carried beyond a certain point becomes a public menace." On this occasion, Abercrombie accepted and, in response, claimed his right to choose the weapons. His specific choice would lend him an advantage over his illustrious adversary; but it surely also testifies, *pace* Pound, to some scintilla of creative genius, for, eschewing both blade and bullet, he proposed that they pelt each other with unsold copies of their books.[27] On that note, it seems right to end this particular book, which is already quite heavy enough.

Notes

INTRODUCTION

1. Guy de Maupassant, preface to *Les tireurs au pistolet*, by Baron de Vaux (Paris: Marpon & Flammarion, 1883), v. Unless otherwise noted, all translations are my own.
2. Gustave Flaubert, *Dictionnaire des idées reçues*, ed. Marie Thérèse Jacquet (Paris: Nizet, 1990), 226.
3. Diego Gambetta, *Codes of the Underworld: How Criminals Communicate* (Princeton, NJ: Princeton University Press, 2009), 262.
4. Ludovico Ariosto, *Orlando furioso*, trans. John Hoole, 2nd ed., 5 vols. (London: George Nicol, 1785), 1:xxxviii, xli.
5. Henry Fielding, *Amelia*, in *The Complete Works of Henry Fielding*, 16 vols. (London: Barnes & Noble, 1967), 7:133.
6. Samuel Richardson, *Sir Charles Grandison* (Oxford: Oxford University Press, 1986), 264.
7. The idea that David and Goliath contested the protoduel was sometimes adduced in works seeking to embarrass modern libertines.
8. Ludovico Ariosto, *Orlando furioso*, trans. Barbara Reynolds, vol. 1 (London: Penguin, 1975), canto 5, st. 84 (p. 218), canto 6, st. 9 (p. 223).
9. James Boswell, *Life of Johnson* (Oxford: Oxford University Press, 1969), 965.
10. Bertram Wyatt-Brown, *Southern Honor: Ethics and Behavior in the Old South* (Oxford: Oxford University Press, 1982), 27.
11. Jules Verne, *Le tour du monde en 80 jours* (Paris: Michel de l'Ormeraie, 1983), 199–200.
12. Stendhal, *De l'amour* (Paris: Cluny, 1947), 39–40.
13. Duelling between instruments seems also to be an innovative feature of music from this period, such as Mozart's *Sinfonia concertante*, K364, in which the viola competes with and ultimately subdues the violin.
14. Lord Verisopht has been shot dead by Sir Mulberry Hawk, who turns out to have a good eye. Charles Dickens, *Nicholas Nickleby* (London: Penguin, 2003), 627–629.
15. Honoré de Balzac, *La peau de chagrin* (Paris: Norton, 1954), 241.
16. Jacopo Gelli, *I duelli mortali del secolo XIX* (Milan: Battistelli, 1899), 13.
17. Andrew Steinmetz, *The Romance of Duelling in All Times and Countries*, 2 vols. (London: Chapman & Hall, 1968), 2:85–98.
18. All the duels discussed are fictional, with one possible exception. Casanova purports to be telling the truth in his autobiographical account, but since it is notoriously difficult to sift out historical truths from his fictional embellishments and he himself writes two differing versions of his duel, he qualifies for a chapter.
19. Micheline Cuénin, *Le duel sous l'Ancien Régime* (Paris: Presses de la Renaissance, 1982); François Billacois, *The Duel: Its Rise and Fall in Early Modern*

France, trans. Trista Selous (New Haven, CT: Yale University Press, 1990); Stephen Banks, *A Polite Exchange of Bullets* (Woodbridge, UK: Boydell, 2010).

20. See V. G. Kiernan, *The Duel in European History* (Oxford: Oxford University Press, 1988); Robert Nye, *Masculinity and Male Codes of Honor in Modern France* (Oxford: Oxford University Press, 1993); Ute Frevert, *Men of Honour: A Social and Cultural History of the Duel*, trans. Anthony Williams (Cambridge, UK: Polity, 1995); Markku Peltonen, *The Duel in Early Modern England: Civility, Politeness and Honour* (Cambridge: Cambridge University Press, 2003).

21. Lord Byron, *Don Juan*, canto 13, st. 11 in *Byron*, ed. Jerome J. McGann (Oxford: Oxford University Press, 1986), 768.528; Irina Reyfman, *Ritualized Violence Russian Style: The Duel in Russian Culture and Literature* (Stanford, CA: Stanford University Press, 1999).

I. HONORED IN THE BREACH

1. See Germain Brice, *Description de la ville de Paris* (Paris: Minard; Geneva: Droz, 1971), 410–13.

2. Such was Voltaire's verdict, *Œuvres historiques*, ed. René Pomeau (Paris: Gallimard, 1957), 1173.

3. See Pascal Brioist, Hervé Drévillon, and Pierre Serna, *Croiser le fer: Violence et culture de l'épée dans la France moderne (XVIe–XVIIIe siècle)* (Seyssel, France: Champ Vallon, 2002).

4. Michel Foucault describes a widespread "illégalisme toléré" in *Surveiller et punir* (Paris: Gallimard, 1978), 98.

5. Jean Frain du Tremblay, *Nouveaux essais de morale* (Paris: Daniel Hortemels, 1691), 312–14.

6. Antoine Furetière, *Dictionnaire universel*, 4 vols. (The Hague: Husson, 1727); *Dictionnaire de l'Académie*, 2 vols. (Paris: Coignard, 1694).

7. Louis-Sébastien Mercier, *Le tableau de Paris*, ed. Jean-Claude Bonnet, 2 vols. (Paris: Mercure de France, 1994), 2: 396.

8. Prince Albert appears to have enjoyed some credit for the decline in dueling in the 1840s. See James Kinsley, introduction to Charles Dickens, *The Pickwick Papers* (Oxford: Clarendon, 1986), xxvi. See again Guy de Maupassant, preface to *Les tireurs au pistolet*, by Baron de Vaux (Paris: Marpon & Flammarion, 1883).

9. Voltaire, for example, dismisses the years between the fifth and the fifteenth centuries as but a "chaos d'aventures barbares, sous des noms barbares." *Œuvres historiques*, 1155. Dr. Johnson defines "barbarous" as "stranger to civility; savage; uncivilized." The supporting quotation from Shakespeare's *Titus Andronicus* (1.1.378) is also telling: "Thou art a Roman; be not barbarous." *A Dictionary of the English Language* 6th edition (London: J.F. and C. Rivington, 1785) [no pp].

10. William Scott, *The Duellist, a Bravo to God and a Coward to Man; and Therefore, Impossible to Be "A Man of Honour"* (London: Wilkie, 1774), xi.

11. Dr. Johnson remarks that "he . . . who fights a duel, does not fight from passion against his antagonist, but out of self-defence; to avert the stigma of the world, and to prevent himself from being driven out of society." James

Boswell, *Life of Johnson* (Oxford: Oxford University Press, 1969), 484 (10 April 1772).

12. European visitors to China, such as Johan Nieuhof and Louis-Daniel Lecomte, noticed that duelling played no part in that society. Instead of the clash of forces in Europe, the Chinese prized subtle, indirect forms of attack, enshrined in the principles of *weiqi* (or Go) and also in *The Art of War*, by Master Sun Tzu, writing at the time of Confucius. Sir Charles Grandison, meanwhile, observes that "the very Turks know nothing of this savage custom. . . . They take occasion to exalt themselves above Christians, in this very instance." Samuel Richardson, *Sir Charles Grandison* (Oxford: Oxford University Press, 1986), 264.

13. For example, Jean-Jacques Rousseau, *Julie; ou, La nouvelle Héloïse* (1761), part 1, letter 57. They are inspired by Montaigne's admiration of the freedom with which the greatest Greeks and Romans insulted each other in Antiquity, when "words were avenged by words alone, with no further consequence." Michel de Montaigne, "On Giving the Lie" ("Du démentir"), in *Essais*, bk. 2, essay 18, 3 vols. (Paris: Garnier Flammarion, 1969), 2:329.

14. Joseph Addison and Richard Steele, *The Tatler*, ed. Donald F. Bond, 3 vols. (Oxford: Oxford University Press, 1987), 1:230.

15. Henry Fielding, *Amelia*, in *The Complete Works of Henry Fielding*, 16 vols. (London: Barnes & Noble, 1967), 7:133.

16. Jean Fougeroux de Campigneulles, *Histoire des duels anciens et modernes*, 9.

17. The duel in 1712 between Lord Mohun and the Duke of Hamilton seems to have been an exception. It is described in Thackeray's *The History of Henry Esmond*, ed. John Sutherland (London: Penguin, 1972), bk. 3, chap. 6, 432–433. See Victor Stater, *High Life, Low Morals: The Duel That Shook Stuart Society* (London: John Murray, 1999), in which the self-destructive fury of the combatants is emphasized.

18. See, for a "remarkable instance" of this, Boswell's inclusion of the poignant testament left by Colonel Thomas the night before he fell in a duel. "In the first place, I commit my soul to Almighty GOD, in hopes of his mercy and pardon for the irreligious step I now (in compliance with the unwarrantable customs of this wicked world) put myself under the necessity of taking." Boswell, *Life of Johnson*, 1228 (28 April 1783).

19. See Michael Macdonald and Terence R. Murphy, *Sleepless Souls: Suicide in Early Modern England* (Oxford, UK: Clarendon, 1990).

20. Pierre Jean Grosley, *A Tour to London*, trans. Thomas Nugent, 2 vols. (London: Devis, 1772), 1:144.

21. Andrew Steinmetz, *The Romance of Duelling in All Times and Countries*, 2 vols. (London: Chapman & Hall, 1968), 1:17. In O. Henry's short story "Roads of Destiny" (1909), the narrator tricks the reader by naming his ill-fated young duellist David. See *Roads of Destiny and other stories* (London: Hodder & Stoughton, 1973), 15–39.

22. Pierre Roques, *Discours préliminaire ou l'on entreprend de montrer que le Duel fondé sur les maximes du point d'honneur, est une vengeance barbare, injuste et flétrissante* (Basel: Jean Christ, 1740), vi.

23. Abbé de Saint-Pierre, *Mémoire pour perfectionner la police contre le duel*, 18 (4 July 1715) [S.I, 1715].
24. *Dictionnaire de l'Académie*, vol. 1. This meaning has, however, lapsed by the time of the equivalent *Dictionnaire* published in 1797.
25. See, for instance, Furetière's definition of "illness" *(maladie)* as "an unregulated affection, an excessive attachment." *Dictionnaire universel*, vol. 3.
26. Michel Foucault, *Histoire de la sexualité*, 4 vols. (Paris: Gallimard, 1976), 1:35.
27. Maurice, comte de Saxe, *Mes rêveries*, 2 vols. (Paris: Desaint and Saillant, 1757), 2: 155–160.
28. François de Fénelon, *Traité de l'existence de Dieu* (1713) (Paris: PUF, 1990), 30.
29. Abbé de Saint-Pierre, *Mémoire*, 33.
30. Jean-Jacques Rousseau, *Du contrat social*, bk. 2, chap. 12, in *Œuvres completes*, ed. Raymond Trousson and Frédéric S. Eigeldinger, 24 vols. (Paris: Champion, 2012), 5: 522.
31. Jean-Jacques Rousseau, preface to *Narcisse ou l'amant de lui-même* (1752), in *Œuvres complètes*, vol. 2 (Paris: Gallimard, La Pléiade, 1964), 971.
32. Jean-Jacques Rousseau, *Lettre à d'Alembert*, in *Œuvres completes*, ed. Raymond Trousson and Frédéric S. Eigeldinger, 24 vols. (Paris: Champion, 2012), 16:551.
33. Lord Byron, *Don Juan*, canto 13, st. 11 in *Byron* ed. Jerome J. McGann (Oxford: Oxford University Press, 1986), 768.
34. I am grateful for Michael Moriarty's suggestion that the "play charts a transition from a feudal to an absolute monarchy, paradoxically achieved by behaviour inspired by the feudal spirit but appropriated by the king." (Personal correspondence, 20 August, 2014).
35. Pierre Corneille, *Le Cid*, *Œuvres complètes*, ed. Georges Couton, 3 vols. (Paris: Gallimard, 1980) 12.1 (1:722).
36. Ibid., 3.4 (1: 749).
37. By contrast, in the epic *Cantar de mio Cid*, he slices numerous Moorish heads in half with his sword.
38. Joseph Conrad, "The Duel," in *The Complete Short Fiction of Joseph Conrad*, ed. Samuel Hynes, 4 vols. (London: Pickering & Chatto, 1993), 4:118; Corneille, *Le Cid*, 4.5.
39. Corneille, *Le Cid*, 4.5 (1: 762).
40. Ibid., 4.5 (1: 763).
41. I am grateful to Joe Harris for this suggestion.
42. Saint-Simon registers his exasperation with Louis XIV's unremitting "préférence distinguée et marquée" for bourgeois over nobles. Evidence for this, besides the antiduelling aggression, was a tendency to appoint to prominent positions bourgeois figures, such as Colbert and Le Tellier. Louis de Rouvroy, duc de Saint-Simon, *Mémoires*, ed. Gonzague Truc, 7 vols. (Paris: Gallimard, 1952), 4:603.
43. Guillaume Thomas François Raynal, *Anecdotes littéraires*, 3 vols. (The Hague: Pierre Gosse, 1756), 2:106.

2. THE COMICAL DUEL

1. See W. D. Howarth, "The Legacy of Farce," chap. 4 in *Molière: A Playwright and His Audience* (Cambridge: Cambridge University Press, 1982), 82–105.

2. La Rochefoucauld, *Réflexions ou sentences et maximes morales et réflexions diverses*, 5th edition (1678), ed. Laurence Plazenet (Paris: Champion, 2005), 175 (maxim no. 326).

3. "I could heartily wish that you may often be seen to smile, but never heard to laugh while you live." Lord Chesterfield, letter 30 (1748), in *Letters* (Oxford: Oxford University Press, 2008), 72.

4. Jean-Jacques Rousseau, *Julie; ou, La nouvelle Héloïse* (1761), (Paris: Garnier Flammarion, 1967), 180 (part 2, letter 17).

5. Patrick Brydone, *A Tour through Sicily and Malta in a Series of Letters to William Beckford*, 2 vols. (Dublin: Ewing and Wilson, 1774), 2:238.

6. *The Duellist, or a Cursory Review of the Rise, Progress and Practice of Duelling* (London: Longman, 1822), 188.

7. *The Spectator*, no. 100, *Critical Essays from the Spectator*, ed. Donald F. Bond (Oxford: Clarendon Press, 1970).

8. Joseph Addison and Richard Steele, *The Tatler*, ed. Donald F. Bond, 3 vols. (Oxford: Oxford University Press, 1987), 1:282.

9. Victor Hugo, *Châtiments*, Bk 7, 9, *Œuvres complètes*, ed. Jacques Seebacher and Guy Rosa, 15 vols. (Paris: Laffont, 1985), 4:187.

10. Vincenzo Marcucci, *Della legittimità positiva o negativa delle pene, principalmente della pena di morte* (Lugano, Switzerland: Ruggia, 1835), 313–15.

11. Concerned to prevent duelling over infidelities, Richardson's Lovelace, ever the romantic, proposes an annual exchange market of spouses and lovers, to be held on Valentine's Day; Leigh Hunt suggests duelling to the sound of music; Xavier de Maistre recommends the drawing of lots to see whether disputes should be concluded in accordance with law or custom, while after a duel, judges are to play dice to decide on their verdict. Samuel Richardson, *Clarissa*, ed. Angus Ross (Harmondsworth, UK: Penguin, 1985), 872 (letter 254); Leigh Hunt, *Table Talk* (London: Smith, Elder, 1851), 81; Xavier de Maistre, *Voyage autour de ma chambre* (Paris: Robert Laffont, 1959), 6.

12. Cervantes, *Don Quixote*, trans. Charles Jarvis (Oxford: Oxford University Press, 1998), 218.

13. Giacomo Casanova, *Histoire de ma vie*, 8 vols. (Paris: Garnier, 1880), 1:119.

14. Jean-Jacques Rousseau, *Les Confessions*, bk. 1, in *Œuvres completes*, ed. Raymond Trousson and Frédéric S. Eigeldinger, 24 vols. (Paris: Champion, 2012), 1: 85.

15. Richard Brinsley Sheridan, *The Rivals*, in *The Dramatic Works of Richard Brinsley Sheridan*, ed. Cecil Price, 2 vols. (Oxford: Oxford University Press, 1973), 4.3. 1: 129.

16. Ibid. Act 5, scene 1. 1: 133, 132.

17. Molière, *Le bourgeois gentilhomme*, in *Œuvres complètes*, ed. Georges Forestier, 2 vols. (Paris: Gallimard, 2010), 2: 291 (3.3).

18. John Locke, *Some Thoughts Concerning Education* (London: Churchill, 1693), § 199.

19. Molière, *Le bourgeois gentilhomme*, 2.2, 276.

20. Ibid.

21. See Larry F. Norman, "Molière as Satirist," in *The Cambridge Companion to Molière*, ed. David Brady and Andrew Calder (Cambridge: Cambridge University Press, 2006), 57–71.

22. Molière, *Le bourgeois gentilhomme*, 3.3, 292.

23. Anthony, 3rd Earl of Shaftesbury, *An Essay on the Freedom of Wit and Humour* in *Characteristicks of Men, Manners, Opinions, Times* (1709), 3 vols. (Indianapolis: Liberty Fund, 2001), 1:93.

24. See the preface to Richard Steele, *The Conscious Lovers* (London: Edward Arnold, 1968), xvii.

25. Ibid.

26. Jonathan Swift, preface to *The Battle of the Books*, in *Jonathan Swift*, ed. Angus Ross and David Woolley (Oxford: Oxford University Press, 1984), 1.

27. William Kenrick, *The Duellist* (3rd edition) (London: Evans, 1773), 2.

28. Ibid., 6.

29. Louis Hurtaut Dancourt, *Jacquot et Colas duellistes* (Paris: Cailleau, 1783), 20.

30. Ibid., 20.

31. Mélesville and Carmouche, *Les duels, ou la famille Darcourt* (Paris: Marchant, 1834), 7.

32. Jean Fougeroux de Campigneulles, *Histoire des duels anciens et modernes* 2 vols. (Paris: Tessier, 1835) 1:viii.

33. In a cross-Channel riposte, William O'Brien's English version, *The Duel* (1772), restored the intended title.

34. Deploying the usual euphemism, Vanderk speaks delicately and plausibly of some "business" *(une affaire)* that is detaining his son. Michel-Jean Sedaine, *Le philosophe sans le savoir*, 4.4 (Durham, UK: Durham University, 1987), 92.

35. Charlotte Lennox, *The Female Quixote* (Oxford: Oxford University Press, 2008), 72.

36. Sedaine, *Le philosophe sans le savoir*, 2.4, 74.

37. G. B. Clarke, ed., *Descriptions of Lord Cobham's Gardens at Stowe 1700–50* (Aylesbury, UK: Buckinghamshire Record Society, 1990), 89.

38. See letter 10, 'Sur le commerce," *Lettres philosophiques*, ed. Olivier Ferret and Antony McKenna (Paris: Garnier, 2010), 97–98.

39. Audiences at this juncture are likely to think back to Jourdain's avowed shame at being the son of a merchant. (Molière, *Le bourgeois gentilhomme*, 3.12).

40. This view, and the tendency to see commerce as a menace rather than as an opportunity, prevails in France well into the nineteenth century (and beyond). See David Todd, *L'identité économique de la France: Libre-échange et protectionnisme* (Paris: Grasset, 2008).

41. Georg Christoph Lichtenberg, *Aphorismen* (first published posthumously, 1800–1806) (Kettwig, Germany: Phaidon, 1990), 105.

42. Sedaine, *Le philosophe sans le savoir*, 3.12, 89.

43. A rare example of a duelling merchant is John Law, founder of the Banque de France and promoter of paper money, but his record in combat seems more

impressive than that in business, for he came to France in 1694, after killing Beau Wilson, and left in 1716, after ruining its finances.

44. Sedaine, *Le philosophe sans le savoir*, 5.11, 104.

45. Ibid., 4.5, 92.

46. Ibid., 4.11, 96.

47. Ibid., 1.1, 63.

48. John Wood describes two honorary laws, published as early as 1742. One restrained gentlemen from wearing swords at Bath; the other prevented "ladies from appearing at the Balls with long white Aprons before them." John Wood, *A Description of Bath 1765* (Bath, UK: Kingsmead Reprints, 1969), 411–12.

49. Sheridan, *Rivals*, 1:115. O'Trigger is goading Acres into fighting a duel with Ensign Beverley, a rival in love.

50. Ibid., 3.4 (1:116–17).

51. Ibid., 2.1 (1:95).

52. See, for example, Sir William Mode's pride in his own uniquely inventive oaths, in Susanna Centlivre's *The Beau's Duel*: "For to use another man's oath, is, in my opinion, as undecent [*sic*], as wearing his clothes." Susanna Centlivre, *The Beau's Duel; or, A Soldier for the Ladies* (1702), in *The Plays of Susanna Centlivre*, ed. Richard C. Frushell (London: Garland, 1982), 12.

53. Sheridan, *Rivals*, 4.1 (1:199), 5.2 (1:139).

54. Ibid., 3.4 (1:116, 118).

55. Ibid., 3.4 (1: 117).

56. Ibid., 5.3 (1: 140).

57. Sir Lucius O'Trigger, and therefore the actor playing his part, is usually the key to the success of the play. Unfortunately, the actor who took the part of Sir Lucius O'Trigger on the opening night was a disaster—Sheridan had made the unforgivable mistake of entrusting the role to a man by the name of John Lee.

58. Sheridan, *Rivals*, 4.3 (1:128).

59. Ibid., 3.4 (1:117).

60. Ibid., 3.4 (1: 117, 118).

61. See Sir Walter Scott's *Guy Mannering* (1815); Sir Edward Bulwer-Lytton's *Richelieu* (1839), among many others.

62. Sheridan, *Rivals*, 4.3 (1:131).

63. Ibid., 1.2 (1: 84).

64. Ibid., 5.3 (1: 142).

65. John Wilmot, 2nd Earl of Rochester, *A Satire against Reason and Mankind*, in *The Complete Poems of John Wilmot, Earl of Rochester*, ed. David M. Vieth (New Haven, CT: Yale University Press, 1968), 100.

66. Sheridan, *Rivals*, 4.1 (1:118). Beaumarchais's *Le barber de Séville*, in which Figaro first appears, dates from the same year, 1775.

67. Ibid., 4.1 (1: 118–19).

68. Ibid., 4.1 (1: 119).

69. Ibid., 4.1 (1: 119).

70. Ibid., 4.1 (1: 118).

71. See John Loftis, *Sheridan and the Drama of Georgian England* (Oxford, UK: Blackwell, 1976), 56.

72. Sheridan, *Rivals*, 5.3 (1:140).
73. Ibid., 5.3 (1: 140).
74. Ibid., 5.3 (1: 141).
75. Ibid., 5.3 (1: 141).
76. Ibid., 5.3 (1:145).
77. William Makepeace Thackeray, *History of Pendennis*, ed. John Sutherland (Oxford: Oxford University Press, 1994), 136.
78. Charles Dickens, *The Pickwick Papers*, ed. James Kinsley (Oxford: Clarendon, 1986), 26 (chap 2).
79. Ibid., 35.
80. Ibid., 36.
81. Ibid., 34.
82. Ibid., 36.
83. Ibid., 34.
84. Ibid., 35.
85. Ibid., 21.
86. See Eve Kosofsky Sedgwick on Dickens in *Between Men: English Literature and Male Homosocial Desire* (New York: Columbia University Press, 1985), 161–201.
87. "'Out of sight, out of mind,' is well enough as a proverb applicable to cases of friendship, though absence is not always necessary to hollowness of heart even between friends." Charles Dickens, *Nicholas Nickleby* (London: Penguin, 2003), 493. A sustained exploration of these questions is best seen in *Our Mutual Friend.*
88. See Sarah Esther Horowitz, "States of Intimacy: Friendship and the Remaking of French Political Elites, 1815–1848" (Ph.D. diss., University of California, Berkeley, 2008).
89. Jules Renard, *Œuvres*, ed. Léon Guichard, 2 vols. (Paris: Gallimard, 1970), 1:894.
90. Dr. Johnson's *Dictionary of the English Language* (1755) defines a "stickler" as "a sidesman to fencers; a second to a duellist." *Johnson's Dictionary: A modern selection*, ed. E. L. McAdam Jr. and George Milne (London: Macmillan, 1982), 400.
91. Dickens, *Pickwick Papers*, 359 (chap 24).
92. See, for a similar figure, Charles de Secondat, baron de Montesquieu, *Lettres persanes*, ed. Paul Vernière (Paris: Garnier, 1960), 124 (letter 59).
93. See James Kinsley's introduction to *The Pickwick Papers*, xvi.
94. John Forster, *The Life of Charles Dickens*, 2 vols. (London: Dent, 1969), 1:14.

3. THE POIGNANT DUEL

1. George Farquhar, *The Beaux-Stratagem*, in *The Works of George Farquhar*, ed. Shirley Strum Kenny, 2 vols. (Oxford, UK: Clarendon, 1988), 2:192.
2. The epithet is James Harlowe's, in Samuel Richardson, *Clarissa*, ed. Angus Ross (Harmondsworth, UK: Penguin, 1985), 119.
3. Ibid., 397 (letter 98), 362 (letter 89). See Dr. Johnson's remarks on *Clarissa*: "if you were to read Richardson for the story, your impatience would be so

much fretted that you would hang yourself." James Boswell, *Life of Johnson* (Oxford: Oxford University Press, 1969), 480.

4. "Rencounter" is a useful term for designating a meeting that, impromptu rather than prearranged, nevertheless seems both improvised and desired. Eventually, the term will become interchangeable with a formal duel.

5. Richardson, *Clarissa*, 200 (letter 44), 136 (letter 29).

6. Lovelace's fiction recalls the stratagem of Aimwell, whose sojourn at a country tavern is explained by a duel in which he apparently left his opponent dangerously wounded. Farquhar, *The Beaux-Stratagem*.

7. Richardson, *Clarissa*, 473 (letter 131).

8. Ibid., 1445 (letter 518).

9. Ibid., 1444 (letter 518).

10. Ibid., 1016 (letter 317).

11. Ibid., 1445 (letter 518).

12. Jean-Jacques Rousseau, *Lettre à d'Alembert*, in *Œuvres completes*, ed. Raymond Trousson and Frédéric S. Eigeldinger, 24 vols. (Paris: Champion, 2012), 16:551.

13. Richardson, *Clarissa*, 1433 (letter 513).

14. Ibid., 1484 (letter 535).

15. Ibid., 1485 (letter 536).

16. Ibid., 1485 (letter 536).

17. Ibid., 1486 (letter 537).

18. Ibid., 1236 (letter 422), 1218 (letter 417).

19. Samuel Richardson, *Sir Charles Grandison* (Oxford: Oxford University Press, 1986), 252.

20. Ibid., 261.

21. Tobias Smollett, Letter 15, *Travels through France and Italy*, ed. Frank Felsenstein (Oxford: Oxford University Press, 1981), 131–38.

22. Delirious and dying, Belton, one of Lovelace's pack of libertine friends, swears that he sees the man he has killed in a duel, years before. Richardson, *Clarissa*, 1231 (letter 419). Sedaine's philosopher, Vanderk, is haunted too, albeit less literally, by the man he killed in a duel, another testimony to the developing eighteenth-century interest in the long-term damage, as well as the immediate impact, left by duels. Michel-Jean Sedaine, *Le philosophe sans le savoir* (Durham, UK: Durham University Press, 1987), 73 (2.4).

23. Jean-Jacques Rousseau, *Les Confessions*, bk. 1, in *Œuvres completes*, ed. Raymond Trousson and Frédéric S. Eigeldinger, 24 vols. (Paris: Champion, 2012), 1: 79. See Maurice Cranston, *The Solitary Self: Jean-Jacques Rousseau in Exile and Adversity* (London: Allen Lane, 1997), 28.

24. Rousseau, *Lettre à d'Alembert*, 502n3.

25. Having previously illustrated *Pamela*, Gravelot perhaps appealed to Rousseau's sense of continuity with Richardson's work.

26. Rousseau, *Julie; ou, La nouvelle Héloïse* (1761), (Paris: Garnier Flammarion, 1967), 239 (part 3, letter 11).

27. Ibid., 180 (part 2, letter 17).

28. In Tennyson's *Maud* (1855), the poet is haunted, after killing her brother in a duel, by his agonized cry: "It will ring in my heart and my ears, till I die, till

I die." Alfred Tennyson, *Maud*, part 2, 1.1.35, in *The Major Works*, ed. Adam Roberts (Oxford: Oxford University Press), 335.

29. Challenged to a duel in 1818, Robert Southey insisted on equal terms. Baron Brougham, who challenged him, should therefore first "marry & have four children." Southey added, "Please to be particular in having them all girls." Recounted in Richard Cronin, *Paper Pellets: British Literary Culture after Waterloo* (Oxford: Oxford University Press, 2010), 4.

30. Pierre Choderlos de Laclos, *Les liaisons dangereuses*, ed. Catriona Seth (Paris: Gallimard, 2011), 432.

31. Ibid., 433.

32. In Bertrand's words, Valmont dies in a combat with *(avec)* Danceny, not against him.

33. The letter in *Clarissa* is sent on the seventh of December under the Julian calendar, or the eighteenth under the Gregorian calendar, to which the former was changed in 1752.

34. Michel Vovelle, *Mourir autrefois: Attitudes collectives devant la mort aux XVIIe et XVIIIe siècles* (Paris: Gallimard, 1974), 195. See Philippe Ariès, *L'homme devant la mort* (Paris: Seuil, 1977), part 4.

35. Matteo Maria Boiardo, *Orlando innamorato* (1482) (Dublin: Hill, 1784), bk. 1, canto 19, stanzas 13–16, pp. 270–71. Laclos was probably aware of the new French translation by Louis Elisabeth de La Vergne, comte de Tressan (Paris: Pissot, 1780).

36. Laclos, *Les liaisons dangereuses*, 433.

37. Ibid., 433, 457.

38. Ibid., 13.

39. Patrick Brydone, *A Tour through Sicily and Malta in a Series of Letters to William Beckford*, 2 vols. (Dublin: Ewing and Wilson, 1774), 1:236.

40. "Longtemps combattue, elle a enfin triomphé," Louis-Sébastien Mercier, "L'inoculation," *Tableau de Paris*, ed. Jean-Claude Bonnet, 2 vols. (Paris: Mercure de France, 1994), 1: 925–29 (chap. 142) (925).

41. Laclos, *Les liaisons dangereuses*, 433.

4. THE JUDICIAL DUEL

1. Heinrich von Kleist, "Der Zweikampf,"in *Sämtliche Erzählungen und Anekdoten* (Munich: DTV, 1978), 240.

2. Ibid., 244.

3. "Unmittelbar." Ibid., 261.

4. "Anekdote" [Baxter], in *Erzählprosa, Werke und Briefe*, ed. Siegfried Streller 4 vols. (Berlin: Aufbau, 1978), 2: 353–354. See the discussion of this late story in Rüdiger Görner, *Gewalt und Grazie: Heinrich von Kleist's Poetik der Gegensatzlichkeit* (Heidelberg: Winter, 2011).

5. Samuel Richardson, *Sir Charles Grandison* (Oxford: Oxford University Press, 1986), 255.

6. The Holy Roman Empire ceased to exist on 6 August 1806, five years before the publication of this story. The story's first readers may have been primed by recent history to expect both such an antiquated practice and the hesitant response to it.

7. Heinrich von Kleist, "Von der Überlegung," in *Über das Marionettentheater* (Frankfurt am Main: Insel, 1989), 40.

5. THE "ROMANTIC" DUEL

1. "Io son uomo di pace, e duelli non fo, se non a mensa," *Così fan tutte* (New York: Schirmer, 1952), 1.1., 17.
2. Louis-Sébastien Mercier, *Tableau de Paris* (1781–88), ed. Jean-Claude Bonnet, 2 vols. (Paris: Mercure de France, 1994), 2:396.
3. Jean Fougeroux de Campigneulles, *Histoire des duels anciens et modernes*, 2 vols. (Paris: Tessier, 1835), 1:320.
4. See Robert Nye, "Bourgeois Sociability and the *Point d'Honneur*: 1800–1860," chap. 7 in *Masculinity and Male Codes of Honor in Modern France* (Oxford: Oxford University Press, 1993), 127–47.
5. "For since every body that has money enough, sets up an equipage, a gentleman ought to find out some other way of distinguishing himself." Susanna Centlivre, *The Beau's Duel; or, A Soldier for the Ladies* (1702), in *The Plays of Susanna Centlivre*, ed. Richard C. Frushell (London: Garland, 1982), 12.
6. Jane Austen, *Emma* (1816; repr., Oxford: Oxford University Press, 1988), 81. Benjamin Disraeli characterized Britain as two nations "as ignorant of each other's habits and thoughts, and feelings, as if they were dwellers in different zones or inhabitants of different planets; . . . ordered by different manners, and not governed by the same laws." Benjamin Disraeli, *Sybil; or, The Two Nations* (1845; repr., Oxford: Oxford University Press, 2008), 65–66.
7. Friedrich Schiller, *Die Räuber* (1781), *Werke und Briefe*, ed. Klaus Harro Hilzinger, 12 vols. (Frankfurt am Main: Deutscher Klassiker Verlag, 1988–2004), 2: 22 (1.1).
8. Xavier de Maistre, *Voyage autour de ma chambre* (Paris: Corti, 1984), 20–21.
9. Alfred de Musset, *La confession d'un enfant du siècle*, Pt 1, chap. 3, *Œuvres complètes en prose*, ed. Maurice Allem et Paul-Courant. (Paris: Gallimard, 1960), 81–83.
10. 'Nous nous battîmes; je le blessai dangereusement, je fus blessé moi-même'. chap. 5, *Adolphe* in Benjamin Constant, *Œuvres*, ed. Alfred Roulin (Paris: Gallimard, 1957), 76.
11. Stendhal, *Armance* (1826) (Paris: Garnier Flammarion, 1967), 131–32.
12. William Shakespeare, *Twelfth Night*, 3.2.
13. It is the "hell within" the murderer into which "we are to look." Thomas De Quincey, *On the Knocking at the Gate in* Macbeth (1823), in *On Murder Considered as One of the Fine Arts* (Oxford: Oxford University Press, 2006), 4–5.
14. Johann Wolfgang von Goethe, *Clavigo*, act 4, in *Sämtliche Werke*, ed. Dieter Borchmeyer 40 vols., (Frankfurt am Main: Deutscher Klassiker Verlag, 1993), 9: 487.
15. See notes on the reception of the play, Ibid., 927.
16. Writing from Spain in 1830, Mérimée describes assassination as "the poor man's duel", but he too thinks it more impressive in that assassination generally results in two deaths, rather than the few scratches left by a Parisian duel. Letter 2, *Lettres sur l'Espagne*, in *Œuvres complètes*, ed. Pierre Trahard and Eduoard Champion, 8 vols. (Paris: Champion, 1933), 8: 278.

17. Sir Walter Scott, "The Two Drovers," in *The Two Drovers and Other Stories* (Oxford: Oxford University Press, 1987), 221, 257–58. See, for similar sentiments, Scott, *Rob Roy* (1818), (Oxford: Oxford University Press, 1998), 298–299.

18. Sir Walter Scott, *The Antiquary* (Oxford: Oxford University Press, 2009), 188–200, 295–96. Scott features a theologically inspired onslaught against duelling in a subsequent novel, set in the 1730s, *The Heart of Midlothian* (1818), (Oxford: Oxford University Press, 1990), 110–11.

19. Denis Diderot, *Jacques le fataliste* (first published in French, 1796) (Paris: Flammarion, 1970), 91; John Cleland, *Fanny Hill* (London: Penguin, 1985), 206.

20. Jules Verne, *Voyage au centre de la terre* (Paris: M. de l'Ormeraie, 1982), chap. 33, 178–85.

21. John Lyde Wilson, *The Code of Honor or Rules for the Government of Principals and Seconds in Duelling* (Charleston, SC: James Phinney, 1838), reprinted in Jack K. Williams, *Dueling in the Old South: Vignettes of Social History* (College Station: Texas A&M University Press, 1980), 89.

22. Charles Mackay, *Extraordinary Popular Delusions and the Madness of Crowds* (1841; repr., New York: Farrar, Straus and Giroux, 1986), 647.

23. J. Maynard Smith and G. R. Price, "The Logic of Animal Conflict," *Nature* 246 (2 November 1973): 15–18.

24. Charles Darwin, *The Descent of Man, and Selection in Relation to Sex* (2nd ed. 1879) (London: Penguin, 2004), chap. 17 "Mammals—law of Battle," 573.

25. See Mark Twain's *Those Extraordinary Twins*, a farce, naturally featuring a duel, that they inspired. Published alongside *Pudd'nhead Wilson* (Harmondsworth: Penguin, 1969), ed. Malcolm Bradbury.

26. Alexander Pushkin, *Eugene Onegin: A Novel in Verse*, trans. Vladimir Nabokov, 4 vols. (Princeton, NJ: Princeton University Press, 1975), 1:136 (chap. 2, st. 14).

27. Lord Byron, *Don Juan*, canto 13, st. 42; canto 4, st. 45.

28. Pushkin, *Eugene Onegin*, 1:201 (chap. 4, st. 11).

29. Ibid., 1:175 (chap. 3, st. 39).

30. Ibid., 1:98 (chap. 1, st. 7). Adam Smith was, of course, not exclusively an economist.

31. Ibid., 1:135 (chap. 2, st. 13).

32. See Nabokov's notes, Ibid., 2:115.

33. Ibid., 1:231 (chap. 5, st. 45).

34. Ibid., 1:243 (chap. 6, st. 7).

35. Ibid., 1:245 (chap. 6, st. 21).

36. See Nabokov's notes, Ibid., 3:26.

37. Ibid., 1:246 (chap. 6, st. 22).

38. François Villon, "Ballade des dames du temps jadis", *Poésies*, ed. Jean Dufournet (Paris: Garnier Flammarion, 1984), 108–110; Alexander Pope, Epistle 1, Stanza 10, "An Essay on Man," *The Poems of Alexander Pope*, ed. Maynard Mack, 6 vols. (London: Methuen, 1950), 3.1:51.

39. Andrew Steinmetz, *The Romance of Duelling in All Times and Countries*, 2 vols. (London: Chapman & Hall, 1968), 1:105.

40. Pushkin, *Eugene Onegin*, 1:247 (chap. 6, st. 24).

41. Ibid., 1: 247 (chap. 6, st. 24).

42. Ibid., 1:249 (chap. 6, st. 29).

43. Ibid., 1:250 (chap. 6, st. 31).

44. Ibid., 1:210 (chap. 5, st. 3).

45. Ibid., 1:212 (chap. 5, st. 6).

46. Ibid., 1:203, 210–11 (chap. 4, st. 45).

47. Ibid., 1: 262 (chap. 7, st. 24).

48. Seamus Heaney, "Faith, Hope and Poetry," in *Preoccupations: Selected Prose 1968–78* (London: Faber & Faber, 1984), 217.

49. Alfred de Vigny's *Chatterton* (1835) celebrates a misunderstood hero. Eighteenth-century contemporaries were less inclined to appreciate the poetical properties of a suicidal fraudster.

50. Pushkin, *Eugene Onegin*, 1:133 (chap. 2, st. 9).

51. Ibid., 1:272–73 (chap. 7, st. 22).

52. Serena Vitale, *Pushkin's Button: The Story of the Fatal Duel Which Killed Russia's Greatest Poet* (London: Fourth Estate, 1999), 251.

53. Ibid., 287.

54. Ibid., 262–63.

55. Théophile Gautier, *Mademoiselle de Maupin* (Paris: Garnier Flammarion, 1966), 146.

56. Prosper Mérimée, "Le vase étrusque" (1830), in *Carmen*, ed. Maxime Revon (Paris: Garnier, 1960), 267.

57. Ibid., 268.

58. Ibid., 269.

59. Mérimée emulates writers of the period such as Keats ("Ode to a Grecian Urn" [1820]) in placing an ornament center stage. With thanks to Andrew Brown.

60. Mérimée, "Le vase étrusque," 245.

61. With another genuflection to Mérimée's story, one of the seconds is called Prosper. Villiers de L'Isle Adam, "Sombre récit, conteur plus sombre" (1877), in *Contes cruels* (Paris: Garnier, 1989), 215.

62. Dorian Gray's maternal grandfather had his new, unwelcome son-in-law (Dorian's father) killed in a contrived duel of this sort. See Oscar Wilde, *The Picture of Dorian Gray*, chap. 3, vol. 3, *The Complete Works of Oscar Wilde*, ed. Joseph Bristow (Oxford: Oxford University Press, 2010), 196.

6. THE DUEL AND SELF-REALIZATION

1. For more details of the failed Jacobite rebellion, see Jeremy Black, *Culloden and the '45* (Stroud: Sutton, 1993).

2. See *Oxford English Dictionary*, s.v. "Random, n."

3. Tobias Smollett, *The Adventures of Roderick Random*, ed. Paul Boucé (Oxford: Oxford University Press, 2008), chap. 66, 410, 416.

4. Ibid., 47.

5. Ibid., 25.

6. Ibid., 53–54.

7. Ibid., 54.

8. Ibid., 106.

9. Ibid., 124.

10. Ibid., 141.

11. Ibid., 155.

12. Ibid., 210.

13. Ibid., 227.

14. Ibid., 227.

15. Ibid., 246–47.

16. Ibid., 247–48.

17. Ibid., 272.

18. Ibid., 281.

19. Ibid., 290.

20. Ibid., 318.

21. Ibid., 362.

22. Ibid., 364–65.

23. Ibid., 25.

24. Ritchie Robertson, *Mock-Epic Poetry from Pope to Heine* (Oxford: Oxford University Press, 2009).

25. The butts of some eighteenth-century pistols were provided with a spike-dagger, known as a "skull-crusher," but the application of the hilt to finish off a duel was, of course, highly irregular. See Howard L. Blackmore, *English Pistols* (London: Arms and Armouries Press, 1985), 69.

26. In 1757, a new Militia Act was passed in order to meet the demands for a more robust civil force. See Linda Colley, *Britons: Forging the Nation, 1707–1837* (New Haven, CT: Yale University Press, 1992), 86–87.

27. Smollett, *Roderick Random*, 371.

28. Ibid., 430, 432.

29. Giacomo Casanova, "Turbolenze della Polonia", *Opuscoli miscellanei* (Venice: Modesto Fenzo, 1780), 18.

30. Luigi Costantino Borghi, *La legislazione della repubblica veneta sul duello* (Venice: Visentini, 1898), 17–19.

31. Giacomo Casanova, "Il duello," ed. Elio Bartolini (Milan: Adelphi, 1997), 33.

32. Giacomo Casanova, "La vergogna, opera postuma di G.C.V.," in *Opuscoli miscellanei*, 84–96.

33. Charles-Joseph, Prince de Ligne, "Casanova," in *Caractères et portraits* (Paris: Champion, 2003), 226.

34. Giacomo Casanova, *Histoire de ma vie* (Paris: Garnier, 1880) 8 vols., vol. 6, chap. 16, 458.

35. Ibid.

36. Prince de Ligne, "Casanova," 51.

37. Casanova, *Histoire de ma vie*, vol. 7, 179.

38. Casanova, "Il duello," 45–47.

39. Ibid., 44.

40. Casanova, *Histoire de ma vie*, vol. 8, 397. With thanks to Marine Ganofsky for these ideas.

41. Ibid., 500, 513.

42. Casanova, "Il duello," 69.

43. In iconographical traditions, curved swords tend to be wielded by devious men. See *L'épée: Usages, mythes et symboles*, ed. Almudena Blasco, Fabrice

Cognot, Christine Duvauchelle and Michel Huynh. (Paris: RMN, 2011), 80.

44. Casanova, "Il duello," 75.

45. The Jesuits were suppressed by Clement XIV in 1773—between the duel that took place in 1766 and the narration of it in 1780.

46. Immanuel Kant, *Was ist Aufklärung?* (1784; repr., Hamburg: Felix Meiner, 1999), 20.

47. Casanova, "Il duello," 82. The exchange recalls Casanova's triumphant confrontation with doctors in the case of Bragadin. Casanova, *Histoire de ma vie*, vol. 2, 27–28.

48. Casanova, *Histoire de ma vie*, vol. 7, 191.

49. Casanova, "Il duello," 83.

50. Casanova, *Histoire de ma vie*, vol. 1, 56.

51. "Il duello," 48.

52. Horace, *Epistles*, 1.2.62.

53. See Niccolò Machiavelli, "To what extent the Romans avoided a middle course of action in passing judgments on subjects for some incident requiring such a verdict," *Discourses on Livy*, trans. and ed. Julia Conaway Bondanella and Peter Bondanella (Oxford: Oxford University Press, 1997) 215–219 (Bk 2, chap. 23).

54. Casanova "Il duello," 21.

55. Edward Bulwer-Lytton, *Richelieu, or the Conspiracy* (London: Saunders and Otley, 1839), 39.

56. Generously, Voltaire includes Richelieu (the author of a tragicomedy called *Europe* and of a tragedy by the name of *Mirame*) among the French writers he catalogues, only to conclude that "the finest of his works is the dyke at La Rochelle." Voltaire, *Œuvres historiques* (Paris: Gallimard, 1987), 1199. Even in Bulwer-Lytton's more charitable play, père Joseph remarks, "Strange that so great a statesman / Should be so bad a poet." Bulwer-Lytton, *Richelieu*, 22.

57. Victor Hugo, *Marion de Lorme* (1829), in *Théâtre complet*, ed. J.-J. Thierry and Josette Mélèze, 2 vols. (Paris: Gallimard, 1963), 1: 1082.

58. Marc Fumaroli, "Richelieu, patron of the arts", in *Richelieu: Art and Power*, ed. Hilliard Todd Goldfarb (Montreal: Montreal Museum of Fine Arts, 2002), 26, 25.

59. Ibid., 982.

60. Ibid., 988. The early decades of the seventeenth century indeed saw a great vogue for duelling. Caravaggio may have fled from a fatal duel, because an impulsive murder is less likely to have caused him to seek exile. Andrew Graham-Dixon, *Caravaggio: A Life Sacred and Profane* (London: Penguin, 2010), 321–23.

61. Hugo, *Marion de Lorme*, 993.

62. Ibid., 1009.

63. Ibid.

64. Hugo wrote the play in June 1829, under the repressive Restoration of Charles X, but then after the July Revolution of 1830, he "censored himself," claiming that he did not want it to be staged. It was, finally, first performed in August 1831. See the introduction to the critical edition of *Marion de Lorme* by John J. Janc, (Lanham: University Press of America, 2013), xi.

65. Hugo, *Marion de Lorme*, 982.

66. Ibid., 1087.

67. Ibid., 1064.

68. Ibid., 1081.

69. John Milton, *Areopagitica* (1644), in John Milton, *The Major Works*, ed. Stephen Orgel and Jonathan Goldberg (Oxford: Oxford University Press, 2008), 247–248.

70. Hugo, *Marion de Lorme*, 1109.

71. Bulwer-Lytton argues in his preface that "to judge the author's conception of Richelieu fairly, and to estimate how far it is consistent with historical portraiture, the play must be *read.*" Bulwer-Lytton, *Richelieu.* Hugo, by contrast, communicates his ideas in an emotive, visceral drama.

72. Hugo, *Marion de Lorme*, 1032.

73. Ibid., 1123.

74. See Eric Zafran, *Cavaliers and Cardinals: Nineteenth-Century French Anecdotal Paintings* (Cincinnati: Taft, 1992).

75. Hugo, *Marion de Lorme*, 996, 998.

76. Ibid., 1144. Hugo sometimes deprives his audience and readers of the pleasure of seeing these patterns for themselves. Or, rather, once we have seen them, he then flatters us that we were right to have done so.

77. Hugo, *Le roi s'amuse*, in *Théâtre complet*, 2: 1337.

78. Mary Magdalene is a figure particularly favored by poets throughout the nineteenth century. The church of La Madeleine was built, as a monument to national reconciliation, in the 1820s before consecration in 1842.

79. *Siècle de Louis XIV*, in *Œuvres historiques* (Paris: Gallimard, 1957), 617.

80. Hugo, *Marion de Lorme*, 1140.

81. Hugo, *Marion de Lorme*, 1003.

82. "La mort a mille aspects," ibid., 1120.

83. Tobias Smollett, *The Expedition of Humphry Clinker* (Oxford: Oxford University Press, 1984), 13.

84. Marc Fumaroli, "Richelieu, patron of the arts", *Richelieu: Art and Power*, ed. Hilliard T. Goldfarb (Montreal: Montreal Museum of Fine Arts, 2002), 25.

85. Anthony Trollope, *Thackeray* (1879; repr., London: Routledge, 1996), 70.

86. John Carey, *Thackeray: Prodigal Genius* (London: Faber, 1980), 9.

87. Indeed, both names are etymologically connected to the color red.

88. William Makepeace Thackeray, *The Memoirs of Barry Lyndon, Esq.* (1844), in *The Works of William Makepeace Thackeray*, ed. Edgar F. Harden, vol. 6 (Ann Arbor: University of Michigan Press, 1999), 15.

89. Ibid., 25.

90. Ibid., 28.

91. Ibid., 30. The unconscionable act of burning a house down functions as a proleptic, ironic detail, as it turns out.

92. Ibid., 36.

93. Ibid., 74.

94. Ibid., 52. Carlyle's history of Frederick would follow in 1858.

95. We may now recollect the implausibility, not to mention the bad taste, of Barry's earlier suggestion that he would "as soon have thought of burning the house down as calling for a bottle of claret."

96. Ibid., 94, 140.

97. Ibid., 155–56.

98. Ibid., 81n.

99. Ibid., 147.

100. Oscar Wilde, *An Ideal Husband*, act 3, *The Complete Plays*, ed. H. Montgomery Hyde (London: Methuen, 1988), 185.

101. "The counties of Tipperary and Galway were looked up to with a fond pride as the universities of the science of duelling." Andrew Steinmetz, *The Romance of Duelling in All Times and Countries*, 2 vols. (London: Chapman & Hall, 1968), 1:51, 54.

102. Thackeray, *Barry Lyndon*, 132.

103. In the preface to his play *Nothing Worse than a Fright (Quitte pour la peur)* (1833), set in the eighteenth century, Alfred de Vigny is similarly disconcerted by the union of a rigorous honor code with a relaxed moral outlook.

104. Thackeray, *Barry Lyndon*, 102.

105. William Makepeace Thackeray, *The History of Pendennis* (1848–50; repr., Oxford: Oxford University Press, 1994), 134–35.

106. Thackeray, *Barry Lyndon*, 224.

107. Ibid. 224.

108. Ibid., 225.

109. Ibid., 225.

110. Ibid., 180n9.

111. Ibid., 182.

112. Dumas, *Les trois mousquetaires* (1844; repr., Paris: Flammarion, 1984), 89.

113. Ibid., 65.

114. Friedrich Schiller, *Die Räuber* (1781), *Werke und Briefe*, ed. Klaus Harro Hilzinger, 12 vols. (Frankfurt am Main: Deutscher Klassiker Verlag, 1988–2004), 2: 267 (4.16).

115. Victor Hugo, *Hernani* (1830), in *Théâtre*, vol. 1, 550.

116. Dumas, *Les trois mousquetaires*, 31. This transgressive enthusiasm for duelling has said to have earned Dumas's novels their place on the Papal Index. See John Pappas, "La campagne des philosophes contre l'honneur," *SVEC* 205 (1982): 40.

117. Dumas, *Les trois mousquetaires*, 33.

118. Italo Calvino, "Tirant lo Blanc," in *Why Read the Classics?* (London: Penguin, 2009), 57.

119. Milan Kundera, in *The Art of the Novel* (New York: HarperCollins, 1988), examines common ground between Cervantes and Descartes and its effect on the novel.

120. Dumas, *Les trois mousquetaires*, 163.

121. Ibid., 287.

122. George Farquhar, *The Recruiting Officer*, in *The Works of George Farquhar*, ed. Shirley Strum Kenny, 2 vols. (Oxford, UK: Clarendon, 1988), 2:81.

123. Dumas, *Les trois mousquetaires*, 214.

124. The same idea can be seen in *Ettore Fieramosca* (1833), by Massimo d'Azeglio, in which disparate individuals from different regions of Italy are brought together by a common love of duelling. See chap. 4 (Naples: [no publ.], 1844), 63.

125. Dumas, *Les trois mousquetaires*, 331, 83.
126. Ibid., 155, 156, 267, 280.
127. Ibid., 163.
128. Ibid., 371, 506, 284, 446.
129. Comte de Chatauvillard, *Essai sur le duel* (Paris: Bohaire, 1836), 31.
130. Ibid., 42.
131. Dumas, *Les trois mousquetaires*, 309, 423.
132. Gustave Flaubert, *L'éducation sentimentale* (Paris: Gallimard, 1968), 249.
133. Dumas, *Les trois mousquetaires*, 483.
134. Ibid., 494.
135. Ibid., 641.
136. Ibid., 749, 761.
137. Ibid., 434.
138. Ibid., 51.
139. Ibid., 408, 451, 54.
140. Ibid., 519–20.
141. Ibid., 524.
142. Ibid., 517.
143. Drake, so legend has it, decides to finish the game before responding to the imminent approach of the Armada. See the disenchanting but salutary information in Harry Kelsey, *Francis Drake: The Queen's Pirate* (New Haven: Yale University Press, 2000), 322.
144. Dumas, *Les trois mousquetaires*, 581–82.
145. Ibid., 160.
146. Ibid., 167.
147. Ibid., 177.
148. Ibid., 807.
149. Gustave Flaubert, *Madame Bovary* (Paris: Gallimard, 1972), 446.

7. THE GROTESQUE DUEL

1. Mark Twain, "The Awful German Language," in *A Tramp Abroad* (1878; repr., New York: Hippocrene, 1982), 413.
2. Jerome K. Jerome, *Three Men on the Bummel* (1900; repr., London: Penguin, 1983), 183, 187.
3. Twain, *A Tramp Abroad*, 22.
4. Ibid., 23.
5. For such information, see Kevin McAleer, *Dueling: The Cult of Honor in Fin-de-Siècle Germany* (Princeton, NJ: Princeton University Press, 1994).
6. Twain, *A Tramp Abroad*, 27–35.
7. Ibid., 42. Twain's principal shares his name with Léon Gambetta, then the most prominent Republican in the aftermath of the constitutional crisis of 1877. The duel therefore perhaps offers an analogy to a wider conflict, the French love of a duel mirroring the internecine violence of the Commune, when Prussians need really to be feared.
8. Jules Renard, 'Le duel' (1895), in *Roman impromptu* (en collaboration), *Œuvres*, ed. Léon Guichard, 2 vols. (Paris: Gallimard, 1970), 1: 894–98.

9. Ambrose Bierce, *The Devil's Dictionary* (London: Folio Society, 2003), 61.

10. Twain, *A Tramp Abroad*, 43.

11. Ibid., 44.

12. Ibid., 44.

13. See Bertram Wyatt-Brown's invaluable study on duelling in the southern states, *Southern Honor: Ethics and Behavior in the Old South* (Oxford: Oxford University Press, 1982).

14. Mark Twain, *Pudd'nhead Wilson* (1894; repr., Harmondsworth, UK: Penguin, 1969), 57.

15. Ibid., 57.

16. *A Connecticut Yankee in King Arthur's Court* ed. Allison R. Ensor (New York: Norton, 1982), 225–227. Galton published *Finger Prints* in 1892, the first of three studies aimed at promoting anthropometry.

17. Twain, *Pudd'nhead Wilson*, 159.

18. Ibid., 159.

19. Ibid., 229, 233.

20. See Justin Kaplan, *Mr. Clemens and Mark Twain* (London: Cape, 1967).

21. Henry B. Wonham, "Mark Twain: The American Cervantes," in *Cervantes and the English-Speaking World: New Essays*, ed. Darío Fernández-Morera and Michael Hanke (Kassel: Reichenberger, 2005), 159–68.

22. Frank O'Connor, *The Lonely Voice: A Study of the Short Story* (London: Macmillan, 1965).

23. Guy de Maupassant, "Un duel" (1883), in *Contes et nouvelles*, ed. Louis Forestier, 2 vols. (Paris: Gallimard, 1974), 1: 951.

24. Ibid., 1: 947.

25. See Joris-Karl Huysmans, chapter 11, *A rebours*, ed. Rose Fortassier (Paris: Imprimerie nationale, 1981), 211. The narrator marvels repeatedly at the obesity of Londoners in Joseph Conrad's *The Secret Agent* (1907) (Oxford: Oxford University Press, 2004), 10, 99, 115, 163, 202.

26. Alain Corbin, *Le village des cannibales* (Paris: Aubier, 1990), 91.

27. Guy de Maupassant, "Un lâche" (1884), in *Contes et nouvelles*, 1: 1159.

28. Ibid., 1: 1160.

29. Henri Bergson, *Le rire* (1900; repr., Paris: PUF, 1989), 29.

30. Maupassant, "Un lâche," 1161.

31. Ibid., 1162.

32. Ibid., 1164.

33. Ibid., 1165.

34. Ibid., 1: 1165. His indecision is also betrayed by a previous, almost identical example of that opening phrase 'Donc il fallait se battre' (1: 1161).

35. Ibid., 1166.

36. Ibid., 1166.

37. Friedrich Nietzsche, *Jenseits von Gut und Böse* (1886; repr., Stuttgart: Kröner, 1953), 88 (§ 146).

38. Ibid., 24 (§ 17).

39. *The Duellist, or a Cursory Review of the Rise, Progress and Practice of Duelling* (London: Longman, 1822), 113.

40. Ibid., 114.

41. André Breton, *Manifestes du surréalisme* (1924), ed. Jean-Jacques Pauvert (Paris: Gallimard, 1972), 74.

42. Richard Brinsley Sheridan, *The Rivals*, in *The Dramatic Works of Richard Brinsley Sheridan*, ed. Cecil Price, 2 vols. (Oxford: Oxford University Press, 1973), 1:112 (5.3).

43. Jean-Jacques Rousseau, *L'Émile; ou de l'éducation* (1762) (Paris: Garnier, 1964), 450.

44. Arthur Schnitzler, "Leutnant Gustl" (1900), *Gesammelte, Werke*, 6 vols. (Frankfurt am Main: Fischer, 1962), 1: 343.

45. Heinz Kohut, "Thoughts on Narcissism and Narcissistic Rage" (1972), in *The search for the self: selected writings of Heinz Kohut, 1950–1978* ed. Paul H. Ornstein (New York: International Universities Press, 1978) 2 vols, 2: 615–658.

46. Guy de Maupassant, "Sur l'eau," (1876) in *Contes et nouvelles*, 58.

47. Gustave Flaubert, *Dictionnaire des idées reçues*, ed. Marie Thérèse Jacquet (Paris: Nizet, 1990), 269.

48. Joseph Conrad, "A Duel," in *The Complete Short Fiction of Joseph Conrad*, ed. Samuel Hynes, 4 vols. (London: Pickering & Chatto, 1993), 4:69.

49. Ibid. 4:69.

50. Ibid. 4:69.

51. Conrad drew on a historical account: "Two Captains of the Champagne Regiment, La Fenestre and d'Agay, had been mortal enemies for twenty-eight years, and had met seven times on the field of honour. La Fenestre had his head blown off by a cannon ball at Vellinghausen, but his partisans noted with a point of pride that a fragment of his skull put out d'Agay's right eye." Lee Kennett, *The French Armies in the Seven Years' War* (Durham, NC: Duke University Press, 1967), 69.

52. Conrad, "A Duel," 77.

53. Ibid., 131.

54. Conrad described himself thus in *Letters*, ed. Frederick R. Karl and Laurence Davies, 8 vols. (Cambridge: Cambridge University Press, 1983–2008), 3:89.

55. Conrad, "A Duel," 114.

56. Ibid., 80. See also Dumas, *Les trois mousquetaires* (Paris: Flammarion, 1984), 91.

57. Ibid., 91.

58. Ibid., 95, 125.

59. Ibid., 98.

60. Ibid., 111.

61. Ibid., 131.

62. G. K. Chesterton, *The Man Who Was Thursday: A Nightmare* (1908) (London: Penguin, 2011), 91–106.

63. Ibid., 9.

64. G. K. Chesterton, "The Duel of Dr. Hirsch" (1905), in *The Penguin Complete Father Brown* (Harmondsworth, UK: Penguin, 1981), 207. See also Schnitzler's play *Fink und Fliederbusch* (1916), in which two quarrelling journalists, drawn inexorably into a duel with each other, are at length revealed to be the same man.

65. Like Chesterton and Twain, Arthur Conan Doyle in "The Tragedians" (1884), and Hilaire Belloc in "The Duel" (*On Everything*, 1909) set their duelling

stories in Paris. These duels evidently distill an Anglo-Saxon view of French civilization as stylish but hopelessly frivolous. Conrad's account is rather more nuanced.

66. Prosper Mérimée, "Le coup de pistolet" (1856).

67. Andrew Steinmetz, *The Romance of Duelling in All Times and Countries*, 2 vols. (London: Chapman & Hall, 1968), 1:82.

68. Remy G. Saisselin, "Poetics of the Western," *British Journal of Aesthetics* 2 (1962): 167.

69. See J. P. Stern's suggestion in the introduction to his edition of Schnitzler's *Liebelei, Leutnant Gustl, Die letzten Masken* (Cambridge: Cambridge University Press, 1966), 1. For a study of the innumerable duels in Schnitzler's works, see Andrew C. Wisely, *Arthur Schnitzler and the Discourse of Honor and Duelling* (New York: Peter Lang, 1996).

70. Jan Morris, *Venice* (London: Faber & Faber, 1993), 141.

71. Arthur Schnitzler, *Casanovas Heimfahrt* (1918), in *Gesammelte Werke*, 5 vols. (Frankfurt: Fischer, 1961), 2:231, 233.

72. Ibid., 2:41.

73. Casanova was indeed bitterly opposed to Voltaire, such that he professed the wish to assassinate Voltaire and regretted not duly doing so. See Gérard La-houati, "Assommer Voltaire?," in *Casanova: La passion de la liberté*, ed. Marie-Laure Prévost and Chantal Thomas (Paris: BNF/Seuil, 2011), 176–79. Schnitzler is unlikely to have known a story by Pushkin, "Joan of Arc's Last Relative" (1836), in which one of the heroine's descendants challenges Voltaire to a duel, but he was, of course, familiar with Schiller's *The Maid of Orleans (Die Jungfrau von Orleans)* (1801).

74. Schnitzler, *Casanovas Heimfahrt*, 2:257.

75. Ibid., 2:259.

76. Ibid., 2:269.

77. Ibid., 2:269.

78. Ibid., 2:270.

79. See the stage directions in Schnitzler, *Gesammelte Werke*, 6 vols. (Frankfurt am Main: Fischer, 1962) 3: 243, 252, 253, 255, 257, 264.

80. Ibid., 2:280.

81. Ibid., 2:274.

82. Ibid., 2:307.

83. Ibid., 2:310.

84. Ibid., 2:310.

85. Ibid., 2:310

86. Ibid., 2:312.

87. Ibid., 2:313.

88. See the memorable distinction in Kenneth Clark, "The Naked and the Nude," *The Nude* (Harmondsworth: Penguin, 1964), 1–25.

89. Voltaire, *La Pucelle*, in *Œuvres complètes*, canto 8, 7:400–401.

90. See Freud's letter to Schnitzler, 14 May 1922, in *Letters of Sigmund Freud, 1873–1939*, ed. Ernst L. Freud, trans. Tania Stern and James Stern (London, Hogarth Press, 1961), 344–345.

91. Schnitzler, *Casanovas Heimfahrt*, 2:241.

92. Ibid., 2:314.

93. Stern, introduction to *Liebelei, Leutnant Gustl, Die letzten Masken*, 11–12.

94. Luigi Pirandello, *Il giuoco delle parti*, in *Maschere nude*, ed. Alessandro d'Amico, 3 vols. (Milan: Mondadori, 1997), 2: 147.

95. Ibid., 2: 185.

96. The principal characters in, respectively, Turgenev's *Fathers and Sons*, *Liebelei* and *A rebours*.

97. Ibid., 2:205.

98. Honoré de Balzac, *Le Père Goriot* (1834), in *La comédie humaine*, ed. Pierre-Georges Castex, 12 vols (Paris: Gallimard, 1976), 3: 290.

99. Jean Genet, "Comment jouer *Les Bonnes*," *Les Bonnes* (Paris: Gallimard, 1976), 10.

100. Theodor Fontane, *Effi Briest* (1895) (Frankfurt am Main: Suhrkamp, 2004), chap 28, 273–78.

101. See also the bizarre duel in Wyndham Lewis's *Tarr* (1918) Part 6, Chapter 5 (Harmondsworth: Penguin, 1982), 271–85.

102. Saki, "Reginald at the theatre," *Reginald* (1904), in *The Complete Works of Saki* (London: Bodley Head, 1987), 13.

8. PARADOXES OF THE DUEL

1. J. G. Millingen remarks in his "Introductory Observations" (1–8) that "the very origin of duelling should make us blush at its permanency,—springing from the darkest eras of barbarism." Yet his subtitle already promises "narratives of the most remarkable personal encounters." *The History of Duelling*, 2 vols. (London: Richard Bentley, 1841), 1: 2.

2. Max Beerbohm, "Dandies and Dandies" (1896), in *The Works of Max Beerbohm* (London: Heinemann, 1922), 12.

3. Steven Pinker, *The Better Angels of Our Nature: The Decline of Violence in History and Its Causes* (London: Allen Lane, 2011), 248.

4. Joseph Addison and Richard Steele, *The Tatler*, ed. Donald F. Bond, 3 vols. (Oxford: Oxford University Press, 1987), 1:220.

5. Ibid., 1:203.

6. Mikhail Lermontov, *A Hero of Our Time* (1840; repr., London: Penguin, 2001), 141.

7. Pinker, *Better Angels of Our Nature*, 23.

8. Leigh Hunt, *Table Talk* (London: Smith, Elder, 1851), 90.

9. G. K. Chesterton, "The Sins of Prince Saradine" (1911), in *The Penguin Complete Father Brown* (Harmondsworth, UK: Penguin, 1981), 114.

10. Théophile Gautier, *Critique d'art: Extraits des salons, 1833–1872*, ed. Marie-Hélène Girard (Paris: Séguier, 1994), 239–44.

11. François Villon, "Ballade des dames du temps jadis," *Poésies*, ed. Jean Dufournet (Paris: Garnier Flammarion, 1984), 108–10.

12. Francis Haskell, "The Sad Clown: Some Notes on a 19th Century Myth," in *French 19th Century Painting and Literature*, ed. Ulrich Finke (Manchester: Manchester University Press, 1969), 2–16.

13. Théophile Gautier, *Capitaine Fracasse* (1863), in *Romans, contes et nouvelles*, ed. Pierre Laubriet, 2 vols. (Paris: Gallimard, 2002), 2:840–73.

14. Villiers de l'Isle Adam, "Le convive des dernières fêtes," in *Contes cruels* (Paris: Garnier, 1989), 97–127.

15. Villiers de l'Isle Adam, "Sombre récit, conteur plus sombre," in *Contes cruels* (Paris: Garnier, 1989), 206–17.

16. Samuel Richardson, *Clarissa,* ed. Angus Ross (Harmondsworth, UK: Penguin, 1985), 1051 (letter 333).

17. Denis Diderot, *Supplément au voyage de Bougainville* ed. Antoine Adam, (Paris: Garnier Flammarion, 1972), 176.

18. Abbé Raynal and Denis Diderot, *Histoire philosophique et politique des établissements et du commerce des Européens dans les deux Indes,* 4 vols. (Geneva: Jean-Léonard Pellet, 1780), 2:11.

19. Augustine, letter 130, in *Letters,* vol. 2 (New York: Fathers of the Church, 1953).

20. Jean-Jacques Rousseau, *Julie* (Paris: Garnier Flammarion, 1967) 512 (part 6, letter 6).

21. Geometers alone, argues d'Alembert, could be sure to work in the same way on a desert island, away from the sway of fashions and the pressure of opinion. Jean-Baptiste le Rond d'Alembert, "Essai sur la société des gens de lettres et des grands," in *Mélanges de littérature, d'histoire et de philosophie,* 4 vols. (Amsterdam: Zacharie Chatelain, 1764), 1:335.

22. Bertolt Brecht, "Kleines Organon für das Theater," in *Gesammelte Werke,* vol. 16 (Frankfurt am Main: Suhrkamp, 1967), 688.

23. Some fictional accounts, such as Chesterton's "The Sins of Prince Saradine" (1911), do feature a duel designed to avenge an injustice that has rankled over many years.

24. Robert Warshow, *The Immediate Experience: Movies, Comics, Theatre, and Other Aspects of Popular Culture* (Cambridge, MA: Harvard University Press, 2001), 111.

25. Addison and Steele, *The Tatler,* 1:205. After Lord Mordaunt's suicide, Parisians observed that this was a typically English expedient *pour passer le temps.* Quoted in Immanuel Kant, *Anthropology from a Pragmatic Point of View,* trans. Victor Lyle Dowdell (London: Feffer & Simons, 1978), 134.

26. So says Axël, having killed his cousin Kaspar in a duel. Auguste Villiers de l'Isle-Adam, *Axël* (1890; repr., Paris: La Colombe, 1960), 249.

27. Thomas M. Kavanagh, "Gambling as Social Practice," *Enlightenment and the Shadows of Chance* (Baltimore: Johns Hopkins University Press, 1993), 29–66.

28. Jean Fougeroux de Campigneulles, *Histoire des duels anciens et modernes,* 2 vols. (Paris: Tessier, 1835) 1:121.

29. Tobias Smollett, *Roderick Random,* (Oxford: Oxford University Press, 2008), 291.

30. Gautier, *Capitaine Fracasse,* 2:868.

31. Addison and Steele, *The Tatler,* 1:194–95.

32. Thomas Holcroft, *He's Much to Blame,* in *The Plays of Thomas Holcroft,* ed. Joseph Rosenblum, 2 vols. (London: Garland, 1980), 2:33 (2.10).

33. Henry Fielding, *Tom Jones,* (Harmondsworth: Penguin, 1968), bk. 16,744.

34. Dion Boucicault, *London Assurance* (1841), in *London Assurance and Other Victorian Comedies,* ed. Klaus Stierstorfer (Oxford: Oxford University Press, 2001), 86.

35. Addison and Steele, *The Tatler,* 1:194–95.

36. Andrew Steinmetz, *The Romance of Duelling in All Times and Countries*, 2 vols. (London: Chapman & Hall, 1968), 1:76, 95, 114. When a man *deloped*, he was seen to acknowledge his guilt.

37. Charles Dickens, *Dickens's journalism: sketches by Boz and other early papers, 1833–39*, ed. Michael Slater (London: Phoenix, 1994), 389–405 (397).

38. Richardson, *Clarissa*, 1481 (letter 535: 2).

39. Richard Brinsley Sheridan, *The Rivals*, in *The Dramatic Works of Richard Brinsley Sheridan*, ed. Cecil Price, 2 vols. (Oxford: Oxford University Press, 1973), 4.3, 129.

40. Tobias Smollett, *The Life and Adventures of Sir Launcelot Greaves* (1760–62), ed. Robert Folkenflik (Athens: University of Georgia Press, 2002), 190.

41. Sheridan, *The Rivals*, 5.3, 140. He may be inspired by *Hamlet*, 3.1.75.

42. Charlotte Lennox, *The Female Quixote; or, The Adventures of Arabella* (1752; repr., Oxford: Oxford University Press, 2008), 128.

43. William Shakespeare, *Twelfth Night*, 3.4.

44. Smollett, *Life and Adventures of Sir Launcelot Greaves*, 17.

45. Pierre Choderlos de Laclos, *Les liaisons dangereuses*, ed. Catriona Seth (Paris: Gallimard, 2011), 477.

46. Ibid., 477.

47. "La lumière des lettres n'a-t-elle pas plus fait contre la fureur des duels, que l'autorité des lois?," in Axel Duboul, *Les deux siècles de l'Académie des jeux floraux*, 2 vols. (Toulouse: Privat, 1901), 1: 546. It is tempting in more recent ages to see the eclipse of the duellist coincide with the rise of tabloid journalists as the new self-appointed custodians of private, often sexual conduct, beyond the law.

48. Smollett, *Life and Adventures of Sir Launcelot Greaves*, 190.

49. Unfortunately, the original source is not attested.

50. Charles Dickens, *The Pickwick Papers* (Oxford: Oxford University Press, 2008), chap. 44, 502.

51. Voltaire, *Candide, Romans et contes*, ed. Frédéric Deloffre and Jacques van den Heuvel (Paris: Gallimard, 1979), chap. 30, 230; Richardson, *Clarissa*, 1489 (conclusion).

52. Kavanagh, "Gambling as Social Practice," 42.

53. Charles Burney, *Music, Men, Manners in France and Italy 1770* (London: Folio Society, 1969), 164.

54. Jonathan Swift, letter to Alexander Pope, 29 September 1725, in *The Correspondence of Jonathan Swift*, ed. Harold Williams, 5 vols. (Oxford: Oxford University Press, 1963), 3:103.

55. Edmund Burke, *Reflections on the Revolution in France* (1790; repr., Oxford: Oxford University Press, 1993), 76.

56. Arthur Schnitzler, *Liebelei* (Cambridge: Cambridge University Press, 1968), 103.

57. Théophile Gautier, *Mademoiselle de Maupin*, 75.

58. Smollett, *Roderick Random*.

59. Lennox, *Female Quixote*, 128.

60. Smollett, *Roderick Random*, 281.

61. Jean-Jacques Rousseau, *Lettre à d'Alembert* (Paris: Garnier Flammarion, 1967), 151.

62. Susanna Centlivre, *The Beau's Duel; or A Soldier for the Ladies* (1702), in *The Plays of Susanna Centlivre*, ed. Richard C. Frushell (London: Garland, 1982), 8.

63. Tobias Smollett, *The Adventures of Roderick Random*, ed. Paul Boucé (Oxford: Oxford University Press, 2008), chap. 49, 292.

64. See Louvet de Couvray, *Les aventures de Faublas* (1787), ed. Michel Delon (Paris: Gallimard, 1996), 729–33, for an unusual duel between Madame de B**, in disguise, and Rosambert, whom she injures. Marquise Du Châtelet, *Discours sur le Bonheur*, ed. Robert Mauzi (Paris: les belles lettres, 1961), 19.

EPILOGUE

1. Denys de Rougemont, *L'amour et l'occident* (Paris: Plon, 1939), 226. The evolving terms with which an apparently ordinary soldier, Private James Beatson, records his experiences may be typical. In 1915, he reports, rather conventionally, a "fierce artillery duel" between the two forces, but, within months, these terms are wholly superseded when he describes the enemy as horribly present and absent at once, like a "cloud you cannot seize." James Beatson, *Private Beatson's War: Life, Death and Hope on the Western Front*, ed. Shaun Springer and Stuart Humphreys (Barnsley, UK: Pen & Sword, 2009), 76, 103.

2. Thomas Mann, *Der Zauberberg* (Berlin: Fischer, 1954), 867.

3. Such, in their polysyllabic splendor, are the rival patients, Sonnenschein and Wiedemann.

4. Mann, *Der Zauberberg*, 867, 869.

5. That analogy between war and duel has been implicitly present in a number of earlier texts, and the latter, "private war" tends to be favored in the comparison. Indeed, in Dr. Johnson's opinion, "it is exceedingly clear that duelling, having better reasons for its barbarous violence, is more justifiable than war, in which thousands go forth without any cause of personal quarrel, and massacre each other." James Boswell, *Life of Johnson* (Oxford: Oxford University Press, 1969), 520 (19 April 1773).

6. Joseph Roth, *Radetzkymarsch*, in *Werke*, ed. Hermann Kesten, 4 vols. (Cologne: Kiepenheuer & Witsch, 1975), 2:113.

7. Ibid., 2:256–57. See also Gyula Krúdy's short stories, "Last Cigar at the Grey Arabian" and "The Journalist and Death" (both 1927), which each turn on one duel, the same duel. They too are set in a period not long before but indisputably prior to the First World War, when the Habsburg Empire yet lives on, precariously, but unsuspectingly. They are available in translation by John Batki, in *Life is a Dream* (1931) (London: Penguin, 2010), 1–58.

8. As Steven Pinker notes, puzzlingly, "a category of violence can be embedded in a civilization for centuries and then vanish into thin air." Steven Pinker, *The Better Angels of Our Nature: The Decline of Violence in History and Its Causes* (London: Allen Lane, 2011), 23.

9. Gregor von Rezzori, *Ein Hermelin in Tschernopol: Ein Maghrebinischer Roman* (Hamburg: Rowohlt, 1958), 167.

10. Ibid., 185–86.

11. See Paul Fussell's discussion of Northrop Frye's cycle in *The Great War and Modern Memory* (Oxford: Oxford University Press, 1975), 311–14.

12. Evelyn Waugh, *Officers and Gentlemen* (1955; repr., London: Penguin, 2001), 220.

13. Rachele Mussolini, *Mia nonna e il duce* (Milan: Rizzoli, 2011).

14. Richard Hillary, *The Last Enemy* (London: Vintage, 2010), 15, 97.

15. The overwhelming wish among writers to escape Europe and its degradation in the aftermath of World War I is explored in Paul Fussell, *Abroad: British Literary Traveling between the Wars* (Oxford: Oxford University Press, 1980).

16. Alan Hunt, *Governing Morals: A Social History of Moral Regulation* (Cambridge: Cambridge University Press, 1990), 121–30.

17. Lord Byron, *Don Juan*, canto 4, st.41, line 325, *Byron*, ed. Jerome J. McGann (Oxford: Oxford University Press, 1986), 529.

18. Rainer-K. Langner, *Duell im ewigen Eis* (Frankfurt am Main: Fischer, 2001).

19. Geoffrey Winthrop Young, "Knight Errantry," in *Collected Poems* (London: Methuen, 1936), 43.

20. See the letter from Felice Tocco, included at the end of Vittorio Imbriani, *Pena capitale e duello* (Bologna: Fava & Garagnani, 1869), 43.

21. Robert Warshow, *The Immediate Experience: Movies, Comics, Theatre, and Other Aspects of Popular Culture* (Cambridge, MA: Harvard University Press, 2001), 111.

22. Leslie A. Fiedler, *The Return of the Vanishing American* (London: Paladin, 1972), 142. Earp himself was, finally, shot in the back.

23. W. G. Sebald, *Austerlitz* (London: Penguin, 2001), 260.

24. Guy de Maupassant, *Sur l'eau* (Paris: Marpon & Flammarion, 1888), 113 (10 April).

25. *Les traites négrières: essai d'histoire globale* (Paris: Gallimard, 2004).

26. See the account of this imbroglio in George Steiner, *Errata: An Examined Life* (London: Phoenix, 1998), 127–28. See also Allen Tate, *Collected Poems 1919–1976* (New York: Farrar Straus Giroux, 1977), 20–23.

27. Quoted in Anthony David Moody, *Ezra Pound: Poet; A Portrait of the Man and His Work*, vol. 1, *The Young Genius, 1885–1920* (Oxford: Oxford University Press, 2007), 206.

Acknowledgments

My greatest debt is to Ian Malcolm, my editor at Harvard University Press, whose support, guidance, and insight have been indispensable in shaping this book and bringing it to publication. I wish also to record my gratitude and appreciation to Heidi Allgair, Joy Deng, and Andrew Katz, who have been extremely perceptive and patient in working on the text of the book. I am also very grateful for the care and consideration invested by the two anonymous readers of the manuscript in its early stages.

I am indebted to the staff of a number of libraries and institutions in which research for this book has been carried out: the University Library, Cambridge; Fitzwilliam College, Cambridge; the Ecole normale supérieure, Lyons; the Bibliothèque municipale in Lyons; the British Library; and the Marciana in Venice. I wish also to record particular thanks to the Cini Foundation, Venice, for allowing me to use their resources.

I am particularly grateful to Donald Lee not just for reading my manuscript, but for years of sympathetic conversational sparring. I would like to thank Marine Ganofsky, Joe Harris, Richard Marks, and Michael Moriarty for reading all or some of the text and for commenting so helpfully. All translations in the book are my own, except those from Russian, where I have not only relied on existing translations but also been able to call on the Slavonic services of Valentine Bolam.

For their suggestions, comments, or encouragement of different kinds, I wish to thank Kasia Boddy, Andrew Brown, Caroline Bugler, Robert Douglas-Fairhurst, Rosalind Esche, Nick Hammond, James Harriman-Smith, Richard Harris, James Hester, Dominic Keown, Niall Mackenzie, Jenny Mander, Rita Marks, Justin Meggitt, Silvia Mei, Michael Minden, Peter Tregear, Catherine Volpihlac-Auger, Tracy Wilkinson, and David Woodhouse.

Finally, I wish to thank Yseult for keeping me going.

Index

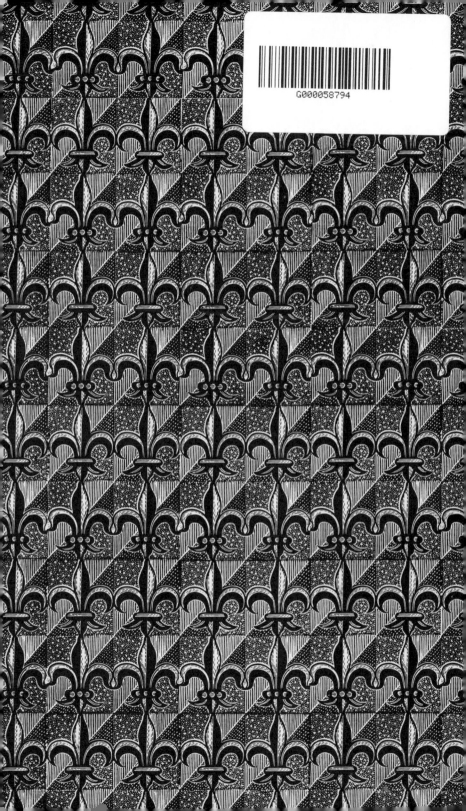

Approaching
Priests

Dearest Liam, Dearest Margaret.
I wish it were a finer thing — you
both deserve the best.

Mary —
October
1951

Approaching Priests

by

Mary Leland

SINCLAIR-STEVENSON

First published in Great Britain by
Sinclair-Stevenson Limited
7/8 Kendrick Mews
London SW7 3HG, England

Copyright © 1991 by Mary Leland

British Library Cataloguing in Publication Data
A CIP catalogue record for this book is available from the British Library.
ISBN: 1 85619 065 X

Typeset by Selectmove
Printed and bound in Great Britain by
Butler and Tanner, Frome & London

To
W.H. and C.B.
FERRY

Approaching
Priests

Part
One

Chapter 1

Before finally, if not formally, renouncing her religion, Claire Mackey found herself wishing that Catholics had been encouraged to read the King James Version. Tonight, at this Legion of Mary Meeting, she heard the Legionaries slew their tongues around *Yahweh*; *Yahweh*, they tried to say, was their shepherd.

'We are in a trial period,' the Spiritual Director told them. The gas fire punctured his words with its ancient, labouring hiss where they sat eager and listening in the too tall, too narrow, damp-patched room. Claire sat towards the back. She was only visiting, she had said in excuse. Just dropping in, and she took a chair behind the ring of chairs at the long, stained table where Damien Sebright presided. He smiled at Claire before going on to explain his use of the new rites.

'What I thought was, we should begin with the most familiar verses in the liturgy. You see, the rites themselves are not new; the Vatican Council made that very clear. Very explicit.'

Had it? All he could find was a linguistic turmoil. The accepting faces in front of him seemed shadowed by the same doubt.

'We should find our way, using these familiar steps, to the new language. We should realise that there is no one language for our approach to God; Latin is not the only tongue in which to celebrate the mysteries of our faith. Of course –' he couldn't help the reflection. He really liked Latin. '– of course it would be a pity to lose it altogether, because it links us to a, to a tradition . . .'

Why was he stumbling? He hadn't meant to say this, that was why. His business was to appear, at least, to know what he was doing. Or saying.

'Well, I'm sure that won't happen. No, the thing we must realise is that language, words, are only a device for coming closer to the desired object, which is the fuller, more immediate awareness of God in our everyday lives. And, nearly as important' – the trouble was, he kept on leaving this bit out, and it really *was* important, – 'by using the everyday language for our church practices, for our sacraments and devotions, we learn to share, we learn how close we are, to the devotions and practices of other churches.

'Now that is *really* very important.' He was uncomfortable with the stress he felt he had to put on the words. The little flock gathered around him, already disconcerted by Yahweh, suppressed the qualms his emphasis aroused. Missionaries every one, dedicated in Mary's name to the promotion of the one true Catholic and Holy Roman Church, they could not readjust without dismay, but had been prepared to try for some months now; they understood at last that doubt was the sacrifice Pope John XXIII had demanded of them. It was an insidious offering, though. Nothing clean, like immolaion or isolation, but a kind of licence – not to disbelieve, but to tolerate disbelief.

Who could tell where that might lead? Fr Sebright could see the anxiety beginning again as his listeners seemed to aquiesce. Why had he started this? Why hadn't he just read the Bishop's pastoral on liturgy and ecumenism and the Vatican Council and asked them to talk about it, the way he had intended? What was this free-fall approach – not really his style at all, these days. Now he had them worried again. These were very tricky times, defining and explaining the small print of Vatican Two.

'It's as if we're finding a new path towards a new understanding, not just of ourselves, but of what we should call our sister churches.'

Much better, that, than our separated brethren. He had to admit that that was a distinct step forward.

'Yes. These are steps we are taking, stepping-stones. A way forward, onward to new heights. Like a kind of Simplon Pass.

'Or Suez Canal,' he added helpfully, hopefully. They remained silent, the young men, the greying women who would find no mates here. But they also remained eager. They would try it. Weren't some of them *Viatores Cristi* – travellers for Christ? They would try anything, those of them who had already knocked on doors in Iceland, gathered head-scarved women around them in Russia. They would even get, some of them, a Jerusalem Bible of their own, if Fr Sebright was sincere in his recommendation of Yahweh. Although that could be a bit expensive if it really was only a trial period. What if it was not a successful trial? Given the way Yahweh was going, success did not appear to be guaranteed.

'Sure, none of them ever heard of the Simplon tunnel.' Claire teased him when the meeting was over, the sweaty winter smells dissolved.

'Them?' He looked at her quizzically, kindly.

He was right. What was she doing here, if she was so confident she didn't belong?

'Ah – I only came to see you. To see how you were. They know I'm not a member any more, that I wasn't a very good one even when I was enrolled. I was only useful for taking the minutes. I'm no loss to you – especially now that you've got Yahweh.'

It had been no surprise to the members of the Legion that she had remained behind after the meeting. She liked this kind of freedom which her own disengagement had given her, a freedom to ignore what others might say, their possible misinterpretations. She was not old enough, yet, to recognise how her freedoms could be the cause of restrictions for other people – as in Damien Sebright's case, here and now, who could not match her implied declarations, and who must remain, for scandal's sake, circumspect.

'*Yahweh.*' Jeering, she softened the word with amiable contempt. Just to draw him out. Just to remind him she was different.

'Come on, Damien. Why not have a regular comparative religions session? They'd take it from you – you could give them the Torah, the Koran, they wouldn't whimper, the Bishop need never know –'

He didn't always enjoy these deft little taunts. Now he was aware that someone else was waiting for him, someone her cynicism could hurt.

'All right, Claire. I agree it's a bit rocky at the moment – but it's not something the King James Version is going to wipe away. Still, if it would please you to know about it, I'm quite prepared to introduce readings, of that and other translations, Duoai for example. And we're not stuck with the Jerusalem Bible, either. Now listen – it's all very well for you to mock this whole thing, but Raphael is out there on the landing waiting for us, and I don't want him to be upset.'

'Upset?' She lifted a lively, mischievous face to him. 'Raphael will be delighted with you if he's allowed to give a reading or two. In fact that's one part of the new liturgy which is going to really please him: out with the Latin, in with the lay readers –'

She saw Damien's face tighten. She knew he was right to be concerned. 'It's all right – it's all right, I'll be good. I won't say another word; I'm sorry – I was really only showing off.'

He was disarmed again. Sometimes, he reflected, she could describe herself quite accurately.

He had seen something of self-knowledge in her the first time he had seen her at all; something of that sympathy for others which comes from a sense of one's own ability to suffer, one's own capacity. She had been the unlaughing one in a clutch of giggling, knowing, schoolgirls; those were the days of Apologetics and doctrinal studies and the penitential missions of young priests to secular private schools. He had been warned about such visits.

'Ravening wolves, they are,' fellow ordinand Johnny Trant had told him gloomily.

'You know the boys are out to get you, and they try, they do try. But at least you can use their own language back to the pimply little buggers, and that shocks the shit out of them. But *girls*! Jesus wept!'

Damien had sisters. He wasn't too worried.

'Ah, Damien, bless your innocence. Sisters aren't in it at all. Not that I've much to say for them, either, but at least you can see them improving as they get older, and in the meantime you can keep yourself a step ahead of their games. No – girls are all right up to about seven, say. First Communion age. After that –'

'A nunnery?' Damien was laughing at him.

'*God!* No. They're even worse. Oh, God protect me from convents! No – a sterile environment for about twenty years, something from Azimov, science-fiction land, that kind of thing. Then let them out, adult, educated up to a point, and so anxious to breed that they won't even see any man in a clerical collar – and I tell you, Damien –' they had been arguing about clothes – 'priests and nuns may be given permission right now with all this upheaval from the Council to wear what they damn well like – have you seen the get-up of some of the nuns? – but the day will come, I tell you, when you'll be bloody glad of the dog-collar itself. Protective colouring, I call it, and we'd be awful fools to abandon it. But with it or without it, we're just sitting ducks for the little bitches in the schools, especially the private schools. I swear, sometimes in those senior classes, I think they're aiming their tits at me, ready to fire.'

Entering that one classroom full of expectant girls to whom nubile was a feeling rather than a word Damien's eyes went immediately to the blank gymslipped chests. He groped for an invocation to Holy Purity, the ejaculation which would ease his soul, and found instead the measuring gaze of a girl sitting under a framed reproduction of a picture he knew to be familiar but could not place. There were tumultuous clouds in it, and mountains like scratched silver and a small grey lake. Yes, a Connemara landscape. Paul Henry.

Knowing the painting, letting recognition strike a note against his own panic, he calmed enough to look around the room and then back again to the quiet face beneath the picture. Just enough of a hint of pity reached him to make him latch his words to her eyes. He had been going to be genial, pretending to a bluffness which he had seen older priests assume with young girls. But it wouldn't sit on him at all. He was vulnerable to their awareness of him as a man, startled by it. He hadn't thought he was as male as all that, not masculine enough to cause this quite overt enjoyment of some incongruity in his presence among them, or his role among them. It made him suddenly grossly uncomfortable when they started laughing, not as boys did with sniggers and leers, but openly, enjoying his embarrassment. He might want to talk about religion, about love of God, about the right way to read the Gospels, and he might be sure, he was sure, that this could be done without any reference at all to human sexuality; but these girls knew how to make it impossible.

'You saw me coming,' he said at last, conceding their supremacy. It was only that they were more adroit than he was, less aware of any strictures against giving offence.

'Ah, but Father – you're gorgeous!' a big lusty girl told him, to the shouts of her companions. He had to laugh then himself, and told them they'd get him in terrible trouble, and indeed the door of the classroom opened and the Head Mistress looked at them all with one stiff grey eyebrow raised. Only Damien Sebright looked uneasy in the calm which followed her entrance. He didn't know that the Head had been timing her intervention, gauging from the relieved free tone of the laughter pealing along the landing that the blooding was over and she could interrupt.

Turning to her with the laugh still on his face, the young priest again found himself outclassed. Every curve of her short abundant figure was rigid with distaste. Running a private school in a Catholic country she had to tolerate these occasional diocesan inspections; they soothed the more conformative parents and gave her otherwise undenominational establishment some small claim to the city's prevailing ethos. Yet she knew how to express her resentment that classics had to be justified in this society by the blessing of catechetics.

'You seem to be very popular with my young ladies, Fr Sebright.'

The young ladies had quieted into no longer appropriate angelical composure on her arrival. Not a breath, not a hair, stirred the still-warm silence into which she dropped her words.

It was the sweetness of her scorn that he remembered when he saw Claire again, not quite remembering the first meeting, the quiet, pitying eyes, this time to the rear of a group which had gathered for a meeting of the Legion of Mary.

'Suffering Jesus!' Johnny Trant had almost cried when Damien told him about the new job.

'What does it take in this bloody diocese to get a good guy into a good place? You'll be down in that feicking hall for years on end now. Leaking ceilings, peeling plaster, jacks running like sewers, with five hundred boy scouts marching up and down over your head on the last bit of second-storey flooring left in Paul Street. There isn't any TB in your family, is there? You might try to get out of it like that – say the conditions might affect your health. Otherwise, I pity you!'

His pity had taken the form of sherry in a half-pint glass.

'It's the only thing in the feicking house. *Nuns!* Sherry and lemonade – that's all they know about. And altar wine. Sure no Christian on earth should be asked to drink altar wine. But that's it now. That's what you're in for. Total abstinence spiked with altar wine.'

Sadly they sipped at the thick brown liquid.

'Virgins too. Every one of them. In the Legion I mean.'

Johnny Trant was getting even more despondent.

'Only thing is, Damien – you won't have to worry about what the Pope's going to say about family planning. You'll be let out of that one, down there.'

'Ah, come on, Johnny. There's a lot of married people in the Legion –'

'Yeh. That's what I mean. Virgins every one of them. No trick questions for you, anyway.'

Damien didn't mind trick questions by then. He told himself he didn't, knowing that it was really a case of not putting himself in the way of them. He had learned that caution, at least, in the first few years of his ministry; he was also beginning to feel that he might some day catch up with Johnny Trant's worldly wisdom without succumbing completely to misanthropy.

He had found himself enjoying the simplicity of the job with the Legion of Mary. A Spiritual Director could interpret the title with some freedom, and in his parish the members, grouped as a Praesidium, included none more knowledgeable than himself. There was a shared desire for holiness, although that in itself was a quality about which there was little or no unanimity. Let it be, then, that they shared some desire to do good, to be good. He could give point to their very ordinary lives – although as a priest he was slowly beginning to understand how very *not* ordinary such lives could be – and he learned to enjoy the gradually unselfconscious readiness with which they listened to him.

There were other consolations; the occasional visits of Claire Mackey, by then grown rare indeed as her job as a reporter on the provincial newspaper provided her with the inoffensive excuse she needed to let her attendance lapse. In her place, as if to fill it – Damien now knew that she was capable of that kind of premeditation – she had brought Raphael Brady.

Eighteen years old, tall, with black, awkwardly growing hair, clumsy in his long-limbed movements, with the large, glutinous eyes that betoken an over-active thyroid, Raphael throbbed with emotions and energies, prayed with devout pleasure, his fervour unashamed and tolerated even by those who were embarrassed by it.

'Do you know, Raphael,' Damien had teased him early on, before he knew the boy was insane, 'you're my first religious maniac?'

Raphael had burned with happiness.

'"How beautiful upon the mountains are the feet of him who bringeth good tidings" – isn't it true, Father?'

'"That publisheth peace, that publisheth salvation" – it *is* true, Raphael.' Damien had not yet learned to be wary of enthusiasm. Looking at the boy's narrow shoes, their soles unravelling from the unpolished imitation leather, he thought that they were beautiful indeed, and smiled with the pity of the image.

Claire Mackey had said 'be careful of him' – not in warning, but in entreaty. She had said that even his name seemed to shine, to burn. There was a background of not poverty, exactly, but some kind of deprivation, some quite deliberate limitation to his schooling, to his imagination. 'Religion is what gives colour to his life; not just the consolation of his belief, his faith in God, but the radiance he needs, the feeling of something outside himself infusing his whole life.'

Because he did not trust her yet, Damien disputed Claire's fanciful analysis. He could not voice his distrust, he could not even identify it properly. It had something to do with his recognition of her as a memory of discomfort.

'Good Heavens,' he had said, his tone touched with sarcasm. 'You're making very large claims for the Catholic Church.'

She had not been impervious, he had seen her skin darken. But her voice was steady and impersonal when she answered, 'No. I wouldn't do that. It's just that I do recognise its liturgical values – or what will be left of them after the Bishops finish their translations. That's all.'

'Liturgical values?' He didn't mean to scoff, he only wanted to challenge her, to get her to declare herself and then show her how vapid, how vague, her ideas of religion were. 'Don't tell me *you* appreciate liturgical values – I thought you did not have time for such sentimental, emotional things.'

It caught her. He saw, with surprising satisfaction which he was ashamed of later, that she was stung.

'You're quite right; I don't have time for them. I specially don't have time for them when they are used to hide poverty, or degradation, or misery, or to keep people suffering in the belief that they are meant to suffer, that this world's lot is atonement, although for some strange reason not everybody suffers in the same way or for the same length of time. I can understand that where squalor or ill-health or deprivation are endemic, like in some African or South American countries, or even, indeed, in the west of Ireland – I can see that the Church can help people to bear what can't be changed – no, I don't have much time for a church that keeps things the way they are, just because it's easiest!'

Damien wasn't old enough to be amused by this. He was angry, and forgot himself.

'Like what? What are you talking about? Sure you don't even go to church any more, to Mass or Confession or Communion. How can you presume to know what's going on – your very occasional visits here to the Legion won't keep you in touch, you know – and why you continue even to come here, when you do come, I can't understand at all.'

His heat cooled hers. She used his own anger against him.

'You're angry now because you know in your heart and in your soul that I'm right. I know you haven't been a priest for very long, that you haven't even done much chaplaincy work yet – not in hospitals, I mean, or really taxing places, places which will challenge your own convictions. So I can accept your ignorance – yes' – she had seen his rage that she should call him ignorant – '*yes*. You *are* ignorant, that's the only reason why your complacency is excusable. And yes, you *are* complacent – much too complacent for a young man. You nestle inside your faith as though it were a carapace, like a crab.'

She had shocked him. He had never been spoken to like this, attacked like this, in his whole life, or at least in that part of it spent outside the seminary. The sensation which was chilling him was the prelude to an absolutely murderous rage. He began to grow hot as though his blood were frothing; that heat gave way to frigid lucidity; he could feel his eyes narrowing with determination to slaughter her with scorn, with status, to savage her with contempt. But the only effective words which rose to his tongue were the street-boy obscenities of Johnny Trant. He could not say them.

'Look,' she had said, appeasing. She put her hand on his arm and he shook her off as if it were a claw about to pierce his skin. He turned quickly away from her, going to stand at the window of the meeting room. He wanted to end this row. He wanted to get out, away from her, from her voice. He wanted to get his hands around her neck and throttle her, to wring her neck as he had seen his grandfather do with chickens. He wanted to get his hands on her, shut her up, frighten her with his own force, to thrust himself at her, on her. In her. His whole body flared, shockingly.

She was silent. Everything in him quieted. His blood still throbbed so that he could almost hear it. He stayed at the window, willing calm on himself. His mind strove for comfort. 'Remember O most gracious Virgin Mary that never was it known that anyone who fled to thy protection, implored thine aid or sought thine intercession was left unheeded . . .'

Her voice said 'I'm sorry.' He waited, and she went on: 'I should not have said those things to you, those personal things. I got . . . carried away. But will you let me explain – not about you, about *me*?'

She had taken his brief nod as consent. He went on staring through the window, his vision blurred by shame and the dirt on the panes of glass . . .

'Please believe me I *am* sorry. I do apologise – with an earnest desire not to sin again –'

There it was again. He spun round on her. But she had started to laugh. 'I can't *help* it: it's years of conditioning – "a *firm desire for repentance"* – sure you had to go to confession the same as I had – come on, forgive me for that, it wasn't a jibe, it's just built into me so that in some situations certain phrases come tripping out, I can't help it.'

She saw, with some relief, that he had begun to smile. He did know what she meant.

'Well, I know I'm younger than you, but I've been around a bit more; in some ways I'm older. And I'm less patient. I'm not so well educated in formal terms as you are, but my job is a sort of short cut to experience. And I can't help seeing the contradictions. No, don't worry, I won't go into them here – but you do hear confession, after all, and you must know, just for one example, you must know about the problems of birth control and what the Catholic Church is saying about all that – or *not* saying. You must hear through those voices that whisper into the sieve of the grille in the confession box that *Humanae Vitae* has induced a kind of despair in so many good-living Catholic lives, people who thought they could use the pill, people with six children already – now the Pope has condemned them to an absolutely monastic life if they want to avoid further pregnancies.'

He stirred: 'There are other ways . . .'

'Do they work? Can you honestly say that you believe they work? Or can they be of any use at all to poor or uneducated people, or to women whose husbands don't much care?'

'You keep on switching the context of your argument.' He would dismay her with logic.

'I know that. It's just a way of showing you – if you don't know already and I think you do – how wide-ranging the effect of the Encyclical must be. And of course you are alienating just those Catholics who want to remain a real part of the Church –'

'We have been instructed: when we hear confession, if penitents come to us with problems about family planning, we must show Christian compassion in our response.'

'And that's another issue – who decides what compassion is, Christian or otherwise? The Vincentians might say, "I understand, but do try not to continue with this practice";

the Augustinians could say, "I feel sorry for you, but this is forbidden and you will be in a state of mortal sin if you dare to continue". Every curate and parish priest in the country will have a variation on those two versions. In that context, "compassion" is a very nasty word, it seems to me.'

She was speaking with real conviction, this was something thought about, not instant, not fashionable. He heard the deepening of her voice, the light mockery gone from her. He noticed again the thick sweetness of her tone.

'Do you sing?' he asked her suddenly, and she burst out laughing.

'Oh, that's just like Dylan Thomas: remember in *A Child's Christmas in Wales*? The firemen rush in to put out the fire, and the place is swamped, and they're all standing around when Mrs Protheroe comes down the stairs and goes in to the firemen and the chaos and says "Would you like something to read?" "Do I *sing*?" What on earth has that got to do with anything?'

Damien had to laugh himself. 'It's just one way of putting a stop to your gallop, I suppose. Although you were beginning to run down naturally. The next time we talk, let's keep it to Dylan Thomas; I've never even heard of *A Child's Christmas in Wales*. I have a lot to learn.'

She had recognised this as a concession. She wanted to accept, to yield, but she also wanted to finish what she was trying to say.

'Let me just get back to where all this began –'

He thought he had been patient enough, and could not remember, anyway, where it had all begun.

'With Raphael,' she told him. He remembered then that it hadn't stayed with Raphael for very long. He began to close up again.

'I don't have much time right now, we should have been out of this building long ago. Won't it keep?'

'Ah, well. It's a case of "when shall we three meet again –"'

'All right,' he said, 'even I can recognise the odd bit of Shakespeare. Get to the point.'

'Raphael does find a kind of glory in ritual. He loves bands, processions, parades. He loves Midnight Mass, May altars, Corpus Christi. He loves benediction, the Tantum Ergo, *O Salutaris hostia, Qui caeli pandis ostium*; his is a soul which can feed on these riches, he really does sing for joy. And he can be blinded by it to other things.'

'Like what?' He was again impatient.

'To this room, for instance.' She hadn't meant to speak with force. She hesitated, and Damien saw her long eyes brush the dingy room, the grey fly-filthy windows.

'That's the one thing I'll do for the Legion before I retire – clear this up a bit. What I can't understand is that I'm the only one who noticed it, or cared about it. Or rather, I do understand – but I won't go into all that again.'

'Thank you for that, at least.' He had feigned a vast relief, but couldn't help noticing that she had said that she would be resigning.

'Oh, yes, I think so. You asked me why I bothered to come here at all. And you're right, I can't treat religion as if it were a supermarket, where I could pick what I wanted from the shelves and leave all the rest. I know it has to be a matter of the whole shop, or nothing. Right now, I think I'm ready for nothing. Except that I'll be taking away the one thing that kept me here – the prayers.'

He was startled but interested too. 'The *prayers?*'

'That's not so strange. I was brought up in a convent, mostly, educated there at any rate. I learned the Latin Mass, acted scenes from the New Testament – all deadly serious; I did Apologetics, we got it all: *Sicut erat in principio, et nunc, et semper*. And I'm like Raphael – I find delight in words, and their images. So, here I really enjoy the prayers, just the sound of them. Especially *terrible as an army set in battle array* – I especially like that because it's about a woman.'

'It's about the Blessed Virgin.' He was indignant.

'A model woman, Fr Sebright; a model for Irish womanhood.'

He couldn't argue with her. 'Do you know what it is,' he said at last, 'you're so sharp you'll cut yourself.'

Her father always said that; so did her mother. In this unity at least, they prepared to part. Still Damien felt he had some duty towards her, now that she had admitted both her enthusiasm for some aspects of their Church, and her intention to quit it altogether. He was a priest, after all; he couldn't just let her go, there must be some effort he could make.

'We must go.' He took her obedience for granted, and she didn't argue. 'But I wouldn't like this to be the last time you came here. And even if it is, I could recommend some books –'

'Oh – do you like reading, yourself?'

The animation of her question alerted him; her face was bright, unpretending. Johnny Trant's voice came back to him:

'Don't let the bitches ever get you on to books,' he had advised. 'After the soul's awakening, that's the next worst time waster. They'll read what you tell 'em to read, they'll know more about it than you do yourself, and they'll never be short of an excuse to talk to you. Oh, keep away from books.'

Confused, Damien lied:

'Theology, that is. Veritas have some nice explanatory pamphlets about, you know, paths to faith, and purpose in living the Catholic life. Direction-finders to spiritual fulfilment, you might call them. A big help to you, I'd say.'

Her eyes had glimmered with fun, her full rather short mouth had pursed into a laugh.

'Come on, Fr Sebright, I thought you meant *real* books – novels, history, poetry; even if you don't know much about Dylan Thomas, there are direction-finders in those too, you know. Anyhow, you're the man on the spot at the moment here, *the* Spiritual Director?'

She had left the question hanging in the musky room as they switched off the light, locked the door.

'Not,' she added with a sly slant glance at him as he bent to the crumbling old mortice, 'not that I'm absolutely beyond the reach of theology, either. I have heard of Teilhard de Chardin, you know –'

As he made a muttered sound against the recalcitrant key she said –

'Well, I know he's not completely recommended either. But there's Jack Dominian, and his attitude to Christian marriage – what do you say to him?'

He swore frankly, nicking a fingernail on the lock and feeling again that mixture of anger, heat and amusement her company had already evoked.

'You're teasing me now.' He could afford to be entertained by her, he was beginning to recognise her tricks. 'I admit it, perhaps I asked for it. Let's keep Dominian for another time. And don't stop coming here yet; remember you have put your hand to the plough, you can't turn back now.'

She had not turned back then. With Raphael she had cleaned the room, and one of the toilets.

'Men and women too?' Raphael had worried when she decided that one lavatory would be enough even for evangelists. Claire scolded him into acceptance by reassuring him against scandal. He trusted her. She might not share his enthusiasm, but she understood it, she could speak his language.

Except for Yahweh. And all Yahweh stood for.

'I don't know,' she had admitted at last to Damien Sebright. And it was at last, at this last Legion meeting, she acknowledged that perhaps he could tell her something, help her with something.

'You must have done a lot of Latin in the seminary. Maybe to skilled Latin scholars the language of the Mass is very prosaic Latin, trite and banal and linguistically sedate. Except if it is, why is the language of the Gospels, in English, so attractive? And then, why change that too to such bland English? People have never been so well educated – so why is the Church so intent, so determined, to simplify even the vernacular?'

This was also to be the meeting, after all, at which Damien realised that he could not help her. Her questions by now were his questions. The answers he could supply: the International Committee on English in the liturgy had been tried already.

Were there no poets? No one who understood how language has special ways of carrying special meanings? He saw that she had wanted a kind of seduction of her unbelief, and the Church at least was being honest in not attempting to provide this.

He said it all again. Claire smiled, and shook her head, and they went out to Raphael waiting, as so often, as if time passing had no importance of its own, in the dingy hall.

He joined them eagerly, they were the purpose of his waiting. He was eager, too, because he knew what came next for him: Damien was bringing him to a meeting at St Dominic's to try out for the choir under a new conductor who was looking for recruits.

'Maybe, now, that's the answer for you, Claire.' Damien stood at the doorway to button his coat to the collar. 'Are we talking about the true vernacular? Have you tried' – and he leered at her like a salesman – 'have you tried the Mass in Irish? Come with us, and you'll get a blast of the real thing.'

Claire took him seriously, underneath the jibe he was serious.

'I must get back to those Irish classes. It's something I keep on meaning to do and never quite manage it, and it seems more important, now, with the Language Freedom Movement making such progress against it. Until I know Irish a bit better – well, a lot better – I suppose I can't say what the value of an Irish-language liturgy might be, but I imagine I could respect it, at the very least.'

'Ah,' teased Damien, 'but would your respect be for the Mass, or for the language?'

Raphael heard the censure beneath the jest, and worried. In his sparse and poorly tended life he depended on the priest's certainties for sustenance, building his own on their borrowed authority. With so much changing – and he knew Claire was right, it wasn't only a matter of words – he needed to know what was going to stay the same.

'But Claire – you know enough Irish, from school, to know the Mass, don't you? Come and hear us, come and hear me, I'm going to sing in Irish tonight, will you come with us?'

Where Damien had been teasing, Raphael was earnest. Claire couldn't go with them and knew she wouldn't have been welcome anyway – no onlookers were welcome at auditions. She took Raphael's arm, telling him that he, too, should close his jacket at the collar.

'Or you won't be able to sing at all. No, I have to go to work, but I'll hear you, Raphael, and Fr Sebright too, some Sunday when you don't expect me.'

'At last, at last!' Damien punched Raphael's arm conspiratorially: 'A victory for Mother Church!' And he swung the boy out on to the pavement so that Claire had to hurry after them.

'*Mother* Church!' she exclaimed as she walked between the two of them. 'That would be a fine thing,' and they all laughed together, at a recognised but unembittered contention.

All three walked contentedly close for warmth against the showery gusts that swept along the street by the river. Although the winter lay ahead Claire felt suddenly comforted, and lifted her face to the brush of rain.

'I love this weather.'

She spread out her arms in her red coat, a bright blur against the November mist. Dislodged, the two men stepped back as she sprinted ahead of them, her face to the sky, her arms clasping not their arms but the drenched breath of the air. She turned to face them, her light curls blustering around her berry-red cap:

>Come hither, come hither, come hither:
>Here shall he see
>No enemy
>But winter and rough weather.

'I love it!' she cried out to them. 'I love it, winter and rough weather.'

They saw her radiance, felt it, while she waited for them to catch up.

Chapter 2

In the office the suicide was waiting for Claire. 'River job,' the night news editor said. 'It came in too late for the evening edition, so it's all yours. Get something by eleven, a couple of paragraphs will do.'

Claire liked Night Town as a duty; rarely exacting, a matter of routine calls to hospitals, fire brigade, police, a culling of bigger or smaller stories from earlier editions for updating, yet it had the potential for sudden excitements and it allowed the kind of telephonic detective work she enjoyed, getting strangers to tell her things.

'Got one for you, Claire,' a photographer stuck his head around the newsroom door: 'Radio, ten o'clock bulletin – the Labour Court has been the brunt of criticism from the unions all week – thought you'd like it.'

'Love it,' she called her thanks after him and scribbled the meaningless words on a page of her notebook. 'Irish indeed,' she scoffed to herself, 'and we can't even talk English properly.'

Yet, as she settled to the typewriter, the telephone and piled copy paper, she thought with some regret of a jibe she had cast at Damien like a stone, sharp enough to tear what she regarded as the too-confident bubble of his faith: 'Necessity,' she had mocked, 'is the mother of conviction; is that what you're trying to say?'

She enjoyed his outrage too much; it was too easy for her, and she acknowledged to herself that of course, glib as it sounded, this was not at all what he had been trying to say. He thought that Claire suffered from a spiritual snobbery, that she insisted on being different, distant, to the congregation of her life. It was true that words carried meaning, but the meaning itself was true, and would endure. Claire could not accept that, or would not, yet. She felt confident enough to separate herself from the multitude of faith, awesome in the multiples of its numbers, its centuries and generations. All she could say to this was that she had never asked to join them and now that she had a choice preferred not to belong.

Anyway, she thought as she dialled the Bridewell, reporters shouldn't be joiners. Of anything. So I won't, ever again. Not even a film society.

'Hallo?' She began her night's work.

Off-the-record: the *garda* at the other end said the words as a slogan. Suspected suicide, a man, not yet formally identified, but she could have the name to work on. A sad story – he had been married, had left a baby.

Any address? A widow?

An address, yes. No widow, not that they knew of, although they were in touch with the Salvation Army. No known relatives.

'So where's the baby now? What is it, a girl or a boy?'

The voice at the end of the line hesitated. 'I'd better put you on to the sergeant altogether. And mind you now, I only told you about the drowning.'

The sergeant didn't trust Claire's temperate, sympathetic voice, her 'dealing with minor officialdom' voice.

'A male body was removed from the river Lee late this afternoon with the assistance of the *garda* sub-aqua team. The name will be released on identification and after next of kin have been informed. An inquest will be held. That's it.'

So it was, so it was, but Claire wanted a little more.

'Thank you, Sergeant, very much indeed, for all that. What's worrying us here' – she gave the impression that the newsroom already had a little bit of information of its own, but wasn't going to get too excited about just another suicide, common enough in a city with two waterways. 'What's worrying us here is the question of the child . . .'

He didn't like the hint of indecision at the end of her question: it might be taken as his indecision.

'The child has been taken to an orphanage for the night,' – Claire scribbled 'check the Good Shepherds' on her piece of paper – 'until suitable arrangements can be made for her.'

'Taken from where, Sergeant?' This could give her the address, and a story: was the child left alone, found alone crying in her cot while her father was floating . . .

'Taken from here.'

'From there? From the *garda* station?' Her surprise was giving the game away, revealing her ignorance.

The sergeant was curt: 'Yes.'

'Just one more thing, was this before or after the drowning?'

'Before.'

Frantically Claire scratched big letters on a fresh sheet of paper, signalling the copy typist to take it to the newsdesk: CHILD IN GARDA STATION AS FATHER DROWNS.

'Sergeant, you'll appreciate I don't want to get this wrong, so can you tell me, who brought the child to the barracks?'

'The father.'

'That is the man who drowned?'

'Yes. That seems to be the case. It was before I came on duty, that would be at six p.m. So there's nothing more I can tell you now –'

She could feel his anxious impatience. He had told her too much. But she couldn't let him go, not yet.

'Sergeant, when you arrived, was the father himself there? And Sergeant, how old is the child?'

'She was there. In the care of a *bean-garda*. She – the little girl – is about two years old. The father was gone. That's all I can tell you now, you understand. That's all I know. I wasn't on duty when it happened.'

But Claire could hear, behind his voice, the fog of conjecture, of reported sightings and sayings, the damp gossip of the duty room. She sat for a moment with the empty telephone in her hand, her ear aching from its pressure.

Tom Morely had come back to write up the anti-EEC meeting he had been reporting; overhearing the last of her questions as she searched for more information he offered the name of a woman police officer. From there she got to the *bean-garda* who had been on duty in that station that afternoon.

'I won't be quoting you. I won't even hint at a source. All I want you to do is keep me right, you know?'

'Oh God.' The woman was frightened, they would know it was her, she couldn't say a word.

'Give me a name, someone who could talk to me, someone, a social worker, who made the arrangements —'

That was easier. She could do that:

'Anselm Daunt. Fr Daunt. In the community centre there. He knows the family. But don't tell him I spoke to you – *please*.'

But Claire had heard of him. He was a friend of Damien Sebright.

It was late, and Damien was reluctant.

'He's not really a social worker, Claire. He's just a curate, although yes, he is involved in poverty relief programmes. But I think he prefers to work away without drawing too much attention to himself, you know?'

Claire knew. Working away without drawing attention to oneself was a skill developed by many young priests in the diocese. It meant giving quiet and unsurprised absolution for 'marital' sins involving birth control, persuading drunken husbands into institutions for a drying-out period of indefinite length, giving character references and going bail in the district courts, keeping itinerants and the settled community away from each other, getting pregnant single girls either married or sheltered and their babies adopted where necessary or where possible. That Anselm Daunt should be one of these men, keeping his head down, was all to the good, surely?

'Well, now, Claire, he doesn't like talking about his work. And certainly he won't be very keen to give any confidential information – even if you *do* say you're a friend of mine.'

She hadn't time to explain to Damien that she would promise discretion. Nor could she tell him that there was something coming from this incident which seemed to be more than just a story for a paragraph the following day. She rang the number he had given her.

The cold voice of the presbytery housekeeper told her that Fr Daunt was not at home. 'At home' – how could these men be at home in a presbytery? Claire could feel its tiles and brown paint in the rigid refusals at the end of the line, its formica and leatherette and unlined curtains, for this was a new house in a new parish, bleak with concrete. Initiate trees had been planted in rows along the wide new street – too wide for dogs and children to cross in safety. The children were knocked down, the dogs killed, the trees broken in a ritual refusal of growth. It was a suburb familiar to ambulances, police cars, chip and ice-cream vans. Even in daytime the few shops wore grilles on their windows.

Yet it was not near a river, and the dead man had chosen a city-centre garda barracks for his child.

All she could write now was a straight report: a body of a man in his twenties taken from the river near the South Gate Bridge. No need here to mention the child. She scribbled 'update' on the copy before handing it in to the sub-editors, and entered the story against her own initials for the following day's schedule. Already pencilled in the space was a query against the word 'Fota' and she remembered – there was a concert there, some agricultural charity needed funds, no, maybe it was only the Pony Club or the South Union Hunt, no, that couldn't be, it was the Orchestral Society, after all, which was arranging the programme. Well, she'd find the invitation later, and then think about getting there.

If that man, the name she had been given was Nicholas Barry, Hazelwood Avenue, had been found near the South Gate Bridge, where had he gone into the river? He must have gone upstream, up the Western Road, maybe even as far as the university, where the southern channel of the Lee seemed to flow in a privileged and dulcet fullness, rippling sweetly beside tennis courts, under the pointed pile of the Aula Maxima, behind the great, laced gateway near the Mardyke. If he had gone to the other bank, on the northern side, he might have had to wade among the swans by the Maltings or cast himself from the steps of the Coal Quay or the Sand Quay, and that would have brought him under the patient eye of the Virgin on the portico of the Dominican church.

Yes, that was how she had heard of Fr Daunt. Damien had been talking about the choir at St Dominic's. Not everyone, he had said, could match the kind of fervour that Raphael Brady was showing at the prospect of joining. Fr Daunt, now; he had been a member for quite a while, but wasn't turning up these days.

'And it's never been so important, Claire.' He was weary with the responsibility of it, idling a spoon in a cup of coffee. With some fascination Claire watched him drink the murky grey liquid as though he really wanted it. It had been a surprise to her that, meeting in the street, he had asked her to find time for a chat; it was no surprise that he thought this dim cafe with its unswept alcoves and plastic furniture was a suitable place to talk in.

Younger than him by several years she thought how young he was, and found this unexpected gaucherie endearing, something to tease him with, and change. So she listened, smiling but none the less attentive.

'You know John Trant – Diocesan Secretary? Well, Johnny says that Irish people only sing in public when they're drunk. He says that nothing that all the liturgical conferences, the Cardinals, the Curia and Maynooth itself can come up with will change that, and trying to get an Irish congregation to sing during Mass will be like asking a donkey to run in the Grand National.'

'Except that it won't be the Grand National, will it?' Claire had her own indignation: 'It will be a donkey race. It is a donkey race, you have to admit that. The whole thoroughbred idiom has been changed, there's no nobility left. So even if your friend Trant is right, what does it matter, now?'

'Ah, Claire –' Exasperation made his eyes sharpen. Actually, thought Claire, he had rather nice eyes. Blue, a kind of dark blue darkened by the iris, the whites clean and milky, unveined. The envelope of lid and lash was narrow, wrinkled and kindly curved. Actually, thought Claire consciously for the first time, attractive.

'No, listen –' He saw her attention wander, and leaned forward to grasp it back.

'What we have got to do is to help people to learn a new way of celebrating. That's all – Trant or no Trant. In fact I'm beginning to think that it's the priests who are going to let the people down. I'm looking at our group now, in the choir. Who turns up? Nearly everyone – and not just the Raphaels of this world. *Except* my own colleagues. Look at Anselm Daunt, for instance. If ever a man needed to help people to celebrate, he's the man. And over at St Dominic's we're really working at it. It's exhilarating. It would do Daunt a lot of good. But can I tell him that?'

He took another surge at the cool coffee.

'Can I tell him that? Not unless I want to get a lecture on special classes for itinerants, the need for a daily health clinic, what will happen if girls are allowed to join the youth club, and what will happen if they're not, how to start a credit union, how to screw the corporation in funding any one or indeed all of these projects.'

Claire knew that because he was himself underemployed, part of Damien's irritation was envy.

'Well,' she offered carefully, 'if he's trying to do all you say – and you have to admit that out there all those things need to be done – maybe the best approach would be, not to ask him to go to something, but to bring that something to him. For what else, after all, was your Legion of Mary established?'

That was the conversation in which she had first heard of Anselm Daunt. His name had come up again since then; Damien had spoken of him, for, while at the time he had raised sceptical eyebrows at Claire's use of '*your* Legion of Mary', the suggestion had been taken up and he had found himself for a month or so getting involved in Daunt's parish work.

That had not been long ago; only quite recently Damien had said something briefly about Daunt almost inviting martyrdom. His parish priest was approaching senility, and all the administrative work of the place had been taken on by the senior curate, which left Anselm Daunt responsible for a new church and a new school. As well as for his own programme against urban poverty: 'He's caught now between planned giving and planned parenthood and doesn't know which he hates the most,' Damien had told Claire.

Yet when they had spoken tonight, on the telephone, Claire had felt that Damien had been almost protective of Daunt. Had their friendship revived? And had he been protecting Fr Daunt from her?

Shouldering into her coat while she waited for a taxi, Claire knew that although Damien usually approved of what she wrote, even enjoyed her tenacity and sometimes relished what he called her lack of respect – which she defended as only a lack of fear – he might prefer not to encourage her questioning or exposure of people he respected himself.

He accepted that she wasn't casual about her work, about the licence it conferred to inquire, to persist, to interrupt and survey, to release into the stream of social awareness or knowledge. 'Consciousness', Claire called it. 'Publicity', said Damien.

Tomorrow – if she managed to get to Fr Daunt tomorrow – he might have the same accusation to make. He might accuse her of investigating private grief, exposing family intimacies. Her answer would have to be that she had no intention of doing anything of the kind. It might happen, but it would not have been her intention. That little bit of casuistry was not quite what she meant, but it would do for Anselm Daunt, who would surely be familiar – what priest now was not? – with its application to his pastoral duties.

Her intention would be to find out what had happened to bring that young man from his own neighbourhood, pushing his infant daughter in a stroller, her food, bottles, clothing packed for the use of other hands, to the surely inhospitable doors of a police barracks. He had had no criminal history, she had discovered that much; perhaps no history at all. Yet there must have been a time for him, as for the parents of Jane Fairfax, 'of fame and pleasure, of hope and interest' – even if nothing now remained of it except this child in a convent cot tonight.

What had happened to bring the father to the lip of this long river-mouth, to leave his footprints invisible on the shoreline mud as the winter day closed down, as he walked into the tide in his weighted shoes, his clothes wettening, flattening to his shivering skin, the foul water with its wastes and oils and weeds holding on to him so that at the last, even if he had wanted to turn back, he could not loosen its grip, and yielded?

Was God there then? Yahweh?

Is death terrible when it happens? Is it less terrible when it is invited, welcomed? But he must have hated it, the slime of it, the suck of the mud, he must have wanted to be saved, to be loved enough by someone to be brought back. Had he thought no one would mourn him, except a child from whose memory he would within weeks be extinguished? That was two deaths, surely: the complacent tide flowing because it had to, covering him because he was there, and the dank loneliness of it with no arms outflung except those of the tolerant Virgin at St Dominic's.

> Look homeward Angel new, and melt with ruth,
> And, O ye Dolphins, waft the hapless youth.

Claire remembered her schoolroom *Peig*, where Tomas gathering heather for fuel fell from a Blasket cliff and was found, not on the broad ocean, but on a smooth, slippery stone, hollowed out so that there was no more in it than the length and breadth of his body, and '*é comh coirithe is comh socair is dá mbeadh dáréag ban ina fheighil*'.

As rightly settled, Tomas had been, in that rock as if twelve women had laid him out there. They would have been keening women, wailing. At the news of his death his father had let out a shout – '*an liú uafásach bróin*' . . . 'a terrible scream of sorrow'. Who would lament this man, this Nicholas Barry, and weep for him?

In the over-scented cabin of the taxi she crossed the river where its two streams became again one flood. The mist had tightened into fog, the river lurked with all its mysteries submerged and silent. She thought of *Little Dorrit*, 'where a wretched little bill, FOUND DROWNED, was weeping on a wet wall –' Her way home lay along the edge of the water which flowed with glossy certainty beyond the city, between its guardian castles, its cluster of watchful islands, to the pallid waiting sea.

Chapter 3

Damp had brought out the waning smells of the garden, fading in colour and virility but yielding still its essences to the rain-wet dark. Although it was winter, there was the summer smell of grass and even in this after-midnight dark Claire could see the soft dim globe of a Casino rose; its bare stems were trained through the trellis of the porch, but there were buds there still and this one bloom, luminous as cream. What was it her grandmother said – 'A green December fills the churchyard'? Well, it wasn't December yet, although she expected that even when it came there would be a poor perished rose or two somewhere in this garden.

As she put her key in the door Claire felt the bush of rosemary tremble. Alerted by the taxi and the muffled warning bark from Bran inside the house, the cat was a fast black shadow on the blackness of the path, leaving his fragrant hideout under the spreading shrub for the chance of sleeping on Claire's bed.

The dog was used to these late-night arrivals, keeping his growl low and thick until he swallowed it entirely in his joy at her entry. They were partners in a friendly conspiracy of silence, of fondling and whispers: while Claire bent to rub his ears, to tell him what a good dog he was, the cat sneaked past them up the stairs. To Bran it was as if the bones of his body lay up there, where Della and Frank went every night and where now Claire would go too, leaving him to his rug in the kitchen. Yet the cat could go there; Bran knew this as some injury of restriction for he obeyed rules that the cat ignored. He did not understand how it was that Gluic achieved his purpose by wile and sleight while he, Bran, waited for an invitation that never came, and grieved when he remembered the grievance. He forgot it again as Claire's hand tugged at the tufts of hair around his ears and rubbed the shallow dip on his chest. He closed his eyes to catch the pleasure completely until she straightened up and gave the final pat to his head, telling him at last to go to bed, to mind the house, and he sighed, and went back to his rug.

There was a tinge of spice on the air of the hall. Claire loved this, the way the house, dark and silent and sleeping as it was now, still sent out its messages. On the brown table in the hall the missals lay side by side, red-edged and leather-bound for her father, Frank, gold-leaf and hand-tooled for Della, her mother. Tomorrow was not Sunday – so why this readiness? She could take advantage of it though, it meant her mother would be out of the house before Claire herself got up, so she took a hurried page from her notebook:

'Choral Concert plus cheese and wine at Fota 6 to 9 pm tomorrow (Friday)'.

Yes, that was it, of course it was Friday, the first Friday in the month. Frank and Della were going to the First Friday devotions, and with November being the month dedicated to remembrance of the dead, beginning with the feast of All Saints and then with the Feast of All Souls, well, of course they would both be off to Mass in the morning.

'Would love Mum's company but have to admit first reason for asking is that I need the lift there. Love to you both; C.'

In the kitchen the spicey smell was stronger: it was curry, surely? That meant Granny had been down for supper. Claire remembered there had been some talk of Della wanting the car if Frank wasn't using it, so it had probably been to take Gran somewhere. She remembered more – to take her to

Angela, Claire's sister, married. Adored. Beautiful, and now rich.

Claire loved the curry smell. Indeed, she was even beginning to enjoy curry, although she still thought that nothing tasted so exotic and delicious as her grandmother's habit of sprinkling the pungent powder on her plate of Irish Stew; the mutton tender and mauve as a flower, the potatoes collapsing into their own white sediment, the translucent segments of onion and the sweet orange and yellow fingers of carrot, all these steaming in their pale liquid burnished to something else entirely as the narrow, heavy-knuckled fingers rubbed the fiery dust on to the air above them.

How early had Claire and Angela known that mango chutney was an ideal gift for Gran? Or Gentleman's Relish – they must have got the ideas from Della, who had never quite explained, or told any complete story, but who had said that of course Gran loved curry and spicey foods, hadn't she spent so much of her life in India?

India! – but they had not wondered then, those two little girls, what had brought their grandmother from that extraordinary location to the house which they found thrilling and strange enough, the British Legion house, set in a park of others, with its latticed porch and its peonies bulbous and red as blood, and its long green timber box under the sink in the kitchen where the meal for the hens was stored. India they accepted as related to the person they knew as Gran in the same mysterious way as she was related to the brown-tinted photograph in her sitting room; a slender, black-haired young woman, a flat but not unbecoming hat on her head, neat in her long-skirted suit, looking steadily, gravely back at whoever looked at her.

Was that a photograph taken just before, or just after, her wedding? Wasn't there, somewhere, a picture too of her husband, Claire's grandfather, Della's father, in his British Territorial Army uniform, the sepia face looking untouched, the eyes pale and level? It was curious how uncurious they were, both Claire and Angela, even as children. Granny was not a loquacious woman, there was something dry, reserved, about her, a kind of acerbic privacy. Even now Claire didn't feel very sure of her approval, although she knew Angela had won that long ago, maybe from the first. But Gran had never given any hint of a difference between the two girls; they were both scolded about holes in their gloves – 'What: would you expect the busman to take a penny from gloves like that!' But they were both allowed to help feed the hens, to run their hands through the sour-smelling grain in the box or mash the wet bread and mix the scraps.

They had never asked what had happened to their grand-father, for they had never known him. The world they knew as belonging to their grandmother did not belong to him, was not a world he had known, with its pear tree and rhubarb, the black iron railings on which the children sat to talk to the woman next door – another army widow – and eat the fruit of the blackcurrant bushes trained against the fence. For all they knew their grandfather belonged to the other world, to the land of cumin and chilli, cardamum and coriander, garam marsala and turmeric. Yet Della prayed for him and he would be remembered among the dead.

Really it was amazing how little they knew about him; she must ask Della about it, or Angela. Since her marriage Angela seemed to have entered some special and acknowledged grouping – as though, if it were long ago, she would have worn a lace cap indoors – and now was privy to the shared experiences of Wifehood.

For Angela now Granny's love had changed from the thick-ribbed patterned mittens of childhood wintertimes to the pick of the first batch of pear chutney, the smallest, brownest eggs from a laying, or, in September, the sweetest of the cherry tomatoes grown in frames beneath the kitchen window. And secrets, what seemed like secrets, although now that Claire thought about it there were no secrets, just questions that had never been asked.

It was curious – her job was asking questions. She loved finding out, being in the know. She had to admit now that for all the facts of her childhood, for all the information about the past, Angela was the one in the know. Or said she was.

Next to the telephone the light had been left on, showing the notepad and its messages: Fr Sebright had rung to say Fr Daunt would meet her the next morning in his office at the President Kennedy Road centre; Leon Dowden would ring back.

Claire's heart jumped at the coincidence; it was a week since she had seen Leon, or heard from him. Now there was no way in which she could anticipate his call. The message was logged in her mother's curling hand, carefully, as if there were no contention. That was the worst of living at home, the absence of privacy. She wondered how they had spoken to one another, her mother and Leon. Guarded, anyway. Della had liked him – so had Frank at first. But really, as Della had tried to explain to Claire, so that their concern would be seen to be reasonable, selling *The Thoughts of Chairman Mao* on Patrick Street, and trying to get the Students' Union to pass a motion supporting Ho Chi Minh, and opening a communist bookshop – quickly closed again – next door to a city-centre church: all this was behaviour they could not condone. There was something wild about it, deliberately provocative.

And they had seen the books he was giving Claire to read, some of the things she was bringing in to the house.

'It's not as if we were expecting you to read nothing except the *Legion of Mary Handbook*, Claire,' Della had said. 'You know we both love books and have never questioned anything we saw lying around. But some of that American anarchist stuff is really a bit much. We can't stop you reading it, and we can't stop you seeing Leon. But we do worry about it. We worry about you.'

Claire could understand her mother's attitude, or thought she could. Leon didn't fit in. He wasn't the kind of young man Della and Frank had expected to meet when they decided to welcome the boyfriends visiting the house in pursuit first of Angela and then, although in smaller numbers, of Claire.

'Gentlemen Callers' Frank had called them because of *The Glass Managerie* – and indeed Angela had built up her own collection of tiny crystal animals since her childhood – and to Claire's grandmother they were 'followers'. Claire delighted in that: it had seemed to her as a teenager that there was something lemming-like about the teams of rugby players, tennis players, even the occasional student who knocked on the Mackey door; they had their uses, though – they gave lifts in their father's car (Frank regarded with suspicion any young man who had a car of his own before he was either twenty-five or married, whichever came first) or did odd jobs around the house or garden, stayed to give company, praised Della's cooking and tried the process known as 'drawing her out' on Claire's grandmother, who knew exactly why they were being kind to her.

Leon wasn't kind to her. Leon, when he met her having supper with Claire one evening, asked her how she felt about having been a part of the colonial domination of India. As an Irishwoman, after all, she must have found it ironic?

Claire hadn't thought of that until she heard him questioning her grandmother. Yet it was true: Onora Motherway had gone with her soldier husband to India to support him in his service of the British Empire. Like many another Irishman of his generation, Patrick Motherway had been a coloniser. Not just a soldier. He had been a soldier, had fought in the Boer War – on the wrong side, Leon had said, but Claire wasn't sure that there had been any right side in that war. But at least that had been a war. India was different.

'India?' Onora had considered Leon's question. 'I must say it didn't bother me at all. It wasn't easy to live there, you know, not with small children. Very hot, you had to be careful of so many things. Dirty, too. The natives had some very dirty habits.'

She made it clear that with a husband and several children – there had been five altogether – to care for on low wages in a withering climate in a foreign country she hadn't been inclined to give much attention to the political implications of her life there.

'Then there was Egypt.' Claire could not remember when her grandmother had volunteered so much information about herself.

'That was even dirtier, and hotter. And such thieves – you couldn't call your soul your own, in Egypt. Cairo, that was.'

Leon said that when people were so poor, when a government tolerated, even encouraged, poverty for the great mass of the people –

'Yes.' She acknowledged the point. 'They were poor in India, too, of course.' Her tone implied that poverty did not necessarily turn people into thieves.

'And then we came back: first to Scotland, to Stirling –' Claire knew that; her mother still sang the songs she had learned there, in Stirling, where she had been happy, where her brothers had grown up – 'and then back here to Cork. Where we were the ones who were poor.'

She turned her bright, dark defiant eye on Leon Dowden. She knew about poverty. Colonialist or camp follower. She knew that over him she had the only kind of supremacy he envied: the glamour of under-privilege.

For an amazed second or two Claire had realised that Leon was ashamed. So far his great struggle in life had been to dissent from the family of merchant princes to which he had been born, to abdicate his right to a career at the Bar rather than the counter, to tear up a birthday present of membership of the Muskerry Golf Club, and to go to university under protest and only on condition that he would study history and economics rather than law or medicine. 'Even *Engineering*,' his father had been heard to say, 'even *Engineering* would have been preferable.'

So Leon had gone his own way – a way of which, like so many other ambitious parents in Cork, Della and Frank could not approve. Onora Motherway did not approve either. She believed in making the most of what you had, if you were lucky enough to have anything.

Even Angela was reluctant to encourage Leon. He made her feel uncomfortable.

'He always wants me to get upset about things I can't change,' she complained to Claire; the point – if she would only see it – was that she could change things if she wanted to. Leon was only trying to make her want to.

No, Della had said, overhearing this conversation or one of the similar conversations the sisters had on this subject, the real point was that Leon wanted people to be different to what they were.

'In order to do what he wants us to do we would have to be what he wants us to be; then we could change what he wants us to change, or try to at least. But we're not like that, which is what he can't accept.'

Frank just thought that both Leon and Claire were very young and that it would all pass over. A lifelong member ot the St Vincent de Paul Society, up to his neck in corporal works of mercy, a founder member of the local Credit Union and the Housing Aid Association, he wasn't inclined to take much notice of any youngster preaching about the claims of the proletariat.

Both Claire's parents had to notice, however, when Leon found his platform: membership of the European Economic Community was the most immediate issue, and Leon spoke, incandescent with energy, from flat-backed lorries in Patrick Street. The country would sell its socialist heritage, inherited from the martyred James Connolly, for the price of membership to a capitalist cabal. Its native language would be abandoned for the language of commerce and conglomerates. Its unfinished nationalist struggle, its claim for unity and total autonomy, would be suppressed in the surge towards economic aggrandisement. As for defence – did the Irish people realise what would happen to the country's single most important article of foreign policy: its neutrality?

It was some help to Claire when she had to deal with her parents' reaction to all this that Damien Sebright didn't think Leon completely wrong.

'It's not all wrong, what he's saying,' he reassured her. 'We do have a lot to lose as a nation. I believe we're not being given the whole story. Anselm Daunt, now – he goes along with a lot of what Leon has to say. And he's not the only one.'

Claire knew that Damien's measured reactions might soothe her father, who would also expect a priest, even a priest as young as Damien, to have some anxieties about what might be the new moral climate of an Ireland annexed and to some extent addicted to European lifestyles. It was no surprise to Frank or to Della that a priest should be among the young men and women sitting in the drawing room, playing cards, smoking, although it was unexpected that it should have been at Claire's invitation that he was there. They had learned to be surprised at nobody who turned up: Leon, at first, was accommodated.

Even Raphael Brady found a place there, brought by Claire who was his friend, but held by Angela, welcoming and generous as only a lifetime of accumulated loving tenderness, earned at first for her loveliness, could make her. He had not known how to hide his adoration, so she did it for him, making his protestations unnecessary, letting him see that, in some way more than just because he was a neighbour's child, he belonged.

To Claire he had said that Angela was like a painting, a holy picture; so she was, a Levantine Madonna in her darkness and brightness. Like an evangelist Raphael had wanted to speak about love, to offer it as an apostle might have done, as if its meaning were always pure, always charity. As holy as that, and with no other meaning.

'You know that boy is mad?' There was no unkindness in Della's question. To her it seemed as if Raphael had been born without a skin, so that everything that happened to him touched the quick of his flesh – all that he felt, and he was all feeling, flared outwards from his core and its heat flicked everyone who knew him.

'He's too intense,' she spoke about him to Claire and Damien together, trusting them as Raphael's friends, 'you'll have to take great care of him. All his friends will have to take great care of him.'

Angela was a friend. Quiet herself, she understood Raphael's discomforts, and eased them, and shared with him her own acceptance of certainties. It seemed to Claire to be so strange: Angela, all her life the favourite, the chosen one, never asked for anything more than the kindness of her beauty, and therefore always confident of goodwill, of eventual happiness: and Raphael, properly a rural child, ungainly, solitary, unsure of everything and especially of affection; yet his intense anxieties found some ease in Angela's passivity. He had never disturbed her with talk of love; she absorbed his emotion painlessly and gave it a resting place. He had never spoken to her about passion; now, since her marriage, he never spoke to her at all.

It had amused Claire – perhaps because Leon had seen some humour in it – that Stan Coupland had not been drawn from the shoal of eligible men netted in Della's and Frank's drawing room. He was a tennis-club acquaintance, whose courting had been carried on at concerts and at dinners in seaside hotels. He had come to the door for Angela, but she had never kept him waiting and so he went no further into the house than the hall. He had been assiduous; by the time Della and Frank knew he was serious about Angela the pair were engaged to be married.

Stan was a non-Catholic, a member of a declining Church of Ireland congregation in an adjoining suburb. He was devout. He had loved his church of clean grey limestone, its square simplicity set among tombstones and yew trees, its steeple square, pointed and unequivocal. He had loved the hassocks worked in Berlin wools, and the marble plaques set in the walls, sacred to the glory of God and the memory of all the Couplands since time, or the parish, began, and the stone font inscribed with the names of the Coupland brothers who fell beneath a regimental flag in the Crimea. He loved the Book of Common Prayer. He loved Angela.

'I suppose he worships God just as much as any of us do,' was Angela's sullen response to her father's dismay.

Without her mother there would have been anger, perhaps even prohibition.

'She's right, Frank.' Della had pitied both father and daughter. 'He's a practising Christian, and a very good young man. He'll be generous to Angela, and let her practise her own religion just as much as she wants.'

To Frank that was the problem. Angela was unlikely to want what Stan didn't want as well. He knew that neither of his daughters was devout, although Claire had once shown signs of interest. He knew that Angela would have no difficulty in becoming a member, in spirit if not in fact – maybe even in fact – of the Protestant community.

'Apostate is a big word for a small thing, Frank.' It had hurt Della, that word. She had heard her own mother use it once, bitterly, to describe a cousin in Bandon.

'And isn't it what we're all supposed to be about, right now? The Vatican Council, and the new liturgy – aren't we all supposed to be coming closer together?' Della had heard Damien and Claire discussing an inter-Church conference he was going to: 'He was talking about sharing. It's ecumenism. We're all God's family, that's the important thing.'

To Frank there was still a big difference between God's family and *his* family. He had muttered anxiously about that being all very well and fine, but what would happen when there was to be a christening or two? It wasn't until Claire told him, with some glee, that Stan's own family were distressed by the impending marriage that he became reconciled to it, as if an equality of disapproval would ensure its religious stability.

Although discomfited by her parents' reaction, Angela had not even noticed the dismay on the other side. Stan had not told her about it either, so the good manners of his family protected her from any surprised discovery of dislike. Because of course, as Claire and Della and Frank acknowledged – even Leon had agreed with this – as soon as the Couplands met Angela they would see she was out of the common run.

Damien became crucial to the wedding plans, for Angela, rarely obstinate, refused to ask for the dispensation from the

Catholic Bishop necessary if she was to marry, as Damien called it, 'within the walls'.

'I'm getting married, I hope in a church, to a church-goer. They don't know how lucky they are, and there's nothing that I have to get permission for. Stan and I are quite capable of deciding for ourselves what to do about the children, if we have children; we can work that out for ourselves. It's all open and honest and holy and if they're not satisfied, I am.'

Damien could only laugh. Even Leon saw the funny side of Angela's revolt, although he derided its substance. Damien agreed to officiate at the University Chapel where he was chaplain. He would probably have agreed to anything she proposed, Claire thought; he delighted in Angela, in the gorgeousness of her beauty, the bright black hair, the eyes of a smoky, freckled grey under brows that arched in a delicate query on the pale velvet of her skin.

'Like a rose, at midnight,' Raphael had breathed to him once in the pain of his thrall, and Damien had not laughed then, but had put his hand on the boy's shoulder, and wondered what it must be like to be, not in love, but in adoration, like a mystic. To him Angela was a joy to look at, and after meeting her with Claire he began to relish the slow determination which formed her purpose, and the calm hardening with which she met opposition. It had been some relief to Claire to realise – she never could have asked – that Damien in fact believed that Angela was stupid, not in any gross or malicious way but in her lack of tension, in the calm with which she made tolerance into a kind of resistance. If it had been Leon who expressed such an attitude Claire might not have been surprised, but he had dismissed her quickly as someone beautiful and idle and rich, thrice denounced.

'But she's not rich,' Claire had protested in her shame that Angela was not a rival.

'She will be, when she marries Stan Coupland,' was Leon's response, and Claire said no more, for the Couplands and the Dowdens were of a kind and Leon could not bear to be reminded.

Damien said that Angela's stupidity was the safe, unhurtful kind. 'Because she doesn't think very much, she works on instinct, and her instincts are towards kindness – and towards faith, too. That's one of the reasons why she's so good in the shop, why Egans think so much of her. Who else will wait while a priest or a nun ponders out loud on the relative merits of St John of God or St John of the Cross? She really doesn't mind whether they buy the books or not, she just hopes they can solve that particular little difficulty. Sure every priest in the city knows her – they all think she's the Blessed Virgin, of course, but they bring in a lot of extra custom to the shop, just for the pleasure of having her look after them.'

The trade in Egans was in monstrances and vestments, chalices and missals and rosary beads. There were Hummel figures petrified at wayside shrines, there was the Waterford Glass and the Cork Silver, there was Spode and Wedgwood and Royal Doulton: in the glass-fronted cabinets pearls and diamonds rested on plump velvet cushions as if breathless from the shock of their own beauty. Angela had worked among the books. She hoarded the Pastorals and Encyclicals for the Canons from Dunmanway and Tallow and Butlerstown, the Mother Superiors from Doneraile and Castletownbere.

The news that Angela Mackey was marrying a Protestant must have shot around the city like those little cash-carriers in the Munster Arcade, Claire thought, remembering the childhood thrill of the pulleys and cylinders accepting payment and returning change from some invisible accounts department. The bulletins of breathless gossip – it might even have been considered scandal in some quarters, Claire thought indulgently – must have slammed from presbytery to monastery in every parish in Munster. Now the old men who stood patiently at the counter for her lovely kindness would know no more of her, except, perhaps, in their saddest dreams or prayers.

Egans, though, imperturbable in its facade of white stone, its huge windows still blazing with the star-burst of a eucharist monstrance – Egans would know of Angela, and would enjoy her transformation from staff to customer. The Couplands had family jewels – *The Eustace Diamonds*, Claire had mocked Angela gently – and family silver, and these might be taken to Mangans or to Hilsers for re-setting and cleaning, but Angela would go to Egans for her china and her glass. The furniture would come from O'Connells, on Lavitt's Quay, with a few pieces, or a few pictures, from Marsh's Auction Rooms, down a tunnel on the South Mall.

Taking Claire with him for advice, Damien had gone there to find a wedding present. 'It's like caves,' she had said, loving it, and was quickly lost among the writing desks and leonine hall tables, unerringly uncovering the pillars of books lurking behind the floor-bound gilded mirrors and dulled prie-dieux.

His chaplaincies brought Damien requests for Masses: Masses to be said, votive prayers and intercessions for the dead, the dying, the despairing. At five or ten shillings each, sometimes a pound, this income was his own, although he had not yet lost the consciousness of where it came from, what it was given for, as he spent it. On this occasion he had felt it contributing warmly to something that had to become more than a gift, that must be an offering in itself.

'Look,' he called to Claire, dusty behind her book-stacks.

'It's an astrolabe.' He squinted at the brass-bound mahogany base. 'Not an old one, I think. Not antique, anyway. It was for finding sightings, for mariners. Finding the position of the stars and planets.'

'If it's not antique, forget it.' Claire was enjoying an exaggerated appraisal of the Coupland heirlooms; she teased the imperturbable Angela with the grandeur into which she was about to marry – 'It must have been like *The Spoils of Poynton*,' she had said, relishing the supposed Coupland horror at the coming of the barbarian. Angela had only replied that 'they', meaning Stan's family, were not like that. The truth was that she and Claire both knew, as Stan did if it mattered, that Angela would cherish anything that came to her through Stan; he was the only provenance she could recognise, as yet.

'If you're that flush, get it for Raphael, you know what he's like about astronomy.' Claire went back to her cobwebbed corner, leaving Damien to smile at the quivering needle, astray without its space, its stars.

These alleyways glinted with mirrors and the mirrored lakes of old pictures. Faces to the wall the watercolours faded from the future, their delicacies too tender to survive separation from the drawing rooms of their time, where the grizzled family dog shown on a named worn rug was known and loved, and the hands which had planted the white lilies in the glowing herbaceous border were the hands that had painted them. But suddenly among these forlorn witnesses to a life long stilled, Damien, handling them with the reverence he gave to all dead things, found a trembling whiteness lambent through the dusk of neglect. A stroke, and another, with his handkerchief – thus rendered unusable for all other purposes – turned the whiteness into light, and the dark above it was blue, or purple, and the dark beneath it brown.

Bog brown. Damien turned the tacky canvas over to see if what he thought could be true – could it ba a Paul Henry? The unvarnished frame was held to the picture by nothing more than glued-on brown paper, stained and cracked. There was no glass, and there was no inscription. Somewhere there, among the right-hand reeds, should float the capital letters. Instead the little lake shone empty of everything except a sapphire shadow. It lay at the base of the picture; its shore was a brown and golden line with turf-stacks darker in the distance, with the golden thatch and white gables of cabins balancing the other corner, and above them the grey and purple stone, ridge upon ridge of the mountain, and above them billowing, heaped upon heap, the creamy clouds and the sky. Lake and lakeshore, water-reeds and tremulous cumulus, all sang from the frame in Damien's hands, their masses radiant with coherent light.

'Who's that other man, the one who died about twenty years ago? He's in the School of Art.' Claire had come to his side, not empty-handed but riveted, as he was, with the wonder of the question before them.

'Craig,' Damien answered. 'James Humbert Craig. But I don't think so. They were really totally different painters. I don't know what to do.'

Claire did. She had a friend among the aproned men between the alleys. She had written so glowingly about the firm's handling of an antique auction of the residue of an old Ascendancy estate that she was remembered by the staff. The important thing was to find out if the picture was going to auction – and it wasn't, or not immediately. So, what was the price? Well, nobody quite knew who the painter was, and it was in poor condition. They had been going to send it over to the curator at the School of Art –

'We'll do that,' Claire assured them. 'We're quite happy to take a chance on it. How much?'

They thought, about £150.

'Good Lord!' Claire remembered she was arguing on Damien's behalf, and was circumspect in her indignation.

'In that condition! Unsigned! Sure it might only be a copy. It really is a big risk; Fr Sebright wants to get something very special for my sister – you know my sister Angela?'

Indeed they did. And liked the thought that they might see more of her, in future, than of either Claire or Fr Sebright. They thought, perhaps, £100?

Claire said it still seemed a lot; at an auctioneers in Oldcastle, she said, she had seen a Lady Dobbin view of Cork, Coburg Street, with cattle and a drover, in a misty rain, and Shandon steeple behind the tiered roofs. And that was signed, and only £60.

Ninety, they said at last.

'Done,' said Claire, before Damien could quibble. The excitement in her voice both appeased and worried him – maybe it was a bargain but at £90 it was a bargain he couldn't afford.

'I hadn't quite bargained for that,' he began mildly – then he heard her making arrangements for payment. Forty pounds now, twenty-five in a fortnight, twenty-five after that. A priest's credit was always good.

'And for this?' Claire held a book in her hand.

A pound, they said, not looking beyond the dull green cloth of the cover. A pound – 'to *you*', they added meaningfully, and Claire took the meaning and smiled her thanks and paid the money, then almost pushed Damien out of the cavernous balustraded room.

'What are we doing?' he said on the street. 'Are we going to go over to the School of Art immediately?'

No, Claire had to go back to work. Anyway, she said, she didn't think they should get the picture attributed. 'Let's get it cleaned. Whoever painted it, I think it's beautiful. If it is a Paul Henry it has a value which will embarrass Angela; if it isn't, it will embarrass you. I think it would be much nicer just to leave the question there with it. What you're giving then is not just a present, with a price tag politely taken off, but a gift of a possibility. Do you see what I mean? It's more exciting, somehow, isn't it?'

He saw what she meant. In the year or so since he had met her as an adult, at the Legion, since he had begun to join the group of young people meeting at her home, Damien had learned that although she could be irritating at times, or downright provocative, Claire had a curious ability to invest things, even places, with a mystery beyond themselves. In her hands something spoke of an unseen history, an unforetold future. What might have been, what might yet be – possibilities pleased her, and even mundane things, enriched by her imagination or sympathy, took on a lustre and became significant.

In the arched limestone shadow of the doorway Damien looked again at his picture. The black slice of bog established it, the shining lough, and the clouds, luminous with hidden light from the sky behind them – they reminded him, just as they made him feel certain, of the painter. He remembered seeing a Paul Henry print in a schoolroom, and a schoolgirl looking at him; why was he giving to Angela a painting which reminded him, suddenly and vividly, of Claire?

'I wouldn't like to cheat anyone,' he said slowly, anxious at least not to have paid less than he should have done.

'Cheat, how are you!' Claire's disdain was robust. 'They're a tough old crew in there, wouldn't let you get away with anything, even if you *are* a priest.

'They let *me* get away with something, though . . .' and her voice trailed off into mischief.

'They were probably glad to get rid of you.' Damien in fact could imagine that the men considered themselves lucky that Claire's visit hadn't cost them more.

'My book – it's *Mount Music*, Somerville and Ross. Well, more Somerville than Ross because Ross was dead when it was finished, but the inscription by Edith Somerville says they planned it together. Look!'

The two sets of initials, E.OE.S. and M.R., were entwined through Celtic coils on the back of the title page. Dated 1919, it was a first edition.

'A first edition of Somerville and Ross. For a pound –' Claire was capering along the pavement. To Damien's relief she sobered quickly. 'It's beautiful, isn't it? And I love that inscription, that loyalty between them. I don't care what the source of it was, it's a real thing, a good thing.'

Damien didn't like to reveal that all he knew about Somerville and Ross was that along with being Anglo-Irish Protestants there was some idea, somewhere, that they also had been lesbians. And that Somerville, in the end, had become something of a spiritualist, or dabbled at least. He followed Claire, his painting wrapped in thick brown paper, and caught up with her near the entrance to her office on Patrick Street. Two massive doors under a fanlight gave on to a stairway rising from street level in a single flight to the glass-fronted commercial offices and editorial departments, the printing works filling the rest of the block on to the narrow street behind, obvious only by the light taint of oil, and lead, and the tang of newsprint. Claire waited for him there, in the dim hall, looking up from the pages of the book only to say that the Boss was in; she could tell by the warm reek of cigar smoke still on the air. She had to hurry.

'But look at this,' she held the book out to him, open: 'It's all set in West Cork, some of it is about Coppingers' Court – did you ever see Coppingers' Court? Near Glandore? It's a ruin, from Cromwell. But here they make it a real house, an estate.'

Some instinct had made her change the page from the one with the words which had first caught her eye. Those words spoke to something private in her, something she had no idea she could ever share with Damien Sebright. She might have shown it to Leon Dowden, but with fear, or else without thinking:

> . . . but she had discovered her soul, and had discovered also that it had been born on the farther side of the river of life from the souls of her brethren, and that although, for the first stages, the stream was narrow, and the way on one bank very like that on the other, the two paths were divided by deep water, and the river widened with the passing years.

Tonight as she climbed towards bed, Claire touched out of habit the blank space on the landing wall where Angela's fluted marble font had been. An austere impression of the Virgin, it was the single religious thing for which she had a vivid affection; Della had put it with the books Angela wanted to take with her to her new home – 'Just in case, I suppose,' Angela had said in a rare attack of wit, kneeling on the floor with Della and Claire as they bundled and packed.

Touching the wall there brought Claire back into touch with that small event, only months ago, the three of them together laughing at some shared notion of complicity. The memory lay in her mind like a shawl comforting the complexities of the day to come. On her bed the cat was curled precisely over the bump in the blankets where Della had put a hot-water bottle. Nudging him with her feet as she got into bed she heard his breathing change to a rough, enthusiastic purr, before he settled into silence again.

She reached for *Middlemarch* and in the glow of her lamp read with all her usual hunger for assimilation. She stretched her being to intervene in the marriages between Rosamund and Lydgate, between Dorothea and Mr Casaubon, between Frank Vincey and Mary Garth. The unsung love of Mr Farebrother awoke some difficulty in her mind as the words began to blur – tomorrow – she had that appointment to keep, Anselm Daunt. And the telephone call to Leon, to the unlicensed pleasure. In the evening, what time was it, to Fota with her mother, yes, for the Carolan concert to be given by the National Association for the Blind. Would Damien be at that? Her mother liked him, but there was poor Mr Bulstrode, and that man drowned in the river, she had to find out all about that. The cat lay inert across her feet; her finger slipped from its place in the pages, the bolster sank behind her head, the lamp dimmed and she dipped and swayed and fell at last into the tide of sleep.

Chapter 4

'Yer mother left a message for you.'

Mrs Cummins spoke laconically around the cigarette dripping from her mouth. Sitting back from the ironing-board in the kitchen she worked her domestic magic at arms' length: on one hand stood the diminishing pile of laundry, on the other the increasing pile of recognisable clothes and cloths, while in between she sprinkled water on the surface before her and steam billowed as if from a censer, the fragrance of cleanliness and warmth filling the room as Claire quickly browned toast under the grill.

'I'll get it in a minute, Mrs Cummins. How's Mr Cummins these days?'

Claire knew well that although her husband was the bane of Mrs Cummins's life, he was also the apple of her eye. Chronically unemployed – unemployable, Frank said with uncharacteristic sourness – he was fed and tended by Mrs Cummins as though he were one of his own prize greyhounds.

'That fellow! I haven't been next, nigh or near him this whole week. He went off fishing on the river with a couple of his cronies from Blackrock and the next thing I hear is a message from Cobh – *Cobh*, if you don't mind – to say they were waiting to get a tow back up against the tide. Fifteen miles in a row-boat! The man's mad. And not a word about any kind of fish to be catched.'

Claire thought that they must have had a motor.

'Divil a motor! Oars is all they ever used, that crowd from the fisheries. Oars -- and bottles of stout from the pier.'

The iron hissed along a sheet. Claire offered tea, some toast.

'I'd be glad of it. The sup I had before I came out was weak enough to be anointed. I was that bothered. And me with four slices of lamb's liver keeping for him, *and* rashers.'

Della had long ago explained that sympathy for Mrs Cummins in these recurrent situations must not contain a single hint of criticism of Mr Cummins. Claire sometimes found it hard to keep this rule; this morning she was able to oblige:

'I suppose he's not the worst. I mean, he wouldn't have known that you had something special for his supper, would he?'

A small woman, and squat, Mrs Cummins had her own dignity.

'He would have known what to expect. I always put a good plate in front of him, never mind what it cost me.'

It did cost her. Claire knew that no one else in the Cummins household ate like the head of it, or drank like him either. She wondered if the children shared Mrs Cummins's devotion to him and, if not, what was the distinguishing thing which kept his wife in such thrall. He was an unlikely hero, but, she supposed, there must have been something.

'Did you hear, Mrs Cummins, that a man was taken from the river yesterday?'

It was almost an idle question, but some part of it was on her mind.

'There's more men, and women too, still in the Lee than was ever taken out of it, if all were known.'

Mrs Cummins was never loth to make a bad thing worse.

'I heard of it; 'twas on the wireless this morning, and yer mother left *The Journal* there when she came back from Mass so I had a gawp. No name though, but they were saying in the village 'twas a boy from the Grove; his mother came in from Bandon and she lived in Factory Lane for a time without, in respects to you, a lace to her stays. That's what they were saying anyhow.'

She sniffed, put the cigarette in a saucer, and took her tea.

'But I wrote that story last night, Mrs Cummins – I didn't give the man's name.'

'And why would you, if you didn't know it? But they knew it in Blackrock.'

'And did they know much about him, himself?' Claire was always ready to take information from any source without, if possible, giving any in return.

Mrs Cummins put down her cup with a deliberate hand. It clicked in its saucer where the cigarette still smouldered.

'Was I ever a one to be listening to that kind of talk? And where would I get the time, and me on my way up here, and no sign of that man of mine down in Cobh still for all I know, to be *stracauling* in the street with the likes of them?'

Claire dared not smile – and anyway it was true. Mrs Cummins sitting here drinking tea was not a usual sight, nor was she a likely member of any group of gossips. What she heard she overheard, being otherwise always occupied, rarely seen even as idle as waiting for a bus. No, she would not be likely to be stracauling, as that kind of easygoing, open-air talkative attitude to life was described.

'Although –' and Mrs Cummins took a deep significant breath. She drained her cup, took it to the sink and washed it, then went back to the table and her cigarette, tapping the fading ash into the saucer, all before continuing the sentence.

'They did say – Minnie Crowley from Rope Walk it was said it – that he was the boy Barry. His mother married at the last, to Paddy Barry from the Marsh. They're dead now, *and* buried. There was three of 'em in it – this lad, and two girls who went to England. Nothing has been seen of 'em since. No. Minnie Crowley said that one of 'em did come home to the Marsh once. They found out she had a baby and they sent a message saying she was to come home if she could: they thought she was married. And she *was*. But when they went to meet her at the station there was only herself and the baby. And now, Claire, don't let on to yer mother that I told you this – but when she got out of the train wasn't the child as black as yer boot!'

Now Claire couldn't prevent herself laughing. Mrs Cummins sniffed, and took up the iron again.

'I'm not a one to spread scandal, mind you. 'Twere better that a millstone be hanged around my neck. But they said that that was the family he came from. Barry, Nicholas Barry. He was married, too, but the wife is gone this year or more. They said he was a nice lad, poor child.'

'Did they have many children?' Claire was thinking she need never make another phone call if she could keep Mrs Cummins as informant.

'I came away out of it after that. What would I be doing wasting my time listening to it? Isn't it sad enough, God help us? And him without another sinner now to get his Masses said?'

Claire could give something back: she would ask Damien to pray for the dead man. She could also try to write about his death so as to give it some meaning – but that was her own business and would not interest Mrs Cummins, or gratify her.

Mrs Cummins wasn't finished.

'Before I came away this morning, Claire, Minnie Crowley said another thing. There did a guard come into her shop yesterday. One of the Heffernans from Dunmahon he was, a grand lad. I knew the seed and breed of him. He said there was a fair bit of war going on down at the settlements, that a new crowd had come in from England. Two of the priests of the parish have been run out of there, he said. 'Twas them gave the news. I suppose, now –' and she put the iron down, this was what she was getting at. She rested her hands on her knees and looked straight at Claire: 'I suppose now yer father can take care of himself. But I wouldn't want yer mother to be drawing any of that crowd on her. I seen her walking down there the other day, of a Tuesday it was, with only the dog for company.'

Claire's mother was not an organisation woman. What charities she performed she did alone, and without suspicion.

Frank worked with the homeless, the jobless, the hopeless, but Della had no use for categories and gave her help with her own hand where she found it was needed.

'Everybody in the parish knows Mum.' Claire was indignant that anyone, even Mrs Cummins, might feel a need to warn Della in her own neighbourhood.

'Isn't that what I'm saying! This crowd aren't from the parish at all. Yer mother, God reward her, goes everywhere and anywhere without a soul except the dog to take care of her. And even the dog, same: they have fights down there with any animal they can find, and they wouldn't be above stealing one if they fancied him. Since I seen her a Tuesday 'tis on me mind. I wouldn't like to say it to her, herself. *Nor* to Mr Mackey – he knows his own know. But you might find a way to say something. The likes of them has no nature – they wouldn't say thank you for a pound.'

Della had left several messages for Claire: Leon had rung; a Fr Daunt had rung; in a radio programme a reporter had said: 'By your own admittance this cannot be achieved.'

There was a postscript: 'Delighted about Fota concert; let me know the time and I'll collect you at the office, but try to be early so we can have a little look around.'

Smiling at her mother's optimism – how much of a look around could they have late in a November afternoon? – Claire scribbled a reply: she should be ready at about 5 p.m. That meant that to get the story done she would have to spend most of the day in the office, from where she could try to reach Leon also. But first she had to get to Anselm Daunt.

Dressing in her room she noticed that the cat had disappeared at some time in the night through the slender gap in her casement window. She saw him now crouching in the garden, half-hidden under the spread of the fir tree, dry on the matted needles of its floor. Beyond the garden, and the parallel gardens of the other houses in the sprawling avenue, lay the last remaining fields of a farm, the dwelling itself exposed by the loss of leaves from the limes behind the high stone wall. The farm was caught in a right angle between the avenue and the river, and its western boundary, where its westernmost fields had been, was a spacious estate of villas, various but all well-built, so elegant that it had made the whole neighbourhood elegant by association – and yet it was true that those suburban householders considered their greatest amenity was the farm itself, the smell, sometimes perhaps too strong, indeed, of the countryside. It was almost, they assured themselves, as if one were living altogether outside the city.

From her window now as she opened it wide, seating herself sideways on the inner sill, Claire saw the irregular black roofs of the farm, one white gable. Rising above this was the wall of the byre, what she and Angela as children had called the byre, where they climbed the unrailed steps to enter a gloom sweetened in spring by the breath of stumbling calves. That had been the first hint in their unstartled lives that they themselves were a threat, unwelcome in their humanness although they meant so kindly. The cow had been fearful; huge to them, and soiled, and malodorous, the charm of the calves uncertain.

Farmer Brady had muttered soothing commonplaces to the cow, and the children had stood still and quiet, and the rolling eyes grew less wary until the red-brown bulk shifted kindly around so that the two new animals could be seen, wondering, in the straw. There was pain in their beauty. Claire still remembered it, responded to it still: she recognised then that her sister and herself, so secure in their own world and so eager to discover others, were intruders, frightening to these creatures incapable of harm themselves, yet with instincts warning them to be afraid.

'Suck! Suck!' Farmer Brady initiated the little girls to the language of the byre. They offered their reluctant fingers to the pink stippled mouths, fearful of teeth but too proud to ask: Farmer Brady approved of courage, what he called boldness, a strange way to them of using the word. Raphael had been with them, his eyes big and soft as those of the calves, long-lashed and anxious. He held Angela's hand, not that of his father, and stood waiting for the girls to move before he moved, not afraid as they were, afraid of something else. In their suspicion of strangeness the sisters, without talking to one another, both knew there was a strangeness in the Bradys' house, that there were silent rooms, and doors Raphael would not open.

Now Claire could see smoke drifting from one of the farm chimneys: Raphael would have put a match to the kitchen fire. It was a long time since Mr Brady had died, since Mrs Brady had abandoned his habit of keeping the fire in at night. In the flush of premarital furnishing Angela had exclaimed over the disused range in the farmhouse, but Mrs Brady had been terse about the trouble it gave and the need for a strong arm to bring in the coal and slack. With a slanted glance at Raphael stroking the collie by the scullery door, she had said that there were some with too much brains for work, fit only for books all day and prayers all night.

The farm was broken up by then, its fields sold to roads and houses, its trees casting too much shade on ambitious gardens and cut down, its cattle a limpid memory, a smell that had come from Mr Brady with his milk-cart and churns and docile old pony at the door, offering the required pints and a tilly for the cat.

Trees must have been cut down for this garden too, although perhaps a hundred years ago, Claire thought. The limes on the Brady side had been left to flourish, and Frank had planted a silver birch and, in another corner, the fir tree which now waved its ferny branches in the rising wind. Although she shivered, Claire stayed at the window for minutes longer. On the last fine day Frank had cut the grass, the chugging old rotary mower leaving the sward in surprisingly trim strips of green; there was even now a smell of the grass, biting but sweet, and Claire could see where it had been lightly piled, then pressed, around the roots of the acacia which felt the cold so keenly. Apple trees, which seemed ancient to Claire because they had been there all her life, but which were not an orchard, divided the lawn and borders from the vegetable garden. Beyond them, at the last corner of the garden where again it touched the Brady wall, stood the great venerable pear tree which yielded in September pound upon pound of hard brown fruit and, for week after welcome week in the spring, a vast white pyramid of blossom, achingly, immutably beautiful.

It was only now, in her early twenties, that Claire was recognising the true dimensions of this garden which had seemed to herself and Angela as children to be huge, offering shaded corners for secrecy, the spaces between the thorny gooseberry bushes dark and promising. Behind the tool-shed they had found an abandoned kitten – not Gluic, but his great-grandmother, according to Angela's careful note-taking. The garage had been a stable once and its wide arched doors held a mystery in their very shape; it was at the end of the garden, away from the house, and the bowered path that brought them to it seemed to them an avenue to another world. Frank's meticulous motoring equipment was there, Della's trugs and shears and secateurs, paint-cans with just a little paint which might come in handy were kept on the dusty shelves, there was nothing there that was not familiar. Yet in among the wire and the paint-brushes and the brown broken-framed prints of another occupation – including a stained reproduction of the Proclamation of Independence of 1916 – hung a horseshoe, shared for six months each for years afterwards by the sisters. They never took it to the house; it belonged, they promised one another, in the stable.

Which of them had been the first to forget it? Claire would have liked to blame Angela, but looking at the garden now and accepting again its new size accepted too that she herself had probably forgotten first. Was it still there? Which long-ago animal had it belonged to? Perhaps one of those stout carriage-horses which Farmer Brady had once told them had drawn the ladies of the house about in a fly. Or something trimmer, like Glencora Palliser's ponies Dandy and Flirt – but that was for a carriage wasn't it, and the ladies of Tower Road had not been grand enough for a carriage. So Mr Brady had said. But surely, now she thought of it, they would not have had the Proclamation of Independence either? Who had brought that into the house, and in which era? Who had thrown it out?

Musing, her eyes still roaming the garden, she saw where a

ball had lodged like a nest in the hedge. Raphael, she supposed – calling to do something for, get something from, her mother, and lured by Bran into a game which made light of Frank's efforts with the lawn. It was typical of Raphael to play like that, with enthusiasm, heedless, and to leave the ball there not quite hidden, not easily obtainable.

On the opposite bank of the river a train lumbered past. From its windows she knew the tower which closed the Tower Road could be seen, matching the folly on the other hill, on the other side. Between them the river, and this morning at its city end rested the Inisfallen, the ferry for Swansea and England. Foreign vessels lay there also at these suburban docks, yet Claire remembered, or thought she did, although Angela said it could not be so, seeing the great grey bridges by the City Hall lift and open in a compact arc to let a freighter through. This had been a commonplace of Frank's childhood – Claire wondered if her memory were jealous of a vanished fact, and she had always guarded the idea that these two towers, now alternately washed by the billowing sunlight, darkened by the clouds, had been built together, the pattern for the city's coat of arms, two castles with a sailing ship between – *statio bene fide carinis*. It was not so; the castles of the crest remained only as place-names and Claire knew that. Yet the idea pleased her, and she did not relinquish it.

She had to go to work. The wind freshened again, and the fir tree trembled. Claire saw Gluic dart from under its skirt and run, hump-backed, across the grass to leap to the tool-shed roof, from which he could survey the behaviour of the dog next door. Bran she knew was curled on the mat in the porch beneath her window, and if she called to him now he would run to the path and cower with delight at her voice, looking up at her and begging her to explain how he could get to where she was. It was better to leave him, she would have no time for him today.

The curved handle of the casement shook suddenly in her hand and the wind flooded her room; looking away from the garden and beyond the farm she could see how still the trees on the skyline were, tanned now and nearly bare. These were the elms, the chestnuts and the oaks of the demesnes of Mayfield, Montonotte, Tivoli. The gaunt ruin of Woodhill House was over there, where Sarah Curran had found shelter after the execution of Robert Emmet. There among its lilac walks she had met and accepted the English Captain Sturgeon. Claire could see the mist of the green ornamental trees which must have heard their whispers, and from here, as she twisted to follow the line of the hills, she could see the spire of the church at Glanmire where they had been married. How still, in the distance, everything was, although the same wind tormenting the garden here surely must be soaring through those trees across the river. It was all a matter of distance: the distance of years had diminished her garden; the distance of miles diminished the wind and its energy.

Anselm Daunt's call said he was to be seen at a community centre. Claire supposed it could be called community, that was its hope, but it was just a place where people were living who had nowhere else to live, no choice in the matter. The houses were well-made, but stood in their hundreds. A flat-roofed church with a grotesque triangular steeple was the only elevation, with a raw red school behind and a block of houses for the priests of the parish – one each. Then, prefabricated, grimy, grim, what could only be the community centre.

Walking carefully between the wet smears left by the pressure of rain on the droppings of the wandering tinker horses Claire found a door open and pushed it in. On the smell which rose towards her came the weary remembrances of impoverished meeting places – of poverty itself, for it held dampness indoors, too many bodies not all of them clean, too little space, a kind of nervous sweat. It was the Legion of Mary smell, sharper perhaps than that, but it was also the smell of the lanes off Military Hill which she had visited as a child with her father on Sick Poor duty.

There was a heavy silence in the hall, broken at last by an irregular metallic beat; she followed the noise of the duplicating machine to another unlatched door opening into a small, littered room in which a young man was cranking the handle of the machine.

His face tense with surprise, he made as if to question her, but she was ready with her own question –

'Father Daunt?'

To his quick, interrogative nod she responded –

'Please, forgive me for interrupting you like this. I'm from *The Journal*: Claire Mackey. I rang, remember? I left a message. We have a friend in common – Damien Sebright? I was hoping you might be able to talk to me for a few minutes – give me some help?'

It was a good technique – names, references, a request for assistance, and all couched as queries. It gave too many things to answer at once, a series of options.

'I can see you're busy – I don't mind waiting,' she added, again anticipating his excuses.

'I'll just finish this lot,' he said after a moment. 'Find a seat – I won't be long.'

She sat and watched him. When he brushed a leaf of brown hair away from his forehead a slick of ink was left on the skin. The machine groaned gently with each crank and the smudged thick-lettered pages piled on the steel plate. He worked without looking at Claire, with concentration; she noticed how his short crisp eyelashes defined his eyes and seemed to widen them, giving his unguarded face a boyish, open look which she thought might be misleading. There was a rough-edged shape to him; not the sharp edge which she found so arresting in Leon, but something rougher, more solid – something she felt now she almost didn't like, almost did fear.

The man's clerical vest and collar hung from a chair, and he wore an open-necked shirt from which his smooth white neck lifted the heavy edge of his jaw. Claire had noticed that before: how different the skin of a man's face could look from the flesh of his throat. In Raphael it had moved her unbearably, his unsunned body seeming to her a symbol of another kind of neglect – of which she herself might be guilty. Waiting for this other man, and thinking of Raphael, she wondered if she might not have tried harder to bring the boy along when she and Leon went to the beaches near the city; or even if she and Angela and their other friends, given that Leon and Raphael disliked or at least distrusted one another, could not have included him sometimes. Why had they not done so? But there was more than that on her mind as she dwelt on this physical contrast between skin and skin. It was to her as though the coloured face were open, readable, while the body paled in a special privacy, never to be revealed, never warmed to life by the air and light of summer.

Never? There was a swelling pleasure in her mouth; a taste flooded it, a summer taste of fruit fresh and stinging. Claire knew she had flushed although she was not hot. The room was close, but she was not part of it. She felt, against the surprise of the feeling, simply subdued by sweetness, and smiled at it, and as the young man turned to her at last it was to meet that uninflected smile, her agile face alight with some pleasant thought which included him.

Anselm Daunt was used to welcome. It did not have to spring from liking, from pleasure in his company. He never thought about its source. People needed him. He brought skills as well as solace. The reverence due to him as a priest might have been blunted by his youth, but instead it was honed by usefulness into a sharper respect. Men listened to him, sought him out, his comfort was not just for women, or girls. He was accustomed also to adoration of a kind. He felt a tug of distaste as he assessed Claire's expression.

'Now,' he was abrupt. 'What's the problem?'

She had thought he knew the problem. Perhaps Damien had not given him the details. Now she wasn't sure where to start. With the death, perhaps, it was unmistakable enough.

'A man from this parish has been drowned. Nicholas Barry –'

'Yes?' The priest's voice was tight.

Defending herself against the downright animosity in his tone, Claire said:

'Fr Sebright is a friend of mine. When I knew the dead man came from here I remembered that Damien spoke about your work. I thought you might help me get the story in its proper context –'

'Story!' He almost spat the words at her.

She was amazed more by his anger than by his contempt.

'That's just a term. It doesn't mean –'

'I know what it means. It means that a human tragedy – and it is a tragedy, let me tell you that much – is seen by you and your *Journal* as a story, to be written up. Served up like something in a novel, even in a comic. Easy to read. A Headline. And then forgotten. But who's going to ask what made it happen, why that young man died in that way –?'

'I am!' Claire was gathering her forces. She had heard this kind of thing before. 'That's why I'm here – that's precisely why I'm here; I want to try to find out what made him take his own life –'

'No!' Daunt countered fiercely. 'No. He was driven to do something desperate. Society, this city, people like you and your paper making him feel he was a failure, of no worth, no prospects, no hope, nowhere to go except the dole. He was *driven*. Driven mad, maybe. But he was not responsible for his own death – *we* were.'

Claire let him finish; she sat back more easily now, knowing that he had to let this out. She scanned the notices on the walls – a meeting for mothers to discuss natural family planning; a trade union conference on membership of the EEC and what it would mean for industry in Ireland; information leaflets on Social Welfare provisions were available here or at the presbytery; the Legion of Mary would meet on the first Thursday of every month. The Catholic Boy Scouts of Ireland, the Catholic Girl Guides of Ireland, the hours the medical centre would be open, youth club football fixtures, the Pioneer Total Abstinence Association, the Children of Mary, the Men's Confraternity and the Third Order of St Francis, a sponsored trip to Derry to find out about civil rights in the Six Counties, the St Vincent de Paul Society, classes in Irish for trade union members. *Sceim na gleardcumann*, Alcoholics Anonymous, polio pools.

Nothing much unusual in that lot, Claire thought. It would be familiar enough to Leon, anyway, even to Damien, although he at least might question some of them – but not to her. Now she heard the priest outline something of what she wanted to say herself. His eyes were bright, the lashes like black sparks as his anger fuelled the energetic words. She could see his neck swell and pulse. His skin looked innocent. She wanted to touch it, and smiled, delighted by the outrageous impulse.

Daunt saw her face lighten.

'It's no laughing matter.'

She couldn't help telling him the truth.

'What an old-fashioned man you are. You're giving out the most downright, unhesitating, *easiest* clichés. You're accusing me, without having once heard what I'm trying to do. You know nothing about me, don't even stop to think why I should be a friend of Damien Sebright – you don't even stop to think whether you could make some use of me. And then – *then* you say *this is no laughing matter*! Even my own father doesn't talk like that any more –'

Still in the chair, she sat back. She wanted him to consider something now that she had won his attention.

'Now. I haven't got all day, and neither have you, to sit here arguing society. But if you're not going to help me learn about this event so as to be able to invest it with *some* dignity, *some* meaning, then I just want to ask you this: you blame society, us, the establishment, the newspaper. What about yourself? What did you offer that man that wasn't enough for him? Why did God fail him?

'*And*,' she added, getting up at last, getting ready to leave him while he was still silent, 'it's completely patronising, condescending, not to let the man take responsibility for his own action. Whatever the reasons, *he* did it. He took the action. *He* is responsible.'

'You said you knew Fr Sebright.' He had been going to let her leave without another word. Seeing her stumble where cardboard boxes fouled her step at the door, seeing the colour deepen on her skin, suddenly he did not want her to go like that.

'Yes?' She stood at the door, her head turned at the question.

'I was just wondering how you knew him . . .'

It was a weak attempt, and he knew it. But even after what had already passed he wasn't expecting her furious rejoinder.

'He's a *friend* of mine. He says he's a friend of yours. He said to tell you that you're letting down the choir. But I suppose that's not your fault – you're driven to it. I'll tell Damien that it's his responsibility if you don't turn up. And mine. Everybody's – but not yours!'

On the beginning of his protest she went out. She tried to bang the door behind her but it only made a soft thud and swung open again. She knew she had been childish, both of them had been childish, but she thought her anger was more justifiable. And she didn't need him, anyway. She was sore that she hadn't been able to convince him, and there was a deeper soreness, their misunderstanding had been despite the almost physical expectation with which she had turned to him when she met him, when she saw his substance. That was the disappointment. She thought as she walked to the bus stop of the look of him cranking the battered duplicator, the grimy pages fluttering from the roller. She remembered the changes in his face, open, then taut. There were two lines in Yeats –

> But one man loved the pilgrim soul in you
> And loved the sorrows of your changing face . . .

Well, that was from the French, wasn't it, and a love-song, what was it doing in her mind now?

Her step gathered pace, bringing her to Hazelwood Heights and another line from Yeats – *'I went out to the hazel wood/Because a fire was in my head . . .'* The irony of it! Hazelwood Heights, flat, unbroken by any trees save the thin *prunus* on the main road, the gardens naked except for a coating of grass so thin it might have been painted. The grey rain turned muddy where it drizzled on the broken pavements, and she wondered what had happened to the wind which had risen so freshly in her own neighbourhood only an hour or so earlier. There was no one at the bus stop, there was nowhere to wait in shelter. Broken windows in houses across the road were stopped with hardboard, and in the cluster of shops beyond them the cage-like grilles were worn day and night over the plate glass. Nothing here of the silver apples of the moon, the golden apples of the sun.

She could read the road sign near the corner – Ascál J.F. Kennedy – J.F. Kennedy Avenue. This wasn't far, surely, from the address she had been given for Nicholas Barry, the man she should be thinking about right now? She could go to the house, look at it anyway. She could talk to the neighbours. With her notes, and if she went to the inquest, she could write what might be a really good story. She wouldn't talk about it to anyone else except the editor – and perhaps Frank. Her father could fill her in on the social background, more objectively at least than Fr Daunt. There was a lot she could do, find out more about the little girl – Della might help there, she knew the Good Shepherd nuns.

Taking her notebook from her bag Claire turned back along the road, getting down the patriotic names, the arboreal pretences. She was giving, she told herself, her mind to the job. Tightening the collar of her coat against the wet, heavy air, the taste came back to her of that warm surprise which had risen in her mouth when she watched Anselm Daunt at work.

It was disturbing. 'I was disturbed by him.' The thought was not welcome. This was not the way she was with Leon, who disturbed her too, activating her, challenging her, but consoling her as well, seeming to approve of her. This was different, strange, to have on her tongue a ripe-berry sweetness, not understood but sensed as if she were an animal. To have that, and then with it the words condemning her as insensate.

Her anger rose again. He had been wrong. She would show him how wrong he had been. She became intent on what she was doing, her job. What she had to do was tell a story, and tell it in such a way that it would become as real as this reality which was all around her, which had been the world of

Nicholas Barry and his child. And which was accepted, except by him.

She wondered what he had been like. Young, anyway, a young father. There had been a blunt sympathy in the voices of the *gardai* who had talked to her, they had felt for him. She would go to the city morgue before the funeral, she would look at him. A new feeling overtook her residual anger. She felt purpose strengthening her stride. She had been curious, now she was committed, there was something she had to do. But as she walked along, looking for the sign which would show her the house she wanted out of all these houses, the house from which her story would begin, she knew she was haunted. She knew it was not the dead man, not only him, haunting her.

Chapter 5

The request from Leon had been that they should go to the Film Society, that very night. '*L'Aventura*', the message had said when she pulled his letter from the rack in the Reporters' Room. 'Monica Vitti; Marcello Mastroianni – can you afford to miss them? Can you afford to miss me? *Ciao.*'

It was her own fault. Claire knew the film was coming soon, she should have checked before committing herself to the Fota concert. In that case she had been influenced by Damien's uncharacteristic eagerness for her attention. It was not only that the concert should be noticed by the newspaper, but that it sould be noticed by her. Which had been as intriguing as it was flattering and she had put her name down for the marking. Now that she looked at the schedule she saw she would have been working tonight anyway: there was a meeting of the Charismatic Youth Endeavour – a rally in fact. She would probably have been marked for that if not for the concert, and even though she was disappointed, and refusing Leon would carry its own difficulties, there was some relief that she did not have to report yet another session of respectable religious hysteria.

'Respectable,' Claire told herself, 'only because of all the priests and nuns mixed up in it. And they're only there because they feel abandoned by Holy Mother Church.'

She had held the Reporters' Room breathless with hilarity by her first accounts of Charismatic meetings, but to Damien she spoke with anger. 'They stand up and they pour out a lunatic gibberish which is applauded, and which is then described, quite calmly, as a visit from the Holy Ghost. *Speaking in tongues*. They really believe it! Honestly, Damien – you always say that lapsed Catholics renounce their membership of the Congregation of the Faithful – but faithful to *what*? That kind of extremism?'

Damien, who had only once said anything of the kind, felt that the emotional fervour of the Charismatic Renewal movement was not a very extreme extremism, but knew better than to try to make Claire see that possibility.

'And the thing is – they're all love and brotherhood and sisterhood, and the laying on of hands, and the healing power of love, all that, but in reality they're fundamentalists, like something you'd get in America. Do you know, Damien –' and she had turned to him speaking more slowly to convey the full enormity of this – 'they still believe in the *Devil*.'

Not at all sure that he didn't share the same belief, Damien had had little comfort to offer her. Johnny Trant's words did not seem appropriate:

'Mad whores the lot of them, poor sods: but they're orthodox, Damien – orthodox, and on our side. They're not going to change anything – a little bit of raving, a little bit of holding hands and singing Joan Baez – makes 'em feel good. No harm in it. Mind you, I know there's a couple of us, and a few poor nuns, mixed up in it, and my advice to you would be to steer well clear of the whole fandango. But if the Bishop isn't complaining you needn't either.'

So Damien had not repeated any of that to Claire, not being very comfortable either with the prospect of her getting to know Johnny Trant. And maybe she had a point – not that he would take the risk of admitting that to her – but maybe there was something in her contention that people only felt they needed the gift of tongues when the language they used was inadequate for their experience. And people did seem inclined to live intensely: Damien, even as a hospital chaplain, had not yet grown unsurprised at the passion with which the struggle for even ordinary life was invested.

He thought perhaps that music might explain that passion, and hoped that music would so infuse the new liturgy that the weakness of words would not be noticed.

'Guitars!' Claire had mocked, and even Raphael, worried by her scorn, wondered why no one played the organ any more. Claire said this was because there was a whole new scheme of canonical architecture: choirs now had to be close to the people and to the celebrating priest at Mass so that the front-facing altar meant a front-facing choir as well, and there was no room for an organ. Damien wished furiously she wouldn't use the legal language of religion so carelessly and allowed that irritation to disguise his own foreboding. He had found some relief at St Dominic's, and so had Raphael, and this was why he was so anxious now to introduce Claire to what he hoped would be at least part of the new music of the church.

'It's a plot, of course, can't you see that?'

Leon didn't accept Claire's excuse lightly.

'Sebright is in with that country crowd, rediscovering the ancient purity of the Irish language. Not only rediscovering it, but tying it in as tightly as they can to Catholicism. Can't you see that? There'll never be a way forward with the language – it has to live in a world of nuclear fission, molecular biology, genetic engineering, the modern world – and they're going to kill it by keeping it, enmeshing it, with religion. I'm telling you, Claire, it's a case of Irish Catholic Ireland all over again – that's what they're up to.'

An unhappy feeling that Leon could be right stopped Claire from framing any defence of Damien. That Leon was extreme she knew, and she understood as well that he felt that she had made the wrong choice for the evening not just because of his own disappointment. He believed that she was turning away from Europe and towards the bog culture he despised. She had said he despised it because he was afraid of it, of its attractions. And anyway, she had pursued another idea in one of their many arguments; anyway surely it was only right to try to find one's roots, find the place from which one could take one's stand, find out where one came from, what one was?

'There aren't many of us who don't know that much, Claire,' was the only answer he gave her, and she remembered, often, how he had looked when he said that, his grey eyes tightened and glinting in what was not a smile, the smooth narrow bones of his face set in a grim confidence.

It was *terribly* attractive. Years later, when she thought of him less often, Claire thought most of that conversation, the end of it as it had been, for when after a moment's silence he had suggested that they might go for a drink she had hurried beside him and when in the pub he had met a friend and borrowed his car for an hour and asked – told – Claire to come with him for a drive she certainly had gone along with him.

She never went to confession again after that drive. Leon had not been the first man to kiss her: that had come after a dance at the boat club, under the elms that lined the river. It had been tentative, and then not quite so innocent, but very sweet and must surely be a sin, so she had confessed it and the kisses which followed other meetings. There was an easy formula – for a sin against holy purity absolution was guaranteed with a penance of three Hail Marys or, if she went to a different priest, perhaps a decade of the Rosary. And then when the kisses had become searching, and a rugby player's thickened knee had pushed her knees apart and his warm and friendly hand had reached her thigh, she had confessed again to sinning but to a priest whose probing questions robbed her more surely of her innocence than anything the rugby player had been able to do. After that she confessed only to appease Frank by making her Easter duty.

There was no more pretence after that drive with Leon. In the first place Claire had had her period, and it was a tremendous shock to her that he didn't mind about that at all. It almost put her off whatever it was that they were going to do; but then his fingers had touched her and all the agony of explaining pads and belts had banished in a hot delight. He had placed her hands on himself – his amazing self, ribbed and silky between her palms. In spurts of breath like flame against her ears he had said he would kiss her, *there*, soon, and she would kiss him, she would take him in her mouth and as she reared away from the very thought his teeth grazed the skin of the breast he held, white and as heavy in his hand as a globe. His thumbs pushed her nipples up until they were sore, aching to be soothed by his lips.

He put his mouth on one, his hand on one, and with the other hand pushed suddenly, fiercely, high up between her legs so that she shied and cried out against him. He stifled her with his mouth, and held her, but she could smell her own body on his hand and closed her eyes against the astonishing shamelessness of pleasure.

He whispered: 'Will you let me in to you?' and when she opened her eyes to see if he could be serious she saw that although his face was quiet it was still intent. Excitement licked at her and liquidised but she was afraid, she might get pregnant, and he put his hand behind her head and brought her face close to his and whispered –

'All right. Then, kiss me.'

When he said, 'Claire. Please kiss me,' his hand tightened in her hair. His light voice was rough, there was the roughness of his skin against her face. She felt him shift, awkward in an effort to loosen his slacks. This was all too much for her. She didn't like this at all. But then he had agreed not to enter her, not to go inside, and he could have done it, she had been helpless, he could have put her in danger. How could she refuse this lesser evil, how could she hurt him? Despite the pressure of his hand against her neck she thought she had a choice, and made it, bending to the forked trunk in the shadow where the white branch gleamed. Enveloped by the smell – not altogether unpleasant – the feel, the taste of him, emboldened by his groans, she forgot, if she had ever guessed, that this was surrender.

He jerked against her face. His hand tugged on her hair and then was still. The wetness on her cheek she brushed off against his thigh. She thought she had done it, and panted with relief that it had been so quick, and so – well, uncontaminating.

With her fingers stroking the loosened spheres dangling where his legs parted – 'Touch my balls,' he commanded, and she had flinched at his coarseness but obeyed – she kept her eyes on his face; the tight skin seemed full, as if something had relaxed, and there was a secretive tuck to his lips as if he were thinking of some faraway, forbidden joke.

'Irish girls,' he said, not looking at her, 'are never any good at that.'

It was something she always remembered, but at the time, with him, Claire had felt only dismay, not hurt. Sitting back from him, lifting her hands away from him, she could see from the spread of his body that he was content. She knew that they had to get back to town, to return the car, but she did not hurry to dress. There was something luxurious in her own disorder, something to be savoured. When she had been helpless, held by him against the seat, her breasts so decisively bared by his hands, she had been almost afraid to look down, to see herself, there was something terrifying about it, the abandon. A bed, now, with covers, that would give her a chance to get used to being naked, to enjoy it and to relish Leon's body, not just what it could do. This was all too abrupt – and yet the determination with which it had been carried through was part of its intense excitement. That could not last; although, even this early she already sensed this truth, it could not last, but she could find it again and not just with Leon. It could not last – but what was to last for her was the image she was forming as she lay for these final moments at his side, the image of herself, naked, suspended from his arms, submitting to his gaze and to his purposes, a torso, a nude, white as marble, immobilised yet ready to respond at a touch.

'I really think,' she said on their way back, 'that just about covers it all – thought, word, and deed. A very comprehensive sinning.'

He had grinned as he drove, the headlights showing her again the eased look of his features, but he did not need, she noticed, to keep in touch with her as she did with him, her hand on the crease of his thigh. That realisation, and the memory of those few casual words after what she thought of as her great gift to him – 'Irish girls are no good at that' – these made her think of getting back at him.

She stretched, taking her hand away, sitting towards the door on her side of the car. 'The great thing about this is that I don't have to worry about marrying you.'

He laughed outright, so suddenly that he almost overshot a bend in the road; he slowed and did what she had wanted him to do, put his hand on her knee and squeezed the bone and, laughing, said that certainly it was one of the great things about it. After that she never did worry about marrying him and because she had gained this knowledge of how her body could be made to feel, how she could make another body feel, she gained control of the exchange. Leon was still the most exciting man she had met, but not the most exacting. They became friends. Perhaps they would never again be lovers, but the possibility, despite Leon's numerous girlfriends, the pretty, casual girls who stopped him in the street, the sense that in some private way he was already bespoken – the possibility that they might become lovers sometime was the hidden ingredient in the enjoyment they shared with one another.

It was also a spur to the anger. Her tolerance of things, of people he despised, made him impatient. He wanted to change her, so that she could change what he did not like, and yet he rarely appreciated her own indignation. As a student of history and politics he had tried to inform what he called her nihilism, resenting her claim to journalistic objectivity. As a student of law, when he had already gone to Dublin, he had tried to persuade her that prejudice was not always evil.

'No,' Claire had rejoined, 'not if you're prejudiced towards good. But that's not what you mean, Leon. You really epitomise the principle of the lever – give me a spot on which to take my stand and I will move the world: except that you don't much care which spot it is, you can take a stand on practically any issue and then you get vicious because other people aren't quite so generous with their allegiances.'

It sounded good, satisfying Claire and maddening Leon, who didn't speak to her for weeks, not until he wanted *The Journal* to carry a speech on Fianna Fail under Lemass and its policy on partition. As this was written from a socialist standpoint – Claire had to go through it and delete every favourable reference to communism – he knew publication would depend on special pleading, and had no trouble convincing himself that Claire would have learned her lesson by now.

It sounded good, but it wasn't true. Claire knew that, and found it easy to forgive Leon, as easy at least as it was to taunt him. But she needed, often, to reinforce her distance from him. Her girlfriends had boyfriends. She was discovering a kind of loneliness, and knew that distance was the only way she could avoid becoming prey to a craven anxiety for his company, his approval, and his love.

There was noise in the Reporters' Room, a late afternoon fug of returning men and women, arrangements being made for the night, typewriters hammering to beat deadlines, smoke from cigarettes gathering to thicken the yellow air. Leon's voice on the telephone sharpened.

'You didn't see *L'Année Dernière à Marienbad* either, Claire. You've missed all the highlights of the programme this year so far. I was hoping we might have a few drinks afterwards, I was going to ask my mother for her car –'

He heard Claire's silence, the quality of it. He said –

'It's been a while, hasn't it?'

There was so much she wanted to talk to him about. Standing there at the only cubicled telephone in the room, her working life going on behind her, the indifferent words of the editor still infecting a confused anger at her heart, she thought of the balm of lying in his arms, of being taken outside herself, of loosening and letting go. Leon would listen to her, even after she had pleased him he would listen to her. He would know, he would not denigrate, how she felt about Nicholas Barry and his child. She thought of Anselm Daunt, his pale throat, his eyes accusing her – accurately, as it turned out.

'Claire – it has been a while, hasn't it?'

'Not that I noticed,' she said, and put down the receiver.

In the car on their way to Fota, Claire told her mother about Hazelwood Heights, about Nicholas Barry and his child Sarah. She spoke about the women who had spoken to her, what they had not said, what they had expected her to understand, those who had expected anything of her. Some husbands had been at home, and left the house when she was made welcome in the kitchen, the woman from next door being brought in as witness to the story. But there was no story. Nothing unusual had happened, they said.

'I remember when they got married,' one woman had told Claire. 'That girl was from one of the lanes up there by the North Chapel. She got her wedding dress sent over by her aunt in America and it was that big she had to go out in the lane to put it on.'

There was grandeur, they had said. They said that Nicholas Barry used to work at Denny's in Blackpool, the bacon people. He had been one of the first men to be laid off there. He was very quiet, they said. All he had ever done was walk the greyhounds. When he lost his job he sent the greyhounds down to his uncle in Dungourney.

'But she was a bold strap,' they had said. After the child was born she wouldn't look after it, a lovely little girl. Her mother took it for a while but then her mother died. There was no holding her after that so she went to England. She hadn't been back since. The nuns had the child now, probably the best thing.

'But there's no fairity in it, is there?' they asked Claire.

Della was driving carefully, listening. With the help of these women, who had nothing to offer except kindness and gossip, Claire had retraced much of the dead man's life over the past few weeks. By a cautious engagement of the interest of the *gardai* she had broken down the hours of his life on that last day. There was to be a postmortem, but she had been able to get to the City Morgue and because the attendant there was a son of a cousin of Mrs Cummins she had been able to get in and see Nicholas Barry, cadaver.

'It hadn't occurred to me that I might be frightened,' Claire told her mother. 'But then when I was going in I heard my own voice echo, it's all tiles, and a smell like the baths, and I remembered – do you remember – that scene in Zola is it *Thérèse Raquin*?' where the drowned body of the husband is found, and the water is dripping on all the corpses, day after day, and they begin to disintegrate –'

'That's all right,' said Della crisply, 'you needn't go on about Zola.'

'Well –' Claire smiled sadly – 'it wasn't like that, of course. Just cold. Tiled, and soggy painted walls. He was on a sort of table. Fully dressed, but no shoes. It looked a bit indecent. His bare feet sticking out, yellowish. He had corns. And an ingrowing toenail. All very clean now, of course. Very well looked after, now.'

Seeing nothing, she looked out the window.

'The awful thing about it, to me, was that there was nothing headline-ish about it. Nothing dramatic. I mean, you couldn't look at him and say "what a tragedy" – do you know? It was *sad*; the whole episode has pathos, the child and everything, it's poignant. But there doesn't seem to be anything big about it. Not on the surface.'

Della drove steadily, the new carriageway sweeping beside the river still sheltered on this side by the heavy trees of Tivoli, her dim headlights warming the leaves, weighted by the day's mist and lying in tumbled shoals along the shore of the road.

'I think that must have been where I went wrong with the news editor. I was so afraid of frightening him by talking about my own rage at the quietness of it all, the acceptability, that I didn't give him that angle of it. I know he hates the idea of crusading journalism, he's terrified of libel actions – I think he's terrified of anything that might be said in the clubs, even, not to mind a court case – we all think that there's more influence wielded in the yacht clubs and golf clubs and the

County Club than there is in the Board Room. So, I played down my own anger, which would be my way of reflecting what should be the anger of the whole community.'

'It seems a bit subtle, to me,' Della tried to appease Claire's guilt.

'Perhaps he felt that it really is a private domestic tragedy and must be left at that. Nothing to write headlines about, as you say.'

'Yes.' This was what Claire was trying to say. 'That's what it is. But there's more to it than that – the whole business of his care for the child, that's what takes it out of the ordinary, and that's what makes it not just a domestic, but a community, tragedy. And I wanted to write it like that: I said – and this was probably my real mistake – I said it was like the Patrick Kavanagh poem, about Homer's ghost, remember? *I made the* Iliad *from such a local row. Gods make their own importance.*'

'Ah, *Claire*.' Della felt it was time to lighten the gloom. 'That really *was* too subtle; I'm surprised at you – trying poetry on the news editor.'

'I know. I knew as soon as I'd done it that it was a mistake.' Claire's rue had a smile in it. Then it disappeared.

'I still feel it's a failure, though. I feel as if I've joined the list of people who could have helped that man and didn't, for one reason or another. I know' – she forestalled her mother's protest – 'it wasn't my fault, isn't my fault. But it's surprising how weak it sounds when you say that a thing isn't your fault, in a case like this. And it *is* my fault in that I didn't work round to it properly, I didn't use the right strategy, the right approach.'

'Well, at least it's not your responsibility,' was all Della could offer, and Claire agreed, after a pause, that no, it wasn't her responsibility. She didn't tell her mother about Fr Daunt, nor did she say that she intended to go to Nicholas Barry's funeral as a mourner, not a reporter. There would be other things to write about, Della reminded her, other subjects for investigation and analytical reporting; there was nothing wrong with indignation, she said, the thing was to learn how to use it.

Claire said, as the car moved carefully on to the causeway which brought them to the Cobh road, that she had had a row with Leon. A sort of a row, she amended, about nothing really. She had felt so bad about Nicholas Barry and the news editor that she couldn't take his insistence and had hung up on him.

'You won't be the last to hang up on that young man,' Della said, her dry tone reminding Claire of her grandmother. In the gloaming the thickly wooded mound of Fota Island rose from the lake-like waters of the estuary as they drove on over the wide, high-walled channel towards Belvelly.

The neat little car purred along, and the arching branches of the roadside woods stretched arms against the shadow of the dusk. In this calm Claire felt her own turmoil subside. She heard Della speak of Frank's gift of a new radio to her grandmother, timed and tuned so that the Remembrance Day ceremonies, broadcast by the BBC, could be shared. Della said that Stan had promised to collect the Earl Haig poppies from the British Legion in town for Onorah before Sunday. Wasn't it strange, she wondered, how their different histories and allegiances could come together for November 11th? Stan, with his family name inscribed with armorial bearings and regimental flags in the church at Sunday's Well, and Onorah, with nothing but old photographs of her Colour Sergeant? Protestant gentry and Catholic commonality? And neither of them English.

'Not the difference, I mean that's a difference they share. I mean, it's because they're both Irish that they can come together on all the rest. That cancels out the inherited antagonisms, or it should. And there must be thousands of people in Ireland like Gran, and like Grandad too, still.'

'It's convenient, anyway,' said Della, grateful that somewhere in Stan's past there had been a military connection impeccable enough to quiet Onorah's doubts about his suitability for Angela. She told Claire that Stan and Angela were to take Onorah to visit Grandad's grave at Iniscarra on Sunday, to put a wreath there. She said that next week they were off to visit some friends in Monaghan.

'Near the Border?' Claire tried to show some interest, but Della didn't know where, exactly, not yet.

'They'll tell us the details on Sunday; we're invited for lunch. Can you come?'

'I'll be working,' Claire said. 'A Vietnam war protest in town at midday. And I saw something in the Diary about the EEC campaign.' She spoke as if her words were not worth the weight of air that carried them. Della thought it must be because she was remembering Leon, with the mention of the EEC debate. Or it might be Vietnam.

'Getting worked up about Vietnam,' Della scoffed lightly. 'I'm still trying to catch up with Hitler.

'Did I tell you,' she asked, 'that there was an interview on the radio today with someone from the Language Freedom Movement, explaining why he was prepared to go to any lengths to make sure that compulsory Irish was dropped from school exams? I think it must have been on the Liam Nolan Hour; anyway, when Nolan tried to remind him of what the Gaelic League position was, he said – and I'm not joking – he said: *"That doesn't wash any water with me."* And a few minutes later –' Della had caught the little reviving quirk at Claire's mouth, at least she was listening – 'a few minutes after that he said that it was *"quite within the cards"* that the Movement would take their case to court.'

Della was rewarded with a turn of the head, an open smile. Trees thronged the avenue where they turned off before the humpbacked bridged could take them on to Great Island. The dense vaulting overhead brought the dark down on them, and it was night at last. Yet when they reached the sweep in front of the house there was a lingering brightness on the looming fields, light spreading in from the reaches of the harbour, a drift of the sea smell on the air, the greensward luminous as a tide.

Woods fringed the sky. In the milky blueness where the day still hung a star glistened, solitary, pale, but present, Venus descending, star-like, as the curve of the world turned away from her.

Leaning at her ease, her back against the back of the car, Claire felt the breathing quiet of the gloaming. The land lapped at her, the pastures swelling to the disappearing distances as though space itself had colour, had islands of copse and hangar, had contours even in its shadows, where sheep gleamed among the clouds of oak and beech. This demesne, which Claire had seen stretched in radiant summer foliage, lush, enticing, warm with self-content, seduced her utterly. She put Hardy to the task, and Clare, and the statelier verse of Yeats, but no borrowed, beloved words could solace the ache at the core of her fervour. She had felt before, as she felt now, hearing a raucous peacock cry into the urgent silence, that there was no solace but assimilation, that if there were some speaking way she could sink into the gathering green and mossy banks of earth that made up these flowing fields, she would yield her own matter to the soil and become subsumed, a part of it, a trace element.

'I always think this place is so typically *English*,' Della said behind her. 'It's not really grand enough to be a stately home, but it is the typical ornamental estate. I don't know anywhere like it in this country.'

She sighed as she stretched, then gasped as pain struck her like a blow in the small of her back. Claire heard the surprised, stopped exclamation and turned to her, but Della, puzzled by the attack, shook her head and said that it was nothing, she must have quirked a muscle or something, it was gone now. She had done a lot of driving today: she needed a walk. They could follow the path to the railway station, to the folly, that should be far enough.

There were other cars on the gravel, lamps in the hall gilded the portico. As they passed Della and Claire could see through the windows of the gallery where the concert would be given that logs were already burning in the ornate, enormous fireplace. They walked on, not quickly, for this was private land and their visits were rare, to be savoured. It was too dark now to go through the coachyard, past the stables lined with timber, grilled with iron, the stone-stepped mounting block set in the cobbles. Even in the dark, as Claire reminded her mother, if it were spring, even in the dark they could have found their way to the gardens at this side of the house by the scent alone of the wisteria under which, once, they had stood enraptured, their faces lifted for the kiss of the flowers which hung, heavy as grapes, in clouds of cloudy blue.

It was a calm night now, and dry. Claire felt the lift in the air as the wind began to drift against them, she heard the dim rattle of the ewes. The cattle were in the further pastures, invisible. Her mind saw them in their summer colours, bronze, black, a dappling of chocolate on white, a lustrous grey on a creamy white, the horns bent like question marks above the dreamy, pacific eyes. All these acres were railed, and fences grew around the shrubby islands of trees where the grass rolled in waves unbroken until they reached each impervious cluster.

If Della said it was English, and if she was right, why did Claire make this demesne beloved in her heart? With each visit she asked herself the question, and although the visits were few the question came again and again – was there never to be a way of claiming its perfection as part of Irishness? Even if the model was foreign, and if to be English was to be foreign, surely this reality lying innocently under the sky could only be Irish?

There was a sense, of course there was, in which her mother was right. Claire knew that: it was a landscape of imagined memory, she could imagine having known it because she remembered reading about it in novel after novel, and not all English novels, surely. That reading had also given her some idea of its vulnerability. She knew, and laughed at the fact as her mother and father laughed, that she identified too strongly with those pastoral idylls which from Goldsmith to Yeats, from Coleridge to Virginia Woolf, had surged green and timbered from page after page. Now when she read in the magazines and newspapers about an old house, an arboretum, a pleached walk, an alley between limes, her mind set up the irritant question – were there sons, were there daughters, was there money? For it not, what might survive? Even in Ireland there were those homes that had passed for great:

Adare Manor, Westport House, Mount Juliet, Doneraile Park, Powerscourt, Straffan, Coolmore. History said, and it was popular to remember the saying, that such mansions were the debris of a system of oppression, colonial exploitation, that they were hated and reviled by a peasantry their inmates themselves hated and reviled. And yet they were beautiful. And Claire had no faith in history; it might explain, it might vindicate, but it had never protected, and it had no argument in favour of loveliness.

> The light of evening, Lissadell,
> Great windows, open to the south. . .

Had Yeats, truly then, been writing only of a class? Not a house? Or in fiction – why had Somerville and Ross set so securely their theme of *The Big House of Inver* in a mirrored obsession – that of the Anglo-Irish? 'And there are very few of us, surely,' thought Claire, 'who are not Anglo-Irish now.'

Once she had hinted at her thoughts in that direction to Leon, who had dismissed them so roundly that she had not followed through. Her mother could have told her that Leon had to banish some ghosts of his own before acknowledging any others, but even without that advice Claire knew that Leon's denial was based on an uneasiness similar to hers.

'I'm a political historian,' he had said. 'I have no philosophy. I can't change the past, and so I don't want to dwell in it – or on it. The future is what I want to influence. The past has no claim on me.'

Listening to this, and more of the same, Claire did not utter the disloyal thought that he had not yet finished his college examinations – who was he to speak of being a political historian? They had been walking through fields by the river, and the bright spring air around them had been ruffled by the wind-beat of a pair of swans flying stretched over the water. Standing to watch them disappear in a distance of hazy waterside trees, knowing that their journey was upriver to the widening stream of Carrigrohane, Claire felt a sweetness grasp her consciousness and turned to Leon, offering the exhilarating loveliness which was yet so ordinary, as part of that rapture of association with the physical world which she felt at that moment was holding them like a cup. Turning, she realised Leon had not waited, but was walking on.

'What kept you?' he asked when she caught up with him.

'The swans,' she said, as simply as that, adding nothing, and he had nothing to say. So, on this evening at Fota, loitering along with her mother, knowing that Della smelt the air as she did, hungered for the wisteria spring as she did, Claire wondered if life with Leon would always be without fragrance, if a future with him would be one without the resonance, the song, of the earth?

Perhaps Leon was right about places like Fota, or Adare on a grander scale? She thought of those words in *Mount Music*, so easily written, it seemed, and yet so possibly, probably true: 'of that special type of old Irish country-house that is entirely remote from the character of the men that originated it, and can only be explained as the expiring cry of the English blood'. Yet surely Edith Somerville knew what she was saying when she wrote that? Was she making an excuse for her own class, her own architecture? And why, even if that were the case, why was it necessary now to pretend to be ashamed of those great windows, open to the south? To watch without lamenting the roof disappear from the shoulders of Woodhill House, and the great walls and woods of Montonotte succumb to the bulldozer, the developer and the civil engineer? Her father could tell her of those two years or three in which the men who were striving to establish the nation burnt such houses to the ground – but there had been, or at least had seemed to be, some reason, some purpose, in that destruction. What had happened since then, Claire felt, had been less inspired, but more relentless – indifference, a casual resentment, a blindness as unseeing as those empty sockets where windows once had been.

Here, as they climbed the lacy iron bridge over the railway tracks Claire and Della looked out to the sleeping estuary, silver in the night, a lake of light spread gently between the darkened shores. They looked back together along what they could see of the path by which they had come this far, and it led their eyes to the massed cumulus of trees around the house, itself invisible, though it stood on the rim of a bowl of unbroken meadowland and a primrose glow showed the cluster of its waking, waiting windows.

Under the porch Raphael Brady stood, irradiated by his consciousness of the link between Carolan the harper and the sponsorship of the concert by the League for the Blind. Through the glass panels of the doors Claire could see Damien Sebright talking to a group of people in the hall, but her immediate attention was caught by Raphael.

'Look,' he was saying to Della, his big hand spread on her elbow. 'I'll show you, Mrs Mackey: come away from the lights here, and look westwards. Wait for a minute, let your eyes get used to the dark.'

Della went without protest, although Claire knew that by now she was feeling the chill of the evening outside. Following the couple, she was led by Raphael's voice, high, anxious, inspired:

'There: *Venus*. And *Jupiter*. I've been watching them and watching. It's a conjunction. They've been coming closer and closer together, and soon, tomorrow or the next night, they'll pass one another. If you watch, you'll be able to see it. About this time, no later. Later, Venus will have disappeared.'

Claire looked at the two faces lifted, absorbed by the sky. Raphael was rapt, his eyes bright as he searched the planets, aeons away from him. Della frowned slightly, anxious to satisfy him, absorbed by his determination to read the universe.

Against Raphael's ruddy profile, Della's skin was white, her ashy hair shadowing her brow. Claire saw a tightness at her mouth, a hollowness around her eyes. It was time to bring her indoors.

'Is it good, or bad, Raphael, a conjunction?' She spoke softly, the moment was tender.

'I don't know,' he answered, his face still bright with his

vision. 'I don't know. But it's beautiful, isn't it?'

He thought, he said, that if Carolan had been able to see such a wonder there would have been a composition about it.

'A stellar slide?' Claire teased him as they moved back towards the house, busy now with arrivals, a conversational hum covering the mildly demented sounds of a harp being tuned.

'At least it isn't raining,' she thought, remembering Damien's telling her once that damp played the devil with a harp. It was Damien, coming towards them through the *enfilade* of yellow pillars in the hall, who remarked on Della's pallor.

'We were looking at the stars,' Claire told him, and Della, anxious now only to sit down, smiled at Raphael and said –

'A conjunction.'

Seats had been reserved for Claire, and she took the press notices off them and found places nearer the fire where Della could sit with a glass of red wine until the concert began. It was time, Claire realised, that she remembered she was there to work. The programme startled her: she looked for Damien to translate the Irish titles, to illuminate the dates. A small platform had been constructed at the far end of the gallery, and upon it stood not a piano but a harpsichord, its panelling painted, the patina webbed with fine cracks. Nearby was a harp, shoulder-high to the player, a young woman with her head bent forward across the strings, the fingers of one hand plucking gently, the other hand twisting and correcting the bevelled pegs as the note slithered in and out of tune.

Searching for Damien, concerned about Della without knowing why, Claire looked back at her mother and noticed that another fireside seat in that row was being taken up by the critic for *The Irish Times*. That meant, if Mrs Neeson was there, it meant that this concert was important. It would be reported in the national press – she dare not get it wrong. Damien was standing, also with a glass of red wine in his hand, between the pillars in the dining room, listening to a man whose face seemed to Claire to be familiar – should she be able to remember the name? Yet she was sure she had never met him.

Damien noticed her efforts to attract his attention without breaking into his conversation.

'Claire,' he said, 'I was sure you'd be here. Do you know Jarleth Tattin?'

God! the Poet Jarleth Tattin, turning to face her now, the big head heavy with hair, the eyes very brown, very round, very bland. She had seen him only in photographs, once a portrait on a programme cover, always looking contained, ungiving. Now he seemed about to smile:

'*The Journal*, is it? Are you a Miss or a *Ms*?'

He emphasised the last word, cutting into Damien's introduction with the sly query.

Claire had to laugh, although she knew she was blushing.

'I agree, I agree,' she acknowledged at once. 'It's terrible, what's happening to the language –'

'Jarleth, be warned, don't start her off on that tack!'

Damien's injunction was so fervent that Claire felt herself blushing again. It made her awkward, conscious that she was in need of help, a need she didn't want to admit in front of Jarleth Tattin.

'I have to do a bit of work on the programme,' she said. 'I was going to ask Damien to fill in a few of my gaps, just to make sure I don't make a *hames* of the job tomorrow.'

She felt Tattin saw through her attempt to disguise her need.

'I'm sure,' his voice was silky, very smooth, 'I'm sure you won't make a *hames* of it. *The Journal* is hardly the most exacting representative of native Irish music in the country, is it?

'No,' he said, before she could answer, or try to answer. 'No – Claire, isn't it? – a little bit of Carolan goes a long way for *The Journal*. But if you are anxious to do something worthwhile about what you're going to hear tonight' – and he folded his arms, and leaned back against the cold, mottled pillar, his gaze not on her although he was talking to her, but reaching over the heads of the moving crowd of which they were themselves a little part – 'tonight listen carefully, and then, if you can, get your friend Damien here to introduce you to his friend the conductor.'

Tattin turned sharply to Damien. 'He is your friend, isn't he, Sebright? Briain Ó Cathasaigh? Isn't he doing a lot these days with the choir at St Dominic's?'

To Claire he said: 'Watch him tonight. Listen to what he can get out of the group he has here, those singers from Inchigeela –' he pronounced it *Inse Géimhleach*, his voice, his attitude suddenly more animated, as though he were concerned despite himself, his interest, or devotion, overriding his reluctance.

'– if you listen, you'll hear a sound which is authentic, although you won't recognise it. Ó Cathasaigh is bringing that sound back – listen when they sing *Cath Chéim an Fhiaidh* – if you know the song you'll know you've never heard it sung like this before, and yet this is the way it has always been sung, where it happened.'

'In Keimaneigh.' Claire thought it was time she let him know she knew something. Conversations like this were always happening to her. No matter how sympathetic she tried to be to people who loved and endorsed and committed themselves to the Irish Language, as Tattin had done by deciding to write only in Irish, no matter how readily she admitted to her own defective skill, her lack of fluency, no matter how carefully she reported their opinions and demands, these people always ended up lecturing her with a disdain which sometimes amounted to distaste. As though there were a supremacy to the Irish which few could match.

She wondered if Ó Cathasaigh would be the same. Directed by Damien she saw him at the harpsichord, a tall, gaunt man, sallow-faced, black-haired, with eyes so dark as to appear black. He was wearing a dark suit, formal, yet looked out of place among this growing gathering of people. Everyone was out of place; this was a private house, but it was also a mansion. Damien's clerical suit probably was not the first to darken its doors, certainly a Church of Ireland minister or two would have visited here many times, but Catholic priests were unlikely guests, she thought. And Raphael would not have been there by invitation, nor she herself. Even Carolan, had he lived to the date of this building, might have been on sufferance, a novelty. The singers, as she saw them assemble, might have been estate workers, asked indoors at Christmas or harvest-time.

Jarleth Tattin was talking to Damien about the programme, saying something of what Claire had been feeling, that perhaps Briain Ó Cathasaigh had been too generous in his expectation of the audience.

'Carolan is all very well, Sebright. Better than that, I know. A few decorous slides, the concerto as a rouser, Fanny Poer for pathos, Bridget Cruise for romance – do you remember, *This is the hand of Bridget Cruise?*'

Although he was not asking her the question Claire thought she remembered: the blind harper was on pilgrimage to Lough Derg and helped to steady passengers on the boat which took them on the lake. Taking the hand of one of them he is said to have declared – '*This is the hand of Bridget Cruise*'; recognising by touch the woman he had once loved dearly. It would do to fill out her review; she would also remember Tattin's other comments, his feeling that the rest of the programme moved away from the harp and the harpsichord to a much fuller medium, the human voice, giving the men such songs to sing as the hardy, tragic or comic ballads of the countryside.

'Briain's point, I think, must be that such melodies were the background, the common artistic expression, of the people among whom Carolan lived. And indeed they were – but this is a drawing-room event. Decorum, I think, is the requirement; nothing less decorus than Thomas Moore, I suspect, has ever sullied these walls.'

Claire, who could sing or recite Thomas Moore until, as her grandmother said, the cows came home, felt inclined to resent this, but she thought she knew what he meant. The gallery was in fact a library, its carpets removed for this occasion, its desk and armchairs nestled into alcoves in the hall where indeed, tonight, they were needed.

To Claire's eyes there was no doubt that the people now filling the hall, walking from its worn exquisite rugs into the green-painted, white-plastered dining room, the sparse rosewood and mahogany re-positioned at the great window facing the dark lawns and fields outside, those people were more inclined for Moore than for Raftery, or Carolan. Yet – 'We're all Irish,' she reminded herself – 'they'll remember the poetry of Raftery from school, they'll remember *Tigh Molaga* just as I do, the only strangeness here for us is this house. And that's part of us too.'

But she would not say any of that to Jarleth Tattin. She studied him as he talked on to Damien and saw that of them all he was completely at his ease in these surroundings, completely at home. A heavy, printed screen stood behind him, behind the pillars against which he leaned, and the dark tweed of his jacket echoed the mottled scenery depicted there. A coloured shirt was matched by his knitted green sweater and a scarf of green and brown silk was knotted, like a cravat, at his throat. Was there something affected about this? In Patrick Street, Claire might have thought so: here it looked right, so right as to make her aware of him as somebody who, for all his apparent familiarity, was not at all familiar to her.

In the gallery the books still coloured the low shelves, the standard lamps had been moved into corners where they shed a friendly glow as people took their seats, shifting the loose chairs and changing rows as they saw friends in the throng, searched for places by the fire which crackled and spat with freshly piled logs.

On her way to join her mother, Claire saw that Raphael was there before her, his head bent over Della's programme, explaining, Claire thought hopefully. Of course he would be doing that – he too had joined the choir at St Dominic's, he too knew Briain Ó Cathasaigh. Damien had been close behind her as they parted from Tattin, but now she saw him back again by the door, squeezed out of the way of people still coming in, talking eagerly to someone else in a black suit, someone who had only just arrived, his hand running hastily through untidy brown hair thick on his forehead. Her heart jumped. It was Anselm Daunt. If he saw her, what would he say to her? What would she say to him, if she had to speak to him?

The air was perfumed, there was the press and softness of furs among the women in the audience, their hair coiffed, they were an elegant display of their husband's wealth. They had stood, Claire thought, unseeing among the splendours of the hall, even those who had gone as far as the wide stone stairway had not looked out through the great window on the half-landing to see what they could not see in the dark, the shallow flights of steps to the terraced lawns, the memorial gate of black arching iron lace to the Italian garden, the trees, the countless trees clustered and apart, not even the leafy edges now of the exotic arboretum perceptible from the house.

She took her place, Raphael moving clumsily, quickly, to accommodate her. All she had to do now was listen, not think. The white-shirted men sitting on the stage were silent, their faces set. The conductor was at the harpsichord, the harpist at her instrument; even the garlands of rococo roses along the mantelpiece were held in the breathing stillness, waiting for the note, the signal.

Chapter 6

'He used to be a wonderful pianist, Brian Casey,' Della said. For a moment Claire was puzzled.

'Briain Ó Cathasaigh? Did you know him?' Most of her mother's youth had been spent abroad, following the drum, as Onorah said, although Stirling had been given most of that time, and Della had no recollection of ever having seen India, or Egypt.

'Your dad knew him. Casey was in the Civil Service for awhile, in the Post Office, I think, before he decided to go into teaching. He was doing some courses at the School of Commerce at the same time as your dad.'

Della squinted up her eyes, praying under her breath for those drivers who did not dip their headlamps as they approached. Claire thought what a small place the city was, how lives could touch and part and stay apart for years and then re-touch. Could it happen, she asked herself, to people who had mattered to one another, been close, been lovers, could it happen that they would separate, depart, then find one another again in the street, in someone's house, at a party or a concert? Could it happen, and how would it be – would it be like Coventry Patmore, 'with tears of recognition never dry'? Or like Carolan – 'This is the hand of Bridget Cruise'?

Raphael was with them, sitting in the back. He lived so near them Della had offered to take him home, not expecting Damien to agree. But both he and Raphael seemed glad of the invitation, and now Raphael sat back, not listening to them, hearing his own music.

'Some of that was really rousing stuff,' said Della. 'I was absolutely fascinated with their version of the "Our Father" – it seemed to have both dignity and pathos, and the way they sang it – just standing there, no accompaniment, just those unadorned masculine voices. It seemed very honest, somehow.'

'A far cry from *Yahweh*, anyway,' Claire was tart, not caring if Raphael heard her. With her ear to an extent accustomed to the plaintive harp, with her imagination stirred by the plangent, plucking harpsichord, it was her soul which had responded to the singers, their voices rough yet still melodious, their harmonies, however delicate, however chosen, sounding firm, and ready, but also grained, as if they would taste of salt if harmony could be tasted.

'I wonder if everybody liked the singers,' Raphael spoke out of his own silence. 'I wonder will they like us when we sing the whole Mass at St Dominic's. Would you say, Mrs Mackey, that they liked the singers tonight?'

Claire sighed, she began to say what did it matter if some people didn't understand, but Della knew that was not the kind of reassurance Raphael needed.

'They were a very polite audience, Raphael,' she explained. 'They weren't the kind of people who get carried away by a tune, you know. They were probably more comfortable with the harp. They would have been more comfortable still with a piano, and with music which would be more familiar to them, Strauss, and a little Liszt perhaps.'

'A touch of Beethoven,' Claire interrupted wickedly, 'a bit of Bach but only a very little bit, a spoonful of Mozart, and lots and lots of "The Merry Widow" or "The Gondoliers".'

She noticed Della did not smile at this familiar mockery, quite unfounded, they both knew that, in any greater musical knowledge or appreciation on Claire's part. In the grey light cast back from their headlamps Claire saw her mother's face had a grey sheen on it, the skin lined loudly.

She had not been uncomfortable during the concert, had she? Claire couldn't remember noticing, and now asked, with some shame at her own lack of awareness, if Della was feeling all right.

'Yes. Fine.' Della was short about it. 'Just a bit of backache. Hard chairs.'

Claire remembered that Della had been stiff after the drive down to Fota, there had been that exclamation in the dusk. A thread of worry began to weave itself into her thoughts about the evening, about the morrow, as she listened to her mother.

'It was a very interesting audience, too, Raphael. There was a lot of money there, builders, stevedores, auctioneers, a lot of solicitors, several butchers, two anaesthetists, two physicians and three surgeons –'

'– But no GPs,' Claire interjected again as if in a game – 'no parish priests, no one from the National Teachers Organisation –'

'At £5 a head, Claire, what would you expect –?' Della knew her city, knew what to expect at any price. 'There were several stockbrokers, and two professors from the university . . .'

'History and music,' Claire reminded herself. 'But no Leon. And one poet. And Damien. And Anselm Daunt.'

'The city's finest,' Della finished, 'and that means, Raphael, that it was a successful evening. All the "right crowd" was there, all the tickets were sold, and that choir has made its way past its first performance in that kind of company, and that's progress. So don't worry about St Dominic's. Just think – if they could be so impressive with the "Our Father" in surroundings like those at Fota, how will the entire Mass sound when it's sung in a church?'

Raphael retired to think about it; would his choir do as well as the singers from Inchigeela, and how would a city congregation react to the Irish – Irish all through from *Introibo* to *Ite Missa Est*?

Claire thought it was funny that Briain Ó Cathasaigh had slipped in the 'Ár nAthair' at all into the programme for that evening. Nothing, she thought, was as it seemed: Ó Cathasaigh had had a reason for every item in that programme, from the cultured pleasantries of Una Halpin's harp to his own pungent playing, not all of it Carolan. 'In his own way,' she thought, 'he was lecturing us. But perhaps he had a right.' She still wasn't sure about how she would write her review, what phrases would come to add to her notes, how much of Damien's commentary she could use without having to endure his subsequent mockery. She had the weekend to think about it, although she knew that if she thought about it too much she would do a bad job – make a *hames* of it, as she had predicted to Jarleth Tattin.

Now there, as her grandmother would have said, was 'a queer hawk'. The appellation was accurate, Claire sensed something predatory about him, an ability to move swiftly, strike silently, for all his big frame, heavy, grey-maned head. And an ability to take on a protective colouring: camouflage.

'I couldn't help thinking,' Della was continuing her thoughts aloud, 'what Mrs Cummins would have said if she'd seen some of the people there tonight. Bridie Conway – did you ever know her? All fur and Sybil Connolly now, but, as Mrs Cummins would have said, "It's far from Fota she was reared." That's the worst thing about this city, no one ever forgets where you came from.'

'I think its one of the best things,' Claire was laughing at her mother's recovery of spirit. 'It can make life very easy for me, sometimes, even if I can't use all the personal information I'm given.'

'Whenever I come to something like this, which is mostly thanks to *you* –' Della was being kind to Claire – she knew that her invitations were often spurred by Claire's need for a drive to a particular job. '– I remember, I can't remember who said it – *always be nice to the girls, you never know who they'll marry . . .*'

'Like Angela.' Claire was not kind in that, but she did not mean to hurt. She loved her sister, but resented, Cordelia-like, having to seem to be part of a consensus of adoration.

'Yes,' said Della, smugly enough to make Claire grin.

'I wish,' Della said, stretching her head beyond her steering wheel, 'I wish I could get away from this slow coach in front of us, we'll be on the road all night.'

'Are you very tired?' Claire was amazed by the sound of those words, slow coach; she had never thought what they really meant before, they had always come glibly to her tongue, *slowcoach*. Differently accented, separated as her mother had separated them now, the words were alive with a meaning beyond this usage; they rang with the weight of a coach, with the jangle of harness, with the rocking, head-bent gait of a draught horse, dragging its load of passengers.

'Well, it's been a long day.' Della would admit to no more. To Claire it seemed as if she led a secret life, mapped in its obvious limitations – Mass, as on this morning, with Frank, then shopping and a coffee in town, in The Green Door, perhaps, where 'the girls', all now over fifty, would be waiting for her. Then an hour or so with Onorah, home for Frank's dinner at 1.30, then housework and the garden and often Angela, a walk with Bran, and in the evening some charity gathering, or a visit to one of her 'cases', or a whist-drive with Frank. Seasons of the year and of the Church changed these elements around, yet they remained otherwise unvarying components of her life. How was it, wondered Claire, that around these predictable shorelines flowed the stream of the other life, the life reaching back to the time of coaches which might be slow, must often have been slow, she had never heard anyone talk of a quick coach. Della would not have been reared to carriages, yet often in her childish play on the streets or in the laneways of Calcutta or Cairo she must have had to skip out of the way of some lumbering vehicle, ox-drawn perhaps, or waved at a glistening equipage on its polished route to Government House.

She said she did not remember. All she remembered, all she ever told Angela and Claire about, were her brothers' pranks with a donkey-cart in Stirling. But those same brothers, time-changed into uncles, delighting in Della's effortless assumption of middle-class ease after her marriage to Frank, delighted also in threatening, with each visit, to tell the patiently amused

Frank, the always-thrilled children, what Della had got up to in her girlhood in Scotland. To 'spill the beans', they had said, and Claire remembered wondering what beans they were, how they might spill like little glossy nuggets of information from a bag made of thicknesses of paper, stitched with twine up the sides, like the flour-bags from Woodford Bourne's on Fridays, or the grain-bags for her grandmother's hens.

Finding her way clear on the clear stretch of road, Della sped past the dawdling cars, and changed gear to cruising speed. When she spoke it was to revert to the earlier conversation.

'If anything happened to me,' said Della, who did not often confide in Claire, 'I think that's what I'd resent most of all, not being around to find out what happens to people. And to places.'

Claire was still too young to understand how often Della and Frank must be surprised at the way things had turned out, not least their own lives.

'Do you mean the girls? Who they marry?'

'That,' Della nodded. She belonged to a generation in which a woman's success in life was publicly measured by the success of the man she married. She had been able to understand why Wallis Simpson had wished to marry the King of England – what else could a truly ambitious woman do? In Ireland it was still possible for a woman to achieve renown of a local kind through the fame of her sons. She began to smile as she remembered the story of the woman who runs out of her suburban house screaming for help – 'My son the engineer is drowning!'

'I didn't tell you I was at St Brigid's today with Gran, visiting Mrs Bracken.'

Claire thought that this might be why her mother was weary; St Brigid's, a private nursing home, confined its ancient patients to a regime of ruthless uniformity, against which only their geriatric waywardness offered any resistance. She knew that despite reassurances, Onorah's fear as her age advanced was that she too might find a place at St Brigid's – 'a bed', was how it was described; not a room, not a home.

Della and Frank and Angela and Stan and Della's brothers – less fervent in their case because of wives – all had promised Onora that this could not, would not happen. Claire had overheard one of these attempts to lull Onora into quietude:

'Don't worry, Gran,' she had said cheerfully – 'I promise you now that I'll hit you hard on the head with a very heavy hammer rather than let you go anywhere other than into a hospital or a grave.' In the appalled glance of her mother she read unsurprised condemnation, but from Onora Claire met a gaze of startled gratitude. Onora could not tell her children or her grandchildren that she would rather be dead than 'cared for'. It was some consolation, as she prepared for that time in which she would not be allowed to decide what to do for herself, in which she would be encouraged, then quickly forced, to relinquish all control over the smallest aspect of her life, it was some help to know that one member of her family understood the terror of it.

'No,' Della was responding to what Claire had not said. 'It wasn't bad, today. Mrs Bracken's son had been down earlier – he came down from Dublin, I gather, just to visit her, and she was much better than usual. No – what I was thinking of was the way the old ladies were talking afterwards. Liam Bracken is a priest, and of course Mrs Bracken's stock went up several points when he arrived, even the Matron went in to see him with his mother, offered him tea, all the doings. By the time we got there all the old dears were talking about it, and I heard Mrs Carlisle – you know she's deaf, and she forgets that everyone else isn't – she was asking if anyone else had priests in their family. And poor blind Mrs Barriscale, over in the corner by herself, you know how little she ever has to say, she spoke up for once: "*No*," she said, and I'll swear she was being sarcastic, "*no priests in our family. Just bank managers* . . ."

'And *that*,' Della concluded with a grin, 'put what Gran would call the kybosh on the general conversation for a while.'

Claire was laughing too – she relished the savagery of the indomitable old ladies, shorn of everything except some need to keep alive, yet finding from somewhere the venom with which to do harm, to affect, to make their claim to notice. She endorsed, when she knew of them, her grandmother's acts of minor rebellion, her surges of independence, of defiance. What would be so terrible, she had challenged her mother, if Onora went on the bus to Mass, and fell, and broke her hip, and died of pneumonia? Onora was old, she expected to die. It would be better, surely, to die while still active, still, for this was true of Onora as of Della, curious about what was going to happen, how things turned out. Della acknowledged that her daughter had a point, but she had no intention of applying that attitude to her care of her mother.

It was a terrible thing, Della knew, to have nothing but death to wait for, but sudden death, untimely death, she could not welcome either. Except, perhaps, as a release – Irish people were always great at identifying what they called, at funerals, 'a happy release'. Pain might make you want to go, but death should not be the only means of escaping pain. If pain made you welcome death, maybe it could be said to have its uses, making the inevitable acceptable, even yearned for, as death was supposed to be, as it was said to have been for the saints. Driving past the heronries, the great woods at Dunkettle, Della could not imagine herself wanting to die.

'I think,' she said to Claire's easy silence, 'I'd feel really cheated if I never found out what happens.'

'But you might disapprove of a lot of it,' rejoined Claire, whose own sense of curiosity was very highly developed, 'and then what could you do about it? I like Gran's old age, where she's not surprised by anything any more, and not inquisitive either. That must be a state approaching peace, I think.'

'And not surprising, if it were true, given that she has survived two world wars, a revolution, an economic war, a civil war, and the granting of independence in several countries, including her own –' Della believed in reminding young people of the endurance of the old. She thought it might comfort them, or in some cases, Claire was an example, remind them that all they knew was not all there was to know.

'And isn't it true?' Claire was not indifferent to the reminder, although she thought she had no need of it.

'That Gran has no curiosity any more? I don't know. It would be nice to think that it could mean she's not afraid any more, has nothing left to be afraid of. But there's that old thing about hostages to fortune, children, you know – as long as you have children you'll fear what might happen to them.'

Sweeping smoothly up the dual carriageway, Della relaxed her grip on the steering wheel, her knuckles flexed, her fingers lighter, more open on the corrugated rim.

'I mean,' Della said, 'I can't imagine a state in which I wouldn't want to know about what happens to Angela. Or to you,' she added in time.

In the back seat Raphael began to sing. The lights of the city bloomed into white flowers on the river, a strong black current flowing under the bridges.

> Agus thart le Roth na Maoile,
> Agus síos go Cruach na Caoile,
> An Cloigeann lena thaobh sin,
> 'S Trá Bhríde 'na dhiaidh –
> Nó gur dhóirt muid le fána
> Thrí fharraige 's i cáthaidh
> Go ndeacha muid don Rátha
> Mar is ann a bhí ár dtriall . . .

He was singing 'Caiptín Ó Máille', a ballad of a disaster at sea, among the islands of Mayo and Connemara. It was only vaguely familiar to Claire, although the men at the concert tonight had sung it, one man rather, the others rowing in – and how apposite the phrase had been for this strong rhythmically surging melody carried on the stark male voices – as the danger and the terror overwhelmed the crew. Now Raphael was singing the Captain's part, the last desperate verse, as the men have tried to swim for it and the Captain is alone hauling on the ropes in an effort to swing the sail around on to the wind.

Agus tá mo lámha stróiche
Go síorraí 'tarraingt rópaí,
Tá an croiceann is an fheoil
Is á tarrangtha 'mach ón gcnáimh.
Ach más é an bás a gheall Mac Dé dhúinn
Cén mhaith a bheith dhá shéanadh
Ach ag gabháil go Flaitheas Dé dhúinn
In aon staid amháin.

Raphael's voice, raw, unexpectedly hard, made the words of resignation harsh. The agony came through: hands striated, ripped from hauling on the rigging, the skin and the flesh torn from the bone. Ah, said the Captain, if this was the death the Son of God had chosen for these men, what was the good of denying it; better to go to the Heaven of God, all of them, all in the one state.

The little world of the car began to fade under the regular flash of the street lights as they passed. Della said that the song she had liked most, after the 'Our Father', had been the one about Keimaneigh, although she had not understood it, except to know because she had been told, that it was about a battle, or a massacre. Claire had liked that too; it had a strong internal rhyming pattern which made the sound of it compelling. The men had sung it with a textured sweetness, because the melody lifted and swung and sank again, a sweetness that denied the song's stark hatreds. It was a song of their district – 'in Uibh Laoire 'sea bhímse' – set in the valleys they knew. They might have made the song.

'I mean,' Della said, 'history is what we live through, even if we don't always notice it. It's our life. It's only later when we can see from a different time that we can see from a different point of view, as well.

'I mean,' she wanted to explain herself, to herself, 'I mean – look at Dubček. Did the Czechs know what was happening when he began his reforms? Not enough of them, anyway. They must see it differently now, with the Russians encouraging them. That's what I mean: if anything happened to me, I'd miss not having the opportunity to find out what happens in the *end*.'

Claire was reminded of a book she had been given to review by *The Journal*; written by an émigré Hungarian noblewoman, it told of the vast changes in her family's fortunes through the tides of the First and Second World Wars. It also told, in passing, of one of the author's aunts who had decided, when offered a means of escape, to stay on, just to see how it would all turn out.

'Let me know,' Della said as the car panted quietly at the traffic lights, 'if you see any more about public events at Fota coming up during the next few months. When your dad and I went down with the Garden Club in the summer he was really taken with it. We wandered off by ourselves at one point, and got into the orchards, the real thing, you know, cordons and espaliers, he was delighted. And then a small gate leads into another garden where there are rows and rows of greenhouses, some built like enormous cold-frames, very low, with steps going down into them. He was like a child. We both were.'

Claire could imagine them, clucking and exclaiming among the vines and terracotta, sharing, like children indeed, the joys of furtive exploration.

'I suppose Dad was putting Latin on everything,' she said lightly, her mind sheering away from an imprint of secrecy. It was inconsequential, it should not be disturbing to picture her parents hand in hand, gleeful middle-aged conspirators. Interlopers.

'The thing was – is – that Latin is on everything already. The whole place is wonderfully kept up in that way – a bit untidy, you saw the borders yourself, wonderful plants but quite a lot of weed as well, but it's all labelled, not the weeds, I mean, but the shrubs and the seed trays, even the pears and the plums, they all have little tags.

'What I liked most, though,' Della had come to the new turning for the avenue which gave on to Raphael's home, a gap in a lane of trees. Moving slowly, the car crunched on leaves, the headlights shining on the blackening boles, the weathered, striated trunks.

'What I liked most was the potting sheds – *were* the potting sheds –' she had heard Claire's indrawn breath – 'they were so tidy, and still they had a smell, an odour of earthiness, and of manure. Your dad said that was the secret – *muck* – and I suppose he's right. And then, on the wall of one of the sheds, the one with the rows and rows of upturned clay pots, and wooden wheelbarrows, up on the wall were pinned hundreds of prize-cards, First Prize for pelargonium, second prize for paeony – did I tell you what Mrs Cummins said yesterday when she saw your dad lifting the two old clumps near the garage?'

She lowered her voice, making a quick nod behind to see if Raphael was listening; she supposed this wasn't really *suitable*.

'Mrs Cummins was bringing in the washing, last thing before she went home, it must have been about six because your dad went into the garden the minute he got in from the office, he was worried about a frost. So they passed one another on the grass, and she left the line to go up to have a chat with him, and she saw what he was doing, and she said – "Oh, Mr Mackey, what a shame to dig them up, them penises is gorgeous!"'

A loud laugh, quickly stifled, merged with the mirth of Della and Claire. Raphael had been listening, he had felt the car slow down, he knew he was home. He was still sniggering when he left them, half-ashamed of his enjoyment of the joke.

Driving quickly away while he stood waving at them in the yard, Della said aloud what she had often thought – why could not Claire's friends, those young fellows, that Fr Sebright, other men in the choir, come and give Raphael a hand to clear up the squelching yard and rotting outhouses? When Claire said that Mrs Brady wouldn't allow what she called 'Christian or Turk' into the place and that Raphael couldn't go against his mother, Della still urged her to try to do something.

'It can't be good for him, Claire, to live like that. And I hate to think of what the inside of the house might be like. I must say

I thought several times tonight that it must be some time since Raphael washed himself – it isn't fair to let him get into that kind of condition, he's too good, he tries too hard to please.'

'That's the trouble.' Claire knew that something should be done. 'It's so easy to hurt him; if I said anything like that to him he'd never talk to me again, or maybe to anyone else, he'd just retreat; and that would make him even more dependent on anyone who seemed to approve of him totally, or else on his mother.'

'Well, I always said she wasn't the full shilling, even when Mr Brady was alive. I don't know, but you should at least ask the others about it, before it's too late to help him to change.'

There was nothing that Claire could say, but a burden settled on her mind, made more tangible by her mother's next query:

'Where did you say that little girl was taken – the little girl you were telling me about, whose father drowned? Where is she?'

'They said she was with the Good Shepherd sisters in Sunday's Well. Peacock Lane, isn't it? Where the laundry is?'

That was an orphanage, as well as a refuge, of sorts, for prostitutes, what Frank called 'fallen women', who worked the laundry run by the nuns. Della said no more, but Claire was glad, as they swung back on the riverside roadway and the deep valley of the tide could be seen tossing in their light, that her mother might take an interest in the child, might not let her be forgotten. It was some antidote to her own sense of failure.

Her sharp cry made Della stamp on the brake:

'Stop! There's Bran – he must have got out.'

The dog had run frantically towards the car, almost throwing himself, in his welcome, against its wheels. When they came to a violent stop Claire leaned behind to let him in, scolding him, praising him, that was no way to behave, he was a wonderful dog, what was he doing out on the road, and he whined and writhed on the back seat. Laughing with relief, she looked at her mother, and saw her face was bleached, her eyes staring, her lips drawn tightly against each other.

Frightened, she touched Della's hand, tight on the wheel.

'Mum,' she said, the word softening her touch. 'Mum – he's all right. It's all right.'

For a few more terrifying seconds Della was immobile. Very slowly then she moved her head around so that she could look at Claire. She sighed, deeply, helplessly, as if her body were collapsing.

'Yes.' Her voice was very light, the word was only a breath. 'I got a fright. I thought he was done for. You shouted – I thought he was gone.'

She did not look at Bran, who had subsided into an anxious silence. Very carefully, she let in the clutch and drove with great concentration down the remaining stretch of road to the avenue. Claire went to get out to open the doors of the garage, but Della said no, she'd leave the car in the avenue tonight, it would come to no harm, it wasn't cold enough for a heavy frost, Frank wouldn't mind.

Before she opened the car door she reached back to Bran, and fondled his ears, and told him with caresses that he was a mad creature, a demon, a villain. How had he got out, she said, so far down the road, the rogue. The dog squirmed, his moans rising into yelps of ecstasy and adoration. With every inch along the path to the house he grovelled, ready to leap into Della's arms if only she would let him. Della walked slowly, Claire had the door open before her, the light on in the hall casting a latticed shadow on the paving. Frank was in bed, and Claire wanted to make tea, something hot to revive her mother, so subdued there was a suggestion almost of absence. But Della said no, she would go straight upstairs, and she clutched the banister, calling goodnight to Bran who was gulping water in the kitchen.

The dog came to the foot of the stairs, and watched Della climb, before curling into an abject heap, his bearded chin resting on the lowest stair. He would stay there all night, Claire knew, his ears alert for any sound from the bedrooms, any suggestion that Della might come down again.

What must it be like, Claire asked herself in her own room,

to be feeling ill, or tired, and to have to lie down next to another body? Married people did it all the time – what must it be like? As a child there had been a delicious cosiness in fitting between her mother and father, although Angela had ofter been there before her. It had been all warmth and softness, a powdery smell from her mother's skin, a rasp of beard when she touched her father's amazing, sleep-ridden face. Once she had slept in Onora's bed, placed right underneath the small, small-paned window; there had been a window at each end of that wonderful bedroom. That had been for Angela's Confirmation; the treat was that Angela would sleep at Whitethorn, given for that one night the mysterious room used only by uncles. And Claire, not to be left out completely, had slept with Onora. There was a distinct smell in that whole house, the red soap that Onora used to wash the floors and sinks, and at the top of the steep stairs there was a window where the sun came in to make scented powder of the dust. This light and sweetness met the soapy smell, and then there was the meal in the hen-box adding its own pungent odour. All these smells she knew, could recapture still when she visited her grandmother, but there was nothing anywhere to describe, or to reproduce, the smell of the sitting room, where things were kept for 'good', where no one ever sat, where a maidenhair fern shivered in a corner, where a vanished grandmother, unknown aunts and uncles stared back solemnly, where the cabinet stood from which, on Sundays, Angela was allowed to take the tea service, its violets shaking in her shaking hands, wistful against the white iridiscent ribbing of the china.

Claire could remember waking that night to see her grandmother at the dressing-table, disguised by a nightgown so white and so encompassing she thought at first it must be a tablecloth. In the light of the candle which Onora for some years after that had preferred to gas in the bedrooms Claire watched the long coil of hair slip from its pins, curling against the white shoulders. Her grandmother used a tortoise-shell comb to free each crackling strand, black at the end, black too but greying at the scalp, and then her fingers braided the hair so that it lay across her shoulder, against her breast. When she doused the candle there was light in the room, and Claire saw her stand at the far window as though she were looking out; for minutes without moving she gazed beyond the glass, not as though she were watching, Claire thought, but as if she were waiting.

At her own window Claire drew the curtains back. She would go to sleep without reading tonight, she would not turn on the light. Lifting the latch she looked into the dark, and saw the sinking stars, and thought of Raphael's incantation, *Arcturus, Sirius, Betelgeuse.* From the river came the peeking exclamations of the colonies of birds on the mud-flats and estuary shores, they always made a noise as if they were jostling one another, shifting for room. Over this noise, but nearer, feathering the air, came the ripple of a curlew's call, its echo drifting until it too sank into obedient sleep.

Chapter 7

Because her report of the alleged beating-up of two young members of Sinn Fein by the local gardai had shown a sympathy unusually consistent with the known facts of the case Claire had been offered an outing, a sign of approval.

'Do you mean they asked for me, specially?' She was dismayed when the news editor told her about the marking.

'I'm not sure their approval is all that important to me. *And*' – she had a decisive point – 'my Irish isn't good enough. You know when they get on the campaign trail they're very pure.'

The problem was that the diversifications of the political process towards entry to the European Economic Community were stretching *The Journal's* resources beyond its never very flexible limits. The major political parties had to be given the space, the time, they thought they deserved; then there were the interested groupings. There were hidden partnerships of consensus. Affiliations undreamed of in the previous half-century suddenly appeared not just possible but right. Europe had been discovered; it was accepted that there were more cities than Rome on the Continent.

Claire had lingered in the office, waiting until she could run across to Woolworths to be picked up by Frank for the trip home. Her day had been calm, setting up an entertainments page, finding photographs, going to the stone with a sub-editor, finishing a column of copy explaining, or extolling, the important attractiveness of French film-making. That was work she liked. Although it had no stretch in it, it took her to the machinery and to the men who worked the machinery, from the blocks in the picture editor's office and the gangling photographic apprentice to the massive drums of the presses, the men here shirt-sleeved and hearty, sitting at keyboards as big as pianos. It was dirty, but it was the dirt of work, of oil and steel and the congealed, nostril-tightening smell of grease and newsprint. Claire liked to walk along the gang-plank above the presses, to go from the light-filled atrium of the main commercial office through a door, down half-a-dozen steps, and into this cavernous, littered engine room, like the engine room of a ship, the bowels of the power which drove them all at *The Journal*. She liked the words the men used – the slugs, the chase, the flong, the rotary hoes. Sometimes, when her copy was questioned for an insertion or a typed confusion, she would stand by the linotype machine and see the sorts rattle from the magazine on to the line: she enjoyed the sense of a machinery which could select letters to match her words, spurred by the man's fingers on the keys. The lines were framed on the great polished bench called the stone; the cliché line left intact, the frames tightened around the columns of metal, the impression taken and sent to the castors, to the mould, to the molten lead, to the trimmer, to the rollers and clamps and finally to the clean wheels of newsprint, crisply odiferous of fir, of pines mounting in green ranks to a cold northern sky.

In here, among the fertile spray of steel and skill, somewhere in here were the processes which gave the word that meant her work – the press. In usage, even by herself, Claire saw the distance there was between the groan as tons of pressure to a square inch squashed the flong, and what was meant by the word: Press Barons, Press Council, a free Press, Pressman, the Press. It was an easy word, accepted, put to use. That day it had been put to the use of a woman who had come in to the Reporters' Room with the photograph of her daughter's wedding. Claire was on duty, took the photograph and the barely intelligible paragraph of information which accompanied it.

Smiling for the camera were a woman in white, a man in a dark suit, neither of them young, both of them, on this evidence, happy. Their names were given, their unmarried addresses were in London although the bride was a local girl. The picture was to go in *The Journal* with the added information that the groom had been received into the Catholic Church at Brompton Oratory two weeks before the wedding. Claire tried to explain that it was unlikely that this fact would be published; it was private, wasn't it? Was the bride's mother sure that the groom wanted everyone to know? The bride's mother had no doubt at all that everyone should know. Her daughter, she said earnestly, had 'turned' him. It had taken years, she said in a whispered confidence; *years*, and praying all the time. For the sake of the children: Claire would understand. Looking at the couple, sensing through the picture the stiff, expectant white of the dress, the scented silk of the petals around the veil, the sweat of the roses too tightly clutched, Claire understood that if this pair had wanted children, they should not have waited for him to 'turn'.

Crusades, Claire thought, something she already knew, were very queer things. And people would indulge in them. The superiority of her disdain for the mother of the bride had smudged a little – those sweet expiring roses must have done it – by the time she was told of this next assignment. The Sinn Fein crusade against the Common Market deserved its press. The news editor said it wasn't altogether Sinn Fein, but a combination of Republican interests – 'shooting each other six months ago' was Claire's comment on this cohabitation – taking their message to the south-west, to the fishing towns and smallholdings of that indented coast. Claire's job would be to report the speeches, assess the local response, describe the atmosphere.

'More of a colour piece,' the news editor said. 'Although' – as he saw the first gleam of interest in her eyes – 'we don't want you to get carried away. It's their polemic, not yours, that we'll be printing. Or some of it. And it's not so much that they asked for you, as that they liked your coverage of the Duffy case.'

Claire was not appeased. Journalistic anonymity was a valuable discretion in a small city. But there had been no mystery about her reporting. She had been seen at the police station, and at the hospital. She had been the first of the reporters to find Diarmuid Duffy's sister, to sit in the weeping kitchen near the Sand Quay and hear out the evidence from the closest she could come to a witness.

'There was a priest there, wasn't there? Going to give evidence? He's in charge of this trip, maybe he's the one who knows you.'

The news editor knew that Claire's story on the Duffy assault might have got them all into trouble – all meaning *The Journal* – were it not for the endorsement by that priest.

'A Fr Daunt. From The Grove?'

Claire knew where he was from. 'Yes. He was there.'

She had seen him striding through the hall of the North City hospital. She had followed him, herself at a loss, unable to think of a way to get beyond the bodies of uniformed gardai, the plain-clothes Special Branch men. Daunt had not noticed her, or seemed not to notice her, as she joined him where he talked to a detective; then she simply followed him through the cordon, head bent, clutching the handbag with its notebook to her chest, saying only 'I'm with *him*,' in a tragic mutter as the police made way. They had not known her, they were not the men who had seen her at the police station. They had known Anselm Daunt, and saluted him. And she had known him and had followed him.

The two bandaged men had lain in a two-bedded ward. All those guards outside and these two, helpless, in here. It was as if all the force of which the law was capable had been coerced into a massive fraud, some trick of deployment by which the decoys would engage the attention while the evil would be done nakedly with no one looking. A conjurer's trick, with the same unreality. What was real was that the men inside, the men outside, and Claire learned more of the truth of this as she listened to Diarmuid Duffy talk to Anselm Daunt, calling him 'Father' – those men were on opposite sides of an ancestral hatred. She had heard her father speak of it, had listened while other men explained to one another how it was, yet she had never understood the survival of that deadly inherited animosity to this point; the remnants of a Republican, thirty-two-county Irish-speaking Catholic Ireland faction refusing to recognise the twenty-six-county English-speaking Catholic State or its officers, while the officers of the State recognised more than was there, surely much more than was really there, translating the slogan-daubing, the maudlin speeches, the selling of Easter Lilies, into the very flower of revolution, hot, palpable, and deadly dangerous.

'That's all you know about it,' Leon had taunted her some time before. He had stayed away long enough for her to notice that he had difficulty finding a reason to pretend that nothing had happened. Accepting her metaphor, he said that what the State did recognise accurately were the seeds of the flower of revolt. It was suspicion which would not die away. Suspicion bred fear, fear bred hatred – and here the hatred had lain before her, sutured, bound, and fervent with victimisation. In Diarmuid Duffy's voice as he spoke of being hammered, in the bright eyes of his silent, broken-jawed companion, a jubilant hatred flourished. Listening, writing down what she heard, Claire heard the priest console the men with a grim slogan – '*Tiocfhaid ár lá*' – Our day will come.

Amazed at the openness of it Claire looked directly at Anselm Daunt and saw that he had known what he was saying, had known that she was there to hear it. He met her startled eyes with something like a smile, a question in his face – 'What are you going to do about this, then?'

She had done what she could. She had not resorted to poetry, had been unemotional and fair to both sides, and had scraped past the *sub judice* embargo with just enough room to spare to satisfy *The Journal*'s lawyers. And that was her reward.

'Mind yourself with those Shinners,' one of the court reporters warned her with a leer.

'They've great sex appeal, those gunmen. Great *charisma*.'

'Oh, the purity of the gun,' another man taunted, although he grinned. Claire had no answer to this innuendo. She tried a cryptic comment and achieved meaninglessness and fled down the stairs wondering, as she took them two at a time, when she would have what Onora called 'words at will' with which to defend herself against the glib, the snide, and quite possibly the accurate.

The city was gilded with spring, with unexpected warmth, and Frank took the long road home, along the riverside, under the lime-green, tender trees. He spoke thoughtfully about Claire's trip to the west, sensing it was worrying her, believing that there was nothing for her to worry about.

'You should know from your friend Leon that these people are part of this country's life, rightly or wrongly. They're here, and perhaps they're here to stay. No harm in getting to know what they're like, what they're up to, even. If you don't know already, that is.'

The sidelong glance he gave her with this didn't take the harshness out of it. Claire had no way of counteracting her father's dislike of Leon. It was distrust, not as cryptic as Della's, not as amused as Onora's tolerance, but more pointed in its meaning, if more oblique in its expression.

'What you have to ask, Claire,' said Frank as he made the turn to reverse into the garage, his voice coming from over his shoulder, from the shadows of the walls, 'is whether these people, in their cry for freedom, are looking for freedom, or for power.

'Now,' he said, his hands resting on the settled steering wheel. 'We are living in a time of great change, and great opportunity. This could be the time when all that crowd, *Saor Eire* and *Sinn Fein* and the *IRA*, decide to abandon their military pretensions, to stop calling themselves an army, and to take the political path. This could be the time for it to happen – and this could be your chance to watch it happening, and to reveal it.'

'Your friend Leon Dowden,' he said, the slam of the car door behind him giving an unfair emphasis to his words, 'will agree with me there. But he's looking to the left, he could get sucked into the Maoist agitation, what there is of it, and inexorably he could find himself on the extreme edge of radical reform in Ireland – and that can be very extreme indeed. So watch that, too.'

Why was Frank talking to her like this? Claire stood beside him on the path between the apple trees and the clumps of wide-leaved reddening rhubarb. Frank never did talk to her like this – had someone been saying something to him about Leon? Should she tell him that she didn't think she'd be seeing so much of Leon any more? No – she hadn't made up her mind about that, yet. And anyway that wasn't what he was talking about, it wasn't her and Leon, it was Leon himself. Stan must have been talking to Frank; politically the two men were tuned, as Leon said, to the same frequency if that, said Leon, could be called politics.

'It's economics, Claire,' he had protested, persuading her of his analysis. That had been only a week ago, after the Duffy case.

'Stan comes from a long line of merchant princes, and of landowners. Your dad – he's a bureaucrat, a civil servant, committed to the viability of this State. They can't help themselves, they see the left as an invasion, like the Vikings – but, as with the Vikings, they'll come to accept the need for change. It's been done before. This is our opportunity to do it again, to begin to make it happen, as a political counterweight to the EEC, a socialist argument against the capitalist amalgamation. Capitalism is uneven – that's our great truth; it doesn't work for everybody.'

'Socialism,' Frank said, ushering her in front of him, their steps accustomed to the tulips, the serried narcissi, the burgeoning blue canopy of the ceanothus in a corner by the tool-shed, 'doesn't work for everybody, Claire. It pretends to – its creed is equality. But I know' – and he stood by the green timber door to the backyard, his words blurred by Bran's staccato welcome on the other side – 'I know how unequal equality really is, how jealously people will guard their differences, how fiercely they will fight not to have to share. Your friend Leon won't ever be able to do very much about that, Claire. Not in this country.'

He turned the handle on the door and flailed at the leaping, ecstatic dog, the clamour not bringing Della to the window. Her absence was explained when they reached the kitchen, its saucepans murmuring on the cooker. The sounds came to them there of a great orchestra being led by a human voice. In the hall, filled with the light of the spring evening, with the vibrating shadows of the leaves of the limes in the avenue trembling through the glass of the front door, the voice was closer, stronger, filled with anguish and with joy, the words in German, the music of Strauss, the voice of Schwarzkopf. The 'Four Last Songs'.

'Fr Sebright brought me down for the afternoon,' said Raphael, getting awkwardly to his feet from the sofa where he sat at Della's side, explaining, exculpatory. Frank went to turn down the music, his eyes sharper as he looked at Della, who had put her hand on Raphael's worn sleeve, soothing him. Claire noticed her father's narrowed eyes and spoke, not to Della, but to Raphael: it was lovely to see him, it was great he had been allowed out, she would just fix things up in the kitchen for their meal, would he like to help her?

'It was only because Fr Sebright said that Mrs Mackey wasn't very well, that she couldn't visit me, that's why I came. And Fr Sebright rang Mrs Mackey to see was it all right, and then Mrs Mackey said would I stay to eat something, so I'm waiting for Fr Sebright to come down for me –'

Claire put her arm around his as she brought him into the kitchen. The awful thing was, she thought, that when Raphael had begun this descent into mania the flow of his words had had a terrible radiance, as if they might burn to the touch, but it was an irradiation, illumination bursting from the centre, very bright, most beautiful. He had seen Christ in Patrick Street. He had been consumed by a vision of the loveliness of ordinary things. At Mass one Sunday, at the elevation of the Host, he had left his place in the choir and stood before the altar, rapt, transcendant, waiting for his feet to lift him from the terrazzo steps, to begin the ascent into Heaven. When it did not happen he wept, stumbling through the queues of only slightly daunted faithful waiting to receive Communion from the unperturbed but watchful priest. Damien reached for him, his arms outstretched for pity, and held him until the sobbing fervour faded in the sunlight of an echoing porch.

It was Claire who was called to take him away from a meeting of Pentacostalists – he was too charismatic for them. He had prayed with loud exaltation, he had stood while everyone else was kneeling, he had prostrated himself in an agony of abasement and submission on the missionary carpets of the convent in which they held their meetings. This was extreme, but fervour was acceptable. Even those who were not embarrassed, however, found that they could not tolerate what Raphael meant by speaking in tongues. The trouble was, they had understood the words. This was not the gibberish of the Holy Ghost, as a raging Claire said viciously to Damien afterwards, this was, they thought, much worse – this was *language*. He told them their sins. Somewhere in his life he had picked up an idea of the romance of mundane experience, he had learned to listen for secrets. These he now told with spellbinding vigour, his joyous eyes burning as the Paraclete spoke through him, urging repentance, threatening damnation. He knew who the unmarried mother was, he knew who had left a wife, who had left a convent, the treasurer who had been quietly banned from his sports and social club he knew, he knew the alcoholic and the spoiled priest. He did not condemn them, the Holy Ghost did not condemn them, but tongues of fire illuminated the bent heads which heard, horrified, their sins being radiantly forgiven. Was not she who was taken in adultery forgiven?

An adulterer who had not been taken – or at least not quite as the Bible had it – decided that this had gone far enough. *'For we wrestle not against flesh and blood,'* shouted Raphael as two men wrestled him to the door, *'but against principalities, against powers, against the rulers of the darkness of this world, against spiritual wickedness in high places!*

'Wherefore,' he shrieked against the obdurate door they had shut on him, *'take unto you the whole armour of God; That ye may be able to withstand in the evil day. And having done all – to stand!'*

He had stood with his forehead pressed to the wall of the room they had found for him. His skin was hot, he was burning. When Claire came he had stopped shouting, but he was not exhausted. She put her hand to his brow, dismissing the by now half-ashamed murmurs of the men who had telephoned for her at *The Journal* office. The bulb of tissue in his throat jerked when she spoke to him, saying only his name. His skin was dry, but his eyes were lambent. At her touch he took her hand and put it to his lips, kissing it. She did not recoil from the hand with its red bones, from the moist, over-ripe mouth.

'They are not ready to welcome me, Claire.' He was not denunciatory, though he spoke with an energy which convinced her she had better not try to take him away with her just yet. She listened to him as they were left alone.

'Ah, Claire,' Raphael said, still holding her hand. 'We must love one another. *"He that loveth not knoweth not God"*. We must make our way to Heaven by loving one another. And we must not let ourselves be confused into thinking that love is only a matter of the prick and the cunt, for *all flesh is grass and all the glory of man is as the flower of the grass, it withers and falls away, and we wrestle not, we wrestle not against flesh, against blood*. The prick and the cunt are innocent. *We wrestle against principalities.'*

Claire drew away from him, shocked into laughter.

'Did you say those words, Raphael? You ought to be locked up.'

For the first time since she came his eyes, stretched to hers, lost their glow and wavered. Doubt softened his face, he released her hand.

'Yes,' he said sadly. 'They seemed to me to go to the heart of the matter. I wanted to get to the heart of the matter,' and he struck his forehead with his fist, hitting it repeatedly. 'There's something in here, in here, I have to reveal, for we like sheep have gone astray –

'Oh Claire,' and he turned to her with tears of terror, 'what will become of me? Why am I here? Have I not been sent, after all? What will become of me?'

She could comfort him, but there was no consolation. She said that Damien knew a priest who would be glad to listen to him, to try to help him understand his own delusions. Even that would be to take away his delusions, which were his bliss. Besides, as Raphael said, having by now been gently escorted away from several altars during several Masses, 'I can't always be approaching priests. They are the anointed ones. I am only one of the many who are called, they are the chosen.'

Claire thought that in another age – perhaps an age in which she would have been burned as a witch – Raphael might have been considered a saint. His mania was visionary, it produced a state of ecstasy. Although he had no wounds, his words bled like stigmata, corrosive as flame, beaten through the furnace of his soul to sear his tongue, his lips, as if the very taste of them scalded his mouth. But they were propelled by the intensity of his truth, and who could bear the inspired denunciations with which he attacked the world?

Without trying to counter the thrust of Raphael's exhortations, Damien could listen to him, could try to appease the helpless questing spirit which he saw tormented in Raphael. But Raphael began to avoid him, he was a priest, Raphael had no mission to priests.

Anselm Daunt, too, Damien told Claire, had begun to take an interest in Raphael, employing him in the Youth Club at The Grove, walking around the city with him on fine evenings after choir meetings. Yet he, also, was a priest, and Raphael, demented, tried to keep away from him. 'I mustn't,' he insisted to Claire, 'I must not be always approaching priests. I must avoid them. They already know what I know. They are no help to me, but *are set as thorns in my side, rocks in my path*. They are good to me, but they cannot help me. *Distance. I must keep my distance.*'

By the time that Damien, encouraged by Claire, had begun to think that perhaps something should be done about Raphael, Della had intervened. Taking one of her increasingly rare walks to the village she was told by Mrs Crowley at the shop that Raphael Brady's mother wouldn't be long in it. What was going in one end was coming out the other as fast as you could swallow – 'with respects to you, Mrs Mackey', said Mrs Crowley, apologising for the necessary crudeness of the image. She had misunderstood Della's wince of recognition.

When Della, taking the car for the five-minute trip from the avenue to the farm lane, walked in through the Brady's wide-open door that spring morning, she had found Raphael on his knees beside his mother's bed, a large brown bottle in one hand and a tablespoon in the other. 'Another sup, Mammy,' he was saying. He had not heard Della's light footstep on the flags of the hall. So wet with sweat that it looked youthfully black again, Mrs Brady's hair fell in tacky strings around her pallid, uncomplaining face. The room was like a grotto: the walls were covered with a mosaic of religious pictures, overlapping, edge to edge, some sliding from their tacks towards a floor already littered with the crumpled faces of the Infant of Prague, the Virgin of Guadaloupe, Blessed Martin de Porres, St Theresa the Little Flower.

The window overlooking the Brady's remaining field was letting in a green grime as the only light. Even in this dewy murk Della could see how the bones stood out under the flesh of Mrs Brady's face, how her nose arched as if the skin, too tight, was ready to crack open and let the skeleton through. Taking it from Raphael's surprised hand she saw that the bottle, at least, was of a prescribed medicine, which meant a doctor had been to the sick bed. 'One teaspoonful three times daily after meals', the label said, and Raphael explained, across his mother's silence, that he had wanted to go out for a while and was giving her a bit extra to keep her going.

Della wasn't long sorting all that out. Mrs Brady died in a clean bed in a white hospital, meticulously cared for by strangers, far from the stench and saintliness of her own home. 'What else could I do?' Della, weary, had asked Frank, telling him about Raphael's anguished and finally violent protests as his mother was taken away, his shrieked abuse of the ambulance men, his hands clawing at the discreet blankets covering her stretchered, diminishing body, his howls.

'Who will repent me of my sins?' he had screamed as he fell to the floor, pushed firmly, too firmly, away by one of the men. 'Who will leaven my soul, who will exalt me?' He had fallen sobbing, indifferent to Della's frightened, soothing words. 'She hated me,' he wept. 'She was my expiation. Now how can I be redeemed?' He quietened at last in Della's arms; she was able to persuade him to the car, to her own doctor, and at last to another hospital, the breadth of two rivers away from where Mrs Brady lay quietly awake, waiting for death which came without too much fuss.

All that had happened and was over, and Raphael spoke these days with the tongue of the visionless man, flat words distinguished only by their anxiety. He was docile in the kitchen, spilling cutlery on to a tray where Claire had put the tablecloth, the side plates, what her grandmother still called Delft, the jug and glasses, the little glass and silver condiment set Frank had given Della for Christmas, napkins in the bone rings Onora had unearthed at the same season, another year. Every Christmas, short as she would always be of cash, Onora rooted among the few chests in her attic. 'Look what I found,' she would announce a week or two before the festival, showing Della and Angela and sometimes Claire a length of shimmering damask clouded by blue tissue-paper, a tobacco box still pungent with the odour of fifty years before, or a thin, filigree brooch from which Onora, her mouth twisted with memory, had taken earlier the brittle frond of heather. 'Wrap it up! Wrap it up!' they would exclaim – 'It's just what I want for Christmas!' Once, waiting for Angela, Onora had exposed to Claire's young eyes a necklace of moonstones, square, mauve-veined, milky as a moon. Valueless, Onora said, she had only worn them once, perhaps twice. In India. Her long fingers, the knuckles flattened, had strayed for an instant to the throat of her blouse, to the pale hollow where the stones had gleamed against the pale silk skin of her breast.

Claire wondered how Onora could manage it, how each year she must turn over the little treasures in her store, valuable only because of their age, yet able to serve her still. Both distant sons sent money which she saved so that each year, as they and their children grew beyond the need for knitted gloves, she could send slippers and scarves and boxes of Afternoon Tea biscuits. 'Maybe,' Claire had offered once, 'Uncle Denis would like this?' With her thumb she had rubbed the raised profile of an Emperor on a medal, and touched the roughened, fragile silk of the striped ribbon.

Onora had known that those two men and their wives had other things to prove before they allowed themselves the luxury of a stowed-away heritage. Once upon a time there had been a military ball in Cairo; she had shown its dance-card to an unfamiliar grand-daughter, placatory. There was the trace of the vanished names pencilled in the spaces on the thick, faded paper. The child was restless, uneasy with this grandmother whom she could not know; she fiddled with the card. It tore; she tore it up. On Onora's tasselled maroon table-cover she left neatly a pile of creamy shards, kept in place by the pin-thin pencil on its silken cord.

At the quickly prepared meal which had been left in readiness by Mrs Cummins, Della took her napkin from the ivory holder. To Claire her hand looked as if it were transparent. Shock made her mouth dry. Then she piled food on to Raphael's plate, endorsing each item with Frank's provenance of the garden, Della's (with Mrs Cummins as her proxy) of the market. The fish, they smiled, had been swimming in Ballycotton last night. The potatoes, too, were Ballycotton's best, small, dry and floury; the spinach was still coming from that row Frank had put down last June. The rhubarb tart, running with clear pink juice and sparkling with sugar – Mrs Cummins had made as she had seen Della make it, using what Claire, thinking of Lucia and Miss Mapp, called 'garden produce'. The cream was from one of the city's big dairies; as Claire lifted the pitcher to pour its velvet stream on to his plate, Raphael's face lightened for a moment, and he turned eagerly to Della – did she remember, did she remember?

Frank had taken Della's plate away. She sat with a tea-cup beside her, her favourite china still full with cooling liquid. Now she raised it to sip; Claire saw how dark her lips were as they touched the Jacobean flowers.

'Of course I remember, Raphael,' Della said. 'Your father gave us lovely cream, only the best. Do you remember –' and she turned to Frank – 'the shine in that little dairy, how clean it was? And the smell? And the wide blue bowls Mrs Brady used for letting the cream settle?'

Frank was grateful. He was astounded at how little there was for him to do now that what was happening was happening. All he had to do was to carry on, to carry on. But it was easier when Della was the one to insist on normality and to break that insistence, sometimes, with a smile at reminiscence. He didn't remember being terribly impressed with anything about the Brady's set-up; he couldn't recall exactly being in the dairy, or noticing the cream clotting in the shallow basins on the mottled, marble shelf. Yet it must have done so, cooling and thickening, and certainly he had seen that shelf, because Della had wanted, and he had found for her, something like it for pastry-making in her kitchen. So it was easy to aquiesce, to reassure Raphael, who was reassured and who began to eat again as though he were eating in a dream.

Chapter 8

It was Frank who answered the knock on the door.

'There's a plain-clothes priest here,' he called out as a welcome to Damien, giving notice to Claire. He wasn't sure at all, as he told Della frequently, that he liked this modern idea, these young priests going around in civilian clothes. It could be misleading after all. It could lead a young woman astray, not knowing a man was a priest only to find out too late. If he thought Claire might be the young woman he didn't say so – although he had ideas about that, too. After all, as he was to say mildly to Della later, while he was helping her to get undressed for bed, needing to talk about something to take his mind off what he was doing, what was happening, after all, wasn't there anyone else who could have given Claire driving lessons except Fr Sebright? Leon was too obviously the answer so he didn't mention him, but he wondered, he said, why she wouldn't wait until Stan had taught Angela, and then Angela could teach Claire. Della only said that teaching anyone to drive was a tricky business for both tutor and student, maybe Claire had picked the best teacher, or at least the one least likely to swear at her. Frank would not have understood why Della had encouraged Damien Sebright to instruct Claire, why when the two young people had joked about it she had said it wasn't a joke, really, but a very good idea, and they could have her car, *the* car, sometimes. Well, Frank would have understood if she had explained to him; but how could she explain?

She needed now to be understood without explanations, even without words, now that she was driven to set things right, to complete what she could of anything she had started. Frank had wondered at the speed, the recklessness with which she had settled the matter of Mrs Brady. There had been, at the same time, the very same day, that trouble with Raphael, yet Della had not waited for Frank's help.

He would have wanted to help. Hearing the story afterwards, hearing Della tell, tiredly, what had happened, he had imagined himself on the scene, making the telephone calls, he had fitted himself into his picture of what she was saying had happened, and making it happen differently, because he was there. But Della now had a new sense of finality, a terrified awareness of time. She was frantic to put to rights what she could of the things, of the people, of her world. Thus Stan and Angela she had made by deference, as well as inference, the special guardians of Onora. She knew she had no hope of settling Claire, but Fr Sebright as a friend, even a critical friend, would keep the girl straight, she hoped. Why should she think Claire might run crooked? It wasn't that – but Frank had fears, and Della had come at last to share them, and saw Damien as the shield against the snares of the world. Against the Leons of the world, she would have said, indeed she had said, to Damien himself, neither of them knowing that Claire had encountered the snare already, had sensed the trap, and was poised to escape it.

'And how is Leon, and his Little Red Book?' Damien asked her when, Raphael deposited without surprise or even reluctance in the grey gothic hospital to the west of the city, they drove in Damien's car, Damien at the wheel, towards the east. He asked the question to tease her, to distract her from her fear for her mother, and was diverted himself when she rejoined with a quick, defensive taunt –

'And how are you, and your little *Blue* Book?'

At his laugh she laughed; she was absolved of any blame for her taunting reference to his Breviary, which she knew was unkind of her, but she wanted to be unkind. Leaving Raphael she had stayed in the car, safe from the viscous smell of the hospital, protecting herself from Raphael's despair, although, as Damien told her when he came out of the building, Raphael seemed unconscious of, or at least undisturbed by, the present conditions of his life.

They drove east, towards the harbour villages of Saleen, Aghada, then inland to Cloyne. Damien wanted Claire to take the wheel, even on the high road, he said she was good enough. But when she said her mind wasn't on it he did not insist. They had talked about Raphael; in that way at least the journey had served its purpose, for Claire had said nothing about Della. Her rage was for Raphael, for the subjugation of his spirit, of his tongue. He lived now, she said, in a kind of ordered dirt, a regulated, organised, drenching despair, wet floors, sodden beds, immured among men who were, some of them, only half-human, cared for by men who only half-cared, who themselves had no hope for the inmates of this bedlam.

Damien knew that this was not all true; the violent radiance of Raphael's condition when he was admitted meant that he was shut up among the violent, the demented, the incurably insane. But drugs had brought him down, released him to the hope of therapy.

'His psychiatrist –' he began, and was surprised by Claire's gasp of laughter.

'That sounds just like the way Angela says "my gynaecologist".' Claire always enjoyed possessive titles. Damien smiled, but went on:

'Raphael's psychiatrist – *yes*, I did go to see him, just as you asked me – he says that Raphael will get better, that he'll be moved out of that ward in another week or two. He said the electric therapy worked well enough and that once the disorienting effects have worn off Raphael should be stable, and should stay stable, especially if he is able to take the drugs himself, for oh, for years, even.'

Claire said nothing. She felt empty; empty but not light. She had seen Raphael after the first course of ECT treatment, had felt his terror, the raw fear of instinct. He had not been wearing his own clothes, but sat, abject with apprehension, in unbelted trousers too long for him, too loose. Damien and Anselm had both looked for his clothes in the bulbless gloom of the farmhouse, deciding together, but not doing it, that the only solution to the problem of Raphael's home would be to burn it down, eradicating its filth, its accumulations, its dour, potent maladies, in one quick conflagration. They diverted themselves in their dank search with plans for the perfect fire, the perfect crime. They had found nothing, except old shoes which could still be worn, but nothing clean, nothing that they could handle without distaste. With Frank's help they had bought garments for Raphael but had not delivered them, not yet, not until Raphael was in a ward where there would be some hope his laundry would be returned to him, his clothes not at risk from his fellow-patients.

Claire had been glad, almost relieved, when Raphael, on seeing a hesitant Angela coming in to the long, blank room where he was kept, had stopped swaying backwards and forwards, had stood slowly upright and, shedding with his unfolding body the aquiescence of shock, had proclaimed, his voice trembling with pleasure and recognition, those words learned long ago when they had lit up for him and for others too, Claire would never forget that, the dust and dullness of the Legion of Mary rooms:

'*Who is she*,' he called out, his voice rising to a joyous inflection as he repeated the invocation:

'Who is she that cometh forth as the morning rising,
'Fair as the moon, bright as the sun, terrible as an
      army set in battle array?'
'My soul' – he sang it out –
'My soul doth magnify the Lord, and my spirit doth
      rejoice in God my saviour
'Because He hath regarded the humility of His handmaid
'For behold from henceforth all generations shall call
      me blessed . . .'

Angela had put a stop to that. Her face was white, and very still, and Claire went to catch her hand, to bring her to a chair next to Raphael who had not moved from his place under the high mullioned window. Angela told Raphael, holding him with her other hand, to stop that, he would be giving her ideas above her station, and Claire gave her credit for making a joke out of Raphael's use of the incantation, of the paean of Elizabeth's greeting to Mary in the house of Zachary in the hill country of Judea. But how clearly Raphael saw things, she thought then, and thought now as she considered Raphael whom they had once again left behind, once again as they headed for the sea, for the villages of the coast. Angela had told Raphael of her pregnancy, Claire did not know what words she had used, but she had done so at the same time as she had told him what she had come to tell him, of the death of his mother. Neither fact had disturbed the stupor of quietude to which he had been reduced at that point, as a preliminary, Claire was told, to further treatment. Since then he had never spoken about his mother, never called for her, she had at last merited his silence. But Angela: on that shared visit Raphael had at once remembered what else he had been told.

Claire thought of the words of the Gospel: in the house of Zachary, when Elizabeth heard the salutation of Mary, she was filled with the Holy Ghost.

'I know this is selfish of me, I'm only noticing my own preferences, but I do feel it's some kind of loss that in getting better – if he *is* getting better – Raphael has to be made dull. As if lack of resistance were more important than –'

As Claire hesitated, Damien was impatient:

'More important than what? Passion? Raphael can't contain passion, that's the problem. That's his problem. Can't you imagine what it would be like for him, to *feel* everything, all the time?'

Claire thought she could imagine what it would be like, but did not want to say it. It was an uncomfortable thought – the possibility that if you could manage it, it would be a good way, even the right way, to live.

'I just wonder, if it weren't so embarrassing sometimes, I mean if it's *only* that it's embarrassing sometimes, if there wasn't some way to mind Raphael, to let him as he is? I mean that time with Angela in the hospital. It was uncanny, it was eerie. It was like – you remember, that play, *The Tidings Brought to Mary*? Like that, as though you were hearing a voice from another time, another world, almost.

'I mean, Damien –' and she turned eagerly towards him – 'you must feel it, don't you, sometimes?'

They were beyond Cloyne now, they had not stopped to exclaim at the round tower, to shield their eyes from the reddening sun in an effort to see through the leaded windows of the Cathedral. They were beginning to turn homewards, away from sea-light and the shore, but it was still day, bright although the sky was closing, bright with the green of the trees along the little roads.

'Don't you feel it?' Claire was persistent. She wanted some recognition from him that while he might not share her perception of Raphael's madness, he could recognise it, at least, give it some credence.

'Damien – you couldn't not feel it. That day with Angela, he just sang out the *Magnificat*. I looked it up afterwards, you know what it is yourself, the Ember Friday in Advent. "*Elizabeth was filled with the Holy Ghost*" – do you see what I mean? The way it ties in, the speaking in tongues, the Pentacostalists, the Holy Ghost – you do see what I mean, don't you?'

Damien turned off the road, along a track between old walls, old trees, into a clearing where the rutted floor was sprung with ferns. Through the rolled-down windows they heard the chuckles of wood-pigeons snuggling in the warm accustomed trees, and they could see how a brake of ferns and brambles had not just grown naturally, untidily, into its shape but looked like, must have been, a hedge around a shed, or what might once have been a cabin, whatever this small stone thatched structure had now become.

In taking his pipe from his pocket Damien's fingers touched the string of brown beads, his Rosary.

'I do, Claire. I know what you mean.' His aquiescence was reluctant: to give her argument credence might also be to give it status, and he would not do that.

'But to be blunt about it, Claire, so what? The boy is ill, unmanageably ill, and he is being cured. Isn't that what we want to happen? Isn't that the best thing for Raphael? There really isn't and shouldn't be any other way of looking at it.'

'No. That's what has to be done. Of course I see that.' That was not Claire's point. 'The point is, *my* point is, that psychiatrists seem to be the wrong people to be dealing with what's wrong with Raphael. He's a visionary –'

'He's a schizophrenic who's hallucinating,' said Damien crisply, tired of Claire's nonsense.

'Yes, he *is*, but he's using the language, the metaphors, of religion. Psychiatrists don't use that language, they even pretend, perhaps they prefer, not to know it. But psychiatry is about the soul, isn't it? You're the one who did the classics – doesn't *psyche* mean soul? Priests are the people who know that language. And poets, perhaps. The language of the soul. Why can't priests help Raphael? That's my point!'

Having made it, she was content, and smiled at Damien, meeting his eyes openly, turned towards him as he turned towards her, cramped as they were in their seats, with her ease, her satisfaction breathing in a soft current between them. Was this what it would be like, Claire wondered as she smiled at Damien, to have a brother? To be able to argue like this, and yet be at ease, familiar enough to disagree, even bitterly, yet not to fear the going too far, the breaking of something which held them together for what held them together could never be broken? She thought with a spurt of affection how good it would be to have Damien as a brother and then thought how she would miss him in the coming year, the coming years perhaps, now that he was committed to going away.

'Yes.' Damien felt suddenly uncomfortable, constricted in

the car. 'Yes – he's using that language, and you say that we're the ones who can help him, but we're also the ones, according to you, who are changing it, brutalising that language.'

'That's true, that's true – Dad's *New Sunday Missal* calls Zachary Zechariah and the Holy Ghost becomes the Holy Spirit and when Elizabeth cried out with a loud voice it says "*she gave a loud cry*" and blessed art thou among women becomes "*of all women you are the most blessed*" – I think it's crazy, especially as the prayer of the Hail Mary has kept "*blessed art thou*".

'And then –' Claire had more to say, a clincher she thought – 'they're spending years, and probably millions of money, making a *hames* of the liturgy, and at the same time they produce something like "*Humanae Vitae*". Trying to modernise the language, while bringing theology safely back to the Middle Ages. And" – she drew a quick concluding breath – "and because priests like you try to argue that *perhaps* a mistake has been made it becomes impossible, it's made impossible, for you to stay here, in your own diocese, in your own country: so you're off to the missions, back to the Black Baby days.'

All that was true also, and its truth, and the confinement of the car, made Damien open the door, get out. Claire's words were an unhappy echo of Johnny Trant's advice: 'You're anathema to the Bishop, now, boy. And because there's a few like you there's a few like him, and he's more important, and he can make sure life is insupportable for you. What kind of a parish will he send you to, or do you want to spend your life as a chaplain and nothing else? The Yanks need men for their missions in South America, and this guy will be glad to see you go.'

Rotund in his study in the Seminary, Johnny Trant had taken on authority with a teaching job: his exposition on exile rang with the conviction of the man who had no intention now of ever leaving home, a man who saw his way to making home his success, his domain. 'South America, boy. Latins, Indians. The poor – it's a great mission field. Peasants, no worry about "*Humanae Vitae*" there; they keep on fucking because there's nothing else to do, keep on dropping kids because so many die

– you won't have to worry about theology there!'

Damien had been devastated then; Trant's words had not made him more angry, but more desolate. He still believed that he could not have done other than he had done, he could not have insisted, even using the compassion of which the hierarchies spoke so complacently, on the glacial certainties of the Pope. He had argued, pleaded through dawns, hungered fearfully for and had found his fellows; but they were few, too few, and their voices, like his, had been raised to no effect except to hint at schism, to give scandal. That hint alone was ruinous to him.

He leant against the car, the outside air soft against his face, the drift of wind lifting the hair at his temples, the smell in it of damp, of dew. Claire stood at the other side, looking beyond the rough-walled cabin, her silence a balm to him. He had come to know her well enough at least to be able to perceive her sympathy, to understand that her words, her taunts, were not always, not even often, an end in themselves, but a spur to another end, another truth. Their disputed truths had brought them closer; close enough most recently for her to thank him, with no laughter in her voice, for his gift to her mother of *El Amor Brujo*, the record sleeve glowing with the sunflowers of van Gogh, the disc a circled skein transfigured into music, a small exquisite miracle wrought from the piercing, redemptive power of love.

She had said, her hand lightly, self-forgetfully, touching the black cloth of his sleeve, that his Spanish lessons were already beginning to bear fruit – 'and flowers', she added. Della had appreciated the sunflowers, their bursting radiance foretelling the beauty held within the whorls as the black wheel shone, ready for release by her hand at a switch. In saying good things to him Claire was offering Damien consolation, soothing the soreness of his decision to depart, mollifying, with reported tendernesses, this sense of tearing, of ripping, which had almost overcome the assumed equanimity with which he had given the gift, and with it the news of his going.

Angela had been there on that giving afternoon a week ago, and Onora, brought out into the spring garden to admire the vigorous Fruhlingsgold, thickly-budded already for its wide-petalled creamy torrents in May. The cat on the wall blinked through its branches, as Frank, delighting in the lovely consanguinity of rose trees and white cherries, positioned Della, Onora and Angela beneath the fronded arches for a photograph, what he still called a snapshot. Claire and Damien watched from their arrival at the gate where Bran squirmed with welcome; he was not in the picture, but then neither were they. Damien kept a copy in his wallet and when he looked at it recalled that of the women who heard his news in that verdant garden, only one, only Claire, had asked when he might return.

Well, they had been right, the prelates, he reflected as he reached in his pocket for his tobacco, his pipe: 'No change will disturb the even tenor of your Christian lives,' the prelates had said, after Vatican Two, a reassurance. No change: it was not from Vatican Two that the changes had come, but from other edicts, *ex cathedra*, encyclical. His Christian life had been put in jeopardy, the force of his spiritual energy, that part of him which Claire had ceased to mock – that had been jeopardised, dulled by the shadow of doubt. How was it, how had it come about that it could only be reasserted in the mountain villages of Chile, the pueblos of Peru? *His* life – *there*, in heat, in drought, in an isolation from which his soul quailed?

It was to be there; here was the cool trickle of a field-edge stream, the gurgle of pigeons in the hawthorn, the sun setting gently, lingeringly in a pink and primrose sky.

Beside him now Claire watched him cradle the bog-brown square of tobacco in his hand; with a sliver of knife he peeled the curls of bark and then with his knife again he scraped quickly around the bowl of the pipe before packing it with the shredded tobacco, pressing it firm with his thumb. This was something she liked to watch; from the first blow to clear the bowl, the puff of harsh breath into the brown bulb, to the scraping, the peeling, the tamping with the thumb, the set of his lips around the lipped stem, then the sharp fume of the match catching and the tang of the blue and aromatic smoke as he breathed, sucked, inflamed the tiny fire, his eyes in the light absorbed, intent on this ritual, this little office. There was a masculinity in it which touched her, and a completeness.

She was seeking this quality of completion, some reassurance that life came round again, that its circles met where their meeting was ordained. There was a fish-bone itch of panic in the throat of her life. She thought of Yeats – 'the centre cannot hold'. She thought of Onora, nothing was happening that had not happened before, that could not be contained, accommodated. All Claire had to do was see how other people let fear through a window into their lives so that when it broke down the door they could deal with it as if it were no more than a difficult visitor. But all her doors and windows were still open, unguarded, defended by nothing except her own instincts. She had a sense of part of her life closing. A date was coming. There would be departures. Leon had already gone to Dublin. Raphael was in hospital. Damien was beginning that circle of visitations which were all farewell: to his own mother in Lismore who could recognise bad news no matter how carefully it was packaged, to cousins, to aunts already distant, always judging, to friends, a few of them, whose sympathy was all they had to offer.

She stood beside him as he held the warming corm of the pipe in his palm. The first deep replete inhalations satisfied, she leaned her arm, her shoulder against him as they leaned against the car. She thought of the masculine rituals: the whisk of Frank's razor against the strop in the bathroom and the bone-handled brush which had seemed to foam of itself into a luxuriant lather when he used it, stirring with it the hot water he poured from the kettle into the shaving mug Onora had given him. In the bathroom Claire still liked to let the bristles tickle the palm of her hand, recalling her practice as a child, separating the hairs with a tingling fingernail.

Many Christmases had taken care of the razor, the strop, although the mug was still on the bathroom shelf; now Frank used a slick Gillette, and sometimes there was an emanation almost like perfume which allowd Claire to tease him. He never smelled, as Leon sometimes did, of whiskey, that other masculine odour which had in her mind and memory a sharp delineating power. Once that smell on Leon's breath had frightened her; he was drinking *spirits*! But her nostrils had become less apprehensive, more tolerant. That clean acidic smell was the smell of sex, of intimate dealings, the breath of darkness, whispers, wetness, of something Claire had thought might well be love. It was a night-time smell, but she had caught it once in daylight when she met Jarleth Tattin in the street and he had introduced her to the tall brown-haired woman at his side.

'Pauline,' he had said; he had wanted, when he saw Claire, to stop and talk to her, to recover where he had seen her before, what it was that he thought he had missed then: the introduction should not be avoided. Although she stood aside from his greeting the woman had not left him. On the winter street she was dressed in matching rusty browns; not smart but with a soft elegance which Claire had recognised as good taste with individuality – *style*, she thought, looking at the close-cut brown hair, its little peak at forehead and nape, the distinction of the outlined skull.

As the women began their polite assessments Tattin drew them closer to him to protect them from the press of people on the pavement.

'Pauline,' he said to Claire. 'My wife.'

He put his arm along her shoulder as Claire watched, joining her to his body.

'My Pauline Privilege,' he said to Claire, his lifted eyebrows expecting her recognition. She caught the exhalation of his smile, caught the racy tang, the whiskey smell. *Dangerous*.

Here with Damien, close to him without danger, she remembered that meeting as a hint of meetings during the coming few days, days when she would travel; first south and west for *The Journal* with Sinn Fein, then north and east for *The Journal* with an international charity sponsoring a fund-raising ball in Dublin. South and west she would be near the cottage in which Tattin said he wrote his poetry. In Dublin she would be near Leon. Near him, she thought, perhaps for the last time. It was what she had thought she wanted. Even that night, that night when she had not gone to the Film Society with him, when she had gone instead to Fota.

What had she lost by not going with Leon that night? The sub-titled film, cool grey undertones, subtlety in an Italian twilight. Monica Vitti, an irresistible beauty being resisted by Marcello Mastroianni, tones of fluctuating desperation, the acceptance of the ordinary miseries of life. What image would she have taken away with her – that of a male hand, long-fingered, speaking as it rested without closing on the female shoulder, the silence invested with all that sympathy could say to the vast recognition of unending loss? Would she, herself, Claire wondered, fear such loss enough to be unable to encourage it, to help it make its entry into her life at last? If she separated now from Leon for how long would she live longing for the sight of him, for how long would her ears quicken at the possibility of his name? Would her perceptions forever remain alert: *'This is the hand of Bridget Cruise'*?

Stirred by a premonitory anguish, she looked around her. There were primroses growing late where rusty branches of briar and thorn shielded a ditch, and by the pier of a broken gateway there were the tangled stems of a rose-bush, the tiny coral roses of these cottages. Beyond the gate was an improvised dog-run with a kennel built like a hen-coop, slatted and corrugated but so far as she could see quite waterproof. Planks laid with straw were raised on concrete blocks inside, two black-spotted tin dishes with water in them set outside the opening, the run itself floored with earth and ashes and enclosed with chicken-wire, a painted bedstead, buttressed with staves, bits of timber, wire and rope and heavy branches.

Claire followed Damien to the house, to the dark-green door, its paint clotted, its latch rusted and tied with twine. The grass grew long to the walls, to the two small windows. Although no bigger than a shed, it was not a shack, but it was poor, there was something makeshift about it, it did not seem even as weatherproof as the kennel. Damien called to her from the door, where he had bent to the big keyhole.

'Look,' he whispered.

His hand on her shoulder guided her as she stooped. She felt its comforting weight as her eye adjusted to the inside dark, then found what Damien had wanted her to see. A deep window let in the evening light, holding it in a sunset frame. On the sill, in the light, and tender as the gentle light itself stood a slender statue of the Virgin: her blue cloak, the white folds of her gown as benign, as suppliant, as her little outstretched hands. On the sill before her had been placed a tin mug frothing with the roses of the gateway, richly pink, coiled tightly petal upon petal as if one fingertip touch would spring the blossoms open and release all their poignant fragrance in an incense on the air.

The roses at the Virgin's shrine; the kennel empty of greyhounds – this was Dungourney. They had come on this circular journey from the city and the burgeoning roses of its gardens to the geranium villages of the coastal plain. With the spring sun behind them and the promise of the lengthening, warming evening ahead they had travelled inland again, turning back on the wheel of whim to the narrow roads of Cloyne, to the cottage in Dungourney.

There had been so much they had meant to speak about. There was so much to be said – about Della, the operation which was to come, about Damien, what his mother had said when he told her about going to South America, about Anselm and the row there had been with Briain Ó Cathasaigh. Damien had hoped to make Claire laugh with his story of Anselm trying to insist on less Latin, more Irish, and Ó Cathasaigh who, God knew, needed no encouragement to keep Irish as the vernacular in any liturgical events at St Dominic's but who had a weakness – he admitted it – for the Gregorian phrases of his faith, resisting with a cold civility quite foreign to his nature. For Damien to tell her that story would also be to let her know that he was on her side. He had decided he would like her to know that much. And he had been going to tell her about Johnny Trant talking on about authority, the need for what Trant had called 'authoritive' statements.

All the way home he listened. The miles took them from one diocese to another. From dusk to dark past the woods of Fota until the river ran beside them. A translucent cuticle of new moon hung like a hinge in the faintly-starred night, a comma among the clouds. He listened to the story of Nicholas Barry, and his greyhounds, and his child. He heard the story that Claire would never write, the story of that death. He heard her tears. He could do nothing to console her. He knew that her grief was for many things, things over and done with, things yet to happen. He knew that it included him.

Chapter 9

For all the rest of her life, Claire would remember that day, that West Cork day, as one of balmy, indifferent benevolence. When the different strands of its conversations came back to her they brought no remembered premonitions, although they proved to be premonitory. No; when she said those words to herself as she was to do, so many times, in the years to come, *Sinn Fein* – we ourselves – when she said these words in her head they carried a different weight, different to the burden of the syllables as she spoke them through the first following years so often, so heavily, until their meaning grew fixed and inexorable, incapable of alleviation or diminution, and she spoke them no more. And even then, even in those impervious years to come, the silent words, internalised, spelled out this echoing balm.

It had begun with irritation: her period had come out of turn, which would make for awkwardness on the journey, she couldn't wear the slacks she had planned as she would be padded to the hilt and it might show, so that put her into a skirt and nylons and shoes which were really unsuitable for any prolonged walking – she had to hope there wouldn't be any prolonged walking. She would be at a disadvantage immediately as she certainly didn't want to have to ask for special consideration or draw attention to herself in any way. On the other hand she had to welcome this menstruation as it meant she wouldn't be bothered with it in a week's time when she went to Dublin. Perhaps on the whole she had nothing to complain about.

Leaving the house early in the morning to get the first bus into town for what Frank satirically called her '*rendezvous* with the Soldiers of Destiny' – she welcomed his satire, it took the onus of irony off her own approach – Claire found Della in the garden, on the path between the drooping tulips and the first fragrant plumes of lilac. The light was clear although cool; 'nippy', Frank would have said. To Claire it had a sparkle; it was fresh, the scents of the grass, of the blossom scattered among the apple trees, the bitter green on the gooseberry bushes, even the damp where her skirt had brushed against the dewy bristling roses had a scent. Air and odours together sparkled and shone on Della, where she stood waiting for Claire, beneath the arching, slowly opening wisteria.

Bran was with Della, and barked once, mildly, at Claire's approach. Gluic was there too, supine as a panther along an apple branch, narrowing his eyes against the fervent staccato of a robin, both of them keeping a wakeful, watchful distance. Della was stroking the striped discarded petals of a tulip; she held them out to Claire and together they bent over the stem, examining the flower's intimate exposed anatomy, the flanged stigma thinning, contracting, the six filaments naked without their exactly, miraculously matching corolla, their painted lobes adherent as a bruise, each bruise precisely tuned to the calyx while the calyx lasted which, for these tulips in this garden, had been quite a long time.

'I feel so sorry for them,' said Della, thinking of the ovary, anther and filament, pistil and carpel. 'Except, of course, that they will come back again.'

'And that they give so much pleasure,' said Claire, who was in a hurry but reluctant to break from this rare moment of sharing: what was it they were sharing? It didn't matter, it was simply that they were together, with no one else.

She was not surprised to find her mother out so early. Della was restless these days. She had been reprieved by pain, by two days of baffling, embattled agony in hospital where the surgeons – Claire had overheard Frank telephoning Stan so that a diluted version would reach Angela – the surgeons had decided that nothing should, or could, be done. They would try drugs to get it under control, they had said, Frank said. And Della, bewildered, had come home and immediately had begun to get better. But restless. Unable to settle to anything for long, even to sleep. She had taken up her embroidery only to let it down to glow like an embossed moon wherever she had been sitting, her sewing-box spilling silks and wools in ribbons of twisted colour, her fingers briefly, beautifully busy among the flossy skeins. She listened to music; even now Claire could hear the spinning spiral of harmony from the sitting room where the windows were open so that the sound could follow Della: Bach. A violin. A sound thin but resonant, its melodic consequence clean as an incision.

Leaving her mother, Claire looked back down the garden; a rose bush climbing untidily beyond the wisteria had put out a lusty purple branch. Its thorns caught Della's dress, lifted a tendril from her hair, clung to her as if unwilling to let her move away. Claire blinked; she felt that discomfort in her vision as if something too bright had dazzled her and left its imprint on her eye, blurring the edge of all else she looked at, but only for a while, a moment or two.

Anselm Daunt was the driver. 'Fr Daunt,' the men said, introducing him. They were old men; in retrospect Claire would realise that they had not been old, not so old as to be harmless. They were gnarled, weathered, humorous. Peadar was the youngest, forty or so, but wore a shiny pallor to his face, the sheen of prison and the imprisonment of tuberculosis. This was the time of miracles in Ireland: a man like Peadar might cross the Border, raid a customs post on the wrong side, escape his incarceration and live to fight another day in the South. He might get TB, consumption the people called it, and dwell for a year in a pallid hospital miles from any city, ringed by fir trees foreign to the native landscape but essential, somebody must have believed, to the psychology of cure. He might lie there and read *The Magic Mountain*, dream of the icy pines of Switzerland

and Austria and become well again and live to fight another day until he died of something else.

Claire knew all that, and read something of it in Peadar's face, although she could not have said, as Onora would have said if she had met Peadar Cullen, that he would not make old bones. Yet for all his apparent langour Claire was to discover on this journey that Peadar had the confidence of the reckless, self-educated man. He had inherited whatever there was left of whatever there had been of a socialist tradition in Ireland. Like Leon he spoke of Connolly, but he spoke as if Connolly had been his father, his martyred, tortured, irretrievable but omniscient father.

Conor Herlihy and Barra Brown were older, men whose memories ranged without effort to 1916 when, they admitted with a candour which disarmed Claire, they had not been born. What they remembered, they said, was what their fathers remembered. As all five of them drove steadily into the western uplands they remembered without passion, with some sense of the comedy of time. The man Claire called Conor spoke with a grin she could see as she turned to look at him from her front seat, he remembered his father recalling with despair how things had gone wrong, how messages had not got through from Dublin and those that had got through had been misinterpreted or countermanded.

'And all the time my dad said the men were ready. And all that was happening, my dad said, was happening in Dublin, and down here there was nothing doing at all, except for Terence MacSwiney walking up and down reading the *Imitation of Christ*.'

Claire caught the quick look Brown shot at Anselm Daunt: 'In respects to you, Father,' Herlihy apologised fluently.

However uneasy this temporary alliance might be, Claire thought, they were practised in one another's sensibilities.

'How are the classes going, Father?' Barra Brown asked the priest, and for miles after that the men discussed Daunt's parish, and the work going on there for the Irish language. The narrowing roads climbed among the rocky outcrops beyond Macroom, into Baile Mhúirne and Béal Átha an Ghaorthaidh, names the men said in Irish, ripening them as they spoke.

The trouble with the Cló Romhánach as a spelling device, they said, was that it made the language *look* so unwieldy; the words looked too intricate, all consonants. What on earth had been wrong, they said, with the old system of aspirates and accents, the *séamhú* and the *síne fada*? Claire remembered Ó Cathasaigh saying something like this to the choir, waiting for Damien one night after work. They were singing *Duain Croí Íosa*, and their social tones were infiltrating the sound Ó Cathasaigh was trying to produce. Their slurs were masking the elisions he craved to hear. He stopped the singing, his eyes fevered.

'Say the *words*,' he commanded. 'Don't sing! You can't sing until you understand. It's not just the spirituality of the meaning – it's the spirituality of the *words*!

'Listen!' he said.

Gile mo *ch*roí do *ch*roíse a *Shlán* aitheóir
is ciste mo *ch*roí do *ch*roíse *d'fh*ail *i m'*chothaire

He took breath, then plunged on again, his white hands breaking the silence of listening. '*Im – im!* Listen to the way they come together. If it was French it would be *liaisons*, and you'd all be mighty proud of them. Will you *hear* it! Will you hear the way the *h* strengthens the *co* of Chroise, the emphasis it gives. Don't you all remember that from school, the *c*-séamhaithe, the *séamhú*? The *m*-séamhaithe, the *d*, the *f*, the *g*? the *síne fada* is only an accent, a stress. But the séamhaithe!

'What is the point of the language if you're not going to use it?' He turned away from the shifting men, opening his arms to the altar of the side chapel where they sang, spreading his hands out as if to beseech some explanation from the altar itself.

'What is the point of the language if you're not going to use it? You cannot ignore its perfections! Its ornaments!'

That had been, Claire realised, in what Protestants would have called a Lady Chapel. The floor was of black and white terrazzo, the pews some foreign timber glazed by usage into a composite of dampness, darkness and hardness, the kneelers uncushioned. Yet the little oratory had its richness in the frilled marble of the altar, its niches and crevices pungent with flowers, always fresh, replaced daily by a few devoted women who were not all old. This was a grotto for St Anne, mother of the Virgin. The altar cloth was crisply white, its entwined initials brilliant with gilded embroidery, and among the flowers the brass candlesticks glittered with devotion. Above the waiting men the roof vaulted into its own grey depths, which now echoed and whispered back the pleading exasperations of Briain Ó Cathasaigh, as fervent, as desperate, as any supplicant.

Could it be true, Claire wondered now, that a country without a language had to be a country without a soul? Those were the words of Patrick Pearse, *'Tír gan teanga, tír gan anam.'* It was more like a threat than a prophecy – except that prophecies often *were* threats. She had tried. She had gone to the night classes in Dún Laoi, her presence sponsored by Leon and, if he was not always there, Raphael kept her company. But she had been too eager, too ready to ask questions, to attempt a joke. This was not the poetic language she had imbibed during her school years, forsaking the demands of declension, compound, gender and cognate accusative and cleaving only to Diarmuid and Gráinne, or Tigh Molaga, or Una Bán. If these poems and legends carried some spiritual truths, and Claire, accepting the encouragement of her teachers, believed they did, she was content to ignore the exigencies of the language itself, or to be irritated by what it expected of her.

This was the sentimental imperfection despised by Leon which she tried to repair at Dún Laoi. But she had, as Mrs Cummins had once said in her hearing, 'too much ould talk'. And she had not had the time, either, to settle down; her job made demands on her that the other students did not share, so her attendance was broken, became erratic, and she was so ashamed of her own excuses, genuine though they were, that she went along for the last time and formally resigned from the class. She had explained it only to Damien. Leon's jibes she had met with a bright defiance, but she had wanted Damien to understand, to accept that she had acted out of self-knowledge, not impatience. He had absolved her, but she was careful to say nothing here in the car as the men spoke around her.

'Whatever happens to the language now is our own fault,' Peadar Cullen said, as if he didn't care. 'We've had it now for fifty years in our own hands entirely, and if we haven't made any progress in that time, if the Language Freedom Movement can defeat any signs of progress we've made in that time, then there's no one to blame but ourselves.'

The others didn't like that. At the wheel Anselm Daunt seemed to wince, tightening his mouth and eyes together quickly.

'But it's not the LFM that's making the real changes,' Barra Brown retorted. 'It's the Government, the Commissions, the people involved in Irish studies – they're the ones with all the learning, they're the ones who know best. They're the ones.'

He lapsed, despairing of seeing the sense in it all.

Conor Herlihy had a savagery about him.

'There's no easy way to make a revolution. And it is a revolution – bringing back the language. Giving the people back the soul the British took away from us. Compulsory Irish has to stay in our examination system, in the primary schools, in the secondary schools too. It must stay as an entry requirement for all university courses, Art as well as Archaeology. Make it part of what people want – it's the only way.'

Anselm Daunt said the problem was, essentially, that the language had been badly taught.

Herlihy had a laugh like a bark.

'You're right there. We've boys and girls coming out of the schools speaking French like *gendarmes* – but the only place people are learning to speak Irish quickly and fluently is in Portlaoise jail or the Curragh camp.'

They all laughed at that. With satisfaction. It wasn't any of their own 'lads' as they called them – even Claire had fallen into the trap of that affectionate appellation – who were in prison these days, except in England; it was the communists, or the free-range gunmen of Saor Éire, the latter-day freedom fighters who, like demented Diarmuid Duffy, had found that they could not wait for their day to dawn.

'Well, it's all of a piece in the end,' Daunt said lightly. 'We won't want to be beholden to any government departments for making this country truly Irish – even if they could do it. Let them try what they can. We'll hold hard to our own principles, for we know where the real truth of Irish nationhood lies. And we'll take advantage of anything good that they do, and eradicate everything bad.'

Claire thought, without saying so, that this implied compulsion too. She thought, and did not say, that sometimes, in certain mouths, the speaking of Irish carried some other meaning with it. Putting words on it in her mind, remembering an argument with Leon, she thought of this other ingredient as a licence to hate, an endowment of victimisation. Below the cream of that richness of imagery – '*Gile na gile do chonnac ar slí in uaigneas/croistal an chroistal a goirmroisc rinn-uaine/binneas an bhinnis* . . .' – brightness of brightness, crystal of crystal, sweetness of sweetness – oh, it was *rich*, it frothed – but below its creamy luxury of consonant on consonant ran that stream molten with vengeance, as if all future excess must now be forgiven, understood, accepted, everything absolved for ever, because of those eight hundred years of domination by another race, another culture, another creed. To think of it, to dwell on it, made her unhappy. Yet she was not unhappy now, with the sun suddenly striking richly into the car and the men, elated with the warmth and their own unanimity, began, in this surprising equilibrium, to tell stories of one another.

Conor Herlihy said, grinning, that the language would never come back until the people understood the breadth of its sexual vivacity. It was as bawdy, he said, as it was religious. He was not afraid that Daunt might contradict him because he knew

Daunt knew it to be true and he was satisfied with the shrug he saw Daunt give in acknowledgement. But Barra Brown misunderstood him and began to talk of the couple he had overheard at a Fleadh Ceoil.

In Ennis that was, he said. Marvellous. All the men nodded – *marvellous*. *That's* where you heard the language. Well, it was, all right, Barra Brown said with a mischievous hesitation. You might say that, he said and, intrigued, everyone was silent. Not much of a story, really, he said, it was just the casualness of it, if they were talking, and they were talking, weren't they, about the uses of language, like the way the vernacular of one language could accommodate another – wasn't that it? It was just on the street, there by the Old Ground, the boys and girls were sitting outside the pubs, on the walls of the gardens, you couldn't help hearing them as you passed, their fiddles, their accordions in cases by their side, and two of them, a boy and a girl, were talking so naturally in Irish that for a minute he didn't even realise it *was* Irish. So he listened away, he stopped, he said, as if to fasten the strap on his *bodhrán*, and then he realised they were talking about someone else: '*Agus nuair a thánaig sé cugham, nuair a chonaic sé mise in aice an doras, ag feithimh air, cad a duirt sé ach* fuck off.'*

Everyone laughed. Daunt at the wheel let out a delighted trill, boyish and innocent. Claire laughed at his laughter, and thought how it changed him, how his face lightened and sharpened.

'Well,' he said, grinning – 'at least it proves that the language is still a cultural reality.'

Herlihy said that that was more than could be said these days for English. He heard someone on Radio Eireann talking the other day, about Vietnam, it was an American who was against the war, and he said – Herlihy's voice took on a ponderous accent – 'He said – "I know the difference between a war, and I know the difference between a game, sir –" Sure if you ask me he didn't know the difference between one word and another.'

* 'And when he came, when he saw me next to the door waiting for him, what did he say but –'

They all joined in. Claire, apart from them, considered with contented surprise the clutch of men in the back seat, their voices loosened, their faces relaxed although their bodies had to be pressed against one another in that space. They were men who had found, were finding, different paths to their own political truths, and those truths too were different, conflicting. But there was no conflict here.

Peadar Cullen – Claire thought Leon had known him at the university – said that 'between' was a great word. He had heard it used at home in Blackpool in the pub after a County Championship – 'Who won between The Glen?' – as though the other team could not possibly matter enough to be mentioned. The understanding of the parochial exclusivity united them all, and Claire said that one of the things worrying her was the way people were forgetting the difference between few and less. They were saying, she said, not that, for example, people were earning less money, but that people were earning less amounts of money. They were forgetting the distinction between number, weight, and size.

But they all said that this was not a confusion between less and few but between less and lesser. That was true, she agreed – she couldn't quite explain what she meant, except by giving examples, and although Peadar Cullen quoted Fowler to Claire's discomfiture, she stuck to her point: in the manner of usage, it was becoming commonly accepted to apply 'less' to numbers, or to plurals, where 'few' was more correct. Brown agreed with that – even Fowler would agree with that, but Claire had her spirit up by now: 'Don't throw Fowler at me,' she retorted – 'I couldn't care fewer.'

The hilarity this provoked almost embarrassed her. She was not used to being a success at close quarters. Daunt's laugh rang out helplessly, the car swerved, the men fell against one another to one side and they laughed louder and Claire reddened, aware she couldn't repeat this trick too often, aware too of the hot pulse of blood against the pad between her legs.

Herlihy said that what he was fascinated by was the way in which English people couldn't manage multi-syllables.

They couldn't say 'particularly'; even radio and television announcers – not that he heard them too often, just now and then, by accident – even they stinted on the word, 'particuly', they said, or 'arbitry'.

'Or terrism,' said Daunt.

No one spoke for a while. The car ran smoothly on. They had been silent too, miles ago, miles after Macroom, when the car swung through the rocks of the defile at Keimeneigh. In the pass before she recognised it, Claire saw the sun strike shadows off the piled stones until it vanished in the elongated curve of the roadway. It came to her then, where she saw the boulders rear to reach in a bridge over the path, widened by the County Council but once no more than a gap, a gorge grown sonorous with history. This was the site of the song, the song of the battle, *Cath Chéim an Fhia* – the battle of the leap of the deer, the song she had heard in the marble halls of Fota. Its melody crept to her lips, she could feel the notes tremble, *Cois abhann ghleanna an Chéama in Uibh Laoire 'sea bhímse*; but she would not attempt to master those intricately flowing words in this company, the liquidity of the language was beyond her, she would sound like a recruit.

And yet why *couldn't* she sing if she wanted to? Any song she wanted to? The language wasn't anyone's private property. But no, she reasoned with herself, it was a declaration too, sometimes. Here, with these men to whom Irish was a code for something else, she would not use it even innocently, there was no innocence with these men.

They were sweeping southwards towards Ballylickey, diving through the Shehy mountains, the little hills quaking with evocations, oh, Claire would have liked to stop here, to talk of Daniel Corkery, to see in the hollows the little lakes on which Frank O'Connor had listened to boatmen and silence. She made promises to herself, she would return with Damien, with Leon. She would walk the hills where Sean O Faloain had lurked and listened to midnight secrets in houses gaunt and grey and solitary. As the heights bloomed before her with banks of broom and bracken, rising into gullies brilliant with cascading water or undulating from the green down of a half-hidden valley, Claire lifted them over in her mind like leaves from a book. That was how they lived for her, these landscapes, these sodden ditches thronged with the delicate stalks of cow parsley and St Patrick's Cabbage: *The Silence of the Hills, A Munster Twilight* – tenebrous, page after tender, darkening page.

Beyond Glengarrif Anselm Daunt himself drew in his breath when the road crested the slopes above the Beara peninsula and looped on until it lost itself in the block of the Caha mountains. This was new country to Claire, but the men knew it well and they hailed it, they halted, it was theirs in the same way the language was theirs, as if they alone identified the symbolism of the territory they surveyed, as if, although it belonged to other people, those smallholders of some ancient lease would recognise, without argument, a superior spiritual right. Understanding this much at least while she leaned against the bonnet of the car, Claire guessed too at the subdued friction there must be in these four hearts which were one against another even there, even in that very identification. This, with Caha and Slieve Miskish looming massive and austere, with Hungry Hill a threatening peak to the south, was the land of darkest poverty, of grimmest injustice against race and religion, of exploitation, of poetry, of resistance. It was a heartland, to be shared only with those who had proven their claim in vengeance, or in victimisation.

The men had loosed themselves in the rocks of the roadside; Claire wondered if they thought she wouldn't notice what they were doing, and then remembered what she had learned from Leon – they didn't care whether she noticed or not. Nothing, she told herself – she had told herself this before – would make her disappear without a word, and certainly not *with* a word – in order to relieve herself on the mountainy shingle. Relieve herself – it meant what it said; listening without wanting to, hearing, rather, the gushy streams of the men whose backs were turned to the roadway but not to one another, Claire felt that it must be a relief, a release, like a bag being punctured. She had done it as a child on long walks home from Knockraha, finding the space among the gladed trees where no one would overlook her, encouraged to privacy by Della and accompanied sometimes by Angela but not if either of them had any choice in the matter. She knew and had liked the tickle of grass, even the more exciting pinch of gorse, against the skin of her bottom, and had not found the warm green smell of the wet ground distasteful.

But here? Among the men? She didn't need to, anyway, although she was conscious of the itch of the pad with its weight of blood. She must remember to buy Kotex in Woolworths when she got home; she had brought enough with her for an overnight trip, and plenty of clean underwear, but she recalled the light feel of the box this morning. She tucked the thought away and turned to the voice at her shoulder:

'Looking for Sliabh Luachra?' Peadar Cullen had come back to the car. The other men lounged against the wall of rock, smooth as slate. They rested with cigarettes in their hands, collars open. Daunt, even at the slouch, was taller than his companions; he had turned so that his back was to Claire, he faced the men as he spoke to them. The ease of his body belied the tension of his speech. She could not hear it, but Claire saw its rigour, the emphasis his hand, fisted, gave his words against the stone.

Although it was a mountain name, it meant a valley. Looking west, Claire saw she could not see that valley beyond the valleys before her.

> Now I shall cease, death comes, and I must not delay
> By Laune and Laine and Lee, diminished of their pride,
> I shall go after the heroes, ay, into the clay –
> My fathers followed theirs before Christ was crucified.

'Ah,' Cullen's smile dismissed her. 'O'Connor – and Yeats. Not bad, I suppose, not bad as an introduction to Ó Rathaille. Although I wonder what he would have made of Yeats's usage – and, indeed, of O'Connor's translations? And there he is –'

'Cullen stretched his arm, palm down, the fingers in the loose, powerful pose of the enchanter. 'There he lies, in Killarney, with the McCarthys. How his life must have surprised him. He never got ahead of it. *Gile na gile*.'

He brought back his hand, empty. He had left his jacket in the car, and the cuff of his shirt was loose, without a button or a link. Was there no one to mind him, Claire wondered, or was he one of those men, Leon would be one without his mother, was one in Dublin now, those men who never hesitated when dressing themselves, never fearing to put on what was to hand, not noticing its condition. 'The cut of him,' would be Mrs Cummins's comment, and Della, Claire knew, never failed to notice things like that. She felt suddenly almost sorry for Cullen as her mother would certainly have done, instinctively, at first.

'No,' she said, 'I wasn't thinking of Ó Rathaille.'

She turned to him, to this man with the closed committed face, eyes luminous but set deep into the hollow pallor of brow and cheek-bone, she turned to him knowing that she had only to get through this day, and tomorrow's return journey, until she would be free of him and his mission. Of all their missions. She found an impulsive, convincing lie, and laughed with it:

'I was thinking of how lovely it all is. I was thinking, remembering, Raftery, my favourite –

> Anois, teacht an Earraigh, beidh an lá dul chun síne,
> Is tar éis lá Fhéile Bhríde ardóigh mé mo sheoil
> O chuir mé im' cheann é, ní stopaidh mé caoitheadh –

'*Go seasaidh mé síos i lár contae Muigheo*'

They had all joined in, coming back to the car, hearing her carefree lilt of the familiar rhythms, enjoying with her the incantation they could all recite in common, common to them as the Hail Mary.

And in the car the words rearranged themselves in her unlistening head. Now, with the arrival of the spring, the day will be getting longer; and following the day of the feast of Brigid I will rise up my sail – from the time that I got it into my head I will not stop ever – until I stand below in the middle of the county of Mayo.

It sang through Claire's consciousness – now, with the coming of the spring, I will hoist my sail, I will keep going until I land in the middle of Mayo. Now, that the spring has arrived, has come, is here, now, I will keep going, I will never stop, I will go on for ever –

The day lengthened before her. Daunt drove on south, under the Caha mountains to Adrigole and Castletown Bearhaven – Beara, they called it. Tomorrow they would assault the farmers and fishermen of Allihies and Eyeries and Ardgroom before swinging homeward through Bantry, south again to Skibbereen and eastwards to Clonakilty and Bandon. Claire heard their voices plotting the route, the strategy, heard the whittling towards the consensus they were trying to define for the sake of the public which belonged to no single one of the several groups they represented. The men noticed her silence. Cullen said that reporters never had much to say anyway, their job was to take everything in. That would be all right, Herlihy said, so long as she gave it all out again, as long as *The Journal* gave them a good show. But Claire said, and saw Daunt give a quick nod of resignation, that she had no control over that.

Daunt said, and Claire never forgot in her life that he had said it:

'Claire's the reporter, she tells what happens. She's the onlooker at life. She doesn't participate. It's what *we* say, today for example, and tonight, it's our words which decide hers.'

She thought he said 'define'; decide wasn't quite so brutal, and it was accurate. He was getting back at her, she supposed, for not agreeing more passionately that she would make sure, do her very best, to get *The Journal* to carry everything that happened, everything they said. She looked at Daunt, who could talk about her without looking at her because he was the driver. His black shirt with its short sleeves showed up the whiteness of his unaccustomed arms, the skin glinting with a fine gold mesh of hair. She had never resolved the antagonisms of their first meeting but now, as then, what she was beginning to accept as a kind of fearfulness, almost unconscious, was overcome by his physical wholesomeness, wholeness.

'I'm not sure I agree with that,' was all she could say in response, and he nodded –

'I didn't think you would. You like to place people, to define them, but you don't like to be defined yourself. Definite, yes –' and he slanted a mocking glance at her, almost smiling – 'I'll grant you that, you can be very definite. But not defined.'

Claire wondered if what she felt about this man, all that complex sensation of disturbance when she was near him, was nothing more complicated than dislike. The possibility freed her spirit. Yes, he did have presence, you could not ignore him, he made you feel as if you did not want to ignore him – but maybe he wasn't a particularly nice person underneath all that. And maybe he aroused such mixed-up emotions in other people – in her, anyway, and Damien too found it hard these days to talk about Daunt as a friend, they were so disparate now – because he was a bit mixed-up himself.

They were all a bit mixed-up, Claire decided then. And although she felt some kind of sympathy for them, and although she heard in their speeches that night echoes of the half-demented litany of woes and wrongs, real and imaginary, cherished and invented, learned, loved and longed for, all those fevered, unforgotten epic horrors of past and future which gave these men their fire, and their focus – although she heard and recognised all they said and understood too why they were saying it, it would be years before she could amend that liberating judgement: they were all a bit mixed-up.

'Crazy, aren't they?' said Jarleth Tattin, who had come to stand beside her in the water-lapped square at Castletown-beare. Startled by his smooth voice at her ear, Claire had no time to hide her astonishment that he should be here, in the cool dusk of the evening, among the farmers and shopkeepers of Beara, and the trawlermen, their pipes sending dubious quivers of smoke into the salty air.

'Are you travelling with them?' and he nodded at Cullen, and Herlihy, and Brown. Daunt had not spoken. He sat on the only seat on the open trailer, his collar a white rim to the dark mass of him, a sombre presence which the shifting crowd had accepted with stillness, with attention. He was the *imprimatur* on these speeches. He was the signal that whatever might be the opinions of the farming organisations and the fishermen's representatives and the trade unionists – what few of them there were down here – the Church in Ireland was not at all sure that the Common Market was a good thing.

Claire explained. Jarleth Tattin offered no explanations of his own but stood with her, listening. He lived, she remembered, somewhere near Skibbereen, a cottage he had said, or someone had told her. With his wife. Pauline, the brown-haired, tall, young woman. How old was he? She measured him beside her in the gloom; the springy hair was greying, she remembered that, and the strongly drawn features, the big straight nose, the sharply cut, long-lipped mouth, were stretched, as if to sit better on the big face. He must be forty, she thought, surely too old for that young woman, his wife.

'I can't stand too much of this,' he said. 'They're saying what the people here, these people, want to be true, but know isn't true. These farmers, these trawlermen – the word they hear is *market*. And they're right. They want to live here. Not in Birmingham, or Springfield Massachusetts, with their uncles and their sisters.'

Claire felt his hand on her elbow.

'And I can't stand too much of this place – I always feel there's blood here, mayhem. It creeps in on you – do you feel it?'

She was ready to feel it. His voice was silky, and knowledge-able. She could respond to his perceptions of this place which was strange to her. What she had been feeling was the tired resentment of old slogans, shaken like tattered flags in the face of modern life, modern progress. She had begun to get angry; her notes drew arcs of incompatibility, of contradictions. Around the town lay abandoned mines, ruins of castles and cabins – fishing boats, flayed and peeling, hung on the shingle, waiting, waiting.

'This is a place of death,' Tattin said. Claire began to laugh, to say she hadn't thought it was *that* serious, but his face was not turned towards her, and the turn of his head was not attentive to the voices on the lorry.

'Fifty-eight men died here, maybe sixty. Hanged. Can you imagine it? All in one day – and twelve more a few days later. That was after Dunboy – have you read your Froude?'

He saw the pen on her notebook.

'You mustn't read Froude as history – only as fiction. I'll let you have something. Come along, we'll have a drink.' And his hands closed over her notes, put the cap on her pen, passed them both to her, closed.

The directness of these commands and assumptions amused her, and beguiled her, too. It was pleasant to be taken charge of, just a little. It was exciting to find, in this nameless crowd, a name which recognised hers – no, what was exciting was that it was Jarleth Tattin who had seen her in the press, in the dark, and who now wanted her company, and would loan her books which she would have to return. Perhaps she would meet Pauline Tattin, see their cottage, meet their friends.

And so it was. All those things did happen, beginning with this hour she spent in a small brown pub with Tattin, drinking her innocuous ginger ale and listening to him talk about Beara and Dunboy, of T. S. Eliot and Martin Ó Cadhain, of Flann O'Brien and Briain Ó Cathasaigh. He did not say much about his work, but she knew that he worked exclusively – except when a piece on Ireland was required for *Vogue* or the *New Statesman*, and that didn't happen very often – in Irish. Did Pauline speak, know, Irish? If not, it must be like having a secret world within his own domestic interiors. She could imagine the cool silences of open doors, of tiled spaces where it was accepted that a man would work, remote and undisturbed, while the urge to work drove him on, where nothing would be expected of him but this work. And the woman would polish the silence, knit and keep bees, make wine and answer letters, the telephone, his needs.

That was what Leon would like, Claire thought now. It was as well he'd given up on her. She could see its charm, even for the woman, the life of the handmaiden, like Augustus John's Dorelia. Dedicated. And then those women could write books about their husband, or be written about themselves. There was a sheen on that prospect, but Claire did not see her own fate reflected in it. No – she would be the writer, but from a different perspective. She promised herself that, and her goodbye to Tattin when she left him to keep appointments Anselm Daunt had made for her in the town was cool, unexpectant.

He noticed it. 'Someday I'll get you drunk, Claire Mackey. And then we'll see!' But it was a teasing threat, and if she felt a little thrill, a little spurt of a promise to be kept, it lasted no longer with her than the following day's reminder, as she travelled with Daunt and Cullen and Brown and Herlihy back to the city through Carbery and the baronies of the southern peninsulas, that down here, somewhere, was where he lived.

Down here. They were returning on the southern ring, climbing the narrow coastal roads over Roaringwater Bay, passing Castletownshend, Union Hall, making for Leap. Claire thought of Edith Oenone, playing the organ at the church of St Barrahane until her death – oh, only a few years ago – and of Martin Ross, dead much earlier, it was said, of an injury in the hunting field – where she jumped everything she came across because she was too short-sighted to see it properly. Seeing the signpost Daunt said – 'A bundle of rags and a cough – that's the way they described an old woman from the town who called to the door – that's what Somerville and Ross were like.'

They passed that turning too, but the men suggested a stop, soon, a pint and a few sandwiches, what did Daunt think? Would Claire like a break? They turned sharply south to Glandore where, as Conor Herlihy said, they were fed and watered. Peadar Cullen held open the door of the car for Claire as they went to get back in, and this gallantry induced an admission from Herlihy – 'I always love it when there's a girl in the car – everything smells so nice.'

Claire grinned back at him; she had sprinkled Blue Grass all over her underwear when she dressed that morning in the damp-smelling guest-house. Smells were startling adjectives to life, she thought, but perfume was like a lie, you could buy it, a secretion which was not your own. As a child she had savoured Midnight in Paris found among Della's nightgowns; when she uncapped the flattened sphere of the dark blue bottle, so dark as to be almost black yet glinting blue against the whites and pinks in the drawer, when she had taken out the little stud of rubber which kept the essence trapped within, the whole person, face, voice, hair, hands of her mother flooded her attentive senses. What had been subtle became pervasive, it was as if a genie had escaped, cancelling by its declamatory presence the gentler mystery of her mother's smell.

From Paris Della had brought home later the aromatic texts which banished for ever the Muguet du Bois Claire had once bought for her in Woolworths. Claire had resisted their heady fragrances. It surprised her that Della no longer shared her own preference for the fresher flowery tones of Old English Lavender or Apple Blossom, or the acidulous clean tang of Eau de Cologne which she and Angela had given for years to Onora as their own, own-pocket-money bought presents. For Claire these were true smells; they were not concoctions, they were essences, as in Bendemeer Stream, Frank's song:

> . . . a dew was distilled from the blossoms that gave
> all the fragrance of summer when summer was gone.
> Thus memory draws from delight ere it dies
> An essence that clings to it, all through the years –

She could hear his voice soaring to it, lingering on the word essence, up to reach clings, hovering there. So many of her visions of calm and restorative beauty were infused with the notes of his voice, the light Irish tenor, untrained but musically very well read.

Only a couple of days ago she had heard him – 'I'll sing thee songs of Araby, and tales of old Kashmir.' He was washing the dishes for Della, after the dinner, stately in an apron. From the bathroom where she hurriedly prepared to go out Claire had heard him – 'o-old Kash-meer'.

'And dreams of delight will on thee break, and vis-hons wa-a-ander there; And *all* my *soul* will *strive* to wake sweet *wonder* in thine eyes' – then slower – 'And all my soul will strive to wake, sweet wonder in thine eyes.'

And that was more of it, Claire thought now as the car spun her towards home. You could be illiterate – people *had* been illiterate – but if you heard good hymns in church, or if you could remember songs and ballads, even if you couldn't sing them, and people had been able to hear all that, well then you were experiencing a quality of language which was ennobling. Country folksongs had it: she remembered hearing on BBC long wave an old farm labourer singing about a maiden who appeared like 'a virtuous bride'; she had heard, in the village of Blackpool among the factory workers, the men singing a refrain – 'then give to me the parting glass and we'll sing in bonds of love'. People accepted and used that kind of language; why should the churches, which of all institutions should be the most ennobling, abandon it?

'They want us to believe in miracles, but they won't offer us miraculous words' – and she felt a kind of angry despair, that she would prefer not to have to worry about it, not to think about it any more, except with scorn.

The day was still bright as they traversed it, soon they would be in Rosscarbery. A dip in the hill showed them the fields spread out below, a valley between the road and the sea. She saw gables, eaves, high chimneys, a roofless ruin still ornate and imposing, but wrecked, abandoned. The signpost arrowed in green lettering for tourists – 'Coppingers' Court'.

Claire exclaimed. The car hesitated, Daunt began a question, she said no, nothing, just something she had seen and they gathered speed again and stopped only once more, at the edge of the woodland along the Bandon river, where bluebells had broken from the banks of trees and streamed in an abundant tide along the edges of the road.

'There's some colour for your colour piece,' said Daunt, but he was not sneering, and when Claire, knowing that her colour would come from the square at Castletownbeare, and from the gorse that triumphed above the ragged fields of Allihies and Adrigole, said only that she would pick some of the flowers for Della, he bent to pick them with her.

At the car Herlihy was waiting. 'That's a smell, now,' he said, 'that reminds me of a church.' He put his face to the limp blossoms he was holding across his arm.

'New suits and First Communion!' he exclaimed with a laugh, and handed the flowers to Claire. He sang:

> Bluebells we'll gather
> Take them and be true
> When I'm a man,
> My plan,
> Will be to marry you.

They all laughed, relaxed, ready for the evening of meetings and marching before them. They hurried towards the city, the sky above it still blue, clear and cloudless. The car filled now with the light, sweet scent of the bluebells. Claire put some newspaper pages under their weeping stems as they lay, dying, in her lap.

Chapter 10

There was a magic about Damien. He had never looked more the priest, gowned in what Della used to refer to as his 'canonicals' – the loosely waisted cassock with its full skirt, the lace-fringed surplice crisp and snowy, its starched purity echoing the sharp white collar at his throat. He had only been an assistant at the Mass and had not spoken; all that had been done by the parish priest which was, Frank had said when he remembered to tell Claire about the arrangements, what Della would have preferred. And that was probably true, because it was what was fitting, and Della had always believed that what was appropriate was also what was right. So mild-mannered, mild-voiced, kind Canon Feerick had celebrated the Mass at the vocal distance imposed by his distrust of the recently installed microphones and his worried dislike of the new liturgy.

He hadn't objected to Damien's presence on the altar, Angela had told Claire, although he had asked that the two Dominican fathers from the city parish and the Capuchin priests who represented the Third Order of St Francis should not expect to concelebrate: they must be content with front pews and a place in the formal recessional. They had a magic too, although they wore only their habits – habitual robes which gave their unhurried pace on the aisle a stateliness which was in itself some kind of comfort.

But Damien: on the altar he wore the simple black and white

clothes which had their own grace, duller than the matted silk of the vestments of the Canon, but appropriate.

Assisting, Claire thought. Perhaps that was what Damien was meant for – assisting. As a chaplain helping people to die, as a priest of the diocese helping to fill gaps, even with the Legion of Mary he had not seemed fully fledged. He never seemed to her to have a central role in anything. He didn't look, now, as though he were aware of that. He looked, now, as though he understood life's purpose in having him assist at the events of death.

The coffin was in the hearse. Angela had made sure that Mrs Cummins's plastic roses of white and blue were as close within the glass walls as those of the family; other wreaths and sheafs carpeted the roof of the hearse, held in by the chrome rail. Small knots of people stood around, apparently irresolute. Onora was inside the first funeral car, Frank and Stan standing at its door. Hands were being shaken, there were some smiles. When the passing bell had ceased someone in a group at the door of the church laughed, and it did not seem incongruous in this shifting, meeting, clasping of people.

Claire's uncles, Della's brothers, were there. One of them turned up alone at Whitethorn – his wife did not travel, he had said. Onora had repeated this assertion to Claire, knowing it to be an excuse, acceptable because she didn't care, but knowing it also to be an extraordinary thing to say, and saying it to Claire because then they could both smile at it – that one of them sitting with Onora in the car, holding her hand, and indeed, Claire had admitted to herself when she saw him come slowly down the aisle with Onora, he did look shaken: 'very low' was how he had described himself.

And Damien: in the Sacristy, she knew, he would take off the cassock and reappear for the burial in his simple clerical suit. But here he stood, robed, within a knot of friends, his hands hammocked in the low-slung pockets of his skirts, and he was not informal. There was a presence here, an appearance of absoluteness. He was not a copy of the Canon; his magic was his own, yet he shared its source with the Canon.

Holy Orders. Claire thought it must be the magic of ordination, of the rite. In common life he was a common man, although not commonplace. On the altar vested, he was remote; a dream, or part of a film sequence, yet tangible. Claire had seen the Canon pause to allow Damien to offer the host to Angela's open mouth, to Frank, to Onora; she too had received – a gesture to the occasion – but placed herself so that the Canon's spotted hands held out the Eucharist. Kneeling she had watched Damien stoop over each communicant, she had seen his fingers spread around the sacred vessel, the inducted touch with which, with second finger and thumb, he caught each wafer. She had remembered those fingers spread with confidence along the rim of the steering wheel, brushing once, smoothly, over hers when she failed to correct her grip. She remembered them tamping down the tobacco in his pipe when they stood together in Dungourney, outside the cottage with its roses, its statue. Those fingers, square, capable, and white with a softness which showed them kept for pure mysteries, dipped the cup of incantation closer to her; she turned towards the ciborium under the Canon's hand. The silver pattern blazed with colour as the sun strengthened through the high, stained windows. The glare sharpened the tears in her eyes so that the Canon hesitated at her bowed head. As her accepting mouth closed again it allowed his knuckles to touch, for an instant, the blurred rim of her cheek.

The small group of singers which Damien, with Raphael's help, had got together for this week-day morning had softened the bones of the new rubric by singing the Gloria, as if for High Mass, in Latin. The music spread itself over the long phrases: *Gratias agimus tibi, propter magnam gloriam tuam.* It should not have been there at all: the Canon had allowed it as a hymn, rather than as part of the liturgy. Claire found its familiarity a solace in itself, but knew that Frank had hesitated, agreeing only when Angela had reminded him of how much Della had enjoyed – and that was the word she used, 'enjoyed' – the Gregorian chant the girls had learned to sing in school. How moved she had been at Mount Mellary, listening to the monks at their devotions. Della had never been as devout as Frank, had always kept the distance of humour between herself and his piety, but she had valued some of the more gracious commonplaces of religion. And Damien, irritated by Claire's irreverence, had appreciated Della's subjective orthodoxy, and recognised the rhythms which had linked her heart to her faith, or thought he did. These unvarnished but mellow cadences were an offering to what he understood.

Claire, suffering through a ceremony with no Introit or Collect, Epistle or Gradual, Offertory or Lavabo, Secret, Preface, or Canon of the Mass, had to remind herself that she wouldn't have wanted to suffer through all those episodes either, it was just that she had been used to them, and had had to learn them, and now wanted them to be there, liturgical punctuation marks which concentrated the attention. She supposed, she said to herself this morning, that none of it mattered, really. If Fr Feerick could live with it she, who had no intention of needing this religion, or of caring any longer than today's length how it was delivered to its adherents, had no right to criticise. Except that she felt, somewhere inside her, a kind of caring, a longing that the substance of things familiar should not be reduced, that their hidden essence should not be diminished or damaged by change. The liturgy, she remembered the old slogan about corporal work of mercy, should be an outward sign of inward grace. How could she think these things, how could she care, with Della's coffin at the altar, the lid closed, tight and irrevocable? How, when she watched the fearful steps of Frank, of Stan, of her uncles Oliver and Edward shouldering the dead weight down the aisle, out on to the sun-lined steps, conducted by the backward-pacing undertaker, steadied by his aides, how then could she think, watching Onora walk with Angela, that it was some relief that for once Onora wore a coat longer than her skirt? How could she ponder the fact that this coffin-bearing, pall-bearing task was undertaken only by men, that women never carried coffins, dug graves? How could she be gratified – as she was – that Stan's mother and sisters had come to the church? It was not their church, and it was not their custom – but they had come, for Angela, to show that they accepted Della's *place* in Stan's life. And it could have been no pain to them, Claire reminded herself on a little spur of bitterness, no pain to sit through this transmogrified Mass; at times they must have thought they were at home up in St Luke's.

Claire saw Raphael, silent, in the group around Angela, next to the two Good Shepherd nuns. The faces were differently composed. Angela looked burnished, her hair glossy and immaculate under a black tam-o'-shanter, her body only slightly engorged by pregnancy and decently cloaked in grey, a black ruffle of collar stiffening her neck and clouding the helpless sheen of her skin. She listened to the nuns as though she were interested. Claire saw her nod, her eyes downcast, her mouth soft and full. Raphael was listening too, nodding more emphatically, his face calm, almost austere, Claire thought, surprised at the thought: it was as if his feelings were put away. Not hidden, not concealed by the fragile skin, the taut bones of his face, but deposited out of sight, put away for some reason. Masculinity, she supposed, thinking of the politeness with which Frank hid his anguish.

She could not see the nun who was talking, the white coif bent towards Angela, the black veiling lifted lightly at her shoulder by the breeze of her own speech. Her companion was holding Angela's hand, her small round face full of that expression so familiar to, so dreaded by, post-*Humanae Vitae* Catholics – compassion. As Stan approached, ready to take Angela to the waiting car, anxious, with Frank, to get 'things' under way, the nun dropped Angela's hand and retreated, just a step or two, but enough. That nun Claire remembered seeing with Della in hospital. There had been whispers. Something to do with the child Sarah, the little girl whose father had drowned, the man Claire had written about, Nicholas Barry. Della had taken some kind of interest – hadn't she known the Reverend Mother, something about the convent where the child was to be reared? Something. Claire would ask Onora about it later.

Onora was not seeing this, she was safe for the moment, held in the car, held on to by one of her sons. 'Why am I seeing this?' Claire was conscious all at once that she stood alone, that her passion for observation had isolated her. 'How can it be like this?' How could she stand, thinking how lovely Angela looked, despite it all, how young Raphael looked, untouched despite everything; how lucky that Damien hadn't had to leave yet. How right she had been to pick the last of the Fruhlingsgold, how good, how real, how appropriate they were now, still fresh, still fragrant, pale as primroses and flushed with pink, trembling on the bones of the branches, held in a fronded sheaf on the coffin's lid.

She stood alone. Colleagues from *The Journal* had come, taken her hand, spoken to Frank. Friends were there, neighbours. Mrs Cummins was among some of the people from the village, from the Fisheries, from Rope Walk and Factory Lane, neighbours who sympathised with her, who said they were sorry for her trouble. Her husband was there, the bould Christy, Della would have said; she would have been surprised and gratified that for this, at last, he had turned out.

Claire stood alone because she could not bear to be with anyone. She could not bear the acceptance, the civility, the balm of custom. She was left alone, she could observe without hindrance, she could think without interruption, because it was not grief she was keeping at bay, but the ignominy of consolation; it was not sorrow she was trying to contain, but anger.

It was anger which had inflamed her since that early call to the Dublin hotel, catching her then in the little lie with which she had protected her visit to Leon's flat; she had not wanted Frank to know she would be seeing him. Or perhaps the anger had begun to flare earlier in that last few days; had it begun when on sitting in Frank's car to go to the railway station she had been briefly delayed by the arrival of Angela, bringing Onora to stay for the weekend?

No, surely that had been merely annoyance. Claire hadn't insisted on going away as planned, it was the others, Frank especially, who had said that everything was fine, that she had a job to do, dammit, and if the job was taking her to Dublin for a night or two then off she had to go. Nothing was happening at home – 'nothing is happening', he had insisted – to make her change her plans. Had Claire been too ready to accept that? She had wanted to go; the charity ball was to be a spectacular event, the first of its kind in the country, internationally funded, minor crowned heads among the guest list, Grace of Monaco the Guest of Honour. There was a newspaper strike in Dublin, *The Journal* would be the only daily paper covering the event. And Della was still the same, no worse, if no better. There was nothing urgent, was there?

Nothing, they had said; Onora, Frank, Angela. From her bed Della had directed Claire to a high, forbidden drawer, a pair of kid gloves, long, unsoiled, the texture of petals. Putting them on slowly, stretching the febrile skin along her arms, flexing her fingers under the tight but softening coating, Claire saw herself for an instant in the pier glass – a blur of blue tulle and lace. She took Della's bristle brush and stroked it through the Amami-stiffened waves of her hair, then turned with a smile to her mother.

At the foot of her bed Della saw the girl in blue. The dark, relaxed hair curled almost to the white shoulders: there was nothing in Claire of Angela's creamy radiance, yet this whiteness exposed by the tracery of the lace *fichu* had both charm and vulnerability. The dress was gathered at the waist, and then azure billows of tulle were let fall to the lace-edged hem at the floor. Pale suede shoes had been found, Angela had loaned a strand of pearls. The gloves – Claire lifted her hand to her nose, savouring their stored-up scent – gave a finished look, curbing the enthusiasms of the fabric, balancing the indulgent blue with their own pale rectitude.

This girl in blue, standing at the foot of Della's bed, the friendly light of the spring garden illuminating her colour, her glow, her vitality – this did not look like a girl going off to work. This looked like a girl in a dream, floating, beautiful, happy. But Della had no dreams remaining for her daughters:

that they were there, concrete, touchable – that was enough, now.

'I'll be back, Sunday or Monday, Mum,' Claire whispered, coming closer to the bed, sitting at Della's side, her skirt a drift of blue against the white pillows, the coloured spread. Her shining head bent to Della's hair, which had thinned, grown grey. Yet it smelt of Della, and the ruched skin of her neck, so strange, so unlikely, the pallid hand she laid in the ebullient cloud, tasting its texture with her fingertips – these were all truly Della, what Della was, what she had become. These were known.

'This is the hand of Bridget Cruise!' The thought sprang into Claire's mind like a shock. She took Della's hand in hers, and sat there, her head still touching Della's head, her eyes thick with tears.

'I do want you to go, Claire.' Della's voice was thin, but firm. Claire nodded. She would change her clothes, get ready. In just a minute of two, there was time.

So much was just as usual. The usual sun spread itself through the casement, the dressing-table looked the same, one side for Della, one for Frank. The pictures – an old bridge somewhere in Holland, vibrant pansies in a latticed basket, sheep in snow with a sunset, and an Italianate crucifixion – all the same. Gluic, as usual, had sunk into a hollow of the eiderdown. On the bookcase beside the bed a stem glass held wallflowers, bronze, gold, ruby-red. A petal stirred and fell.

'You mustn't mind so much,' Della said. She sounded unfocused, as though the words were not exactly what she wanted, not what she meant to say, but came close enough. Then she said: 'I don't mind.'

She was weary. She had no more reassurance to offer. She wanted her gone, this girl trailing yards of untidy tulle; she wanted her off, away, enjoying herself, busy. She wanted not to have to think about her.

The Journal had a transport concession; its reporters went first class, which meant curtains and antimacassars and waiter service in the carriage. Leon derided Claire's liking for the comfort, the privacy. Once he had surprised her there, diving into the seat next to hers just as a ten-second tunnel came up, and he kissed her suddenly, fiercely, in the dark, grinning at her, delighted with himself, as they emerged.

'I believe in taking advantage of every opportunity,' he forestalled Claire's protests, confident that her rosy, half-indignant smiles accepted his daring.

Would tonight be an opportunity? They had not met for several months now. They had left things unfinished, but there had been letters, brief but friendly. He was not going to the ball with her; that would be Dan Smylie, the paper's Dublin photographer. Claire liked him, they had worked together, got on together, before this. They were both ambitious, and had a good-humoured tolerance of one another's priorities. But tonight she would meet Leon, she was only checking into her hotel tomorrow to get ready – ironing the dress, having a bath, getting her hair done – for the ball.

After all, she would be glad to see Leon again. She flexed her feet against the opposite seat, let her book lie open, ignoring Felix Holt, the radical. She looked instead into the green distances of small fields, the flat rich midland acres clotted with the cream of clover, the thick abundant ditches frilled with cow parsley, elder flower, dog daisies and still, here and there, she could see when the banks ran close to the train, tufted with primroses, their scorched centres fading at last as the blackthorn and whitethorn twisted above them, laden branches bursting with May blossom, brilliantly white and pink. A horse stood alert in a field, beside a foal furled in the grass like an unsaddled snail. Cows drowsed along the shallows of a stream, their horned heads lifting as the train passed, their hides burnished red or black, grey, white or roan, patterned with indeterminate freckles or great white and black Friesian patches.

What *was* that, Claire tried to remember –

When the dark cow leaves the moor
And pastures poor with [something: greedy?] weeds
Perhaps he'll hear her low at morn
Lifting her horn in pleasant meads.

Ledwidge, that was it, the *Lament for Thomas McDonagh*.

What did she mean, *'I don't mind. You mustn't mind so much'*? What had Della meant by it? In the wider fields the lambs stretched with woolly langour beside their complacent mothers, content with the day that they knew, unquestioning. Clouds like fleeces dappled the sky, still blue, still friendly, here where it was still the south.

But racing towards Dublin, through the carpeted fields of Laois and Kildare, the sky thinned and darkened. After the Curragh it was black, with a curious white fringe under its northern hem, as though a storm was being stirred into it from the edges. Ragged castles pierced the meadowlands. It would be raining and cold in the city. Claire shivered, the train becoming bleak as its last stops slipped away behind it.

Leon was waiting for her at Kingsbridge, wearing small round glasses which made him look, Claire told him, like Trotsky, and he smiled, contented. She was glad to see him, that he had cared to come for her. She told him about Della, quickly, in the taxi, not knowing what she was telling him, except that it made it seem better, somehow, more manageable. She said she thought Della had liked seeing her in her ball-gown.

Leon would not see her like that, but he put his arm around her and drew her close to whisper: *'My love in her attire doth show her wit/It doth so well become her/For every season she hath dressings fit/For winter, spring and summer/No beauty she doth miss/When all her clothes are on/But Beauty's self she is/When all her clothes are gone.'*

Which indicated his plans for the evening and Claire, caught on the surprised pleasure of his courtesy, his fun, aquiesced with a speed which astonished them both. So they went straight to Leon's flat in a red-brick old house on a tree-lined old street, near the canal. Tomorrow, Claire promised herself, she would walk its suburban length, thinking of Kavanagh,

> O commemorate me where there is water,
> Canal water preferably, so stilly
> Greeny at the heart of summer. Brother
> Commemorate me thus beautifully.

For all her poetry, it had been very direct, once they got indoors. Leon kissed her at once, rasping his face against hers, determined against her gasped protests when she came up for air. She had a glimpse of a kitchen, not messy. With shrinking nostrils she allowed herself to be propelled to the bedroom, but the big sash windows were open, the room smelt only different, not stale, not threatening. A frantic glance at the bed promised clean sheets – 'Should I even be thinking these things?' Claire waited for the gush, the loosening flood of excitement. She gulped the wine Leon poured, it had been ready: 'It is already,' he said '*chambré*,' emphasising the pun, and she laughed and choked and took another glass quickly, easing the dryness in her throat, the throb in her breast almost hurting. She began another question as he closed in on her, his shirt open, his hands at her skirt, thrusting under her blouse, and his tongue stopped her.

'The bathroom,' she panted, 'I have to –'

'No,' he said, 'I have them, I'll take care of that,' and pulled her down on the bed.

'No!' she was almost wailing, 'I have to go to the bathroom. *Leon!*'

'Hurry,' he said, only that, but it made her hot, and she did hurry, she relieved herself, then washed hastily between her legs, noticing that the toilet bowl was clean, the wash-basin untidy but not slovenly, the bath unstained. But where had he got 'them', the condoms? From England or Belfast she surmised; smuggled, wouldn't doubt him! Towels were heaped on the floor, but fresh ones hung behind the door; there was a cupboard, open, with more towels, more toilet paper. All very reassuring.

She went back to him in her slip, her skirt and blouse folded. He was lying on the bed, bare-chested, his shoes off. She wasn't sure how to start again, but Leon simply brought her to lie beside him, ran his hands over her shoulders, along her neck, through her hair, held her and brought his face down close to hers.

His glasses slipped along his nose, he took them off, put them on a little table beside the bed. His face changed. That was the thrill, for Claire. The removal of the spectacles, the intimate gesture which revealed his face, made him briefly vulnerable, made her breathless with tenderness. His tongue, his teeth at her ear, that was not new, that was part of their journeys before. It was great, but the new thing was this newly-shielded face, newly revealed. She rolled easily under him, her eyes open, happy. She helped him out of his trousers, didn't touch his underpants, striped she noticed, and not baggy. When she went to kiss his penis he said no, later, he wanted to make her ready.

'I'm ready!' Now she was at his mercy, loving it, open, yielding, panting. He was huge, he seemed to twitch, she could see him before Leon moved decisively on to her stomach. How could she have held that in her mouth? Her mouth twisted, her eyes squeezed against the roughness of Leon's hand, Leon's penis, both down there, pushing. Could she keep her legs up? Leon's other hand was at her shoulder, hurting, his mouth was at her breast, sucking on her, *that* didn't mean much, everything was happening down there. Wasn't it? She felt fluid, a hole being filled in – that was why some men called it that, so – your hole.

Then Leon reared above her, his head over her, his eyes shut, he began to move, to shove, almost to rotate. Her body began to fill, to expand and palpitate. 'My goodness,' she thought, 'I can certainly feel this all right. This is certainly something.'

She became wildly exhilarated, she began to move herself, she thought she had found the rhythm of his thrusts. Leon put his hand over her mouth. He said, 'Be still;' as though she were interrupting something. He shuddered, moaned once, stayed poised above her, then opened his eyes and grinned. With a sharp pull he came out of her. Claire felt tears pricking her eyelids. Why should she want to cry – because it was over too soon?

Leon said – 'I'll be back,' and went to the bathroom. He returned, diminished. Claire, cold and self-conscious, had covered herself, but he drew back the quilt, looked intently at her face, and kissed her gently, with kindness, saying 'lovely girl, lovely girl' over and over.

They ate, quickly, in the not untidy kitchen. He was taking her to the Abbey Tavern in Howth for the singing. Ballads, he said, and when she asked 'Sean Nós?' he looked quizzical and said maybe.

They got to Howth with friends of Leon's, sat with them at a rough-edged table, sweltered with them in the crowded heat, gasped with them in the smoke-drenched atmosphere.

'It is a great atmosphere, isn't it?' Leon was enthusiastic, not at all cryptic or withdrawn, wholeheartedly enjoying the *'craic'*, as he called it, slapping his hand on the table in time to the bodhrán rhythm from the group singing itself hoarse and unharmonious on the stage.

It was rollicking ballads they roared out –

> The sea oh the sea is grádh geal mo croidh
> Long may it stay between England and me
> It's a sure guarantee that one day we'll be free
> Thank God we're surrounded by water!

Everyone joined in. They sang 'The Rocky Road to Dublin' and 'McAlpine's Fusiliers' – 'When the going is rough, ye must be tough, with McAlpine's Fusiliers!'

As I was a-walking one morning in May, they sang, everybody sang. One pleasant morning in the month of June: early one morning just as the sun was rising; it was on a summer's morning all in the month of May. They sang farewell to Liverpool, Yarmouth, the Holy Ground while they hunted the bonny shoals of herrin' and drank strong ale and porter. They were all off to Dublin in the green, in the green.

Claire sang. She was lifted by all this, there was a freedom in it, a rousing uncritical friendliness and fellowship, something very masculine. She felt close to Leon, closer to him than ever before, none of the people here, none of his friends, knew her except as his companion, she was there only because he was there. She was a part of his life. Did she want to be? Here, now, *yes*. She wanted to be the woman on whose shoulder he would spread his hand as he left to go to order more drinks at the bar. She wanted to be the woman who could look at that sharp-edged clever face, the confident eyes, knowing that if she took off his spectacles, if she just reached across now and unhooked them, she would recognise the briefly bewildered look in his eyes. She really wanted that, she decided, watching Leon moving carefully among the throng, on his way back to *her*. And he looked good, he looked in command, enjoying himself but independent. As he came nearer to their table he caught her eyes on him. He returned her gaze, deepening it, so that other senses became alert in her and she said, when he reached her side – 'Can we go soon?'

Apparently absorbed in the arrangement of pints and half-pints he slanted a look at her: 'After this,' he said, indicating the arrival on the platform, to knowledgeable applause and stamps and shouts of acclaim, of a young man who adjusted the microphone to his liking and then stood before it, thumbs in the pockets of his jeans, and pitched his voice at it.

> By the margin of the ocean, one pleasant evening in the month of June
> When all those feathered songsters their liquid notes did sweetly tune.
> 'Twas there I spied a female, and on her features the sign of woe

Conversing with young Bonaparte, concerning the Bonny
Bunch of Roses, O.

He sang without adornment or accompaniment. His voice
was not sweet, yet it had more musicality, more tone and
tune to it, than those other voices which everyone accepted
as singing. He clenched his eyes, Claire could see his fists
clenching, when the notes had to be raised or lengthened, or
when long words had to be cornered in a single bar, and then
other men murmured praise, or said 'Good on you!'

His open eyes were cool, almost colourless. He had the high
cheek-bones of a natural charmer, and there was something
attractively dangerous about the character that his voice, his
features, his pose suggested. Claire thought that the women,
too, who stood on this platform, who sang songs like these,
had this rakish racy look to them, the skirts long, the hair
loose, a personality flamboyant yet contained. But they were
not raucous. They always found the song and gave its truth to
the audience – as this young man was doing now.

In the din of acclaim as the song ended Claire and Leon
got up to leave, but this brought them suddenly next to the
singer. There were quick introductions, both Claire and Leon
enthused, and Claire heard, and hated, her own gushing words.
She tried to excuse herself to Leon, who said, 'He's probably
well used to it by now' – but that wasn't what Claire had meant.
'He was a medical student,' Leon added, 'but he's given all that
up now; now he writes traditional ballads.'

Claire wondered if, after all, she wasn't inclined to over-
estimate Leon's intelligence. But she was still caught in that
security of male friendship which Leon seemed to spread
around her by his familiarity with all these men. Men who
enjoyed being together, who had made music their expert,
energetic thing, whose loud, witty collaboration drew people
into their extrovert gaiety, yet men who also shared the mystery
of accomplishment and made people like them, want them in
some conspiracy of communication which Claire, suddenly,
was coming both to admire and distrust. It seemed connubial,

a partnership finely balanced and understood, of which the offspring was music and its pleasures.

In the taxi she held herself away from Leon, storing up the excitement, keeping it at bay by reminding herself that there were things she wanted to tell him, she needed help, and the first, urgent source of help would be to be in his arms, in his bed, and she held him off now with promises. 'Later,' she whispered, 'wait.' She was hungry for him and he knew that, his own excitement held amusement too, she was turning out to be great fun, really.

He fumbled paying the taxi fare, struggled with the door keys. Claire felt the rain softly on her face and ran down the steps back to the empty street. The lamplight made a halo of the wet green trees. The night smelt of the coming summer, it smelt young: *'Leafy with love banks and the green waters of the canal'* she remembered. Thinking about tomorrow and tonight she turned back to where Leon stood, watching her, waiting for her, still on the steps by the open door. When she reached him, reaching out for him, he kissed her roughly, his hands on the damp of her hair. They got to bed very quickly after that, there was no time for talking, nothing that had to be said.

The morning came early. Claire wakened to the shock of knocking at the front door. What time was it? She felt Leon struggling awake beside her, it was – what? Eight o'clock? What could it be so early on a Saturday? He got his trousers on, a shirt, told Claire to stay where she was, went to open the front door. Through her fright Claire heard voices, a girl, then footsteps to the kitchen, the sound, she could identify it, of the kettle being put on. She felt cold. Leon came back after a while to finish dressing. He sat on the end of the bed and said *'Shit!'* He shook his head, as if to clear it of surprise. When he looked at Claire he was embarrassed.

'It's –' He got up, went over to the window. A clear dawn shone obediently into the room when he pulled back the curtains. 'It doesn't matter who it is. The thing is, she's someone who thinks I'm alone. And I suppose she has the right to think so. If anyone has.' He stopped.

'I'm giving her breakfast. But she's exhausted, she's been travelling all night, she needs, well, to sleep . . .'

Claire behaved, as she told herself afterwards, absolutely beautifully. Just give her a few minutes, she said calmly, and she'd be gone. She would need a taxi, there was her bag with her dress in it. She could leave that at the hotel, although it was still too early to check in. But she would go into the city centre, get her hair done, have coffee – she would be fine. He need not worry about her.

No indeed, Claire thought now, as she watched Leon moving towards a car with friends around it, waiting for him. He need not have worried about her, and had not. She acknowledged to herself that it had been thoughtful of him to come to the funeral – and daring, given the circumstances of their last meeting. But nothing in his behaviour suggested embarrassment, or awkwardness. He had found her quickly outside the church, put his arms around her, kissed her cheek, and left her alone. He had said nothing. And she had been touched, for a minute, that he had come – and grateful too, when she saw him shaking hands with Frank, and then leaning into the funeral car to speak to Onora.

'And now he will be gone,' Claire told herself. She saw already his right to be away from this gathering on this day. It was in his face – a preoccupation, a distance. There was a sense of his life gathering pace, closing around him like a net of demand and estrangement.

'He will always say he's one of us,' Claire realised, 'and he won't be, ever again. He will always turn up at funerals, always do his part, but that won't make him one of the people whose funeral it is. He will always have to get away, and be glad he has to.'

But they were all selected lives, the young faces turning away from her, turning towards the appointments of their future. Some of them would see this funeral through, but they would, all of them, they would all be somewhere in a day or two, maybe tonight even, where they would say – 'I was at Claire's mother's funeral the other day' or 'I saw him at Claire's mother's funeral.' And their lives would go on.

'Oh, this is not the worst part of it, Claire,' Onora had said. They were together in her dining room, waiting. 'The worst of it is that nothing, after this, will seem to have changed. She'll be gone, that's all. No more than that. No more than that, at all. Everything else – everything else will go on.'

'But not as if she had never been here,' Claire said, her words desperate. 'She made things different for people, she added something to the world she lived in. Didn't she? Didn't she, Damien?'

She turned to him, sitting at the other side of the fire he had prepared for Onora. They were here because it was close to the hospital where Frank and Angela and Stan were keeping vigil. Frank had said it would be better if Onora were at home, had something to eat. Damien had been at the house when they got there, he was cutting the grass. He had met Claire at the train and brought her to the hospital, that was what he had been asked to do. His impending departure had released him from other duties, he could do everything, anything, they asked of him, things no one thought of asking. On each of the last three days he had taken Bran for a walk, thinking Della would have liked that, and the puzzled but amenable dog had frisked and retrieved in the riverside fields and that, somehow, had made Damien feel useful. Cutting the grass, lighting Onora's fire, those things helped him.

Meeting Claire had not helped. When she saw him at the station she had thought Della was dead. 'What!' she had cried out at him. 'What!'

She had quietened then, seeing from his face that it was not what she had feared. Not yet. He had brought her wherever she needed to go, he had brought Mrs Cummins to the hospital and home again, wearing casual clothes to take the fright out of being given a lift by a priest, but that was wrong too because Mrs Cummins quite liked being given a lift by a priest.

'Is this all I can do?' he had asked himself, doing all he could. When Claire turned to him he wondered what she expected from him: why should she expect the conventional words of consolation?

'We must remember she's not gone,' he said, hesitating, but he meant it, he didn't want to anticipate the death which he knew was inevitable. Claire nodded, but she was impatient:

'But her life had *meaning* – things will go on, of course, but some things will be different, won't they, because she was here?'

'Yes, things are different. She helped other people, made their lives better.' He thought – '*Our birth is but a sleep and a forgetting: The Soul that rises with us, our life's star . . .*' – but left it, he couldn't offer it.

'I don't believe,' he said, surprising himself, 'that the dead are lost to us.'

He saw Claire wince at the words, 'the dead'.

'I mean, dead to *us*. The people that we love live on with us, within us. And God has promised us so much, the Resurrection – I believe he allows us, if we want it, the relief of knowing that a beloved life continues after death. It's like that Bidding Prayer, they said it in Stan's church, "*all those who rejoice with us but upon another shore and in a greater light*" – I believe in that.'

He believed in many things; he believed in the usefulness of his own ministry, although he had not ministered to Della. Frank had thought she might have more faith in Canon Feerick. In the event it was the unknown hospital chaplain whom Della had woken to see, his hand raised in a mute Benediction, standing at the railed foot of her bed, black and white against the veiled window. A nun was kneeling at the bedside; Della awoke on her whispered 'Amen'.

'Amen' to the prayers against the gates of hell, to the lighted candle and its murmuring flame. Amen to the imposition of hands, the invocation. Amen to the holy angels, archangels, patriarchs, prophets, apostles martyrs confessors virgins and all the saints. Amen. Amen to the holy oils, the odourless unguent touched on her eyes, her lids felt damp and heavy, her ears, her nose, her mouth, her hands and feet, against the sins of the senses. Where she walked, where her hands rested, had she touched sin? Had her nostrils inhaled the odours of evil, she who breathed most deeply of flowers?

For a second's time the nun was the nun who had shaken her head at a Della of long ago, who had said – 'Della Mother – way, what will become of you!'

Oh, *this*, thought Della, terror trapping her thought as she looked, wordless, at the sibilant priest, his office eliminating every other scent, sight, sound in the spare white room – oh, *this* is what was going to become of me, *this* is what was waiting for me!

Oh where are they, the people who were to protect me from this, who would not let this happen to me? The clangorous panic in her brain brought the word – 'Mother?' on a despairing, questioning breath. The nun beside her heard it, and leaned closer to her ear, and said quickly, deeply – 'Mother of Christ pray for us, Mother of divine grace pray for us, Mother most pure, Mother most chaste, Mother inviolate, Mother undefiled, pray for us –'

The familiar words filed into Della's stricken, faltering consciousness. 'Mercy,' she gasped and the nun responded immediately – 'Hail Holy Queen, Mother of mercy, hail our life our sweetness and our hope, to thee do we cry poor banished children of Eve – to thee do we send up our sighs – turn then most gracious advocate thine eyes of mercy towards us and after this our exile –'

It was like being at home after the Rosary. Where was Frank? Where was home? Whitethorn where she said the Rosary with her eyes fixed on the two red swans on the mantelpiece, her bare knees faintly branded by the indented linoleum on the floor? The Avenue, where she caressed her mother-of-pearl beads with her palms, passing them sometimes to Angela, sometimes to Claire, to stop them from giggling. It was always Frank who gave out the decades, the mysteries. He liked to precede it with a little invocation – in memory, tonight, of my father, he would say, of *my* father, remembered Della. Will he say the Rosary in memory of me? And after this our exile –

'Memorare,' she whispered, and the nun answered: 'Remember O most gracious virgin Mary that never was it known

that anyone who fled to thy protection, implored thine aid or
sought thine intercession was left unaided. Inspired with this
confidence I fly unto thee, O Virgin of virgins, my Mother –'

My mother, thought Della, where is my mother? She opened
her eyes wide, conscious. She wanted her mother.

Frank came. It must have been raining, his hair, his
shoulders, were damp. Della wanted to touch the rain, to
feel. She felt nothing, there was nothing in her body to distress
her, it was empty, weightless, she was floating. She lifted her
hand to touch the droplets on his collar, the wet that would
bring her the touch of the world outside, the wet of the weather.
He caught her hand, held it to his mouth, held it like a long
shell against his face.

She felt tears. 'I don't know what to do,' she said plaintively.
It was her only complaint. She reiterated it to Onora, brought
by Damien.

'Am I doing the right thing? Am I doing what they want me
to do?'

There was no rain on Onora. Damien had brought her to the
hospital door, parking his car afterwards.

'I don't know what to do about Angela,' she said to Onora.

'She's coming,' Onora told her. 'She'll be here any minute.'

'Yes,' said Della. She said nothing for a little while, then –

'What am I to do about Angela?' Suddenly her voice
brightened, she looked directly at Onora, interested. 'It's so
difficult, isn't it? Wanting to know how things turn out? But
where would it all stop – worrying about your child, then about
her children, then their children, you couldn't go on, sure you
couldn't?'

'No,' said Onora, looking at her child. 'No, you couldn't go
on.'

'But Angela,' Della's voice had become vague again. 'I love
to think of her in that lovely house, so big. It suits her. And the
sloping gardens. I love to think of her.'

She was drifting. But she was cold. 'Is it raining?'

Frank was pressing her scapulars into her hand. Her fingers
touched them; no sin there. The light was fading, but she knew

it was Damien who had come into the room. 'You're drenched!' she said joyously. She could smell the rain on him: the sins of the nostrils. When he came close to the bed he saw that she wanted to touch him. He dried his hand quickly against his shirt, but she grasped his sleeve, she could not hold it, but she held up her wet fingers, she could see them, the sheen of the living outside weather, it was at her fingertips.

Triumphant, she closed her eyes. She could smell the flowers in the room, the roses Frank had brought, there was lilac somewhere, lovely. She could hear the silence. She was cold, but she wouldn't worry them with that.

While she slept, there had been nothing for the others to do but wait. A doctor had spoken quietly, finally, to Frank. There was nothing to be done.

'It's the Feast of Pentecost,' was all Raphael had said to Claire at the church. 'Sunday was.'

He said, quite calmly, Claire thought, considering – 'The Spirit of the Lord fills the whole world. It holds all things together and knows every word spoken by man.'

Funny. Claire watched as Raphael went off. Damien has none of that carry-on. After all those years of learning, after Bible study and apologetics and Canon Law and ritual and rubric and liturgy, he never reminds you of what you should know. With his breviary, now, and his Office, he could have religious platitudes for every occasion, especially this kind of one. But he doesn't offer them.

I wonder, she thought, are people disappointed?

Frank and Della had always known they would be buried in the small local graveyard above the estuary. To get there the funeral procession passed the Avenue, and halted there. Some people who had not gone to the church were waiting, and crossed themselves as the hearse paused. Last night they were among the people who had waited there again, there where the laburnums shed their golden racemes on the pavement, where the chestnuts reared their pinnacles of white, where the limes blushed green with new growth.

Last night those waiting people had joined the procession,

walking behind the hearse from the Avenue to the church, gathering more waiting groups at each corner. 'Brought to the church,' Mrs Cummins called it – 'he was brought to the church last night' – as though there was compulsion in it, as indeed, indeed there was.

Now as they halted in observance of the place of Della's life, her hinterland, Claire thought of the garden, stilled; of the flowers, and the trees that grew there yet, the life that it contained, its careful, cared-for beauty, the seedlings. Coming out that morning she had seen a gobbet of brown fur suspended from a stalk of lavender. At her touch it exploded into tens, hundreds, of tiny spiders, so tiny she had to look closely to be sure they *were* spiders. They hurtled into the shelter of the bush, frantic for safety, but ready to begin life.

And Della's house; when she got back to it that evening, after the day spent with Angela and Stan and Frank and Onora, with the friends who had been welcome at Angela's home to eat and drink, to weep furtively in the bathrooms or in the sloping shadows of the garden, to bring family gossip up to date, to retell, to recount, to spend the hours of this first day together – when Claire got back to her own house it seemed to palpitate expectation. Nothing had changed: Gluic yawned in his Sultanesque pose beneath the rosemary, the Casino rose shone green and glossy, proud of its long buds.

There was no bark: 'Is Bran out there?' she called to Damien, who was locking the car. Twilight coloured the hall. White lilac sprayed in heavy sheaves from the Waterford glass vases beloved of Mrs Cummins. On the table in the dining room pleated campaniles of columbines arched from a column of Spode; they stood on a shield of lace: Claire saw Della's hands hesitating among the pins as the white web had grown between her fingers.

Damien said – 'Tea? A drink? I'll do it –' and went into the kitchen. Perhaps Bran, left to his own devices, had gone upstairs. The house must have seemed strange to him, once Mrs Cummins had left it clean and flowery and ready for visitors who, as it happened, did not arrive. Just in case, she had said to Frank, you'll never know who'll turn up, she said, and he agreed while she hacked at his lilacs with the kitchen shears.

Claire searched the bedrooms. Only one door was closed, Frank's and Della's room. She opened it, slowly, she did not want to go in, she felt it was more private now than it had ever been. But there was nothing there. Frank's pyjamas, folded, on the quilted bed. One of his black ties cast like a question mark along the turned-down sheet. Freesias, from Angela's greenhouse. Nothing.

It was evening, growing dark. Claire opened out the window, leaned on the sill, calling to Bran. He must be hungry, although Mrs Cummins had fed him in the morning. Claire saw a light across the field where Brady's farm had been; Raphael must be home, then. He had not gone to Angela's house. He had never been inside it.

She turned in the window, sending her voice up the Avenue into other gardens. There was the moon, slight, but fuller than the moon at Powerscourt, when she had waltzed from the ballroom out on to the long terrace. She had not danced at all at first; both she and Dan Smylie knew that they had to work well on this marking, it was fun, but it had to be well done, they would take their time about it. They liked the look of one another, though, and Claire, relieved by their uncomplicated partnership, read from Dan's smile that they would have time for one another later on.

Claire had dressed, that night, with a careless fury. In her bath she had seen the bruises of Leon's kisses on her breasts, and knew they would not feel his lips again. It did not matter, she told herself, and stood before the mirror in a mist of blue; she saw she could look beautiful. She felt the rage settle in her heart, and hide there. Dan Smylie's eyes had widened when he met her in the hotel foyer, and she had laughed approval of his own evening dress, and they had gone off well satisfied with one another.

In her soft, slim purse Claire had her notebook and several slender pencils. 'Not exactly a dance card,' she thought ruefully, remembering Onora's mementos, the tasseled pencil painted gold. And only once during that radiant night-time had she thought of Leon: only once, when on a surge in the splendid music she had spun herself out of the grasp of a young French diplomat and said she wanted to go outside, she would be back, she was too hot to keep dancing. A tide of Strauss drowned his protest, but she saw him smile, and bow acceptance as she moved, still in step, through the long open window.

Flowered urns flanked the long stone flights that led from level to level, to the fountain with its great bronze horses rearing above the spray. She turned her back to the lights and the music of the house, the happy graceful shadows in its fulfilled windows. She looked instead into the valley which spread from the garden terraces to the mountains ranged against the Wicklow sky.

There was the moon, a twist, a shard, a shred of it. Invincible, inviolate: though man might touch it, it remained untouched. What could not be bridged was the chasm between it, its place in the sky, its unalterable cycle, and this fragile reckless earth.

> Yon crescent moon, as fixed as if it grew
> In its own cloudless, starless lake of blue.

The words smarted in her mind:
'*I see them all so excellently fair, I see, not feel how beautiful they are!*'
Where was he? Leon should be with her. She wanted to share, to share in order to feel, to seal the moon in that blue void by sharing it with him. She was full of the sense of herself, of the silken sound of her skirts on the paving, of the moonlight on her hair, on her skin, of the night air cool and dewy, and sparkling, here, with faint iridiscent harmonies as music floated lightly from the house. She sobbed against a fluted balustrade, the rough stone grazing the skin of her arm. She wanted to feel, to strike into this bitter absorption the passionate pattern of herself.

The sky was midnight blue – like 'Midnight in Paris', and

on that thought Claire turned back to the luminous house, its perfumed people already captured in her notebook, its bands and orchestras, caterers, florists and chauffeurs listed most dutifully. The quietude of the gardens and terraces, the infinity of perspective which linked them to the furthermost landscape, these she left behind. She left behind the unchanging, unchangeable core of the countryside, the challenging moon, and to the hiss of her own skirts she joined again the hot multitude of enjoyment. Becoming part of the house, entering under its roof, she left behind that vision of its ecstatic architecture illuminated from within; she saw the moon only through its windows.

There was the moon. It had not disintegrated.

At Della's window Claire thought she heard a sound from the garden. 'I think Bran may have got locked into the garage!' she called as she ran past Damien in the kitchen. Running up the path the thought of the dog waiting for her, hoping for her return, his rescue, blotted from her mind the thump of earth thrown on the coffin, the sight of Onora's clenched face, the mounded mass of flowers.

She wrenched open the door, calling, relieved. Frank's car was there; he was staying with Angela and Stan tonight. The car, and silence. No bark, no scurrying, frantic welcome.

Perhaps he had soiled somewhere and waited, cowering, for her anger. But even then his tail would have been thumping. Although never angry with him, Claire had seen him like this with Frank. Her voice husky with forgiveness Claire called – 'Bran? Old boy?' – but there was silence.

Quickly she found the high-up light switch. In the pale glare she saw the shadow suspended from the furthest rafter. It moved in the draught from the door. The head was turned helplessly towards her, the gross tongue lolling, the eyes huge and bulging from their sockets. The limbs dangled, limp as if he had been a pup held by the scruff, the tail fell, abject, between his legs.

She whispered a scream of terror and pity – '*Bran!*' – and tore frantically at his unresisting body. She could not reach his head, his neck. She looked desperately for something to stand on, the ladder was too high up, weren't there steps, a stool, an old chair! The deckchairs hanging from the wall were no good, there were hooks with ropes and hammers and long-handled secateurs. Among the half-empty stagnant paint-pots and the jars of nails and screws she saw the cobwebbed shape of an old horseshoe.

No good, nothing was any good, her breath rasped like a file in her throat. She stood on the fender of Frank's car, it was turned the wrong way, she would have to get on to its roof. Leaning from there she saw the bright raw gleam of the garden wire twisted around the timber. The other end was nearer her; it was noosed under the dog's sideways chin, slicing into the flesh in a mess of fur and tissue which Claire tried and tried to release. The weight of the hanging body tightened the wire against her palms. She began to understand how the dog had died, how long it had taken. Her nails broke, her hands began to bleed.

Jumping down she saw the little lumps of excrement, of blood. She felt, not saw, the cracking skin of her hands, her own blood. She heard Damien calling her, was anything wrong? 'Here!' she shouted. '*Please!* Here!

'Oh, God,' she cried, reaching for the long arms of the secateurs. 'Oh, God, oh God.' Today of all days. Who could have done it?

She reached the wire, the blades split it and the dog fell flatly on the dirtied floor. The thump of his body hit her brain. She bent to cradle him. '*Tá mo láimhe stróicthe,*' she thought, '*go síorrai 'tarraingt rópai.*' My hands, my hands are ripped. Oh, God, oh, God, if this is the death destined for us; if this is the death, what can we do? Only go to Heaven, all of us, all of us.

Groaning with anguish she dropped her head on to the lifeless mass in her lap. 'Oh!' she cried out to the astounded Damien. 'Who! Who!' She swayed on the floor, in a trance of despair.

Damien crouched beside her. 'Let me,' he begged her, 'I'll look after him now.'

She did not hear him. '*Who?*' she moaned. 'Who could have done it?'

'Claire,' he said, his arm tightening around her shoulder. 'Claire, my dear.' He touched her face, drawing her head back up closer to him. He fondled the sluicing tears on her cheeks.

'Claire, my poor little girl,' he said. 'My dearest.'

She did not hear him. Her head sagged down to the stiffening corpse in her arms. Without heed, without restraint, she wept into the staring, crested hair.

Part
Two

Chapter 1

'Pure Constable,' said Pauline.

Joining her at the gate, where the small black dog had already hurled himself into the field, Claire had to agree. Pure Constable.

The gate itself was rusty, hanging on one pier. Beyond it stretched a meadow of matted grass, hedged by rising ground and a palisade of brown untidy shrubs, straggling one into another, without shape, but with some substance of outline which suggested form; even the brown was not flat, there were variations, as though the tangled branches were striations tinted by the painter's finest hair. Beyond again perspective pressed another field into a golden-brown stripe edged with a hangar of trees, leafless but with green showing in their shallows, and rising in smoky ranks to the summit of the hill they made invisible, cloaking the church whose spire, caught in the light of the dull November sky, shone translucent and stony above hill, trees, fields, shrubs, the black burrowing dog and the two watchers at the broken gate.

'A symmetry as effortless as that should not surprise us,' said Pauline, walking on. Her voice came back to Claire who stood at the gateway, waiting for the dog.

'If we saw it at a greater distance it would be even more graceful – there would be these trees, along this bank, and the river, all giving it depth, and a little mist for mystery.'

'Perhaps we have been looking at it for too long,' said Claire, who halted at the gate every time she took this walk. 'If we give it too much distance it will disappear altogether: we will see only the trees, only the river. The vista disappears.'

'But that's what I've always said about you, Claire.' Pauline was smiling at her over her shoulder, waiting for her to catch up. 'Isn't it what I've always said about you – that your sense of perspective is reversed? It's the further you go, the easier it is to see clearly. Distance is like time: it changes the way we see things.'

'I've been wondering about that.' Claire was thoughtful. 'I've been wondering – I don't know why it should be something of a surprise to me. Time, distance, even absence, I agree they can change the way I think about things, but not the way I feel. And I get tired of feeling. I keep on waiting for people to grow up, I say and I mean it, even about awful things, awful people – I say: they'll grow out of it. Life will fix that for them! It makes me impatient. I keep on waiting for old age, as if it were an island, somewhere where I won't have to care any more, where I can respond to what happens with my head, not with my gut.

'And then I think of my grandmother. She always seemed so contained. I don't think I ever saw her cry. Not ever.'

Pauline said nothing. 'Not ever' was saying a lot.

'But she was cryptic. As if her feelings were pared down, made minimal. As if she had got to a stage at which she no longer had to react obviously to very many things. But those that remained, she cared about intensely. But even then, you'd only see it in the dryness of her comments, perhaps, or in no comment at all. Or in something bitter. Even savage.

'And she saw things from a distance, didn't she? She was eighty-four when she died. So much of what was important in her life had happened such a long time before.'

'That's what you'd think,' Pauline said gently, after a little quiet. 'But life does keep on surprising us, doesn't it? Even with the way we can accept things, even the worst things?'

They were silent. Their worst things had been different, but each had shuddered at the other's pain.

'As for Onora – how do we know what sustained her at the end? There had been joys in her life; she must at least have learned how to measure them against the grief. And that's what it is, isn't it, so much of life? A balancing act?'

Claire looked at her suspiciously.

'That's a bit too flippant for you, Pauline. It has the distinct ring of the wrap-up about it. You're afraid, now, that I'm going to build a dogma on this, aren't you?'

'No, no – not at all.' Pauline was laughing. 'I just don't think we should let it get too boring, that's all.'

'Oh, God, Pauline!' Claire tucked her arm under Pauline's elbow. 'You're very good for me.'

She called the dog away from the noisome margins of the river, and as he scurried to catch up with them the two women walked on, heads amicably bent against the gusts of weather.

'Do you remember,' Claire asked as they neared the car, 'the first time I met you, Jarleth called you his Pauline Privilege?'

'Yes.' Pauline's voice was clipped. 'I used to hate that. He doesn't say things like that now.'

'None of us says things like that now,' said Claire, taking out the car keys. 'We're afraid nobody will understand us.'

Opening the hatchback door she gestured to the dog – 'Snoopy! Get in!' – and he jumped on to the rug laid on the floor of the boot for him. Letting Pauline sit in the car before going round to her own side, she stood for a moment by the door, feeling the weather on her face. It would be dark when they returned this way after shopping in town. Claire liked it in the dark, although she agreed with Frank that the riverside road was dangerous at night; she liked it because the clustered lights on the hill, those further, mounting ones above the industrial fluorescences of the oil depot and tanker wharves – they had a star-like quality to them. Although they were only windows, or street lights, they offered an orange constellation fringing a new highway over the hill.

'Is that where Woodhill House used to be?' Pauline asked, clicking her seat belt. She could see the pink flattened piles of rubble among the empty trees and red and white bungalows across the river.

'Ah,' said Claire, driving away from it, 'that's it, that's all that's left of it. Usually I don't walk down quite this far – I hate looking at it. It's like a wound, every time I see it.

'Do you ever,' she asked, the little car speeding into the city, the dog asleep in the boot, 'do you ever get tired, just plain tired out, of feeling? Of caring?'

On a better day she wouldn't have asked Pauline that question – Pauline, whose trip to town for some shopping was accepted by them both as an open-ended flight from Tattin's latest escapade; she could arrive when she liked, she could leave when she liked, she had a key to Claire's house, and Frank, when he was there, knew better than to be surprised.

'Why don't you leave him?' Claire had asked once, exasperated, stricken by Pauline's tense, accepting smile.

'But I leave him three times a year!' was the answer. And it was true, departure had become Pauline's protest. She made it gracefully; there were no slammed doors or angry telephone calls now – whatever there might have been in the past. Sometimes in their nights together Pauline would tell Claire – no, tell was not the word. They might be talking of something else, someone else, even of Claire herself sometimes; about making jam, or during the autumn walks along the headlands gathering blackberries – then the words would colour in the contours of Pauline's career as a wife. More wife than mother, Claire believed, and said so. She had discovered that it was all right to say what she thought to Pauline; although she never, now, wanted to hurt her, she had become less afraid of hurting her. Once she had asked Jarleth Tattin – 'Doesn't Pauline know? Doesn't she care? How can she be so indifferent?' and Tattin had said that it wasn't indifference, it was serenity, calm.

'Luckily for you,' Claire had said, mischievously. 'That must really suit you – so long as you don't get confused between calm and just not caring.' But she had known he wouldn't get confused – even then she had known, then when she hadn't known Pauline.

And when she did know her, she had said – not worrying about hurting her – one of the things she had said had been that Pauline was concentrating more on being a wife than on being a mother. It seemed to Claire that Pauline's function was to facilitate Jarleth, to make his life entirely possible. That might even have been why he had married Pauline, her Quaker money smoothing the floors of the small house in the west, tiling them, stretching them into the furthest possible corners, embroidering the simplicities of his life there with polished timbers, with patchwork hand-worked quilts, with trees and blue hydrangea and cloches covering strawberries and sea-kale, with asparagus – in which he took some pride, it was not easy to grow there – with a patio.

When a visiting lectureship had been offered at a university close enough to New York to be acceptable – although small – Pauline had made the important decisions. Not about accepting it – Jarleth made that, an immediate affirmative. But about what to do with the children, the two of them, boy and girl, travelling each day to school in Skibbereen. They had been sent to boarding school, their fierce, accusatory indignation handled by Pauline as a childhood ailment as predictable as measles. Just think, she had promised them when they accepted that she would not yield – 'just think, for this one year, only nine months really, of boarding school, you'll get three weeks in New York – New York at Christmastime!' And that came true – she made it come true for them. But all their remaining schooldays were spent at boarding school. It made such good sense, she had told Claire when she returned from America. 'It gets them out of Jarleth's way, and turns them into affectionate visitors. And it gives me freedom of movement, almost as much as Jarleth has. And I need it.'

Had she known then what she had needed it for? These flights, less regular now, less frequent, when she closed her joint accounts, took away with her her Access, Visa, Diners' Club, American Express cards, her cheque book, when she left her honeycomb of sweet-smelling rooms and asked a neighbour's child to feed the cat. And what, Claire had wondered, and once had asked her – 'What does the child think – what does your neighbour think – when they meet the latest blonde having breakfast on the patio?'

'They're not always blonde,' answered Pauline, who knew that Claire had once been one of those transient waifs sucking up a sense of some kind of life with the coffee Jarleth ground for them – all part of the real thing.

And Claire, wincing at this, Pauline's strongest rebuke, was silent then. But they had travelled further on from that in the days that followed. Now she knew that to Pauline lack of curiosity was the first courtesy; where she lived there were few neighbours, but among them, or those who mattered of them, it had been understood that her reticence was not a blameless disguise for passivity. It what what they often called Protestant good manners – for, asking no questions, she had sheltered their children with her own, herded their straying cattle into her own acre, rescued them from flat tyres and burst pipes just as they had rescued her. The essential reciprocity of country life was no effort to her, for although she did not give much of herself, she gave of everything else she had.

It was this bewitching placidity – it had bewitched Claire, she knew it had bewitched Jarleth – which allowed Claire to use Pauline as an emotional Thesaurus. There were always alternatives, she had learned. However bad it was, it could be worse, might have been worse, indeed, for both of them, had been worse.

'I would like,' she said now, continuing her question, 'to be impervious. To wear emotional impenetrability like an anorak. To live, as though I were on an island, surrounded by the milling seas of human concerns, touched by them even, but only around the edges. In the core, where the palm trees lean above the little well, where water, shade and shelter are all I want of life – there I would be untouched.'

'Would you?' Pauline looked, making sure Claire saw her glance, at the small brown pits in the skin of Claire's arm, where the soft woollen sleeve had fallen back as her hands held the steering wheel. She had seen Claire's fingers pick at the innocent flesh of her wrist, of her heel, of her upper arm. The skin would be unblemished, softer than the skin of her face. Claire, as if not aware of what she was doing, would scratch it and produce blood, a lesion. A scab would form, to be picked off. Another scab would dry and harden, but the questing fingers would find it, prying it, not without pain, from the clinging skin. She knew Claire knew what she was doing, she had seen her efforts to hide, or disguise, the scars. She had wanted to say – why do you hurt yourself so much? But then, if there was a reason, Claire would either give it – or else keep it a secret. Pauline felt she could not justify the question – but she could not pretend, either, that those punitive fingernails, those narrow scars pink as a membrane with their soft purple edges, were not a sign, and were hidden.

'All right,' Claire amended equably, 'a plateau. And that way, of course, you could also see what's going on. My mother always said she'd miss knowing what's going on – and so, I think, would I.'

Her mother had only said anything of the kind once, that Claire could remember, but Claire preferred this suggestion of a more boisterous characteristic. When she spoke about her mother she liked to say 'always', she liked to give this illusion of constancy, now that she was no longer so sure of what her mother's characteristics had been.

The light rain of the river had drifted eastwards away from the city by the time they found a space in the high-rise car park. A wind, cold enough to make Pauline insist that Claire wrap a warm scarf around her shoulders, had lifted the clouds and pushed them down river so that they hung resentfully above the grain silos, the warehouses, the factory roofs, the turreted domes of the oil exploration ships, the hay-baled decks of the Galloway Express.

From their tier of the car park, the city unfolded terrace on terrace, a pink warmth suffusing every surface, every facade, as if despite itself the town was blushing. It was the onset of evening, the onset of winter; the narrowing streets disappeared in a vapour of smoke and mist and orange-tinged dusk, the tall old houses on the hillsides taller and thinner in the soft crepuscular light than in full sun or in glooms of rain. The subdued sky had a yellow skin of fragility, as if it could not hold the crowded mass of roofs and steeples, of trees and streets swept into its western corners. It trembled like a mirage, lofty, remote, its colours fading to deeper, darkening blue, unassailable, lovely. Her hands cold on the concrete shelf of balcony, Claire felt the bruise around her heart wince at the imperturbable skyline, its offer of immolation.

Leaving a window slightly open for Snoopy's comfort, Claire was humming as she locked the car.

Time and time again I've said that I don't care,
That I'm immune to gloom, that I'm hard through and
    through,
But every time it matters all my words desert me,
So anyone can hurt me,
And they do . . .

But turning to Pauline, who waited with the shopping basket once favoured by Onora, she caught her gently derisive smile and smiled herself, apologising. Taking the basket she said only that she still thought it was the best song from *Evita*, far better than 'Argentina'.

'Do you ever think,' she asked, as they descended into the town, 'of the things we've lived through, the changes we've seen?'

'Do you mean,' Pauline was uncertain, 'things like, well, the Anglo-Irish Agreement? Or the Falklands War?'

'Something like those – although what I remember most from the Falklands War is how it suddenly became necessary to call people from Argentina "Argentines" instead of Argentinians. But I mean things more like, well, Aids, for example. Or the first family-planning clinics. Or decimalisation. Or joining the EEC and the other kind of CAP – the common agricultural policy. And the EMS and the SEA and GATT – things which have changed our language.'

'Fax?' offered Pauline. 'HRT? Videos? Quiche? Duvets? Swatch watches? The multiple heart by-pass? Compact discs?'

Three army jeeps trundled past them with a surly whine, soldiers inside with rifles laid innocuously across their knees. It was Thursday, Claire remembered, they must have been patrolling the Securicor transfers at the main banks.

'All those things. Exactly –' Claire's face was bright beneath the neon signs of the cinema complex. 'Like the acoustic couplers on my main frame operator. Intervention beef. The Ayatollah. Chernobyl. *The Deer Hunter.*'

'Anal intercourse,' said Pauline, adding at Claire's gasp, 'on the radio, I mean. On Radio Eireann.'

'Oh, yes. And gays. And the ozone layer. Moving statues. Acid.'

'And in regards to that – as Mrs Cummins used to say –' Claire clutched at Pauline's arm as they went up the steps to the covered market – 'I heard a woman on the radio yesterday talking about an optional illusion. Isn't that lovely, as if you could have your choice of mirages?'

The fish was fresh that morning up from Castletownbeare, they were assured in the market. In French Church Street they walked on Huguenot flagstones, and found a delicate gilt necklace Pauline wanted to give to Claire's niece Emily; the angled lamps in the ceiling of the shop window enriched the gleam of the light, linked filigree.

'It's not *la vraie chose,* but it's pretty enough to need no excuses.'

Pauline consciously satirised Jarleth. It was a source of some relief to her, Claire believed – this dismissive appropriation of the coinage with which Jarleth had reinforced his intellectual superiority, his knowingness. Perhaps, for all they knew, he still did so in those same terms. Pauline when she mocked him to Claire was never bitter, but knowing in her own way. It was a kind of ownership – and Claire accepted it. She did not deride the subtle effulgences with which she, after all was said and done, had once been captivated. No, parody was Pauline's prerogative; Claire was content to relish it.

'And that's another thing.' Pauline turned to her, adding the slender package to the shopping basket's bulbous load. 'Debs: the Deb balls – there were none of them when I was at school, or leaving it. To me they're as new as microwaves, or microchips, or Silicone Valley – but at least with all those things there's some developmental logic. Science always seems to have that logic. But social things – the way a fashion becomes a tradition, that's really disturbing, it's so mysterious, so thoughtless.'

'And so absolute,' said Claire, whose mind had been ticking off another list, the names, the initials, she would not repeat. The SAS; Claudy; the Miami Showband; the Dublin bombs; H-Block. Hunger strike. Crossmaglen. Captain Nairac. Shergar.

Two men were urinating noisily in the doorway of a warehouse in Bowling Green Street. Claire closed her ears to the splash of their bodies, pinching her nostrils against the imagined odour. The shops were closing, but she made a determined rush into the store where she hoped she might still be able to get the taffeta Emily had decided she wanted for her ball gown. She defended herself to Pauline: 'I'm going to all this trouble because she does really want a ball gown. Remember – she could have chosen to wear black leather and Doc Martins; I'm so relieved I'm even prepared to go over Stan's budget – and anyway, you're taken by it yourself, getting her that necklace.'

In the shop Claire asked if there wasn't some brown paper in which to wrap the wave-indented fabric. It was a shame, she told the reluctant assistant, to bundle its creamy folds into a plastic bag along with the zip, the spools of thread, the pads for the shoulders. The paper found, the parcel wrapped – did she want twine, the assistant asked sourly, or would sellotape do? – they returned to the car, to Snoopy's leaping, snuffling welcome. Their descent floor by floor took them to the level of the quayside, the river fluorescent with all its drifting lights, the flush of illumination on the portico of St Dominic's, the wreath of stars around the head of the Virgin.

'I think religion is Dad's plateau,' Claire said, driving. 'It isn't so much that it isolates him – it insulates him. He can say – "I'm doing something – I am a convinced ecumenic. I am on North/South commissions, committees, bridging groups. I am in the St Vincent de Paul Society and do good works among the poor – "'

'"I give tithes of all I possess,"' said Pauline. 'I know, I know – but you have to admit yourself, Claire, that he believes in them. He is the most devout man I know, and I don't mean pious, or anything ostentatious. I've been with you – wasn't I, once – when you went to meet him at that big Italianate church, the Franciscan one. It was after a meeting, a confraternity, was it? And I saw them all coming out of the church, old men – Frank was one of the youngest, certainly one of the ablest of them. They were all old men, some were tottering along, clutching at the pews to keep them upright. Frank must know that all that's on the way out, but he's loyal to it, he *believes* in it.'

'But they all believe in it.' Claire felt a puzzled tenderness for those old men, their numbers diminishing month by month, their voices weaker in the old anthems. 'And you're right, Frank is devoted. Things like the Third Order, or the First Fridays, things which are almost personally Catholic, those are the staples of his practised faith. It's as if by keeping so loyally faithful to them he can do everything else asked of him, from going to Sunday Mass on Saturdays (did you ever hear of anything so ridiculous? The Catholic church has lost the run of itself entirely) to taking Holy Communion from a woman to accepting that the Archbishop of Dublin will bring the Eucharist personally to a member of Sinn Fein on hunger strike in jail!'

The acceleration through a set of traffic lights which accompanied this last enunciation threw Pauline back in her seat. She tucked her hand under the grip of the seatbelt across her chest, ready for another swerve.

'And honestly, I think he found it harder to take the arrival of women as Ministers of the Eucharist than to forgive any of the asinine things the Cardinal has been saying about Sinn Fein and the IRA. I mean he knows that the Cardinal equivocates, he agrees with me that the Cardinal has never understood that he's Primate of all Ireland, not just south Armagh, but everything else he forgives him. He just says "poor man, poor soul".

'And I will say this for him –' Out of the city, Claire was more relaxed, lighter on the steering wheel. She drove cheerfully, usually; she loved the sense of power and independence having her own car gave her, and Pauline knew only too well how she enjoyed speed. But today there was a dimness about her, something not quite focused, so that a weary bitterness showed through.

'I will say this for Frank – he was sad about Damien, but only because, he said, it was a great loss to the Church to be without men like Damien when men like Anselm Daunt were becoming notorious. That consoled me, the fact that he didn't seem to be blaming Damien, but rather the Church itself for insisting that he had to go.'

'And there's something else you must say for Frank,' said Pauline, 'all that he's done for Stan and the children. His care for them as a unit, something which must not be broken up. He just made everything possible. I remember you were thinking of giving up work, remember? And he said that no, he was at retirement age, and between himself and Stan and Stan's mother and you things should be able to go on as normally as possible. I remember you telling me about all that, and how what it really meant was that Frank became a kind of surrogate mother.

'And although it might not now seem like much of a compliment to you, either, Claire, I have to say that between you all you've brought off a great achievement – normality.'

Claire smiled in acknowledgement of the tribute. She would not have thought, ten years ago, that normality was an achievement. Now, watching the lengthening distance between herself and the children, seeing Emily and her brothers Hewitt and Lyle finish school and take off – Hewitt was already in Trinity, Emily would finish school this coming spring, Lyle was only a year or so behind her – Claire could admit that something had been accomplished.

'It isn't over yet,' she reminded Pauline, 'but I agree with you. And I'm glad you feel we've brought it off, or nearly.

'What I have to wonder, though,' and she twisted the car in under the wall by the gate, 'is how normal life has been for the rest of us? I mean Stan, really, I suppose. I mean – is it normal, do you think, that he never remarried? I've wondered about that.'

They sat for a moment under the gaunt remaining lime trees. The early darkness was gentle around the metal space which contained them quietly. Its atmosphere held Pauline's perfume, a vaporised, flowery dew. It held Claire's scarred fingernails, the slight downward pull of her pale mouth. Pauline, who had wondered also, let the silence hold, gentle as the dark. Her eyes could reach through the gate to where the massive Casino rose twined branch over branch above the trellised porch, a faint wet gleam among its cords to show where its last late blossoms still shone. There was no light on in the house, the door lay in shadow, but crouched on the sheltered window sill above the bush of rosemary, she could see the humped impatient shape of Sammy, the cat Claire had nearly called Hodge before deciding that would be too pretentious.

Claire's eyes had a silver metallic sheen when she turned to Pauline.

'An optional illusion . . . I've wondered about drugs. How hard it must be, if you give them up. Not just the pain of addiction, the agony of it. But the loss of your visions. Do people remember them years after? Mourn for them?'

If Pauline had answered she would have said yes. She would have said that was why she was so sorry for Jarleth. But she did not answer.

In the car Snoopy, who knew he had come home, became restless, and Claire stirred, looking at Pauline with a pursed, rueful smile at her lips, her eyes admitting uncertainty. She had tucked the car in too tightly, leaving space for Frank, she said; she had to get out at Pauline's side. Laughing together at the discomfort, the ungainliness of this, they left Snoopy to rustle in the garden and went into the empty, lightless house.

Chapter 2

'It's all the identical same,' said Mrs Cummins, placing in front of Claire a bowl of porridge, crusted with sugar.

'If we fly out from here or if we fly out from Dublin we'll still be going to the same place and they tell me we'll still be paying the same price. Not that November –' she turned away to swish the laser knife through the bread and brought back two thick brown slices to the table – 'November was never my idea of the right month to think about holidays, even if it is the All Grave. But she will have it, "book it now" she says, "before you get stuck into Christmas" she says, "because you won't have a penny piece left after" – and do you know, I suppose she's right in that.'

Claire knew that for weeks to come she would hear about the progress of plans for another of the holidays Mrs Cummins was now in the habit of taking with her only unmarried daughter. The death of 'himself' from heart failure during a bronchitic seizure had left her in unchallenged possession of the family home, his insurance money, and her own time, and she had been able to combine her sense of an annual duty to her daughter in Dublin with that daughter's determination to give her mother what both she and Mrs Cummins agreed year after year to have been a good time.

'I always had an inkling for the Continent,' the daughter had assured Claire once, meeting her at the airport when

Claire had gone to collect Mrs Cummins. 'And now Mam agrees with me – there's nothing like the sun.'

'To tell you the truth,' Mrs Cummins had subsequently said to Claire, 'it's all them churches I like. And the shopping – the fish. The kinds of them; and the colours of them. And the way the people do go on – you'd have to laugh if all belong to you were dead. But I don't say that to herself – she thinks the sun is what's in it, that it do me good.

'But I love them fish,' she said. 'You'd think they came lepping out of the sea on to your plate, silver and blue and pink, and the bright eyes daring you to eat 'em.'

Claire could understand her relish; she remembered the years spent waiting for the grey catch of estuary mullet, the toil of the rowing boats pushing against the wind and the tide of Lough Mahon, the hushed jubilation of the silver illegal stripe of a salmon, the labour of net-mending, the terror when sudden squalls of rain and wind beat the boats down into the lower harbour, the anger at their eventual return, safe but without their cargo. All that was the past, the river was too dirty for fish or fishing, the boats were beached for ever. The Fisheries pier was crowded only for regattas, or for the annual visit of the harbour yacht clubs to the city's marina.

'Your friend Mrs Tattin has gone down to the village to get *The Journal* – she took the dog with her. She said,' and Mrs Cummins sniffed, half-past ten was no time for a working woman to be getting out of her bed in the morning, 'she said not to wake you. But everything's done here now, and if you just put your things into the dishwasher and turn it on it'll all be grand. The fire is laid if you don't want to turn on the heating. Your father won't be back, he said he's spending the weekend at Sunday's Well, and I'll go up there now to look after them all.'

Acknowledging the instructions, suggesting that if she could wait a few more minutes either she herself or Mrs Tattin could run her into town, Claire thought as she helped Mrs Cummins into the warm tweed jacket she and Frank together had bought for her last Christmas that the daughter was probably right –

the sun did do her good. Mrs Cummins no longer as brisk as she had been, took a taxi home if she went shopping in town, and rarely spent more than a couple of hours a week in Claire's home unless Frank was there. Her duty now lay altogether with Stan and his children, drawn there by her allegiance to Frank, Frank's allegiance to them. Her loyalties were not misplaced; there had been great need of her, and Frank and Stan jointly had paid not just her wages but state insurances and taxes so that now, in her early seventies, she had more money than ever in her life before.

'She must be in her early seventies.' Claire poured coffee for Pauline, who had spread the newspaper across the table. 'She doesn't spend all that much time up there any more with the children grown up. I think she just likes having somewhere to go, somewhere she can say she *must* be. And she always liked that house. I can remember my mother took her up to it when Stan and Angela bought it first – she was *very* impressed!'

They had all been impressed – all the Mackeys. Onora had said that going into the hall was like entering a chapel, what with the terrazzo floor and the stained-glass windows. Della had reported the remark to Claire, thankful that Onora had not said it in company which would be mixed as the marriage was mixed. She had sighed as she spoke to Claire; they had been sitting together – where? In the garden? On a wall – yes, on that low stone wall at the edge of the grass, Della had been speaking of what would be Angela's garden as she looked at her own. She had sighed: Onora, she felt, had not been wholehearted in her approval. She told Claire that Onora's response seemed to be that it was all great while it lasted, but who knew how long it was going to last? Claire said that she was ready to bet that her grandmother had said one predictable thing – how times changed, and people too, how her ears were used to the clatter of clogs going up, and the rustle of silk coming down.

The remark had won a smile from Della. Thinking of her now, and of how her long fingers had tickled the rough hair behind Bran's ears as the dog sat leaning against her, Claire looked at Pauline's fingers, narrow articulate digits which handled the turning pages with a white spread as fluent as the wing of a stretching swan. She could picture them hovering with balletic infinity over bowls and basins, the most ordinary occupations, pointing to different seeds, selecting beans for storing, holding up to the light as she had done yesterday the filigree necklace, its magic metallurgy cushioned on the pads of her palms.

'Do you want a look at this?' Pauline folded the paper neatly, but Claire shook her head.

'Not today, or not yet, anyway. I've heard all I want to know about from the radio: a booby-trapped body in the North – that man who murdered his wife given a suspended sentence because he was drunk at the time, and queues outside the St Vincent de Paul offices for EEC beef – no thanks!'

'Have you heard from Damien?' Pauline's question was quick and sharp and startled Claire.

'No!'

To Pauline's uncritical silence she added: 'I haven't heard from him. Not since he went to California. But I didn't, don't, expect him to write. Maybe – I don't know, but *maybe* it's that I don't want him to write to me. He has too much to get straightened out. I don't think I've anything to offer to that process. I did send a little note to say I'd be in San Francisco in the spring.'

Again she added – 'No – he didn't answer that. But he'll probably send a card at Christmas. And I'll write then too and give him more details about my trip, where I'll be and for how long, that kind of thing. And leave it up to him.'

'You're leaving it all up to him, aren't you?' There was no criticism in this. Pauline was trying to relieve Claire's misery, to reach its source, to understand it.

'I know. I have thought about it, maybe I'm doing all the wrong things. But it's all so confused. Now that he's actually left the priesthood he has to figure the next part out for himself, what he's going to do for his life, for his living.'

She smiled in a half-ashamed acknowledgement of Pauline's derisive eyebrow.

'I know that too: it *is* a kind of cop-out. I feel like those women who decide to have their baby under anaesthesia – wake me up when it's all over. But at least I won't claim the result as my own work. I may not claim the result at all. He may not claim me.'

She was laughing: 'I may not be here to be claimed; San Francisco beckons; normality has been achieved, I'm free as a motherless child. I *am* a motherless child!'

Despite this hilarity, Pauline's suggestion of a walk before she began the next part of her journey, on to Dublin, was refused.

'You haven't seen the shoreline below the Tower. It's unspeakable. The tide washes up these carcasses – dogs, all swollen with gas and Christ knows what else. Sometimes they're in bags, bloated and shiny, and live dogs sniffing among the lot. No one comes to take them away. And further down, where that grass margin has been left between the river and all those new houses, it's all littered with old mattresses, and bits of washing machines and fridges. So the people in the houses, if they look out on the river, have to look over a beach of dead, corrupt, corroding matter, the grass growing through canisters, rusting spokes and springs. Unspeakable. Even the trees left there – the plastic bags get caught high in the branches and flutter there like gigantic, noisy, white unnatural leaves.'

'I feel I *have* to go and see it,' Pauline was an energetic conservationist. 'Snoopy has already had a walk so we don't have to bring him. But if it's that bad surely someone should be trying to get it cleaned up?'

'Honestly, Pauline, I know I sound like someone out of *The Fall of the House of Usher*, but I have tried, a few of the people along this side and some people from the new housing estates did try to get something done about it, but the authorities blame the tide. I swear, if they could cover over the river they'd probably be happier. No, let me alone today, Pauline. I've two articles to write, both for America, both about the comely maidens and beauteous mountains of dear old Erin. I can't do that kind of thing for weeks after a walk down the Tower Road.'

But after Pauline's departure Claire did not settle to work immediately. The glossy photographs spread on her desk seemed to her to breathe more of a selected reality than she felt any words of hers could do.

It was not that she had lost her faith in words, or in her ability to use them. That ability had done too much for her to be undervalued. It had brought her a livelihood, praise, travel, friends, satisfactions. She trusted language, but she used sometimes the syllables of her own tongue as if they related to exotic declensions, as if they had no connection with that commonplace usage which seemed to her to leave language like a carcass on the beachhead of communication. Her name, therefore, appeared in no native magazine or newspaper. Her reputation lay abroad; the cheques came in dollars and sterling. She had developed a healthy interest in several exchange rates.

Now she loitered through the house, doors opening at a touch, the cat surprised on Claire's own pillows. Nothing else moved; there would be no other sound but her step, her breath, unless Snoopy barked at the postman. With Frank's encouragement, she saw the house as hers. He had made his home in Sunday's Well, he and Stan had agreed years ago that the house up there on the hill, its balconies and terraced lawn, its half-hidden secretive delightful steps leading like a stone ladder among the shrubs right down to the willows that bent and trembled above the velvet river – that house was to be Frank's home, the family home.

From her bedroom Claire looked across the teeming roofs which, although still separated from her road by the high wall, had obliterated all trace of Brady's farm and Brady's field. The glass of the window was streaked; she would have to wash it. Or she might leave it until the spring, then she would get a proper job done on all the windows inside and out. Afflicted with her usual reluctance to get to her typewriter until the last possible minute, she found a cloth and milky window-cleaning fluid and drew idle patterns in circles and loops on each small pane. Opening the casement she sat on the sill, her back to the road. The air was cold, the light without sparkle.

Beneath her the grass was edged in its clean green spread with the heathers and shrubs and prostrate conifers which Frank had said would keep things tidy. But they had defeated him. They couldn't help but grow, indulged as they were. The lavender had grown into a hedge, the heaths into trees. A canopy of ceanothus leaned happily against a wall, cyclamen corms coiled in its shelter, the ropes of white jasmine were wrapped around a fuchsia, skimmia and viburnum disguised the November skeleton of a guelder-rose, hollies hid the corners and a broad, golden cypress kept the wind from the shorn branches of the acers, the lilacs, from the tender abutilons and the mimosa which Frank had said would never take.

'November is come and I wait for you still'. Claire wiped the smudged solution from the glass, satisfied with the sheen. She curved her fingers into the corners of each square, catching little flakes of paint under her nails. Particles. Pain as she stubbed them to the quick. Outside as far as she could stretch her arm she spun light into each frame, the small squares dazzling the grey sky, the reflective river. The edge of the window cutting against her legs, her hands clutching the angle of the open casement, she glanced downstream to see Dunkettle House, marooned on its island of greensward above the raw red seams of road and roundabout swooping against its hill. Concrete ellipses swerving with traffic where the marshland had been, and the birds. The herons, the curlews.

On Damien's last visit he had slept in Frank's room. That had been in this past spring. It would be a year before she saw him again. He had been troubled then. The intimacy of his visit made him uncomfortable. Claire felt almost as if there were something for which he needed to forgive her. Or forgive someone.

'Think what he is leaving,' Pauline had counselled. 'All that certainty.' But what did Pauline know about it that she, Claire, did not know too, even better?

Those letters. Pauline knew something of those, of the later ones. The first had come in courses; acclimatisation, adjustment, challenge. Then – the people. The Church and the people and the poverty. Could she send him D.H. Lawrence? He was not coming home on leave, he was taking his holidays in Mexico and Texas and then going on to a retreat house with some of his colleagues in Vermont.

The passages of her career seemed vapid when Claire set them down – her own letters gave her a perspective on her life, and she wrote about it less and less, telling instead of Angela and Stan and their children, the births and deaths of the diocese, of Frank and Onora, and Mrs Cummins. Of *The Journal* and her work with it she wrote little, sending him cuttings sometimes of an item in which she took some pride, her story of the refugees from the North she sent him, her account of a trial following an arms find, of a funeral following a mistimed bomb. She wrote to him – things she could never write for *The Journal* – about the Church, the miasma of ambivalence in which, it seemed to her, the country was trapped. Gradually she wrote about being afraid.

She had no conception, he replied, of what terror meant. Of what bombs could do. Of police brutality. Of the ambiguities of doctrine. She had no idea, he wrote – and he wrote as if she had not written at all.

Their lives enlarged and grew more separate. She was going north, to Dublin, to Belfast, and eastwards, to London. He was going south, to little dusty towns or towns where the dust had obliterated everything that might be called life. Yet life remained, black-eyed, impassive. He was sent only where it would be found. He found it further and further from the places to which he was sent. He became absorbed in its resistance to deprivation.

'There is a kind of resistance there,' Claire wrote to Damien when she had left Belfast, 'which denies all the words which are used to describe the place, the conflict. Killing after killing, funeral after funeral, the words ascend the pulpits of their churches, the same words mount the headlines. But the words belong to another culture, they are another language. They have no meaning, and no power, up there.'

She wrote to him that it was Anselm Daunt who had made her understand the limits of her language. 'You don't understand the Brits, Claire,' he had said. 'You like them, though. And you don't understand *us* – you're afraid of us. But we are your people. So you can't align yourself.

'I can understand,' he had said, 'why you think it would be a good idea to take up this job in Belfast. You think that by settling there, by getting to know the scene, the score, the people, you'll be able to figure it all out.

'But I can tell you,' and he had leaned forward closer to her across the china cups, the hotel's damask napkins, 'you're not that kind. You're no war correspondent. You like this kind of thing too much, the airs and graces; what was it they called your friend Leon? A smoked salmon socialist? You're a cucumber sandwich Republican – but we're meat eaters!

'No, Claire,' he had said, his fingers flexing the metal spine of her notebook on the table. 'You'll be much more useful down here. We need people here who can present our case socially, without getting excited about it, who can express it in rational terms – no! Not an apologist –' he raised his hand against her laugh of recoil – 'just a friend. A *friend*, with access to newspapers, to the radio, to television, to good company, to society. That's what we need, down here.

'And Claire,' he had said, a smile of amusement meant to make his words appeasing, 'you can do it all *intellectually*. We'll keep out of your way. We won't ask you for a safe house. You need not be uncritical. All you need to do, all you need to be, is *on our side*.'

His voice was close to her. She could feel the gush of his breath. When he rang her at *The Journal* to arrange the meeting he had said he was in Dublin on business. She had heard rumours; she had seen his photograph, taken at a protest march. Then there had been a death, a young man blown up by the bomb he was inexpertly planting. Two other people had been killed, but Fr Anselm Daunt was credited with officiating at only one of the consequent funerals, that of the boy placing the bomb. He was photographed too with some Americans in Derry, some American priests. In all those photographs he had been wearing his clerical collar.

Here, in this tree-shaded hotel, the location of his choice, he was attended with deference, even though he wore nothing to indicate his priesthood. They either knew him to be a priest, Claire thought wryly, or they suspected that he was a terrorist; it was only slowly dawning on her that he was both. And she had been deferential too.

Her mind had been made up already about Belfast. Hardly was she off the plane at Aldergrove than *The Journal* – Claire learned subsequently it was under pressure from a more ambitious man who already had experience of working in the North – asked her to take on a senior position in the Dublin office. She was offered a world of politics and diplomacy, national and international, of High Courts and race meetings, of universities and fashion shows and literary evenings. She took it.

But for this meeting, in this sunny, gardened hotel, sitting away from the windows but with the calm light of ordinary day seeping even to their corner, Claire was still too close to the decision to be sure that it had been a good one, the right one. It would suit her, she knew that. It could be made significant, for the times, as the radio in her car had reminded her as she left the office that afternoon, '*they are a-changing*'. The long-drawn vowel sounds of that last word pleased her. There was relish in its animosities, the cadence was unforgiving.

The question was – were they changing faster in the North or in Dublin? Where was there going to be the most excitement, the challenge, the best stories? The danger? There – up *there*, the North. If she had insisted she could have kept that posting. She had not been quick enough to see the reasons for the Dublin offer, she had not been suspicious enough. Flattered, she had moved out of her colleague's way. And so she was here, caught in the light of this man's mission, listening.

If she had ever wanted his good opinion, she could have it now. If she had ever felt worthy of his attention, it was here, now. She looked at the neat pale hand touching the edges of her notebook. What was it he had said one day, a day of bluebells, that day of Coppingers' Court, yes, that day which had ended with Jarleth Tattin in the pub in Castletownbeare, she remembered, in the car, he had said – 'She's only a reporter.' He had said – 'Our words are what she writes.' – No, it was more than that, it had more meaning, more definition.

'Our words define hers,' he had said to those men. To Peadar Cullen, who was dead, his suppurating body found in the heather of the Wicklow hills. The survivor of TB, the escaper from Port Laoise prison, the man who had stood at her shoulder at the edge of the valley of Sliabh Luachra – shot in the back of the neck like a Nazi victim, probably by Conor Herlihy, she had been told at the time, Herlihy the man who had gathered bluebells. *Take them and be true.* He was in prison in Scotland, Claire couldn't remember now what for. Brown had been shot dead in Derry by the British Army; Anselm Daunt received his coffin at the church, his welcoming hand resting on its covering flag.

That hand tipped the edges of the unopened pages on the table between them. She had brought her notebook as an explanation, as a defence. It was her *carte d'accès*, more potent than the NUJ card, more an extension of her questioning, reflective mind than her tape-recorder. At this time she kept all her notebooks – she had been right in her anticipation of what Dublin had to offer, the leaves were packed with the small histories of the weeks as they went by, with the meetings, the people, the interviews, the events. She would grow out of this habit; or rather she would cease to hoard these little journals, so precisely dated. She would lose faith in the notations, the letters of record. They had been written, she would believe, by someone else, and in another time, as if the continuum of her own existence had splintered into episodes.

She had drawn the notebook back across the table. He read the gesture as an indication that she was ready to leave, and his hand touched hers, his fingers at her wrist. They were warm, and the rough whorls of what she suddenly thought would be his fingerprints grazed the shrinking surface of her skin.

'The thing is, Claire,' he said, leaning a little closer. 'You'll be in good company. There are some important people – you haven't been long enough in Dublin to know yet just who is really important – some really important people here know why all this is happening, and they're on our side. They can sense, as we can sense, that the time is right. *This* is the struggle. We must make it now. Look at it' – and his fingers closed on her wrist.

'Look at it – I could say to you now that if you in the South do nothing, and if we in the North only defend ourselves, this will go on for years. We want to make it fast. We are not going to let the Unionists win this one. This is the fight the Irish people are going to win. At last.

'We're going to win. Remember that, Claire. We're going to win. Be with us, be against us, or stay somewhere in the middle – it will only make a difference in terms of time. We're going to win. The Brits will go. We're going to live to see Ireland free as she has not been free for eight hundred years.'

His voice had not risen. The emphasis of his words contracted the grip on her arm, closing and relaxing, but not letting go. She had yielded so far; she wanted to understand his purposes; she did not want to alienate herself from him. But she couldn't let him think that she agreed with him. Could she? After all it might be wise to prevaricate. He could be a good source, and she had her way to make.

She moved her arm, straightening back from the table so that he had to let her go. The warmth of his grasp flushed for a second beneath her skin, and then he said:

'The plan is offensive, Claire. They'll move, plot, plan on all fronts. I'm no terrorist. I don't want lives to be lost. I have people in my care. Souls. I have a pastoral responsibility – don't think for a moment that I forget that I'm a priest. I never forget that. My priesthood makes me more sure, more convinced that rebellion in the name of justice is exactly that – a just war.'

'A religious war?' She flashed the question at him, her only show of fire.

'Maybe.' He considered it. 'That would be unfortunate, though. That need not be the way at all. Politics does that to people. Politics has always made the people of the North fear one another; the politicians, not the people, were the ones who would not let those old loyalties die out, they were too useful. No, it need not be a religious war.'

He was silent. The sun slanted across the room to them. Claire heard the birdsong from the garden, a siren wailed in the industrial distance, a long way away. '*Lointain*,' she thought, far far away, the sound in her head giving a lonely meaning to the word.

How simple he could make it seem. History, the past was a record which could be simply understood. The future, too. That could be predicted. He spoke, perhaps he thought, as if diplomats had never existed, as if Shakespeare's versions had never been challenged, as if America had not lost the war in Vietnam. Sinn Fein could do better than this. She had been at their meetings, she knew there were strategists among them, men and women who comprehended the complexities of motive, or thought they did; people who knew as this man before her seemed unable to acknowledge, that life, even in its most direct causes and effects, did not run according to plan. They engaged in counter-effect. They computed coincidence, they accepted the logic of responses which had or seemed to have no logic, they read mistakes like lessons, they evaluated, with considerable accuracy, the power of hatred, of fear; they perceived vulnerabilities which gave them power, they played on loyalties faceted as life-blood which glistened as the leaders moved ahead.

This man, this priest, was not one of them but would be used by them. He was not at all sophisticated. Claire saw him as she had seen him once before, sweating, frustrated, alone with a machine which did not work properly, alone with a girl who was too efficient for him. Yet he had stirred her then. There had been – what? Some tremor of recognition, and of resistance. Was she wrong – had she not enjoyed some affirmation in his personality that acted on hers at that first meeting? 'Did you take pleasure in it, my child?' The innocent query of the confessional came back to her.

Something else came back to her: a note in his voice when he made a reference to Damien in South America, a sneer, light, but acid, something about 'liberation theology' and new definitions of pastoral responsibilities. Damien had been wrong to trust his doubts and conflicts to Anselm Daunt. Claire had known that then, although she had merely overheard the comment, it was made among other priests at some ceremonious event.

'You used to be all against liberation theology,' she suggested, at last, smiling as if with surprise.

'In South America? Of course I was. I am; there's no contradiction in that – I'm surprised that you even think so. No – the people I support are engaged in – or are the cause of – a straightforward resistance to colonial oppression. There's no theological conflict there at all.'

He was looking across the room, out the window at the grassy slopes, the tidy recommended shrubs.

'No, Claire, it's a different thing entirely. We don't want to rewrite the rules of the Church, we want to enforce them. In the Catholic republic which will be in place after this is over we *will* enforce them.'

He heard her quick breath –

'Among Catholics; Protestants can go their own way. We respect freedom of religion; right now, right at this minute, the Protestant militia is our enemy on the ground, but once they're dispersed, the Protestant people will be welcome to live with us as citizens of our country.'

'You make it sound so simple.' Claire knew of no way to stop him. It must be utterly releasing, she thought, to see one's way so clearly, to be so confident of the outcome. A great cause; a conviction of righteousness; a knowledge of one's enemies; a brotherhood of comrades – they solved all the complexities of life. They licensed the arrogance, the absolutism, the conviction that in making his request he was doing her a favour. She might, by his invitation, be one of the chosen – *we few, we happy few*'.

He had spoken easily about Raphael, working among the poor of Daunt's parish, manning a community advice office, helping to distribute funds.

'Can't you see it, Claire? It's all coming true, the comrades coming from afar, the Spanish wine, everything promised in *My Dark Rosaleen* – it's all coming true! Yes, money instead of wine, and America instead of Spain, but we can all see it, this path to justice and to peace was laid out for us generations ago. Raphael understands that – don't you?'

She asked, unkindly, if he wasn't afraid that Raphael might embarrass them all some day, and for the first time he was angry, sitting back from her.

'There's a thing called discipline,' he said quietly. 'And if things do go wrong, we'll take care of him'.

In the silence she let her eyes dwell on what she had already seen in the wide, sunny room. The fireplace, with its wreathed marble, its brasses, its turf-box spraying flowers into the grate. Beneath the loose rugs the floor shone like burnished tweed, its parquet patterned, its lustre a patina of many years' usage, dancing perhaps, slippered feet gliding through measures as precise as the parquet itself. There were light-bulbs where the sconces had held candles, but the sconces were still there, and candelabra on the mantelpiece at each side of the great, gilded mirror which now showed candle after candle, window after window, a receding succession of light. And in the light they sat, receding also, their quiet words opaque as the blinds which in the great houses such as this were drawn down against the sun, shielding the carpets, the portraits, the Sibthorpe stencils.

How had she left? Without saying anything much more, she did remember that. Without, certainly, committing herself. Or so, at the time, she had thought. But he had known she was not with him. And he had known, he must have known, why she didn't want to say so, why she would not declare herself. She would not pretend to sympathies she did not feel, but neither would she admit to the sense of creeping revulsion flickering behind her brain. Keep it cool, she had counselled herself before this meeting. She was keeping it cool, she must keep the lines of communication open; if he thought perhaps that she didn't believe him, didn't believe that the plans he was talking about would work, that would be enough. It would be a challenge to him; he might be amused.

'Well, Claire?' His question, formed as he read her gestures of departure, did have a lift to it, as if, although seeming to look for an answer, he wasn't expecting one.

'I know,' he said, 'that all this must seem hard for you to understand. I suppose it's hard for you to feel sure that you're doing the right thing. And you've always liked to be sure of that, haven't you?'

His smile was reminiscent. Cosy. They shared, he was telling her, the same refusal to accept injustice. He was reminding her of Nicholas Barry. That one death, so long ago, so lonely, in the river by the church where the Virgin's hands were held outstretched.

'It's a question,' he said, 'of allegiance. Of knowing where you stand. The struggle has begun, and cannot be turned back. You must make up your mind, Claire, now. At this moment in time.'

What was a *cliché*? A metal casting of much-used words, a set of phrases kept in type, always ready to hand in the case-room or printing-floor. Always ready to hand.

Not even as she waved a salute from her warm little car to where he stood, solitary but confident in the doorway of the house which was now a hotel, not even then did she grasp how unlikely it was that he would be amused by any challenge, any resistance, on her part. He was in earnest. It was all real. Perhaps he could not know for certain what would happen, what did, indeed, come about, but he had accepted what would have to be done. Simple. It was what made him a good priest.

Simplicity. It bound him to the most oppressed of his people, and to the most extreme.

The post had come. Claire ran downstairs to catch Snoopy, trying to restrain him from flinging his whole body at the front door, or chewing the envelopes which the unsurprised postman seemed to pitch at the letter-box. She saw with some relief that there was a cheque for her, sterling. Nice – this time the difference between the Irish and English pound was running in her favour. And there was a copy of the German magazine which had translated her series of articles about the Burren.

In the polished pages, flowing with currents of wind-swept colour, the dry yellows and greens of stone embroidered with lichen, the sweeps of limestone cushioned with tufted flowers, brilliant gentians and saxifrages, lanced by legions of orchids, she saw that all the botanical names she had given lay in heavy parenthesised legends along the bottom of each page. There was a photograph, taken at some accommodating sunset, of the Poulnabrone dolmen. The Germans loved that kind of stuff, she thought thankfully. And the photographer had done his best with the crosses at Kilfenora and Dysert O Dea, picturing them in monochrome and through the angle of his lens finding the depth of the relief, darkening it, strengthening it. The effect was of looking at something which was not at all accidental, but deliberately crafted so as to speak, and to remain. The camera had found the power in the stone. Working on the flowers, the skies, the seashore and mountains, the photographer had dutifully reproduced their loveliness, the spaces in which their colours and forms and involuntary relationships to one another settled into harmony.

But the crosses – they had given a different excitement. Although time had beaten a softness into the outlines, the lens had redeemed the chiselled purpose. Christ had entered Jerusalem. Christ had died on the cross. Christ had lived as the men and women in those surrounding graves had lived. Christ had risen.

Faith.

She turned another page. A warm blue mist, and deeper blue and silver on the farther edge of Galway Bay, the massed peaks of the mountains of Connemara. Beneath them the brush-strokes of green for pasture and woodland. Claire knew the trees were not so thick as distance made them. This soft abundance lied – and hid another betrayal in the abandoned stones of Coole Park, that house behind whose curtains, among whose avenues, Yeats and George Russell had gossiped or intrigued with or about Shaw and Douglas Hyde and Sean O'Casey, even, for such is the way of artistic guests, about the hostess herself, Augusta Gregory, that laurelled head. And they had written there; it had infected them, it became part of the legend of their lives . . . Bought by the State, demolished by the State, Coole Park was gone. Some of its timber remained, shade for its ghosts.

She had not written it in her article, but looking at the concluding photographs Claire remembered the words cut into the parapet of Adare Manor: '*Unless the Lord bless the house, the labour is lost that built it.*' Had the Lord not blessed that house of Coole so blessed by its keeper and her visitors?

Faith. All that was left of Coole now was romance. And something for her, and others like her, to write about. To make money from. But faith – was that why she had been thinking of Anselm Daunt? Father Anselm as they spoke of him in the North, in his parish? That charisma, that had struck her even at the time. No sophistication – although that had come. Journalists could nowadays refer to him as a polished performer on television, on radio. And he had his uses, Claire could not deny that. The Irish media, forbidden by law to broadcast the speeches or comments of the para-militaries or their support groups, were always delighted to find clean apologists. Daunt had never joined anything except the priesthood itself; his politics, officially nonexistent, were impeccable. White as a host. His was the charisma of deceit.

The odd thing – or one of the many odd things – was that nowadays Daunt was more transparently a socialist than any other Irish priest Claire could think of. Funny, the way it had gone. Those early years of groups for this, classes for that, all that anger he had about the way people were left to live their lives as best they could, all his zeal for resources, the shanty club rooms offering classes, pre-school education, free legal advice, housing aid or action or activity at the very least – all the intention of his work, that had all been Catholic. Troublesome – she remembered Damien's awe – but fervent.

That was what had inflamed Raphael, drawn him to Daunt's cause, whatever it might be. All that fervour. Not just the holy words on the altar: *My brothers, do not try to combine faith in Jesus Christ our glorified Lord with the making of distinctions between classes of people . . . Listen my dear brothers: it was those who are poor according to the world that God chose, to be rich in faith and to be the heirs to the kingdom . . .* Not just the holy writ, but that absolution Daunt offered. It's not your fault. It is the fault of your circumstances. It is not your responsibility.

What a creed that had become, applied to the young fundamentalists of the North. What a solace, offered in kitchen and pub and funeral parlour: the circumstances of your time have forced this response, these deaths, from you. You are absolved.

That was not sophisticated but socialism was. Did it mean that Daunt, after all these years, saw a tide turning and was ready to swim with it? From that remembered day to this, Claire had never spoken to him. She had never declared her rejection, he had never demanded an answer. And that day was fifteen years ago. Only once had they come close enough to let their reckoning be made. They had weighed the meaning of the history of those years without speaking. They had looked at one another, full face, unsurprised, trapped by crowds in the doorway of the courtroom where the inquest on Angela Coupland had been adjourned.

'*Work,*' said Claire to herself. It was a fierce admonition. '*Work!*'

She left her room, collecting the sheets from Pauline's bed on the way, putting them and anything else she could find into the washing machine. What was it Mrs Gaskell had advised the aspirant woman writer? 'First put the washing down to soak . . .'

Snoopy unrolled himself from his post at the foot of the stairs and she opened the door for him, making sure the garden gate was secure. The little room she called her workroom was scented by the freesias Pauline had brought with her a few days ago. Enriched by flowers, Pauline had still seemed tentative, as if she never could believe the warmth of Claire's unfailing welcome. Considering the subject once, Claire had decided that Pauline was someone who would look the same in bed, even making love, as when fully clothed; her face, that is. Claire's idea of rapture then had been those secret changes in the eye which transfigured hope into certainty, which made the alluring face suddenly, excitingly, that of a stranger. But there was something raw-boned about Pauline, a nakedness, an honesty as endearing as it was demanding. Her face in love would be alight, but unchanged. Pauline, Claire had decided, had no art. It was what had made Claire trust her. When you opened the door on Pauline, what you saw was what was there. Intrinsic. The real thing.

Chapter 3

Claire resisted her own suspicion that this room, here, where she worked, reflected that of someone else. It was only, she had reassured herself, that she had followed his example in making one place unchallengeably her own. Yet it held echoes. She had had no design, but had an impression of what she wanted it to be. If it spoke to her of someone else the voice she heard was less insistent now. And less recognisable. And here were Pauline's freesias, a fragile radiance of white and gold and cold pale purple, their fragrance banishing the room's reminders.

She had been sure when she amassed what was here, when she added to it as the years went by and the work came in, she had believed she was creating an essence of herself. The photographs – Della and Frank, Onora and Della and Angela, Bran, Angela and her children. There were no photographs of Raphael, or of Leon. Nothing of Damien. Many things about the house were precious to her, she hoped she would have them for all of her life, wherever she might live. The clock in the hall – the framed old prints of the city, of the Tower Road itself, the damask stored by Della, the piano at which Frank still played out old melodies with one hand: *When in thy dreaming, moons like these shall shine again* . . . In here the choices were hers, not just the possessions. Those photographs hung on the wall, stood on her bureau, through an act of affirmation on her part. There was no Leon, no Raphael. And Damien.

When had she had a photograph of Damien? There was one, sent during his first months in South America, wearing clothes she had never thought likely – jeans, a cotton T-shirt. A beard, a broad, bright grin.

No Damien. Yet this was where she wrote to him. Did the location of her letters matter? What could it mean that when she tapped out the words: 'Raphael has been sentenced to twenty-five years. It's a lot, isn't it, just for gun-running?' – they sped from her fingers on to a screen, green characters jogging like a monitored heart-beat; that she sat in an old Windsor chair, that thick velvet curtains framed a corner of the garden, that Della smiled down at her, that her own paintings, pictures she had purchased herself, daring herself to a display of taste or acumen, hung from their striped Regency background. That all these things, her books, Fowler and Brewer and the Shell Guide to Ireland and the poets and *Middlemarch* and *Mount Music* – her property, summoning her. Did they add up to something? Did they even add something – to her? To her sense of herself?

This was a room which did not enter into the life of the house, although it was a room Claire loved. The cat no longer tried to enter it. Snoopy had never been allowed. Frank knocked on the door and opened it tentatively always. Mrs Cummins was banned. But why? It was not just that her work had to be left about, that lay-outs and roughs and page designs might sometimes litter the floor, that letters were stacked in an order to which disturbance would be fatal.

Had she been trying to re-create something?

No. Sitting at her table, pushing back into its alcove the intrusive evidence of new technology, Claire could let herself acknowledge the ambition of the room. This was not the room which would re-create, for her, the dedicated space in which Jarleth Tattin worked. It was the room to which, on that day, on that night, when he would arrive unannounced at the door, she would introduce him. Introducing, at last, her self.

It would not happen.

November is come and I wait for you still. That was an advent she did not visualise. Not now. Once it had been the focus of her intention: that he would scan this room, approve the music centre ('What is love,' he had whispered, 'without music?'), be curious about her photographs, complimentary about the pictures, envious of the books and of the pretty fireplace wherein, of course, a log or two would be prettily burning.

Pauline liked the room. She saw no dislocation there, no area of it which Claire did not fill. Some of its components might match elements of the room she had provided for Jarleth, but she was unconscious of her own investiture of that space, thinking instead, but only occasionally, of its curtains, the rug brought back from Morocco. In her eyes Jarleth's room spoke of Jarleth. Claire's room spoke of Claire.

Yet surely, surely, some sense of other presences must have sprinkled the calm light when Pauline, in Jarleth's absence, entered his room? Although she knew that Pauline had no curiosity about it, and knew also that Pauline must have known, no need for guessing, that Jarleth confined his amorous activities to what he termed, for newcomers, his study – being more certain of successful seduction there – Claire could not believe the room had no evidence to offer to the wife of the man who worked there.

Look at what that location had become for her! On her first visit, an interview for a Dublin periodical, it was just a studio. But what glamour! The antique desk, that rug, the French stove, the record player and shelves of discs, the books – one complete wall lined with them, all bound or hardback at least. French windows opening on to shallow steps above a lawn, trees and birdsong at the edge of the grass, at the margins of the water, where a swift deep stream ran among rocks below the house.

At that interview Tattin, who had welcomed her call, and made the appointment willingly, was irritable. They were speaking in English – Claire could not do otherwise. She had thought he understood that her Irish couldn't match his. And anyway, as she reminded him when she recognised the cause of his impatience, he was the one who had the political statement to make, not her. He was the one who had made the choice between English and Irish as the medium of his work, who had chosen Irish as the path to the national consciousness, despite the fact that the vast majority of the nation spoke nothing but English – and that, not very well, as she pointed out with an acidity which made Tattin laugh at last.

He had relaxed then, been more gracious. Making coffee for them both – real coffee, Claire noted, he ground the beans in a mangle like the one she had at home for mincing meat – he had explained that Pauline, his wife, was in America, with the two children. Claire had been right about the silences in the house, the polished floors, the windows warm with light even as they looked towards the sea. Knowing too well how fated she was to misquote, Claire had asked him only enough about his poetry to draw him out, to find references she could look up and copy later. They had spoken about religion: he had once been a Catholic, but now, he didn't know, he said, shrugging his shoulders in the long Aran sweater.

'Mass, I mean. The miracle of it. But it has to be preceded by the blood sacrifice. No transubstantiation without the blood of the lamb. Being reminded of that every week – I don't know. It's a little bit too much for me.'

But could there be an ethnic Irish poetry, an indigenous one at least, without religion, Catholicism? Claire had been reading Seàn Ó Riordáin, trying to grasp the contemporary function of the poet.

'There must be. There always has been – what have you been reading, for heaven's sake? Haven't you read Seàn Ó Riordáin? Móire Mac an tSaoi, Seàn Ó Tuama? And before – the great debaters such as Ó Rathaille, Ó Brúadair, Raftery? But now – ask me did religion ever do any service to poetry? What do we owe to it? Ask me that.'

Cowed, she obeyed, and wrote down his answers, and saw how he liked her obedience, the diligent pen. When she said 'But –!' he stopped her. At last she interjected – '*Adoramus Te, Christi*? Or that one, the poem to the Heart of Jesus –?'

'Yes,' he said. He looked away from her. She saw the lines in his cheeks, pulling the skin down, the sag of his mouth.

'Am I repudiating something precious? Valuable in terms of truth, the only value there is?'

Because she was still so young, Claire was able to say that she had always believed that the poet should repudiate nothing. He wasn't under an obligation to write about everything – his smile made her defiant – but while it was one thing to repudiate a language, which after all was only like a different kind of typewriter – she said things like that in those days – it was another thing to close off a whole continent of human experience, human exaltation.

Wasn't it? And wasn't it also, suddenly she was sure of this, impossible?

She had thought, driving back to the city, that she should have reminded him of the commonplace beauties he, as well as she, must once have known. '*Gratia agimus tibi*', she thought, and imagined singing it to him there in his room, her voice shining among the glistening discs on his shelves. '*Propter magnum gloriam tuam*', she sang in the car, letting the window down, letting the chant float into the night as she pounded past the slender towns, the villages whose names would never be released in her lifetime from this web of exultation.

Then what had happened? Yes, then, there could be no doubt about it, then Briain Ó Cathasaigh died. That was another letter to Damien, the fact of the death. Not what followed it, for her. What followed it was to be a story for the future. Yes. And this also was when the murmurs of the job in Belfast, the job in Dublin, began to ripple among her colleagues, when with Damien gone, Leon gone, Della gone for ever, Claire found herself repeating silently the bracing injunctions of women's magazines. 'Time to take stock', they said. 'Don't be afraid of change' – even if it only meant changing your lipstick. Time. And Claire began to see time as something to be used, change as a welcome arbiter, life. LIFE! the magazines said – having properties more malleable than she had courage to admit.

'I think,' Frank had said, 'if you opt for Belfast – and I'm not saying it wouldn't be a good move in career terms – but if you do agree to go, try to have a term put on it. It must be hard on reporters there. I'd say you'd find yourself in a burn-out condition.

'Literally,' he added, with a slight smile of apology.

It was with amusement too that Claire interpreted Angela's cautious recommendation of Dublin. She quoted Stan's conviction that it would be safer, all things considered. Claire knew that she was considering Leon, last heard about, not from, operating a pirate radio in Derry. And Raphael, known to be helping Anselm Daunt run a boys' club somewhere in Belfast.

Onora had said nothing, just 'be careful', but expressed no surprise when Claire, for months after that, travelled without explanation around her own county, impatient of questions, claiming attention only by her absences. They began the night of Briain Ó Cathasaigh's funeral.

Nicely timed for a Saturday, a full-fleshed autumn day, caught at the far edge of summer and still warm and ripe. A day with colour in it, and time available, no need to rush back to the city to file the story, Sunday would do. She didn't write like that to Damien, but she did send him a clipping of her report: she was proud of it, she had gathered assessments of the dead man from those men who valued him, who had helped his sons carry his coffin. She had written their word into her record, and mingled their grieving praises with the smell of the smitten heather, the turf flowering under the feet of the mourners. And the report did not betray her.

Claire herself had been mourning. Admiring the man, she had attended his concerts, had not been immune to his rhapsodic visions. 'A little naive, perhaps,' she had acknowledged as she came to understand the purity of his love for language and its music, as she watched, and several times wrote about, his efforts to change education, religious worship, to make a citizenry know itself at its best. In those days she had listened to the men who, knowing Briain Ó Cathasaigh, were

• *230* •

more comfortable dismissing him. With sympathy, of course – but a sympathy more dismissive than indifference.

Had she taken her position among those delicate detractors? Worse, had she ever let that be known? Confidence could blind you to the truth of life, she told herself as she drove; regret made you question your own thoughts, words and deeds, the sins of omission. Her mother had known Ó Cathasaigh – hadn't she said so, one time? Brian Casey, she had called him. That would not be the name on the coffin. The silver plaque had its inscription cut in the thin vowels of the Irish version. Under the simple appellation was the one word – *Amhránaí*. Singer.

Who would not weep for Lycidas? The word stung Claire to the heart, her feeling rushed into appropriate phrases. And the wrong ones, she realised as the choir, filling the timber gallery of the church with coughing sounds, the noise of boots on the uncarpeted floor, swept without more ceremony than a surprised wheeze on a harmonium into the awesome solemnity of the requiem.

Who would not *sing* for Lycidas! Claire felt a blush creeping up – she might have said that to someone afterwards – and from her carefully chosen seat near a door (good sight-lines to see who was there, easy exit to get to the graveyard early) she noticed, the blush heating her senses, that Jarleth Tattin stood in a side aisle with fellow poets, faces she recognised from Dublin magazines. Yet if there were many here representing other more exalted offices and departments of national life, names she would be sure to spell correctly, it was also true to say, and she would say it, that the greatest part of the congregation was composed of friends, good neighbours, plain people, in whose plain souls Ó Cathasaigh had struck a chord. But of what? Claire could suspect that he had offered them a chance, through music, to express themselves more as what they thought they should be than what they knew they were. But was it true?

Requiem aeternam dona eis Domine, et lux perpetua luceat eis . . . She had expected something more homespun. Yet why should she be surprised? Ó Cathasaigh, now she thought about it, had been tutored by those choir masters imported to the city in the early years of the century. She remembered Frank talking about Herr Gmuerr, of Herr Fleischmann, the bell-ringer Gebruers, the Germans and Austrians who made the great choirs of Saints Peter's and Paul's, the North Chapel, the choir at St Dominic's itself, the carillons in Cobh.

Give him eternal rest, O Lord; let the perpetual light shine on him; a hymn, O God, becomes Thee in Sion; and to You a vow shall be made in Jerusalem. All flesh comes to Thee, *Requiem*. The men sang with tenderness. This was the music, Claire saw from the printed sheet in her hand (someone had been very busy getting all this ready), of a French composer, Duruflé. She could look him up in her *Penguin Dictionary of Music* when she got home.

The men sang in Irish, the cadences of their countryside making the words of the Mass their own, as Ó Cathasaigh had taught them. *Ár nAthair*, they sang, freeing and lifting the words. Our Father. At the *Agnus Dei* Claire shivered as the voices muted into the sad descant: *A Uain Dé, tabhair dhúinn síocháin*. Lamb of God, who takest away the sins of the world grant unto us – peace.

The congregation had joined the singing. Give us peace, they sang. Peace – did they mean it? There were people there – Claire did not know if Ó Cathasaigh might have been one of them himself – who she knew did not want peace. Raphael was not there, although he must have yearned to be; he could not easily come South these days, he could not cross the Border.

Claire saw who was there; already, on her way into the church she had acknowledged smiles from women whose husbands explained explosions and death; she had shaken hands which had held guns, which for all she knew had fired them. They would have had her believe that much at least, and she did believe them. Grant us peace, they sang, and opened their mouths for the Host which was not denied them.

She did not go to the altar. Being a reporter, her job was to observe, not to join. It was convenient: sometimes she had a professional excuse for not doing what was expected of her. Today she observed, and saw, watching the men of the choir who were the last to receive Communion, that one of them passing the bier on his way back to the loft walked slowly, and put out his hand to the coffin, and touched with his fingers the grooves of the silver lettering, learning them through the layers of his skin, indelible. His face red, he hurried to his fellows, embarrassed by the delay but not by the reason for it.

The gesture of love released in Claire the throb of her own pain. She saw again the Fruhlingsgold on Della's coffin, Onora's blighted face. For all its wonders, time had done her no service there. Anger rose to her brimming eyes. While the congregation knelt for the final prayers she made her way apologetically through the crowded door, calmed at last by the sunshine and the quiet and the little whispering knots of those mourners who had been unable to get inside the church.

As silence gathered within, Claire wondered if *In paradisum* would be sung. She had heard it in the Fauré *Requiem*, longed to hear it again. *Chorus Angelorum te suscipiat*: may you be received by the choir of angels; may you have eternal rest with Lazarus, who once was poor.

Lazarus – what lies we tell ourselves! Claire sat in her car, facing away from the churchyard, still angry but ready for the road into the hillside, to the cemetery among the fields.

Before she drove off, the coffin was borne out into the daylight. The men of the choir ranged themselves around the hearse, they were going to walk with it to the graveyard. In the church Claire had seen that one of their own number had acted as conductor for the more formal singing, the Duruflé, for instance, but out here they seemed to be without a leader. Well, so they were. From the car she heard one voice strike out an anthem. Roughly, others strengthened the song; it rose and spread like a mesh of lamentation, its stern sequences animated by a single voice, the men mustering for the refrain, martial:

Sé mo laoch, mo gile mear,
Sé mo Shéasur, gile mear . . . the song for the bright hero.

Claire left the song behind the gates and sped to the hill, to
the readied grave. Cars followed hers, again men and women
grouped in murmuring folds, she heard their laughter, joined
them to hear the stories being told, not all lies. She found
Jarleth Tattin had come up to her. Was she all right, he asked?
He had noticed her leaving the church.

'You must go to some interesting funerals,' he teased, and
they smiled together while he said that he had been quite
satisfied with the publication of her interview with him. He
had meant to write, but she knew how these things went . . .
Relieved that it was he who was in the wrong, Claire responded
to his mood, and chided him for a recent review: the author of
a new book had been his friend, and although the book was
disturbingly bad, Tattin had found excuses for much praise,
and room for no criticism.

'Oh, for goodness' sake!' The mild rejoinder left her in no
doubt of his embarrassment.

'I review his book, he reviews mine – it's all a game. You
know that!' He scuffed the tufted grass with his shoe, not
looking at her.

'But how do you feel when he writes about you as if
it were an exchange of pleasantries? Don't you want to
have a disinterested intellect considering your work? Doesn't
anybody's opinion, or approval, matter to you?' Claire was in
earnest, quite shocked.

'I mean, I thought there was a kind of scholarship; when
I read the *Observer*, or see reviews by A.S.Byatt or Anthony
Burgess, I mean, even if you read the American critics – you
don't get the feeling that all they're really doing is paying one
another's debts. Which is what you're saying!'

'Yes. That's what it sounds like. But I'm referring only to
this country. And remember that I've chosen the better part
– my own work uses the tongue of the Gael. There's a kind

of immunity in that. It's not acknowledged, perhaps, but it's there!'

Now he was deriding himself for her amusement. Condescending to her. He might play the game as he described it, she accepted that, but he took no consolation from his own remoteness. And critics who wrote in the Irish language had his measure, because their literary context had few fashions and immense exemplars. He had not simplified his creative life, but made it more complex, more demanding, and more lonely.

'Listen!' he said, his touch at her shoulder – 'They're coming!'

What had he heard? She heard nothing, yet the waiting groups were still, there was a signal travelling on the air. Between the little valleys a sound crept upwards. Claire heard it without knowing, but Jarleth Tattin's hand slipped under her arm, he drew her close to his side.

'Listen. Do you hear?'

It was as though the trees were sighing, and the bushes, things green and fronded rustling with air. Slowly, lightly, it came towards them, becoming clearer only, no stronger, as it neared. The voices of many women, lamenting. The keen for the dead singer.

Where the furrowed old path to the cemetery met the main road the hearse was halted. Between hedges voluptuous with blackberries the men shouldered the coffin, flowerless, to the hill. The chanting followed them, seeming to have no corporal source, no mouths opening on the wailing wild crying stream of voiceless grief which eddied around the cortege, swelling and fading as the hills absorbed it.

'The *caoineadh*,' Tattin whispered, his face close to hers. 'The keen. The true keen, the real thing. You won't hear that again.'

She would not wish to. Once, said Claire to her startled heart, once was enough. But it was an imprint. She closed her notebook, she had put down all she could, all that would mean anything. She had had enough, and would not look at the bone-white family faces beside the heap of earth.

Tattin felt her impatience.

'I must wait,' he said. 'A few of us are having a drink at The Mills after this. Would you join me there?'

She saw the lines on his face had tightened. He was no longer bland, he had business here, and would not leave before his time. She had some sense of change in him, that he was not resilient. His presence was not a gesture, but a commitment. He could not leave.

'Yes,' she said. 'I'll be there.' She turned quickly away, feeling the waning sun on her hair, hearing in the new silence the song of nothing but the birds, bright, defiant, irreducible.

Chapter 4

'Touch me,' the poet crooned, and every woman in the audience dreamed of touching him, every man dreamed of being touched. There were more women than men, Claire noticed. And maybe she was wrong. These were women who dreamed of being poets themselves – who had that been? George Eliot – *'she wished, poor child, to be wise herself . . .'* Yes – *Middlemarch*, Dorothea's earnest assistance for Casaubon with his Guide to all the Mythologies. Something like that.

No. Looking around even in the dark she could see that the attentive faces had a considering look, judgemental even. The women at this reading were feeding fantasies not of making love with the poet, if that once had been the ultimate fantasy, but of sharing the platform with him, or reading to an audience which included him. And reading, as Claire already knew, poems about poets like him, writers like him, and their failures.

Aha!

She shouldn't gloat. And indeed she was only moderately amused. She didn't attend many readings of this kind any more. Robert Graves had been worth going to hear, and John Heath-Stubbs. Some of the major Irish names, a very few of the minor. None, none at all, of those who had supported the H-Blocks Campaign during the hunger strike. Not that she could be sure that these women tonight, when they got the confidence of their own written words, published words – she could not be sure, could not even guess which of them would or would not align themselves in sympathetic signatures.

'There are black flags everywhere,' Claire had written to Damien.

'The country waves with these emblems. It's as if evil were floating above our heads, triumphant. Everywhere. If they are taken down they reappear as if magic currents in the night nailed them again to the telephone poles, the rooftops, the monuments.'

In her distress, she wrote: 'We are to believe that the men on hunger strike are not criminals. Must not be dressed as criminals, must not associate with other criminals. The other demands too – they all have this faceted substance, so you can never be sure what the argument is about. It's subtle. Subtle and perverse. You'd get tired if you were here, trying to understand it.'

She wrote: 'It's a national malaise. The country is coming down with this sickness, this disease. I'm frightened by it. It makes me angry, and I want to do something desperate, to show I'm not fooled by it, that I haven't succumbed.

'You'll be amazed by the enclosed,' she wrote. 'I'm amazed at some of these names. That they're willing to keep this kind of company. Look at them!

'Do you know, Damien,' she wrote, 'what I think about it now? When I read those names, and when I listen to some of the people I have respected, some of them I even admired, when I listen to them on the radio, I think to myself that they're glad they have an opportunity to show some kind of support for Sinn Fein – just in case the Provos win!'

In her bitterness, in her bewilderment, Claire wrote – 'I am demeaning them – I mean it is demeaning to them to attribute such motives. It's easier to do so – and yet, what do I know? Remember, I never went to live in the North. I never worked there, among its people. It can truly be said – and it is said, when I make one of my proclamations, that I don't know what, or who, I'm talking about. And, of course, I have to recognise also that I'm not talking the same language either as the people of the North, or at least the nationalists, or as these people here, these names on the newspaper advertisements.

'And hatred,' she wrote, 'is a wonderful excuse. It relieves the conscience. You'd be struck dumb if you knew the people, the quite attractive, intelligent people, who have turned Anglophobe. There's something cathartic about having an enemy at last. I feel it, because the hunger strikers have become, in some way, *my* enemies. And yet I know that if anyone, in all of this, can really claim to be a victim, it must be each man on hunger strike. How can I hate them?

'There are priests everywhere,' she wrote to Damien. 'And Americans. All righteous, dealers in holy death. All holy, holy, holy.

'Bobby Sands,' she wrote, 'is not only martyr, and hero, and saint – he is also a man of letters. Or was. God help him. I wonder how many more will die? I'm enclosing the Cardinal's statement on the death of McCreesh. At least you'll know what you're coming home to – are you coming home?'

He had not come home. Not then. Claire wondered if she herself had put him off – her letters had been so full of anger, of despair. And there had been such grief.

'It doesn't matter,' she had written during those continuing years, 'how beautiful this country is. It doesn't matter how thickly the harebells grow on the Burren, how dense, how sweet their blueness. It doesn't matter how the moon rises like an eggshell over the cliff-coloured sea, or that the sun fades in a torc of faceted gold, shimmering on the lichens, the webs of flowers, the gentle waves which rush in their long loving unbroken crests towards the stones near Ballyvaughan. It doesn't matter. We will always find words for these things.

'But what words do we find for the people who claim them as so much their own that they have turned the country into a magazine, who have layered it with explosives, with rockets, with ground-to-air missiles, with armalites and ammunition and trip-wires? We who walk above ground walk over these things, these traps.

'Every time there is a death,' she wrote, 'the same words

come squirming out like blood itself. No one is too shocked to speak, there is no outrage that cannot be described and thus absorbed, assimilated. So the words are there: words for the evil-doers, words for the evil that they do. But those men and women, and the carnage they so readily inflict – they have become indescribable. They have defeated language, they have enshrined the cliché, it is the only resource for those of us who have to say something – and it implies a kind of acceptance. Although every death is a victory for the murderers, an attainment of the precise objective – we find words for it, and so accommodate it. Language itself, it seems to me, has been subverted.' What relief could she have offered Damien then? A change of war zones? And he would have had to take a position; she had not yet learned indifference, and would have demanded from him commitment, instead of consolation.

She ran her hands up under the sleeves of her blouse, feeling for the abrasions inflicted by Rosa Gallica Complicata, by Climbing Compassion, by the Fruhlingsgold and Fruhlings-morgen. She wore a jacket. The blood would not show through. Her skin winced and reddened under her touch. A tiny sliver peeled away in one piece, and she rolled it under her thumbnail, pressing it, holding it there, stealthy but safe in the darkness.

Jarleth Tattin had stroked her arm when, after several drinks at The Mills, friends had asked if she was going home that evening. Would she not stay on? They were going to make a night of it, the widow and family would be coming in.

Jarleth Tattin stroked his finger along the downless under-side of her arm. Looking at her he said aloud: 'We'll have one more drink. Then, she's leaving with me.'

She sipped at sweet white wine while he downed a black pint. When he leaned his head in close against hers she could smell the stout on his breath, sour but full-bodied.

'Come on,' he said, 'let's leave this before the singing starts.'

When she found her jacket he held it for her as she reached for the sleeves. Her back was turned to him, her head bent away. She felt there was something almost servile in her obedience. Yet even as she struggled into the coat, shifting her handbag from arm to arm, conscious of his breath, his waiting, holding hands, there was excitement too. She smiled at those she was leaving behind, as if she knew exactly, exactly, what she was doing.

The night had darkened, the air had the chill of the coming winter, and in the blackness Claire stumbled against Tattin as they left the inn. But winter was a long way in the future as she felt his steadying hands on her shoulders.

'Stand still!' he said urgently.

'Stay there, just there!' His voice moved away from her. She saw his outline on the road, the pale hair.

'You are exactly, just like that, precisely under Orion.' His arms opened to catch the shape of the stars spread out above them both. She looked away from him, up to the glistening sky, discerning the outspread constellations, the approaching Orion, the pulsating Betelgeuse. For the second time that long day her eyes stung sore with tears. Tattin's image dissolved. The sky with all its burden closed in above them, the country road was luminous. She thought of the quiet graves, the flowers repaired each month on the flat grass where Della lay, the newly-dug clay that covered Briain Ó Cathasaigh.

She brought her gaze to ground, and reassembled Jarleth Tattin, who stood smiling down at her, a finger tender beneath her eyelashes.

'You'll have to drive me,' he said, 'I have no car.' It was a matter of thirty miles. The distance to his home gave reason enough, then and forever after, for that first spurt of astonished doubt. It would be so *convenient*, she had realised, if she fell in love with him.

Later, when her powers of reduction had become more efficient, Claire reclaimed that doubt and worked it into the past. How like him, she allowed herself to consider, to start an affair because he had wanted a lift home from the pub. To believe that was to smear Jarleth Tattin with the same brush of contempt she used for those who took up easy political postures. Yet she held no political posture at all. To smear him was to smear herself, and all that happened between them, and all that she had once believed, once reassured herself, was true between them both.

And what was true? She could look at this mythologising poet now, raggedly wrapped in some creation of himself, a cable-knit sweater which Claire categorised as American issue, and considerably beyond its best, doing its duty as required reading costume, ethnic and manly. And seedy, frayed as the poet's reading voice. 'In need of a serious jar,' she thought, gauging the grip on the lectern, 'to judge by appearances.'

Yet appearances were not the truth – and she would have to rescue some truth from this performance if she were to write about it adequately. A small notice was all she had been asked for, but she wished to make it worth reading.

Appearances were not the truth: 'Where do we see the truth about one another, and ourselves, if not in love?' The question was Jarleth's, his voice moulding her to the shape of his mystery and her own. She had succumbed to that as much as to his power over her senses. From that moment beneath the stars, his fingers tender beneath her eyes, from that first kiss in the car – her car – parked beneath fragrant bushes outside his door, her mind as well as her body had opened to some version of a vision of herself. He had been proprietary, and she had welcomed his insistence.

And that was what had assuaged that brief premonitory question in her mind when they stood outside the pub, beneath the stars – his physical assertion had besieged and bewitched her. In the weeks, the months, which followed, she had felt the intense charm of his claim on her. She heard her name on his voice when he spoke to other people. 'I've been looking for you,' he said sometimes, and he had been looking for her, among crowds at a writers' conference, among rocks on a deserted beach. When they went separately to functions in the city, when she still lived in that suspended territory between one job and another and filled attractive engagements which brought them together among friendly strangers – then she would feel his touch on her shoulder, at her elbow. It would be time to leave, time to go away. Together. It was the kind of thing she had seen Stan do, with Angela, possessive, confident, not secret, yet with a secret destination contained within it for them both. They had to attend to those ties which bound them. It was like a promise.

That was like Stan and Angela; the stars – that starburst, that conjunction – had she felt when it happened that the excitement of its timing, its significance, was an echo not of the future but of the past? Of the great house, its windows, its skies, open to the south? Nothing new under the sun – or under the stars. She could think that now. Now, Claire believed that. But then – then it had seemed new. It had been revelatory.

They made love to music.

The operas, *Fidelio*. Fidelio! – and where was Pauline? The question lingered too amongst the arias of Verdi, taking on melodic mystery as pleasure foamed through her body, seeping from that moist site where his unexpected kisses flicked the tissues of sensation into unquestioning, obedient delight.

'Pauline,' he had said on her second visit – her third? – 'is *my* concern. Because she likes to take the children to visit their American grandparents, she spends some time out of this country. She will not be here when you are here. Ever.'

A concerto shimmered through the house. Wide awake, staring blankly at the pastel-coloured ceiling, its edge of stencilled leaves matching the brown and gold of the studio's carpet on which she lay, naked, spread out, Jarleth a clothed shadow beyond her eyes, Claire waited for his will. There was the chink of glass against glass. The shadow deepened, his dark shape shut out the tranquil colours of the room, his mouth when it covered hers was wet with whiskey.

'We're safe,' she thought, her eyes straining around his head to where the windows, curtained, were closed, the studio door locked, the house doors, she always asked him to do this, locked front and back.

His fingernails ridged her puckering breasts, his hands unfolded and held and stroked the stretched weight.

'Put your arms over your head,' he instructed, the words crisp. 'Clasp your hands together.' She felt his eyes cool on her skin as she flexed, the tightened breasts lifting, her joined fingers closing in the security of his intention. 'This will be a long one,' she thought, the music melting into her brain. 'Oh, this will be a long one.'

'There's a nice long crescendo coming up,' Jarleth said, still cool, amused. 'And it's all for you.' His hands were under the fold of her bottom. 'Lift,' he said, and she moved her hips from the floor, feeling the draught against her spine. She bent her knees, knowing this was next, and his hands were between her thighs, separating the flesh between the top of her legs and her vulva, that slim rift which his fingers had discovered for her. She closed her eyes, not seeing him, concentrating on this, this waiting, the hinges of her body taut, her skin untenanted.

'I think we'll have a little bit of squirming, will we?' The words were distant. 'A little bit of writhing? Yes?'

His hand was on her pubis. He pulled, not hard, at the hair.

'Oh, *yes*,' she breathed, a gasp. She was suspended on his hand. His finger found her, probed, and deepened its reach and stirred the soft membranes like a mixture, rasping so that her moans had a choke of extremity in them. Slickly, quickly before she was expecting it, he withdrew, and waited while she sobbed her broken '*Please!*'

'Keep your arms stretched,' he commanded, and on his order her body seemed to liquify, yielding as his wet finger stroked the anal ridge before the single forceful stroke admitted him.

Her howl was drowned by percussion. Karajan doing his bit. He moved his hand as she flailed against him, but her fists gripped his shirt, her breasts strained against the rough fabric, her body latched to his, her eyes closed to hide the smile on his face. He moved again, 'switching', he called it. The plunges deepened, hurting her, not filling her, but the escalation tore the imploring words from her – '*Ream me!*' '*Core me!*'

Sometimes if he were not drunk, he would stop when she was at that point. He would take his hands away, sitting back on his heels, watching as she undulated towards his smeared, wide-spread fingers. It was part of his game with her, part of one of them. And sometimes, if this happened, she would relax, and laugh, and turn her back so that he had to catch and kiss her, cajoling her with embraces and contrition. And once when he had sat back to view her frustration she had flung herself at him, hitting him viciously on the mouth, across his cheek, before he toppled her under him, swearing, clutching her hands, stilling her with his weight while he undid his clothes and rammed into her enraged and hostile body, crushing her mouth with his, forcing his tongue between her teeth as she grunted with fury, her nails scoring his shoulders, leaving red welts on his back, anywhere she could reach his flesh. Her triumph came with his orgasm, a helpless thing in itself which reduced him, he moaned and trembled and dropped his face into the waiting curve of her neck. She shifted away from him, letting him lie face down on the floor, feeling in herself a deadly contentment which for a while disguised the pulse of bruises.

She need not be his creature. Anger, resistance, reaction – these could arm her against his powerful claim on her senses. Bold with this confidence she had less fear of his sexuality, less fear of her own which answered his so readily. Location mattered too: she was more compliant, more abandoned, when they were together in her own flat in Dublin. Some other danger was absent. In his home, she was truly submissive, because fear of discovery was part of the price of rapture. She had to trust him. In Dublin, it was her territory, and more anonymous. She had a consciousness of lack of restraint. Before he started drinking heavily they went together sometimes to meetings or parties. And then – the word mouthed across the room – 'Home?' – and their leaving separately, still discreet, to meet by her car.

The intermissions in their relationship gave her confidence too. He lived for months as a married man. Once they avoided each other for half a year. Even when in Dublin her work took her to publicity functions marking his publications or those of other poets, a smile and a nod was all they had for one another, and she would not let herself look at him with anything except amused affection.

Claire still wondered if they had fooled people – but they must have done, no one ever spoke to her about Jarleth Tattin as if she might have any extra knowledge or depth of acquaintance with him. But if she had contained it all so well, so very well, all that moaning and passion and secret, flooding pleasure, all that shameful luxuriance of physical engagement, the intense determination they had for one another's pleasure, separately or together – if none of this had overlapped to swell against the plateau of their individual lives, could it have mattered? Could it have continued?

When Claire looked back and saw herself on that floor, on Pauline's carpet, pinioned and beseeching, she wondered if the she who had been so accurately evoked by Pauline's husband was now a vanished being. That she who had indeed existed. He had been completely confident of her. He had played games with her, but never played tricks. He always stated his intention – it was part of the thrill for her. And she grew audacious, and stated hers. They heated together, on one another's words. In Dublin they had disagreed as they left a political meeting. His Irish verses had been mined for republicanism and a selected few had been read, an attraction for a nationalist campaign, they were applauded with more enthusiasm – and probably more comprehension – than was usual for public readings of his work. He was titillated, she grew angry, and said she admired more, for their honesty, the poems of another writer in Irish, a woman. Furious, for he was threatened only by writers in his own acknowledged tongue, he said he would not go home with her, he would want to beat her, she deserved it.

'Why not?' she responded, and looked him boldly in the face. They were in a pub. He put down his drink, and put his hand at the back of her neck, spreading it between her shoulders and her skull. 'Why not, indeed?' he said slowly, and steered her before him to the door. They walked in silence to the tall house she lived in, less squat than the one in which Leon had once slept with her, and more formal, more expensive. Her hand shook as she put the key in the door, and Jarleth whispered – 'Quickly!' – as she inserted the key again, her imagination a cold light in her brain. In the hall, up the stairs, at her own door, she wanted to hesitate. Why had she said what she said? What would he do? In her small sitting room she pressed her face against his coat and said – trying to laugh – 'Not too hard, now, Jarleth, I didn't mean –' but he kissed her gently on the lips. There was an edge in his voice when he told her to go into her bedroom, to take off her clothes. He took off his own jacket, she heard him in the kitchen, the smell of coffee – coffee? She wondered as she stripped quickly, switching on the heater, the cold would make her reluctant, she tried not to think but to wait for him, for his will, she made herself think of submitting to him, with her own hands she stroked her body – why coffee? The aroma softened the air, its homeliness relaxed her.

When he came in she was still standing, the curtains closed, her bedside light a glow of normality. He put his arms around her, he whispered, his tongue dipping in her ear between the words, 'You've been a hussy, haven't you? A brazen little hussy? Haven't you?'

Breathless, she nodded, the words were his permission. He pressed his hands against her bottom, lifting each buttock, straining her against his loins, she could feel the long bulge and as she tried to put her hands there he stopped her and led her to the bed where he sat down and positioned her across his legs.

'You should be punished, shouldn't you?' It was all a formula, she knew it was. But if he said the wrong words she would laugh, the excitement of it would be over, they would both be embarrassed.

'Yes,' she said, her head turned away. She could see the gleam of his shoes. Her voice was small, childish. His hands found her breasts, fondled them, then he put one hand again at the nape of her neck, not caressing her, but as a kind of force, a coercion. Warm and light the other hand moved slowly down her back, rippling her spine like a piano.

That was what the coffee was for, she realised, he was absolutely sober. The thought was cut from her mind by the first slash of his hand, so hard she jerked and said quickly, terrified, 'No!' but he held her head down and slapped again, in the same place so it didn't feel so bad, and then the blows cracked all across the upraised offered skin and heat spread to her face and chest and although she could still feel the graze of his flannel trousers against her belly she felt also the damp trickle of readiness between her legs. She moaned that it was enough, she'd had enough, she was sorry, and the slaps ceased, there was a lull into which his voice said, thickly, that no, she hadn't had enough, he would say when she'd had enough, he was taking his belt to her.

She struggled as she felt his hand unlatch the buckle, she twisted her head in an effort to dislodge his grip, but he put one leg across her back and held her bent over, and she submitted again – imagine it! It was all very well to subside in a well-timed orgasm as von Karajan uncoiled his frenzy on Beethoven and battered an orchestra into tremendous silence, but this! Although she trusted Tattin and believed he would not damage her, Claire understood from then on that he liked to hurt her in some way, even in deepest, warmest, most tender love sometimes there would be that little pinch, a sudden roughness, a command.

Until he got too drunk. Then there was real danger. That began, when did it begin? The intermittent meetings grew further apart, his life seemed to have settled down, he was working and travelling, he wrote to her. In these absences her disquiet muttered, slimy as a gutter alongside the main road of her life. So much of that affair was wrong, there was Pauline, seen only in the distance, in a photograph, heard in the overheard remark of someone who knew Jarleth and Pauline as a couple, and who did not know her, Claire, at all.

'You're not taking anything that belongs to someone else,' Jarleth had said, to quieten her. They were not committed to one another, they were just friends. They made love, they weren't *in* love – these were the significant distinctions, and

Claire accepted them. Even in his garden, picking loganberries, his tongue licking the scratches on her arms, even in his kitchen, opening a fresh pot of jam, she accepted that; yet the fruit was grown, the jam poured into the shining jars, by that someone else. It was his dexterity of distinction which appeased her; even the uninterrupting skill with which he used the condoms essential to Claire's peace of mind was part of the smooth-flowing arrangement of his life and, by association, of hers.

The drinking, though – that did not seem to be calculated. At first there was something mischievous about it, he knew Claire was disturbed by it, he said only that it made him loosen up. It did; there were extravagant moments, excesses which made her wary. But not enough to make a difference, not in time.

He became more voluble about the conflict in the North. Once, she had hardly listened. Once, they had lain together after love, looking at the television screen in the discreet corner of his room, looking at the ferocious couplings of police and protesters, seeing in one camera shot a priest, a streak of hair like blood across his forehead, his eyes alight.

'Do you know his name is Anselm Mary Daunt?' Tattin murmured. 'You should always be wary of men with Mary in their name: it sets up an equivocation. If you know what I mean . . .' and they had laughed together, derisive, safe. She felt safe with Tattin, saying with him, for him, the clever, cynical comments, the little jokes that made a mockery of other lives. She worked on that lightness to secure her position, to remind him it was safe to love her, she was making no demand.

Then Jarleth began to break that cynical security. She was away from him often enough after a time to know the patterns of his need of her, and she was gradually able to discern also the stability of his ego. He muted his Republicanism with her, because they spoke in English, and his meanings were too clear, too unpoetic. But Claire had seen the ease with which he could let himself feel at home among those who spoke a more rabid language, who quoted Pearse and balladry and gave rough evolutions when they thought some sources were required. And among those who reasonably, articulately, rejected those attitudes, revoked the inherited permissions – among these he appeared to be a reasonable articulate man. And even in his cups he could pretend: he could hold the pose – erudite, smilingly regretful that history had turned bloodily obscure, oozing with quotable explanations.

Completely drunk, he could meet her rage with tears, he could defend himself by his own helplessness so that she would kiss him to tearful sleep without forgiving him.

'I don't need to be forgiven,' he had cried, circling her living room with a bottle of whiskey raised above his head. 'I only need to write!'

Over two years Claire had watched all this develop. He could not write dry. Pauline could not understand. She left him if he began serious drinking. Pauline would not watch Jarleth drink himself to death, Jarleth reported her as saying.

'Do you think I will?' was Claire's response, but his instinct was right – it would be easier with Claire, they could leave one another readily having by now grown accustomed to doing so. But his emissions stained her life. Was it a lack of love which made her reluctant to be the one who had to clean up after him? Vomiting, incontinent, he fell one night between the toilet and the bath in her bathroom and she could not release him. She left him there, returning only to pin to his jacket the savagely worded note – 'Jarleth Tattin, the Real Thing'. In the morning he was gone. She did not see him for months, but read of him on platforms, signing petitions, giving readings in Derry. There was a radio programme – she had to laugh: 'You'd have to laugh,' as Mrs Cummins would say, 'if all belong to you was dead!'– in which he was interviewed by Leon.

But nothing new was being published. He was performing, not working. Claire missed him, her body tormented her, she began to seek him out where he could not be, she allowed herself to think he was important to her in some elemental way. Could it be, she allowed herself to think, that she was essential to him? She heard of his drunkenness, she heard his wife had left him. She saw him, once, in Merrion Square, walking with a woman who was not Pauline. She wrote to him care of the Arts Club. She would have holidays soon, would be going to the south-west, could they meet? A week after she posted the letter he was on her doorstep. They would travel south together, taking days to it, they would walk around Monasterevin and Durrow and travel every by-road that spread from Abbeyleix, they would picnic on the canal banks, they would cancel time, the past.

Claire cancelled those promises she had made to Angela, to Onora and Frank. She would see them, she told Angela, on her way 'through'. She had some business to do in the local office, she had colleagues to consult, she would leave a phone number in case – she made it clear that it should be only an urgent case – someone wanted to get in touch with her.

There was a note in Angela's voice Claire had not heard before: unexpectant. The only thing, she said, was to make sure that Onora wasn't disappointed. If Claire could see her, spend a little time with her, she'd see Onora was failing, both Frank and Mrs Cummins thought it was time she went to live with Frank, Claire might help her towards that decision. If she had the time. It was a pity the children would be away on various summer courses while Claire was passing through: the baby would be with Stan's mother, and Angela and Stan were going to have a small break themselves, going north to their friends across the Border, Claire remembered them?

Claire remembered, and made her promises. She would be travelling back alone, she would see Onora then. She chattered obligingly for a little while longer, disguising her impatience, holding back the swarm of happiness aerating her spirits. They were going, not to his home, but to a house on a hill in a distant mountainy town, she would be doing the driving, she would be in charge.

Jarleth Tattin was aware of this lilt of joyous supremacy and did not disengage from it. Claire had brought tapes to play in the car – *Don Giovanni*, and *Le Nozze di Figaro*, and Bruch and Tchaikovsky and the Berlin Philharmonic. In sunny daylight the journey roved fearlessly through the successive plains. In the long evenings they played the tapes of The Chieftains, or copies she had made of old recordings, Ceoltoiri Chualainn, O Riada with Carolan's Concerto, Sean O Sé, *Do Bhí Bhean Uasail* . . . shadowed, love-lorn songs which cushioned them in sentiment, and encouraged Claire's confidence that this time, this one time surely, she herself understood the nature of the real thing.

'I love these midland towns,' she confided. 'Although the road goes through them, they seem to be undisturbed, and carry on their own life at either side, down those little streets we can only glimpse.'

She loved, she said, the way church spires announced the towns. In the distances the steeples rose above cornfields, pastures, broke through the hillocks of cloud. It was as though the first announcement to be made about a place was that God was there. The first commandment.

The trouble with Jarleth, she decided to say, was that he was afraid of sentiment. It made him feel uncomfortable, and so he disparaged it. But sentiment, she said, was a way of describing what was acknowledged to be true. It was the truth which made him uncomfortable.

In the guest-houses, at night, they saw the news bulletins.

'I wish they'd bomb a bloody American,' Claire said. 'That would put those opportunist politicians in their place. Take it home to them. The Berrigans. The Indians. I really do wish the IRA would make a mistake in America, or with Americans.'

She looked for no affirmation from him. She had become alert to the simple fact that on this journey, most of the time, he was parched for a drink. She put no obstacles in his way, stopped when he indicated a useful-looking pub, bought wine for their picnic meals, whiskey to shorten the nights. In bed he moaned above her, fruitlessly, and sobbed in her arms. His endearments were bilingual, and gradually, from this foreshore exploration of his being, she began to perceive his hinterland, and its barren terror.

He had to write – why couldn't he write? Had his language been stolen from him and put to other uses? Why did she think he allowed himself to identify with the nationalist struggle in the North – they were the people who saw his language as real, as vital, as powerful. They were the believers. If he was not to write for them, who would be his people? And yet – they had destroyed his faith in the language by using it for their own purposes, as if it had no intrinsic, mediumistic value of its own.

Claire, who that very day had heard a trade union representative explain on radio that a gesture from the employers had been anticipated in advance, wondered if perhaps that wasn't the fate, perhaps even the cause, of all language? And anyway, wasn't he confusing his audience with his 'people'? Did a poet have to have prosaic allegiances? And didn't a writer have to write without reference to the nature or number of his readers?

As they drove slowly southwards he said that English was a useless language now. It was corrupt, gone beyond its true meanings, deviant. Irish was pure, uninflected by popularity. English, living, was the dead, lost language. Irish, the hidden but impeccable tongue.

'And it's the mother tongue,' he said one night as they neared the Blackwater. 'We must not forget that. The mother tongue – it's a source, and it's a route to that thing poets, male poets, male writers, find so elusive. The feminine. The feminine in *ourselves*.'

'Treat me like a woman,' he whispered to Claire that night in bed. Dismayed, she kissed his breasts, and took his penis in her mouth until it stiffened and tried to breach his clenched anus with her finger, trying to be rough with him as he sometimes was with her.

'I don't know what you want,' she said helplessly at last, looking into his dry tormented eyes and stroking him from shoulder to calf.

'I want birth,' he said, 'and renewal! And a drink to be going on with.' So she fed him whiskey, and held him while he wept and fell asleep.

From Lismore, Damien's mother's home, they were driving straight all in one day to the western, coastal hills, but they breakfasted among the flat-topped tombs around the Cathedral and then went inside to read again the sisterly eulogy to Jonathan Henry Lovatt Esquire, 'this excellent young man'.

> Then for remembered Lovatt drop a tear
> Arrested in his transient bright career . . .

'Now that's pure sentiment,' Jarleth pronounced.

'But very feminine,' rejoined Claire, who went to look at the tablet to Olivia Martha Hillier of Mocollop Castle, *'where she lived among her own people to whom she being dead yet speaketh'*.

All that day they travelled through countryside brimming with ardent woods, then out of the valleys of the Blackwater and Bride and along by the shores of the Lee. They were a day later than they had proposed, and it was a clear, lightly-tinted twilight when they reached the small house, bare on its buttress of rock, the telegraph poles lurching beside the track to the door. As Jarleth opened it, the telephone rang with an exhausted air, as if it had been ringing and ringing, all day.

Jarleth lifted the receiver, gave the number, then passed the handpiece to Claire.

To this day, to this night, here in this peopled auditorium, Claire could remember the feel of the instrument, weighting her hand. It was Frank. Had she been listening to the news, had she seen the television? Was she alone?

'No,' she had said, 'no.' She trembled.

'Is it Onora?' she asked. 'Has something happened?'

'It's Angela,' Frank said, his voice very close. 'Angela.'

'Sit down, Claire,' said Frank's voice, very close to her. 'It's bad. Are you sitting down? Is someone with you?'

'Yes,' she said, standing at the telephone.

'It's very bad.'

She waited, her heart rocking in her breast. Jarleth stood beyond her, blocking the light from the door still open, letting birdsong in, and the sharp sweet smell of clover which spread like down over the little fields below the house.

'She and Stan were in the North. You knew that? They were with those friends of theirs. Last evening, last evening, the men went out. It's a farm, they went out to look at some fields. The girls were in the house.'

His voice came in gusts, snatches broken on his breath. Last evening. She had cradled Jarleth to sleep. They had drunk red wine by a Blackwater stream, sung inconsequential songs.

'*And they kissed so sweet and tenderly as they clung to each other/They went arm in arm along the road like sister and brother/They went arm in arm along the road till they came to a stream/Then they both sat down together love, to hear the nightingale sing.*'

What was the song Della used to sing – '*O list to the tale, of the sweet nightingale, as she sings in the valley below, below, below below, as she sings in the valley below . . .*'

What was he saying?

'They were both. Angela, Angela is dead. They were both killed, the two girls. Betty Millar.'

To her silence he said:

'They don't know yet who did it. It could have been either side, it could have been one of the maverick outfits.'

He said: 'I'm going up there in the morning. Can you come home here? Onora – and there's the children, Stan's mother is with them, but we've been trying to find you.'

There was no accusation in his voice, there was no room for it. Claire put the receiver back slowly, carefully. The telephone squatted, she noticed, on the marbleised top of that kind of little table which had once been a sewing-machine stand. Her hand was sore and scored with two parallel welts where she had held the receiver.

Jarleth had turned on a radio somewhere while she was listening to Frank. 'Widespread expressions of shock and horror have come from both sides of the political divide . . .' she heard, words she could have written, had written, herself. She groped for her handbag, her keys. She held her hand out to Jarleth, formally: 'Goodbye,' she said. 'I'm sorry to rush away like this. But something has happened.

'Elsewhere,' she said, standing at the door, looking at the placid pool of sea between the horizon and the shore. He walked to the car with her, told her to drive carefully. He did not try to detain her, to make her eat, to do something for her own sake: she had been in charge all along. It had been her journey.

She never spoke to him again. He wrote to her once, not then, about a year later. During the H-Block Campaign. He wrote knowing she would have seen his name among the supportive signatures. 'I have a collection coming out,' he wrote. 'In English. But I cannot be unaligned. Forgive me.'

Did she still have that note? Claire thought she remembered putting it away, eventually, between the pages of the undoubtedly slim volume which arrived one morning in her post. She supposed it was there still – but where was that?

A quietly falling cadence brought the poet to his conclusion. He blinked in the light, acknowledging the applause with some surprise. It was more than polite. He must be so relieved, thought Claire, without a single twinge of compassion, hitching her handbag over her shoulder, folding away her notebook. He would be taken for the obligatory drinks to the obligatory pub, then given a lift to the guest-house (it was always guest-houses for poets of his status: not obscure enough to be grateful for somebody's boxroom, not eminent enough to justify the expense of an hotel), but if he was lucky he would be driven by one of these bright young women here, some aspiring writer still apologising for her own ambition; he could charm her to his temporary will and, who knows, it might all begin again, for him.

Murmuring quickly to a friend or two Claire went out into the street. She had a lot to do in the coming weeks, America, Damien, Emily's final school examinations. But at her car she hesitated for a moment, hearing her own name like a throb in someone's voice. No one. It was not true.

Chapter 5

 This was one of Pauline's maxims: identify what is important, and then get on with it.

     'Sometimes,' she added sadly, 'it can be surprisingly easy.'

What was important about this particular news item in the black-leaded column of *The Journal* which lay under Claire's hand on this early-morning train? It reported – there would be plenty of interest in the item, small as it was – that the marriage had taken place, in prison, in Northern Ireland, of Raphael Brady (sentenced for importing guns and ammunition and explosive devices) and Sarah Barry (18, convicted last year of attempting to carry an explosive device through the airport in Belfast). The ceremony was performed by Fr Anselm Daunt – *who else?* was Claire's bleak reaction – and the couple who shared tea and cakes with several relatives were separated an hour later and Mrs Brady was returned to Armagh Jail.

What was important was the link. All the lives contained on this one island were not running in parallel, as Claire had once allowed herself to think, but had contours which met, involuntarily. No matter how determined the original separation, how intense the antipathies, there were conjunctions. 'Do what we will,' Claire thought now, 'life brings us into touch with one another. It is as though there is some absolute rotation, some rule, so that nothing is coincidence. And yet it seems so random; things happen which we never have intended. People, like stars, meet on some unknown, unplanned trajectory. A conjunction.'

Claire wondered, but without wanting to know, how Raphael and this Sarah had met; he must be, surely he was, twenty years older than her, if not more? How had it been contrived, this marriage? The news column said that Sarah Barry had been orphaned as a child and reared in England by relatives. When the nuns had said goodbye to that baby, into whose arms had they placed her? Tied together as they were now, Raphael and Sarah had been linked all those years ago through Della, whose loving hands had reached to both of them. Would Raphael remember that? So much had happened in between – to him, to them all.

When he had been ill, his recovery had coincided with Della's illness; Claire remembered, willing herself to break back into that little cell of anguish, how strange his grief had been. Cursory, that was the word for it. She could remember finding him in the house before Della died – then he had been frightened of change. But the hospital had done its work, and Raphael, adjusted to grief, began to live by the appearance of things, not feeling them as he once had done, but acknowledging, if not sharing, the feelings of others.

He must have changed since then, Claire decided. He had found a surrogate family in his fellow militants, sharing their cause, their danger. Perhaps they had been kinder to him than she had been, or Angela, or Leon, or Damien? She thought she could remember his lost look as he was left behind; was there something from those years which he remembered, and would not forgive?

And that girl was lucky. She had been caught coming off an Air France jet. If she had been caught in Paris, getting on – she would still be waiting for trial, with nobody inclined to get worked up about her and no chance of extradition with a guiltless legal system courteously ignoring the official representations of consuls and ambassadors. In the North, instead, the plan was already in operation. This depended on the general acceptance (and it would be accepted) that

Sarah Barry, while not too young to carry a bomb on board a plane, was certainly much too young to be punished for doing so. After all, the story would go, she could not have had any evil intent towards the people on the plane, as these would be her fellow-passengers and anything that happened to them would happen to her. And even if the bomb was timed to go off in the airport, the point was that the security staff would be given a warning and if they didn't get everyone out in time that would be their fault – not hers. She would only have planted the bomb. Its detonation, and its effect, were nothing to do with her. So really, in a way, she was innocent.

This marriage would make her a romantic as well as a pathetic little figure, and it would be no time at all when, with the help of a politician or two, and maybe some bishop or other, Anselm Daunt would arrange a weekend parole for Sarah and Raphael and *then*, in a carefully timed announcement, the Northern Ireland Office would find it had a pregnant teenage political prisoner whose lying-in would get more media attention than the Nativity. And when Sarah was released early – having been a model prisoner, no 'dirty' protests for her! – she would write a book about it all and appear on television all over the world. Beginning right here at home, Claire acknowledged. She might even become a member of the NUJ and write for national magazines. And there would be endearing photographs of a little toddler visiting Dad in jail. And then, another twenty years on, it would all start again, another Brady joining the ranks of Death.

'Oh,' sighed Claire as she turned to look out at the country revealed by the dawn, 'why can't they ever blow *themselves* up?' She was forgetting for a moment how many of them had done exactly that. She made a list in her mind of the people who had not been killed, although they had surely been suitable targets. Was there some pact, so that the leaders on all sides would be untouched, the really prominent people who would go on being prominent? And the victims would continue to be the bricklayers, and the soldiers, the policemen and the census-takers, the farmers and the company directors, the labourers, the bystanders, the neighbours who are worried that the man next door hasn't been seen for a few days and who go anxiously up the path to the door and press the bell, which has been wired.

'Everything that happens here now,' Claire had written to Damien when he was still in America, 'has to be strained through a kind of moral sieve. To get the rights of it, you know? They have this trick of making people afraid to do the right thing, the good thing. And then they can work it the other way around: they make threats which depend for their success on *your* having the correct, charitable, humane responses.

'Very few people here,' she wrote, 'are either able, or have the courage, to define these conflicting moral impulses. There are Northern priests, and Northern bishops, who do continually and courageously try to remind their people of what is happening, or what could happen if it continues – but then, they're comprehensively against birth control and integrated education and women priests and marriage for the clergy. So you can see – it's all very, very confusing.'

The confusion was part of her life now, Claire knew. Most of the time she accepted it. There were moments of rage: she saw, on television, bleak parades of victims, legless, eyeless, jobless. And without anger. No, they all said. 'No, I don't feel bitter. No. I don't blame anybody, it just happened.'

Claire was bitter. She shut her mind to these mouthings, shamed by them, not believing them.

'They're not telling the truth,' she said accusingly to Pauline.

'They can't be telling the truth. I think they're afraid of their own anger. Look at their lives! Confined, dependent, maimed and scarred, unemployable, unable or unlikely to have sex, or children. Robbed of their lives! Or are these specially vetted people, trundled out for the media, laundered, so that while they might shed a few acceptable tears, there won't be any ungainly or unsightly or uncomfortable outbursts?'

Pauline didn't think there was any plan to it. She thought, she said, that perhaps these were people who had genuinely come to accept that however they had become what they were, they were what they were, and they had to get on with it. Hatred, she said, took up a lot of energy. 'An awful lot of energy, Claire,' she had said gently. 'And hatred changes people in another way, maybe even as dramatically as injury. You know that.'

Claire had had the energy for hatred, and she had hated. And she had changed.

'But I got on with it too,' she told herself now, watching the irreconcilable country drifting through the dawn of the window. At the other tables the businessmen, the computer analysts, the company directors and statisticians and solicitors and advertising consultants and politicians and professors had all finished their full Irish breakfasts – Claire always enjoyed the way they held their knives and forks: there was something babyish about their clutch on the cutlery, expectant but protective – and with a concerted unzipping and clicking of briefcase latches they settled down to the documents which were part of their working day. Sometimes a passenger who was too obviously not a super-standard fare wandered into this compartment, and then all the busy heads would be turned studiously away until the ticket-collector had accomplished the embarrassing business of ousting the interloper.

There had been times during the years when Claire had been considered the interloper – the only woman in the class. Now as she took out her own documents from her own briefcase she could hear several female voices, recognising them all. One was that of a politician, eager and voluble, laughing as if she were also as cunning as her male colleagues. Another was what Claire described to Pauline as a 'professional wife', gilded from her nail-tips to her toes, scent like an aura around her, costumed with stunning simplicity: a chairman's wife from Italian kid shoe to pearl-pierced earlobe. Claire remembered her from school, a child of poor parents, distinguished only by her prettiness and her kindness. She had married, quite young, a local lad who had got his commerce degree at the university before being left a public house in a small coastal village not far from the city. They worked this together for several years, selling it at a decent profit just as the national economy began to turn, and suddenly the husband was a property developer, a man of substance as well as status. His wife got out of the kitchen and into Escada, flower-arranging and Ballymaloe cookery classes, with a little bit of discreet vocal training thrown in to the mix which yielded her now, tinted, scented, immaculate, her successful husband's ambassadress – and as kind as ever she had been in those early unexpectant days when Claire first knew her.

She was no rarity in Ireland. She was one of an edition of women whose gloss shone from every newspaper, reflecting the light given off by the men they had married, the managers, the proprietors, the chairmen of the State.

'But something must have worked, Claire.' Damien had tried, during their brief meeting in America, to win an acknowledgement from her. 'Those policies, that indecision, that vagueness, that policy of holding, of doing nothing much, of waiting – it must have worked.'

Claire had wondered how to tell him of the oppression – the depression – she felt; it came from being an intelligent human personality, aware and sentient, and helpless. The armed policemen; the striking teachers; the corrupt politicians; the soldiers with their guns rimming the banks on the city streets. The planning decisions – the very plans themselves, with hotels proposed for marshes which had for centuries been bird sanctuaries, recreation complexes for wild landscapes like the Cliffs of Moher, a theme park for the Rock of Cashel, an airport on a Connemara bog. The judgments from the courts, the extradition shambles – to Claire these seemed to teem in shaming indictments of a shallow, vainglorious and fragile national consciousness. Yet listing them was inadequate – for when she did so Damien said only that the country was no worse than any he had lived in up to now, and a great deal better than most.

'And these are the afflictions of a democratic society, Claire,' he had pointed out, wanting her to believe him. 'All right, a capitalist democracy, a young state. But you can't lose faith in it – in the State. It's too soon. We haven't tried hard enough.'

Standing together on the latticed balcony of her hotel room, willing to acclaim all the sights of the city which she was visiting and which Damien was preparing to leave, they were striving to reach some terms on which to quit their disappointments, some mark of mutual recognition from which they could move on, possibly together. Claire had turned to deny that accusation of not having tried hard enough: living in her country, she had begun to say, took effort. She had committed herself to the nation when it would have been easy for her to leave, to live and work profitably elsewhere.

'I don't want to say that it's not the same thing, Claire, but what you committed yourself to was the family – what became your family, the children. And maybe it *is* the same thing: Stan didn't take them and run away – and he had much better reason than you had to leave. Did you have to make the same act of faith?'

He knew what he was talking about: he believed that Claire's decisions after Angela's death had been instinctive, that she could not claim, much though she might like to do so, that it was intention rather than accident which had decided the past ten years.

'You are misjudging me.' Her voice was quiet, more sad than he had heard for years.

'At that time I acted on impulse. We all did. But our impulses were correct. Within six months I could see that. It is not fair to say that everything I did from that time was ordained for me by circumstances. There were opportunities I could have accepted without blame. You must remember my letters. I tried to tell you, to aquaint you, for a while.'

He did remember them, he thought. Better not say anything in case he got the details wrong. He put his hand over hers on the wreathed metal of the balcony. The impulse undid her tears.

'You *want* to believe that it's better than it is. You *want* to go back, to live there. And you think – even if it's as she says, it can't be as bad as some of the places, some of the countries, I've lived in. And you're right.'

'But Damien –' and she turned to him, taking her eyes from the luminous host of the moon mounting the clouds – 'those countries haven't been *your* country. You haven't been responsible. It's different at home. There's a new kind of reality. I can't explain it. Except – did you know, did your friends tell you – Johnny Trant has been made a professor of Moral Theology? He'll probably be a Bishop soon. And as for the EEC –'

'What about the EEC?' said Damien, who had begun to laugh. Johnny Trant held no terrors for him. Laughing he put his arm around Claire's waist, holding her to his side, bringing his head close to hers.

'It's not funny!' The tears made her eyes shine, large and bright in the dusk. 'People like Trant are on boards of hospitals, on university councils, directing school management. There's some terrible complexity to it: private life has never been so lax, so uninformed, yet the Church has hardened its grip on every area of public influence it can reach. And as for the EEC –'

But Damien had produced a big reassuring man's handkerchief and was gently wiping her face, smiling at her, streetlight and neon and moonlight together painting his skin in ghastly, ghostly hues.

'What about the EEC?' he whispered, his lips on her hair.

'It's just' – he could sense the smile coming into her voice. Her cheek beneath his had creased, he could feel the warming swell of it under his cheek-bone.

'A minister, a commissioner, said last week, he got huge, approving headlines for it, he said that with a little bit more work the EEC would be ready to declare that seventy-five per cent of Ireland was a disadvantaged area! And wasn't that a great achievement?'

Their laughter rang, united them, holding them on that balcony above the foreign, radiant bay.

'Sometimes,' Claire confided, 'I feel there should be a special support group for people living in Ireland. The kind of thing that's growing, something like the Irish Cancer Society offers, a help-line. "If you live in Ireland, and you are troubled and suffering any anxiety caused by life in this country, remember you are not alone; just dial 021 584444 and help will be available . . .'"

'Oh, God, I can't wait to get back!' Damien said, and looked directly at Claire. Mirth had banished the tenderness. He wanted, with a desperation which surprised him, to kiss her, to feel her mouth yielding under his. Taller than her he had to move back a step to reach her face. She was relaxed and close to him, but as he moved she increased the distance and turned away into the soft light of the room.

'It's all fixed up so, is it?' She was nervous, lifting a magazine from the couch, offering it to him as proof of the success of her newest editorial contract.

'Yes,' Damien answered, wondering how to get back to her. 'I'll be right there again on your doorstep. The only thing is,' he said, trying for a light tone, 'will there be room for me?'

She didn't answer, her face was blank.

'I'll go now,' he said, 'I know you have an early start in the morning.' He tried to be decisive in his stride towards the door but he was waiting, hoping for some hint of that closeness they had shared on the balcony, for some revival of that spirited affection she had shown in all her letters, not in words but in the arrangements of words, the pleas she had made for herself through those years, the shine her letters had put on some days of his life, the sense of a continuum they had achieved. He was hoping, too, to put his hands on her again, to see what would happen.

Her voice came thinly. 'It will be different. You'll be – just a man. A lecturer at the university, Frank will be delighted about that. But it won't be the same.'

He came quickly across the room to stand in front of her.

'How could it be the same? Who wants it to be the same? And you know I like Frank, admire him, but that's not what I'm on about. I'm on about *you*. Will there be room for me, with *you*? And if I were still a priest I couldn't ask that question. I *am* just a man! I'll never be anything even approaching a priest again – I'm just a man!'

'I don't know why you're so pleased about that!' She was cross because she was confused. 'You had to wait until your mother died before you left the priesthood! Was that manly?'

'We've been over that.' He was starting to laugh again. This was a Claire he could enjoy. 'And you're not to throw it up at me any more – do you hear?'

'Now, Claire,' and he put his hands on her shoulders, making her look straight into his face. He saw in the lamplight the ineradicable lines at the corner of her eyes, the crease like silk at the edges of her mouth, the fold of skin beneath her chin. He saw the blades of grey beneath her hair's gloss, lightly striping the brown waves which fell at either side of her face. He knew what she must see – the thin scalp, the white in eyebrows and beard, the harassed skin. Clearly as he saw it all, he saw too the spring of her hair, the poise and confidence of her step, the bright charm of her eyes, her smile, and within that frame the person he had known for so long, whom circumstances and choice together had made inaccessible, and who now was within his grasp. His covered flesh craved the substance of her; the excitement simmering under his skin was controlled, as his arms were controlled – but they were ready to form themselves to fit her shape. His hands knew where they would fit and waited, ready for their right to curve and cup her body. In her, he sensed, there was a readiness also. He could act without being sure of it. For Claire, he knew, the instinct was no longer enough. He remembered a meeting, a purchase, in an auction room, it must be twenty years ago, he held an astrolabe in his hands and watched its trembling lance, seeking without light, without space, without its stars, to find a direction, its pole.

'Now, Claire,' he slipped his hands down along her arms to take both her hands in his.

'We're not young, but we have a long way to go yet. I think it would be good if we were together. I think –' he stopped, conscious of a hot lump of pity in his throat, remembering some essence of spiritual optimism which once had attracted them one to the other, although then they had not understood.

He knew he was blushing, he felt tears at the edges of his eyes.

'I think – I didn't mean to say this, perhaps I shouldn't say it, perhaps it's too soon – but Claire, my dear, I think we could love one another. Just as ordinary people.'

His mouth touched her forehead, the paler hairs. There was no resistance there.

'I liked you when you were a priest,' she said stubbornly.

'You despised me when I was a priest.' His hands tightened over her fingers. He saw where this was leading, she wanted to be forced. He would not allow that. He could make his life without her, even in her city, in that proximity which must make them friends or enemies. He knew that he wanted her, and wanted her bodily, and he sensed that if he insisted now she would let him make love to her. But that was not the way he wanted them to go, not yet. It was a decision he wanted, not acquiescence.

'There are things you need to know. About me. My life.' She had raised her eyes to his, he felt the biting tension of her hands clasping him. He saw her eyes were clear, and steady, and hard. A pang of love burst inside him. He rested his lips for an instant against her rigid mouth.

'No,' he said, releasing her hands. 'There is nothing I need to know. I'll write to you, I'll give you the exact dates I'm finishing here and getting back to Ireland. We could meet for a few days in Dublin, if you like, and then we could go home, together. But there is nothing you have to tell me, Claire. Not a thing.'

He had gone. He had written, his dates had coincided with a planning meeting Claire herself had scheduled for this week in Dublin. She was making the journey now and could tell herself it was for several reasons. It was convenient. A nice coincidence, and she would make it a happy one. But it was not a commitment.

Ireland, implacable, flashed past in vivid emerging fields.

Where the Blackwater swung towards the town of Mallow Claire saw the brown shallows clear in the sun, and felt through her Italian shoes the satin of the stones, the cold of the water, the slide and the stubbed toes as she gripped for a hold, feeling the white wrinkles ribbing the soles of her feet, hearing the shrieks, the laughter, of some companions – Angela? Raphael?

May-flower and dog-rose burdened the ditches of the diminishing counties where the pastures were small and thronged with sheep. A nonchalant tractor leaned rakishly against the brow of a brown-ribbed hill. Through the flat fields a girl rode among a slow-moving herd of Friesian cattle, her pony switching its tail. A dog, a collie, ambled along in their path, or almost, head down between the spires of weeds. The cattle, Claire noticed, had very short tails – they had been cropped for some reason. In the warm weather they would have nothing with which to dust the flies away.

Plantations of forest pines flanked the rail, blue efflorescences powdering the branches. The girl, the pony, the dog, the cows disappeared, as much a dream as those remembered voices by the shallows of the river. A house of exquisite Georgian purity stood alone on an eminence of lawn, with a little white-painted gazebo at the edge of the garden, a gravel sweep leading to a pillared front door. Below its gentle slope had fallen the steel and aluminium rubble of a generation's abandoned cars. Piled crazily as mating cattle, heaped in a mouldering shambles of rotting elements and alloys, the metals leaped in the sun, all their colours vivacious as a shattered pageant. Two piebald horses, hobbled at the neck, had found the thick lush grass which grew among the corpses. Heads arched towards the ground, their manes brushed the rubble, their pocked soft lips flickering against the rotting, perished tyres.

Why did that hurt so much? Claire smoothed the lay-out pages on her table, adding measurements she would discuss at the planning meeting for the magazine which, as she had told Damien in San Francisco, had taken off: it advised

Americans and Europeans about the best of business-like Ireland, softening the straightforward monetary allure with luxurious dollops of ancient castles turned into splendid hotels, pictures splashed with blue skies above vast meandering golf courses, frantic salmon jumping for the terraces of bright, broad and unfrequented rivers.

It hurt because it was true, that rubble, that detritus. It was true that the country's own people could turn it without apology into one big scrap heap. Even these pine forests creeping like a commercial plague across the landscape could not hide the glitter of spent traffic around their tarnished edges. As the train halted in prosperous towns, Claire was reminded of how, in city, town and village, householders were ripping out the old windows which had been built with their houses, replacing them with rigid plastic frames in shapes and sizes which betrayed any claim the domestic architecture of the country might have had to its own character. All this was part of modern Ireland, progressive but blind to itself. And yet, some part of her yearned for it. She was falling in love again, as she did every spring, with her own country.

Out of the mountain-ringed valley the train shuddered through the new landscape of prairied acres, clean-shaven and hedgeless, without ditches or trees or shelter. Cows stood in yards hoof-deep in mud, heavy grey animals dehorned and alien, Charollais, Claire thought, or Blonde d'Aquitaine. But outside her own rushing window a bank blazed molten with furze, and she could see in the unmanicured distances the bounding outlines of obdurate elder, blackthorn and whitehorn and crab-apple still fringing some unruly patch. And where once she had wondered why all the long-horned cattle had disappeared to the western counties, and why the Kerry cow was seen no more, now she was glad to spy a drift of grey on black, white on black: Friesians still among the heavier herds and once, near Abbeyleix, a calf as brown as caramel.

While the train hissed and squealed in Portlaoise Claire could see the life of the town going on beneath the scaffolded, netted high-security walls of the jail, dominant as the Cathedral. A man walked on the road below the station, four stilted greyhounds at his side, innocent through the glass. They walked on their own way out of her sight. She made a note to mention that as another sport – not coursing, but racing, what they used to call 'the dogs', there should be some interest in that, and it would yield terrific photographs. Hadn't there been, what was it she had seen, where had she been with Damien, something about greyhounds? Leading back, in some way, to Raphael – no, to Sarah Barry. Well, and then to Raphael. She would think of it again. Perhaps she would remember.

Her heart surprised her by twisting in the socket of her chest. She was going to meet Damien. In his letter he had said that he would be at the station when she arrived. She had some idea, now, of how she would feel when she saw him. She still wanted to stand back – but perhaps the time for standing back was over. 'It's late, it's late,' she told herself, but knew it was not too late. And they had rehearsed this compromise of their lives, their own coming together.

During that uneasy holiday of Damien's last year they had rehearsed, seeking what had lain behind, or beneath their advances and retreats, their diligent, mutual fact-finding conversations covering those years of absence and of change, of grief and acclimatisation. They had gone to Fota, and walked through the restored rooms of the house with other tourists, seeing from the upstairs windows the swaying giraffes which ranged, aloof but accustomed to the terrain, across the opened fields, caged only by the ha-ha.

The cheetah were fenced in, she reassured Damien, but not the ostriches or zebra or wallabies. The monkeys and the lemurs swung and chattered across a group of new islands built into the shores of the lake. Also fenced in was pets' corner, with its pigs and hens and rabbits and goats. They would save all that, Claire had decided, for another day. It would be enough for them both to wander around those acres of the estate which were for sale with plans being made to build hundreds of time-share homes among the woods on the estuary banks, a hotel was to be built, a golf course. It would give employment.

Slowly circling the arboretum, they made their way to the coachyard, strolling beneath the dense blue plumes of wisteria. From there Claire knew a way into the old orchards. She found the door, warped, the paint withered, but it was not locked, and Damien helped her push it open. The great thing about Damien these days, Claire realised, was that he never bothered any more to wonder if permission were needed for anything he wanted to do. It was as if it didn't matter – but that wasn't the case. No, it was that he didn't worry if what he was doing was incorrect; he could not be embarrassed by being at fault. He could be apologetic, but not ashamed. Now, unquestioning, he followed her. They stood together inside the door, the high stone walls around them, grass thick and trenchant and almost knee-high obliterating any shape, any order, which might have been here once. The surviving trees were twisted in their struggle to bear fruit, their bark cracked and mossy. Leafy strands against one wall remained to bear witness to the pears of long ago, and in here, between these walls, all the brightness of the day which had encouraged their journey was dimmed to faded, shadowy light.

They went on. There was no one to challenge them as they climbed through the grass to the wicket in the furthest wall. This too they opened with a combined push, and Claire, who had been thinking of those furtive visits her mother had once described to her, suddenly recalled instead an earlier Damien bending to a door, a hasp, an ungainly key. So long ago; it was at the beginning of their joint lives. Not joined; although she saw now how much there had been to unite them. She thought of that young man, a priest, eager, sturdy with his conviction, ready always both to explain and to understand, his youthfulness unable to hide that hint of what Onora would have called the tearaway, something still ungoverned despite all his acquiescences.

Damien saw her thoughtful eye on him and grinned.

'Not what you expected, is it?'

She looked at the ranges of ruined glasshouses, lianas thrusting through broken roof panes, light occluded by a mould of blown dust and soil and tacky matted cobwebs. Where there had been order and intent there was litter, abandonment. Where there had been fruition, fertility, there was desolation. The pots, whole or in rusty shards, lay overlapped like tiles beside the derelict cold-frames. The dereliction was everywhere in the garden, the brick-faced raised beds collapsed, their rubble thronged with weeds, the paths hidden as if in a field.

But in the potting sheds the barrows, the hoes and shovels and spades, these all stood neatly where they had been stored. Had there been one day when it had been decided – no more work is to be done in this garden? Had there been a date for it, that decision? Or had someone tried to carry on, to do so much, the 'at least' factor? At least keep the weeds down. At least keep the frames watered. At least keep the door locked.

In the largest potting shed the pots were stacked like miniature Babels, row upon towering row. The rolls of twine, of labels, the secateurs with their thin curved handles, the trowels and hand forks, the trays, the bundles of canes – all had been finally laid by, in their correct place, as if they would be taken up again within the week. As if, were they not to be used again, never to be put to their tasks again, they would rest in an honourable quietude in the murk of silence, of green light deep and deepening, in the faint but faithful smell of soil and roots and manure and dry and earthy implements. On the wall where the light from door and window shone Claire saw the cards, the telling pinks and blues and reds now rendered to one faded pastel tone: First Prize for Pelargonium, Second Prize for Sweet Pea, First Prize for Cucumber, Second Prize for Pear, Third Prize for Gooseberry. Witness to the trowel, the hands that wielded it, the many years of diligence and delight, the little triumphs of an ordered, cloistered, devalued world.

Damien had come to stand beside her. During this short visit they had spoken of all their lives: of his decisions which had brought him now, unvested, laicised and unaligned, searching for employment in his native country; of her decisions which she had not made, of the things she had allowed to be decided for her, the feeling which came upon her sometimes, especially when she met some friend of years ago in the street, that she had lived through most of her life without noticing it, that she had been living in a dream.

She had not told him about Jarleth Tattin. He had asked her why she had never married, or even come close to marrying, and she had said that she had been too involved, through several years, with a man she could not marry. And would not, she had added after a pause, even if it had been possible. And then, after Angela.

She did not add the other lurking reason – Damien himself. She would not tell him yet that when his letter brought the not unexpected news that he was leaving the priesthood, that he was moving permanently to a teaching post in America and would not be returning to the missions, that then a twist from that skein of neverness with which she hardened all her thoughts of herself had broken loose. Her responding letter to Damien had been so cheerful she had had to apologise in case its tone seemed unsympathetic, or insensitive to what she knew, of course, she assured him, she *knew*, must have been a bitter struggle. But try as it might it spilled joyous congratulations, bright and insubstantial as sequins, into his tragic consciousness. Its very inappropriateness was a message. He might not read that message immediately, but it would keep until he was ready.

Now Claire felt him at her side, in the gloaming of the shed, tracing her thoughts to the witness on the wall.

'It was good while it lasted,' he suggested mildly, turning her around to move outside again. 'And perhaps that's all there is. Several linked lives shared all that the house, the gardens, the stables, the farmyard, all that these offered, and demanded. Through generations, I know. But the fact of those generations doesn't enshrine them, and if they haven't ensured their own continuum then that's it – they can't continue. So now other generations are linked here, through the house, the land, for other reasons, in other ways. Nothing is lost – it's just changed.'

'I feel a loss,' she said, thinking of Della and Frank like children escaped into the fruit garden.

'Yes,' he said, misunderstanding her. 'You have an idea of a house, an estate, like this. It's the kind of thing you like to read about, all tennis parties and wills. But in reality people had to slave to keep these lawns so smooth, those marble halls so clean and shining. You assume that you would have been the lady of the manor, had you lived then – but what if you had been the scullery maid, or the governess?'

'I know,' she said, smiling, 'I know all that. And if I place myself in that scene I usually give myself the role of a poor relation, a niece of the family, perhaps, invited for longish holidays when the children are fractious or because I'm so good at doing the flowers. But that wouldn't have prevented me from seeing it, physically, and loving it.

'These days,' she added lightly, 'you're not supposed to love places like this. It's still true that you're not supposed to feel any affinity for them, you're supposed to despise the class structure which allowd them to flourish – and I do. In a way. But –'

She had turned to his laughter. 'I *do*! But that doesn't prevent me from feeling that the good things about that way of life at its best had some value which we are too eager to deny.'

'Even if that were true,' Damien said, 'true about those houses and families which were what I suppose you could call the genuine article, they existed only in Britain. They grew in Britain, from Britain. Here they were an imposition, they had nothing to do with the people of the country, with the natives. That's where the tension, the conflict lies, I think. You should be able to see that. It's not that the Irish people now despise these houses, it's just that they're not relevant.' They had come back to the terraces. A peacock swished gloriously away from their quiet footsteps, his gait contemptuous, his tail a sumptuous train. Claire knew that Damien was right, but she was right too.

'They are relevant because they're here. We've been left them, like bequests. It's what we do with them – that's what's relevant. Can we value things, can we take care of things, of people, of expressions of ideals, or dreams, of history even? What value, what values, do we possess as attributes? – It's relevant, because it's what we are!'

They walked beneath the drapery of trees towards the estuary, talking about Leon in his job with a commercial television company in London, making significant documentaries. They talked about San Francisco, and Aids, and by a route which Claire distrusted they got on to feminism and women in the Catholic Church and what ecumenism could, or should, really mean. It was not that they came to any agreement on all these issues or on the others they touched in their talk; all they were doing was clearing some of the conversational scrub which had grown between them during the absences of the past twenty years. They left the pathway and went through the fields to the knoll from which Claire could show Damien the silver panels of the sky-tuned solar energy unit which provided power for the farmyard

'It has its own beauty, though, hasn't it?' said Claire, willing to be wise, and Damien put his hand in hers and led her back through the shoreline woodland to the folly, the little railway station, the trellised bridge, and across the curtailed walks to the car park shimmering in the sun. Sitting in the car, her foot on the clutch, hands ready on the steering wheel, Claire looked at the children scattered among the thin trees, their parents folding push-chairs back into luggage-boots, a hatchback commonality feeding on ice-cream and cola and crisps, as amazed by the pig and goat as by the flamingo.

'They look happy, don't they?' she asked Damien. 'They look as if this suits them, as if it is a good way of being entertained. I must bring the children here again, before things change.'

His assent endorsed their fragile peace. Claire drove, her spirit lifting, although she knew that this was to be their final day together before his return to America. It was enough, she thought then.

She thought now, as she was borne at speed towards him once again, that it had not been enough. She thought now, with trepidation, that they had not covered enough ground in their scrub clearance. The sketched pages waiting for her confirmation, the newspaper with its information adding another bracket to her life, the diary in her briefcase with its ledger of the year to come – where would this free-wheeling, self-directed Damien land on the map of her life?

The quickening memory of a month ago in San Francisco charged her heart like a battery. She remembered his body standing next to her, before her, against her in that hotel room of which she now had so little recollection – a smell perhaps of powdered fabric which had been dusted with floral freshener, not a unique smell. The balcony, yes, where Damien had stood with her, the railing, his hand over hers, enfolding it. His beard under her ear.

A sodden blush pushed her senses to the surface of her skin – just her luck to be gripped by the menopause at the very point of a change in her life! Reminding herself that the sweat did not show on her face she tried to think, to think, as Pauline advised, of what was important. But what was important? What he was? What she was? Which identity was the less perplexed?

She must not panic. Fear was admissable; if she decided now that she did not want to lose this chance of a life with Damien, then she could become afraid that the chance was at his disposal and he might not offer it to her. Fear was less demeaning than panic, and she had learned to live with it, fear in the compulsory modern sense of being afraid of violent death, afraid of the telephone call, of being frightened of the news item on a bomb blast in central London knowing Emily would soon be somewhere in that city – that fear she knew well. The other, this new tension in her brain, in her stomach, the tightness of her hands – this was the fear that Damien at home would at last be lost to her.

There were things he did not know about her. He did not know about Jarleth Tattin. And yet, in that hotel room, oh, let her remember this! he had said – 'I do not need to know.'

He had said – 'There is nothing you have to tell me. Nothing.'

He had kissed her. She could not remember the pressure of his kiss, the taste of it, it had been tender, leaving no imprint. She could not reach her arms, feeling the itch to score them, to lift the tiny dryly-decaying scabs. For weeks she had worn long-sleeved, tight-cuffed shirts, even her nightgown made it awkward to reopen her wounds, she was determined to beat this need to draw blood from her own flesh. She might go to him scarred, but not bleeding. If she were to go to him. Cold with the doubt she looked out at the plain of the Curragh, at the prancing silhouettes of horses and jockeys where the turf rose towards the gallops. She thought of Shergar, a folk mystery now yielding to time, a question as intractable as who killed Michael Collins but almost as answerable, the evil was known, the end of the poor, abducted beast as familiar to his killers as that of the hero was to all his countrymen.

Claire hoped still that at some point in that brutal episode the horse had kicked, and bitten, and shown all the temper of his blood by striking with his flashing hooves, by seizing with his great teeth an unwary hand or arm in a sluicing, slicing grip which could not be released without agony. If that exquisite, unmourned animal had been terrified to death she lusted to hear that he had inflicted terror in his turn on his captors, to whom his heart and beauty and power meant nothing except a weapon for their hatred.

Her fingernails curved to shred the cuticle of her thumb. She straightened her hands, she had cared for them in the past few weeks, painting the nails, using cream for her skin. Would he notice that her hands were softer, prettier? She looked at them, the nails neatly curved, the pink polish a soft colour, the skin still firm, hands which he would hold. No matter what was to come, he would take her hands, she would offer them. '*This is the hand of Bridget Cruise.*' The memory consoled her.

After all it was he who had said there was nothing she needed to tell him. When she thought of them again the words sounded so firm: not wiping out all that might impede her, but making it of no further importance. Like an absolution. Her brain remembered the learned words: *Ego te absolvo.*

Pauline had said something like that, like Damien. In Claire's garden, at just that point in the evening when the heat of the summer day was waning to a balmy residue of warmth, before the midges and flies began to swarm around the little china teapot, the remaining crustless sandwiches, the cream-smeared bowls emptied of raspberries and sugar. Pauline, hearing the note in Claire's voice which suggested the onset of a fit of confessional honesty said, with enough quiet warning to silence Claire altogether, that Claire was to be careful.

'Stop it, Claire,' she had said. 'Don't tell me what I don't need to know – just because of your need to let it out.

'You'd be surprised,' she added lightly, 'how very little I need to know in order to stay happy. And Claire –' she put her hand on Claire's arm to convince her by touch – 'friends can have secrets from one another. In fact, if they really *are* friends, there will be many things they won't say.'

Perhaps it wasn't an absolution, like Damien's, but it offered Claire some escape from the burden of betrayal. She could keep her secret not from shame, but as a loving duty. But how much had Pauline known of Claire before she met her? For all her calm she was shrewd – not a graceful attribute perhaps, and Pauline possessed it only to a delicate degree. She was not a fool. She had explained to Claire that she understood her husband's infidelity. She had explained it as if she were speaking in the abstract. It was like the alcohol, she had said. He needed drink to spark some madness in his brain, washing away the inhibitions of insecurity or of despair, releasing his consciousness of conflicting realities, reducing his fear of naming them to the world. If alcohol was like fuel to the engine of his mind, women, sex, the repeated challenges of love – these revived his ardour for the scientific principle, the theory of combustion which drove him to find bursting words for the energy reborn, time after time, conquest after conquest.

'It is a kind of rebirth of something in himself; it is not just sexual gratification he is dredging from these encounters. It's like faith, he needs to be reminded of his power by the constant demand of the faithful, those women who find in his words, in his seductive intelligence, the best part of him, and who go to bed with him to prove their allegiance.'

Claire had thought of all this in the garden where they had been talking about those women, not Tattin's women specifically, but those women who had found themselves celebrated in verse, or through their part in a poet's life, an artist's life. They had spoken of Tattin, Claire listening.

'He needs a sense of the possibilities of life. All these renewals – these are renewals of himself, and a promise that even as he ages he remains alluring. And that reinforces his creative confidence, he remembers who he is, what he is, and he goes on.'

Claire wondered if the understanding of this indulgent process was enough to wipe out the hurt.

'No. Even when you are used to this kind of thing it is hurtful. You know I don't pretend about that. I may not say very much – but I feel it. It's why I go away. But then, when I go back, for a while *I* am the renewer, the reviver.'

Thinking that all this must call for miracles of precision timing, Claire thought also that there must be a risk that at some time some woman would capture Tattin imaginatively. She would not be a functionary only, but a source.

'Someone did, I think, once. It lasted for a few years. But it's over. He changed during that time, it was unusual. And he started to drink heavily too, then. But look what's come out of it all – those two last collections after he decided to go back into English, opening up that huge British readership, the Americans. I think –' and there was a lightness in her voice as she spoke – 'I think he's decided that it's better to be international than just ethnic. I can't disapprove.'

Had that someone been Claire? But how could it have been? She had not praised Jarleth's words, their provenance had not lain within her spirit, or what he perceived of it. She had drawn from them. She had recognised both his vocation and his submission to it. In him she had heard some echo of a national soul which appeased her own. By his sacrifice of one language to another she had been enriched. She believed then that she had been enriched. It was the idea of him, not the substance, which had charmed her. She had been receptive to him, lulled by the words as tokens of what he was, even before she met him at that funeral.

Lying in his arms she had only half-listened when he translated his own words to her – and half-listening, what did she hear? In the languor of those hours it was the alchemy of the process which enchanted her. Away from him, thinking of him, then she could feel what she knew his words to mean floating like a tentacle to grasp and pull her emotional attention back to him. She had invested him with inherited nobilities; an aristocrat of language, a lyricist of the harboured past, the singer of a vernacular which, banished and despised, had survived its dispossession through the dynamic of its metaphors. He was an incarnation; words made man. But not his words. Hearing only their ancestry, she had been deaf to their evocations. She had been deaf to him.

Had he known it? Was that what had allowed the growth of the intimate violence they shared for a while? It was safer to believe that those half-shameful habits of their last year had grown from other frustrations – his because of Pauline, perhaps. Pauline, Claire had known from the time she got to know her, would never play games. Pauline, in the truest sense of that phrase Jarleth Tattin had fixed so mockingly in her brain, Pauline was the real thing, the true coin, unvariable.

Looking at her there, sitting back against the timber of the old garden seat, her long legs stretched and browning in the sun, her hands relaxed under the delicate cup and saucer, sunglasses perched on her dark brown head, the Sunday papers strewn with pleasurable disregard on the grass, the whole dappled by the shading pear tree – looking at her, Claire could see that attenuation of line, of bone, which made her look so vulnerable and yet so unmistakably complete. It was how she had recognised her when they met, it was only for the second time, at the inquest. And that had been something true for both of them; although Claire had met her only once before and many years ago, she had never feared or suspected Pauline's motive for being there, for presenting herself, at the end of that day, at Claire's side. From that day of despair and terror so hallucinatory that Claire had always had to squeeze it into a recess of her normal mind if she were to have any hope of continuance – from that day had come this friendship, its unlikelihood an unspoken amusement to both of them.

Pauline confessed later that she had been driven to attend the inquest by what she had heard earlier of the horrors to be officially disclosed. They were the breathless gossip of the city. Remembering the gaiety of the girl she had met, once, in the street, she had not been able, she said, to ignore what was now to be inflicted on her. She had wanted to be here, if help were needed, she might offer it. Or something, whatever might be needed that she could provide.

There had been a moment at the end of that day when Claire, waiting for Frank to bring Stan to the door of the courthouse in the Northern county, had stood alone beneath the bleak lights of the drab, moist-smelling hall. Racing through her brain were the words, not of the evidence she had heard, but of the Compline prayer by John Henry Newman: '. . . until the shadows lengthen, the evening comes, the busy world is hushed, the fever of life is over and our work is done – then Lord in Thy mercy grant us a safe lodging, a holy rest and peace at the last . . .'

'A safe lodging' was stuck in her brain. She had heard of the dinner among friends, the decision the men had made to walk together to newly aquired fields, the dogs following them. The two women had remained sitting in the orchard behind the house where they had taken their after-dinner drinks, basking in the lingering sun and in the silence from the childrens' rooms. And then the shadows lengthened and the evening came.

They must have heard the crunch of a car on the drive, because the gravel when examined was scored by furious wheels. The body of Betty Millar had been found in the kitchen garden where, according to the evidence at the scene – that meant footmarks, a sandal in the asparagus bed – she had been trying to reach the lowest point of the garden wall. In her struggle to escape she had dislocated a shoulder; there were abrasions on feet and hands, some teeth were broken. She had been shot at close range. The measured details of contusions, wounds, and injuries were given, as precise as those for the bullet, the type of gun, the cause of death. The halting pathologist spoke about the left eye and cheek-bone; damage to the teeth suggested that some type of gag had been applied, or perhaps – he agreed politely with the coronor that this was a possibility – one side of the face had been pushed so roughly to the ground in order to silence screams that the lacerations and breakage had occurred in that way.

A thick plastic bag had been tied over the head of Angela Coupland. This would have caused suffocation and death, but the body had also been beaten with a weapon such as a hammer or a metal bar about the head, face and torso to such effect that the cause of death had been ascribed to head injuries including laceration of the brain. The litany of measurements was read out, the list of fractures to rib, wrist and collar-bone, haematoma on the inside of the legs indicating both forcible sexual penetration and attempted resistance, there were bruises – described by length and weight – indicating manual and penile assault of such strength as to suggest frantic haste. 'Manic' was a word the coroner offered to the pathologist, who agreed; there was a conciliatory tone to their exchanges which diminished the savagery of the sentences they uttered.

Claire was not unused to the language of the court, the autopsy findings; these had been familiar enough in her young days with *The Journal*. In those days, as with subsequent hearings and trials, she had wondered why certain questions had not been asked: then as now she wanted to hear that the victim had been dead – or please, at least unconscious – before the gross indignities of this death had been inflicted. There was no such solace here. Grass and soil and blood and shreds of plastic had been found under Angela's torn fingernails. Her feet in their light sandals were bruised, the skin of the heels ripped, grass and gravel embedded in the gashes. She had been fighting, she had been thinking, she must have known her life was ending in this fury of terror and humiliation. She had died, drowning in her own captured cries. What words, what sounds, had anointed her convulsing senses? There were signs, the pathologist said, of considerable resistance.

The two husbands, who had understood immediately that they had been the original target of the attack on the house, gave evidence of finding the bodies. They had returned at dusk, preferring not to walk on to the nearby village pub as they had agreed it might not be a good thing to leave the women alone for too long. They had been absent, they said, for approximately an hour. They had approached the house from the laneway which led to the fields so they had not seen that the gates at the end of the driveway were open. They had gone into the house, Stan to go to the bathroom, Brian to set out some drinks. Nothing had been disturbed, the children were still asleep, nothing was unusual. They had gone back into the orchard to look for the women; Brian in his evidence helplessly referred to them, only once, as 'the girls'.

They had said all they had to say about all that to the investigating police; here they had merely to concur and corroborate. Claire had already heard Stan, who for days afterwards could not stop talking, telling Frank how he had tried to lift the bag from Angela's face, the plastic clinging to the wet flesh, how puzzled he had been by the little scraps of matter sliding on to his hands, the blood and flesh congealing and sticking to the shining material, he had seen her mouth, the lips drawn back, agape. He had seen an eye. Just like that,

that was the way he talked about it, that was what he had seen.

Brian had run sobbing through the orchard searching for Betty, discovering her where she had fallen for the last time, bleeding into the asparagus bed, a mist of flies and midges hovering above her hair. There was enough, just enough, of her face left to make the official identification a matter of course. As for Angela – Stan, who had never taken a detailed interest in Angela's clothes, had identified her by a necklace she was wearing: moonstones.

Neither Stan nor Brian, who had delved with their shaking hands into these horrors, were expected to seek out and destroy the murderers, and they did not do so. Claire reminded herself – 'Vengeance is mine, sayeth the Lord' – but would these husbands ever question the justice of that inhibition? When they saw the bunkers of semtex exposed on television, when they saw technical irregularities prohibiting extradition, would they not wonder what the Lord was up to?

After all that had gone on in the court Claire found herself in the hall looking at two people whom she recognised. One was a tall woman, brown-haired, awakening a memory which heated Claire's cold skin. The other was Anselm Daunt who, as he moved towards her, seemed to grow acolytes like wings from the shadows behind him. Turning slowly and unmistakably away from his approach, Claire clutched the hand of the woman who had come close to her.

'I must get out of this,' Claire had said, and together the two women had moved carefully into the street. It was clear that Pauline had been for several years the woman in Claire's life. Her presence here did not seem immediately to be a mystery. The question Claire asked herself for a long time after was – what had Anselm Daunt been doing there? The rector from Sunday's Well had come North to be with Stan and Frank, who were bonded by this grief into a mutual, accepting dependence. A clergyman from Brian's parish stood with the Millars, and with them too was a young priest who, as he told Claire when he was introduced to her, had pastored Betty.

Whom did Anselm Daunt represent? He had been going to

speak to Claire, that was plain, but why? She never discovered the reason. It was enough that she had escaped him, that Pauline had rescued her.

'How can people forgive?' She had stopped in the street and grasped Pauline's arm.

'Did you hear all that in there? How can we live with it? Even the priests, the clergymen, they had no words for us. And they know, we know, the police know, that nothing will come of this! There will be no charges. No convictions. And in time, in a short time only, people will nod to one another and say – yes, that Coupland killing, the Millar woman, they've known all along who did that job. Nothing to make it stick, of course. It will be just one more forgotten incident – all this grief, all that agony and horror, those hideous deaths, just part of what makes us Irish!'

And all that came true: no charges, no convictions. The journalist who had got the Belfast job instead of Claire had told her a few years later that yes, up there certainly they knew who the killers were. Everyone knew – but there would never be any evidence. Nothing, he had said, would happen about that case unless one of the men was taken for something else and put in jail and found God there and felt the compulsion to confess. 'And that could happen,' he said. 'I wouldn't discount that possibility at all.'

Pauline, thought Claire now, as the train slewed through Sallins, and the curves of the Wicklow hills gathered towards Dublin – Pauline had understood about forgiveness, the necessity for it if life was to go on. And she had achieved it, too, as a power of her spirit, a serene manifestation of her own grace. Normality though – that was less measurable. Pauline had claimed it as an achievement for Claire and Stan and Frank that the frenzied and hysterical sense of loss had been quietened to the calm of bereavement, that life, which will go on, had gone on unchallenged.

Claire had wondered about the validity of that great cause – the imperative on-goingness of life. What she had had to help Angela's children to learn was that time heals all wounds, that no one is indispensable, that even the traumatic and clamorous event which had engulfed their family would reveal itself to be a nine-day wonder. As it did. Claire who had had to deal with her own embattled feelings about Angela, transformed from sister to saint in the space of a weekend, cared for the children with an imaginative assiduity which she hoped for their sake and for her own might replace the maternal comforts which they were denied. They talked of Angela often at first; when Onora died – without fuss, and after promising to let the doctor see what could have caused the attack of breathlessness and lethargy which had brought her early to bed one evening – Hewitt had admitted that he knew that they all meant to keep Gran's memory alive, and that she would live on wherever those who loved her thought of her, yet he was afraid, he said in his new, manly voice, that memories didn't live. He was afraid, he said, that he wasn't always able to remember his mother's face. Her voice, he said, yes, he remembered that. He remembered her voice calling down the garden steps, he remembered things she had said to him. But her face. What she had looked like. Did it mean, he had whispered, that he would forget her altogether, that she would be finally gone, entirely lost from his life?

Holding him, smoothing the tears from his cheeks, Claire had said that no, it was simply that memory was absorbed so as to become a part of you, not just something that could be flicked on or off like a light bulb. It would grow deeply into your brain, not always near the surface, but always within you. And it would surprise you, cropping up sometimes, disturbed by a word, or a gesture, or a smell. And then, when you were older, you would find another thing happening: in a way, throughout your life, you would be looking for that beloved person. And you would always find her, because she was part of you.

All sentiment, thought Claire, mulling over those early years. But not necessarily untrue. Or unhelpful – it had helped Hewitt then and although both Emily and Lyle had that cryptic tendency they must have inherited from Onora – certainly none of their paternal relatives had it – Claire believed that the softer, less demanding explanations allowed them to find their own way to the harder truths. That was her theory anyway; she would have to wait and see how it all turned out.

A crooked line of caravans bordered a road at the edge of the city. Dogs and goats were tethered, hens struck at the worn grass in a reflex of hunger. Straps of withered plastic hung lifeless on untidy bushes, and Claire sent her brain on a by-pass around Angela to reach Emily instead, who had gathered only last night with her classmates for her school's Parting Mass.

This was to mark the departure of the senior girls from the community of nuns and teachers, and from one another; they were facing into the first hurdle of their adult lives, the examination which would determine for them the course and the location of the next three or four or six years; even, indeed, their future. Pass or fail, they were wearing their school uniform for the last time. Smiling to herself, Claire recalled the almost ceremonial disrobing Emily and three of her friends had staged in Claire's garden the previous afternoon, when school was out, over and done with. Ties were discarded or turned into headbands, shirts opened, skirts hiked up at the waist.

At Emily's instigation they had each chosen a single, different rose: Claire had watched with rueful pleasure as Emily led the girls gaily to each bush and shrub, naming the blossoms with a familiarity Claire had not suspected, and with an affection which she could only take as some kind of compliment.

They plucked a long yellow bud from the Casino climber at the door, a creamy frill from Alberic Barbier, a cup of deep and blushing pink from Zephirine Drouhin and, for Emily herself, the paler, fuller, quartered bloom of Fantin-Latour. Decked with these they jumped in turn on the old garden seats, they sang songs to each other, using the uncoiled garden hose as a microphone, they held hands and swayed as they sang on the lawn, burnished by the sun, released to energy and optimism and an intense commemorative awareness of one another.

'*We met as soul mates/On Paris Island*', they sang, arms linked, feet naked and dancing on the grass.

We left as inmates
Of an asylum
And we were sharp
As sharp as knives . . .
And we will all go down together,
Yes we will all go down together
We say we'll all go down together!

They spun on each other's applause, in love with themselves, dazed with this arrived freedom. The shrubs, the trees, the roses drank in their laughter. Claire saw the sun ripening on the swelling pears, the plums budding on the arching branches. The happy voices sang on, and sang well, they were all members of the school choir and singing was like breath to them. All their sweetness climbed among the petals, drifted into the fragrances of the garden as they embraced one another, oblivious of Claire and Mrs Cummins smiling in the kitchen, conscious only of the life, the living they had to do, the future that was stretching out its arms to their welcome.

Don't you know – talking about a revolution, sounds
   like a whisper [*they asked the delighted air*]
While they're standing in the welfare line,
Crying in the doorsteps of these armies of salvation,
Wasting time in the unemployment lines,
Sitting around waiting for a promotion –
Don't you know – talking about a revolution!
Don't you know – you gotta run run run run run –

And they ran gleefully around the garden, clasping each other.

Finally the tables are starting to turn [they chorused]
Finally the tables are starting to turn,
Talking about a revolution . . .

But they were angels again, or at least angelic, when they assembled with all the other girls for the Parting Mass. The school orchestra played, there were violin and flute solos, and to these graces the nuns had added pedestals of flowers to bless and brighten the small convent chapel. An aged priest invoked the future by referring to the past. Feeble and shaking as he made his way to the front of the altar, he spoke with a voice which had no tremor in it, no hesitation.

His life had been spent in great public service. Now it was nearing its end. But through all his work, he told the rapt young faces before him, he had been surrounded in this country by a vast and mighty flame of social love and social justice.

'I have come into contact with great and noble souls,' he said. 'They have lifted me up, they have led me on. And whatever good I did, whatever I have given – it has been returned to me a hundredfold.'

Claire, sitting with a proprietorial Stan among the other parents, felt the priest was offering assurances to the good that was in all those young people, making a promise to them in the language of his heart, speaking to them as if to equals, not of experience, but of aspiration. The hopefulness, the courage he saw in them he had seen in his own life bearing rich fruit. He wanted them to know how possible goodness could be.

Gathered for the last time, the girls sang their songs of faith, of hope, of love. '*Bind us together, Lord, Bind us together, in bonds that can never be broken*'.

They offered their gifts at the altar, the symbols of their talents.

And they offered themselves: '*Here I am, Lord. Do you hear me? I have heard you calling in the night.*'

Before the communion they sang the O Riada 'Our Father', their voices sliding down to the wistful plea – '*agus saor sinn o olc*'. And liberate us from badness. Everyone sang united in this embracing request. Deliver us from evil: *sed libera nos a malo*.

Maybe, thought Claire, looking at all the young features, the shining eyes, the exuberant gestures, maybe there is something there to be going on with? Maybe the Irish were not done for yet, had not yet done themselves in? She knew that among these children were those who, like Emily, would be taking a route far away from this convent, these songs, this land. She and Stan together had encouraged Emily in this, as they would encourage her brothers. But perhaps they would take that path only for a while; there would be homecomings.

The train curled in alongside the industrial yards, the housing estates. She grouped her pages into coloured sheaves to lay them in the briefcase, her eye dawdling on the glistening swing of a salmon, the spire of Lismore Cathedral silver above its trees. Pictures of grace. The words would lie beside them, beneath, with justified margins. She was a journalist: justified lies were part of her skill, what she lived on. But not what she lived by.

Damien, she thought, had said so little in his note arranging this appointment; what would he think of her when he saw her now, for real? The hasp of her heart tightened. She felt again as if she had been a bystander all her life, while Damien had made his own journey to this place at which they were now to come together, this conjunction unattended by stars.

'We're like those Polynesian boatmen,' she decided, 'finding one another as they found islands uncharted on any map, by non-cognitive recognition.'

With a quick hiss of perfume she shocked the skin at her wrists, her throat. As she stood to put on her jacket a stone flung at the train from a pavement split the window into fragments. Clasped to the frame the glass was held as a square of prismatic iridescence, silicone separation transforming it to rigid spray, imprecise yet crystalline, exquisite as a snowflake, blinding her to the world outside.

'Mother Ireland,' she thought, not despondent. 'It's part of our lives, let it be what it will. Like a birthmark.

'Once,' she remembered, standing by the automatic door as the platform crept nearer and nearer, 'once I imagined myself interfering in the stories I read, changing the end because I knew the end. Now I am living in a story, one of the stories that make up this country. And I want to change it – but I don't know what the end will be. How it will all turn out.'

There might be no turning out. Just a continuing, a going on with life, taking it more or less as it came, not interfering. Or at any rate, not too much.

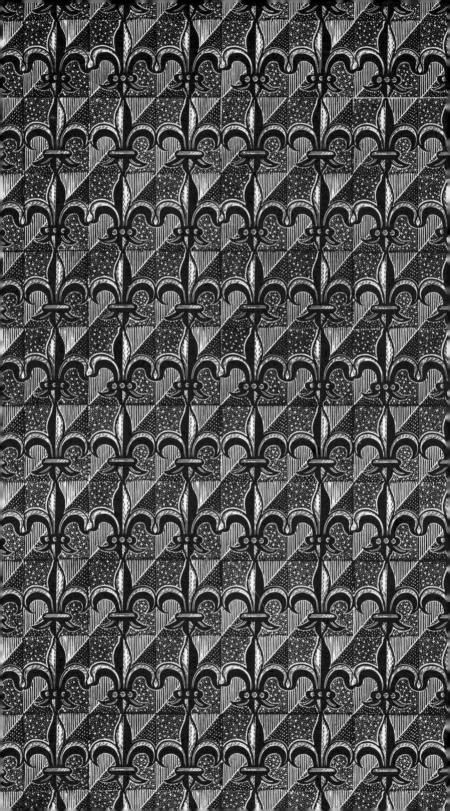